To Mary —

Best wishes for success
in your graduate program.
I've really enjoyed having
you in class.
Keep in touch

DH Nina

The Rise and Fall of an Urban School System

The Rise and Fall of an Urban School System

Detroit, 1907–81

Jeffrey Mirel

Ann Arbor

THE UNIVERSITY OF MICHIGAN PRESS

Copyright © by the University of Michigan 1993
All rights reserved
Published in the United States of America by
The University of Michigan Press
Manufactured in the United States of America

1996   1995   1994   1993   4   3   2   1

A CIP catalogue record of this book is available from the British Library.

Library of Congress Cataloging-in-Publication Data

Mirel, Jeffrey, 1948–
    The rise and fall of an urban school system : Detroit, 1907–81 /
Jeffrey Mirel.
      p.   cm.
    Includes bibliographical references and index.
    ISBN 0-472-10118-8 (alk. paper)
    1. Urban schools—Michigan—Detroit—History—20th century.
I. Title.
LC5133.D48M57   1992
370.19'348'09774'34—dc20   92-38551
                                                   CIP

To my father and mother,
Allan and Ida Mirel

Preface

The Rise and Fall of Urban Public Education

Urban schools are the most troubled part of the American educational enterprise. Daily, the barrage of reports on staggering dropout rates, rampant violence, demoralized teaching staffs, and declining academic achievement have convinced many observers that urban public schools are the worst in the nation.[1] Adding to this perception is the continuing failure of attempts to solve urban educational problems. Regardless of how well thought-out and well intended solutions might be, their goals are rarely realized, caught between the competing demands of local school boards, state departments of education, federal agencies, federal courts, teacher unions, and community groups, to name only the most visible participants in modern urban school politics. The "organizational theorist's nightmare" that David Tyack and Elisabeth Hansot see engulfing all of American education is at its worst in the nation's urban systems.[2]

This dismal picture stands in stark contrast to the exalted position urban school systems had throughout most of American educational history. Writing in 1919, Ellwood Cubberley claimed that America's urban systems were the best in the nation and had been for nearly half a century. The cities, he argued, "have been able to draw the keenest thinkers and the most capable administrators engaged in educational work."[3] These leaders instituted reforms that gave urban systems unrivaled reputations for administrative efficiency, innovative educational programs, and educational quality. When compared to the rural and suburban schools of the era, there is little doubt that Cubberley was correct. Indeed, as late as the 1940s, urban schools still set the standard for excellence for all of American education.

What went wrong? For a quarter-century, Americans have been passionately and often acrimoniously debating the reasons for the rise and fall of urban public education. Central to this debate is the 1966 study, *Equality of Educational Opportunity,* better known as the Coleman Report. In this massive survey, Coleman found that, in terms of available resources, black and white children essentially attended separate but equal schools and that the level of resources channeled to these schools made little difference in determining student achievement. Explaining the differences in achievement levels between these children, Coleman argued that families and peer groups had a significantly larger influence on student outcomes than did teachers or school environments.[4] One Harvard professor succinctly summed up the report, declaring, "Guess what Coleman found? . . . Schools make no difference; families make the difference."[5]

The Coleman Report profoundly affected educational thought in the United States. Former assistant secretary of education, Chester E. Finn, Jr., described it as "probably the best known and most influential piece of educational research ever published."[6] The report transformed the debate about educational policy in this country, greatly strengthening some points of view while diminishing, almost effacing, others. Policy analyst Henry Aaron notes that the Coleman Report severely undercut the liberal faith that equalizing educational resources would ultimately equalize educational outcomes. As a consequence, the report encouraged a thorough reanalysis of American education by critics from both the left and right.[7]

Left-wing scholars and activists used Coleman's conclusions to bolster their arguments that public schools are a tool of American capitalism. Because schools did not mitigate the importance of family factors in determining educational outcomes, these scholars argued that the actual purpose of public education was to reinforce or reproduce social and racial inequality. Denouncing most reform efforts as superficial, these intellectuals and activists challenged Americans to seek more fundamental structural changes in our society.[8] In contrast, conservatives used the report to support their arguments that family structures, core values, and cultural norms are central to educational achievement. Conservatives also questioned the utility of many educational reforms, particularly calls for additional resources to improve public education.[9]

The Coleman Report appears to have had an equally profound effect on how educational historians have conceived of their work. Apparently convinced by Coleman that resources were, at best, a secondary factor in explaining the problems of American public schools, educational historians have pursued several lines of inquiry that roughly correspond to the larger theoretical debates about public education. One of the most extensive analyses of public schools, generally, and urban schools, in particular, has come from a group of left-leaning, "revisionist" scholars who have tried to illuminate the mechanisms through which schools perpetuate social and racial inequality. Revisionist interpretations trace the problems of urban education to the actions of upper-class, business-oriented reformers who, in the late nineteenth and early twentieth centuries, transformed urban school systems in order to satisfy the changing nature and needs of American capitalism. Turn-of-the-century school reform, the revisionists argue, placed power in the hands of economically and socially elite school board members, reproduced social inequality through biased testing and tracking procedures, and socialized children into the norms and values of a bureaucratic, corporate society.[10]

As a consequence of these reforms, the very structure of urban school systems came to work against the needs of poor and minority children. Rather than being Horace Mann's "balance wheel of the social machinery," modern urban schools have contributed to the creation of a hopeless urban underclass. As Bowles and Gintis argue, public education has been more likely "to justify and reproduce inequality rather than correct it." Moreover, Bowles and Gintis claim, during periods of wrenching economic and social change, schools have become an "admirable safety valve for the economic pressure cooker . . . a monument to the capacity of the advanced corporate economy to accommodate and deflect thrusts away from its foundations."[11]

In response to this revisionist critique of American education, another group of scholars rose, more or less, in defense of public education. As with the revisionist critique, however, this defense is situated well within the parameters that the Coleman Report defined.[12] Nonrevisionist scholars argue that, in the 1920s and 1930s, despite the elite takeover of the schools and the racial, ethnic, and class bias of many of the Progressive era reforms, urban systems still provided an avenue for upward mobility and integration into the American mainstream for large numbers of poor, immigrant children. In her study of the New York City schools, Diane Ravitch criticizes revisionist scholars for

> inevitably los[ing] sight of the monumental accomplishments of the public school system of New York City. . . . The descendants of the miserably poor European immigrants of the nineteenth and early twentieth century are today the prosperous middle class of the city and its suburbs. Without the public schools, despite their obvious faults, this unprecedented social and economic mobility would have been inconceivable.[13]

The key question that these scholars ask is why, amid similar types of demographic and economic changes, were urban schools a means for mobility and equality in the 1920s and 1930s and not in the 1960s and 1970s? To answer this question, these historians focus on changes in school curricula, the shifting function and purpose of the high school, and the growing dependence on the schools to solve major social problems. In the 1920s and 1930s, they argue, urban schools had a straightforward mission, namely to transform the diverse ethnic population of our cities into American citizens. Educators had no doubt about what that mission entailed: fundamental literacy and mathematical skills, knowledge of a "core" curriculum including a strong emphasis on literature, American history, and American values, and, above all, mastery of the English language. While this approach to citizenship education often provided teachers with a self-righteous cloak for racism and the denigration of ethnic cultures, it nevertheless resulted in upward mobility for many immigrant groups.[14]

The modern problems of urban education, these scholars argue, developed as educators abandoned the straightforward inculcation of skills and values necessary for success in American life. Since the 1930s, Ravitch contends, American schools have become agencies of social adjustment designed to "meet the needs of youth" rather than institutions committed to providing access to a common culture. The consequence of these curricular decisions have been particularly disastrous for children in urban systems. Rather than obtaining the same high-quality education that children of immigrants received in the 1920s and 1930s, children of the new black and Hispanic urban immigrants have entered schools in which educators have softened curricula and lowered standards and expectations. Given these conditions, the massive failure of urban schools should come as no surprise.[15]

For the last two decades, the debate between the revisionists and their critics has dominated discussions about the history of urban schooling in America. Recently, however, a group of "postrevisionist" historians has tried to move beyond that debate by offering another perspective on the development of urban schooling. These scholars have concentrated on the one apparent flaw common to all of the previous interpretations, namely the assumption that urban minority and working-class communities have been largely passive, uncomprehending victims of vast social or educational changes.[16] According to these scholars that view of minorities and the working class seriously distorts all the earlier interpretations. As Katznelson and Weir put it, "We take issue . . . with the disappearance of the working class from educational analyses and the glib dismissals of education from the agendas of democratic and egalitarian movements and aspirations."[17]

This new group of historians perceives schools as contested institutions in which working class, ethnic, and independent civic organizations have clashed with more established interests over the direction of educational policy and practice. While their studies differ in emphasis, these scholars all share a dynamic vision of the politics of twentieth-century urban education. Their main theme is that women's groups, progressive politicians, ethnic and minority organizations, and organized labor have had a substantial, generally positive, influence on the development of urban public education.[18]

Of these studies, Katznelson and Weir provide the most sweeping vision of urban educational decline by linking labor activism, urban politics, and demographic change. Briefly, they contend that the rise and fall of urban education has been strongly associated with the degree of working-class involvement in school issues. Throughout the Progressive era, they note, the working class played an important role in shaping urban educational policy, but, in the 1930s, working-class interest and influence on the schools began to wane. As Katznelson and Weir put it, "Social class ceased to be a basis of mobilization in school politics in the 1930s. In the very decade when labor emerged as a mass interest group on the national level, working-class self-images, political language, and assertions of interest with regard to education contracted." By 1950, working-class influence on urban schools had "disappeared entirely."[19]

This "domestication" of organized labor occurred at roughly the same time that industrial cities began experiencing major demographic changes. As organized labor paid less attention to educational issues and as white, working-class families abandoned central cities, urban school systems began their long slide into bureaucratic stagnation and educational ruin. By the 1970s, these trends had transformed the basis of educational politics from class to race, pitting largely minority cities against white suburbs, and leaving the beleaguered civil rights movement as the last champion of the ideal of equal schooling for all.[20]

As in many of the postrevisionist works, Katznelson and Weir are sensitive to "the politics of money," the perennial issues of school finance, taxes, and expenditures. Yet even studies that have provided the most extensive treatment of resource issues have not conveyed the almost overwhelming obsession urban school leaders seem to have had with funding problems.[21] "During the entire 100 years of our public school system," the president of the Detroit Board of Education declared in 1942, "the Board has never experienced a time in which its schools had sufficient seats for all who sought its service." Overcrowded schools, overcrowded classes, and an almost perpetual financial crisis have dominated the history of urban education since the nineteenth century.[22] Reformers and school leaders frequently campaigned for specific changes in the hope that such innovations as centralization, the junior high school, the Gary plan, age-grading, and standardized testing would enable schools to serve more children, more efficiently. School leaders fought, bitterly and repeatedly, with city councils, state legislatures, and powerful interest groups over levels of funding. Racial and ethnic groups routinely clashed over inequalities in the allocation of school resources. Yet educational historians often downplay these battles over financial issues, seeing them as secondary to more fundamental struggles over school governance or the curriculum.[23]

My study of the Detroit Public Schools argues that issues of governance, curriculum, and resources are inextricably intertwined. Shifting levels of available resources have had an enormous impact on the development of urban public schools, and political battles about resources have been one of the driving forces shaping virtually every aspect of urban public education. This argument about the role of resources in the history of urban education does not deny the importance of Coleman's and subsequent researchers' conclusions about the relationship between resources and educational outcomes.[24] Nor does the argument question the profound impact that social class, race, culture, curricular change, family structure, peer groups, or values have had on education. Rather, it contends that, by downplaying the importance of resource issues, educational historians have focused on only half of a dynamic process. In a sense, we have been considering schooling as an abstraction, as an enterprise unrestrained by material demands and uninfluenced by the actual conditions in which educational policymakers, community activist groups, teachers, parents, and students must operate.

There are four main reasons for focusing on resources. First, at the most fundamental level, the amount of money available to a school system is one of the crucial material constraints on public school development. In many ways, these material constraints define educational priorities, shape the organizational plans of school districts, and even influence changes in schools' curricula.

Second, the level of support for urban schools has rarely been steady. In modern American history, such catastrophic events as wars, depressions, and civil unrest have caused major disruptions or changes in the flow of school resources. In every case, these events have compelled major adjustments in school life.

Third, the struggle for resources is invariably a political struggle. As such, the alignment of interest groups and the shifting balances of power among these groups play an enormous role in determining both the level of support for schools and the power these groups have to influence school policy. Urban educational politics, especially in regard to school finance, have frequently been as fierce as any political conflict in American life. It is only by downplaying the importance of these controversies that Tyack and Hansot can argue that "public education has differed from other sectors of society where competition and conflict have been taken for granted and treated as part of the natural order."[25] Indeed, school politics since the 1930s may have more in common with larger national politics than historians have heretofore suspected.

Fourth, the amount of resources that school systems have is often a good indication of the level of commitment that a community or, at least, the most influential interest groups within a community, has for public schools.

Any investigation of the ebb and flow of educational resources and the ongoing struggles about them must take a long perspective that analyzes the connection between actual educational policies and practices and the social, political, and economic dynamics of a given place. Ideally, historians should research educational systems in different cities, each representing different economic and political contexts throughout the country. Unfortunately, efforts to achieve that ideal, even when aided by substantial grants and teams of research assistants, have fallen far short of the mark. The reasons for that failure are simple—the amount of material that is necessary to consider in studying the history of even one large urban system is enormous and the factors involved in the decline of any urban system are tremendously varied and complex. The sheer magnitude of available records, for example, forces even well-funded projects to concentrate on specific, important events rather than the processes and patterns of change. Yet the only way to truly understand the rise and fall of urban school systems is to identify and analyze those processes and patterns. For the time being, individual case studies may be the only feasible approach to longitudinal research on the history of twentieth-century urban education.

In many ways, Detroit is an ideal place to undertake such an investigation. For most of this century, it was the fourth largest city in the country and one of the great manufacturing centers of the world. Detroit has gone through virtually every significant economic and demographic change that Americans associate with large industrial cities. No city felt the impact of the Flint sit-down strike more profoundly, and, in 1943 and 1967, Detroit was shaken by two of the worst race riots in American history. Few places in the country offer a better perspective on the interaction between industrial capitalism and the politics of class and race.

The history of the Detroit Public Schools also offers a unique opportunity to explore the rise and fall of a great urban school district. Virtually every major educational reform and innovation of the twentieth century took root and flourished in Detroit. In a classic example of Progressive era reform, Detroit shifted from a ward-based to an at-large form of school board elections and became a national leader in Americanization, standardized testing, and vocational education. The school system suffered severe retrenchment during the Great Depression but emerged, in the early 1940s, as the national center of wartime training and education. During the late 1940s and the 1950s, the school system struggled to accommodate the flood of baby boomers and wrestled with problems of race as the African-American community also grew substantially. By the 1960s, the city and the schools were engulfed in racial tension that ultimately led to the extensive decentralization of the school system and to two of the most important Supreme Court decisions on desegregation, *Milliken v. Bradley* (1974 and 1977).

In searching for a site to explore the history of urban education, no city is perfect because each city will have features that undercut generalizations. The rise of the Democratic political machine in Chicago in the 1930s, for example, a development that was not widely repeated, must temper conclusions that historians draw from case studies of the Windy City. Detroit also has drawbacks as a site for this research. The rise to prominence of the United Auto Workers (UAW) in the late 1930s that transformed Detroit into a bastion of industrial unionism insured organized labor an unusually important role in city and state politics. In few other cities was union power so substantial. In addition to the rise of the UAW, since the 1940s Detroit has had a large, politically sophisticated African-American community. This factor also precludes hasty generalizations one might draw from Detroit. Yet, in many ways, both these factors can be seen as strengths as well as weaknesses in focusing on the Motor City. The combination of relatively clean local politics and the fact that organized labor and the African-American community have been unusually strong in the city means that Detroit offers a superb opportunity to explore how issues of class and race have been played out in the public schools.

I attempt to describe how Detroiters struggled with the task of building and supporting a vast urban school system amid seemingly constant change and conflict. Chapter 1 presents the battle between elite reformers and members of the ward-based board of education for control of the schools. That battle lasted from 1907 to 1916, ending with the replacement of the ward-based board with one elected at-large. Chapter 2 focuses on the political and educational implementation of the reforms that followed that change in governance, particularly the emergence of broad-based consensus in support of the expansion and improvement of the Detroit schools. In chapter 3, I discuss how the Great Depression shattered that consensus and how educational politics came to resemble the larger political configurations abroad in the land during the New Deal years. Chapter 4 focuses on the 1940s, when the political alignments of the Depression became institutionalized in state and local politics and when the Detroit Federation of Teachers and the growing African-American community began to have an impact on educational policy and politics in Detroit. Chapter 5 explores the rise to prominence of the liberal-labor-black political coalition in the city and its effort to recreate a consensus on educational issues in the 1950s and early 1960s. In chapter 6, I analyze the collapse of that coalition in the late 1960s and early 1970s, demonstrating how racial issues fragmented organized labor's support for public education, a development that nearly bankrupted the school system and left the system racially and political isolated. In the epilogue, I assess the impact these political changes had on public education in Detroit and address some policy issues that are implied by the arguments in this book.

NOTES

1. See, for example, Carnegie Foundation for the Advancement of Teaching, *An Imperiled Generation: Saving Urban Schools* (Princeton, NJ: Princeton University Press, 1988); Chicago Tribune Staff, *Chicago Schools: "Worst in America"* (Chicago: Chicago Tribune, 1988).

2. David Tyack and Elisabeth Hansot, *Managers of Virtue: Public School Leadership in America, 1820–1980* (New York: Basic Books, 1982), 246.

3. Ellwood Cubberley, *Public Education in the United States* (Cambridge, MA: The Riverside Press, 1919), 465–67.

4. James S. Coleman et al., *Equality of Educational Opportunity* (Washington, DC: U.S. Government Printing Office, 1966). A good, short summary of the findings of the report can be found in James S. Coleman, "A Brief Summary of the Coleman Report," in *Equal Educational Opportunity*, ed. Harvard Educational Review (Cambridge, MA: Harvard University Press, 1969), 253–59.

5. Quoted in Godfrey Hodgson, "Do Schools Make a Difference?" *Atlantic Monthly* 231 (March, 1973): 35.

6. Chester E. Finn, Jr., quoted in the introduction to U.S. Department of Education, *What*

Works: Research About Teaching and Learning (Washington, DC: U.S. Department of Education, 1986), 3.

7. Henry J. Aaron, *Politics and the Professors: The Great Society in Perspective* (Washington, DC: Brookings Institution, 1978), 77.

8. See, for example, Christopher Jencks et al., *Inequality: A Reassessment of the Effect of Family and Schooling in America* (New York: Harper and Row, 1972); Samuel Bowles and Herbert Gintis, *Schooling in Capitalist America* (New York: Basic Books, 1976).

9. Department of Education, *What Works*, 2–3; A. L. Ginsburg and S. L. Hanson, "Values and Educational Success among Disadvantaged Children," Contract No. 300-83-0211 (U.S. Department of Education, Washington, DC, 1986, photocopy); Andrew Oldenquist, "The Decline of American Education in the '60s and '70s," *American Education* 19 (May, 1983): 12–18.

10. In identifying revisionist scholars and key revisionist ideas, I am using the criteria established by Diane Ravitch (Ravitch, *The Revisionists Revised: A Critique of the Radical Attack on the Schools* [New York: Basic Books, 1978], 36–37). Examples of revisionist scholarship include Bowles and Gintis, *Schooling in Capitalist America;* Clarence Karier, Paul Violas, and Joel Spring, *Roots of Crisis: American Education in the Twentieth Century* (Chicago: Rand McNally, 1973); Michael Katz, *Class, Bureaucracy and Schools* (New York: Praeger, 1972); Joel Spring, *Education and the Rise of the Corporate State* (Boston: Beacon Press, 1972); Paul Violas, *The Training of the Urban Working Class* (Chicago: Rand McNally, 1978).

11. Bowles and Gintis, *Schooling in Capitalist America*, 102, 4–5.

12. David Angus, "The Politics of Progressive School Reform, Grand Rapids, 1900–1910," *Michigan Academician* 14 (Winter, 1982), 239–58; David Angus, "Vocationalism and the Blueing of the High School, Grand Rapids, Michigan, 1900–1920" (paper presented at the History of Education Society annual meeting, Pittsburgh, October 1980); Diane Ravitch, *The Great School Wars* (New York: Basic Books, 1974); Ravitch, *Revisionists Revised*.

13. Ravitch, *Great School Wars*, 403.

14. See, for example, Nathan Glazer, "Ethnicity and Education: Some Hard Questions," *Phi Delta Kappan* (January, 1981): 387–88; Glazer, "Black English and Reluctant Judges." *Public Interest*, no. 62 (Winter, 1981): 51–52.

15. Diane Ravitch, *The Troubled Crusade: American Education 1945–1980* (New York: Basic Books, 1983), 43–80, 155–57.

16. The works by "postrevisionist" scholars include Ronald Cohen, *Children of the Mill: Schooling and Society in Gary, Indiana 1906–60* (Bloomington, IN: Indiana University Press, 1990); David John Hogan, *Class and Reform: School and Society in Chicago, 1880–1930* (Philadelphia: University of Pennsylvania Press, 1985); Michael Homel, *Down from Equality: Black Chicagoans and the Public Schools, 1920–41* (Urbana: University of Illinois Press, 1984); Paul Peterson, *The Politics of School Reform, 1870–1940* (Chicago: University of Chicago Press, 1985); William Reese, *Power and the Promise of School Reform: Grass Roots Movements During the Progressive Era* (Boston: Routledge and Kegan Paul, 1986); Julia Wrigley, *Class Politics and Public Schools: Chicago, 1900–1950* (New Brunswick, NJ: Rutgers University Press, 1982); Ira Katznelson and Margaret Weir, *Schooling for All: Class, Race and the Decline of the Democratic Ideal* (New York: Basic Books, 1985); Tyack and Hansot, *Managers of Virtue*, esp. pt. 3.

17. Katznelson and Weir, *Schooling for All*, 14.

18. Many of these studies have also moved beyond the limits of the Coleman Report by paying more attention to what Tyack, Lowe, and Hansot have called "the politics of money" and the allocation of resources. Yet, because these works have other historiographic priorities, these discussions of resources invariably have been relegated to a supporting role in the unfolding drama of urban education (see David Tyack, Robert Lowe, and Elisabeth Hansot, *Public Schools*

in Hard Times: The Great Depression and Recent Years [Cambridge, MA: Harvard University Press, 1984], 42–91).

19. Katznelson and Weir, *Schooling for All,* 134, 120.

20. Katznelson and Weir, *Schooling for All,* 122–23, 178–222.

21. The works by Peterson and Homel have been the most sensitive to resource issues, yet even they focus on such issues in a very narrow way. See Peterson, *Politics of School Reform,* 72–95; Homel, *Down from Equality,* 58–87.

22. DBEP, 1942–43, 2. On the nineteenth-century fiscal crises, see David Angus, "Conflict, Class, and the Nineteenth-Century Public High School in Cities of the Midwest, 1845–1900." *Curriculum Inquiry* 18, no. 1 (1988): 7–31.

23. See, for example, David Tyack, *The One Best System: A History of American Urban Education* (Cambridge, MA: Harvard University Press, 1974).

24. Eric Hanusek, for example, has argued that research over the past two decades has shown that "performance in many different educational settings provides strong and consistent evidence that expenditures are not systematically related to student achievement" (Eric A. Hanusek, "The Impact of Differential Expenditures on School Performance," *Educational Researcher* 4 [May, 1989]: 49).

25. Tyack and Hansot, *Managers of Virtue,* 11.

Acknowledgments

One of the pleasures I have been looking forward to upon completing this book is thanking all of the people who helped make it possible. Anyone who has undertaken such a project knows that, despite the solitary nature of writing, the work that goes into reaching that stage is a genuinely collective effort. In the nine years that I have been researching and writing about the Detroit schools, many people and institutions have provided me with aid and support. The Rockefeller Foundation and the John M. Olin Foundation played indispensable roles in providing funds for the completion of this project. A residency fellowship from the Rockefeller Foundation allowed me to spend nine extremely productive months at the Walter P. Reuther Library on the Wayne State University campus in Detroit. A John M. Olin faculty fellowship gave me a crucial year away from my teaching responsibilities that enabled me to research the final chapters of the book and to write most of the manuscript. In addition, the Earhart Foundation funded my preliminary research into the last sections of the book and the Henry J. Kaiser Foundation provided travel funds for me to return for short research trips to the Reuther library on several occasions. I would also like to thank the Joyce Foundation and especially its former president, Craig Kennedy, for supporting the publication of the book.

Dean Jerrold Zar of the Graduate School of Northern Illinois University, and the Graduate School Committee on Research and Artistry provided indispensable research and travel funds over several summers. Dean Charles Stegman of the College of Education and L. Glenn Smith, chair of the Department of Leadership and Educational Policy Studies, aided my research in many ways and generously provided funds to sustain the project, even during difficult financial times. My colleagues in the Foundations Faculty, especially the faculty chairs whose terms coincided with my work on this book, David Ripley, Wilma Miranda, and Homer Sherman, have been unfailingly supportive of my efforts.

I have been very fortunate to have done my research at some of the finest archives in the country. I am particularly indebted to Philip Mason and the staff of the Walter P. Reuther Library at Wayne State. During my year in residency at the Reuther, and in my subsequent visits, they went out of their way to make my time there productive and enjoyable. I would particularly like to thank Warner Pflug, associate director of the Archives of Labor and Urban Affairs, and archivists Patricia Bartkowski and Carrolyn Davis for their unfailing help in finding sources, answering my innumerable questions, and making the time I spent at the Reuther a pleasure. Francis Blouin, Jr., and Nancy Bartlett of the Michigan Historical Collection of the Bentley Historical Library in Ann Arbor also greatly aided my research and routinely went out of their way to facilitate my work. Alice Dalligan and Mary Karschner of the Burton Historical Collection of the Detroit Public Library provided valuable aid in using several collections that were crucial to this manuscript. Geraldine Frenette and the staff of the Religion, Education, and Sociology section of the Detroit Public Library helped me in numerous ways, often going above and beyond the call of duty in their efforts to get me materials. Gerald Dorfman and Aurelia Hanna of the Paul and Jean Hanna Collection at the Hoover Institution on War, Revolution, and Peace at Stanford University were quite gracious and helpful during the time I spent at Stanford working on the final chapter of this study.

Over the years, a number of administrators in the Detroit Public Schools, including Michael Albert, Stuart Rankin, and Alan Zondlak, aided this project. I especially want to thank Charles Partridge, who first introduced me to the "school archives," actually a large closet near the professional library in which he had gathered and protected a marvelous collection of materials.

I have also been blessed with a large number of friends and colleagues whose advice, criticism, and support has aided this project tremendously. Diane Ravitch has inspired and encouraged me throughout my work on this book and has provided valuable assistance along the way. Guy Senese has offered thoughtful criticism and ready wit, both of which helped me through many difficult spots. Over the years, Richard Altenbaugh, Barbara Finkelstein, Fred Goodman, Thomas Hoffer, David Kamens, Phil Kearney, Elizabeth Schulman, Jordan Schwarz, and David Tyack took time to discuss the study as it progressed and guide me to new sources and interpretations. Richard Angelo, Robert Bain, Virginia Brereton, Ronald Cohen, Paul

Kleppner, and William Reese read and commented on various sections of the manuscript. Arthur Jefferson, former superintendent of the Detroit schools, graciously agreed to critique my work and gave me the benefit of an insider's point of view. I am most deeply indebted to Lawrence Berlin, Sidney Fine, John Rury, and Maris Vinovskis, all of whom took time from their busy schedules to read and extensively criticize the entire manuscript. Their suggestions helped me improve the book immeasurably. Most important, I cannot begin to thank David Angus enough for his continuing friendship and support. This book began as a dissertation under his direction. As the project expanded beyond the scope of that original study, his help and commitment to it never flagged. David's good influence is present on every page. Mary Erwin, of the University of Michigan Press, has been a pleasure to work with and has been endlessly forgiving as I "met all of my delays." These friends and colleagues saved me from numerous errors and inaccuracies, those that remain are my responsibility alone.

My family has endured the writing of this book with great patience and goodwill. For almost their entire growing up, my children, Josh, Lisa, and Diana, have had to compete for my attention with a shapeless rival known only as "the book on Detroit." That they have successfully transcended this sibling rivalry is testament to their resilience, strength of character, and sense of humor. Throughout the duration of this project, my wife, Barbara, has regularly taken time from her own academic career to critique, edit, and refine every section of this study. Her strength and love sustained this project and much, much more.

This book is dedicated to my parents with love and gratitude.

Grateful acknowledgment is given to journals for permission to reprint portions of the author's previously published material.

History of Education Quarterly for material from "The Politics of Educational Retrenchment: Detroit, 1929–1935." In Vol. 24, February 1984, pp. 323–58.

Journal of the Midwest History of Education Society for material from "'Out of the Cloister of the Classroom': Political Activity and the Teachers of Detroit, 1929–1939." In Vol. 11, 1983, pp. 49–82.

Contents

Abbreviations

AE Papers	Arthur Elder Papers, Archives of Labor History and Urban Affairs, Walter P. Reuther Library, Wayne State University, Detroit, MI
ALHUA	Archives of Labor History and Urban Affairs, Walter P. Reuther Library, Wayne State University, Detroit, MI
CR Papers	Carmen Roberts Papers, Michigan Historical Collection, Bentley Historical Library, University of Michigan, Ann Arbor, MI
CS Scrapbook	Charles Spain Scrapbook, Wayne State University, Archives, Walter P. Reuther Library, Wayne State University, Detroit, MI
DBEP	Detroit Board of Education Proceedings
DNLB Scrapbooks	Detroit News Lansing Bureau Scrapbooks, Michigan Historical Collection, Bentley Historical Library, University of Michigan, Ann Arbor, MI
DFT Papers	Detroit Federation of Teachers Papers, Archives of Labor History and Urban Affairs, Walter P. Reuther Library, Wayne State University, Detroit, MI
DM Papers	Detroit Mayors Papers, Burton Historical Collection, Detroit Public Library, Detroit, MI
DNAACP	Detroit National Association for the Advancement of Colored People, Archives of Labor History and Urban Affairs, Walter P. Reuther Library, Wayne State University, Detroit, MI
DPS Archives	Detroit Public Schools, School Center Building, Detroit, MI

DPS/DCR Papers   Detroit Public Schools, Division of Community Relations, Archives of Labor History and Urban Affairs, Walter P. Reuther Library, Wayne State University, Detroit, MI

DUL Papers   Detroit Urban League Papers, Michigan Historical Collection, Bentley Historical Library, University of Michigan, Ann Arbor, MI

EG Papers   Ernest Goodman Papers, Archives of Labor History and Urban Affairs, Walter P. Reuther Library, Wayne State University, Detroit, MI

LFO Papers   Laura F. Osborn Papers, Burton Historical Collection, Detroit Public Library, Detroit, MI

MFT Papers   Michigan Federation of Teachers Papers, Archives of Labor History and Urban Affairs, Walter P. Reuther Library, Wayne State University, Detroit, MI

ND Papers   Norman Drachler Papers, Paul and Jean Hanna Collection, Hoover Institution, Stanford University, Stanford, CA

RGR Papers   Remus G. Robinson Papers, Archives of Labor History and Urban Affairs, Walter P. Reuther Library, Wayne State University, Detroit, MI

WPR Papers   Walter P. Reuther Papers, Archives of Labor History and Urban Affairs, Walter P. Reuther Library, Wayne State University, Detroit, MI

A Note on the Tables

One of the biggest frustrations in researching the history of the Detroit schools is that, over the past eighty years, school administrators rarely used the same criteria or categories to report statistical data about the system. Even such basic figures as enrollments fluctuate dramatically, depending upon whether the administrators listed just K–12 students, K–12 plus students in special programs, or all students in the system, including those in adult programs, the city colleges, and so forth. In addition, administrators, at times, shifted from listing students by grades to listing them by divisions (elementary, junior high, and so on). When reporting by divisions, however, they did not note that many seventh and eighth graders, for example, who should have been in junior highs according to school policy, actually attended elementary schools and were thus counted as part of the elementary enrollments. In other words, one could not assume that the enrollments listed in either the elementary or junior high school divisions represented the number of students in either grades 1–6 or 7–9.

In financial reports, administrators rarely indicated what they included in creating categories of revenue or expenditures. This was particularly troublesome in terms of capital expenditures, which were often listed in several conflicting ways. In addition, administrators occasionally revamped statistical reporting procedures without making clear how the old and new figures might correspond. In annual budget reports, this problem was acute. In 1965, for example, the board totally changed how it figured all its revenue and expenditures, and even such fundamental aspects of the budget as the annual amount of local tax collections did not match the data from previous years.

In the tables contained in the Appendix, the data are drawn from those sources that reported the most consistent sets of figures over sustained periods of time. The tables only go as far as such internal consistency allows. Even among these figures, however, there are discrepancies that I cannot explain. I have simply chosen to report the numbers as I found them, inconsistencies and all.

Chapter 1

"Beer and Pedagogy," 1907–19

On November 14, 1907, the women of the Twentieth Century Club marched into a Detroit school board meeting demanding that the board fire a recently appointed principal. For nearly four years, members of the club had denounced Superintendent Wales Martindale for creating a corrupt, political machine that put patronage before pupils. Now they had an incident to force his hand. The previous month, the *Detroit Journal* had reported on the appointment of Ralph Treppa, a Polish bar owner, as the principal of the Campbell Evening School. Sensing an issue that combined two of the most potent political issues of the day, temperance and school reform, the women called for Treppa's ouster. Led by Laura Osborn, a suffragist, temperance advocate, and wife of a prominent Detroit businessman, the women argued that a "saloonkeeper" was morally unfit to lead a school. The women cheered as Hiram Goldberg, one of their allies on the board, chastised his colleagues for allowing Treppa "to mix beer and pedagogy."

Unfortunately for the reformers, most of the board members, including Treppa's brother, Anthony, were unmoved by the protest. Amid shouts, insults, and a near fistfight, the board refused to reconsider the appointment. As the women left the meeting, some weeping tears of rage, Osborn declared, "We are heartsick. The spectacle we have witnessed tonight shows why the public school system of Detroit is the laughingstock of leading educators all over the United States." Osborn vowed to return, as did representatives of the Detroit Board of Commerce and an association of Protestant ministers.[1]

In many ways, this was a classic Progressive era confrontation—an alliance of elite women's groups, Protestant ministers, and a prominent organization of businessmen challenging the policies of a largely middle-class board of education that had strong ties to the growing ethnic communities of the city. Indeed, behind the charges of corruption and immorality was one of the great educational issues of the day, school governance. Osborn and her allies were not merely seeking the removal of one Polish night school principal or even the dismissal of Superintendent Martindale. Their ultimate goal was to replace the large, ward-based board of education with a small, "businesslike" board elected by the city at large.

Generally, historians have interpreted similar events in other cities in two different ways, depending on their theoretical perspective. On the one hand, one might portray Osborn and her supporters as heroic reformers who worked to liberate the schools from the depredations of a corrupt political ring. On the other, one might see them as representatives of monopoly capitalism who sought control of the schools in order to mold the values and skills of urban children according to the demands of modern industry and to reinforce social inequality. Yet neither of these two interpretations nor any of their more recent refinements do justice to these events. There is more here than any earlier interpretation of the Progressive era allows. First, school reform in Detroit was strongly tied to religion and the temperance issue, a situation few educational historians have explored in other settings.[2] Second, what class conflict there was in these events generally pitted upper-class insurgents against middle-class officeholders. During the first part of this century, Detroit's working class, at least as represented by organized labor and the local Socialist party, did not play a major role in school politics. Third, the issue that dominated the reform campaign in Detroit generally concerned the ethics and character of the superintendent, particular board members, and the process of selecting board members, *not* specific educational policies or practices. During most of these years, educational politics in Detroit were marked by broad agreement about important educational policies and practices, with both reformers and antireformers supporting such initiatives as Americanization programs and a differentiated high school curriculum. Finally, in 1916, the reformers mobilized a substantial political consensus that succeeded in replacing the ward-based board with one elected from the city at large. This chapter focuses on how educational politics in Detroit moved from conflict to consensus in the Progressive era.

The Birth of Reform

People called it "Detroit the Dynamic." From 1900 to 1920, few cities in the nation could match the dramatic increases in population, the industrial élan, and the sheer exuberant expansion of Detroit. During these years, the city grew from 23 to 79 square miles and its population leapt from 285,704 to

993,675.[3] The obvious cause of this growth was the rapid concentration of the American automobile industry in Detroit. At the turn of the century, Detroit was just one of many cities engaged in the production of cars. By 1903, however, with the establishment of Cadillac, Packard, and Ford, the city quickly emerged as the national center of the industry. In 1909, Detroit accounted for almost 40 percent of U.S. auto production, by 1914, 75 percent.[4]

Lured by the promise of plentiful jobs and relatively high wages, immigrants from eastern and southern Europe flocked to the city, transforming its demographic character. In 1904, the city's Polish, Russian-Jewish, and Italian communities numbered 13,000, 1,300, and 904 respectively. In 1925, the Polish community had grown to 115,069, the Russian-Jewish to 49,427, and the Italian to 42,457. Overall, between 1904 and 1925, the proportion of foreign-born residents of Detroit jumped from approximately one-third to almost one-half.[5]

In many ways, the growth of Detroit public schools was more dramatic than the growth of the city itself. Enrollment in kindergarten through twelfth grade climbed from 29,401 in 1900 to 115,389 in 1920, well outpacing the general population increase in the same period. By 1920, almost half of the students in these schools were foreign born or the children of foreign-born parents.[6] As in other booming cities, the problems of accommodating this staggering growth provided the background to the campaign for school reform.[7] Throughout the Martindale era, many children attended school on a part-time basis, in basements and in rented buildings. The city council and board of estimate, which determined the annual tax appropriation to the schools, never provided adequate funds for public education.[8] Indeed, the portion of the local tax levy allocated to the schools averaged 21.9 percent from 1896 to 1905, and *fell* to an average of 15.2 percent between 1906 and 1915. The annual tax allocation fell in absolute as well as relative terms as per pupil revenues dropped from an average of $102.54 (adjusted for inflation) between 1900 and 1904 to an average of $71.37 between 1905 and 1911.[9] Throughout this time, cost overruns and unfinished buildings regularly kept "hundreds from school," with critics blaming the board for incompetence and mismanaging the meager amount of money it did receive.[10]

The school board in Detroit was composed of one school inspector elected in partisan contests from each ward. Allegations of corruption, mismanagement, and malfeasance were nothing new to the Detroit Board of Education. In 1894, following an elaborate "sting" operation, reform mayor Hazen Pingree and a squad of policemen descended on a school board meeting, arresting four board members for taking payoffs on building and furniture contracts.[11] While "throwing the rascals out" satisfied one important part of the reform impulse, many Detroiters argued that Pingree had not gone far enough.

In 1902, a group of elite Detroiters led by State Representative Edwin Denby and School Inspector Clarence Burton began a campaign to change the structure of school governance in the city. The campaign had two main thrusts. The first focused on breaking the power of school Superintendent Wales Martindale, who reputedly controlled a political machine that reached from the precincts of Detroit to the very heart of the state government in Lansing. The second aim of the campaign was to destroy the ward and precinct base of the machine by creating a small school board elected at large.[12]

Spearheading the reform campaign was the Detroit Municipal League, an organization led by such prominent businessmen as J. L. Hudson, the department store magnate, and Henry Leland, founder of Cadillac. The actions of the Municipal League and its successor, the Detroit Citizens League, illustrate the complex interweaving of religion, temperance, and political ambition that marked progressive reform in the Motor City. Both organizations drew their support from wealthy, Protestant businessmen, many of whom were temperance advocates. These men linked political corruption with "saloon politics," and, according to Raymond Fragnoli, they saw their opponents as the "organized forces of evil."[13]

In 1907, the members of the Municipal League had some reason to believe that the winds of fortune were blowing their way in school politics. Two years before, Delos Wilcox, executive secretary of both the Detroit Municipal League and the Grand Rapids Civic Club, engineered a total transformation in school governance in Grand Rapids, replacing the large, ward-based board with a small board elected at large. The following year, in the first election to that new board, elite citizens of Grand Rapids won eight of the nine seats. The campaign for the small board in Grand Rapids was punctuated by many of the themes that would soon become common in Detroit, particularly the joining of temperance, educational reform, and allegations of corruption in the purchase of textbooks.[14]

While the Municipal League drew inspiration from events across the state, by far the most important development in school politics in 1907 was the emergence of Laura Osborn as the leader of the reform campaign. Linked to the Municipal League by her husband, Francis, a wealthy inventor and a member of the League's education committee, Laura Osborn quickly proved to be an effective educational politician.[15] With her ties to the Municipal League and her base of support in the Detroit Federation of Women's Clubs (DFWC), Osborn rallied hundreds of Detroit women to the causes of temperance, women's suffrage, and school reform. As William Reese has pointed out in his study of progressive reform, women were among the most important participants in school politics of the era.[16] Osborn, in fact, was the primary leader of the reform campaign, and the women she inspired were instrumental in transforming the Detroit schools.

Religious leaders, primarily Protestant ministers affiliated with the Detroit Pastors Union, joined the Municipal League and the women activists as the third group pressing for school reform in Detroit. Like the latter groups, the religious leaders initially concentrated on ousting board members linked to the liquor dealers. As one Baptist minister put it, "Our political life will not be free until the saloon power is broken. The saloon must keep her dirty hands off the school system." Throughout the era, the ministers and, at least one rabbi, Leo Franklin, repeatedly used their pulpits to denounce the influence of liquor dealers over public education and to demand an end to ward-based control of Detroit schools.[17]

On the periphery of the school reform effort were a number of other important organizations and several newspapers. The Detroit Board of Commerce, the leading businessmen's group in the city, was an early advocate of school board reform as was the Detroit Civic Association.[18] Similarly, three of the leading daily papers in the city, the *Detroit Journal, Detroit Times,* and the *Detroit Free Press,* a strongly antiunion paper, all endorsed the campaign against Martindale and the ward-based board of education.

Martindale stood fast against the reformers by drawing support from two main groups, people who benefited from the status quo and those who recoiled at the tactics of the Municipal League and its allies. People closest to the system tended to be Martindale's strongest advocates, with his major support coming from the majority of ward-based school inspectors. Martindale, however, also received the enthusiastic endorsement of many teachers and administrators. As attacks from reformers increased, principals and teachers cheered Martindale at mass meetings called to support the embattled superintendent.[19]

Three newspapers criticized the attacks on Martindale and provided additional evidence of the complex nature of progressive educational politics. The *Detroit News,* a politically moderate paper, gave such solid support to Martindale that Laura Osborn called the *News* "the school board organ." Yet James Scripps, editor of the *News,* was a founder of the Municipal League and Scripps supported at-large school board elections.[20] The *News*, however, was bitterly opposed to the tactics of the reformers and the paper routinely denounced them in many of the same terms that the reformers used for the board, accusing them of lies, obfuscation, and misrepresentation. The stand taken by the *News* may have had as much to do with personalities as politics, since Scripps intensely disliked Anthony Pratt, who had succeeded Delos Wilcox as the executive secretary of the Municipal League. The *News* repeatedly accused Pratt of employing unscrupulous tactics in the school reform campaign, and it pointed out that as long as the key issue was the character of school leaders, the league needed to get its own house in order before attacking the school board.[21]

The *News* was the only pro-Martindale daily, but two weeklies, *Detroit Saturday Night* and the *Little Stick,* also routinely denounced the Municipal League and blasted its campaign tactics. *Saturday Night,* a paper that appealed to the city's upper-income groups, supported the concept of a small school board, but the paper ran lengthy articles detailing the duplicity of the reformers in seeking that goal. The *Little Stick,* a generally proreform paper, was also no friend of the large board of education, but it directed particular venom at the Municipal League, which it called a "fake reform body" led by a group of "self-seeking hypocrites."[22]

Although deeply committed to the public schools, the fledgling labor movement of Detroit remained on the outskirts of this conflict with an attitude of "a plague on both their houses." The *Michigan Union Advocate,* the official voice of the Michigan Federation of Labor, suspected the intentions of the reformers because several reform leaders were also active in the open-shop movement. The paper editorialized that if the reformers gained control of the board they would employ nonunion workers in school construction. The unions were not pro-Martindale, however, since at least one open-shop advocate also supported the superintendent. In the 1909 school board election, for example, the *Union Advocate* urged labor to vote for the Socialist candidates rather than support men pledged to either the pro- or anti-Martindale factions.[23]

With the unions sitting on the sidelines and the Socialists too weak to have a significant impact on the outcome of the election, class conflict in this contest generally pitted upper-class reformers against middle-class office-holders. Early on, the reformers set the tone of the debate by defining the issue of school governance in terms of the character of the men who ran the schools. The reformers sought to remove men who, they claimed, were morally unfit to guide the young and to replace them with men of "high quality." As the rector of St. Paul's Episcopal Church declared, "Next to our religion, our educational system is the most sacred thing we have. And yet it is possible for men who have not the slightest conception of the responsibility that rests upon them as school inspectors—men who are nothing more than ward heelers, cheap politicians, and saloon keepers—to sit on the board of education and say how our schools shall be conducted." The reformers routinely appealed to the voters to elect instead men of "fine sympathies" or, as reform leader Samuel Mumford put it, "big and better men."[24]

These sentiments also reveal the nativist bias of many of the reformers. Throughout the country, the temperance issue and school reform often cloaked anti-immigrant sentiments.[25] Detroit was no exception to that pattern. Nothing better underscores these underlying attitudes than the zeal of the reformers in the Treppa incident, where their target was a Polish principal of a largely Polish night school. After failing to get the board to fire Treppa, one reformer noted that this appointment highlighted the desperate need to get the "best" men to lead the schools, because only such men could be proper American role models for the immigrants. Another reformer chided the Polish citizens of Detroit, telling them that supporting such a man as a night school principal was not in "the best interests of the Polish people."[26] But when one of Treppa's defenders tried to point out that, "It is our duty as Americans to get the aliens into the schools [and] Mr. Treppa has shown that he can get them there," the reformers responded with disgust.[27]

The reformers' obsession with character demands the qualification of one widely held interpretation of Progressive era educational reform. David Tyack and Elisabeth Hansot argue that this era saw a fundamental shift in the nature of school leadership as the "aristocra[ts] of character" of the nineteenth century were replaced by the "social engineers" of the early twentieth century.[28] The controversies in Detroit seem more suited to the nineteenth century than twentieth, since educational reform in Detroit turned almost entirely on questions of virtue and venality, not efficiency or social engineering. Indeed, reformers and antireformers in Detroit supported all the educational innovations geared toward creating a modern, "socially efficient" school system. One of the supreme ironies of the battle over school governance in Detroit was that Wales Martindale and the ward-based board of education introduced "progressive education" to the city.

While the reformers hurled allegations of autocracy, corruption, and mismanagement at Martindale, his defenders pointed to a dramatic record of educational reform and innovation. Martindale became superintendent of the Detroit schools in 1897, having served previously as principal of one of the city high schools. No more than a high school graduate himself, Martindale was vulnerable to the attacks of the reformers that he lacked the necessary educational qualifications to lead a modern school system.[29] Yet Martindale had an almost unerring eye for both modern innovations and for talented individuals to implement them. During his fifteen years as superintendent, Martindale introduced key elements of the progressive educational agenda, including child-study, a more child-centered curriculum, expansion of the secondary curriculum, vocational education, and standardized testing. Specifically, Martindale implemented playgrounds, kindergartens, summer schools, a committee for child study, annual age-grade surveys, and programs for crippled, blind, and mentally retarded children. He supervised a revision of the English curriculum, bringing greater relevance and efficiency into the English classroom by separating the teaching of composition from that of literature and stressing oral communication and dramatics. He changed basic approaches to arithmetic by including commercial math in the eighth grade curriculum as a means of encouraging children to stay in school.[30]

Martindale also broadened the high school curriculum by adding courses in manual and vocational training and physical education. Edwin L. Miller, who became a nationally renowned advocate of the differentiated high school curriculum, justified these changes in decidedly progressive terms, citing them as evidence of greater equality of educational opportunity. "The object of public education," he stated in 1911, "is not to produce an intellectual aristocracy, but to train the community as a whole in such a way that the largest possible number of individuals shall be raised to higher levels of efficiency and happiness." By that year, Central High School offered courses in pattern making, forging, machine shop, domestic science, and laundry work.[31] Martindale also expanded the Detroit vocational program with the creation of a commercial high school and, under his auspices, construction began on Cass Technical High School, which was destined to become the "jewel in the crown" of the system's vocational program. In addition, during these years, schools were increasingly used for evening and weekend community centers and the system greatly expanded its evening program, intended primarily to Americanize immigrants.[32]

Martindale also introduced standardized testing to the Detroit schools. In 1910, he sent two Detroit teachers to study with H. H. Goddard, who had pioneered the use of the Binet intelligence tests in the United States. These teachers returned to Detroit and, under Martindale's supervision, set up a psychological clinic for the school system.[33] Martindale also hired Stuart A.

Courtis, a prominent Detroit educator who went on to become a nationally renowned figure in the standardized testing movement. Courtis increased the use of the Binet-Simon intelligence tests in Detroit schools, introduced a battery of his own arithmetic achievement tests, and modernized the teacher training program for the city schools by teaching the techniques of "scientific pedagogy" in the Detroit Normal School.[34] In addition to Courtis, Martindale also hired a number of individuals who would play a central role in establishing Detroit's reputation for efficient and scientific educational practices. These included Charles Spain, David Mackenzie, John F. Thomas, Byron Rivet, and Edwin L. Miller.[35]

The commitment of Martindale and the members of the large board to innovative educational policies and practices challenges two important assumptions historians currently hold about educational progressivism. The first concerns the identity of the "real" progressives, and the second concerns the timing of pedagogical reform in relation to changes in school governance. The typical historical interpretation of progressive educational reform maintains that, in most American cities, a clearly identifiable group of elite, business-oriented reformers wrested control of the schools from ward-based boards of education and swiftly implemented the key elements of the progressive educational agenda.[36] Events in Detroit challenge this interpretation because both the elite reformers and their ward-based opponents were "progressive" on educational policy and practice. The ward-based board of education introduced all the basic elements of educational progressivism *before* the elite reformers either achieved a majority on the board or reduced its size.

Detroit offers a more complex picture of progressive reform because both sides in the conflict agreed on specific policies and practices of the progressive educational agenda but differed on the nature of the leaders and on the form of school governance required for implementing and overseeing that agenda. As David Plank has cogently argued, support for one element of progressive reform, such as changes in pedagogic practice, does not necessarily imply support for other elements of reform, such as changes in school governance.[37] The conflict in Detroit centered almost entirely on who should rule, not on specific policies or practices. As the *Detroit News* noted, "[The reformers] stood before the people as advocates of nothing beyond what the school board has always stood for. They advanced no plan, they advocated no new departure."[38] Perhaps nothing points more surely to the widespread agreement about the pedagogic changes introduced by Martindale than the fact that, during this period, the city's unions and the Board of Commerce both applauded the "progressive" character of the Detroit schools.[39] Beneath the raging political controversy over Martindale and the ward-based board, there was a bedrock of consensus about the nature and direction of educational policy and practice in the city.

Sober Reformers versus the Saturated Machine

"Scandal," the *Little Stick* shrewdly observed, "is the food of any self-righteous organization such as the Municipal League."[40] Indeed, allegations of scandal *were* the basis for the reform campaign in Detroit. In the two most crucial school board elections, held in 1909 and 1911, cries of "boss rule," "corruption," and "mismanagement" resounded as the reformers tried to capture enough seats to deny Martindale another three-year term as superintendent. In both elections, the reformers built their campaign on allegations that Martindale ran a corrupt political machine tied to the liquor dealers of the city and that the machine was cheating the people in the purchase of textbooks.

The appointment of Ralph Treppa in 1907 had given the reformers an issue and had broadened the political base of the reform coalition by drawing in temperance advocates. Unfortunately for the reformers, the Treppa incident came too late to influence the 1907 school election, but the reformers kept the incident in the public eye for the next two years. In 1908, for example, Laura Osborn and Clarence Burton reminded Detroiters of the Treppa appointment as they launched a campaign to fire another educator that they charged was tainted by the liquor interests, in this case an Italian night school teacher who worked days as a bookkeeper in a brewery.[41]

As the 1909 school board election drew near, reformers redoubled their attacks against the "saturated" school machine. Reporting on the Republican primary for school board candidates, the *Detroit Times* noted that "the better people, the business and professional people and the thoughtful workingmen" favored the reformers while "the Martindale faction has uniformly made a saloon campaign and its dependence lies in the votes of those who can be swayed by prejudice or ignorance or by the influence of patronage."[42] Unintentionally substantiating that charge several weeks later, supporters of one pro-Martindale board member showed up at a saloon and announced, "Mr. Miehm is going to buy everybody a drink. He wants you to vote for him April 6." Customers cheered as they surged toward the bar, one yelling "Miehm's as good as elected now if he keeps this up."[43]

The reformers had no doubt that a nefarious organization known as the Voteswappers League was behind this saloon campaign. The Voteswappers

League was a bipartisan group of precinct bosses who stole elections in exchange for graft and payoffs. Many of these precinct bosses were saloon-keepers or bartenders who sported such colorful nicknames as "Squangee" Rosenberg, "Mose" Jacobs, "Batty" McGraw, and Billy "Boushaw" Bouchard. All of them were closely tied to the Royal Ark, the association of Detroit liquor dealers. The reformers routinely charged that only the manipulation of the Voteswappers League kept Martindale in power.[44] They alleged that, in exchange for rigging the election of pro-Martindale school board members, the superintendent gave the precinct bosses patronage jobs within the school system. Moreover, the reformers claimed, the power of the Martindale "ring" went all the way to the state capitol. There, the superintendent's brother, Frederick C. Martindale, used his position as secretary of state to quash every attempt in the legislature to abolish the ward-based system and to ensure that "any legislation favorable to the Board [goes] through without a halt."[45]

The truth of all these allegations is hard to determine. Certainly, vote fraud was common, and the Voteswappers League did steal elections in Detroit. Some school board members were saloonkeepers, some campaigned in saloons, and these campaigns were often raucous and indecorous. In addition, some school board members got jobs for friends and relatives and violated proper procedures in the process. Indeed, in 1906, a board member was arrested for accepting bribes for janitorial positions.[46] Yet a conspiracy linking the Voteswappers League, saloon politics, corruption in the school system, and a statewide political machine is more difficult to find. The statements of the reformers, particularly those of the Municipal League, were supported more by innuendo than by fact. The only independent inquiry into the school board during this era, a three-month grand jury investigation in 1908 into charges of corruption and malfeasance brought by Hiram Goldberg and Clarence Burton, totally exonerated the board and castigated the reformers. Following the investigation, the prosecuting attorney declared, "The gravest and most serious charges came from them [Burton and Goldberg] with a freedom that, considering the groundlessness of the accusation, was abhorrent and shocking to the sense of justice."[47]

Like the allegations of widespread corruption and boss rule, the other great issue of these campaigns, textbook purchasing, was also based on questionable evidence. The reformers, however, had good reason to believe that claims of impropriety in regard to book purchases could be an effective political tool. In Grand Rapids, the successful 1905 reform campaign centered on accusations that antireform school board members had accepted bribes and payoffs from the American Book Company.[48] Indeed, Delos Wilcox, who had masterminded the Grand Rapids reform effort as executive secretary of the Municipal League, specifically urged his successor, Anthony Pratt, to look for "any positive scandal . . . involving corruption in connection with the American Book Company" in order to oust Martindale and his "coterie."[49]

On the eve of the school board elections, Laura Osborn made just such an allegation, announcing that Detroit was paying 20 percent more for its textbooks than Cleveland. In a front page article, the *Detroit Journal* applauded Osborn's "sensational discovery" and accused the school board of mismanaging textbook purchases and wasting thousands of taxpayer dollars annually. Hinting at a still larger conspiracy of corrupt textbook companies and liquor dealers, the reformers pointed out that Anthony Treppa was chairman of the board's textbook committee.[50] These allegations, like so many made by the reformers, were based on ad hominem arguments, half-truths, and innuendos. The *Detroit News* countered the *Journal*'s accusation by pointing out that Cleveland paid less for its textbooks because Ohio law mandated that school boards pay no more than 75 percent of list price for all books. In addition, the *News* argued that, despite the law, Detroit actually paid less than Cleveland for its elementary school texts.[51]

Unswayed by these arguments, the reformers reiterated their charges right up to election day. The voters, however, were unconvinced. Despite strenuous efforts by Laura Osborn, the activist women of the DFWC, the Municipal League, and even with police watching for vote fraud at several polling places, the pro-Martindale forces retained a slim majority on the board. The reformers *did* score some notable victories, particularly defeating Anthony Treppa, but they failed in their ultimate mission of electing enough board members to deny Wales Martindale another three-year term.[52]

In assessing the election, Laura Osborn had no doubt about what went wrong. Writing to William McAndrew, who, the reformers hoped, would replace Martindale as head of the Detroit schools, Osborn attributed the outcome of the election to the strength of the "foreign and liquor element" in several key wards. She was particularly exorcised at the "betrayal" of an anti-Martindale candidate who had run with the backing of the Municipal League but who later switched his vote in favor of retaining the superintendent. Here, Osborn saw the dirty hand of the "ring" manipulating behind the scenes. As she revealingly put it, "A roll top desk and other considerations caused a Pollack we elected to vote for Martindale."[53]

Over the next two years, the reformers marshaled their forces, refined their tactics, and determined to make that appointment of Martindale his last. They reminded voters of the Treppa incident at every opportunity and continued to smear Martindale with claims that he was "Saturated with Cheap Politics."[54] Late in 1909, Laura Osborn again raised the question of the moral fitness of the board members after a brewer spoke against prohibition to students at Detroit Central High School. Neatly tying the brewer to the "saturated" school board, Osborn declared that the speech at Central was the "boldest and last attempt of the liquor element to force its way into our households, take our children out of our hands and educate them to the support of the saloon."[55] Beyond pressing the liquor issue, the reformers also redoubled their efforts to paint the Martindale "machine" as fiscally irresponsible and guilty of gross mismanagement. Perhaps their most important tactical decision was to use their considerable financial resources to determine the issues and spread their message.

The issue that dominated the 1911 school board election was the cost of textbooks. As the campaign began in March, Laura Osborn announced that, since Martindale took office, the board had overpaid more than $50,000 for textbooks. She pointed specifically to a crucial vote on January 27, 1910, in which the Martindale "ring" showed its true colors by defeating a measure that would have cut the cost of book purchases.[56] In this campaign, Osborn directly accused the pro-Martindale board members of collusion with the American Book Company. Strengthening this accusation, the reformers invoked the specter of Anthony Treppa, the former chairman of the textbook committee, alleging that the "Polish saloonkeeper" was a central figure in the collusion.[57]

These accusations were virtually the same as those in the 1909 campaign, yet the manner in which they were publicized was markedly different. As the primary elections approached, the Municipal League ran a series of full-page advertisements in the *Free Press,* the *Journal,* the *News,* and the *Times.* These ads stood out dramatically under the headline "Voters, Attention" and recalled both the appointment of the "saloonkeeper Treppa" and Osborn's charges about overpayment for texts. The ads highlighted the January 27th vote on textbooks, listing the men who voted for cheaper books and those who opposed them.[58]

These advertisements were a brilliant political stroke but they were also part of a deliberate campaign of distortion. Just prior to the general election, *Detroit Saturday Night* ran a long, angry analysis of the textbook controversy. *Saturday Night* found that, from September, 1909, to September, 1910, every important vote on textbook purchases had been unanimous except for the one on January 27, 1910. Indeed, the resolution passed by the board in September, 1910, was precisely in line with what the reformers had been seeking since it enabled the board to purchase textbooks directly from publishers (thus reducing the cost). Nevertheless, soon after the board passed that resolution, the city's assistant corporation counsel informed the members that the board could only act on it if the school system had "funds which can be made or are available." Four months later, at the "fateful" January 27th meeting, Clarence Burton moved that the board spend $12,000 that it *did not have on hand* to purchase the books. In accord with the city attorney's opinion, six inspectors voted against the motion and defeated it. *That* vote was the basis of the Municipal League's massive advertising campaign. The League failed to note that two weeks later, when the board had sufficient funds, the same resolution passed unanimously.[59] In other words, every school board member voted for purchasing cheaper textbooks. The only disagreement among them was over fiscal responsibility, and clearly, in this case, it was the Martindale faction that acted responsibly. In a bitter editorial, the *Little Stick* denounced the campaign of distortion by the League saying, "Where there is nothing of a grave or serious nature to be dug up much must be made of little things."[60]

Such charges notwithstanding, the reformers hammered their opponents with allegations that the Martindale machine was responsible for gross fiscal mismanagement. Their particular electoral target in 1911 was the school board president, Dr. Charles Kuhn. Ironically, in many ways, Kuhn was a model progressive reformer, at least in terms of the curricular and programmatic changes that he espoused. Kuhn was "a leading physician and surgeon" in Detroit as well as the founder of the city's Samaritan Hospital.[61] His interest in education arose out of his commitment to children's health, and Kuhn used his position as board president to push for a broad agenda of reforms, including a civil service–style examination for school engineers and janitors to eliminate patronage, programs to make teachers more conscious of children's health problems, the expansion of playgrounds, the introduction of public baths, the use of schools in the fight against juvenile delinquency, the replacement of bolt-down desks with moveable classroom furniture, and the creation of a department of special education within the school system.[62] Although he was elected to the board in 1907 as an independent, Kuhn eventually supported the embattled superintendent, thus earning the enmity of the Municipal League and its allies. The reformers focused much of their campaign on Kuhn, linking him to the textbook "scandal" and ridiculing him in their newspaper advertisements as "a little waif, snared by stronger hands and helpless in the grasp of stronger intellects." Members of the Twentieth Century Club went door-to-door in Kuhn's ward urging voters to defeat him. Kuhn doggedly tried to defend his record against these attacks, arguing that, like all the other inspectors, he had voted for cheaper textbooks. Yet Kuhn's responses and those of his defenders were often relegated to the letters to the editor section of the *News*, a far cry from dramatic, full-page ads demanding "Voters, Attention!"[63]

By far the most important incident of seemingly underhanded politics in the campaign was the ban against women voting in the primary elections. After the 1909 board election, the legislature revised the state election law and barred women from voting in primaries. This was a serious blow to the reformers because, during these years, the Republican party so thoroughly dominated politics in Detroit that the primary elections held the key to control of the school board. Reformers saw the revised law as clear evidence of "ring" manipulation of the state legislature since the change had disenfranchised a large anti-Martindale constituency. On the eve of the primaries, as efforts to lift the ban against women voters by emergency legislation bogged down in the legislature, Laura Osborn declared, "A certain dominating political machine, having statewide influence, has deemed it not to its interest that the women be permitted to vote at school elections in Detroit, and it has blocked every effort in the present legislature to correct, by an emergency law, the defects in the primary law."[64] Whether the "ring" actually orchestrated these events in Lansing is impossible to say, but the perception of dirty politics was overwhelming. Even the pro-Martindale *Detroit News* denounced the ban on women voters.[65]

Outrage over the disenfranchisement of women voters apparently worked to the advantage of the reformers. Even without the women and despite claims of vote fraud, the anti-Martindale forces defeated Charles Kuhn and placed six out of eight of their candidates on the ballot.[66] The reformers were jubilant, sensing that victory over Martindale was within their grasp. Yet the general election did not prove to be the easy triumph that the reformers had expected. The pro-Martindale forces threw their weight behind several Democratic candidates, making the normally one-sided general election a real contest. Indeed, the races were so close in several wards that, in the first few days after the election, it appeared that Martindale had retained his hold on the board. When the results of several recounts came in, however, the anti-Martindale faction emerged with a two-vote majority and the superintendent's days were numbered. Martindale's contract expired on July 1, 1912. Less than two weeks later, the board voted 10 to 8 to fire him.[67]

While the reformers had achieved one of their primary goals, it was a costly victory. The tactics used by the Municipal League angered even some of its most prominent supporters. Following the general election, the *Detroit Journal* declared,

> The campaign conducted by Pratt in the name of the league and the reputable and excellent citizens who maintain the league was one of the most irritating that this community has ever seen. Where Pratt did not resort to brazen falsehoods he gave out half truths still more insidious and cowardly. . . . In the abused name of "reform," Secretary Pratt and his assistants in this campaign have established a new record for personalities, crude deception and deliberate misrepresentation. His astounding unfairness brought about the inevitable revulsion of popular sentiment. Pratt drove from the Municipal League voters who would have been its friends and friends of the cause which he pretended to represent.[68]

In addition to these complaints, some members of the Detroit Federation of Women's Clubs denounced Laura Osborn for using the organization for what they claimed were her own "partisan" purposes. Such criticism of the Municipal League and one of its staunchest allies undoubtedly played a role in its demise the following year.[69] In essence, the battle between the League and Martindale destroyed them both.

The firing of Martindale and the passing of the Municipal League marked the closing of an era in Detroit educational politics. Never again would character assassination, blatant distortion, and charges of vote fraud so dominate a school board election. While controversy continued over the second major goal of the reformers, the creation of a small, at-large board of education, the overall direction of educational politics in Detroit was toward consensus, not only on policy and practice but on governance issues as well.

The Administration of Superintendent Charles Chadsey

In many ways, the second phase of the reform campaign in Detroit, the establishment of a small, at-large board of education was anticlimactic compared to the battles over Wales Martindale. Dr. Charles Chadsey, whom the board chose as the new superintendent, generated far less political controversy than did his predecessor. During the seven years Chadsey served in Detroit, school politics lost much of its razor edge, although the reformers continued to make allegations of corruption and malfeasance. Despite the ongoing battles over school reform, Chadsey eventually proved to be popular with both factions. As George Condon, a leader of the "regulars" (as the press now termed the antireform bloc on the board), stated in 1914, he and Samuel Mumford, one of the reform leaders, "are worshippers at the same synagogue so far as being friends of Superintendent Chadsey."[70] Maintaining such amicable relations with both sides of the school reform controversy proved to be crucial for Chadsey during the first four years of his administration. In April, 1913, the reformers lost all but seven of their seats on the board and the "regulars" once again returned to power.[71]

Chadsey's willingness to work with both sides of the reform controversy in no way sullied his credentials as the very model of a modern urban school superintendent. An apolitical educational expert, Chadsey was a charter member of what Tyack and Hansot describe as the "Educational Trust," an informal network of university professors and school superintendents who dominated educational policy-making in the Progressive era. Chadsey was a "protégé of George Strayer," had a master's degree from Stanford, a Ph.D. from Columbia's Teachers College, and, prior to coming to Detroit, had been superintendent of the Denver Public Schools.[72]

Upon arriving in Detroit, Chadsey praised the accomplishments of Martindale and set out to build upon the foundation that the former superintendent had constructed. Chadsey focused on three important Martindale initiatives: accommodating the growing enrollment through structural and curricular reform; expanding programs of special education, especially night schools; and increasing the use of standardized tests and measurement.[73] As in the Martindale era, wrangling between the school board, the city council, and the board of estimate was a constant source of frustration for school leaders. Dr. Albert McMichael, a prominent local Republican who served as board president from 1913 to 1916 and was a leader of the regulars, repeatedly complained that the city was underfunding the schools despite the clear evidence about serious shortages of buildings and classrooms. Compounding the problem of limited resources was a soaring enrollment that outpaced any previous period. Between 1911 and 1917, enrollments in regular kindergarten through twelfth grade climbed from 50,105 to 91,790. Between September, 1914, and September, 1916, alone, the board had to increase the number of classes on half-day sessions from 154 to 289.[74]

Half-day sessions, however, were merely a stop-gap approach to the larger problem of insufficient numbers of classrooms and teachers. In addressing that problem, Chadsey implemented several structural and curricular changes. He began dismantling the 8–4 system—eight years of elementary school and four years of high school—introducing instead a 6–6 system in order to provide more classrooms at the elementary level, where the enrollment pressure was the greatest.[75] In addition, in order to use both staff and buildings more efficiently on the elementary level, Chadsey pioneered the use of the platoon school system in Detroit. This innovation, a variation of William Wirt's Gary plan, will be discussed in considerable detail in the next chapter. For now, suffice it to say that in 1918, under the direction of Charles Spain, Detroit began what would become the most extensive use of the Gary plan of any school system in the nation.[76]

Special education in Detroit also took a distinctive turn during the Chadsey administration. The number of classes for blind, deaf, incorrigible, "backward," and gifted children greatly increased. The most noticeable effort in this area, however, was in adult education, particularly the Americanization program. As early as 1904, Detroit school officials reported that several immigrant communities had requested evening schools for English and citizenship instruction. In response, Martindale substantially increased the number of night school classes for adult immigrants. During the Chadsey years, however, the Detroit evening school program expanded even more dramatically. Frank Cody, a former school superintendent whose district had been annexed by Detroit, supervised the Americanization program, which eventually became a model for many other cities.[77]

Two features stand out in this expansion of the Americanization program under Chadsey and Cody. First, the school system ended the practice of hiring teachers from the immigrant communities to teach the Americanization courses. Instead of continuing to hire Americanization teachers from the ethnic communities, Chadsey sought "to place wide-awake, socially efficient American instructors in charge of these rooms."[78] Second, school officials worked closely with the major employers of the city in developing the program. In 1915, members of the education committee of the Board of Commerce, the mayor, and school officials formed the Detroit Americanization Committee to promote learning the English language and the rights and responsibilities of American citizenship. Chadsey quickly doubled the appropriation for Americanization night schools, and employers urged, sometimes forced, their workers to take advantage of the classes. Evening teachers received special training in working with adults, and school leaders prepared a new course of study to facilitate English instruction. School leaders coordinated the work of the evening schools with that of federal naturalization authorities. The results of these efforts were spectacular. Between 1912 and

1922, participation in Americanization classes jumped from 3,000 to 27,000 students.[79] It is worth noting that most of these changes were introduced by the ward-based board during the period in which the regulars held a majority of seats.

As with the curricular and programmatic reforms initiated by Martindale, neither the introduction of platoon schools nor the Americanization program generated much controversy in Detroit.[80] The increased use of standardized testing, however, set off a long, bitter struggle between teachers and the Chadsey administration. In his last report to the school board, Martindale recommended that the Courtis efficiency tests be used far more extensively than they had been and on both the elementary and high school levels. In 1914, Chadsey followed up on that recommendation appointing Courtis as director of the newly created Department of Educational Research with the expressed purpose of implementing his testing program on a wide scale. Courtis immediately sparked controversy by introducing standardized achievement tests to measure the "efficiency" of teachers. Teachers balked at the tests because they feared the results would be used as "a rating of their teaching ability."[81]

Such battles between proponents of the "scientific management" of education and teachers were quite common in the Progressive era. Historians have often described these struggles as examples of elite reformers using the methods of major corporations to strip teachers of what limited autonomy they had maintained under the ward-based systems.[82] In Detroit, the controversy about the use of standardized tests as a measure of teacher effectiveness seems to fit nicely into that argument. Yet three developments in Detroit argue for considerable refinement of that interpretation. First, the Courtis efficiency tests were introduced and heartily endorsed by the archenemy of the centralizers, Wales Martindale. Second, between 1913 and 1916, when most of the controversy about Courtis and achievement tests took place, the board of education was controlled by the "regulars," not the reformers. In other words, an antireform superintendent and a ward-based board largely composed of middle-class officeholders implemented and expanded the use of standardized tests to insure teacher accountability.

Third, teachers responded to these demands for greater accountability by pressuring the board to fire Stuart Courtis and, failing that, by supporting the use of IQ tests rather than achievement tests to guide instruction.[83] In his study of the development of the testing movement in Detroit, Stephen Williams found that many teachers opposed the Courtis achievement tests because these tests assumed that *teachers* were primarily responsible for student performance. The achievement tests demanded a form of accountability that the teachers were unwilling to accept. This resistance to achievement tests gives a curious twist to the interpretive debate regarding teacher autonomy, because eventually many Detroit teachers enthusiastically supported the mass use of IQ tests in order to protect their positions. Unlike achievement tests, IQ tests placed the responsibility for learning either on students or on school administrators. Put simply, with IQ tests, teachers could attribute poor student performance either to "defective genes" or to improper academic placement rather than on poor teaching. While the debate over whether IQ tests or achievement tests should guide school policy and practice continued for nearly two decades in Detroit, it is important to recognize that many teachers sided with the advocates of IQ testing.[84]

The Triumph of Reform

By 1913, the locus of debate over school governance in Detroit had shifted to the state capitol in Lansing. The loss of control of the school board in the April election spurred the reformers in their effort to create a governance structure that would break the power of the "regulars" once and for all. In the subdued confines of the state legislature, the reformers proved that they could use their status and influence more effectively than they had in the turbulent wards and precincts of Detroit. Laura Osborn continued to lead the drive for school board reform, holding the anti-Martindale coalition together in the battle to enact a law abolishing the ward-based board.[85]

In addition to Osborn, three other players on the political stage, Samuel Mumford, Alan S. Whitney, and the Detroit Citizens League, were crucial in this phase of the reform effort. Mumford was an executive with Detroit Edison and a member of the city's social elite. While he had been elected to the Detroit school board in 1907, he did not emerge as one of the main reform leaders until several years later.[86] Whitney was a professor of education at the University of Michigan who had been advising Osborn and other reformers for several years. A trusted ally in the battle for the small board, Whitney became the principal architect and chief Lansing lobbyist for the reform legislation. Late in 1912, Whitney began work on the small board bill, submitting drafts to Osborn, the president of the Grand Rapids board of education, and the Michigan attorney general. The final version of the bill called for a seven-member board to be elected in at-large, nonpartisan elections. In addition, the bill mandated staggered six-year terms for board members, a provision that would make changes in board membership possible but gradual, since no more than three board members would ever be up for election at one time. After ironing out final provisions of the bill with members of the Board of Commerce and the Twentieth Century Club, state senator George G. Scott introduced the bill early in April, 1913. Throughout the legislative session, Whitney regularly traveled from Ann Arbor to Lansing, shepherding the legislation through the House and Senate, securing strong backing from the governor, and orchestrating meetings and rallies. In late April, 1913, his work bore fruit as the legislature approved the Scott bill.[87]

Celebration by the reformers was shortlived, however. Over the next three years, opponents of the small board delayed the implementation of the Scott law through a series of court challenges and, in 1915, they nullified the law by passing an entirely new bill that created a seven-member, partisan board, elected from districts rather than wards. The controversy over that bill provides additional evidence for eschewing a simple form of class analysis for explaining events in Detroit. An "ardent supporter" of the district plan was James Veech Oxtoby, a leading businessman and attorney. As vice president and counsel of Detroit Edison, Oxtoby certainly clashed with fellow Detroit Edison executive Samuel Mumford over this issue. Indeed, such powerful opposition to the at-large plan spurred Osborn and a "train load" of club women to converge on Lansing to convince the governor to veto the measure. The governor cast the veto and the state senate sustained it, thus killing the district representation plan and reinstating the Scott law.[88] But even that effort did not get the Scott law implemented. The court challenges continued for another year, and, when the last of these challenges was exhausted, the law still faced a citywide referendum that opponents of the change had added to the original measure.[89]

The referendum on abolishing the ward-based board of education was an important concession to the opponents of reform. In such cities as New York, Chicago, and even in nearby Grand Rapids, state legislatures had simply abolished the ward system without giving local voters any chance to approve or reject the change.[90] Thus, Detroit offers an excellent opportunity to see how voters responded to these proposed changes when they did have the chance to cast a ballot.[91]

To some extent, the fate of the referendum was shaped by the actions of another new player on the political stage, the Detroit Citizens League. The Citizens League arose in 1912 out of the ashes of the Municipal League. Like the Municipal League, the Citizens League began as a "Protestant men's club" led by ministers and businessmen, including Henry Leland, S. S. Kresge, and Divie B. Duffield. Also, like the Municipal League, the Citizens

League viewed the power of the liquor interests as the most serious political problem in Detroit. In several key areas, however, the Citizens League differed from its predecessor. Most important, Pliny Marsh, the executive director of the Citizens League, recognized that moral indignation was no substitute for effective political organization. Thus, Marsh concentrated on broadening the base of the Citizens League to include individuals from a wide range of social classes and creating ward and precinct organizations based in Protestant churches to directly challenge the Voteswappers League.[92]

The most important early achievement of the Citizens League was on the state level. In 1915, after heavy pressure from the Citizens League, the legislature passed the Scott-Flowers "Honest Election" law, which permitted nonpartisan challengers to monitor activities at every polling place, restricted "aid" to voters in the polling place only to people who did not speak English or were physically handicapped, and provided for the prosecution of corrupt election officials. The law was crucial for school reform, because it broke the power of the precinct bosses and provided for clean elections just as the referendum on the small board was coming to a vote in November, 1916.[93]

From August, when the last of the judicial decisions on the Scott school board law was handed down, to election day in November, the reformers marshaled their considerable resources and energies to convince Detroiters of the benefits of a small, nonpartisan board of education. Laura Osborn and Samuel Mumford spearheaded the campaign, writing letters, answering the charges of the opposition, and exhorting the faithful at meetings and rallies. The women of the Twentieth Century Club and Detroit Federation of Women's Clubs served as the foot soldiers of the campaign, circulating thousands of handbills and brochures prior to election day. They were supported by the Detroit Pastors Union, the Board of Commerce, the Wayne County Equal Suffrage Association, the Federation of Civic Societies of Detroit, the Michigan State Teachers Association, the Michigan City Superintendents Association, and the Association of City Boards of Education. Charles Chadsey, though less vocal than the other partisans, endorsed the changes, as did numerous business and civic leaders such as Henry Ford. Every major daily newspaper supported the small board, including the *Detroit News*.[94]

Unlike the campaign against Martindale, the campaign for the small board dealt more with issues than with personalities. While the reformers still labeled the large board a tool of the American Book Company and a breeding ground of "dirty ward politics," these accusations tended to be less shrill and less specific than in the earlier struggle.[95] Two arguments dominated the 1916 campaign. Pointing to the enormous problems facing the Detroit schools, the reformers declared that the large board had shown itself incapable of providing enough buildings, classrooms, and teachers for the children of the city. They claimed that the small board would run the schools more efficiently, equitably, and honestly than the large board ever could. On the other side of the issue, supporters of the ward-based board argued that the at-large, nonpartisan election would hand power over to an unrepresentative elite.

In many ways, the reformers presented a textbook case for the at-large board. They argued that the school system was a great public business that should be run on business principles. They wanted the small, at-large board to be "similar to the board of directors of a large corporation." Because the small board would be "merely legislative, advisory and supervisory in function" nearly all the standing committees of the large board, which were responsible for most of the work and, the reformers added, most of the corruption, would be eliminated. Finally, they planned to delegate the day-to-day operation of the school system to a qualified educational expert, the superintendent of schools. Each of these changes, the reformers claimed, would enable the schools to run more efficiently and more equitably.[96]

Inextricably linked to the reformers' promise of greater efficiency and equity was their belief that the small board would be free from corruption and political manipulation. Politics, Laura Osborn declared, "is the great evil of the present ward system" because political deals and favors rather than educational considerations shaped school policy.[97] The reformers denounced the ward system not only because it encouraged school inspectors to serve their wards at the expense of the city, but, worse, it encouraged them to serve their political organizations better than the children of the wards. As the *Detroit News* put it, "[the ward-based] school inspector does not represent the people of his ward. Rather, he represents the teachers, janitors, and engineers whom he befriends, and who need his political influence. It is high time that the schools ceased to run in the interests of the teachers, janitors, and engineers, and were put in charge of a board that will see they are run for the children." The rallying cry of the reformers, publicized on thousands of pamphlets, trumpeted "Children First: The Schools Out of Politics—Politics Out of the Schools."[98]

Defenders of the ward-based board, largely incumbent school inspectors, countered these arguments by claiming that the great benefit of the ward system was precisely the proximity of the board members to the people.

While the advocates of the at-large system argued that it would result in greater equity and efficiency for the city schools, backers of the ward-based board claimed that precisely the opposite would be true. On returning from a fact-finding trip to St. Louis to assess the effects of the small, at-large board in that city, Albert Kunz, one of the leading opponents of reform, announced that the St. Louis schools were "languishing" because the school board members were not personally involved in the management of the schools. "School commissioners elected at large," he declared, "cannot give personal attention to the needs of all the sections of the city as can the board elected under the ward system."[99]

Moreover, the proponents of the ward system argued that the small board would silence the voice of the people in setting school policy.[100] As Dr. Charles Kuhn put it several years earlier, "The congested condition of the schools in the different sections of the city, and the ever changing population require constant wisdom and forethought, therefore I believe the Ward representatives, keeping in close touch with the needs of the children in their respective districts are able to render the best service." [101] Proponents of the ward system argued that this diversity was precisely what the reformers wished to destroy. They charged that at-large elections would result in a school board dominated by people drawn entirely from exclusive parts of the city, specifically the wealthy first, second, and fourth wards.[102] Noting that wealthier people often had considerable name recognition before they entered politics and that they had the resources to conduct citywide campaigns, Albert Kunz declared, "I am opposed to the seven-man school board because I believe that the mechanic or laboring man or cattle drover should have as much representation in our governmental system as the rich man who has his name over a dry goods store or who has made his name in some profession."[103]

In making these claims, the opponents of reform may have had a sense of history. In 1880, Detroit replaced its ward-based board with a twelve-member, partisan board elected from the city at large. One of the most striking features of that at-large board was that it was dominated by professionals and businessmen. Critics argued that this experiment "proved to be a dismal failure," a fact attested to by the decision to return to the ward-based system in 1889.[104] The reformers, however, responded that the proposed board would be smaller than the 1880s version, and, as important, the new board would be nonpartisan. Moreover, they pointed out that the ward-based board that came to power in 1889 was the most corrupt in Detroit's history, the very board that Mayor Hazen Pingree "stung" in 1894, when he carted four school inspectors off to jail.[105]

Nowhere was the difficulty of choosing between the competing claims of honesty and efficiency, on the one hand, and greater diversity in school board membership, on the other, more apparent than in the stands taken by the Detroit Federation of Labor (DFL) and the Detroit Socialist party. Many socialists and union members were ambivalent about the reform effort, especially the oft-stated hope of the reformers that the new board would be dominated by businessmen and run according to business principles. But both the Socialist party and the DFL also routinely deplored the inability of the large board to provide an adequate education to the children of Detroit, noting particularly the lack of schools, overcrowded classrooms, and poor salaries paid to teachers, especially those in "working class districts."[106] These inequalities, however, were precisely what the reformers argued the small board would correct. "School facilities should be equally [sic] distributed . . . ," the reformers declared, but, under the present system, "[a] ward-elected board school inspector with strong 'pull' gets more than his share for his ward, or a clique, by vote-trading, gets the lion's share—others must get less." Only under an at-large system, the reformers claimed, would inspectors "consider the city as a whole and treat all sections alike." Caught between the deplorable conditions of the schools and the possibility of elite control, the Socialist party and the DFL, not surprisingly, took no official position on the school board issue.[107]

One leading Detroit socialist, who wrote a weekly column in the socialist weekly under the pseudonym Apropos, however, did find a way to reconcile the party's dilemma on the school issue. Apropos blasted the overcrowded conditions of Detroit's schools, blaming the situation squarely on "the inefficiency of the present large school board." The column continued, "[a]s conditions cannot be worse than they are, it would be well for us to vote for the small board amendment to the charter," adding that "the small board will be of advantage to the Socialist party when we capture political power in Detroit."[108]

The voters finally got the chance to settle the issue on November 7, 1916. In a stunning victory for the reformers, Detroiters voted 61,806 for the small board, 11,342 against it. Despite a prediction by the opponents that the measure would only pass in five wards, in fact, it received overwhelming majorities in every ward. Indeed, voters in only *one* of the 285 precincts in the city voted against the measure and there by only 10 votes. Just prior to the election, the *Detroit News* had asked rhetorically, "Where is the opposition?" The question proved to be prophetic.[109]

Not surprisingly, the measure received strong support in the "wealthy" first, second, and fourth wards where many of the reform leaders resided. But the 92 percent of the vote that these wards gave to the measure was only slightly larger than the 85 percent that it received in the seventeenth, nineteenth, and twenty-first wards, which the *Michigan Socialist* described as working-class districts. In the third and fifth wards, which had large Jewish and black communities, the measure got 85 and 78 percent, respectively. What little opposition there was to the measure came from voters in the seventh, ninth, and eleventh wards, which had large Italian and Polish populations, perhaps because some voters in these wards recalled the nativist tone of the earlier school board campaigns. Nevertheless, even in these wards, the measure received nearly 72 percent of the vote, and, in the thirteenth, sixteenth, eighteenth, and twentieth wards, which also had very sizable Polish communities, the measure got over 75 percent of the vote.[110]

A number of factors combined to bring about the lopsided victory. Ironically, the three-year delay in getting the law before the voters worked substantially to the advantage of the reformers. The November 7th voting was the first general election conducted under the provisions of the Scott-Flowers Act, a situation that insured both a high turnout among supporters of reform and scrupulous inspection of election procedures. The Citizens League, for example, assigned three challengers per precinct to watch for irregularities in this election.[111] A high turnout of reform-minded voters was also due to the presence on the ballot of a referendum to prohibit the sale of liquor in the state of Michigan. Given the strong link between school reform and prohibition, the fact that both of these referenda were on the same ballot was indeed propitious for the advocates of the small board.[112]

More important than either of these considerations, however, is the fact that the reformers had convinced the public that a small, at-large board would do a better job educating the children of the city than the ward-based board. The problems of too few buildings, overcrowded classrooms, and an inadequate number of teachers were obvious to all. The key question many voters may have asked themselves was, who is better able to manage the incredible growth of the city schools, the reformers or the regulars? People clearly had to recognize that once the bitter wrangling about school governance was over, school leaders would have to turn their attention to such basic issues as the lack of buildings and teachers. The overwhelming vote to change the system of governance reveals a profound dissatisfaction with the ward-based system and the emergence of a broad-based consensus willing to allow the reformers the chance to run the schools.[113]

The 1916 election represents more than the victory of the reformers on the issue of how school board members would be chosen in Detroit. This election signifies the emergence of a consensus regarding school governance that complemented the long-standing consensus regarding policies and practices. For the next fifteen years, opposition to the goals of expanding and improving the Detroit public schools was virtually impossible to find.

The Small Board Takes Over

While the 1916 election settled the question of how Detroit would elect its school board members, the long-running conflict about *who* should set school policy continued. The 1916 election was hardly over before interest groups started to vie for control of the small board and plan strategies for the April, 1917, election in which the new board members would be chosen. Less than two years later, in January, 1919, a second controversy over school governance broke out, focusing on the appointment of a new superintendent. Both these conflicts saw some of the old arguments about the control of schools resurface, this time, however, without the vicious political bloodletting that so dominated the earlier struggles.

The April 2, 1917, ballot listed twenty-six candidates for the new school board. On it were several members of the last large board, a black attorney, a seven-person reform slate led by Laura Osborn and Samuel Mumford, and, despite the nonpartisan mandate of the new school law, candidates backed by the Republican, Democratic, and Prohibition parties, as well as a complete slate of Socialists.[114] Coinciding as it did with the Russian Revolution and America's entry into World War I, the school board campaign was hardly the center of popular attention. Yet even if the election had taken place in a less momentous period in world history, it probably would have received scant coverage. The *Free Press* noted that fears about "bitter fighting" over school board nominations proved groundless and that the campaign was strikingly "tame."[115] Indeed, given the great diversity of the candidates, the most notable aspect of the campaign was the remarkable similarity of their stands, with nearly all stressing the need for more schools and teachers. For example, in a column urging support for the Socialist slate, Apropos argued, "There are 87,000 children attending the public schools and there is only room for 75,000, consequently 9,000 have to be content with half-day sessions and the balance are overcrowded, the teachers are overworked and the amount of supplies are inadequate for the needs of the scholars. Capitalism cares little for the schools."[116] On the other side of the class struggle, a spokesman for the Detroit Citizens League also deplored "the crisis of school conditions," noting that such things as the "[n]eeds of teachers, whom I class as martyrs to society, for salaries commensurate with the high cost of living, are causing a scarcity of teachers that makes this a crisis. . . . Our immediate need is to get the right men elected." For the Citizens League, of course, the "right men" were businessmen such as Samuel Mumford and Frank Alfred, who campaigned on the platform that the improvement of the schools lay in imitating capitalism, not abolishing it, particularly in adopting the management techniques of major corporations.[117]

The April, 1917, election proved to be as overwhelming a triumph for the reformers as the November, 1916, election had been. Every reform candidate won, making the election a virtual elite takeover of the Detroit schools. Each of the seven new board members had the endorsement of the Citizens League, each was listed in the Detroit social register, and, with the exception of Laura Osborn, each was a prominent businessman or professional. The socioeconomic status of the new board differed markedly from that of the last large board, which had had, in addition to businessmen and professionals, a number of clerks, tradesmen, and so forth. The essence of the election can be summed up simply: the only incumbent to gain a seat on the new "elite" board was Samuel Mumford, who was the only member of the large board listed in the social register.[118]

The triumph of the reformers confirmed the worst fears of small-board opponents about at-large elections resulting in elite control of the school system. The outcome of the school board election quickly became an important element in the opposition to other at-large election proposals. At year's end, on the eve of another charter election (also engineered by the Detroit Citizens League) to replace the ward-based city council with a nine-member body elected at large, some DFL leaders cited the results of the school board election as their reason for opposing the change. As one labor leader put it, "The present school board is an example of the type of mind we will have for a council if the 9-man plan carries. They are practically all people with the employers' viewpoint."[119]

Interestingly, however, DFL opposition to the at-large system of city council elections did not translate into opposition to the at-large system for electing school board members. Indeed, over the next thirty years, while the DFL actively supported every effort to abolish the at-large city council, only once, in 1928, did the *Labor News* even editorialize against the at-large system of electing school board members. In fact, as the next chapter will show, beginning in the 1920s, the DFL became one of the strongest supporters of most school board policies and practices. Thus, rather than working to abolish the at-large board, the DFL devoted most of its energy in educational politics to a long but ultimately successful effort to elect a prolabor majority on the board of education.[120]

When the newly elected board convened in July, 1917, one of the first orders of business was to change the administrative structure of the public schools. Under the ward system, committees of board members made key decisions regarding textbook purchases, courses of study, and the appointment of principals and teachers. The new board consolidated these powers in the superintendency, giving the superintendent authority over every department in the system. In making the superintendent the chief executive officer of the school system, the Detroit reformers, like their counterparts across the country, were carrying out their pledge to run the schools like great public businesses. The superintendent, of course, was not only a chief executive but also an educational leader whose decisions the reformers hoped would be guided by professional expertise. In Charles Chadsey, the new board members felt that they had the man who could admirably fill both roles.[121]

Unfortunately for the new board, the city of Chicago agreed with that assessment of Chadsey. In January, 1919, Chadsey stunned Detroit by announcing that he was breaking his contract to assume the superintendency of the Chicago public schools.[122] Replacing Chadsey plunged the small board into the most serious controversy of its early years. Conflicts over candidates, who, because of the recent consolidation of authority in the office of the superintendent, would now step into a very powerful executive position, caused some board members to fear that remnants of the Martindale "machine" were climbing out of their political graves and again reaching power. At the center of the controversy was Frank Cody, whom the board had appointed as acting superintendent upon Chadsey's departure and who, subsequently, became the leading internal candidate for the position.

Cody had been the superintendent of the Delray public schools prior to their annexation by the Detroit board in 1906. Following the annexation, he rose through the Detroit system, beginning as a high school principal and moving up to general supervisor for the district of special activities, a position responsible for all night schools, playgrounds, special education classes, and so forth. In 1914, the board appointed him assistant superintendent to oversee the Americanization program, and, in 1919, acting superintendent.[123]

Cody's wealth of experience was tempered by a number of serious liabilities. With only a master's degree from the state normal school, he lacked the academic credentials that were becoming necessary for assuming the superintendency of a major urban school district. In addition, several board members, led by Laura Osborn, believed that he had strong ties to the men and the practices of the Martindale "machine." Osborn's fears were justified. Cody had befriended many of the ward-based board members during his early years in the system, and, beginning in 1912, he had worked closely with them as a liaison for Charles Chadsey. As Cody recalled many years later, Chadsey would not "lower" himself to "even speak to most of the members of the [ward-based] board," and he assigned Cody the task of conferring with them on crucial matters. "So I met them," he explained, "most of the time, I must confess, in the bar of the Ste. Clair Hotel. I could always get a quorum there." At these meetings, Cody smoothed the way for many important initiatives of the Chadsey administration. Nevertheless, the rumors that he was "playing politics" at the Ste. Clair Hotel were so strong that when Chadsey stepped down he specifically urged the board not to appoint Frank Cody as the next superintendent.[124]

Compounding the appearance of political impropriety was the fact that Cody's brother and most trusted political adviser was deeply involved in local politics and had worked in the textbook division of that nemesis of the reformers, the American Book Company.[125] Indeed, as early as 1914, the *Detroit News* reported on rumors that the American Book Company had positioned someone within the school administration ready to take over if Chadsey left, someone who had "a relative who has cut some figure in local politics and who is credited with being the official lobbyist of the A. B. C."[126] The profile fit Fred and Frank Cody perfectly. As far as Osborn was concerned, Cody embodied everything she and the reformers had worked so hard to defeat. In one respect, she was right, Cody was definitely more an educational politician than an educational expert.

Yet it was precisely his political acumen that enabled Cody to outmaneuver his opponents during the seven months of infighting that followed the Chadsey resignation. In the five years that Cody had directed the Americanization program of the Detroit schools, he had cultivated the friendship of many of the leading businessmen in the city. He impressed many of them with his "business ability" in expanding the program, and, as the debate over Chadsey's successor continued, key business leaders, and eventually the Board of Commerce itself, broke with Osborn and endorsed Cody. In spite of their efforts, however, in May, 1919, the board narrowly voted to offer the position to the outside candidate pushed by Osborn. But, in a move that stunned the school board, Mayor James Couzens, a former Ford partner who favored Cody, vetoed the salary appropriation for the new superintendent. The board voted to override the veto, but the uproar over the mayor's actions led the newly appointed superintendent to resign even before he actually assumed the position. Seeing the handwriting on the wall, the board finally ended the controversy on June 26, 1919, by appointing Cody to serve out the remaining two years of Chadsey's term.[127]

While Cody certainly was a politician, he was by no means an ordinary one. He quickly made his peace with Osborn and his other opponents on the board and went on to serve as superintendent for twenty-three years. As the next chapter highlights, with his appointment, the Detroit public schools began a decade of political stability and unprecedented growth. For a while, the great political battles over education were over.

Conclusion

As 1919 drew to a close, Laura Osborn could look back with considerable satisfaction at the transformation of educational politics in Detroit and her own role in the process. The voters had overwhelmingly supported the abolition of the ward system, and a small, nonpartisan board of education now presided over the schools. As one of seven board members, she was the first woman to hold elective office in the city. While the appointment of Frank Cody may have troubled that pleasing vision, Osborn was politically astute enough to know that the old days, when a superintendent could run the school system like a personal fiefdom, were ended forever.

In many ways, this political transformation neatly fits into the pattern of school reform that was sweeping the nation during the Progressive era, namely elite reformers leading a moral crusade against ward-based office-holders for control of the public schools. Yet the events in Detroit demand considerable reassessment of the interpretations that revisionist historians have placed on these reform campaigns. Bowles and Gintis, for example, note that the campaigns to abolish the ward-based boards of education were "aimed at reducing the political power of the 'ethnic enclaves' of the urban working class and small property owners."[128] The conflict in Detroit, however, primarily pitted upper-class reformers against middle-class and, in several cases, upper-middle-class, politicians. Indeed, except for the Dau *Blue Book* listings, the occupational and ethnic backgrounds of the reformers and their opponents is strikingly similar. Such antireform leaders as Dr. Charles Kuhn and Dr. Albert McMichael, both of whom served as school board presidents, were well-known physicians and McMichael was one of the most prominent Republican leaders in the city.[129] George Condon and Albert E. Sherman were prominent lawyers who practiced out of downtown offices. None of these people were either ethnic or working class as Bowles and Gintis use those terms. Even Ralph and Anthony Treppa, the Polish bar owners whose actions precipitated the reform movement, came from one of the oldest and most prosperous Polish families in the city. Only Albert Hely, a livestock dealer, and Albert Kunz, the owner of a clothing store, seem to fit the "small property owner" characterization of opponents of school reform.[130] In Detroit, as far as the battle over school governance is concerned, class conflict was on a very limited scale.

In addition to demanding another look at the ethnic and occupational backgrounds of the opponents of reform, events in Detroit also compel a reconsideration of the chronology of reform. Scholars must reconsider whether the struggle for control of boards of education really was the first step in transforming school systems into institutions whose function was to reproduce the social and economic order. In Detroit, virtually all of the curricular elements that revisionist scholars see as central to the reproduction of inequality (kindergartens, standardized testing, differentiated high school curricula, vocational education, and Americanization programs) were introduced by the ward-based board of education before the reformers took control of the public schools of Detroit. Indeed, between 1907 and 1917, the years in which Detroit became a model "progressive" school district, the reformers controlled the board for only two years (1911–13) and then by the narrowest of margins. The character of the board members, not the character of the curriculum, was the main issue in the political battles about the nature and composition of the school board. In fact, both sides in the conflict agreed on the basic direction of educational policy and practice.

The commitment of the ward-based board to the fundamental elements of "progressive" educational reform also calls into question the notion of reform-by-imposition that has dominated much of recent scholarship in educational history. If, as many scholars have assumed, ward-based boards of education were closer to the people and more representative of the desires of neighborhood constituencies than at-large boards, then we must see "progressive" reform in Detroit as an expression of popular will, not elite imposition. The fundamental direction of educational reform was popular throughout the city. As we shall see in the next chapter, during the 1920s, every major interest group in Detroit demanded more schools, more teachers, and more modern programs.

Finally, nothing belies the notion of reform-by-imposition more than the results of the November, 1916, referendum to abolish the ward-based board. Given a clear choice between continuing with the ward system or changing to at-large elections, the voters overwhelmingly opted for change. Undoubtedly, many voters were suspicious of the motives of the elite reformers who led the campaign for the at-large board, but, when these voters marked their ballots, they indicated their willingness to see if the reformers could keep their promises and improve the quality of public education in Detroit.

NOTES

1. *Detroit Journal*, 11/15/07.

2. Several scholars note the relationship between temperance and school reform in the nineteenth century, but few discuss that relationship in the Progressive era. Victor L. Shrader, however, does raise some issues similar to those I found in Detroit. See Victor L. Shrader, "Ethnicity, Religion, and Class: Progressive School Reform in San Francisco," *History of Education Quarterly* 20 (Winter, 1980): 389; David Tyack and Elisabeth Hansot, *Managers of Virtue: Public School Leadership in America, 1820–1980* (New York: Basic Books, 1982), 73–74; David John Hogan, *Class and Reform: School and Society in Chicago, 1880–1930* (Philadelphia: University of Pennsylvania Press, 1985), 11, 73, 76–77; Paul E. Peterson, *The Politics of School Reform, 1870–1940* (Chicago: University of Chicago Press, 1985), 98, 99, 126, 127. On the relationship between Protestantism and progressivism generally, see Robert M. Crunden, *Ministers of Reform: The Progressives' Achievement in American Civilization, 1889–1920* (New York: Basic Books, 1982).

3. Julian Street, "Detroit the Dynamic," *Colliers*, 7/4/14, 9, 10; Arthur Pound, *Detroit: Dynamic City* (New York: Appleton-Century, 1940); Sidney Glazer, *Detroit: A Study in Urban Development* (New York: Bookman Associates, 1965), 129–30.

4. G. T. Bloomfield, "Shaping the Character of a City: The Automobile Industry and Detroit, 1900–1920," *Michigan Quarterly Review* 25 (Spring, 1986): 168–78.

5. Melvin Holli, "Dynamic Detroit, 1900–45: Introduction," in *Detroit*, ed. Melvin Holli (New York: New Viewpoints, 1976), 121.

6. Detroit Board of Education, *Seventy-fourth and Seventy-fifth Annual Reports of the Board of Education, 1917–18* (Detroit: Board of Education, 1918), 190; Detroit Board of Education, *Eighty-eighth Annual Report of the Public Schools, 1930–31* (Detroit: Board of Education, 1931), 16; Detroit Board of Education, *Superintendent's Annual Report, 1943–44* (Detroit: Board of Education, 1944), 105–6; Department of Special Education and Bureau of Statistics and Reference, "Age-Grade and Nationality Survey," *Detroit Educational Bulletin* 4 (December, 1920): 15; Detroit Board of Education, "Pertinent Facts Relative to the Proposed Increase in Millage" (Detroit: Board of Education, 1949), in DFT Papers [inventoried 1/20/83], box 1, Millage and Government Aid to Education folder, 21.

7. On the relationship between enrollment growth and Progressive school reform in New York, see Diane Ravitch, *The Great School Wars: New York City, 1805–1973* (New York: Basic Books, 1974), 107–58.

8. One comment by the president of the board in the 1895–96 annual report typifies the problem the board had with the other governing bodies. "Year after year," the president noted, "this Board has appealed to the City Council and the Board of Estimates for appropriations for

new school houses in order to meet the demands of the growing population, but the appropriations are kept ridiculously below the urgent needs of the community" (*Fifty-third Annual Report of the Detroit Board of Education, 1895–96* [Detroit: Board of Education, 1896], 12).

9. *Annual Report, 1917–18*, 190; *Annual Report, 1930–31*, 16; Arthur B. Moehlman, *Public Education in Detroit* (Bloomington, IL: Public School Publishing Co., 1923), 162. In computing the per-pupil costs adjusted for inflation, the rate of inflation was based on 1967 = 100. See U.S. Department of Commerce, *Historical Statistics of the United States, Colonial Times to 1970* (Washington, DC: U.S. Government Printing Office, 1975), 210.

10. *Detroit Journal*, 3/15/07; *Detroit Journal*, 9/10/08, in the Laura F. Osborn Clipping File, LFO Papers; *Detroit Times*, 1/19/07, in the CS Scrapbook.

11. Melvin Holli, *Reform in Detroit: Hazen S. Pingree and Urban Politics* (New York: Oxford University Press, 1969), 27–29.

12. Detroit Board of Education, *Sixtieth Annual Report of the Board of Education, 1902–3* (Detroit: Board of Education, 1903), 15; Detroit Board of Education, *Sixty-first Annual Report of the Board of Education, 1903–4* (Detroit: Board of Education, 1904), 13–14, 17–18; Detroit Board of Education, *One Hundred Years: The Story of the Detroit Public Schools, 1842–1942* (Detroit: Board of Education, 1942), 68–69; Detroit Municipal League, *Thirteenth Ward Bulletin*, 2/23/09, 1, in LFO Papers, box 13, Political Miscellaneous folder; William Lovett, *Detroit Rules Itself* (Boston: Gorham Press, 1930), 20–23.

13. Raymond Fragnoli, *The Transformation of Reform: Progressivism in Detroit—And After, 1912–1933* (New York: Garland, 1982), 16–36, 39.

14. Throughout this book, the term *elite* will refer specifically to people listed in the *Dau Blue Book* or the *Social Register*. The campaign to reform the school in Grand Rapids is described in David Angus, "The Politics of Progressive School Reform: Grand Rapids, 1900–1910," *Michigan Academician* 14 (Winter, 1982): 239–58. On the actions Wilcox took in behalf of the two organizations, see *Detroit News*, 2/20/07 and 2/21/07; *Detroit Free Press*, 2/21/07 and 2/22/07; *Detroit Times*, 2/21/07, in the CS Scrapbook.

15. A. N. Marquis, *The Book of Detroiters* (Chicago: A. N. Marquis, 1908), 350–51; Laura Osborn, typescript reminiscences in LFO Papers, box 1, Tributes, Eulogy folder.

16. William J. Reese, *Power and the Promise of School Reform* (Boston: Routledge and Kegan Paul, 1986), 33. See also Ravitch, *Great School Wars*, 154–55; Bryce E. Nelson, *Good Schools: Seattle Public Schools, 1901–30* (Seattle: University of Washington Press, 1988), 42–44.

17. *Detroit Times*, 2/20/07; *Civic News*, 11/23/07, in LFO Papers, box 7, Clipping folder; *Detroit Free Press*, 11/25/07; *Detroit Journal*, 11/25/07, 11/28/07, 3/13/11. The minister is quoted in the *Detroit Journal*, 11/28/07. Rabbi Franklin and School Inspector Hiram Goldberg represented the more assimilated portion of the Detroit Jewish community. For biographical information on them, see Herbert S. Case, *Who's Who in Michigan, 1936* (Munising, MI: Who's Who in Michigan, 1936), 138; *Detroit Times*, 4/2/09; *Detroit Journal*, 12/2/07; *Detroit News*, 4/7/13.

18. Lela R. Hannah, letter to Sir (form letter), 11/27/07, in LFO Papers, box 11-A, Correspondence 1900–1909 folder; William Stocking, letter to Laura Osborn, 12/9/07, in LFO Papers, box 4, folder 4.

19. *Annual Report, 1909–10*, 12; *Detroit Free Press*, 2/22/07, in CS Scrapbook. The alliance of ward-based school board members and teachers against elite reformers was not uncommon in this era. In New York City, for example, this was precisely the alignment that battled over plans to centralize New York schools in 1896 (see Ravitch, *The Great School Wars*, 154–55).

20. Osborn characterized the *News* in Laura Osborn, letter to William McAndrew, 4/18/09, in LFO Papers, box 16, Correspondence, 1903–19 folder. On Scripps, see Fragnoli, *Transforma-*

tion of Reform, 16; J. Elenbaas, "Detroit and the Progressive Era: A Study of Urban Reform, 1900–1914" (Ph.D. diss., Wayne State University, 1968), 120, 122.

21. For examples, see *Detroit News,* 4/2/09, 4/3/09, 4/5/09, in LFO Papers, Clipping file.

22. *Detroit Saturday Night,* 3/6/09, 3/13/09, 3/17/11, 3/25/11; *Little Stick,* 3/11/11, 3/18/11, in CS Scrapbook.

23. Reformers Clarence Burton and Henry Leland were leaders of the open-shop movement in Detroit, while Hinton Spaudling, a pro-Martindale school board candidate in 1907, was also an open-shop man. *Detroit Free Press,* 2/21/07, in CS Scrapbook; *Michigan Union Advocate,* 4/2/09, in LFO Papers, Clipping file; Fragnoli, *Transformation of Reform,* 16.

24. The rector of St. Paul's is quoted in *Detroit Times* 2/20/07. Mumford is quoted in *Detroit News,* 10/24/16, in LFO Papers, box 7, Clippings. See also *Civic News,* 11/23/07, in LFO Papers, box 7, Clippings.

25. On temperance, prohibition, and nativism, see James H. Timberlake, *Prohibition and the Progressive Movement, 1900–1920* (Cambridge, MA: Harvard University Press, 1963), 115–19; John Higham, *Strangers in the Land* (New York: Atheneum, 1975), 41, 267–68; on school reform and anti-immigrant biases, see Ravitch, *Great School Wars,* 134–45.

26. *Detroit Free Press,* 11/25/07; *Detroit Journal,* 11/28/07.

27. Detroit Municipal League, *Thirteenth Ward Bulletin,* 2/23/09, 2, in LFO Papers, box 13, Political Miscellaneous folder.

28. Tyack and Hansot, *Managers of Virtue,* 5–6.

29. A brief biography of Martindale can be found in Marquis, *Book of Detroiters,* 316. Martindale's lack of a university or normal school degree was one of the main charges made against him by Wilcox and the Municipal League (*Detroit Free Press,* 2/21/07, in CS Scrapbook).

30. On age-grading in Detroit, see David L. Angus, Jeffrey E. Mirel, and Maris A. Vinovskis, "The Historical Development of Age Stratification in Schooling," *Teachers College Record,* Winter, 1988, 211–36; on kindergartens, see Detroit Board of Education *Sixty-eighth Annual Report of the Detroit Board of Education, 1910–11* (Detroit: Board of Education, 1911), 91–96; on the introduction of special education programs, see W. C. Martindale, "How Detroit Cares for Her Backward Children," *Psychological Clinic* 6 (October, 1915): 125–30; on ungraded schools for children defined as discipline problems, see W. C. Martindale, "The Separation of the Insubordinate and Incorrigible Children from the Regular School," in *Proceedings of the National Education Association, 1907* (Winona, MN: National Education Association, 1907), 322–26; on revisions of the high school English curriculum, particularly the emphasis on composition, see Edwin L. Miller, "Rebuilding an English Course," in *Proceedings of the National Education Association, 1910* (Winona, MN: National Education Association, 1910), 483–87; on changes in the arithmetic curriculum, see W. C. Martindale, "Discussion," in *Proceedings of the National Education Association, 1908* (Winona, MN: National Education Association, 1908), 559–60; on all other topics, see Moehlman, *Public Education in Detroit,* 158–77; "An Up-to-Date School System," *The Detroiter,* September, 1911, 37.

31. On manual training, see J. H. Trybom, "A Report on Manual Training in the Detroit Elementary Schools, with a Discussion on the Disciplinary Value of Manual Training," in *Proceedings of the National Education Association, 1901* (Chicago: University of Chicago Press, 1901), 250–57; *Detroit Free Press,* 3/2/07, in CS Scrapbook. Miller is quoted in *Detroit Journal,* 4/3/11, in CS Scrapbook. On some of Miller's other views on the differentiated curriculum, see Edward A. Krug, *The Shaping of the American High School, 1920–41* (Madison: University of Wisconsin Press, 1972), 111. On Central High School, see Detroit Public Schools Staff, *Frank Cody: A Realist in Education* (New York: Macmillan, 1943), 320.

32. An excellent overview of strides in vocational education during the Martindale years can be found in J. H. Trybon, "Manual and Industrial Training," in *Sixty-ninth Annual Report of the*

Detroit Board of Education, 1911–12 (Detroit: Board of Education, 1912), 139–43; also see "Up-to-Date School System," 37; on the opening of Cass Tech, see "Cass High School Shows Tremendous Advance in Industrial Education," *The Detroiter*, May, 1912, 14–16; "Cass Technical High School Formally Opens its Many Continuation Classes," *The Detroiter*, November, 1912, 14–15; on the commercial high school, see Moehlman, *Public Education in Detroit*, 170; *Annual Report, 1909–10*, 12; Wales Martindale, "The School as a Social Center," in *Annual Report, 1911–12*, 158–66. For a detailed look at the development of evening schools in Detroit during the Martindale years, see Allan Robert McPherson, "The Introduction and Development of the Detroit Public Schools Adult Education Program: A Historical Study" (Ph.D. diss., University of Michigan, 1988), 120–46.

33. Public Schools Staff, *Frank Cody*, 327. On Goddard's hereditarian and anti-immigrant biases, see Stephen J. Gould, *The Mismeasure of Man* (New York: Norton, 1981), 158–74.

34. Moehlman also claims that Martindale lay the groundwork for the office of educational research by bringing together all the people in the system who did statistics, testing, and vocational guidance. See Moehlman, *Public Education in Detroit*, 172–73; Leslie L. Hanawalt, *A Place of Light: The History of Wayne State University* (Detroit: Wayne State University Press, 1968), 135; a brief summary of Courtis's career can be found in Case, *Who's Who in Michigan*, 84.

35. Moehlman, *Public Education in Detroit*, 174.

36. For example, David Hogan writes of Chicago, "In effect, the same individuals, the same organizations, and the same philosophy—social efficiency—guided both centralization and vocational education to victory. Where one set of reforms insured that businessmen formally governed the school system and that superintendents administered the school system in a businesslike manner according to businesslike principles, the second transformed the school into a business institution, an adjunct to the market economy" (Hogan, *Class and Reform*, 219). See also Michael B. Katz, *Class, Bureaucracy, and Schools* (New York: Praeger, 1971), 113–25; Samuel Bowles and Herbert Gintis, *Schooling in Capitalist America* (New York: Basic Books, 1976), 180–200.

37. David Plank, "Educational Reform and Organizational Change: Atlanta in the Progressive Era," in *Southern Cities, Southern Schools: Public Education in the Urban South*, ed. David Plank and Rick Ginsberg (Westport, CT: Greenwood Press, 1990), 142–45.

38. *Detroit News*, 4/5/09, in Laura F. Osborn Clipping File, LFO Papers.

39. *Michigan Union Advocate*, 4/2/09, in Laura F. Osborn Clipping File, LFO Papers. In 1911, the staunchly anti-Martindale Board of Commerce went so far as to claim that "From an academic standpoint Detroit schools are the finest in the state" (*The Detroiter*, September, 1911, 37).

40. *Little Stick*, 3/11/11, in the CS Scrapbook.

41. *Detroit Free Press*, 10/11/08, 10/13/08, in the LFO Papers, box 13, Biography folder.

42. *Detroit Times*, 2/27/09. See also *Detroit Times*, 3/1/11.

43. *Detroit Free Press*, 3/26/09.

44. On the Voteswappers League, see Fragnoli, *Transformation of Reform*, 13–14; Lovett, *Detroit Rules Itself*, 20–23. In one election, for example, Hiram Goldberg accused Billy Boushaw of vote fraud in the first precinct of the first ward, where reform candidate Samuel Mumford received only 9 votes compared to his antireform opponent who received 189 (*Detroit Journal*, 3/25/11, in CS Scrapbook).

45. Detroit Municipal League, *Thirteenth Ward Bulletin*, 2/23/09, 1, in LFO Papers, box 13, Political Miscellaneous folder; Mrs. George Johnson, letter to the Citizens School Board Committee, 1/23/17, in LFO Papers, box 4, Papers and Correspondence folder. For more on Frederick Martindale, see *Detroit News*, 4/2/13; *Detroit Free Press*, 5/28/14; see also Elenbaas, "Detroit and the Progressive Era," 81, 201.

46. Elenbaas, "Detroit and the Progressive Era," 120–21.

47. *Detroit Journal*, 4/20/08.

48. Angus, "Politics of Progressive School Reform," 243–45.

49. Delos Wilcox, letter to Anthony Pratt, 4/10/09, in LFO Papers, box 4, Papers and Correspondence folder.

50. *Detroit Journal*, 3/20/09, in LFO Papers, Clipping file, *Detroit Journal*, 3/22/09.

51. *Detroit News*, 4/1/09.

52. *Detroit Free Press*, 3/2/09, 3/3/09, 4/3/09, 4/4/09, 4/06/09, 4/7/09; *Detroit Journal*, 4/3/09, 4/5/09, 4/6/09; *Detroit Times*, 3/2/09, 4/3/09, 4/6/09.

53. Laura Osborn, letter to William McAndrew, 7/19/09, in LFO Papers, box 16, 1907–19 folder no. 2; see also Osborn, letter to McAndrew, 6/12/12, in LFO Papers, box 16, 1907–19 folder no. 2; *Detroit Journal*, 7/13/09. *Detroit Journal* 3/25/11. The Municipal League alleged that Martindale had bribed school inspectors to vote for him in 1906, but, following an investigation by the county prosecutor, these allegations were dismissed for lack of evidence (Elenbaas, "Detroit and the Progressive Era," 120).

54. *Detroit Times*, 3/10/11, in CS Scrapbook.

55. *Detroit News*, 11/20/09, in LFO Papers, Clipping file; *Detroit Free Press*, 11/21/09, in LFO Papers, Clipping file.

56. *Detroit Journal*, 3/9/11, in LFO Papers, box 13, Biography-Clippings folder; untitled campaign literature, in LFO Papers, box 4, correspondence folder no. 4.

57. *Detroit Journal*, 3/9/11, in LFO Papers, box 13, Biography-Clippings folder; *Detroit Times*, 3/9/11.

58. *Detroit Free Press*, 3/12/11; *Detroit Journal*, 3/13/11; *Detroit News*, 3/12/11, 3/13/11; *Detroit Times*, 3/14/11.

59. *Detroit Saturday Night*, 3/25/11.

60. *Little Stick*, 3/11/11, in CS Scrapbook.

61. Clarence Burton, ed., *The City of Detroit, Michigan 1701–1922* (Detroit and Chicago: S. J. Clarke Publishing, 1922), 5: 88.

62. *Annual Report, 1909–10*, 12–13; *Detroit News*, 3/11/11; Moehlman, *Public Education in Detroit*, 163–64, 166.

63. The description of Kuhn appears in a *Detroit Journal* editorial from 7/10/09 that was reprinted in a Municipal League advertisement in the *Detroit News*, 3/13/11. (See also *Detroit News*, 3/11/11, 3/12/11, 3/13/11).

64. *Detroit News*, 3/11/11, in CS Scrapbook; *Detroit Journal*, 3/14/11, in CS Scrapbook.

65. *Detroit Free Press*, 3/12/11, 3/14/11; *Detroit Journal*, 3/14/11; *Detroit News*, 3/15/11; all in CS Scrapbook.

66. *Detroit Journal*, 3/15/11, in CS Scrapbook; *Detroit Free Press*, 3/15/11, 3/16/11, 3/21/11, 3/23/11; *Detroit News*, 3/15/11, 3/16/11, 3/23/11; *Detroit Times*, 3/15/11, 3/17/11, 3/21/11.

67. *Detroit Journal*, 4/4/11, 4/11/11; *Detroit News*, 4/4/11, 4/11/11; *Detroit Times*, 4/11/11, in CS Scrapbook. On the vote to fire Martindale, see Detroit *News*, 7/12/12, in CS Scrapbook.

68. *Detroit Journal*, 4/4/11.

69. *Detroit News*, 4/28/11, in CS Scrapbook; *Detroit News*, 5/3/11, in LFO Papers, Clipping file. Fragnoli points to a dispute between J. L. Hudson and Anthony Pratt over municipal ownership of utilities as the immediate cause of the League's collapse (Fragnoli, *Transformation of Reform*, 16).

70. *Detroit Free Press*, 6/21/14. Chadsey's first few years *were* marred by some factional controversy, but, as the Condon quote shows, he eventually won the support of the majority of

the board. In 1915, for example, he was reappointed unanimously. See Moehlman, *Public Education in Detroit*, 176; Public School Staff, *Frank Cody*, 203; *Detroit News*, 8/10/12; *Detroit Free Press*, 8/11/12, in CS Scrapbook; DBEP, 1915–16, 2.

71. There was surprisingly little press coverage of the 1913 school board election, in which the "Martindale men," as the *News* called them, returned to power. The school board election took place during a statewide battle over women's suffrage that overshadowed all other races. In addition to the defeat at the polls, the reformers were rocked by the defection of George Condon, who began his years on the board as a reformer but switched his allegiance sometime in 1913, rising to the position of floor leader of the regulars by 1914 (*Detroit News*, 4/8/13, 4/10/13, 10/9/14; *Detroit Free Press*, 6/21/14). In addition to George Condon, the leaders of the antireform bloc on the board were "The Four Alberts": Dr. Albert McMichael, who served as president of the board from July, 1913, to July, 1916; Albert E. Sherman; Albert G. Kunz; and longtime Martindale ally, Albert Hely (*Detroit News*, 6/30/14; DBEP 1915–16, 1–2).

72. While Tyack and Hansot are correct about Chadsey's "membership" in the educational trust, they are wrong in their description of the events that led up to Chadsey's appointment in Detroit. They state that the reformers had already changed the city charter and abolished the ward-based board of education before they hired Chadsey. Obviously, that was not the case. See Tyack and Hansot, *Managers of Virtue*, 131, 141; see also Moehlman, *Public Education in Detroit*, 180.

73. *Detroit News*, 8/19/12, in CS Scrapbook; Moehlman, *Public Education in Detroit*, 180–86.

74. Detroit Board of Education, *Seventy-first Annual Report of the Detroit Board of Education, 1913–14* (Detroit: Board of Education, 1914), 10–11; Board of Education, *Superintendent's Annual Report, 1943–44*, 105–6; McPherson, "The Introduction and Development of the Detroit Public Schools Adult Education Program," 149–51; Elenbaas, "Detroit and the Progressive Era," 202. Adding to pressure on enrollment was a 1913 compulsory education law that ordered all children between the ages of seven and sixteen to be in school; see Moehlman, *Public Education in Detroit*, 182; *Annual Report, 1930–31*, 16; DBEP, 1915–16, 121; DBEP, 1916–17, 125.

75. Moehlman, *Public Education in Detroit*, 180–83; *The Detroiter*, November, 1913, 22.

76. Moehlman, *Public Education in Detroit*, 195–98.

77. On the history of special education in Detroit, see Joseph Tropea, "Bureaucratic Order and Special Children, 1890s–1940s," *History of Education Quarterly* 27 (Spring, 1987): 35–41. On Americanization, see Edward George Hartmann, *The Movement to Americanize the Immigrant* (New York: AMS Publishers, 1967), 24; Moehlman, *Public Education in Detroit*, 188–89.

78. Charles Chadsey, quoted in McPherson, "Introduction and Development," 195.

79. Public School Staff, *Frank Cody*, 159–63; Moehlman, *Public Education in Detroit*, 188–89; Robert A. Carlson, *The Quest for Conformity: Americanization Through Education* (New York: Wiley, 1975), 112–14; Olivier Zunz, *The Changing Face of Inequality: Urbanization, Industrial Development, and Immigrants in Detroit, 1880–1920* (Chicago: University of Chicago Press, 1982), 313–18.

80. As we shall see in chap. 2, organized labor, which in other cities strongly condemned platoon schools, praised the platoon schools in Detroit. As far as Americanization is concerned, Zunz notes that "most ethnic leaders endorsed the [Americanization] program" in Detroit (Zunz, *Changing Face of Inequality*, 316). For a good discussion of a very popular Americanization program in another industrial city, see Ronald D. Cohen, *Children of the Mill: Schooling and Society in Gary, Indiana 1906–1960* (Bloomington: Indiana University Press, 1990), 27–36, 66–69.

81. *Annual Report, 1911–12*, 167; Hanawalt, *Place of Light*, 149; Moehlman, *Public Education in Detroit*, 184–85.

82. Hogan, *Class and Reform*, 224. See also James W. Fraser, "Who Were the Progressive Educators Anyway? A Case Study of the Progressive Education Movement in Boston, 1905–1925," *Educational Foundations* 2 (Spring, 1988): 14–19; Peterson, *Politics of School Reform, 1870–1940*, 166–69; Ravitch, *Great School Wars*, 229; David Tyack, *The One Best System* (Cambridge, MA: Harvard University Press, 1974), 101–4, 165–66.

83. The leader of the anti-Courtis faction on the board was Inspector Alexander Reinhold, secretary-treasurer of the Reinhold Manufacturing Company. Reinhold took the fight from the school board to the city council but he failed in his efforts to oust Courtis (*Detroit News*, 3/30/17; DBEP, 1915–16, 259; Moehlman, *Public Education in Detroit*, 185; R. L. Polk, *Detroit City Directory for the Year Commencing September 1, 1914* [Chicago: R. L. Polk, 1914], 1891).

84. Stephen Scott Williams, "From Polemics to Practice: IQ Testing and Tracking in the Detroit Public Schools and Their Relationship to the National Debate" (Ph.D. diss., University of Michigan, 1986), 88–180.

85. Laura Osborn commented after the April, 1913, results were announced that "Monday's election emphasizes the necessity for action [on the small school board bill]." Almost immediately, Senator Scott introduced the bill that eventually reduced the size of the board (*Detroit News*, 4/10/14, 4/13/13).

86. Moehlman, *Public Education in Detroit*, 180; *Detroit Journal*, 2/16/07, in CS Scrapbook; *Detroit Journal*, 4/1/15, in LFO Papers, Clipping file; *Dau's Blue Book for Detroit and Suburban Towns, 1917* (New York: Dau's Blue Book, 1917), 100; R. L. Polk, *Detroit City Directory, 1917* (Detroit: R. L. Polk, 1917).

87. *Detroit News*, 4/10/14, 4/13/13; Alan Whitney, letter to Belle Brotherton, 11/20/09, in LFO Papers, box 16, 1907–19 Correspondence; Laura Osborn, letter to Alan Whitney, 12/18/12, in LFO Papers, box 16, 1903–19 Correspondence folder; Alan Whitney, letter to Laura Osborn, 1/21/13, in LFO Papers, box 16, 1903–19 Correspondence folder; Alan Whitney, letter to Laura Osborn, 1/31/13, in LFO Papers, box 16, 1903–19 Correspondence folder; Alan Whitney, letter to Laura Osborn, 4/12/13, in LFO Papers, box 16, 1903–19 Correspondence folder; Alan Whitney, letter to Laura Osborn, 2/7/13, in LFO Papers, box 16, 1903–19 Correspondence folder; Laura Osborn, letter to Francis King, 2/10/13, in LFO Papers, box 16, 1903–19 Correspondence folder; Alan Whitney, letter to Laura Osborn, 3/5/13, in LFO Papers, box 16, 1903–19 Correspondence folder; Alan Whitney, letter to Laura Osborn, 4/2/13, in LFO Papers, box 16, 1903–19 Correspondence folder; Alan Whitney, letter to Laura Osborn, 2/4/14, in LFO Papers, box 16, 1903–19 Correspondence folder; "The Small School Board Law" (brochure marked 1915), in LFO Papers, box 19, Campaign Literature folder. A brief biography of Whitney can be found in Case, *Who's Who in Michigan*, 426.

88. Laura Osborn, letter to State Senators (form letter), 3/8/15, in LFO Papers, box 4, Correspondence folder; "The Small School Board Law" (brochure marked 1915), in LFO Papers, box 19, Campaign Literature folder; *Detroit Free Press*, 4/30/15, in LFO Papers, Clipping file; *Detroit Journal*, 4/30/15, in LFO Papers, Clipping file, *Detroit Times*, 4/30/15, in LFO Papers, Clipping file; *Detroit Free Press*, 4/9/17, in LFO Papers, Clipping file; "Interview with Laura Osborn" (typescript), in LFO Papers, box 1, WDET Radio Program folder; *Detroit Journal*, 11/11/16, in LFO Papers, box 1, Death: Tributes, Eulogy folder. On Oxtoby, see *Detroit Journal*, undated (probably from 1915) in LFO Papers, Clipping file; Burton, *City of Detroit* 3: 69–70.

89. The plaintiff in these court challenges was the city. The city argued that both the Scott school board law and the later Scott-Flowers honest election law abridged powers granted in the city charter. In both cases, the corporation counsel of the city, representing the city election commission, argued the cases. See *Detroit News*, 2/14/15, in LFO Papers, Clipping file; *Detroit Free Press*, 8/24/16, in LFO Papers, Clipping file; *Detroit Journal*, 8/24/16, in LFO Papers,

Clipping file; Lovett, *Detroit Rules Itself,* 92; Michigan Department of Public Instruction, *Annual Report of the Superintendent of Public Instruction, 1912–13* (Lansing, MI: Wynkoop Hallenbeck Crawford, 1913), 2, 5.

90. Ravitch, *Great School Wars,* 156–58; Peterson, *Politics of School Reform,* 139–53; Angus, "Politics of Progressive School Reform," 253–55. On state legislatures unilaterally abolishing ward-based boards in Rochester, Toledo, and Milwaukee, see Reese, *Power and the Promise of School Reform,* 103–12.

91. *Detroit News,* 2/14/15, in LFO Papers, Clipping file. Under the Michigan election law, only men and women who owned property assessed for taxes in the school district and the parents or legal guardians of school-age children were eligible to vote. If Zunz is correct in arguing that substantial numbers of working-class Detroiters owned their homes, then the property qualification was probably meaningless as a factor in determining turnout (Zunz, *Changing Face of Inequality,* 152–76).

92. Raymond Fragnoli, "Progressive Coalitions and Municipal Reform in Detroit, 1912–18," *Detroit in Perspective* 4 (Spring, 1980), 120–21; Fragnoli, *Transformation of Reform,* 19–41; Lovett, *Detroit Rules Itself,* 93–94.

93. Fragnoli, *Transformation of Reform,* 78–83, 96–98; Lovett, *Detroit Rules Itself,* 91–94. The Citizens League was also directly active in the effort to defeat the district school board bill in 1915. The executive director of the league, for example, sent copies of a *Free Press* editorial on the benefits of the small board of education to all state senators and traveled to Lansing to personally lobby against the district plan (Pliny Marsh, letter to Laura Osborn, 4/9/15 and 4/10/15, in LFO Papers, box 19, Correspondence folder, 1915–19).

94. *Detroit Journal,* 3/13/11; Laura Osborn, letter to Francis King, in LFO Papers, box 16, 1903–19 Correspondence folder; Byres H. Gitchell, letter to Laura Osborn, 3/25/13, in LFO Papers, box 16, 1903–19 Correspondence folder; Ralph Stone, letter to Laura Osborn, 4/7/13, in LFO Papers, box 16, 1903–19 Correspondence folder; *Detroit News,* 3/27/15, in LFO Papers, Clipping file; *Detroit Free Press,* 11/17/12, in LFO Papers, box 7, Clippings folder; Education Committee of the Twentieth Century Club, "Children First: The Schools Out of Politics—Politics Out of the Schools" (1916), in LFO Papers, box 19, Campaign Literature folder; *Detroit News,* 3/17/15, in LFO Papers, Clipping file; *Detroit News,* 11/1/16, 11/2/16, 11/3/16, 11/6/16.

95. *Detroit News,* 6/19/14, 6/23/14, 6/25/14.

96. Education Committee, "Children First."

97. *Detroit News,* 3/27/15, in LFO Papers, Clipping file.

98. *Detroit News,* 11/3/16. The slogan appears in Education Committee, "Children First."

99. *Detroit News,* 6/30/14.

100. *Detroit News,* 11/3/16.

101. *Annual Report, 1909–10,* 11–12.

102. *Detroit News,* 3/27/15, in LFO Papers, Clipping file; McPherson, "Introduction and Development," 150.

103. *Detroit Journal,* 10/10/14.

104. David Angus, "Conflict, Class, and the Nineteenth-Century Public High School in the Cities of the Midwest, 1845–1900," *Curriculum Inquiry* 18, no. 1 (1988): 20; *Annual Report, 1903–04,* 14.

105. *Detroit Journal,* 4/1/15, in LFO Papers, box 7, Personal Clippings folder; *Detroit Free Press,* 8/24/16, in LFO Papers, Clipping file; Education Committee, "Children First."

106. Excellent examples of these sentiments can be found in editorials in *Detroit Labor News,* 12/4/14 and 9/24/15; *Michigan Socialist,* 8/11/16.

107. *Detroit Labor News,* 9/24/15; *Michigan Socialist,* 8/11/16; Education Committee, "Children First."

108. *Michigan Socialist,* 9/29/16. Apropos repeats these arguments in *Michigan Socialist,*

12/29/16. For other left-wing criticism of ward-based school boards, see David Swing Ricker, "The School Teacher-Unionized," *Educational Review* 34 (November, 1905): 350, 362, and Scott Nearing, "The Working of a Large School Board," *Educational Review* 38 (June, 1909): 43–51. In a handwritten note on the margin of the one issue of the paper, Apropos is identified as Daniel L. Powell, Jr. Powell was a prominent socialist leader in Detroit who later ran for the school board and for Congress. However, since I did not find any other evidence that he was Apropos, I have not assumed that they are one in the same; see *Michigan Socialist,* 1/12/17.

109. *Detroit News,* 6/30/14 and 11/3/16. The election data were compiled from Election Commission of the City of Detroit, *Proceedings of the Board of Canvassers, November 7, 1916* (Detroit: The Commission, 1916).

110. Characterizations of the wards are based on U.S. Department of Commerce, Bureau of the Census, *Fourteenth Census of the United States, 1920: Composition and Characteristics of the Population by States* (Washington, DC: U.S. Government Printing Office, 1922), 496–97; see also *Michigan Socialist,* 8/11/16 and 10/27/16; *Detroit News,* 3/27/15, in LFO Papers, Clipping file.

111. Fragnoli, *Transformation of Reform,* 108–10, 114–15; Lovett, *Detroit Rules Itself,* 98–99.

112. Paul Kleppner has analyzed the 1916 prohibition referendum in Michigan and found a strikingly high correlation between support for prohibition and support for women's suffrage. Certainly, Laura Osborn and her supporters in the Detroit Federation of Women's Clubs stand as superb examples of individuals who actively supported both these causes. See Paul Kleppner, *Continuity and Change in Electoral Politics, 1893–1928* (Westport, CT: Greenwood Press, 1987), 172–74.

113. Lovett, *Detroit Rules Itself,* 29.

114. *Detroit News,* 3/3/17 and 4/3/17. On the effort by prominent business and professional leaders in support of the reform slate, see Lovett, *Detroit Rules Itself,* 104. The Socialist slate included several people who were prominent in left-wing politics in Detroit for many years, including Dennis Batt, Daniel Powell, Jr., Albert Renner, and Jane Mayer Sugar (*Michigan Socialist* 1/19/17, 3/23/17, 3/30/17).

115. *Detroit Free Press,* 2/27/17 and 2/28/17.

116. *Michigan Socialist,* 3/9/17.

117. *Detroit Free Press,* 2/28/17; see also *Detroit News,* 3/1/17, 3/4/17, 3/5/17, 3/26/17, 3/30/17.

118. In addition to Osborn and Mumford, the new board members were Judge Alexis Angell, son of former University of Michigan president James B. Angell; Frank H. Alfred, president of the Pere Marquette Railroad; Andrew Biddle, a physician; John S. Hall, a dentist; Joseph Stringham, a civil engineer. *Detroit Free Press* 2/28/17 and 3/2/17; *Detroit News,* 3/26/17, 4/1/17, 1/3/17; Polk, *Detroit City Directory, 1917; Dau's Blue Book, 1917,* 36, 37, 42, 73, 100, 103, 123; Ruby Mervin, ed., *The Social Secretary of Detroit, 1930* (Detroit: The Social Secretary, 1930), 33, 35, 41, 82, 122, 126, 149; Lovett, *Detroit Rules Itself,* 104; Moehlman, *Public Education in Detroit,* 189–90.

119. *Detroit Labor News,* 10/26/17.

120. For examples of the DFL opposition to the at-large city council, see *Detroit Labor News,* 10/12/17, 10/19/17, 10/26/17. On the later efforts to abolish the nine-member council, see Fragnoli, *Transformation of Reform,* 336, 376. The only time the DFL called for an end to the at-large system for the board of education came in 1928, in an editorial that criticized the board for being a "rubber stamp" for the superintendent and the business manager; hiring married women teachers when many single women teachers were unemployed; and contemplating the construction of a new teachers college when new elementary schools were needed (*Detroit Labor News,* 2/17/28).

121. Moehlman, *Public Education in Detroit*, 190–91; Tyack, *One Best System*, 144–45.

122. Moehlman, *Public Education in Detroit*, 180, 198.

123. Public School Staff, *Frank Cody*, 37, 101, 153; Moehlman, *Public Education in Detroit*, 203–4.

124. Public School Staff, *Frank Cody*, 515, 203–5, 211.

125. As the *Detroit News* put it, Frank Cody would be hampered in his administration of the Detroit schools because he "has a brother who was for many years connected with a great school book publishing concern while he was at the same time active in the school politics of Detroit" (quoted in Public School Staff, *Frank Cody*, 229). Similar concerns were raised in editorials in the *Detroit Free Press* (6/20/19, in Frank Cody Clipping file, Burton Historical Collection, Detroit Public Library, Detroit, Michigan) and the *Detroit News* (12/3/19, in Cody Clipping file). Fred Cody hampered his brother's chances for becoming superintendent of schools for reasons other than his involvement with the American Book Company. Fred Cody was indicted in the 1918 election scandal surrounding U.S. Senator Truman Newberry, and he was close enough to the notorious precinct boss Billy Boushaw to socialize with Boushaw's daughter. See John C. Lodge, *I Remember Detroit* (Detroit: Wayne State University Press, 1949), 95; Conot, *American Odyssey*, 258–60; *Detroit Free Press*, 6/20/19, in Cody Clipping file; *Detroit News*, 12/3/19, in Cody Clipping file.

126. *Detroit News*, 6/23/14. See also Upton Sinclair, *The Goslings: A Study of the American Schools* (Pasadena, CA: Upton Sinclair, 1924), 185–86, 318–20.

127. Public School Staff, *Frank Cody*, 210–29; *The Detroiter*, 6/23/19; *Detroit Times*, 6/27/19.

128. Bowles and Gintis, *Schooling in Capitalist America*, 187.

129. Elenbaas, "Detroit and the Progressive Era," 202.

130. To a considerable extent, this evidence about the occupational and ethnic background of the opponents of reform confirms the argument, noted by Peter Filene, that "the progressives resembled their opponents in terms of class, occupation, education, age, religion, political experience and geographical origin. The sociological characteristics which have been presumed to be particularly 'progressive' turn out to be common to all political leaders of the era" (Peter G. Filene, "An Obituary for 'The Progressive Movement,'" *American Quarterly* 22 [Spring, 1970]: 30). The occupational background on Hely, Kunz, McMichael, and Sherman came from Polk, *City Directory for 1914*, 1156, 1399, 1539, 2059. As far as the ethnic background of the opponents of reform is concerned, Condon's family were longtime residents of the United States; Kuhn was born in Detroit of German parents; the Treppa family arrived in Detroit during the Civil War, thus both Anthony and Ralph were U.S. born; and Kunz was born in the United States but traced his roots back to Switzerland. For more detailed information on Condon, see Burton, *City of Detroit* 4: 423–24; information on Kuhn and the Treppas can be found in Burton, *City of Detroit* 5: 88, 501; on Kunz, see *Detroit Journal*, 10/10/14.

Chapter 2

One of the Finest School Systems in the World, 1919–29

Throughout the 1920s, Detroit was the shining star of the New Era, the very center of the American economic universe, where capitalism and technology combined to produce the greatest goods for the greatest numbers. Matthew Josephson declared, "Nowhere in the world may the trend of the new industrial cycle be perceived more clearly than in Detroit. In this sense it is the most modern city in the world, the city of tomorrow." In many ways, by the mid-1920s, the Detroit public schools occupied a similar position in American education. In 1923, Alice Barrows of the U.S. Bureau of Education visited the city and observed, "Detroit must be put foremost in the ranks of cities which have made a newer and better education possible." A 1925 survey of school superintendents rated the Detroit schools first in the nation in organizational efficiency and visual instruction, third in "excellence in teaching reading, writing, composition, and arithmetic and fourth in playgrounds." By 1927, the school system's reputation was so substantial that an article in the *New Republic* stated, "[Detroit's] own coordinated school system is one of the finest in the world."[1] What accounts for this rise to prominence?

Over the past two decades, urban educational historians have focused almost exclusively on the great conflicts of the Progressive era. Their studies have raised provocative questions about the relationship between education and social change by examining the battles over school governance, bureaucratization, and curricular reform. Unfortunately, this emphasis on conflict has obscured one of the most obvious and important characteristics of urban public education from the 1910s and 1920s, the overwhelming political consensus in favor of expanding educational opportunities for urban children.[2]

From 1907 to 1917, Detroit endured more than its share of conflict over the issue of school governance. However, as chapter 1 shows, a broad-based agreement about the nature and direction of educational policy developed in Detroit in spite of the fierce political battles about Superintendent Wales Martindale and the abolition of the ward-based board of education. This chapter explores that consensus in depth by looking at three fundamental issues: the struggle for an adequate supply of teachers, the construction of enough schools to accommodate the continuing flood of students, and the introduction of 1920s-style "progressive" forms of school organization and curricula in the Detroit schools. Each of these issues illuminates one powerful theme—every major interest group in the city strongly supported efforts to provide a high-quality, "modern" public education to the children of the city. This support gave Detroit school leaders the unprecedented opportunity to create one of the great urban school systems of the twentieth century.

Educational Consensus amid Social Conflict

In periods of relative political and social calm, agreement on educational issues would hardly be surprising. The most striking aspect of the consensus in favor of expanding and improving the Detroit public schools is that it emerged during a time of enormous demographic and economic change as well as a period of fierce class conflict. Between 1920 and 1930, the population of the city increased from 993,678 to 1,568,662. Many of these new residents crowded into the already sprawling eastern and southern European immigrant communities, utterly transforming the ethnic character of the city. As with earlier immigrants, many of the newcomers sought jobs in the booming auto plants that, by 1929, employed over 400,000 people in the metropolitan area. Nothing demonstrated the strength of this economic and demographic transformation more than the increase in assessed valuation of property in Detroit, which soared from $392,335,600 in 1916 to $2,933,638,350 in 1929. Racing behind this motor-driven economy, Detroit struggled to provide services to a city that grew in area by almost 75 percent between 1920 and 1930. By 1930, Detroit's bonded debt reached $255 million, nearly ten times its level of a decade before.[3]

These changes did not come easily to Detroit. During these years, the city was rocked by the Palmer raids against suspected Bolsheviks; a nativist inspired attempt to abolish all private and parochial schools in the state; violence against the black community (about 41,000 in 1920); the rise of an active chapter of the Ku Klux Klan; the election of a Klan-supported mayor in 1929; and bloody battles between Italian and Jewish gangs for control of the liquor trade during Prohibition.[4] More important than any of these disturbances, however, was the fierce struggle between management and labor over the issue of the open shop. As early as 1910, the Employers' Association of Detroit broke the metal trade unions, and, throughout the boom years of the 1910s and early 1920s, the auto industry ruthlessly fought to maintain an open shop.[5] Throughout this period, the Detroit Federation of Labor (DFL) clashed repeatedly with the Employers' Association and the Board of Commerce over the open shop. Business leaders, for example, issued dire warnings that "The Clutch of Labor Monopoly is at Detroit's Throat Today" and almost every issue of the *Detroiter,* the official publication of the Board of Commerce, vilified unions and labor leaders. On the other side of the struggle, the union leaders and the *Detroit Labor News,* official voice of the DFL, issued equally frightful warnings that "Organized Greed and Reptile Press Plan Attack on Labor."[6] The 1927 mayoral contest was dominated by the open-shop issue, pitting the DFL in an unequal struggle against the combined forces of the Board of Commerce, the Employers' Association, and the Detroit Citizens League. By the early 1930s, the employer groups were so successful in breaking unions that Detroit became known as "the graveyard of organizers."[7]

Surprisingly, for most of the decade, few of these confrontations spilled over to school politics. Those that did, however, are noteworthy because they stand as the rare examples of educational conflict in this era. Three issues sparked particular controversy: the "militarization" of the schools during World War I; the use of school buildings for meetings of left-wing groups and organizations; and the unionization of teachers. Significantly, none of these issues was entirely resolved in the 1920s, and each played a role in the reconfiguration of educational politics in the 1930s.

The first of these issues, the introduction of military training into Detroit high schools, was part of the larger national controversy about U.S. entry into World War I. Early in 1917, the Detroit Socialist party denounced a voluntary program of military drill involving some 400 young men from Central High School. Outraged that these students were being "prepared to be used for cannon fodder to advance and protect the economic interests of the American plutocracy," the socialists petitioned the school board to end this "movement to militarize this educational institution." In a raucous demonstration at the board, the socialists, led by Dennis E. Batt, a former U.S. cavalryman, lectured the school officials on the evils of militarism.[8] The DFL also joined the protests. However, after the American Federation of Labor

(AFL) threw its support to the war effort, the DFL reversed its position, leaving the socialists as the lone opponents of military training in the schools.[9]

On the other side, in support of the training, stood the Board of Commerce. In the spring of 1917, businessmen demonstrated their commitment to the program by providing free uniforms and rifles for the trainees. To oversee the effort, the Board of Commerce set up a Committee on Military Training in the Schools, chaired by school board member Alexis Angell and including school leaders Frank Cody and Edwin Miller. Faced with such well-entrenched support for the program and under enormous political pressure because of its antiwar stand, the Socialist party retreated in its efforts to change school policy on this issue.[10]

While the Socialist party lost its campaign to end military training in the schools, left-wing organizations scored a notable victory in the second controversial educational issue of the era, the use of schools for evening and weekend forums that presented diverse and often radical views. As William Reese has shown, the use of schools as social centers was an important part of the educational agenda of many "progressive" reformers. In Detroit, the small board of education approved an "open forum" resolution early in 1917. The commitment of the board to that resolution was severely tested four years later, when the Socialist party requested permission to hold its national convention at Detroit's Northeastern High School. The board approved the request, and, despite a flurry of criticism, the event proceeded without incident, marking the first time that the socialists ever held a national convention in a public school building.[11]

The Socialist party convention was not an isolated example of the board's liberal policy of building use. Throughout the 1920s and early 1930s, a period of American history when organized labor and left-wing organizations often failed to gain access to privately owned meeting halls in many parts of the country, the Detroit school board routinely provided rooms and auditoriums not only for the Detroit Federation of Labor but also for many radical organizations, including the Proletarian party, a communist splinter group, and, at times, even the Communist party.[12] By far the most important program of controversial speakers was the annual DFL Labor Forum that was held in the auditorium at Cass Technical High School. Beginning in 1925, the forum featured such speakers as Clarence Darrow, Lillian Herstein, A. J. Muste, Scott Nearing, W. E. B. DuBois, and Norman Thomas. Occasionally, the speakers at the Labor Forum outraged individual school board members, who denounced "communistic speeches" in the schools, but the forum continued throughout the 1920s and 1930s, providing an important platform for liberal and left-wing views in Detroit.[13]

The last controversial issue, the efforts by teachers to unionize, reflected the larger battle between business and labor in Detroit. As early as 1914, the *Labor News* urged Detroit teachers to follow the lead of teachers in other cities who had joined the labor movement. The formation of the American Federation of Teachers (AFT) in 1916 and salary increases won in other cities by teachers using union tactics raised DFL hopes for a teachers' union in Detroit.[14] As a front page *Labor News* editorial argued in September, 1919, "[There is no] prospect for the teachers to ever receive their just dues in Detroit unless they follow the profitable experience of teachers in the communities where they have organized. . . ." The *Labor News* promised the full backing of the labor movement should the teachers form a union.[15]

In late February, 1920, these promptings bore fruit as thirty-nine male high school teachers signed an AFT charter. Less than a week later, eleven female high school teachers formed a second AFT local. The DFL was elated and resolved "to support to the utmost the teachers of this city in their efforts to unionize. . . ."[16] Unfortunately for the new AFT locals, DFL support extended no further than these resolutions. Amid a storm of community outrage, the fledgling unions were quickly swept away. The president of the administrator-dominated Detroit Teachers Association denounced the unions as "unprofessional" and labeled their leaders "a small group of radicals." School board member Dr. John Hall urged the board to immediately fire the union members. The *Detroit Free Press* assailed the unions as "class organizations," and argued that, in joining them, the teachers had violated the public trust as surely as if they had preached partisan or sectarian lessons in the classroom. Echoing the conventional wisdom of an era that severely circumscribed the political and private lives of teachers, the *Free Press* demanded that the teachers quit the union, because"[i]nstructors of the youth in this republic are not altogether private individuals." Amid the public outcry, school officials acted decisively. As Superintendent Frank Cody recalled years later, "The teachers who participated were informally but officially notified that their contracts for the following year would be withheld if they became members of the teachers' union."[17]

Unnerved by the angry outcry and the threat to their livelihood, the union members reconvened the locals. After some debate about "unionism versus professionalism," they repudiated the union charters and announced the creation of a new organization, the Council of Detroit Teachers, with no ties to either the AFT or DFL. The council was, at best, a face-saving gesture for the teachers, and it soon collapsed. In all, the first teachers' unions in Detroit had lasted barely a week. The flirtation with unionism, however, was not a total failure. As will be discussed later, the threat of a teachers' union did help spur the mayor and city council to approve a substantial pay raise later that month. Nevertheless, it would be more than a decade before any teachers were willing to risk union affiliation again.[18]

These conflicts over "militarism," the use of school buildings for left-wing forums, and teacher unionism pitted major interest groups squarely against each other in battles that paralleled larger, more intense conflicts raging in the political and economic arenas of the city. Undeniably, the three school-related controversies represented deep divisions in politics and public opinion. Yet the most significant aspect of these controversies is that none threatened the overall support for public education in Detroit in the 1920s. Indeed, business leaders and organized labor probably agreed more on educational issues than on any other issues in city government. Behind that consensus lay the fact that both sides recognized that the schools worked in their interests.

Roots of Consensus

In an insightful essay on conflict and consensus in American educational history, Carl Kaestle argues that "what appears to be American consensus on education is to some extent the result of ambivalence, muted conflict, and trade-offs. The American public school is a gigantic standardized compromise most of us have learned to live with."[19] While that perspective captures important elements of the American educational consensus, it downplays the very positive support that Americans have often given to public schools. The educational consensus in Detroit in the 1920s was marked by some "ambivalence, muted conflict, and trade-offs," but these characteristics were less prominent than the strong current of popular enthusiasm for public education. Different interest groups supported the schools for different and, at times, conflicting reasons, but fundamental support for the schools was something people in Detroit took for granted.

The swift collapse of the AFT locals in 1920, for example, was a blow that surely fueled DFL fears about business domination of the school board. But even this defeat did not weaken the commitment of the DFL to the schools. Labor justified its support for public education ideologically, historically, and economically. Ideologically, labor assumed that education and liberation went hand in hand. As the *Labor News* put it in a 1917 editorial, "Ignorance is bliss for the employer so long as the employe [*sic*] remains ignorant. Education is power which stands ready to serve you after you have acquired it." The editor of the *Labor News* had no doubt that education would lead workers to better understand capitalist exploitation and to realize that only unions could end that exploitation.[20] Another *Labor News* article entitled "Education Will Emancipate Workers" argued, "Education and slavery cannot exist together in one land and as the vision of the toiler becomes clearer to discern the brutality of the economic system that enslaves many but enriches the few, he places his individuality behind the fortress of the labor organization feeling and believing that men cemented together by the ties of class interest can and will usher in a civilization where man, woman, and child will be free."[21]

The DFL, however, did not simply support education in the abstract. Education was essentially synonymous with public schooling. As one *Labor News* editorial in March, 1919, declared, "Education is the bulwark of American liberty. The public school is the fortress of education." This support for the schools was strongly based on the historical belief that working-class agitation in the nineteenth century had created American public education. As a 1924 *Labor News* editorial put it, "Labor was the first to fight for the public schools in America." This interpretation of educational history, today associated with the work of Frank Tracy Carlton and Merle Curti, inspired not only Detroit's unions but virtually every other important left-wing organization to back the public schools. In addition to organized labor, the Detroit Socialist party and even the Communist party similarly articulated their commitment to the schools through this view of educational history.[22]

Perhaps the finest expression of this historical interpretation and its practical consequences appeared in the 1924 report of a DFL committee that analyzed the school board's proposed budget for 1924–25. The committee was composed of three members of the DFL executive board, including Dennis E. Batt, editor of the *Labor News,* a socialist who helped found the Communist Party of the United States but later shifted to the Proletarian party, and William Mollenhauser, who was a leader of the Detroit Communist party in the early 1930s.[23] Their assessment of the budget concluded by stating,

> Your committee believes that the labor movement in the city of Detroit should do everything within its power to see that the children of the community are provided with adequate education facilities. This opinion is in perfect harmony

with the traditions of the American trade union movement. We were the first upon the American continent to demand free public schools. This tradition imposes on the trade union movement the responsibility of endeavoring to protect and develop the public school system to its fullest possibilities.[24]

Beyond reinforcing a strong commitment to public education, this perspective encouraged intense interest in the operation and governance of the public schools. The *Labor News* emphasized the need for workers to "maintain an active interest in the management of the schools," and it ran numerous articles warning about efforts by business groups to influence school policy across the nation. These articles argued that the price for free public education was eternal vigilance on the part of the working class, vigilance that would keep the hands of the bosses off the schools.[25] As a 1916 article in the *Michigan Socialist* put it, "Workers of Detroit—keep your eye on your public schools and don't permit the minds of the children to be poisoned against your own best interests." In short, this perspective encouraged union members and left-wing activists to become engaged with, but critical of, public schools.[26]

Nowhere was this stance more apparent than in efforts by the DFL to elect school board members who were sympathetic to organized labor. As early as 1919, the *Labor News* editorialized that "future school boards [should] be composed of men and women wearing overalls."[27] While achieving that specific goal was long in coming, by the mid-1920s organized labor had succeeded in breaking the monopoly elite Detroiters had on the school board. In 1925, John H. Webster, a pharmacist, and Frank Gorman, an insurance agent, became the first "non-elite" Detroiters elected to the small board. The DFL strongly backed Webster in his race against the incumbent, Dr. Andrew Biddle, who the *Labor News* described as notoriously "anti-labor." While the DFL did not officially endorse Gorman, the *Labor News* reported that he was "well thought of in labor circles."[28] Throughout the 1920s, Gorman and Webster did not rock the boat toward either the left or the right, but both men, who served on the board for more than two decades, eventually sided with the DFL on several key issues in the 1930s and 1940s. By far the most notable change on the board occurred in 1929, when Edward H. Williams, an insurance agent, ended Samuel Mumford's twenty-two years as a school board member. Williams was the first avowedly prolabor candidate to win a board seat, and the DFL trumpeted the election as a victory of the people over the "interests."[29]

While ideology and a sense of history led the DFL to both support the schools and work to limit capitalist domination of them, the economic issue of child labor provided the most direct and tangible reason for union interest in the public education. Indeed, no other education-related issue aroused such passion or so dominated the *Labor News* as the exploitation of children. As one editorial stated, "Organized labor, if it stands for anything, stands for the development of the mind and the protection of the child." Throughout the 1920s and early 1930s, it was practically impossible to read the DFL paper without finding an article or editorial denouncing child labor.[30] A typical editorial, "Sacrificing Our Children," deplored child labor in gruesome terms, comparing it to "grinding the flesh and lives of children into dollars, [a practice] which will bring joy and pleasure to exploiters of labor."[31] As far as the DFL was concerned, nothing characterized the brutality of capitalism as much as the exploitation of children.

Like the American Federation of Labor, the DFL plan for eliminating child labor rested on three principles: gaining a living wage for heads of households so children would not be forced to work, passing and enforcing strict child labor laws to limit the ages and hours of child workers, and enacting compulsory school laws. Throughout the 1920s and 1930s, the DFL urged Michigan legislators to "Guard Our School Laws" against efforts by employers to weaken these laws and enthusiastically backed efforts to pass a child labor amendment to the U.S. Constitution.[32] The importance of public schools and compulsory education in the campaign to end child labor cannot be underestimated. Union support for expanding educational opportunities through building more schools, hiring more teachers, and implementing "progressive" curricula was inextricably linked to the effort to eradicate child labor.

While the issue of child labor certainly galvanized union support for the expansion and improvement of public schools in the 1920s, its deeper, long-range significance was that it inspired an important, unusual political alignment. Abolishing child labor and getting working children into school were perhaps the most important issues on which union members, socialists, school leaders, and elite reformers could find common ground. The DFL, for example, warmly received Charles Chadsey when he spoke to the unions on the need to curtail the employment of children. Similarly, although union leaders were quite wary of Laura Osborn and the women of the elite Twentieth Century Club, the DFL and Osborn found common ground in her involvement in the National Child Labor Committee, the leading anti–child labor organization in the nation. This alliance of labor, school leaders, and elite reformers on the child labor issue foreshadowed the political coalition these groups would form in the 1930s, when the Depression essentially enacted the policies these groups had been seeking, dramatically curtailing child labor and forcing huge numbers of adolescent workers back to school.[33]

Though considerably less self-conscious than organized labor in their views on education, such business organizations as the Board of Commerce and such conservative newspapers as the *Free Press* and *Saturday Night* found several important reasons to strongly support public schools in this era. On an abstract level, these conservative interests ironically associated public education with the advancement of liberty in terms almost identical to those expressed by organized labor. A 1923 *Free Press* editorial, for example, argued "that despotism finds its chief support in ignorance, and that knowledge and freedom go hand in hand."[34] Yet when business leaders or the editors of conservative newspapers got down to specifics, the differences between the right and left on how public education was linked to freedom become quite clear.

Whereas labor viewed education as a means for challenging the status quo, business leaders and conservative opinion makers counted on the schools to strengthen the established order. Liberty, in their eyes, could only be maintained by encouraging patriotism, instilling a commitment to American political institutions, and inculcating the virtues of free enterprise.[35] By far, the most explicit effort to institutionalize these educational goals was the Detroit Americanization program, jointly sponsored by the board of education and the Board of Commerce. But, as the architect of that joint program, Superintendent Frank Cody, once noted, the schools were also responsible for "the Americanization of the American," a job that he believed was "more vital than the Americanization of the alien, important as that is." To that end, the Board of Commerce sponsored a series of patriotic programs in the schools, and the newspapers kept a watchful eye on programs in character and citizenship education.[36]

While ideology may have provided business leaders with the rhetoric of support for schools, like organized labor, the business community also sought to realize some economic gain from public education. If the chief economic benefit organized labor received from the schools was keeping young workers out of the labor market, then the primary economic benefit businesses received was the preparation of young workers for their eventual entry into that market. As one Board of Commerce spokesman stated in 1916, "It is natural for business men . . . to see the work of education as the single problem of educating the young men who will work in the factory or improving the education of those already engaged there." Over a decade later, the

Free Press applauded " . . . the cooperation of the schools with industry to the end that every student upon graduation should be fitted to earn his living in one field or another."[37]

Nothing delighted the business leaders of Detroit more than the superb reputation of the school system in vocational education. Cass Technical High School drew particular praise from the Board of Commerce as "a monumental achievement of education and architecture of which any city would be proud." In addition to Cass, business leaders and conservative newspapers, particularly *Detroit Saturday Night,* took great pride in the "revolutionary" changes in the school system, especially the expansion of vocational and practical courses on the intermediate school (grades 7 through 9) and high school levels.[38] In their public pronouncements, these business leaders and conservative newspaper editors explicitly praised the schools because education was indispensable to increasing the wealth and social stability of the community.

In addition to these ideological and practical reasons, Detroit business leaders supported the schools in the 1920s because they were quite comfortable with the school leadership. Aside from Frank Gorman, John Webster, and Edward Williams, every school board member elected in the 1920s was listed in the Social Register. The other new members included A. D. Jamieson, vice president of the Union-Guardian Trust Company, and Dr. Burt R. Shurly, both of whom began more than two decades of school board membership with their election in 1927.[39] Jamieson and Shurly quickly emerged as the most articulate spokesmen on the school board for conservative positions.

But perhaps more important than the political leanings or social status of any school board member was the influence of Superintendent Frank Cody. Despite taking office under a cloud in 1919, Cody had received strong support from business leaders in his effort to become superintendent. By the mid-1920s, the cloud had entirely dissipated and Cody basked in the acclaim of his allies in the business community. Like the captains of industry in Detroit, Cody directed and nurtured a vast, booming enterprise that rapidly became a model for the nation.[40] Indeed, in 1922, *Saturday Night* bestowed its highest compliment upon him, stating, "Frank Cody is first of all a businessman, an energetic hustling businessman. There is nothing pedantic or academic about him. . . . He looks talks and laughs like a big business man. And that is after all just what he is: one of the biggest in town." Throughout the decade, the Board of Commerce, the *Free Press,* and the *Detroit Times* (part of the Hearst chain) all echoed these sentiments. Cody provided the vital human link between the business community and the schools, and he helped insure support for public education throughout the 1920s.[41]

The fact that business and labor, the two interest groups engaged in the most ferocious economic and political conflicts of the era, could agree upon the need for high-quality public education had important, positive consequences for the Detroit schools, most notably in terms of increased funding. In the 1914–15 school year, for example, $2,341,599, less than 18 percent of the total city tax levy, went to the public schools. Four years later, in the 1918–19 school year, the amount raised for the schools had climbed to $6,137,468, almost 28 percent of the total municipal levy. By the 1920–21 school year, funds for the schools soared to $11,983,671, an all-time high of 34 percent of total city revenue. The increase in local spending for the schools is even more dramatic if we look at spending in the years immediately preceding and following the reform campaign. Between 1910–11 and 1917–18, per-pupil revenue from local taxes adjusted for inflation averaged $102.74. Between 1918–19 and 1931–32, per-pupil revenue averaged $143.94. What makes that per-pupil increase even more impressive is the enormous enrollment growth of the system between 1918 and 1932, from 95,023 to 254,645 students.[42] Although state-level data at this time are sketchy, Detroit clearly was one of the richest school systems in Michigan. A 1920 survey of sixty-six urban school districts in the state listed Detroit sixth in per-pupil operating expenditures. Detroit spent almost 36 percent more per pupil than the average of these districts.[43]

These increased expenditures for public education came from city council allocations rather than from direct taxation by the school board. Like other city agencies, the board of education submitted its annual budget to the city council, which then determined the actual amount the schools would receive. The budget then went to the mayor, who had veto power over the allocations.[44] As the largest municipal expenditure, the school budget was always a potentially volatile political issue. Yet, throughout most of the 1920s, the city council and a series of mayors readily agreed to these substantial increases. In other words, most political leaders in Detroit also favored increased spending for education. And in the rare instances where some politicians did propose cuts in the school budget, they ran squarely into opposition from business and labor alike.

Such unanimity on education encouraged a sense of exuberant optimism among Detroit educators. Surveying the transformation of the school system between 1919 and 1922, Deputy School Superintendent Charles Spain could barely contain himself, declaring,

The last three years in Detroit have been a period of unprecedented educational progress. I am sure that we are justified in saying no other large American city has ever made so much progress in so short a time. . . . The sudden growth of the city, which has brought in a new population including hundreds of well-trained men with progressive ideas and desiring the best and most modern things in the way of education for their children, the new attitude toward education, and the new appreciation of the value of education on the part of the people as a result of the war and the revelations of the war, the habit of looking at things in a large way and of spending money in large sums to carry on great undertakings, the general prosperity of the entire community due to conditions attendant upon the war, the fact that schools were under the control of a forward looking, far-sighted superintendent and a board of education progressive with a large vision, the favorable attitude of the Mayor and the Common Council in appropriation of funds, reflecting as it did the more liberal attitude of the entire public toward education—the combination of all these factors made possible a rapid and well-organized development along all lines of educational endeavor which perhaps has been unparalleled in any city of this country.[45]

The fact that the people of Detroit responded so enthusiastically to increases in the school budget does not necessarily make the case for a broad-based consensus on public education in Detroit. Taken alone, agreement on budget increases is only one part of the story. Political conflict often arises when participants move beyond such vague goals as increased funding for schools and begin discussing concrete programs, expenditures, and priorities. Indeed, many educational historians have described bitter controversies over specific Progressive era policies and practices in other cities undergoing rapid educational expansion. Such issues as raising teachers' salaries, the hiring of married women teachers, the construction of new buildings, and the introduction of such "progressive" innovations as standardized testing, junior high schools, and the Gary Plan all generated serious conflict in major cities across the country.[46] Detroit faced all of these issues, and any assessment of the educational consensus in the Motor City must take them into account.

Hiring an Adequate Number of Teachers

The history of American education in the twentieth century has been punctuated by several periods of severe teacher shortages. The first time the inadequate supply of teachers became a major, national issue was during the post–World War I years. Several factors that would also figure into subsequent teacher shortages precipitated the shortage of the 1920s: a sharp drop in teacher salaries relative to salaries in other fields, a rising cost of living that further depressed teachers' earnings, a large number of teachers who abandoned the classroom for more lucrative jobs, and a substantial decline in the number of students preparing for careers in teaching in colleges and normal schools.[47] In 1920, the Commission on the Emergency in Education of the National Education Association (NEA) found that the shortage reached into classrooms in every section of the country. The commission declared that the nation needed approximately 170,000 new teachers, which was *"more than twice the total number* of graduates of all the private and public normal schools in the entire country."[48] Large urban school systems that had better salaries and working conditions than rural districts had a somewhat easier time finding teachers during this period. Nevertheless, teacher shortages also plagued urban districts, because enrollments in these districts were growing at an unprecedented rate, and teachers in urban areas had greater opportunities for finding better paying jobs outside of education.

Detroit felt the teacher shortage acutely, in part because the city had not been paying its instructors well even before World War I. As early as 1911, *Saturday Night* editorialized against "Starving the Schoolmaster," noting that earnings for Detroit teachers lagged behind other major cities. The *Labor News* also deplored low teachers' salaries.[49] The problem of just compensation for teachers did not become a serious issue, however, until early in 1917, when Charles Chadsey announced that new teachers were refusing to come to Detroit because the salaries in the city were inadequate. Actually, the reluctance of prospective teachers to come to Detroit said more about the erosion of teachers' salaries in general than it did about salaries in the city because in the 1917–18 school year, teachers in Detroit were among the highest paid in the state.[50] During these years, however, teachers' earnings neither kept pace with the dramatic surge of inflation associated with World War I nor with the salary scales of other professions. Between December, 1914, and July, 1919, the cost of living in Detroit shot up almost 94 percent. Teachers salaries during the same period only rose about 49 percent. Moreover, Detroit teachers saw wages rise at a substantially faster rate for people in practically every other occupation. For example, between September, 1914, and September, 1919, metal workers had received wage increases of more than 106 percent, chemical workers 104 percent, and boot and shoe makers 68 percent. Early in 1920, Superintendent Frank Cody reported that twice as many teachers had resigned in the last six months as had resigned in the entire previous year. Their reason for leaving, he noted, was the simple "desire to enter more lucrative employment."[51]

Schools opened in Detroit in September, 1919, with 300 unfilled teaching positions. In a series of front page editorials, the *Labor News* denounced the meager salaries that were forcing teachers to abandon the classroom for other careers. The paper noted bitterly that "when the wages of our teachers will be advanced to favorably compare with those of a scrub woman, there may be some inducement for them to continue their useful function." The *Labor News* saw the low salaries for teachers as part of a larger pattern of capitalist exploitation of workers. Denouncing the business-dominated school board, the labor paper claimed that "no one will be surprised that a business administration most generally manages to get its books to balance and to get 10 cents worth of work out of every one receiving a nickle."[52]

The DFL defined the problem in terms of class oppression, partly to inspire teachers to form the AFT local discussed previously. But the DFL interpretation soon lost credibility as it became clear that support for teachers' pay raises had broad support that transcended class lines. Not long after the *Labor News* series of editorials, Frank Cody, hardly a radical, also implored the city to raise teachers' pay. Cody estimated that Detroit would need 600 more teachers in the 1919–20 school year, and he argued that higher salaries were essential for attracting qualified applicants. These sentiments were quickly endorsed by the Board of Commerce, which issued a resolution stating that "the cost of living has increased more rapidly than teachers' salaries, thereby impairing the efficiency of our school system." The business leaders urged civic leaders to give the problem immediate attention, adding that "the Detroit Board of Commerce thoroughly approves of the principle of higher compensation for the teaching profession in the City of Detroit." The *Free Press* also denounced the "starvation wages" paid to the teachers, and *Detroit Saturday Night* argued that increased salaries were "simple justice."[53]

These appeals coincided with the annual budget deliberations of the mayor and the city council and were obviously designed to influence the process. Amid these deliberations, teachers organized the ill-fated AFT locals in late February. In support of the new locals, the DFL renewed its call for higher salaries for teachers by issuing a strongly worded resolution addressed to the mayor and the city council.[54] While the flirtation with unionism by the Detroit teachers quickly cooled, the threat of unionization may have increased the pressure on civic leaders to compensate the teachers more fairly. Faced with palpable demonstrations of need, a broad, united political front, and the threat of teacher militancy, the mayor and council could hardly avoid increasing the municipal allocation to the schools. The amount they approved, however, must have fulfilled the most ardent dreams of school supporters. The mayor and council almost doubled the total allocation for the schools to $11,983,671 for 1920–21, almost $5.8 million more than the previous year.[55]

All of that money, of course, was not just for increasing teachers' salaries. New teachers needed to be hired and new buildings needed to be constructed. Nevertheless, Detroit teachers received very substantial raises. The board increased starting salaries for kindergarten and elementary school teachers from $920 to $1,500 annually and increased maximum salaries from $1,520 to $1,800. For intermediate and high school teachers, the board increased starting salaries from $1,100 to $1,700 and maximum salaries from $2,200 to $2,500. The new salary schedule had an immediate impact on the teacher shortage in Detroit. Within a month, the board reported a large increase in applications and assured the public that "the new schedule has eliminated any possible danger of teacher shortage in Detroit." That assessment appears to have been accurate. Over the next decade, the number of teachers in the Detroit public schools grew from 4,083 in 1920–21 to 7,525 in 1929–30. Indeed, for the rest of the 1920s, *Saturday Night, The Detroiter,* and the *Labor News* continued to comment on the difficulty rural districts had in finding trained teachers, but none of these publications mentioned the problem again in regard to Detroit.[56]

Having resolved the issue of salaries, late in 1921 the Detroit school board turned to the question of whether to continue its policy of employing married women teachers. In employing married women, Detroit was a notable exception to a national trend, since most school districts in the nation in the 1920s and 1930s refused to hire married women teachers and terminated the contracts of women who did marry during the school year.[57] Early in September, 1921, board member Dr. John Hall introduced a resolution that would have ended Detroit's unusual status in this regard by ending the policy of employing married women teachers. The resolution provoked a vigorous struggle between Hall and Laura Osborn, the only woman on the board.

In addition to her strong views on school reform and temperance, Osborn was an ardent suffragist and campaigner for women's rights. Given these commitments, it is not surprising to find that she believed married women had as much right to teach as married men. Such arguments carried little weight with Hall, however, which forced Osborn to seek additional reasons why married women should continue to teach in the Detroit system. At the urging of Osborn and her allies, the board tabled Hall's resolution until a board committee could conduct a study on married women teachers in the city. The study focused on two key criticisms of the policy: (1) that married women were taking jobs that otherwise would go to single teachers, and (2) that married women were often distracted by familial obligations and therefore were less effective in the classroom than single teachers. The study, carried out by board members Osborn and Campbell, found that neither of these criticisms had any merit. No teachers seeking work in Detroit were denied jobs due to the employment of married women. In addition, Osborn and Campbell found that problems at home rarely interfered with the professional commitments or abilities of married women. Indeed, after surveying the merit rankings given to all the teachers in the system, Osborn and Campbell remarked that "[m]arried women teachers rank as high in professional ability as the general body of teachers." Armed with this new information, the proponents of the policy urged that the report be adopted and Hall's resolution be denied. The showdown came on December 22, 1921, as the board voted, by the narrowest of margins, 4 to 3, to continue employing married women.[58]

The implementation of a more generous salary schedule and the decision to employ married women assured Detroit of a steady flow of teachers throughout the boom years of the 1920s. During these years, most Detroiters seemed content with board policy on these matters. Neither of these issues would emerge as controversial questions again until the Great Depression.[59]

Building the System

Next to salaries, the other great expense in any school system is capital spending. Constructing and maintaining the "physical plant," as school buildings came to be known in this era of business metaphors, demanded huge amounts of money. Like other major cities in the 1920s, the enormous growth in enrollment in Detroit precipitated an unprecedented crisis in school construction. Such reform leaders as Laura Osborn had repeatedly denounced Wales Martindale and the ward-based school board for their failure to accommodate the upsurge of students in the early years of the century. Even organizations like the DFL, which was lukewarm to reform, castigated the ward-based board for its building policies. "Disgraceful is a mild way to describe the condition which exists in Detroit," the *Labor News* declared in September, 1915, "when many children of school age cannot go to school because this city, 'where life is worth living,' has not enough schools to house these yearners after knowledge." One year later, the socialists also blasted the ward-based school board for the inadequate number of schools, claiming that the board was providing "for the education of the children of the wealthy classes at the expense of the city no matter what may happen in the 'overcrowded congested districts' where the workers have to live."[60] If the reformers were to make good on their promises of more efficient and responsive school governance, the construction of new schools was imperative.

The magnitude of the housing problem, however, was staggering. During the American involvement in World War I, school construction in Detroit essentially halted, but enrollments continued to rise. Between the 1917–18 school year, the first year the small school board took office, and the 1934–35 school year, when interwar enrollments peaked, the total number of students in the Detroit system, including those in special programs, grew from 95,023 to 268,323.[61] In other words, in this seventeen-year period, the Detroit board practically had to create two new school systems equal in size to the system in place in 1917–18. In order to meet the average annual increase of students between 1917–18 and 1934–35, the board had to construct buildings at a rate of more than 10,000 seats per year.

In confronting this challenge, the board had to deal with two crucial issues. First, convincing the people and the city government to approve tax increases and bond sales for new school construction, and, second, deciding which form of school organization and which pedagogic practices would best serve the burgeoning student population. Both of these issues had the potential to generate intense political conflict.

In many ways, the effort to convince the city to provide huge sums of money for school construction directly paralleled the struggle for higher salaries for teachers. Initially, both the Socialist party and the DFL viewed the lack of buildings and inadequately housed pupils as part of a capitalist conspiracy to keep the children of workers ignorant. In 1917, the socialist columnist Apropos pointed to the half-day sessions and overcrowded classrooms in Detroit as proof that "capitalism cares little for the schools." Two years later, upon discovering that 15,000 elementary students were attending half-day sessions, the *Labor News* angrily declared, "this incompetence or indifference on the part of the school board to provide adequate educational facilities for our children may be traced to the fact that they are after all only the children of workers." The labor paper declared unequivocally that "the slogan of the working people should be: 'Build New Schools.'"[62]

Yet, just as the DFL was mistaken in describing the salary issue in class terms, so the question of building more schools also failed to fit a class analysis. As early as 1918, *The Detroiter* issued "A Call to Duty" to every member of the Board of Commerce urging them to support city council candidates who favored allocating more money for school construction. *Detroit Saturday Night* also advocated more spending on school construction, declaring that "Detroit's need of schools is notorious." Immediately upon becoming superintendent, Frank Cody pledged that his primary goal "will be to provide proper school accommodations and full day sessions in elementary grades for all children in all sections of the city." Two years later, an article in *Saturday Night* reminded its readers that "we must provide increasing funds for proper education. We must provide many educational buildings for pupil accommodation. We must make it possible for more children to complete the public school course."[63]

As with the salary issue, pressure on city government from the business community, organized labor, as well as civic and school leaders, combined with the obvious need for more schools, resulted in a substantial increase in funding. Capital expenditures that were $2,056,932 in 1917–18, climbed to $3,652,648 the following school year, fell somewhat to $2,796,451 in 1919–20, and then soared to $18,819,019 in 1920–21. While the 1920–21 rate was not sustained, from 1921–22 to 1931–32, when capital expenditures were curtailed because of the depression, capital spending averaged over $5,500,000 annually.[64] Much of the money to fund this building campaign came from increasing the school system's share of local taxes. In addition, the bonded debt of the system nearly doubled from $33,230,894 in 1921–22 to $66,236,617 in 1928–29.[65]

These swift, dramatic increases in taxes and bonded debt generally met with public approval. But the sheer volume of capital spending between 1921 and 1923, more than $31million, made the school board an easy political target. Unlike the salary issue, which was essentially settled in 1920, the construction of new buildings drew some criticism. Yet even the controversy over capital spending, because it was brief and unrelated to class divisions, provides further evidence of the fundamental agreement that undergirded school politics of this era. It also offers another glimpse of how business and labor joined together on this issue to support the interests of the public schools.

The most important conflict over school construction occurred in late 1923 and early in 1924. The 1923 municipal election was dominated by the issue of excessive governmental spending, with several city council candidates targeting the school board as a major source of extravagance and waste. The leading critic was Joseph A. Martin, former commissioner of public works. Throughout his campaign, Martin asserted that Detroit was short of classrooms because the school board had squandered its funds constructing "schools that resemble palaces." The *Free Press* echoed that criticism declaring that "if the millions of dollars that have been needlessly spent in putting up ornate and elaborate buildings had been employed in a frugal, businesslike way there is little doubt that all the children attending the public schools of Detroit today could easily be given seats in good, substantial, safe, comfortably appointed buildings."[66]

While most of the criticism of the board centered on costs, there were hints in this campaign of a nativist backlash, alleging that these expensive schools were going up primarily in "foreign neighborhoods." Indeed, there was some talk of stripping the school board of the right to decide where new schools should be located.[67] Recently, several historians have wrestled with the question of whether school officials in the 1920s and 1930s distributed educational resources equally to various racial and ethnic communities. The nativist allegations of discrimination *in favor* of the foreign born in Detroit provides an opportunity to examine that question. The critics who accused the school board of extravagance most often pointed to the new, platoon-style elementary schools and the intermediate schools as evidence of wasteful spending. These schools will be discussed in greater detail in the next section, but, for now, the most important fact about them is that they did indeed cost more than traditional elementary schools. The new buildings contained swimming pools, gymnasiums, shops, art rooms, music rooms, and so forth. They embodied the progressive ideal of educating "the whole child" and were the best the system had to offer. As such, did some groups get greater access to these schools than others?[68]

A 1921 nationality survey that listed school enrollment by ethnic group and a 1924 list of platoon schools provides some answers to that question. The 1921 survey found that the dominant ethnic groups in the school system were U.S.-born whites, 46.5 percent; Poles, 9.2 percent; Russian-Jewish, 7.1 percent; Canadians, 6.5 percent; Italians, 4.8 percent; Germans, 4.5 percent; African Americans, 4.4 percent; and English, 3.1 percent. By 1924, 67 out of 141 elementary schools were platooned. The racial and ethnic distribution in these schools closely parallels the larger distribution within the system, with U.S.-born whites accounting for 40.9 percent of platoon school students; Poles, 9.5 percent; Russians, 7.6 percent; blacks, 4.5 percent; Canadians, 4.4 percent; Italians, 3.3 percent; Germans, 2.8 percent; and English, 1.6 percent.[69]

This equality of access to platooned elementary schools, however, was not duplicated in the intermediate schools, which served grades 7 through 9. In 1921, the construction of intermediate schools had just begun and there were only four such schools, serving 3,616 students in the city. Of these students, 51.9 percent in these schools were U.S.-born white, 12.7 percent German, 5.6 percent Canadian, 3.7 percent Polish, 3.6 percent African-American, and 3.1 percent Italian. Russian-Jewish students were not present in sizable numbers in *any* of the four intermediate schools. While this analysis of platoon and intermediate school enrollments is hardly conclusive, it does indicate that the nativist allegations of favoritism to the foreign born were groundless. At least on the elementary school level, access to the newest and most expensive schools in the system was essentially equal to all racial and ethnic groups. If anything, the foreign-born communities appear to have had reason to protest the lack of access for their children to the intermediate schools.[70]

Such considerations aside, as election day neared, council candidates attacked "school frills" and promised to rein in the profligate board of education. Since Joseph Martin generally "enjoyed support from upper-income and 'good-government' groups in the city," it is notable that the most vigorous opposition to his attacks on the school board came from the Board of Commerce.[71] In response to the growing criticism of the board on this issue, the *Detroiter* published an article on the national shortage of schools that concluded, "Detroit's position among other large cities is favorable, but until every school child can attend full time the city should not stop in its construction program." An editorial in the same issue dismissed the allegations of "DeLuxe" schools and wasted money as "balderdash." In an apparent reference to Martin, the editorial concluded, "For any individual, no matter what his administrative position, to say that we must stop building schools, is utterly ridiculous. That would be a very neat and effective way of committing civic suicide." As the accusations about frills increased during that latter stage of the campaign, *The Detroiter* again editorially defended the school construction program and disparaged the talk of "frills."[72]

The DFL also responded to the attacks on the building program of the board of education. Just before the election, the *Labor News* joined the construction and frills controversy editorializing that "children are deprived of full time in school and do not have the proper attention while there due to overcrowding. The struggle for a livelihood in modern society has become so keen that the best possible equipment in the way of training is not too much with which to fortify one starting out into life."[73]

Despite such support for the school board, Martin and other advocates of fiscal conservatism won their races for the council. Their victory shifted the controversy about school construction from the campaign hustings to the budget hearings that began soon after the first of the year. In response to the challenge to the construction program, the Board of Commerce directed its Governmental Committee to study the municipal budget and make recommendations. At the same time, the DFL also appointed its special executive board committee that included Dennis E. Batt and William Mollenhauser to study the school budget.[74]

The DFL committee strongly endorsed the proposed school budget despite the fact that Dennis Batt had previously criticized the board about the lack of school construction. In 1921, in an article extolling the educational advances of the Soviet Union, Batt derided Detroit educators for failing to equal the communist efforts in building schools for all children.[75] Nevertheless, after studying the proposed budget for 1924–25, Batt and the other two committee members obviously were impressed with the sincerity of the board in regard to school construction. They dismissed the allegation that the new schools were "too elaborate" and praised such frills as "baths, swimming pools, gymnasiums, and other physical culture features which have become a part of our school system." The committee was particularly angered by the nativist accusations that these "modern" schools were disproportionately going up in foreign neighborhoods. "The critics of such schools seem to more particularly direct their criticism toward the erection of such buildings in the so-called poorer neighborhoods, occupied frequently by Italians, Poles, and other foreign born people. It appears to your committee that it is just such people who are entitled to and need this service from our educational system." Following a detailed discussion of the remainder of the budget, the committee not only strongly endorsed the document but concluded that even "[i]f the proposed budget is granted in its entirety the year 1925 will still find the children of the city suffering from inadequate educational facilities. . . . Under such circumstances the school budget must increase from year to year and we can hope for different until such time as Detroit ceases to grow, a thing which would be deplored by all."[76]

The Governmental Committee of the Board of Commerce came to almost precisely the same conclusion, emphasizing the need for the city to make "every effort" to insure a seat for "every child of primary school age." These sentiments were endorsed by the Citizens League and the Detroit Bureau of Governmental Research, an agency created in 1916 to study urban problems.[77] As the budget-setting process neared its conclusion, the Citizens League, Bureau of Governmental Research, and the Board of Commerce issued a joint statement declaring "that the school authorities must be supported in such expansion of the educational system as would care for the population of a growing city."[78] The *Detroit News* also added its voice to the chorus of calls for more schools. Noting that "Detroit needs all the schools for which the board has asked . . . ," the *News* concluded, "[i]f the Board of Education is extravagant, the people have their remedy—they can refuse to re-elect it. Every election shows on the contrary, that it has the people's support. The people of Detroit want their children well-educated; and they are willing to spend their money in such a good investment."[79]

In response to this pressure, the city council compromised, adding $510,845 to the operating budget of the school board but cutting capital spending by $1,172,776. The drop in capital expenditures, however, was short-lived. The following year, the council approved $6,416,313 for new construction for 1925–26, almost 129 percent more than in 1924–25. In March, 1925, as the budget deliberations concluded, a Board of Commerce spokesman announced with pleasure that "this is the first time in history— recent history at least—that the school board has been permitted to build all the schools it requested."[80] That assessment was fairly accurate for the rest of the 1920s and for the first years of the 1930s. Except for 1928–29, when capital spending fell to $3,394,041, between 1925–26 and 1931–32, spending on construction averaged over $6 million annually. During this period, the issues of extravagance and frills essentially disappeared from the local political agenda and funds for construction flowed to the school board with relative ease.[81]

The results of this building campaign were impressive, to say the least. On July 1, 1917, when the small board of education took office, the Detroit public school system consisted of 126 schools of all types, with eight new buildings under construction. By January, 1922, the system was operating 162 schools. All told, between the 1920–21 school year and the 1929–30 school year, the board constructed 44 new elementary schools, 11 new intermediate schools, and added 5 new high schools. The board also undertook seventy-five major renovation projects at elementary schools, twelve at intermediate schools, and fifteen at high schools, projects that usually entailed the construction of annexes and additions to increase building capacities.[82] Perhaps the best indication of the extent of the building can be seen by considering the half-day sessions that had plagued the system for so long. Between 1919 and 1929, the number of students on half-day sessions dropped from 17,795 to 6,370.[83]

Despite this massive construction program, on the eve of the Great

Depression, Detroit still had not fully met the housing needs of its burgeoning student population. As late as May, 1931, both the *Detroit Times* and the *Detroit Mirror* published a spate of articles and editorials deploring the overcrowded and hazardous schools that many Detroit children were attending. Noting that 23,000 children, nearly 10 percent of the total student population, attended schools constructed in the nineteenth century, both newspapers chastised the board for denying these children an equal opportunity for a decent education.[84] Thus, while the great building program of the 1920s went a long way toward providing a seat for every Detroit child who sought public education, as the impact of the Great Depression bore down on the Motor City, the problem of school accommodations had not been solved.

Progressive Educational Innovations

The last major area of potential conflict that the small board of education faced was over the expansion of progressive educational innovations. As I noted in chapter 1, the ward-based school board introduced virtually every important element of progressive reform, including kindergartens, standardized testing, and vocational education. The reform board simply broadened the reach of these innovations so that they touched the lives of every public school pupil in Detroit. In essence, the reform board rationalized and bureaucratized what the ward-based board had begun.

No actions taken by the small board, however, had more potential for controversy than this expansion of progressive educational initiatives. Because such policies as establishing the Gary system in elementary schools had immediate effects on children, school leaders certainly could expect sharp criticism from parents and community leaders who distrusted these innovations. In Chicago, for example, organized labor vigorously protested against the introduction of intelligence testing, junior high schools, and Gary-style elementary schools. In New York, Jewish parents rioted when the school board implemented the Gary plan, precipitating a major upheaval in city politics. Modern educational historians have routinely described these actions as evidence of class and cultural conflict over important elements of the progressive educational agenda.[85] Given that Detroit had all the elements for a similar type of explosion—deep class antagonism, considerable ethnic diversity, and an elite-dominated school board—controversy over the implementation or expansion of any or all of these reforms certainly could be expected.

School leaders in Detroit were well aware of the serious, even violent, reactions from parents in other cities who protested just such changes as the introduction of the Gary system. Yet, unlike other major cities, the Detroit schools experienced remarkably little controversy about organizational or curricular issues in the 1920s. Four main factors account for the rather harmonious expansion of the progressive educational agenda in Detroit. First, as previously noted, there was little conflict about pedagogical reform during the period of political controversy about school governance. The fact that the reformers and the "regulars" never quarreled over the basic direction of educational policy prior to the creation of the small board of education unquestionably contributed to the continuing consensus about these policies in the 1920s. Second, business leaders and organized labor, the key antagonists over these issues in other cities, shared a fundamental, progressive philosophy in support of expanding the role of the school in the lives of young people. Third, educational leaders in Detroit conducted an extensive, effective campaign of public relations to encourage support for these reforms. Finally, throughout most of the 1920s, the Detroit Federation of Labor, the most likely source of opposition to these innovations, either remained neutral on the new policies or, in the case of the Gary plan, joined the school leaders as an enthusiastic supporter of reform.

Although the first of these factors, the fundamental agreement on policy and practice amid the conflict on school governance, has been discussed, the other three factors bear investigation. The philosophical consensus that underlay the support of progressive innovations in many ways is the easiest to document. By the 1920s, the ideas articulated by John Dewey in *The School and Society* (1900), that industrialization had drastically diminished the educational role of the family and that schools needed to fill that educational void, had become conventional wisdom for opinion makers in Detroit.[86] Thus, in 1924, the DFL committee that analyzed the school budget applauded the expanded mission of the public schools, declaring that it must be kept in mind

> that life in a modern city such as Detroit has undergone a tremendous change within the last generation. The modern industrial system has destroyed home life as known by our fathers and many of us. Crowded housing conditions, heavy traffic in the street, lack of recreational facilities in the home or under the supervision of the parents throws an additional responsibility upon our school system, which is now charged with the training of our bodies as well as the minds of the coming generation. Schools providing these things must be considered a modern necessity.[87]

Later in the decade, the conservative *Free Press* echoed this position in the first article of a series on manual training and vocational education, noting that "the changing conditions of society have placed new burdens on the schools—burdens which earlier the home had of necessity assumed." Organizations as politically opposed as the Board of Commerce and Socialist party also used these arguments to support the introduction and expansion of progressive innovations.[88]

Agreement on fundamental philosophical principles, which certainly existed in many cities other than Detroit, does not, however, guarantee consensus on specific reforms supposedly based on those principles. Yet the major progressive educational reforms that set off political explosions in other cities—intelligence testing, junior high schools, and Gary-style elementary schools—became mainstays of the Detroit school system in the 1920s with little serious conflict.

To a considerable extent, the broad public acceptance of these reforms in Detroit was due to the vigorous public relations campaign that the school leaders conducted. Soon after Frank Cody assumed the superintendency in 1919, the board commissioned a school survey to assess all aspects of the system. In classic progressive fashion, school officials used the survey to justify vastly expanded use of IQ tests, extensive tracking based upon these test results, a 6–3–3 form of school organization with considerable emphasis placed on broadening the curriculum of the intermediate and high schools, and the introduction of platoon schools, Detroit's version of the Gary plan, in all elementary schools. Each of these innovations was thus carefully wrapped in the mantle of "educational science."[89] But more was involved than simply invoking the authority of science. In presenting the new programs to the public, Frank Cody provided ample evidence of his skills as a master politician.

Cody was a tireless booster of public education in Detroit. Delegating much of the day-to-day responsibilities of running the system to a group of talented subordinates, Cody spent much of his time building support for the schools in the community. He once explained his public relations philosophy, saying, "Go out and join organizations! The city is full of luncheon clubs, exchange clubs, friendship organizations. Go out and mingle with these men. Find out what they want. Then bring the information back and put it to work in your schools." Cody, himself a fixture at meetings and conferences of major civic organizations in Detroit, was known for his colorful remarks and sharp wit. He was a darling of the press and a sought after toastmaster at public gatherings. He used these opportunities to tout the progress of the schools and to keep prominent business and governmental leaders apprised of the current developments in the system, a process he once candidly admitted was just "tell[ing] 'em everythings going along fine." Reflecting on this public relations strategy, deputy superintendent Charles Spain stated that "under [Cody's] leadership every available agency is utilized to bring the schools to the public and the public to the schools. The good will thus generated stands as a bulwark behind the school administration when budgets are under consideration, and when the schools are under criticism."[90]

Of the major progressive policy initiatives, Cody and other school leaders probably spent the *least* amount of time defending IQ testing and curriculum tracking. Detroiters were certainly familiar with these innovations, since both had been introduced under the ward-based board of education with the backing of superintendents Martindale and Chadsey. Under Cody, however, the scale of testing and tracking in Detroit expanded dramatically. Beginning in September, 1920, all first graders were required to take the Detroit First Grade Intelligence Test, the results of which were used to place children in one of three tracks: "X" for children in the upper 20–25 percent of IQ scores; "Y" for 50–60 percent of the children who scored in the middle range: and "Z" for the 20–25 percent of the children who had the lowest IQ scores. While these classifications were not immutable (teachers *could* recommend changes based on student achievement), throughout the 1920s, IQ tests played a major role in determining the curricular tracks most students followed.[91]

Despite the extensive use of IQ tests in Detroit, little public criticism of either IQ testing or curriculum tracking appeared during this era. The most likely source of criticism, the DFL, was silent on the issue. The *Labor News* did give front page coverage to the 1925 attack on IQ tests by Victor Olander of the Chicago Federation of Labor, but the Detroit paper never editorialized against intelligence testing or tracking.[92] Indeed, most of the criticism of testing and tracking took place *within* the system in a spirited academic debate that was rooted in the IQ versus achievement test controversy of the Martindale era. Harry J. Baker, director of the Psychological Clinic, and Warren K. Layton, director of the Guidance and Counseling Department, promoted IQ tests as the most accurate means of determining the native abilities of children and the best guide for efficient, "individualized" placement of children in curriculum tracks. Opposing them were Dr. Stuart Courtis, who became director of the Department of Instruction, Teacher Training, and Research and dean of Detroit's Teacher College in

1920, and his colleagues, Walter G. Bergman and Paul Rankin, who advocated broader use of achievement tests to assess student progress, judge teacher effectiveness, and adjust teaching strategies accordingly. During the 1920s, the more rigid, hereditarian views of Baker and Layton held sway in Detroit as they did throughout the nation. But, by the mid-1930s, as leading Detroit educators questioned both the validity of IQ tests and the accuracy of student placements based on those tests, the views of the "achievement" advocates became more influential. Nevertheless, Detroit continued to use IQ tests extensively.[93]

Like IQ testing, curriculum tracking found few vocal detractors during the 1920s. The ward-based board had also laid the foundation for differentiated high school curricula in the early 1910s. The small board of education refined the practice of tracking, first through the use of standardized tests to determine placement and, then, by introducing four distinct high school tracks, academic, commercial, technical, and general. Frank Cody, like so many educational leaders of the era, equated tracking with democracy in education. Cody believed that the differentiated curriculum offered expanded educational opportunities to students who otherwise would have shunned the classical high school of the nineteenth century, and he routinely deplored the traditional high school as an institution that had only served a narrow, intellectual elite. "The watchword of our public schools is 'Equal Opportunity to All,'" he declared in 1922, "until a few years ago that was only a motto." He presented the commercial, technical, and general tracks as the realization of an egalitarian dream in which average students could succeed at what they were best suited.[94]

Although many modern scholars dismiss these egalitarian appeals as mere rhetoric whose purpose was to obscure the undemocratic nature of the reforms, it is important to understand why educators in the 1920s sincerely believed that "individualizing" instruction in these ways would actually increase educational opportunity and fulfill the democratic mission of the schools. Indeed, the arguments for standardized testing and tracking put forth by such leaders as Cody parallel more recent demands for "equity" in regard to the curriculum. In modern terminology, Cody and other educators of the 1920s characterized traditional high schools as "inequitable" because they offered the same curriculum to all students and ignored obvious differences that children had in talent and interests. From the tracking-for-equity perspective, the traditional high school essentially forced students who were not academically inclined to drop out of high school, because too few courses suited them. In other words, critics of the traditional high school argued that the one-track, academic curriculum required of all students actually *denied* equal educational opportunity. Equity thus demanded differentiation of the curriculum since it provided equal access to the high school while accommodating individual differences.[95]

Given that argument, it is not hard to see how such conservative educators as Cody and such liberal commentators as those writing for the *Labor News* could find common ground in support of the differentiated curriculum. Indeed, a long, 1918 article in the labor paper supported changes in the educational system based squarely on the principle of equity.

> Education to be democratic and to equip properly for life must be free as the air we breathe, for every mother's boy and girl, everyone "of the least of my brethren," black or white, rich or poor, bright or dull. Our future bricklayers, carpenters, plumbers and blacksmiths need as much care and as much preparation for life as our future doctors, lawyers, preachers and teachers.[96]

Over the next decade, organized labor in Detroit continued to support that position. In the early 1930s, for example, the president of the Michigan Federation of Labor praised the differentiated curriculum in public schools and advocated "industrial education as a common right to be open to all children on equal terms, to be provided by general taxation and kept under control of the whole people."[97]

More than concern for educational equity was involved in the DFL stand on this issue. Organized labor had long sought to keep children in school and out of competition with adult workers in the labor market. Because educational leaders touted the differentiated curriculum as a way to prevent dropouts, labor saw the policy furthering its interests. In addition, in the late 1920s, the DFL waged a vigorous verbal and legal battle against private trade schools that the unions claimed offered expensive vocational training for nonexistent jobs. It was clear that vocational education offered by the public schools was far more accountable to the DFL in protecting entry into skilled trades than the profit-making, "bunco" schools that sought to circumvent union agreements on such issues.[98]

The lack of conflict about the differentiated high school curriculum probably also explains the general acceptance of the junior high school in Detroit. When Cody decided to scrap the 6–6 plan that Chadsey had introduced in favor of a 6–3–3 system, he sought to defuse criticism by labeling the new institutions "intermediate schools" rather than "junior" high schools. The key idea was for the new schools to be transitional, to provide a bridge from elementary school to either work or high school rather than a "downward extension of the high-school curriculum."[99] As with the differentiated curriculum, the goal of the intermediate school was to keep children in school for a longer time, a goal that again certainly appealed to the leaders of the DFL.

Unlike Chicago, where opposition to the junior high largely came from organized labor, the leading critics of the Detroit intermediate schools were the *Free Press* and fiscally conservative councilman Joseph A. Martin. Their attacks on the intermediate schools came amid the 1923 campaign for city council and focused entirely on what the *Free Press* called the "extravagant" and "undemocratic" nature of the new schools. These charges were based entirely on the fact that intermediate schools cost more than elementary schools and served fewer students. Martin specifically called for more elementary schools and fewer intermediates.[100] As noted earlier, neither Martin nor the *Free Press* appear to have had much impact on school construction policy, and their criticism of the intermediate schools quickly faded from view.

Despite the scholarly attention given to the debates about intelligence testing, curriculum tracking, and junior high schools, if one judges the controversial nature of an innovation by the degree of political upheaval it generates, no educational initiative in the Progressive era was more volatile than the Gary plan. Originating under the guidance of William Wirt, superintendent of schools in Gary, Indiana, the Gary plan initially seemed to answer the dreams of urban school leaders by offering, at once, the most up-to-date curriculum and considerable cost efficiency. In the Detroit version of the plan, children were divided into two platoons of equal size, with each platoon using half the school's facilities for half the day. While one platoon studied the three R's with a single teacher in their homerooms, the other platoon participated in an enriched program, with several teachers taking classes in literature, geography, art, music, manual training, or domestic science, as well as participating in activities on the playground or auditorium. At midday, the platoons would switch, and the children who had the enriched program would get work in the three R's while children in the other platoon would get the enriched program.

The key to the system was the rotating schedule that guaranteed continual use of every room in the building every minute of the school day. The system satisfied three crying needs for major urban school districts such as Detroit—more efficient use of space, lower costs, and curricular reform. Since every room in the school was in continual use, platoon schools could accommodate as many as a third more students than schools organized along traditional lines, thus easing problems of overcrowding. In addition, teachers who supervised the playground and auditorium classes, two elements of the enriched program, supervised 80 to 90 students; therefore, fewer teachers were needed to oversee the larger number of children in the school. Finally, the enriched program allowed urban educators to introduce up-to-date courses taught by teachers who specialized in their subjects. In short, platoon schools seemed to offer the best of all educational worlds.[101]

In 1912, the Gary plan began receiving rave reviews from leading educators across the country. Such commentators as John Dewey to Randolph Bourne applauded the Gary schools for making the most modern educational programs and methods accessible to large numbers of urban children. But the plan also met with severe criticism. The Gary schools had several drawbacks, not the least of which was the unfortunate public association of the schools with Gary, Indiana, and the U.S. Steel Corporation. When the New York City Board of Education introduced the Gary plan in 1916, the reform was met by allegations that the steel trust and the Rockefeller interests were secretly trying to control the schools. As Diane Ravitch points out, the accusation reflected popular concern that the Gary schools were class biased, providing a downgraded, vocationally oriented education to the children of the poor. Critics of the plan repeatedly used the image of students marching from class in disciplined platoons to strengthen the public perception that the ultimate goal of the schools was to regiment children. The issue came to a head in New York in 1917 when Jewish parents and children rioted against the plan, and the city voted the mayor who supported the reform out of office. Criticism that the Gary plan was class biased and militaristic plagued every effort to introduce the system in other cities and formed the basis of the 1924 attack on the plan by the Chicago Federation of Labor (CFL).[102]

Educational leaders in Detroit were well aware of the criticism and the failure to implement the platoon system in New York. Learning from experience, they proceeded slowly and devoted considerable effort to informing the public about the new schools. In 1918, the board converted two elementary schools into platoon schools, added two more the next year, and nine more the following year. Principals and teachers in these schools chose to be involved in the platoon system, and school leaders promised that no policy changes would come without rigorous study of the results of these experiments. As results of these studies came in, school officials proclaimed that children in the new schools performed better academically than children in traditional elementary schools. In addition, school officials repeatedly promoted the reform as a vital element in solving the problem of overcrowding and half-day sessions.[103] After visiting a Detroit platoon school in 1920, a prominent New York educator applauded the manner in which the system had been implemented.

> Detroit did what New York should have done; started for educational reasons and stuck to educational reasons, went slowly, used only those who wanted to try the new plan; fitted the plan to its own pupils; carefully studied the results; did not allow visitors to overrun its experimental schools; politicians and boosters, political and philanthropic, kept hands off; tried no buildings where equipment was lacking; answered questions specifically and criticism by changing the work or converting the critic.[104]

Despite these efforts, the Detroit platoon system did provoke some controversy. By 1922, forty-four elementary schools were platooned, and questions about the system grew. Interestingly, the most vehement local critic of the platoon schools was neither a left-wing leader nor an immigrant parent, but Andrew B. White, a well-to-do Detroiter who served as the superintendent of a Methodist Sunday school. In March, 1922, White appeared at a board meeting with two hundred supporters to denounce the platoon schools as wasteful and immoral because of the enrichment classes in dancing, theater, physical education, and swimming. To the cheers of his supporters, White also claimed that children in the platoon schools were not learning "half as much of the fundamentals of education as children did when he was a boy."[105] The board members at the meeting defended the system but ordered a study of the allegations. Several weeks later, the committee that looked into the matter declared that the charges were nonsense. White, for his part, threatened a popular referendum to force the schools to return to teaching "basics," but nothing came of the threat.[106]

The following year, the Detroit platoon schools came in for more substantial criticism, this time from the left. In December, 1923, nine Chicago teachers visited the city to assess the platoon system and unanimously denounced the schools as "detrimental to the children." They cited one Detroit mother who withdrew her child from a platoon school, complaining, "These long lines of little children—marching—marching—marching—looked to me like nothing so much as the lines of uncompleted Ford cars in the factory, moving always on, with a screw put in or a burr tightened as they pass—standardized, mechanized, pitiful." A group of Milwaukee teachers also visited Detroit and condemned the platoon schools as unhealthy for the children. These teachers claimed that the children became fatigued and nervous due to the change of classes. They added that the system was educationally unsound because it "breaks down the personal and motherly contact between children and teachers." Around this time, Upton Sinclair visited Detroit, researching the platoon schools for his upcoming exposé of American education, *The Goslings*. Repeating most of the criticisms made by the Chicago and Milwaukee teachers, Sinclair labeled the platoon schools "the very latest wrinkle in Ford factory standardization applied to the minds of children."[107]

Surprisingly, however, little of this criticism appears to have influenced left-wing leaders in Detroit. As early as 1916, the *Michigan Socialist* ran a lengthy article that applauded the Gary plan as a welcome alternative to the "medieval military method" in vogue in most American schools.[108] That attitude appears to have prevailed among leftists and labor leaders in the city. The only *Labor News* editorial on the platoon system in the early 1920s chastised a school official for defending the system because it was "cheap" and challenged the board to produce some evidence that the schools were really better for children.[109] Not content to wait for the school leaders to reply, the DFL executive board charged its education committee, the same committee that had analyzed the 1924–25 school budget, to investigate the platoon schools.

In June, 1924, the committee, which was chaired by Dennis E. Batt, issued a lengthy, glowing report on the platoon system. Batt and the two other committee members analyzed studies of the platoon schools, visited several schools, and spent time talking with teachers, students, and parents. Responding to the charges made against the platoon system, the committee found that children in these schools were as healthy as those in traditional schools; that rather than producing nervousness and fatigue, changing classes was a brief, welcome respite from demanding school work; the homeroom teachers had adequate time to "mother" the children; that multiple classes enabled students to gain from teachers who were clearly excited by the special subjects they taught; and that students in platoon schools performed slightly better in basic subjects than students in traditional schools, especially once they reached high school. The committee also found "no connection" between the schools and moral laxity, although it did cite evidence of less emphasis on traditional discipline and more encouragement of individual freedom than in other schools.[110] An "overwhelming majority" of the students with whom the committee members spoke approved of the platoon schools. Finally, the committee turned to the most serious allegations, those of standardization and militarization. Given the strong left-wing and antimilitary credentials of the committee members, particularly Batt, one must assume that this issue was uppermost in their minds. Indeed, Batt noted that the committee

> paid particular attention to the charges that the platoon school was factorized or militarized. Our observations reveal no basis for these charges. In transferring from class room to class room necessary in the platoon system there is no element of militarization. If the introduction into a school of an efficient method and tightening up of loose ends is factorization, then the school has been factorized. We can see no objection to this. Your committee was impressed that the atmosphere of the modern platoon school is that of a club, rather than factory or an army post.

The committee concluded that the critics of the platoon system were either biased or uninformed.[111]

On the level of national controversies over educational policy, the DFL study certainly deserves equal attention with the Chicago Federation of Labor report on the platoon schools, IQ testing, and junior high schools that appeared in July, 1924, just one month after the publication of the Detroit report. Ironically, given current interpretations of the CFL report, the Detroit statement on platoon schools probably represents the views of the *more radical* wing of the American labor movement. A closer look at the criticism of the platoon schools leveled by the CFL, Margaret Haley, and Upton Sinclair reveals a profound educational conservatism. These critics of the platoon schools wanted to maintain the role of elementary school teachers as "mothers" to their students, avoid the specialization of subject matter, and otherwise retain traditional forms of schooling as a refuge from the rigors and regimentation of modern, industrial life. On the other side of the issue, the DFL report argued that schools must accommodate to industrialism. As communists, Dennis E. Batt and William Mollenhauser, two of the three authors of the Detroit study, were neither repelled by industrialism nor put off by criticism that the platoon schools were preparing students to take their place in an industrial society. For them, capitalism, not industrialism, was the bane of modern life. Their enthusiasm for the platoon schools is not surprising at all in light of general communist positions on social efficiency and social engineering. As Richard H. Pells points out, left-wing intellectuals of the late 1920s and early 1930s used many of the same terms for Bolsheviks that they had once used for progressives, namely "consummate technicians—

committed to experimentation, concerned with economic efficiency and expert social control, men who got results without worrying too much over morality or doctrine."[112] From that perspective, the platoon school could easily draw support from individuals on the far left, while more moderate leftists and liberals might resist the innovation.

Indeed, several years after the publication of the committee's report when a battle for control of the DFL broke out between radicals and moderates such educational issues as support for the platoon school played a role in defining the factional differences. The battle erupted in 1926, due to a sharp denunciation of Russian Communism by AFL president William Green. Late in 1927, amid this debate about communism and the American labor movement, moderate leaders of the Detroit Federation of Labor ousted Dennis Batt as a member of the DFL executive committee and dismissed him as editor of the *Labor News*. The next year, in a last-ditch effort to regain his position within the movement, Batt ran against the incumbent, Francis X. Martel, for the DFL presidency. His loss in that election marked the end of Batt's career as a Detroit labor leader.[113] The election also marked a sharp, rightward shift in DFL stands on several issues. The *Labor News,* which had once been the forum for articles by such leading communists as William Z. Foster, now began featuring red-bashing editorial cartoons and articles that denounced communists and open-shop advocates with equal vehemence.[114]

The more conservative drift of the DFL also had a profound impact on two major educational issues—married women teachers and platoon schools. Under Batt's editorship, the *Labor News* had strongly supported the right of married women to teach. In 1928, however, following Batt's ouster, the *Labor News* made a complete about-face on that issue and demanded that the board fire the married women so that unemployed, single teachers might get jobs. In the 1929 school board race, two of the DFL-endorsed candidates campaigned on the promise to enact that policy. In addition, these candidates were outspoken critics of the platoon system, repeating almost verbatim the arguments leveled against the platoon schools by the Chicago Federation of Labor. Upon taking his seat on the board in 1929, DFL candidate Edward Williams began a determined effort to end the employment of married women teachers and to eliminate platoon schools. These positions were among the first indications that the grand educational consensus of the 1920s was starting to unravel.[115]

The emerging controversy about the platoon schools in 1929 should not obscure the fact that, throughout most of the 1920s, the Detroit public schools had drawn substantial support from a broad social, political, and economic base. This support extended to virtually all of the "progressive" innovations in the city and helped gain Detroit a reputation as one of the leading school systems in the nation. That reputation was so formidable that in 1931, when the National Education Association met in Detroit, the *New York Times* editorialized that, " . . . it is doubtful that any session in the six days of reading and discussing papers will be as valuable as the time spent in becoming acquainted with this thoroughly organized and well-administered system which offers a model to other cities."[116]

Conclusion

In the summer of 1929, the *Free Press* congratulated Frank Cody on the tenth anniversary of his appointment as superintendent, noting that these "have been years of harmony and progress."[117] During the decade, the Detroit schools had indeed made dramatic progress in raising teacher salaries, recruiting new teachers, undertaking an enormously ambitious school construction program, and gaining a reputation as one of the most progressive school systems in the nation. All of this had been accomplished with remarkably little controversy. Throughout the decade, a broad-based consensus of interest groups supported almost every move to expand and improve the system. Charles Spain accurately summarized the first decade of the Cody years as an " 'Era of Good Feeling' in education in Detroit. Public sentiment has been solidly behind the schools and serious obstacles to progress have been entirely wanting."[118]

One assessment of the degree to which the schools satisfied the demands of strikingly different constituencies can be had by considering the large number of positions taken by the socialist school board candidates in 1917 that wound up being enacted by the elite-dominated school board in the 1920s. Several of the important items on the socialists' platform, such as shared governance between teachers and administrators and an end to "militarism and military training" in the schools, were not realized. Several others, such as the formation of a teachers' union, the improvement of teachers' pension and insurance plans, and establishment of a program of free lunches for students, had to wait until the 1930s to be achieved. But almost all of the other items on the platform were realized prior to 1929. These items included increasing salaries for teachers, hiring substantially more teachers, employing married women as teachers, constructing new buildings, using school buildings for afterschool public forums and guaranteeing free speech for speakers in those forums, expanding programs of physical training for young people, and introducing progressive curricula, including such subjects as nature study (a key component of the platoon school program).[119] What is remarkable is not only that the school board adopted all of these measures but that almost every important interest group in the city supported them as well. Throughout the 1920s, the expansion and improvement of public education was one of the great areas of consensus in Detroit politics.

To argue that consensus was the moving force behind educational politics in Detroit is not to deny the fierce political, social, and economic struggles that were taking place in the city during this era or that different factions existed in educational debates. Rather, this position maintains that, *in spite of* these struggles and disagreements, major interest groups found substantial reasons to support the expansion and improvement of the schools. These groups supported the schools for different and, at times, opposing reasons, but the consequences of this support were obvious—by 1929, the Detroit public schools were one of the preeminent school systems in the nation. Unfortunately, that grand educational consensus of the 1920s was one of the most tragic casualties of the Great Depression.

NOTES

1. Josephson is quoted in Melvin Holli, ed., *Detroit* (New York: New Viewpoints, 1976), 163. Barrows is quoted in *Detroit News*, 3/27/23, in LFO Papers, Clipping file. On the surveys, see "Detroit Rated First," *Detroit Educational Bulletin* 8 (January, 1925): 4; Cyril Arthur Player, "Detroit: Essence of America," *New Republic*, 8/3/27, 274. Other examples of the acclaim given to the Detroit Public Schools can be found in Albert Winship, "Two Famous School Board Members: Dr. Shurly and Mrs. Osborn," *Journal of Education*, February 16, 1931, 170; Philip Lovejoy, "Detroit the Dynamic," *Nations' Schools* 7 (January, 1931): 63–64.

2. David Hogan, *Class and Reform: School and Society in Chicago, 1880–1930* (Philadelphia: University of Pennsylvania Press, 1985); Ira Katznelson and Margaret Weir, *Schooling for All* (New York: Basic Books, 1985); Paul Peterson, *The Politics of School Reform, 1970–1940* (Chicago: University of Chicago Press, 1985); Diane Ravitch, *The Great School Wars* (New York: Basic Books, 1974); William B. Thomas and Kevin J. Moran, "Centralization and Ethnic Coalition Formation in Buffalo, New York, 1918–1922," *Journal of Social History* 23 (Fall, 1989): 137–53; David Tyack, *The One Best System* (Cambridge, MA: Harvard University Press, 1974); Julia Wrigley, *Class Politics and Public Schools* (New Brunswick, NJ: Rutgers University Press, 1982). Most historians who have noted the educational consensus of the Progressive era argue that the spirit of goodwill did not survive the great struggles surrounding America's entry into World War I. See William Reese, *Power and the Promise of Progressive School Reform* (Boston: Routledge and Kegan Paul, 1986), 249; Bryce E. Nelson, *Good Schools: The Seattle Public School System, 1901–1930* (Seattle: University of Washington Press, 1988), 3–22, 37–44; Ronald Cohen, *Children of the Mill: Schooling and Society in Gary, Indiana, 1906–1960* (Bloomington: Indiana University Press, 1990), 78–107.

3. Robert Conot, *American Odyssey: A Unique History of America Told through the Life*

of a Great City (New York: William Morrow, 1974), 260; Sidney Fine, *Frank Murphy: The Detroit Years* (Ann Arbor: University of Michigan Press, 1975), 96–97, 247, 376; Sidney Glazer, *Detroit: A Study in Urban Development* (New York: Bookman Associates, 1965), 91, 129; Arthur Pound, *Detroit: Dynamic City* (New York: D. Appleton-Century, 1940), 244–47; Detroit Bureau of Governmental Research, *Accumulated Social and Economic Statistics for Detroit* (Detroit: Bureau of Governmental Research, 1937).

4. Fine, *Frank Murphy: The Detroit Years*, 66–69, 97–100, 145–70, 188; Conot, *American Odyssey*, 291–310, 340–44; Timothy Mark Pies, "Historical and Contemporary Analyses of the Financing of Lutheran and Catholic Education in Michigan's Saginaw Valley" (Ph.D. diss., University of Michigan, 1983), 93–110.

5. Sidney Fine, *The Automobile Under the Blue Eagle: Labor, Management, and the Automobile Manufacturing Code* (Ann Arbor: University of Michigan Press, 1963), 9.

6. The best single example of the clash over the open shop in a Detroit paper appears in *Detroit Labor News*, 6/25/26. The quote about "The Clutch of Labor Monopoly . . . " is from that issue, which reprinted some of the antiunion literature distributed by the Board of Commerce. The "Organized Greed . . . " quote is from *Labor News*, 3/28/19. Other noteworthy examples of the DFL arguments on the open shop can be found in *Detroit Labor News*, 2/27/21, 4/30/26, 5/3/29, 5/10/29. Examples of the Board of Commerce positions can be found in virtually every issue of *The Detroiter*, 5/3/26 to 11/1/26; see also *The Detroiter*, 3/14/27, 5/16/27, 11/14/27, 11/28/27, 4/2/28, 4/16/28, 9/17/28, 5/3/29, 9/2/29.

7. Raymond Fragnoli, *Transformation of Reform: Progressivism in Detroit—And After, 1912–33* (New York: Garland, 1982), 326. The quote about the graveyard of organizers is from Fine, *Under the Blue Eagle*, 21.

8. *Michigan Socialist* 1/12/17 and 4/13/17. For a discussion of the Socialists' stand on militarism in the schools in other cities during World War I, see Reese, *Power and the Promise of School Reform*, 238–56; Nelson, *Good Schools*, 107–29.

9. The final vote on military training in the schools took place on April 10, 1917. The vote followed extensive debate on the issue during which Batt and others expressed their views. Despite the opposition to military training, the board voted unanimously to proceed with it. This was one of the last major policy decisions of the ward-based board of education; see DBEP, 1916–17, 417; 472–73; *Michigan Socialist*, 2/16/17 and 4/13/17; *Detroit Labor News* 4/13/17 and 11/23/17.

10. *The Detroiter*, 4/30/17, 5/14/17, 6/4/17, 6/11/17; Board of Commerce, Committee on Military Training in the Schools, letter to Sir (form letter), May 11, 1917, in Truman Newberry Papers, box 348, folder no. 1, Burton Historical Collection, Detroit Public Library, Detroit, MI. See also *Michigan Socialist*, 5/27/17, 1/13/17, 7/27/17. On the national persecution of the Socialist party due to its antiwar stand, see Theodore Draper, *The Roots of American Communism* (New York: Viking Press, 1957), 92–96; James Weinstein, *Ambiguous Legacy: The Left in American Politics* (New York: New Viewpoints, 1975), 19–25.

11. Reese, *Power and the Promise of School Reform*, 186–97; DBEP, 1916–17, 348; *Detroit Labor News* 6/10/21 and 8/5/21; *Detroit Saturday Night*, 7/2/21.

12. For a discussion of the origins of the Proletarian party, see David A. Shannon, *The Socialist Party of America* (Chicago: Quadrangle Books, 1967), 146–47. The school board routinely allowed the Proletarian party to use the Northern High School auditorium for its weekly forums. DBEP, 1931–32, 554; *The Proletarian*, 3/31, in Labadie Collection, Hatcher Graduate Library, University of Michigan, Ann Arbor, MI; *Detroit Labor News* 10/30/31 and 2/5/32; James R. Prickett, "Communists and the Automobile Industry in Detroit before 1935," *Michigan History* 57 (Fall, 1973): 198.

13. DBEP, 1925–26, 211–12; *Detroit Labor News*, 11/13/25, 12/17/26, 2/4/27, 3/4/27,

4/11/27, 11/8/32. On the angry reaction by Samuel Mumford to a "communistic" speech by Scott Nearing at Cass Tech, see *Detroit Labor News,* 5/7/26.

14. *Detroit Labor News,* 5/22/14, 7/17/14, 7/24/14, 8/21/14, 9/18/14, 10/30/13, 11/6/14, 9/17/15, 5/12/18, 4/4/19, 5/2/19, 5/9/19, 5/23/19. Militant action by teachers in this era was extensive, taking place in Atlanta, Boston, Memphis, Seattle, and other cities. On the formation of the AFT, see Wayne Urban, *Why Teachers Organized* (Detroit: Wayne State University Press, 1982), 134–53; on Atlanta, see David Plank, "Educational Reform and Organizational Change: Atlanta in the Progressive Era," in *Southern Cities, Southern Schools: Public Education in the New South,* ed. David Plank and Rick Ginsberg (Westport, CT: Greenwood Press, 1990), 141; on Memphis, see Lynette Wrenn, "The Politics of Memphis School Reform, 1883–1927," in Plank and Ginsberg, *Southern Cities, Southern Schools,* 88; on Boston, see James W. Fraser, "Who Were the Progressives Anyway? A Case Study of the Progressive Education Movement in Boston, 1905–25," *Educational Foundations* 2 (Spring, 1988): 17–18; on Grand Rapids, see George Male, "A Century of Efforts to Improve the Salaries of Teachers in Michigan," *History of Education Journal* 3 (Winter, 1952): 54; on Seattle, see *Detroit Labor News,* 5/21/20.

15. *Detroit Labor News,* 9/12/19 and 10/10/19.

16. *Detroit Labor News,* 3/5/20. See also Florence Estes, "Detroit Teachers—A Selected History, 1920–1965" (seminar paper, Wayne State University, 1980), 2–3; Orin-Jane Bragg Gardner, "A Study of the Role of the Teacher in the Evolution of Administrative Personnel Practices in the Detroit Public Schools" (Ed.D. diss., Wayne State University, 1965), 91–95.

17. Estes, "Detroit Teachers," 4; *Detroit Labor News,* 3/5/20; *Detroit Free Press,* 3/1/20. Cody is quoted in Donald Disbrow, *Schools for an Urban Society* (Lansing, MI: Michigan Historical Commission, 1968), 139.

18. Estes, "Detroit Teachers," 5. Interestingly, the restriction on union membership only applied to teachers. In 1921, the Detroit School Engineers union joined the DFL without provoking any response from the board of education (*Detroit Labor News,* 11/4/21).

19. Carl F. Kaestle, "Conflict and Consensus Revisited: Notes toward a Reinterpretation of American Educational History," *Harvard Educational Review* 46 (August, 1976): 396.

20. *Detroit Labor News,* 12/28/17; for similar statements, see the editorial on 5/18/17 and articles on 8/1/24 and 9/3/26.

21. *Detroit Labor News,* 8/13/20. Nelson quotes very similar statements from left-wing candidates for the Seattle school board in 1914; see Nelson, *Good Schools,* 66.

22. *Detroit Labor News,* 3/21/19 and 9/26/24. For other examples of this historical interpretation in the *Labor News,* see *Detroit Labor News,* 4/23/15, 9/24/15, 3/12/20, 1/13/22; Frank Wade, "Organized Labor Wants Adequate Public Schools," *Michigan Education Journal* 10 (1933): 274; Frank Tracy Carlton, *Economic Influences Upon Educational Progress in the United States* (1908; New York: Teachers College Press, 1968); Merle Curti, *The Social Ideas of American Educators* (1935; Trenton, NJ: Littlefield, Adams and Co., 1966). For examples of the Socialist party's use of that historical interpretation, see *Detroit Leader,* 2/11/33 and 2/18/33, in Labadie Collection, Hatcher Graduate Library, University of Michigan, Ann Arbor, MI. For the Communist party, see Richard Frank, "The Schools and the People's Front," *The Communist* 6 (May, 1937): 432–33, 443.

23. Batt played a very important role in forming the Communist party, serving as editor of the official party journal, *The Communist,* and as secretary of the National Organization Committee of the Communist party. His notoriety increased when, in one of the most famous events of the 1919 Chicago convention during which the party was created, he was arrested for sedition. Batt, however, led the heretical "Michigan group," which quit the party in 1920 over ideological differences (see Draper, *Roots of American Communism,* 160, 165, 167, 173, 175, 182, 184, 210–11; Irving Howe and Lewis Coser, *The American Communist Party* [New York: Praeger,

1957], 39; Shannon, *Socialist Party*, 145–46; *Michigan Socialist*, 7/21/16 and 10/27/16). Batt is first listed as editor of the *Detroit Labor News*, on January 5, 1923. On William Mollenhauser, see U.S. Congress, House Special Committee on Un-American Activities, *Investigation of Un-American Propaganda Activities in the United States, Hearing before a Special Committee on H.R. 282*, 75th Congress, 2d sess., 1294–95.

24. *Detroit Labor News*, 2/8/24.

25. *Detroit Labor News*, 9/26/24. For examples of this engaged but critical stance in regard to the public schools, see *Detroit Labor News*, 2/28/19, 3/26/20, 5/21/20, 10/18/20, 9/2/21, 6/2/22, 7/7/22, 9/21/23, 1/2/25, 10/9/25.

26. George M. Miller, "The N.E.A. Labored Under Mailed Fist of Militarism," *Michigan Socialist*, 7/21/16. See also Arthur E. Holder, "Democracy in Education," *Detroit Labor News*, 9/13/18.

27. *Detroit Labor News*, 10/17/19.

28. *Detroit Labor News*, 3/20/25, 4/10/25, 4/17/25; Frank Cody, "Detroit's Board of Education," *American School Board Journal* 82 (February, 1931): 57. Neither labor candidate was elected in the 1927 school board race (*Detroit Labor News*, 2/25/27, 3/11/27, 4/1/27).

29. *Detroit Labor News*, 3/1/29, 3/29/29, 4/5/29; Leon S. Waskiewicz, "Organized Labor and Public Education in Michigan, 1888–1938" (Ph.D. diss., University of Michigan, 1939), 325–26.

30. *Detroit Labor News*, 3/30/17. For a sample of anti–child labor editorials, see *Detroit Labor News*, 3/19/15, 4/27/17, 6/15/17, 7/20/17, 11/1/17, 11/8/17, 9/6/18, 6/27/19, 3/14/19, 9/12/19, 1/16/20, 8/6/20, 11/16/23, 6/13/24, 8/1/24, 1/16/25, 12/3/26, 2/4/27, 2/25/27, 2/3/28, 7/6/28, 1/25/29. Examples of articles are just short of overwhelming; see *Detroit Labor News*, 4/24/14, 5/1/14, 7/10/14, 11/6/14, 8/20/15, 9/24/15, 2/17/16, 9/8/16, 7/6/17, 7/20/17, 8/10/17, 9/7/17, 9/21/17, 1/25/18, 6/14/18, 7/5/18, 11/29/18, 3/7/19, 1/16/20, 7/2/20, 1/27/22, 6/9/22, 5/26/22, 5/25/23, 7/27/23, 8/17/23, 11/21/24, 12/26/24, 1/16/25, 8/27/26, 11/12/26, 12/10/26, 12/17/26, 8/5/27, 2/3/33, 3/24/33, 3/31/33, 5/5/33, 5/12/33, 5/19/33, 5/25/34, 5/10/35, 6/28/35.

31. *Detroit Labor News*, 6/15/17.

32. Philip R. V. Curoe, *Educational Attitudes and Policies of Organized Labor in the United States* (New York: Teachers College, Columbia University, Bureau of Publications, 1926), 39, 108–9; *Detroit Labor News*, 1/30/26 and 12/4/31; Wade, "Organized Labor," 272; *Detroit Labor News*, 2/4/27 and 12/4/31. Examples of *Labor News* editorials supporting the Child Labor Amendment can be found on 6/13/24, 8/1/24, 11/21/24, 1/16/25, 11/11/32, 3/25/32, 3/29/33, 4/19/33.

33. On Chadsey's address to the DFL, see *Detroit Labor News*, 2/12/15. See also Charles Chadsey, "Child Labor and Our Public Schools," *Detroit Educational Bulletin* 2 (January, 1919): 1. On Laura Osborn's involvement in the National Child Labor Committee, see Owen Lovejoy, letter to Laura Osborn, 2/30/13, in LFO Papers, box 19, Correspondence 1909–14; on the Twentieth Century Club's donation to the organization, see *Detroit News*, 3/6/17.

34. *Detroit Free Press*, 10/7/23.

35. *Detroit Free Press*, 10/7/23; *Detroit Saturday Night*, 8/28/20 and 8/6/21.

36. Frank Cody, "What One Representative American City Is Doing in Teaching American-ism," in *Addresses and Proceedings of the Fifty-Ninth Annual Meeting of the National Education Association* (Washington, DC: National Education Association, 1921), 760. Similar sentiments can be found in Charles Chadsey, "Aggressive Americanism in Our Schools," *Detroit Educational Bulletin* 1 (May, 1918): 1; Frank H. Alfred, "American Citizenship in Detroit," *Detroit Educational Bulletin* 6 (November, 1922): 17. On the Board of Commerce activities, see *The Detroiter*, 5/6/18, 5/19/19, 11/20/22, 5/19/24, 3/9/25, 11/2/25, 11/16/25, 1/18/26, 1/17/27, 1/30/28, 5/28/28.

37. Boyd Fisher, "Board of Commerce," in Detroit Board of Education, *Education in*

Detroit (Detroit: Board of Education, 1916), 152; *Detroit Free Press,* 6/26/29, in Frank Cody Clipping file, Burton Historical Collection, Detroit Public Library.

38. *The Detroiter,* 9/25/20; see also 3/18/17 and 9/18/22; R. J. McLauchlin, "Junior High School Experiment Ended," *Detroit Saturday Night,* 8/14/20; R. J. McLauchlin, "Age of Jazz Forces High School to Modify its Course of Study," *Detroit Saturday Night,* 10/1/21; Donald A. Hayden, "Detroit Public Schools Have Been Revolutionized in Last 20 Years," *Detroit Saturday Night,* 4/15/22; *The Detroiter,* 6/19/22; *Detroit Free Press,* 1/20/27.

39. Ruby Mervin, ed., *The Social Secretary of Detroit, 1932* (Detroit: The Social Secretary, 1932), 92, 138; Cody, "Detroit's Board of Education," 57; Paul T. Rankin, "Board Members and Administration Officials, Detroit Public Schools, 1842–1965," in DFT Papers, box 11, Biographical Sketches folder.

40. *Detroit News,* 3/27/23, in LFO Papers, Clipping file.

41. *Detroit Saturday Night,* 12/9/22. Praise of Cody can be found in *The Detroiter,* 9/18/22; *Detroit Times,* 2/11/23; *Detroit Free Press,* 6/26/29, in Frank Cody Clipping file, Burton Historical Collection, Detroit Public Library. An excellent short biography of Cody can be found in David Tyack and Elisabeth Hansot, *Managers of Virtue* (New York: Basic Books, 1982), 144–52. See also Detroit Public Schools Staff, *Frank Cody: A Realist in Education* (New York: Macmillan, 1943).

42. The enrollment figures include students in special programs that were not normally computed in the regular K through 12 figures. Detroit Board of Education, *Seventy-fourth and Seventy-fifth Annual Report of the Board of Education, 1916–1918* (Detroit: Board of Education, 1918), 190; Detroit Board of Education, *Eighty-eighth Annual Report of the Detroit Public Schools, 1930–31* (Detroit: Board of Education, 1931), 16; Detroit Board of Education, "Pertinent Facts Relative to the Proposed Increase in Millage Election of April 4th" (March, 1949), 29, in DFT Papers [inventoried 1/20/83], box 1, Millage and Government Aid to Education folder; Detroit Board of Education, *Detroit Public Schools Directory and By-Laws, 1952–53* (Detroit: Board of Education, 1952), 122. The adjustment for inflation was computed using the consumer price index with 1967 = 100 (U.S. Department of Commerce, Bureau of the Census, *Historical Statistics of the United States: Colonial Times to 1970* [Washington, DC: U.S. Government Printing Office, 1975], 210).

43. Superintendent of Public Instruction of the State of Michigan, *Eighty-fourth Annual Report, 1919–20* (Lansing, MI: Wynkoop, Hallenbeck Crawford, 1922), 65–66.

44. The success of the Citizens League in 1918 in establishing a city council elected at large certainly played an important role in the dramatic increase in school revenues. Given the close relationship between school board and city council reform, it is not surprising that the large increases in the school budget coincided with the inauguration of the small city council in 1919. Yet the link between the small council and the school board should not be exaggerated. Unlike the school board, elite Detroiters *never* dominated the city council. Indeed, throughout the 1920s and the 1930s, the council was largely composed of middle-class businessmen. See Fine, *Frank Murphy: The Detroit Years,* 92; Fragnoli, *Transformation of Reform,* 137; William P. Lovett, *Detroit Rules Itself* (Boston: Gorham Press, 1930). Other historians have also noted the expansion of city services under reform administrations. See Terrence J. McDonald, *The Parameters of Urban Fiscal Policy: Socioeconomic Change and Political Culture in San Francisco, 1860–1906* (Berkeley: University of California Press, 1986); Judith Sealander, *Grand Plans: Business Progressivism and Social Change in Ohio's Miami Valley, 1890–1929* (Lexington: University of Kentucky Press, 1988).

45. Charles L. Spain, "Three Years of Educational Progress in Detroit," *Detroit Journal of Education* 1 (June, 1922): 3.

46. For example, see Hogan, *Class and Reform,* 138–93; Michael Homel, *Down From Equality: Black Chicagoans and the Public Schools, 1920–41* (Urbana: University of Illinois

Press, 1984), 58–87; Ravitch, *Great School Wars*, 189–230; Tyack, *One Best System*, 214–16; Wrigley, *Class Politics and Public Schools*, 160–87.

47. Michael Sedlak and Steven Schlossman, *Who Will Teach? Historical Perspectives on the Changing Appeal of Teaching as a Profession* (Santa Monica, CA: Rand Corp., 1986), 5–6; Commission on the Emergency in Education, "Teachers' Salaries and Salary Schedules in the United States, 1918–19," in *Addresses and Proceedings of the Fifty-eighth Annual Meeting of the National Education Association, 1920* (Washington, DC: National Education Association, 1920), 537–702.

48. Commission on the Emergency in Education, "Teachers' Salaries," 540.

49. *Detroit Saturday Night*, 3/25/11; *Detroit Labor News*, 8/21/14 and 9/25/14.

50. *Detroit News*, 3/24/17; Michigan Department of Public Instruction, *Eighty-first Annual Report of the Superintendent of Public Instruction, 1917–18* (Fort Wayne, IN: Fort Wayne Printing, 1918), 64.

51. The 1920 NEA study of teacher salaries found similar trends across the nation. In Chicago and Cleveland, the reference points for the midwestern part of the NEA survey, researchers found that union-scale machinists, lathers, bricklayers, glaziers, plumbers, carpenters, and bakers were making substantially more money, in some cases nearly twice as much money, as teachers in those cities (Commission on the Emergency in Education, "Teachers' Salaries," 747–48; Arthur Moehlman, "A Survey of Teachers' Salaries in Detroit," *Detroit Educational Bulletin*, Research Bulletin no. 1 [1920]: 4–7). Cody is quoted in Estes, "Detroit Teachers," 1.

52. *Detroit Labor News*, 9/19/19. The first editorial quoted is from 10/10/19, the second is from 9/19/19. Other front-page editorials on this issue can be found in *Detroit Labor News*, 9/12/19 and 10/17/19.

53. Frank Cody, "Must Increase Teaching Supply," *Detroit Educational Bulletin* 3 (December, 1919): 1–2; *The Detroiter*, 12/29/19. The *Free Press* editorial of 12/6/19 is quoted in Estes, "Detroit Teachers," 1; *Detroit Saturday Night*, 1/24/20. *Saturday Night* also editorialized in favor of higher salaries for teachers on 7/12/19 and 2/28/20.

54. *Detroit Labor News*, 3/5/20.

55. Board of Education, *Annual Report, 1930–31*, 16.

56. "Find Your Salary," *Detroit Educational Bulletin* 3 (March, 1920): 6–7; "Many Teachers Apply," *Detroit Educational Bulletin* 3 (April, 1920): 5. On the growth in the teaching staff during the 1920s, see Detroit Board of Education, *Eighty-seventh Annual Report of the Detroit Public Schools, 1929–30* (Detroit: Board of Education, 1930), 230. On the shortage in rural areas, see *Detroit Educational Bulletin* 4 (December, 1920); *Detroit Saturday Night*, 5/1/20; *The Detroiter*, 9/18/20; *Detroit Labor News*, 10/8/20 and 7/25/24.

57. For more on the issue of married women teachers, see Willard Elsbree, *The American Teacher: Evolution of a Profession in a Democracy* (New York: American Book Company, 1939), 537; "Married Women Teachers and Their Status in 1,500 Cities," *Nation's Schools* 8 (October, 1932), 52; "Forum [on married women teachers in Michigan]," *Michigan Education Journal* 8 (May, 1931): 538–39; Willard Waller, *The Sociology of Teaching* (New York: Wiley, 1932), 45.

58. DBEP, 1921–22, 169, 194, 223, 362–63. On the survey, see DBEP, 1921–22, 223.

59. For press reaction to this issue, see *Detroit Saturday Night*, 9/10/21; *Detroit Labor News*, 6/5/25. In 1925 Hall made a second attempt to ban married women teachers, but that failed also. See DBEP, 1924–25, 448 and 471.

60. *Detroit Labor News*, 9/24/15; *Michigan Socialist*, 8/11/16. Other examples of *Labor News* editorials criticizing the ward-based board for the lack of buildings and the use of half-day sessions can be found in *Detroit Labor News*, 12/4/14 and 4/30/15.

61. Public Schools Staff, *Frank Cody*, 240; Board of Education, *Detroit Schools Directory, 1952–53*, 122.

62. *Michigan Socialist*, 3/9/17; *Detroit Labor News*, 3/21/19 and 9/19/19. The September editorial in the *Labor News* actually underestimated the number of children in half-day sessions. The labor paper protested that 15,000 students attended half-day sessions when, in fact, there were almost 17,000 in such sessions in September, 1919, more than 20 percent of all elementary school pupils (*Detroit Labor News*, 9/19/19; Detroit Board of Education, *Eighty-fourth Annual Report of the Superintendent of Schools, 1926–27* [Detroit: Board of Education, 1927], 16). In addition to such editorial discussions of the issue, the DFL paper also regularly reported on the shortage of school buildings both in Detroit and nationally. See, for example, *Detroit Labor News*, 3/14/19, 4/11/19, 4/20/20, 9/25/21.

63. *The Detroiter*, 11/4/18; *Detroit Saturday Night*, 7/5/19; DBEP, 1919–20, 1; Ernest L. Thurston, "6,000,000 Children Repeaters in School," *Detroit Saturday Night*, 5/7/21. Additional evidence of Board of Commerce support for new schools can be found in *The Detroiter*, 4/14/19.

64. The $5.5 million annual average more than doubled the average annual capital expenditure of the next best period, 1913–14 to 1919–20. Board of Education, *Annual Reports, 1916–18*, 190; Detroit Board of Education, *Seventy-eighth Annual Report of the Superintendent, 1920–21* (Detroit: Board of Education, 1921), 7; Board of Education, *Annual Report, 1929–30*, 227; Detroit Board of Education, *The Superintendent's Annual Report, 1938–39* (Detroit: Board of Education, 1939), 191.

65. Michigan Department of Public Instruction, *Eighty-fifth and Eighty-sixth Annual Reports of the Superintendent of Public Instruction, 1920–1922* (Lansing, MI: Fort Wayne Printing, 1924), 150; Detroit Board of Education, *Eighty-sixth Annual Report of the Detroit Public Schools, 1928–29* (Detroit: Board of Education, 1929), 123.

66. *Detroit Free Press*, 10/2/23 and 10/5/23.

67. The protest about building new schools in "foreign" neighborhoods was quite possibly orchestrated by a rapidly growing Ku Klux Klan chapter in Detroit; see Fine, *Frank Murphy: The Detroit Years*, 98–99; Public Schools Staff, *Frank Cody*, 305; *Detroit Labor News*, 2/8/24; *Detroit News*, undated (probably March 1924), in LFO Papers, clipping file. On a similar attack on "excessive" spending on schools in "foreign" neighborhoods in Gary, Indiana, see Cohen, *Children of the Mill*, 42.

68. Michael Homel finds evidence of substantial discrimination against black Chicagoans, especially in terms of overcrowded schools in black neighborhoods. Paul Peterson, however, finds that school resources generally were distributed fairly among the various ethnic communities in Chicago and San Francisco (Homel, *Down from Equality*, 58–87; Peterson, *Politics of School Reform*, 72–94).

69. Bureau of Statistics and Reference of the Detroit Public Schools, "Age-Grade and Nationality Survey," *Detroit Educational Bulletin*, Research Bulletin no. 7 (January, 1922); Charles Spain, *The Platoon School* (New York: Macmillan, 1924), 251–53.

70. The lack of foreign-born children in the intermediate schools may have had less to do with blatant discrimination on the part of school officials and more to do with the slow pace of intermediate school construction and family choices about child labor.

71. *Detroit Free Press*, 10/6/23 and 10/18/23. The characterization of Martin's support is from Fine, *Frank Murphy: The Detroit Years*, 172, 174, 175.

72. *The Detroiter*, 9/10/23 and 10/22/23. Given the fact that *The Detroiter* was the official organ of a conservative, businessmen's organization, perhaps the most incredible thing about the editorial was its defense of the large debt that the school board had incurred in the construction of the schools. The editorial declared, "Now we hear that they are nine million dollars overdrawn—but we have the schools. We are reported as being five thousand seats short, at that. If the school board had not spent that nine million dollars, try to imagine how many more than five thousand children would not be able to go to school" (*The Detroiter*, 9/10/23).

73. *Detroit Labor News*, 11/2/23. For earlier comments on the construction problem, see *Detroit Labor News*, 3/20/23 and 8/17/23.

74. *Detroit Free Press*, 11/7/23; *Detroit Labor News*, 1/18/24; *The Detroiter*, 1/21/24 and 3/24/24; Fragnoli, *Transformation of Reform*, 296.

75. Dennis Batt, "Soviet Government Great Educator: More Schools Than Ever," *Detroit Labor News*, 12/2/21. This article was one of a series of pro-Soviet pieces by Batt that appeared in the *Labor News* on 10/14/21, 11/18/21, and 12/2/21.

76. *Detroit Labor News*, 2/8/24.

77. *The Detroiter*, 3/24/24. On the founding of the Detroit Bureau of Governmental Research and its relationship with the Detroit Citizens League, see Fine, *Frank Murphy: The Detroit Years*, 96; Fragnoli, *Transformation of Reform*, 283–84.

78. *Civic Searchlight*, March, 1924.

79. *Detroit News*, undated (probably March, 1924), in LFO Papers, Clipping file.

80. Board of Education, *Annual Report, 1929–30*, 227; Board of Education, *Annual Report, 1930–31*, 16; *The Detroiter*, 3/23/25. The Board of Commerce remained a steadfast supporter of new school construction in the 1920s. On that stand, see Fragnoli, *Transformation of Reform*, 299, 300, 315.

81. *Detroit News*, 9/20/27, in LFO Papers, Clipping file; *Detroit Free Press*, 3/24/28 and 4/5/28; Frank Cody, "Statement on Housing [1928]" in the Detroit Mayors Papers, 1928, box 2, Detroit Public Schools folder in Burton Historical Collection, Detroit Public Library.

82. Charles Gadd, letter to James Couzens, 1/30/22, in Detroit Mayors Papers, 1922, box 2, Board of Education Folder no. 2. An excellent summary of all the construction that took place in the 1920s is presented in Board of Education, *Annual Report, 1929–30*, 212–26.

83. Board of Education, *Annual Report, 1926–27*, 16; Board of Education, *Annual Report, 1930–31*, 5.

84. *Detroit Mirror*, 5/9/31 and 5/12/31, in LFO Papers, Clipping file; *Detroit Times*, 5/8/31, 5/9/31, 5/12/31, 5/14/31, 5/15/31 in LFO Papers, Clipping file.

85. Chicago Federation of Labor, "Labor Analyzes Public School Policy," *Illinois State Federation of Labor Weekly News Letter* 10 (July 16, 1924): 1–4. The best discussion of the violent opposition to the Gary plan in New York is in Ravitch, *Great School Wars*, 189–230. See also Ronald Cohen and Raymond Mohl, *Paradox of Progressive Education: The Gary Plan and Urban Schooling* (Port Washington, NY: Kennikat, 1979). David Hogan provides an excellent summary of opposition to intelligence testing and the junior high school by the Chicago Federation of Labor (CFL) (Hogan, *Class and Reform*, 185–92). For other examples of very similar analyses of the CFL positions, see Tyack, *One Best System*, 214–15; Peterson, *Politics of School Reform*, 169–70; Wrigley, *Class Politics and Public Schools*, 160–74.

86. John Dewey, *The School and Society* (1900; Chicago: University of Chicago Press, 1971).

87. *Detroit Labor News*, 2/8/24. In addition to providing the rationale for supporting such innovations as baths, swimming pools, and physical education, this perspective on the changing nature of families and schools also led organized labor to strongly endorse other progressive innovations in Detroit, most notably kindergartens, open-air schools for tubercular children, and free lunches (*Detroit Labor News*, 3/30/17, 4/19/18, 10/11/29).

88. *Detroit Free Press*, 11/20/27; *The Detroiter*, 9/10/23; *Detroit Leader*, 2/11/33. *Saturday Night* echoed this position. See Donald A. Hayden, "Detroit Public Schools Have Been Revolutionized in the Last 20 Years," *Detroit Saturday Night*, 4/15/22.

89. Public Schools Staff, *Frank Cody*, 245; Arthur B. Moehlman, *Public Education in Detroit* (Bloomington, IL: Public Schools Publishing, 1925), 203–8; Tyack and Hansot, *Managers of Virtue*, 145.

90. Public Schools Staff, *Frank Cody*, 493, 495, 503–8. Spain is quoted on 494.

91. Stephen Scott Williams, "From Polemics to Practice: IQ Testing and Tracking in the Detroit Public Schools and Their Relationship to the National Debate" (Ph.D. diss., University of Michigan, 1986), 110–24; Moehlman, *Public Education in Detroit,* 220–22.

92. *Detroit Labor News,* 11/27/25; for more on Olander's criticism of IQ testing, see Hogan, *Class and Reform,* 186–87.

93. Williams, "From Polemics to Practice," 114–68; Paul T. Rankin, "The Division for the Improvement of Instruction," in *Improving Learning in the Detroit Public Schools: A History of the Division for Improvement of Instruction, 1920–66,* ed. Paul T. Rankin (Detroit: Detroit Board of Education, 1969), 1:12–13; author interview with Walter G. Bergman, Ann Arbor, MI, May 5, 1985.

94. Public Schools Staff, *Frank Cody,* 300, see also 236–37, 246–48, 288–91. Another strong endorsement of the differentiated curriculum can be found in Hayden, "Detroit Public Schools," 2.

95. On the theoretical differences between "equality" that implies "sameness" and "equity" that suggests "justice" or "fairness," see Thomas F. Green, "Excellence, Equity, and Equality," in *Handbook of Teaching and Policy,* ed. Lee S. Shulman and Gary Sykes (New York: Longman, 1983), 318–41.

96. Holder, "Democracy in Education," 4.

97. Wade, "Organized Labor," 273.

98. *Detroit Labor News,* 3/11/27, 3/18/27, 4/1/27, 4/15/27, 4/22/27, 5/6/27, 5/13/27, 5/22/27, 9/16/27.

99. Public Schools Staff, *Frank Cody,* 275–76; Charles Spain, Arthur B. Moehlman, and H. L. Harrington, "The Intermediate School in Detroit," *Detroit Educational Bulletin,* Research Bulletin no. 6 (December, 1921): 1–16; "The Intermediate School and Vocational Guidance," *Detroit Educational Bulletin* 4 (April, 1921): 2.

100. *Detroit Free Press,* 10/15/23 and 10/18/23.

101. Moehlman, *Public Education in Detroit,* 195–98; Spain, *Platoon School,* 43–100; Cohen and Mohl, *Paradox of Progressive Education,* 5–7.

102. Cohen, *Children of the Mill,* 51–53; Cohen and Mohl, *Paradox of Progressive Education,* 51, 142; Ravitch, *Great School Wars,* 197–203, 214, 219–39; Chicago Federation of Labor, "Labor Analyzes Public School Policy," 2–3.

103. In making these claims about better academic performance of platoon school students, Detroit school officials apparently ignored a 1919 study done by none other than Stuart Courtis, who found "consistent evidence" in the Gary schools of "careless work, imperfectly developed habits, and marked lack of achievement" (Courtis, quoted in Raymond Callahan, *Education and the Cult of Efficiency* [Chicago: University of Chicago Press, 1962]). On support for the platoon schools in Detroit, see Spain, *Platoon School,* 44–47; Public Schools Staff, *Frank Cody,* 252–54; Moehlman, *Public Education in Detroit,* 195–98; Charles Spain, "The Platoon System," *Detroit Educational Bulletin* 2 (March, 1919): 1–3. An engaging interchange on the pros and cons of platoon schools took place at the 1926 National Education Association meeting. See Charles Spain, "The Platoon School—Its Advantages," in *Proceedings of the Sixty-fourth Annual Meeting of the National Education Association, 1926* (Washington, DC: National Education Association, 1926), 797–800; H. B. Wilson, "The Platoon School—Its Disadvantages," in *NEA Proceedings, 1926,* 800–809.

104. *New York Globe,* 3/11/20, reprinted in *Detroit Educational Bulletin* 3 (April, 1920): 4–5.

105. *Detroit News,* 3/23/22.

106. *Detroit Journal,* 3/24/22; *Detroit Times,* 2/27/22; *Detroit Free Press,* 3/28/22, 9/29/22 in LFO Papers, Clipping file; *Detroit Journal,* 4/4/22; *Detroit News,* 3/31/22 and 4/14/22; *Detroit Times,* 4/14/22.

107. Margaret A. Haley, "The Factory System," *New Republic,* November 12, 1924, 18; Upton Sinclair, *The Goslings: A Study of the American Schools* (Pasadena, CA: Upton Sinclair, 1924), 100, 101–2, 186.

108. George M. Miller, "The N.E.A. Labored Under Mailed Fist of Militarism," 2.

109. *Detroit Labor News,* 3/7/24.

110. Dennis E. Batt, "Report on Platoon Schools Made to Federation of Labor," *Detroit Labor News,* 6/27/24.

111. Batt, "Report on Platoon Schools," 3. The DFL was not the only left-wing or labor organization to endorse platoon schools at the time. Ronald Cohen points out that such influential left-wing leaders as Scott Nearing and Floyd Dell praised the Gary plan, as did organized labor in Gary. In addition, during the 1917 controversy about the Gary plan in New York, Socialist mayoral candidate Morris Hillquit endorsed the plan, although he criticized the way it had been implemented in the city. In January, 1922, a delegation that included the president of the Wilmington, Delaware, Central Labor Union toured the Detroit platoon schools. The union leader was most impressed and announced his hope that Wilmington would also adopt the platoon system (Cohen, *Children of the Mill,* 51–53, 62; Cohen and Mohl, *Paradox of Progressive Education,* 51; "Wilmington Visitors Like Schools," *Detroit Educational Bulletin* 5 [March, 1922]: 9; *Detroit News,* 1/25/22).

112. Richard H. Pells, *Radical Visions and American Dreams: Culture and Social Thought in the Depression Years* (New York: Harper and Row, 1973), 65.

113. *Detroit Labor News,* 10/15/26, 12/31/26, 1/7/27, 3/4/27, 3/18/27.

114. A series of articles by Foster ran in the *Labor News* from 6/24/21 to 7/15/21; anti-Communist editorial cartoons and articles can be found in the *Labor News* on 7/12/27, 8/10/28, and 11/2/28.

115. *Detroit Labor News,* 2/17/28, 3/1/29, 3/29/29.

116. *New York Times,* 2/21/31.

117. Quoted in Public Schools Staff, *Frank Cody,* 528.

118. Charles Spain, "Frank Cody—An Appreciation," *Detroit Educational Bulletin* 13 (March, 1930): 1.

119. "Platform of the Socialist Party of Detroit: For the School Board Election, April 2, 1917," *Michigan Socialist,* 3/23/17. Nelson cites a Socialist-organized labor platform from a 1910 school board race that is quite similar to the Detroit platform (Nelson, *Good Schools,* 41–42).

Chapter 3

School Politics Divided, 1929–40

The broad-based consensus that sustained the Detroit schools in the 1920s weathered every crisis, including such volatile political and economic controversies as the battle over the open shop. During the 1930s, however, that grand school consensus weakened and shattered when faced with the enormous crisis of the Great Depression. Sidney Fine argues that "Detroit was the hardest hit big city in the nation during the Hoover years."[1] Unprecedented levels of unemployment and soaring tax delinquencies in Detroit not only caused widespread misery and despair among tens of thousands of residents, but the downward economic spiral also undercut the widely shared unanimity on school issues. Amid fear and confusion, the powerful interest groups in Detroit challenged one another in the arena of school politics, transforming educational issues into another dimension of the emerging national political realignment.

Recently, scholars have devoted considerable attention to education in the Great Depression, but there is little agreement about the importance of the era in educational history. On the one hand, Tyack, Lowe, and Hansot conclude their comprehensive study of education in the 1930s by arguing that the era did not "constitut[e] a watershed in American public education." Katznelson and Weir, on the other hand, argue that the 1930s *were* a pivotal era in educational history because the working class, particularly organized labor, abandoned its commitment to the public schools during those years. Carnoy and Levin also see the 1930s as a crucial period but, unlike Katznelson and Weir, they maintain that, during the depression, liberal social movements became more effective in achieving greater educational equality.[2]

Unfortunately, these studies either underestimate the great educational changes caused by the depression or they misread the significance of those changes. Moreover, none of these studies illuminates the most profound development that the 1930s brought to public education in Detroit and Michigan—the integration of school politics into the larger political transformation taking place in America at the time. In the Progressive era, as we have seen, school issues became linked to campaigns for municipal reform. That process of political integration went even further in the 1930s, as interest groups in Detroit divided on school issues along essentially the same lines as the national realignment of the New Deal era. By the late 1930s, business and labor, conservatives and liberals were as deeply divided over school issues as they were over a host of other domestic political questions.[3] This local reflection of national political alliances centered on four interrelated educational issues: (1) reducing the local educational budget; (2) eliminating curricular "fads and frills"; (3) organizing a teachers' union; and (4) increasing state aid to education. The economic crisis of the Great Depression created each of these issues and the political dynamics of the New Deal years defined the alignment of interests that determined their development. Most important, the shattering of the Progressive era educational consensus and the transformation of the mission of the schools in response to the Great Depression began the gradual but unmistakable decline in the quality of public education in the Motor City.[4]

Cracks in the Educational Consensus

As with the rest of the nation, the effects of the depression materialized slowly but irrevocably in Detroit through late 1929 and the early months of 1930. By April, however, with over 90,000 Detroit workers unemployed, evidence of economic collapse was unmistakable. In February, 1929, the index of industrial employment, published by the Board of Commerce, had reached a record high of 135 (1923–25 = 100), but throughout 1930, the index plunged to a monthly average of 87. Within a year of the October stock market crash, nearly 28 percent of the 400,000 auto-related jobs in the Detroit metropolitan area had been eliminated.[5]

Each new year added to the economic misery of the city. The industrial employment index continued to slide, averaging 66 in 1931, 56 in 1932, and hitting bottom at 29 early in 1933. Aggregate wages from industrial production, which had totaled about $511 million in 1929, plummeted to $218 million four years later. Retail sales in 1933 were 42 percent of 1929 levels. Some of the most serious economic declines were in the construction industry, which did $183 million worth of business in 1926 and only $4 million worth in 1933. Assessed valuation of property plunged from more than $3 billion in 1930 to $1.8 billion just seven years later. In the one area that most seriously affected the schools, tax delinquencies, Detroit led the nation. Unpaid taxes ran at a rate of 15 percent for 1930–31, 26 percent for 1931–32, and 35 percent for 1932–33, in every instance almost one-third higher than that of other major American cities.[6]

The staggering decrease in assessed valuation and the high rate of tax delinquencies precipitated a major fiscal crisis in Detroit. This crisis was compounded by two factors: the enormous debt for public works amassed by the city in the 1920s and the maintenance of a municipal Department of Public Welfare to provide relief for poor and unemployed citizens. As rising unemployment compelled ever greater relief expenditures, the city was forced to borrow heavily from local banks and divert funds from other city departments. By fiscal 1931, Detroit was spending almost $14 million on relief and over $10 million on interest. Since the schools traditionally commanded the largest share of the municipal budget, nearly $18 million in the 1930–31 school year, the mounting debt and welfare burdens placed the city government on a collision course with the board of education. Educational retrenchment quickly emerged as one of the major political issues of the era.[7]

The conflict over retrenchment marked the beginning of the end of the grand educational consensus of the 1920s. Several months after the stock market crash, a group of businessmen led by banker Ralph Stone persuaded the mayor to appoint a citizens committee to advise the administration on the growing financial crisis. The Stone Committee, as the group became known, was composed of representatives of the Business Property Association, the Detroit Automobile Club, the Detroit Board of Commerce, the Detroit Citizens League, the Detroit Bureau of Governmental Research, the Detroit Real Estate Board, the Michigan Manufacturers Association, and the Woodward Avenue Improvement Association.[8] As the fiscal crisis in the city worsened, the Stone Committee became increasingly more powerful in determining retrenchment policy. Bank loans that were vital to keeping the city solvent became contingent on the approval of the committee. Demanding a balanced municipal budget as the prerequisite for approving these loans, the committee, and ultimately Stone himself, exercised enormous power over the city government.

Throughout the early 1930s, Stone and his allies essentially directed the retrenchment of the city government, repeatedly forcing the mayor, common council, and the board of education to slash spending in the two most costly areas of governmental service, welfare and public education. Although many of the key organizations in the committee, such as the Board of Commerce and the Citizens League, had been enthusiastic boosters of the public schools in the 1920s, in the 1930s their commitment to a balanced municipal budget proved greater than their commitment to the schools.[9]

The demands for educational retrenchment thus provoked a profound change in the relationship between the schools and these allies from the Progressive era. In assessing this change, two factors must be kept in mind. First, occasionally in the prosperous 1920s, some business leaders and conservative politicians in Detroit *had* expressed concern about rising taxes and governmental spending although, as the previous chapter shows, these concerns were rarely directed at the schools. Yet amid the boisterous campaign of civic boosterism and the rising levels of prosperity, criticism of municipal spending was not a widely held political position. Only as the depression worsened and the debate about how to respond to the crisis divided the city and the nation into conservative and liberal camps, did criticism of excessive taxing and spending emerge as a key rallying point for business leaders and conservative politicians.[10] The second factor to keep in mind is that the change in position regarding municipal and school spending by these business and civic leaders developed gradually between 1929 and 1931. Members of the Stone Committee initially recommended minor cuts in the school budget, confident, no doubt, that the economic downturn would be brief and that the funds would be restored within a year or two. As a 1931 *Free Press* editorial praising cuts in the school budget noted, "[The reductions] are necessary, and they will be only temporary."[11] By 1932, however, hope for a quick economic upturn had vanished entirely. In addition, the local, state, and national political landscapes were changing in ways that aggravated the cracks in the educational consensus. Each new battle over educational retrenchment and related issues deepened the cleavage between the schools and their erstwhile conservative allies from the Progressive era.

The political problems faced by the schools in the 1930s were not confined to the right alone. Early in 1929, the Detroit Federation of Labor (DFL) had helped elect Edward H. Williams to the school board. Williams relished his role as the "representative" of organized labor on the board, using his position as a forum for championing union causes and policies. As the economic crisis worsened, the DFL protested every wage cut in both the private and public sectors, and demanded that all available jobs go to American citizens, Detroit residents, and the unemployed. Following the lead of the DFL, Williams repeatedly urged the board to fire aliens, non-Detroiters, married women teachers, and eliminate "fads and frills" courses—central to the platoon school system—rather than cut salaries. These demands targeted key school board policies and practices and greatly added to the political turmoil that gripped the schools in this era.[12]

As serious as the demands of organized labor were, however, they were more than offset by the determined support the DFL and other liberal organizations gave the schools in their battles with the Stone Committee and its allies. On almost every major issue in school politics of the 1930s— slashing the school budget, reducing teacher salaries, organizing a teachers' union, and increasing state aid—organized labor, liberal, and left-wing organizations strongly backed the board of education. The most striking feature about educational politics in Detroit in the 1930s was the deep division along class lines, with organized labor and other left-wing groups calling for increased taxes and spending for public education while the business community and right-wing organizations fought to keep taxes and spending for education as low as possible.

The Battle over Teacher Salaries

Ironically, the areas of greatest conflict in the retrenchment controversy—the reduction of teacher salaries and the elimination of "progressive" curricula— were among the areas of greatest agreement in the 1920s. A quick look at the school budget, however, reveals precisely why these areas were central to the retrenchment controversy. Almost 75 percent of the annual budget in 1929–30 went for salaries and about 10 percent supported such programs as art, home economics, music, manual training, and physical education, with most of that appropriation going for salaries. Planned school construction was the only other item in the budget that accounted for large sums of money. Between 1929 and 1932, the board spent about $6 million annually on construction and maintenance, equal to approximately 20 percent of the total budget.[13] Eliminating new buildings and drastically cutting maintenance services were the only retrenchment actions the board would take that did not generate controversy.

The first major issue in the retrenchment battle in Detroit occurred over teacher salaries. The controversy began in late February, 1930, when the Stone Committee called on the common council and the mayor to eliminate all pay raises from the 1930–31 budget. The committee specifically demanded that the council delete $732,000 in step increases for teachers and more than $326,000 in step increases for other city employees. Following a month of hearings, the council voted to suspend the salary schedule for city employees and to withhold the funds for salary increases for teachers from the board of education. The school board initially acquiesced to this cutback, but an unexpectedly large state aid payment that arrived six months later provided the board with funds to grant the increases despite the actions of the council. The Stone Committee demanded that the board stand by its original decision. The board, however, voted unanimously to raise salaries.[14]

Members of the committee were outraged by this action of the board. Two members, John L. Lovett, general manager of the Michigan Manufacturers Association, and William Lovett, executive director of the Detroit Citizens League, were so incensed that they began an unsuccessful effort in the state legislature to strip the school board of its power to make budgetary decisions. This legislative initiative sparked an angry verbal exchange between the school board and the Stone Committee, an exchange that marked the beginning of a serious breach between school officials and the advocates of retrenchment.[15]

This controversy struck at the very foundation of the educational consensus of the 1920s. Though the Board of Commerce and the Citizens League were once passionate advocates of educational expansion and school board autonomy, these groups now demanded a reduced school budget and threatened the board of education with control by the common council. Stone, himself, provides dramatic evidence of the political shift this issue had provoked. In 1913, as chairman of the legislative committee of the Board of Commerce, Stone staunchly supported efforts to "take the schools out of politics." Yet, as the school board resisted his calls for retrenchment, Stone endorsed the call to strip the board of its budgetary autonomy.[16] The *Free Press,* which, as late as 1929, had lavishly praised the public schools and their leaders, quickly emerged as an outspoken advocate of reduced school spending. Yet perhaps the most dramatic about-face of any participant in this controversy was the editorial shift of *Detroit Saturday Night,* one of the most enthusiastic supporters of school reform in the 1920s. By 1933, *Saturday Night* was shrill and relentless in its condemnation of educators and their expensive fads and frills.[17]

The angry outcry from the business leaders and the conservative press drew an equally impassioned response from groups that opposed educational retrenchment. The *Detroit News,* the largest circulation paper in the city, warned the politicians to "keep their hands off education" and opposed most cuts in the school budget. Similarly, the Hearst-owned *Detroit Times* provided steady support for the school board in the retrenchment battles.[18] By far the most consistent and outspoken opponents of retrenchment, however, were the Detroit Federation of Labor and its official voice, the *Labor News.*

The *Labor News* routinely described the retrenchment controversy as a conspiracy of the rich to deprive working-class children of their right to a decent education. Not surprisingly, both the Socialist and Communist parties in Detroit also analyzed the issue in terms of class struggle. The short-lived socialist *Detroit Leader* vilified the wealthy advocates of retrenchment and strongly opposed all cuts in the education budget. The communist *Michigan Worker* paid less attention to education than the socialist paper, but it also opposed retrenchment.[19]

These pro- and antiretrenchment positions developed slowly in the early 1930s, but they solidified as the economic decline continued unchecked. At the outset of the controversy, it appeared that the Stone Committee and its allies simply hoped to keep the city from defaulting on its loans by reducing city services in order to achieve a balanced municipal budget. While this position was unassailable from a financial perspective, opponents of retrenchment pointed to the devastating human costs that resulted from the reduction of city services. The meager relief payments provided by the city helped thousands of families keep body and soul together during the years of high unemployment. The schools also provided a haven for children, offering not just an education but free lunches for indigent pupils as well as some dental and medical services. Opponents of retrenchment pointed out that every cut in the budgets of the Department of Public Welfare and the schools had painful human consequences. As Mayor Frank Murphy declared in the midst of the worst period of retrenchment, "To sacrifice everything to balance the budget is fanaticism."[20]

Gradually, the practical motivations behind the pro- and antiretrenchment positions hardened into political philosophies abstracted from the initial demands for a balanced budget or more social services. Advocates of retrenchment saw lower taxes and reduced governmental spending on social services as essential means for restoring economic well-being to the city as a whole. Opponents of retrenchment focused instead on the relief of human suffering, staunchly supporting the expansion of governmental services through greater spending and higher taxes. These positions simultaneously evolved on the state and national levels, eventually providing the framework for the New Deal realignment.[21] Caught as they were in this seismic shift in the political landscape, school leaders in Detroit found themselves lining up against their former allies in the business community and good government organizations.

Nothing reveals the growing breach between the schools and these groups more than the renewed battle over salaries that took place early in

1931. In its last meeting of 1930, the school board cut some $3.9 million from its proposed 1931–32 budget, primarily from maintenance and capital costs. The Board of Commerce angrily and accurately described the cut as one that existed mostly on paper, since much of the money was for planned expansion. As unemployment grew and apple vendors began their poignant vigils on city street corners in January, 1931, the battle over school spending was joined in earnest.[22]

Conflict erupted as three separate committees recommended cuts in the school budget. Leading businessmen prepared the first two committee reports advocating major reductions in the school budget. One proposed substantial cuts in kindergartens and vocational education and urged that the school year be reduced by one week, in essence cutting salaries by 2.5 percent. The other report, prepared for the Board of Commerce by two members of the Stone Committee, called for a 20 percent cut in teacher salaries as well as other economies. Both studies outraged school officials, who at one point "dared" the Board of Commerce to show how its recommendations would not cripple the school system.[23]

The final report, the one with the greatest impact on the 1931 salary battle, came from a committee created by Mayor Murphy to specifically study the issue of teacher salaries. Composed of fourteen school and civic leaders, the committee specifically studied the issue of teacher salaries and recommended that the mayor approve pay increases for the coming year but then reduce the education budget by a modest amount.[24] Only two committee members dissented from this recommendation, the most notable being C. E. Rightor from the Bureau of Governmental Research, who represented the Board of Commerce. Apparently convinced by the majority report, the mayor and the common council settled on a 3 percent cut in appropriations to the board and left the matter of salaries in the hands of the school officials.[25] As in the previous year, this decision polarized the city.

The 1931 school board election that coincided with the salary controversy provides evidence of how serious this polarization had become. The salary increase was the only issue in the reelection campaigns of board members John Webster and Frank Gorman. Both Webster and Gorman supported the increase, while their chief opponent, Dr. Albert Krohn, called for the suspension of the salary schedule and for additional cuts in school spending.[26] As the election approached, the *Labor News* defended the salary increases for the teachers and declared, "When educational institutions are assailed, whether it be through hysterical super-economy or any other menace which threatens to curtail the possibility of the people of this country obtaining an opportunity to improve their conditions through education, every loyal citizen should rise in defense of those institutions and American principles." The DFL strongly endorsed Webster and Gorman.[27]

The Board of Commerce, the archconservative Michigan Union League Club, the Michigan Chapter of the National Economy League, the *Free Press*, and *Saturday Night*, however, vehemently opposed the incumbents. These organizations and newspapers sought to defeat Webster and Gorman not merely because of their stand on teacher salaries, but also because they encouraged teachers to participate in the reelection campaign. Invoking the rhetoric of the Progressive era, Clarence Ayres, president of both the Union League and the Economy League, blasted the incumbents and the teachers for "dragging our schools through the mire and degrading them to the level of ward and precinct politics."[28]

Facing a clear choice on the issue of salary retrenchment, the voters overwhelmingly returned Webster and Gorman to office, with Gorman more than doubling Krohn's total vote. The *News* and the *Labor News* interpreted the election as a sign of popular support for the board and the teachers.[29] That popular mandate notwithstanding, salary cuts for school employees soon became inevitable, as the economic situation in the city deteriorated. Not long after the school board election, Ford fired an additional 16,000 employees, and half of those who still held jobs saw their wages slashed 40 percent. Edmund Wilson reported that the auto plants in Flint had cut wages by 33 percent, and Detroit's metal finishers, "the highest grade of skilled labor," had taken a staggering wage cut from $1.10 per hour to 15 cents.[30] In May, faced with growing tax delinquencies, the school board ordered fee hikes at all night schools and colleges, drastic cutbacks in summer school, and, at last, a 3 percent cut in teacher salaries. There were no protests, for the teachers probably appreciated that their wage cut was modest compared to other workers in the Detroit area.[31]

In July, as the city faced the first of many serious cash shortages, Ralph Stone wrote Murphy that it was time for "sharp retrenchment by the board of education." The board responded three weeks later with $445,000 worth of additional cuts in maintenance and services. These actions were merely stop-gap measures. City officials informed the board that its share of the city's tax delinquencies would amount to some $2.5 million.[32] The need for a more calculated, long-range plan for retrenchment was apparent.

On August 11, 1931, board president A. D. Jamieson addressed his colleagues about the crisis. Obviously stung by recent criticism of the board, Jamieson began by discussing the serious split that had developed between the schools and the business community. "Businessmen know that our system is one of the best," Jamieson complained, "yet Board of Commerce officials frankly tell us that we are a 'rubber stamp' for the Superintendent and his staff." Indeed, Jamieson claimed that business leaders characterized the board as "a one-ring circus with the Superintendent holding the hoop for the members to jump through!" Dismissing these allegations as absurd, Jamieson pointed to the superb national reputation of the Detroit schools, adding, "What an anomaly—the School system considered by real thinkers to be outstanding, betrayed and ridiculed in its own home."[33]

These complaints against unjust criticism, however, masked the thrust of the speech, the utter capitulation of the board to the demands of the Stone Committee. The board had to acknowledge the obvious, Jamieson argued, that school revenues were inextricably bound to city revenues, and the school system had to assume its share of municipal retrenchment. At least, Jamieson contended, the means for achieving those reductions remained in the hands of the school board, and he recommended a direction for the board to pursue. Starting with the premise that the system was committed to "modern education—the education of the whole child," Jamieson declared that the schools must try to continue as much of their regular program as possible. He was less sanguine, however, about maintaining salary levels. Although he defended the past actions of the board on salaries, he noted that, as the largest single expense of the board, they were "the obvious source of substantial economy." He added that the cost of living had fallen in the past year, that private businesses had "readjusted" their wages, and that taxpayers who supported the schools were suffering wage cuts of their own. Jamieson made no overt request for salary reductions, but the message was clear. Perhaps hoping to soften that impending blow, he pledged that the board would not fire employees for budgetary reasons. He concluded with a set of cost-cutting recommendations designed to save some $800,000: a hiring freeze, recommended (not mandated) leaves of absence for married women teachers, elimination of paid sick leave, centralization of administrative offices, further fee hikes, sharp reductions in building maintenance, and a moratorium on new school construction. The board approved these proposals unanimously.[34]

This speech by Jamieson was a watershed in the retrenchment controversy. It acknowledged the fragmentation of the political base of support for the schools and perhaps, most important, noted that even Frank Cody could not work his political magic in the face of the continuing economic crisis. In addition, the speech defined the course of school retrenchment for the next three years, first, by emphasizing the financial link between the city and the schools and, second, by prioritizing programs over salaries. The second decision quickly split the board into opposing factions. Within weeks of the Jamieson speech, Edward Williams tried to use the crisis to enact his campaign promises by demanding that the board save money by firing married women teachers and scrapping all enrichment programs, particularly those associated with the platoon schools. Not long after Jamieson's speech, Laura Osborn also changed her position on retrenchment and steadfastly opposed *every* additional reduction in the school budget. With Williams and Osborn in unrelenting opposition to the main thrust of board policy on retrenchment, the board never again voted unanimously on any retrenchment decision.

Ironically, the retrenchment decisions that provoked no controversy, the decisions to defer maintenance on existing structures and to suspend the construction of new schools, may have been the most serious of them all. While the board members could not know it at the time, their 1931 vote on maintenance and construction was to be the first in a prolonged series of decisions that effectively halted the physical expansion and improvement of the schools. The combined crises of the depression and World War II essentially ended school construction in Detroit for almost fifteen years. In the late 1940s, these decisions came back to haunt school officials.

Over the next few months, the financial situation in Detroit steadily worsened. City officials spent much of the fall negotiating a series of short-term loans to cover the ever-widening city deficit caused by delinquent taxes. By early December, unpaid taxes amounted to $13 million out of a total city tax bill of $76 million, with officials estimating that unpaid taxes would increase to $19 million before the fiscal year ended. Of the $57 million that Detroit would collect, almost a third was taken up by the city's massive debts. Faced with rising unemployment, on the one hand, and the looming threat of bankruptcy, on the other, Mayor Murphy entered into an unequal partnership with the bankers whose lines of credit alone could keep the city from default. Ralph Stone was the final arbiter of these transactions and a balanced municipal budget was the prerequisite for his approval. Stone delegated the responsibility of checking on the city budget to Lent Upson and C. E. Rightor of the Detroit Bureau of Governmental Research. By mid-December, William Lovett noted in a confidential memo "that Detroit's financial affairs were being handled by Stone with the aid of Rightor, Upson and Divie B. Duffield, president of the Detroit Citizens League."[35]

As the new year approached, the mayor fired some city workers and introduced an ordinance cutting salaries for the remaining city employees.

In January, the council adopted the ordinance cutting all city salaries 10 percent and slashing an additional 10 percent from salaries over $4,000, an action that came to be called the "ten-and-ten" cuts. It was obvious to most school board members that, this time, the board could not avoid major salary reductions. With the schools' share of delinquent taxes exceeding $2 million, the board voted, over the objections of Osborn and Williams, to adopt the ten-and-ten cuts. Because the school employees had already taken a 3 percent cut, the net effect of this action was to reduce wages by an additional 7 percent.[36] Even this largest cut to date, however, was not enough.

On February 9, 1932, Stone wrote Murphy that deeper cuts in the city budget would be needed to wipe out a projected $6 million deficit. He computed the school's share of the shortfall at $2.4 million. Stone suggested the sum could be trimmed if the board eliminated the last month of the school year or instituted payless pay days to equal a one-month reduction. Several days before, Murphy met informally with four board members and apprised them of the situation. At that time, the board members agreed to reduce school salaries if the need arose. On February 9, after Stone officially made his demands, the board voted "to contribute the same portion of payless days either through contributed service or by closing the schools as that contributed by city departments generally."[37] The February 9 resolution was a natural consequence of the retrenchment policies outlined by Jamieson six months before.

Throughout the spring of 1932, Stone and Murphy continued to battle as Stone and the bankers demanded even greater salary reductions for city employees. With $3.6 million (of a total $20 million package) in loans at stake, Stone demanded further reductions, this time seeking the equivalent of a one-month slash in city wages. Despite fiery rhetoric from Murphy that raised the specter of repudiating the debt altogether, the outcome of the struggle was no surprise. As the city missed its April 15 and 30 payrolls and "welfare recipients were reduced to a ration of bread, flour and milk," the common council voted to cut the pay for city workers by 50 percent for May and June. The school board then had to approve its share of the reductions.[38]

Stone had written Murphy in late March noting his satisfaction with the school board for being more willing to cooperate in reducing the city budget since February 9th. That assessment, however, was premature. The board balked at slashing salaries an additional 50 percent for May and June. In three extraordinary special sessions on May 3–5, with the city's loans hanging in the balance, the board refused to conform to the ordinance. Its opposition this time was based entirely on what the members viewed as the inequity of the cutbacks as they affected teachers. Since teachers worked a ten-month year, the one-month cut cost them 10 percent of their wages, whereas for most municipal workers, employed for twelve months, the loss was 8.3 percent. Hundreds of teachers crowded the board room, booing and hissing at city officials who reminded the board of its February 9th commitment to share the wage reductions. Stone lashed out at the board members, demanding that they live up to their pledge of salary cuts. But the board held firm. On May 5, it passed a resolution cutting May and June salaries only 41.6 percent (amounting to 8.32 percent for one year) and promised to make up the difference in "other economies."[39]

The following months brought no relief to the financially beleaguered city. Facing an immediate deficit of over $6 million and anticipating a deficit of almost $24 million by June, 1933, the city stood on the brink of financial collapse. In addition, advocates of even more severe reductions of governmental spending began a boisterous campaign for a charter amendment to limit the municipal budget to $61 million, a sum, its opponents argued, that would have brought most city services to a halt. Faced with such desperate prospects, Mayor Murphy called together a new committee of bankers and industrialists who could help the city avoid defaulting on its debts. The committee agreed to secure more credit for the city, but they demanded an additional $7 million in retrenchments. As an article in the *Nation* accurately noted, "[Detroit] is today at the mercy of the banks." Murphy agreed to the cutbacks, and the city controller informed the school board that its share of reductions would be $2,814,160.[40]

On July 26, 1932, the board put the necessary economies into effect. The board voted to end school on May 26, 1933, which resulted in a 12 percent cut in teacher salaries. In addition, the board instituted salary reductions of 14.5 percent for twelve-month employees, equal to reductions passed by the council for twelve-month city workers. That was the last salary reduction made by the board in 1932. Combined with the larger municipal reductions, the salary cut helped keep Detroit solvent over the next few months and probably contributed to the defeat of the $61 million tax limit at a special election in early August.[41]

The educational retrenchment of 1932 generated less political and editorial attention than had previous school cutbacks. Only the *Free Press* continued its relentless criticism of the public schools, denouncing, in a succession of editorials, "the swollen condition of local school appropriations," the arrogance of educators, and the impracticality of many college and university courses. Commenting on the decision of the board to cut four weeks from the 1932–33 school year, the *Free Press* glibly assured its readers that school children in Detroit would learn as much in nine months as in ten.[42]

On the other hand, the antiretrenchment politicians, organizations, and newspapers were surprisingly low key in responding to the educational events of 1932. Once the school board decided to tie its salary reductions directly to those of the city, the schools became just another municipal department caught in what the *Labor News* called the larger struggle between "private capital and the public weal." Throughout the year, the labor paper responded to the educational cutbacks with only occasional swipes at Ralph Stone and his "payroll robbers." Frank Murphy continued to defend the schools and teachers in speeches denouncing the Stone Committee, and the Socialist party tried to rally the public at mass meetings "to save the schools from the encroachment of false economy."[43] But amid the economic devastation facing the city, even the friends of public education in 1932 seemed to agree that the school system needed to accept its share of the cutbacks in order to keep the city from bankruptcy.

Such reasonable conclusions, however, could not hide the fact that the reduction of school funds had been severe. During the 1932–33 school year, the city allocated only $12,875,173 to public education, almost 22 percent less than the previous year. Even controlling for the substantial drop in prices that had occurred during this time, the 1932–33 school budget was 17 percent less than in 1931–32. In the same year, school enrollments grew by almost 3,000 students, but, because of the hiring freeze, the system employed 182 fewer teachers. Many school officials believed that the schools could not absorb further cutbacks.[44] In December, 1932, when the budget-setting process began again and retrenchment advocates called for additional educational cutbacks, the bitter contentiousness that had marked the politics of retrenchment in 1930 and 1931 was reawakened.

The "Fads and Frills" Controversy

The winter of 1933 was undoubtedly one of the worst periods in American history. The hopes engendered by the election of Franklin D. Roosevelt in November withered during what Jordan Schwarz has called "the interregnum of despair." By February, the battered national economy hit bottom, beginning with the collapse of the two largest banking groups in Detroit. The Detroit bank failures set off a chain reaction of bank closings across the nation; only a handful of financial institutions were still open when Roosevelt took office in March.[45]

The bank closings crippled the economy of Detroit. In March, 1933, unemployment in the city may have exceeded 350,000. With $2 million in board of education funds on deposit in the failed banks, the schools were inescapably caught in the raging economic storm. The teachers had received, and most had deposited, their paychecks just days before the bank collapse. Thereafter, like other city workers, they received no salaries for more than two months, and then they were paid in scrip. During this period, although totally without funds, the board struggled to keep the schools open. In early March, it sought credit for food and transportation for its employees but was successful only with the transit and oil companies. The grocery chains, already owed large sums by the Department of Public Welfare, flatly refused the credit request of the board. By the end of the month, Detroit teachers joined thousands of other municipal employees in the relief lines.[46]

Adding to the financial woes of the school board was the passage of a constitutional amendment sponsored by the Michigan Manufacturers Association and the state Grange that limited property taxes to 15 mills. Michigan voters had narrowly approved the measure in November, 1932. As a result of the amendment, the Detroit school system stood to lose over $2 million annually, more than 40 percent of its state aid. Over the long run, the 15 mill limit forced major changes in public school finance in Michigan. Its immediate impact on Detroit was felt as the board announced that the ten-and-ten cuts and the nine-month school year would remain in effect throughout the 1933–34 school year.[47]

The bank failures and declining state revenue were not the only problems facing the board. As the municipal budget-setting hearings began, Ralph Stone demanded further cuts in educational spending, particularly in salaries.[48] As the participants in the budget process prepared to do battle once again, board member Edward Williams launched a vigorous attack on the retrenchment policies of the board, an attack that shifted the nature of the retrenchment debate entirely. In two speeches that kicked off his campaign for Wayne county auditor in January, 1933, Williams proposed that the board eliminate "fads and frills" instead of reducing salaries.[49] The ensuing "fads and frills" debate polarized the city once again and widened the breach between school leaders and their former allies in the business community and "good government" organizations.

Edward Williams and Laura Osborn had distinguished themselves throughout 1932 by opposing every salary reduction the board had approved. Osborn was almost indiscriminate in her casting of no votes, taking the position that teacher salaries simply should not be cut. She railed against "the reactionaries" who sought to cripple the schools and blasted "the bankers who have placed the city in receivership." In opposing the salary cuts, Osborn demanded that the banks holding city of Detroit notes cut their interest rates and "accept lower returns."[50]

Unlike Osborn, Williams advocated selective cuts. In his 1929 campaign for the board, Williams had promised, among other things, to eliminate platoon schools. As the 1932 conflicts over retrenchment intensified, Williams redoubled his efforts to abolish the "enrichment" classes that made operation of the platoon system possible. Explaining his vote against the ten-and-ten cuts early in 1932, Williams declared, "I vote no because I think it is highly unfair to assess this reduction at this time, that [*sic*] the Board should just eliminate Health Education, Cooking, Sewing, Art, Music, Manual Training, Children's Museum [and the] Psychological Clinic." His position on eliminating these "fads and frills" remained unchanged throughout his term of office on the board.[51]

Williams received front page coverage for his January, 1933, speeches denouncing "luxury courses," thus sparking a lengthy debate on curriculum policy in Detroit. By his calculations, eliminating enrichment classes and some administrative positions could save between $3.2 and $3.5 million. These savings, he claimed, would make it possible for the board to restore a ten-month school year. At the January 24 school board meeting, Williams introduced a resolution to cut the enrichment program from the budget entirely. The resolution provoked several angry exchanges between Williams and Frank Cody, and it received no support from other board members.[52] Nevertheless, once Williams publicly proposed this alternative retrenchment strategy, other school leaders felt compelled to defend their policies and programs more vigorously and extensively than ever before.

Attacks on what Williams called "luxury courses" were a common feature of the retrenchment debates taking place across the country. A 1933 article in *Harpers* on the "fads and frill" debate nationwide noted that, "Art, home economics, manual training, physical education, trade and vocational classes, and even foreign languages are all being eliminated or curtailed." According to Edward Krug, the impetus to cut these courses was simply the fact that "academic subjects on the whole were cheaper, and more could be saved by cutting out the practical subjects."[53]

In Detroit, however, school officials built their strongest case for retaining the "modern" courses precisely on the grounds of cost efficiency. They argued that the platoon system was uniquely cost efficient and these courses were central to that system. Charles Spain and Frank Cody, the leading defenders of the "frills" courses, argued against their elimination on the grounds that such cuts would diminish the schools educationally and, ultimately, cost the taxpayers more money.

Cody had made precisely that point in early January, 1933, when, as chairman of the White House Conference on the Crisis of Education, he told a subcommittee that Detroit would need 900 additional teachers if the system eliminated their art, music, and health programs.[54] Although this number appears to have been grossly exaggerated, the general assessment of the situation was correct. The $3.2 million savings that Williams sought by eliminating "frills" would have come entirely from salaries. Assuming that the special subject instructors would have been replaced by regular classroom teachers, very little would have been saved. Also, eliminating the platoon system on the elementary level, which accounted for about 60 percent of the "frills" budget, would have forced the board to hire between 300 and 450 new teachers to make up for the loss of the large gymnasium, playground, and auditorium classes.[55] Cody and Spain drove home those points at every budget hearing, in press releases, and in radio speeches.

The heated debates over the nature and scope of additional educational retrenchment revived public interest and concern about the schools. The major interest groups and newspapers once again entered the arena of educational politics. Throughout 1933, the political alignments over the "fads and frills" issue remained much the same as in the previous years, but with a broader base and sharper boundaries. The *Free Press,* which had supported the "modern curriculum" throughout the 1920s, began criticizing "practical subjects" as early as 1930. As the retrenchment conflict intensified, the *Free Press* became the leading advocate of cutting "fads and frills." Shortly after Williams launched his campaign against the "luxury courses," the *Free Press* essentially endorsed his stand, blasting the "Educational Despotism" described by the paper as a "crowd of well-fed and well-paid professional educators who have fallen into the habit of considering luxury education necessary." Several weeks later, as the city budget hearings continued, the *Free Press* strongly endorsed the decision of one school district to go "back to the three R's." In a statement clearly intended to influence the common council in its budget deliberations, the *Free Press* argued that, in addition to cutting salaries and the school year, "an equally practical way to save is to cut from curriculums courses in music, art, manual art, domestic science, athletics and so forth, which in the aggregate create a considerable part of the expense of any school where they are given."[56]

Detroit Saturday Night, which had also heartily endorsed "modern education" in the 1920s, made an equally dramatic about-face on this issue. Beginning in 1933, *Saturday Night* became a vigorous supporter of the Michigan chapter of the National Economy League, an organization of prominent business and civic leaders that was noted for its efforts to slash educational spending. At a December, 1932, meeting of the Michigan chapter of the league, for example, Thomas Conlin, an Upper Peninsula newspaper editor, denounced the educational establishment for burdening taxpayers with "fads and frills" courses "that call for initial outlays for equipment and continual outlays in the way of added instructors."[57] In August, *Detroit Saturday Night* echoed these sentiments in a front-page paean to "The Little Brown School" that strongly urged a return to the three R's. Several months later, a *Saturday Night* editorial applauded Conlin for his efforts to reduce state school aid to a level that would force schools to operate "stripped of all hangers-on, such as athletics, instrumental music, physical education, manual training, etc."[58]

While not specifically calling for the elimination of "fads and frills," the Board of Commerce exacerbated the situation in March, 1933, when it issued its recommendations for the upcoming city budget. The business leaders called for even more massive cuts in municipal spending, including a further reduction of 22 percent in the school budget. The sum the Board of Commerce recommended for the schools, just over $10 million, was lower than any amount appropriated for public education since 1921, when the school system served over 123,000 *fewer* students. Still, *The Detroiter* argued, the schools were well supported "receiving a very liberal portion of the available public funds. . . but they will have to make added economies to keep within their income."[59]

The stand taken by the advocates of retrenchment added considerably to the hostility between the business community and school leaders. A 1933 report to the Department of Superintendence of the National Education Association, hardly a hotbed of radicalism, reveals the depth of the anger educators felt over the "betrayal" by their former allies on this issue.

It appears that there is now an organized attempt by certain vested interests to cripple the public school system in America. This attack is more insidious because by its subtle propaganda it enlists thousands of harassed taxpayers in leagues militantly organized and committed to the task of betraying the best interests of their own children. Tremendous pressure is being exerted for the elimination of the so-called "fads and frills" which in reality constitute the fundamentals of twentieth-century education. Those who direct this campaign, far removed from the front line of attack, desire to force the schools back into the type of institution which they attended in their own school days and which has produced the misguided leadership responsible in part at least for our present tragic plight.[60]

In Detroit, the 1933 retrenchment controversy also provoked some of the sharpest rhetoric that school and civic leaders had yet used. Soon after the "fads and frills" conflict began, Frank Murphy denounced "any cuts in the fundamental services of the schools." In a radio speech, Laura Osborn blasted the "reactionaries [who] have seized this opportunity to become more active in their chronic opposition to modern education and are loudly advocating a return to the good old days of the three R's." Incumbent board members A. D. Jamieson and Burt Shurly launched their 1933 reelection campaigns attacking "the opponents of modern educational methods who would strip the schools of 'fads and frills' and limit education to the three R's, the curriculum of the little red school house of a bygone era." What is particularly noteworthy is that Osborn, Jamieson, and Shurly were all elite Detroiters who, one might suspect, would have sided with the business community in its call for further retrenchment. Indeed, Jamieson and Shurly were probably the most conservative, business-oriented members of the school board, yet, by 1933, they were battling strenuously against further reductions in school revenue.[61]

The *Detroit News* also defended "modern education" against what it saw as misguided attacks from shortsighted budget cutters who sought to return to "backwoods education." The *News* cheered the resurgent opposition to educational retrenchment and debunked the accusations of "educational despotism." "Strange as it seems," the *News* editorialized, "the [antiretrenchment] movement does not come primarily from educational authorities, eager to save their jobs and their income" but rather chiefly from parents. Regarding the controversy over "fads and frills" education, the *News* maintained that "there is something more to education than the three R's, and that the students are entitled to everything that trained educators believe is good for them."[62]

The Socialist party also entered the fray as a solid supporter of "fads and frills." As the controversy raged, the socialist weekly, the *Detroit Leader,* highlighted the class conflict inherent in the debate: "The taxpayers of the city, now largely the banks and the insurance companies, still continue their drive against educational opportunities for the children of workers. For the past two weeks their campaign has been directed against the 'frills of education.'" The *Leader* defended the enrichment courses.

What are the frills of education in 1933? Not health education, for in a society which gives man so little opportunity for healthful exercise which honest toil proverbially brings, training in this department is imperative. Nor are music and art frills for the worker's enjoyment of these is now limited to the appreciation acquired at school. Nor literature—never has man had more leisure for enjoying the treasures of the centuries. Yet, these are the very activities which are being assailed by the enemies of our schools.[63]

The socialist candidates for the school board declared, "Would these businessmen dare admit that what is good for their children is *too* good—or a 'frill'—for the worker's child?"[64]

The only apparent weakening in the antiretrenchment ranks on this issue was the stand of the DFL. Edward Williams, who had sparked the attack on "fads and frills," had been the darling of the DFL since his election to the school board in 1929. In several ways, however, the stand Williams took on this issue placed the DFL in an uncomfortable position. In late December, 1932, just before the 'fads and frills" controversy broke, the *Labor News* declared that "terrific attacks are being made throughout the country on the educational system of the nation by subversive forces, who, by sinister design seek to destroy opposition by the rearing of ignorant children." The labor paper urged its readers to oppose further cuts in salaries *and* programs. Soon after Williams launched his attack on "fads and frills," the *Labor News* repeated its call for organized labor "to champion the cause of the Public Schools" and demanded that there "be no lowering of standards of education or curtailment of services or activities."[65] The ambiguity of that statement as far as the "fads and frills" debate is concerned was undoubtedly due to the role that Williams played in provoking the controversy. Trying to balance its commitments to Williams and to the schools, the DFL simply repeated its opposition to all forms of retrenchment and supported Williams for Wayne county auditor.[66]

Although the DFL essentially avoided the "fads and frills" issue, the renewed controversy about educational retrenchment in general inspired organized labor to redouble its support for public education. The DFL stance can be neatly summarized by the title of one *Labor News* editorial from this period, "Defend the Public Schools." Organized labor in Detroit never wavered from that position. One simple but dramatic example of DFL support for the local schools appeared during the debate over the 1934–35 school budget. From December, 1933, to March, 1934, the period in which the common council deliberated about its annual allocation for the schools, atop the front page of every issue of the *Labor News* (except the Christmas edition) was the statement, "The Best Safety for Democracy is an Adequate Free Public School System."[67]

Beyond supporting the school leaders in the "fads and frills" controversy, the Socialist party also threw itself into school politics with renewed vigor in 1933. The socialists helped organize the "Save Our Schools" campaign, an antiretrenchment coalition of teachers, parents, and students, and socialist candidates for school board ran on a "Save the Schools" platform.[68] During its eight-week existence, the socialist *Detroit Leader* was probably the most militantly antiretrenchment paper in the city, protesting every cut in the educational budget. Drawing on the classical left-wing interpretation of educational history, the *Leader* argued that just as the working class had battled the forces of greed to create the public schools in the nineteenth century, so the workers of the 1930s had to defend the schools from the likes of Ralph Stone and the Board of Commerce. As one editorial put it, the "industrialists and bankers, who never enjoyed paying taxes that the children of workers might get a decent education have seized upon the current economic collapse [to destroy] the system completely. The reduction of the school year to nine months, the overcrowding of classes, and the elimination of socially necessary services from the school system is [*sic*] all part of this attempt."[69]

More mainstream organizations and newspapers voiced their opposition to further educational retrenchment. The *Detroit Times,* for example, though generally ignoring the "fads and frills" controversy, ran a series of editorial comments and editorial cartoons during this period urging city officials to "Spare the Schools." The American Legion also threw its support behind efforts aimed at "preventing the breakdown of the educational system in Michigan." Late in the year, representatives from a dozen women's organizations, including the American Association of University Women, the Detroit Federation of Women's Clubs, and the Wayne County League of Women Voters, formed the Detroit Council on Public Education to defend the schools from further budget reductions and to lobby in Lansing and at city hall for increases in school funds.[70]

The formidable array of interest groups that had assembled by 1934 was able to both end the assault on "fads and frills" and essentially halt the process of budget cutting. The 1933 budget battle, for example, resulted in a municipal allocation for the 1933–34 school year only slightly below that granted for 1932–33. Still, the city appropriation of $12,185,452 was the lowest amount the schools had received since 1923–24. The ten-and-ten cuts remained in effect, as did the nine-month term. Nevertheless, the 1933–34 school year was the trough of the depression for the Detroit public schools.[71]

Vocal opposition to further budget reductions was just one of many factors coalescing in 1933 that led to the end of the period of relentless educational retrenchment. Among the most important factors was the declining political status of businessmen. Following the bank collapse, many Detroiters wondered why city officials should listen to these men of commerce, who obviously could not keep their own financial houses in order. During the budget hearings, council members lashed out at "the rapidly-growing dictatorship of Wall Street over the representative municipal governments of America." The council even eliminated interest payments from the 1933–34 budget.[72]

More important than these political factors, however, was the successful refinancing of the city debt in June, 1933. As a result of this effort, annual payments for interest and the sinking fund were slashed from over $30 million in 1932–33 to just under $9 million by 1934–35. The total city tax budget was reduced to some $55.5 million in 1933–34, thus relieving a great deal of the pressure on such departments as the board of education to cut spending. A second important change in municipal finance that substantially aided the schools was a revision of the city charter in October, 1933, that removed the penalty for delinquent taxes and made it easier for delinquent taxpayers to fulfill their obligations to the city. In December, 1934, Mayor Frank Couzens, who assumed the mayor's office after Frank Murphy was appointed Governor-General of the Philippines, reported that the city had received $15 million in overdue taxes and that pledges of $22 million in deferred payments were in hand. The public schools received a substantial portion of these "windfall" revenues.[73]

The school system also benefited from the gradual improvement of the economy over the next few years. The industrial employment index, which had fallen to 42 in November, 1933, rose to 52 a year later. By 1935, building permits and retail sales were up to 38 percent and 62 percent of 1929 levels, respectively. By 1936, almost 4.0 million cars rolled off Motor City assembly lines, over 2.5 million more than in 1932. Tax delinquencies in 1934–35 were down to 25 percent, and the following year they had fallen to 20 percent. In 1934–35, the city allocated $13,300,981 to the schools, the first increase in the school budget in five years. Thereafter, the municipal allocation rose slowly but steadily for the rest of the decade.[74]

The improved financial outlook for school districts and the reduction of controversy over retrenchment that occurred across the nation around this time has led some historians to argue that the latter half of the 1930s witnessed the return to normalcy in the politics of education.[75] Several developments in Detroit, however, challenge that assumption. Most important, the realignments in school politics in Detroit did not disappear in the latter part of the 1930s despite the somewhat reduced tension over retrenchment. The political alignments and arguments over school issues in Detroit that were established by 1933 continued and increasingly became integrated into the polarization that characterized the national debates about the New Deal. Nationally, as well as in Detroit, these debates centered on determining the proper role and size of government.

In Detroit, school politics witnessed political liberals and moderates uniting with advocates of social welfare, organized labor, and left-wing activists to press for more money for education. On the other side of the issue, political conservatives joined with businessmen, financial leaders, and scions of established wealth to push for lower taxes and lower appropriations for the schools. Only the issue of public relief for the unemployed polarized Detroit more clearly along these lines. As the political divisions in the nation became sharper, these educational positions expanded to cover other issues, hardened, and became institutionalized. School leaders whose personal predilections may have inclined them toward political and economic conservatism found themselves seeking alliances with liberals and organized labor in their struggle to increase funding for the schools. Three interrelated issues in Detroit—political activity by teachers, the development of a teachers' union, and increased state aid to education—highlight how the political divisions created by the battles over salaries and curriculum continued and, indeed, widened throughout the last half of the 1930s.

Teacher Unionism and Educational Conflict

Nothing exacerbated the rift between the school board and its former conservative allies more than the political activities of teachers and the organization of a teachers' union. Both these developments arose in response to the battles over salary cutbacks and "fads and frills." As large numbers of teachers protested the salary reductions and a small but vocal number joined with organized labor, the political polarization over educational issues intensified. Throughout the remainder of the decade, as the struggle between capital and labor exploded in the sit-down strikes, these divisions over educational issues became an established part of the larger transformation of Detroit from the strongest open-shop city in America to a bastion of industrial unionism.

The issue of politically active teachers first arose during the controversy over suspending the salary schedule in November, 1930. As in many school systems across the country, prior to the Great Depression, school leaders in Detroit generally frowned on political activity by teachers. With the conflict over the "Martindale machine" still well remembered by many civic leaders, concern about politically active teachers in Detroit was acute. Indeed, as late as May, 1930, when Frank Cody asked the board to allow teachers to pass out petitions supporting state reapportionment, the board refused the request. Board member John Webster summed up the attitude of his colleagues, remarking that "a teacher's time should be all for the pupil."[76] Thus, when teachers angrily protested the suspension of the salary schedule five months later and then successfully lobbied the mayor into approving the increase in November, such opinion makers as the *Free Press* renewed warnings about the teachers becoming part of a corrupt political machine.[77]

Three events in 1931 kept the issue of teacher activism alive. Ironically, the most important of these events, the organization of the Detroit Federation of Teachers (DFT) in February, received the least attention. Mindful of the quick demise of the American Federation of Teachers locals in 1920, the new union spent its first years as an "underground" organization that attempted to influence educational politics through covert means. Without acknowledging their membership in the union, DFT members played important roles in the two other dramatic expressions of teacher activism that year, the reelection campaigns of John Webster and Frank Gorman and the "Free Speech Controversy."[78]

As I have noted, the April, 1931, school board race was essentially a referendum on teacher salaries. Webster and Gorman strongly supported salary increases for teachers while their opponent, Dr. Albert Krohn, called for salary reductions. Despite earlier pronouncements against teachers in politics by the board generally, and by Webster in particular, teachers turned out in large numbers to campaign for the incumbents. As the campaign progressed, the *Free Press* repeated its accusations that the teachers were becoming "Detroit's New Political Machine," declaring that "even in the old days when members of the board were chosen from the wards and the board itself was frankly up to its neck in politics, the town never saw anything more open and brazen than the present [activities by the teachers]."[79] *Saturday Night* denounced the teachers in similar terms, as did Harvey Campbell, vice president of the Detroit Board of Commerce, and Clarence Ayres, president of the Union League and the Michigan chapter of the National Economy

League.[80] The Detroit Federation of Labor, on the other hand, heartily endorsed the incumbent board members and cheered their reelection.[81]

By far the most dramatic and celebrated instance of teacher activism occurred late in the year at the Detroit City College, one of several institutions of higher learning over which the board of education had jurisdiction. In December, Walter Reuther, then a student at the City College, invited Dr. Walter G. Bergman, a socialist member of the DFT and professor of education at Detroit Teachers College, to address a student meeting about the recently introduced ROTC program. Unbeknown to Reuther or Bergman, board member Burt Shurly sent an informant to the meeting to report on the speech. Upon hearing that Bergman had denounced "militarism" on campus and had urged students to pass out petitions demanding an end to ROTC, Shurly vowed to fire Bergman at the next school board meeting.[82] This action precipitated the most extensive debate Detroit had ever seen on the issue of the civil liberties of teachers.

The Bergman controversy was part of a larger struggle then taking place in Detroit over the issues of free speech and free assembly. As the depression worsened and left-wing protests became more vehement, business leaders and conservative politicians demanded stern measures to preserve public order. Mayor Frank Murphy and other liberal leaders, on the other hand, strongly defended the rights of the protestors. The attack by Burt Shurly on Walter Bergman fits neatly into that larger conflict, since Bergman was well known as a member of the liberal "Murphy crowd."[83] Indeed, in commenting on the incident, Shurly declared that "we had this thing licked once in Detroit, but now, under the patronage of Mayor Murphy, the propaganda is creeping back again, and it is time for another fight."[84]

For the next few weeks, the controversy over Bergman and the constitutional rights of teachers were front-page news. The controversy cleanly divided the city into liberal and conservative camps. The Detroit Federation of Labor, the Socialist party, the League for Industrial Democracy, the Detroit chapter of the American Civil Liberties Union (ACLU), the Wayne County League of Women Voters, and the American Association of University Women strongly backed Bergman and expanded civil liberties for teachers. All of these organizations argued that teachers had the constitutional right to speak out on issues regardless of the stands they took on the issues.[85]

On the other side, the Board of Commerce, the Michigan Union League, the American Legion, the Reserve Officers' Association, a group known as the American party, the *Free Press,* and *Saturday Night* denounced

Bergman's actions, declaring that he had violated the public trust by using his position to indoctrinate students. The response from *Saturday Night* was typical, "The lid is off," *Saturday Night* declared, "[i]t should be no long time till some Communist school teacher who has been keeping his or her real ideas under cover assembles the boys and girls to hear the soviet [*sic*] gospel of revolution preached on public property by an individual living on the public payroll."[86]

The issue also split the school board along liberal and conservative lines. In this fight, the question of firing Bergman quickly took a back seat to a more inclusive "Free Speech" resolution introduced by Edward Williams. The resolution endorsed the rights of teachers "to discuss and to express their honest opinion, outside of the classroom, upon all subjects including social, economic and political questions without fear of official reprimand or coercion on the part of any one connected with the Board of Education."[87] When the roll call vote on the resolution was finally taken, all of the members who had received DFL endorsements, Williams, Webster, and Gorman, voted in favor of the resolution, while the three members who received the strongest support from business and conservative leaders, Shurly, Jamieson, and McLean, voted against it. The deciding vote on the resolution was cast by Laura Osborn, who was increasingly taking liberal stands on controversial issues before the board.[88]

The Detroit free speech resolution drew praise from liberal leaders across the country. John Dewey, Arthur Garfield Hayes, the American Civil Liberties Union, the American Federation of Teachers, and the *Nation* hailed the Detroit school board for its unprecedented action. The resolution also had a profound impact on educational politics in the city by loosening the bonds that had held teacher activism and unionism in check.[89]

The passage of the resolution, however, did not mark a complete reversal in the civil liberty policies of the board of education. Indeed, less than four months after the smoke from the Bergman incident had cleared, another free speech issue, the use of school buildings by radical political organizations for afterschool meetings, found the school board siding with the conservative leaders of the city. Throughout the 1920s and early 1930s, the board had made school rooms and auditoriums available to a variety of left-wing organizations. While some of these meetings occasionally sparked controversy, nothing provoked outrage as much as the "trial" of Henry Ford and Frank Murphy conducted by the Communist party in the auditorium of Cass Technical High School following the violent "Ford Hunger March" in March, 1932. The "trial" found Ford, Murphy, and other prominent Detroiters guilty of the deaths of the four hunger marchers who had been killed by Dearborn police and Ford security guards.[90]

Disgusted by the use of a school building for such subversive purposes, *Detroit Saturday Night,* the Citizens League, and the Michigan Union League demanded that the board end its policy of providing meeting places for "reds." The Union League, however, did more than protest. In April, the group presented the board with an opinion from the attorney general of Michigan, who declared that neither state nor federal law guaranteed that communists had the right to use school buildings for their meetings. With that opinion in hand, the school board voted unanimously to deny requests for school rooms or auditoriums from radical or revolutionary political groups.[91] Nevertheless, the board continued to provide meeting places for other left-wing and labor groups, such as the Socialist party and the United Auto Workers, and the board routinely granted auditoriums for rallies in support of such liberal causes as Tom Mooney, the Scottsboro Boys, and Republican Spain.[92]

Just as the school board appeared to be taking a more conservative stance regarding civil liberties, however, the teachers began testing the limits of the free speech resolution. In 1932, the underground DFT helped engineer the election of E. W. McFarland, a liberal economics professor at City College, to the presidency of the Detroit Teachers Association (DTA). As I show in the next section, McFarland set a more militant tone for that organization, leading the teachers into state-level politics, where battles for increased state aid were taking shape.[93]

Having succeeded in capturing the leadership of the largest local teacher organization in the state, the DFT turned its eyes toward the board of education itself. In the grim early months of 1933, as antibusiness sentiment was at its height due to the bank collapse, the DFT brazenly attempted to unseat incumbent board members Burt Shurly and A. D. Jamieson. The union targeted Shurly and Jamieson primarily because of their willingness to accede to the retrenchment demands of the Stone Committee. The teachers heartily agreed with the *Labor News,* which had labeled the two men the "bankers faction" on the board and accused them of placing the interests of banks above those of the schools. Both men were also considered to be staunchly opposed to teachers' unions.[94]

Since the DFT was still an underground organization, a Saturday study group that met at a neighborhood YMCA served as a front organization in the campaign. In the March primary, the group succeeded in getting Charles Lockwood, a liberal attorney, on the school board ballot. Under the direction of Ethan Edloff, a DFT leader, the study group then set up an extensive ward and precinct organization to work for Lockwood's election.[95] Despite efforts to keep union involvement in the election under wraps, rumors that unionized teachers were directing the campaign soon leaked out. Amid the panic that followed the bank collapse and heightened fears of radicalism generated by a communist-led strike at a Ford supplier, the prospect of union influence over the schools produced one of the most heated school board races in the history of the city.[96]

As in the 1931 school board race, the issue of teachers in politics polarized the city. The added dimension of *unionized* teachers entering politics in 1933, however, considerably sharpened the rhetoric and deepened the divisions over the issue. The Citizens League, which had denounced unions for public employees as early as 1927, solidly backed the incumbents. Not surprisingly, the *Free Press* and *Saturday Night* also strongly supported the incumbents and blasted the teachers for trying to unseat them. Both papers declared that the campaign against Shurly and Jamieson was orchestrated by left-wing radicals within the Detroit Federation of Labor who sought to control the board of education.[97]

By far the most stinging attack on the teachers came from the usually moderate *Detroit News*. In an impassioned editorial entitled "A Political School Teacher Is a Public Enemy," the *News* denounced the teachers for bringing "putrid" politics back into the schools and urged that the leaders of the campaign be fired. Following a flurry of letters protesting the editorial, the *News* responded with another commentary deploring the links between the leaders of the campaign and the DFL. The *News* thus joined the *Free Press* and *Saturday Night* in condemning the prospect of a teachers' union in staunchly open-shop Detroit.[98]

Fears of unionized school teachers also drew the Employers' Association of Detroit into the contest. As "the spearhead of the open shop forces in the city," the Employers' Association had been active for almost three decades in strike-breaking and other antiunion activities. Just the hint of union involvement in the school board race led the general manager of the Employers' Association to quickly inform his membership that Shurly and Jamieson had been targeted by people who "support the organization of the teachers by the A. F. of L." He urged the members to back the two incumbents, arguing that "Dr. Shurly and Mr. Jamieson have demonstrated their ability to stand against the forces of radicalism."[99]

On the other side of the issue, the DFL urged voters to defeat Shurly and Jamieson, who, the *Labor News* argued, "placed the interests of the bankers ahead of the school children." The Socialist party, which enrolled a sizable contingent of teachers (including Walter Bergman and Ethan Edloff), strongly backed the effort to defeat Shurly and Jamieson. In addition, following the "public enemy" editorial from the *News,* the socialist *Detroit Leader* passionately defended the rights of teachers to engage in political action. Such educational organizations as the Southeastern Michigan Teachers Club also entered the fray, deploring what they saw as the effort by the *News* and other critics of the campaign to deny teachers their constitutional rights.[100]

Despite the efforts of the DFT and its allies, however, the campaign to unseat Shurly and Jamieson failed. The election was a clear defeat for the fledgling teachers' union that had long-range repercussions. In addition to widening the breach between liberals and conservatives in educational politics, the campaign also unleashed a torrent of protests against politically active, unionized teachers. More ominously, right-wing newspapers and organizations used the campaign as evidence of radicalism among the teachers, an accusation that would grow increasingly menacing as the decade wore on.[101]

In the year that followed the effort to unseat Shurly and Jamieson, the DFT maintained a low profile, fearing that the board would take reprisals against members in spite of the free speech policy. Despite these fears, membership grew, and, by late 1934, there were enough members to form three distinct factions. The largest faction was composed of liberal trade unionists led by Frances Comfort, Arthur Elder, and Florence Sweeney. Socialists, including Walter Bergman, Ethan Edloff, and Huldah Fine, made up the second-largest faction. The smallest faction was a group of more radical leftists with some ties to the Detroit Communist party. This group included Jane Mayer, Gertrude Mayer, and Elinor Laffrey. Although there was some dissension between these groups—the liberals, for example, complained that the "fellow travelers" regularly used the union to endorse noneducational communist causes—the factions essentially worked well together for most of the 1930s.[102]

By the fall of 1934, the generally improved position of organized labor that resulted from the passage of the National Industrial Recovery Act encouraged the DFT to publicly announce its existence. In late October, following a speech in Detroit by AFT leader George Counts, the DFT officially removed its veil of secrecy and took its place as an active union within the expanded Detroit and Wayne County Federation of Labor (DWCFL).[103] Yet no sooner did the union emerge from underground than accusations of radicalism in the schools resounded. Three days after the Counts speech, the notoriously antiunion commissioner of police, Heinrich Pickert, declared that Detroit teachers were "teaching, living, talking and breathing Communism." The *Free Press* and the increasingly conservative *Detroit Times* quickly called for firings of the "red" teachers, while liberal leaders and the *News* blasted the police commissioner for supplying no evidence of his claim. Indeed, Pickert produced no names and the incident quickly faded from view, but the repercussions from the accusations were serious.[104] According to testimony before the Dies Committee in 1938, the police department stepped up its surveillance of leading DFT members soon after this incident and the antisubversive committee of the local American Legion also began an investigation of suspected radical teachers.[105] Like other unions in the city, the DFT struggled to establish its legitimacy amid repeated accusations of radicalism.

Over the next few years, the DFT did little to mollify the critics who accused it of radicalism. In the spring of 1935, the DFT again participated in a school board election, this time working publicly to reelect Laura Osborn. No cries of "Public Enemy" were raised by any of the major newspapers or civic organizations regarding this support for Osborn, but that may have had more to do with her reputation for incorruptibility than a lessening of fears about unionized teachers.[106] The DFT also opposed the expulsion of communists from the AFT, participated in communist-front organizations such as the American League Against War and Fascism, and marched in the local May Day parades.[107]

Among the most controversial stands taken by the DFT was its vigorous advocacy of increased state and local support for the public schools. As the 1935 budget hearings commenced, the DFT blasted "reactionary" business leaders, whose retrenchment demands had "brought severe suffering to the working class, who, in spite of their poverty, continue to bear the greater part of the tax burden. The demands of reactionary groups are definitely hostile to the ideas of free democratic education and demand curtailments of education which would serve to deprive Labor of the one public service which can be said to benefit the poor equally with the rich."[108] Although the union remained small, enrolling fewer than 150 members as late as 1938, it drew on the increasing power of the DWCFL and, later, the United Auto Workers (UAW) to become an important factor in the local budget battles. Indeed, even during the period when the American Federation of Labor and the Congress of Industrial Organizations (CIO) were feuding in Detroit, both organizations strongly supported increases in the school budget and backed the demands of the teachers' unions.[109]

Indicative of this support was the fact that, throughout the late 1930s, DWCFL president Frank Martel routinely accompanied DFT president Frances Comfort to the budget hearings, at times with a phalanx of Teamsters, to pressure the common council into increasing appropriations for the schools.[110] In addition to seeking larger educational appropriations, in 1937, the DFT and DWCFL initiated a process to force the city to repay the salaries that had been taken from the teachers by the common council in May and June, 1932. While this effort took more than a decade to reach its goal, its ultimately successful outcome boosted the prestige of the DFT considerably. On the state level, the DFT joined with locals from Ann Arbor, Kalamazoo, and Grand Rapids in early 1935 to form the Michigan Federation of Teachers (MFT), which immediately began lobbying for increased state aid to education.[111]

All of these actions were controversial, and right-wing critics used them to claim that a coterie of radical teachers were seeking to take control of the Detroit public schools. As conflicts between labor and capital intensified in the late 1930s, such accusations became increasingly common. But the political context in which these charges were made was changing dramatically. The passage of the Wagner Act in 1935 and the election of Frank Murphy as the governor of Michigan the following year spurred organized labor to directly challenge the powerful, open-shop forces of the automobile industry. In late December, 1936, the conflict between organized labor and General Motors exploded in the Flint sit-down strike, "the most significant labor conflict of the twentieth century." The sit-down strike was followed by scores of other successful strikes that transformed Detroit from one of the strongholds of the open shop to a center of industrial unionism.[112] The strike also propelled the United Auto Workers and the CIO into the front ranks of the political and educational battles in Detroit.

As the educational wing of the labor movement in Detroit, the DFT quickly felt the reverberations from the sit-down strikes. In July, 1937, while the National Education Association was meeting in Detroit and numerous strikes continued to plague the city, Burt Shurly assumed the presidency of the board of education and denounced "communism and unionism" in his inaugural address to the board. Questioned after the speech, Shurly declared that his remarks specifically referred to members of the American Federation of Teachers.[113]

The *Labor News* blasted the speech as evidence of "Fascism on the School Board" and several weeks later a delegation led by DWCFL president Frank Martel and DFT president Frances Comfort attended a board meeting to protest Shurly's speech. In several ways, the July 27th school board meeting was a pivotal event in the history of the school system. As Comfort recalled, more than 200 DFT supporters attended the meeting, including representatives from "every union and liberal organization in Detroit." This turnout, which had been orchestrated by Martel, was ample evidence of the deep commitment that organized labor had to the fledgling teachers' union. In addition, the appearance at the meeting of Clara Van Auken, a member of the national committee of the Democratic party, testified to the growing alliance between organized labor and the Democrats and hinted at increasingly partisan battles over educational issues.[114]

As impressive as that turnout was, the response of the school board was even more striking. Five of the six board members who attended the meeting (Shurly was absent) unequivocally repudiated Shurly's views on unionism, declaring that teachers had every right to join the DFT. Even conservative board member A. D. Jamieson noted that there was much in unionism that he found commendable. While the board did not issue a formal endorsement of the teachers' union, Martel, Comfort, and their supporters left the meeting in triumph. Just three years after emerging from underground, the DFT now took its place as the educational wing of the burgeoning labor movement in Detroit.[115]

In conferring a "recognized" status on the DFT, the board implicitly acknowledged the enormous political and economic changes the sit-down strikes had brought to Detroit. By the summer of 1937, the board members recognized that the DWCFL and the UAW would play crucial roles in the battles over educational funding. Indeed, union leaders who spoke at the July 27th board meeting emphasized the support organized labor had given the schools during the worst times of retrenchment and noted their continued pressure for increased school appropriations during the annual municipal budget deliberations. The board members saw the clear link between maintaining union support for increased funding and recognizing the teachers' union. While such conservative board members as Jamieson may have opposed teachers' unions in principle, the rift between school leaders and the business community over the size of the education budget left these members without much political clout. By 1937, the left, not the right, was the mainstay of support for increased funds for the public schools, and board members such as Jamieson bowed to the emerging political realities.

Other conservative leaders and opinion makers in Detroit, however, were outraged by the pro-union sentiments expressed by the board. In an editorial that undoubtedly represented the fears of many conservative

Detroiters, *Saturday Night* denounced the "polite indulgence" of the board "to men aligned with a movement that would destroy every traditional American institution. . . . Communism should not be allowed to penetrate the American school system at any point."[116] The *Saturday Night* editorial highlighted the vicious cycle that had come to dominate educational politics in the Motor City. As the rift between school leaders and the right widened over the issue of finance, school leaders sought support from the increasingly powerful labor movement and its liberal allies. And every gesture by school leaders toward the left exacerbated the disagreements over educational issues with the business community and conservatives.

Nothing better illustrates this process than the controversy over radical teachers that emerged from the 1938 investigation of the sit-down strikes by the House Special Committee on Un-American Activities, better known as the Dies Committee. In October, 1938, the Dies Committee began hearings in Detroit, ostensibly to investigate charges of communist involvement in the sit-down strikes. But coming amid the reelection campaign of Governor Frank Murphy, the Detroit hearings quickly became a forum for diatribes directed at the liberal, Democratic governor and his supporters in the CIO and the UAW.[117] Investigating radical activity in public education was not a high priority for the committee, but the hearings nevertheless elicited numerous allegations of communist activity within the Detroit schools. As one witness put it, ". . . many [Detroit] school teachers have Communist leanings . . . and at every opportunity forward the cause of un-Americanism to the children of the state."[118]

Three trends are evident in the accusations made before the Dies Committee. First, the chief accusers of the teachers were members of the "Red Squad" of the police department or members of the antisubversive committee of the American Legion. These organizations had been keeping dossiers on a number of teachers for at least four years. Second, most of the accused teachers were members of the DFT, and some, such as Walter Bergman, Huldah Fine, and Elinor Laffrey, were leaders of the organization. Third, none of the witnesses before the committee presented evidence that the teachers had indoctrinated children in the classroom, only that the accused teachers had attended radical meetings, associated with radicals, or, for many of the women named, were married or had been married to leading communists.[119]

During the first few days of the hearings in Detroit, these allegations about radical activities by teachers dominated the headlines. As in previous "red scares," the accusations polarized Detroit along liberal and conservative lines. The conservative mayor, Richard Reading, for example, demanded that the school board immediately fire the accused teachers, a position echoed by the American Legion and the Veterans of Foreign Wars.[120] The *Free Press* blasted the school board, declaring that "there might be considerably less work for the Dies Committee to do in this city today if the local school authorities had a better and more courageous conception of their duty when dealing with loose tongued and impudent persons of anarchistic and communistic leanings on the teaching staff." The *Detroit Times,* which enthusiastically supported the work of the Dies Committee, trumpeted the allegations in its editorials, in blatantly biased news articles, and in such double banner headlines as "BRAND 10 TEACHERS AS REDS/ Dies Witness Lists Names."[121]

The major liberal and labor organizations in the city rushed to the defense of the teachers. In addition, the *News* and its leading columnist, W. K. Kelsey, denounced the allegations. But perhaps the most significant reaction was that of the school administration, which stood firmly behind its teachers. Unlike Mayor Reading, who used charges made before the committee to summarily fire several public aid doctors, the school board refused to be drawn into the anti-Communist hysteria.[122] The attitude of the school administration was summed up by Frank Cody in what became the most memorable and widely quoted statement about the crisis. Responding to a reporter's question about the headline in the *Detroit Times,* Cody declared, "There are 8,000 teachers in our school system, and if 10 of them are red and the remainder well read, I'll be satisfied."[123]

An even better indication of the attitude of the school administration about these charges came several months later, when a special committee of the school board, chaired by Jamieson and including Osborn and Cody, issued the results of its own investigation of radical activity by Detroit teachers. Charged with establishing if any of the teachers were communists and if any had used their positions to spread subversive teachings among students, the committee spent three months reading testimony from the Dies hearings, analyzing police files on the accused, and interviewing all the teachers named and their supervisors. In a ringing reaffirmation of the 1931 free speech policy, the Jamieson Committee acknowledged that all of the accused teachers were active in left-wing politics in the city, but that none were guilty of spreading subversive doctrines in the classroom. Unlike similar investigations across the nation, such as the 1940 Rapp-Coudert hearings in New York City, these conclusions guaranteed against firings or damaged careers. Without a doubt, the Jamieson Committee would have fired any teacher found guilty of "indoctrinating" students in left-wing ideas. Finding no evidence of such actions, the committee accepted left-wing and labor activism by the teachers as long as it took place outside the classroom.[124]

These developments had obvious benefits for the DFT. The conclusions of the committee had, to some extent, removed the taint of radicalism from the union and reduced fears of administrative sanctions against unionized teachers. By 1940, the union had almost 300 members, making it one of the largest locals in the AFT. This increase in membership had a profound impact on local educational politics. Since most of the new members were "bread and butter" unionists who sided with the liberal rather than far-left faction in DFT policy debates, the priorities of the union shifted. Ironically, this movement of the DFT from the far left to the moderate left increased rather than decreased conflict over educational issues in Detroit. The liberal union members of the DFT repeatedly complained that the leftists diverted the attention of the local from the day-to-day needs and demands of teachers. As the far left-wing faction lost power in the early 1940s, the "bread and butter" issues of salaries and working conditions rose to the fore. Since invariably these meant battling for more money from the city and the state, the DFT and its allies in the DWCFL and UAW increasingly locked horns with such fiscally and politically conservative organizations as the Board of Commerce and the Citizens League.[125]

As the result of this focus on economic issues, the patterns of conflict that developed between the advocates and opponents of retrenchment in the early 1930s continued into the next decade under the guise of debate over the size of the school budget. Few events better highlight this continued polarization than the struggle in the winter of 1939–40 over appropriations for the upcoming school year. The battle lines on this issue could not have been clearer, as the Board of Commerce, the Citizens League, and the Bureau of Governmental Research condemned proposed increases in the school budget, and the Detroit Federation of Teachers, supported by the DWCFL and CIO, argued for increases. Perhaps the most striking aspect of the debate over this issue was how little the rhetoric used by the participants differed from the angry exchanges that had dominated the early 1930s. In a series of editorials, including a dramatic front-page appeal entitled "The People's Education in Danger," the *Labor News* reminded its readers of the historic struggle to create public schools and blasted the renewed efforts by "stuffed shirts and wealthy property owners" to deny the children of workers an adequate education.[126]

In only one significant way did the alignment of interests over educational issues change from the early 1930s to the early 1940s. Beginning in

1939, the black leaders of Detroit loosened their ties to the business community and began to play an increasingly important role in school politics. Committed to better funding for the schools and to greater equality in the distribution of educational resources and opportunities, these leaders emerged during the war years as strong and determined supporters of the public schools. The story of the increasingly activist stance on education taken by black Detroiters will be discussed in the next chapter. Suffice it to say that, as with the alignment of other interest groups in Detroit, the changing political orientation of the African-American community mirrored the larger changes taking place in the nation. Much as blacks were becoming an increasingly important part of the New Deal realignment nationally, so, by the late 1940s, blacks would become an important part of the liberal-labor coalition on school issues in Detroit.[127]

The Struggle for State Aid

The final issue that contributed to the persistence of educational conflict in Detroit was the issue of increased state aid to the schools. The 15 mill property tax limitation that Michigan voters approved in November, 1932, delivered a staggering blow to public education across the state. Prior to the 15 mill limit, the average tax rate in the state was over 32 mills, of which approximately 11 mills went to support the schools. In July, 1933, the Michigan Department of Public Instruction reported that, as a result of the limitation, about half of the schools in the state would have to close their doors in January, 1934. The cities of Flint, Jackson, Kalamazoo, and Saginaw projected five-month school terms, and a host of villages and towns followed a similar course. Rural school districts slashed salaries of teachers to $50 and even $25 per month. Two figures summed up the situation most clearly: in 1930, total support for education from property taxes and from the Primary School Fund, the main source of state aid, amounted to almost $90 million; in 1934, the total was just $42 million. Even taking into account the increased value of the dollar due to deflation between 1930 and 1934, the drop was still more than 42 percent. In addition to these immediate problems, the amendment introduced two other restrictions on school finance that had serious long-range consequences. First, millage increases above the 15 mill limit had to be approved by two-thirds of the voters. Second, school districts could only issue bonds with five-year terms. In effect, these restrictions made it impossible for school districts to raise money either for operating revenue or capital expenditures.[128]

The impact of the 15 mill limit on the Detroit schools was more ambiguous. As a home-rule city, Detroit itself was exempt from the limit. Nevertheless, the impact on *state* funding for the Detroit schools was profound. The Primary School Fund, which supplied Detroit with the bulk of its state aid, was based on "the [statewide] average rate of taxation on property assessed for state, county, township, school, and municipal purposes."[129] The 15 mill limit reduced that average so severely that the total Primary School Fund fell from just over $24 million in 1931–32 to only $14.4 million in 1934–35. Since Detroit generally received about a third of the disbursement of the fund, the Detroit schools stood to lose some $2 million annually as a result of the 15 mill limitation.[130]

By the start of 1933, reforming the state system of support for public education had become a top priority for Detroit's public school leaders and their allies. The alignment of interest groups on the issue of increasing state aid to education directly paralleled the alignments that had formed over the issue of retrenchment. In February, Detroit school board member A. D. Jamieson chaired a conference on the crisis in education sponsored by the Michigan Education Association (MEA). Representatives of thirteen statewide organizations, including the American Legion, the Kiwanis Club, the League of Women Voters, and the Michigan Congress of Parent-Teacher Associations, joined the MEA to work for increased taxes and state aid. These organizations formed the nucleus of the state "education lobby." They were eventually joined by the DFT, MFT, the Michigan Federation of Labor, the Detroit and Wayne County Federation of Labor, and the CIO unions, particularly the United Auto Workers, all of which actively supported increased state aid for the public schools.[131]

Almost immediately, the education lobby provoked controversy by supporting the introduction of a state sales tax that was to raise some $15 million for the schools. Although the legislature eventually passed the 3 percent tax, the final version of the bill failed to provide additional educational funding and the school leaders geared up for a new campaign to raise $25 million for the schools through new taxes.[132] This campaign for new taxes immediately drew fire from the same coalition of business organizations and conservative political groups that was leading the fight for educational retrenchment in Detroit. Soon after the educators announced their proposed new taxes, the Board of Commerce denounced the effort and derided the educators for their "exaggerated and unsupported statements relative to the financial needs of the schools." The Michigan Manufacturers Association, the Economy League of Michigan, the Michigan Chamber of Commerce, the

Detroit Bureau of Governmental Research, the *Free Press,* and *Saturday Night* all joined the chorus of opposition to the proposed new taxes. In addition, powerful farm interests across the state lined up against the educators.[133]

This coalition of business, farm, and conservative political interest groups vigorously fought every effort by the educators and their allies to increase taxes and state aid throughout the 1930s. By 1934, the heated rhetoric that had dominated school politics in Detroit in the early 1930s had become a commonplace on the state level. Responding to the opposition to the proposed taxes the legislative committee of the MEA, for example, declared that

> those who are in entrenched places generally have not viewed with favor the public school system. They oppose it, first, because the public schools have been training persons who are capable of replacing those in entrenched positions; second, because all dominating groups attempt as a means of control to restrict the opportunities of the dominated; third because the training of sovereign citizens furnishes a greater degree of independence to the body politic and proportionately restricts the greed of entrenched privilege on the one hand and the rapacity and folly of demagoguery on the other.[134]

E. W. McFarland, the leftist president of the Detroit Teachers Association (the local MEA affiliate), put the situation more succinctly, declaring that educators needed to cast off the naive belief "that the interests of education and especially the costs of education always harmonize with the interests of privately owned industry and its own financing."[135]

Even when politically conservative educators took back the presidency of the DTA in late 1934, the efforts of the organization to increase taxes and revenues for public education did not slacken in the least. Indeed, by 1936, the DTA had become a major force in educational politics, mobilizing large numbers of teachers in support of proschool candidates and focusing considerable media attention on issues deemed vital to the schools. While the more conservative DTA leaders eschewed overtly radical rhetoric, in almost every election, the DTA blasted "selfish interests," code words for business leaders and taxpayer groups who were opposed to increases in state aid. In the 1936 elections, for example, school leaders and their allies waged a successful fight against the Detroit taxpayers association and realtors, who sponsored two constitutional amendments that would have substantially reduced state aid to education. Throughout the 1930s, the typical alignment of interests on the issue of increased educational funding pitted the DTA, MEA, and their liberal and labor allies against the business community, usually led by the Michigan Chamber of Commerce.[136]

In Detroit, the Board of Commerce echoed the stance of the state organization and staunchly opposed increases in state aid, claiming that the "so-called financial crisis" in public education was due mostly to the proliferation of small, inefficient rural school districts.[137] In January, 1935, *Saturday Night* also dismissed the $25 million plea by labeling it a smokescreen for continued expansion of "fads and frills." The conservative weekly demanded that educational funding support little more than instruction in the three R's. Anger about the efforts to increase taxes even touched Frank Cody, who had attempted to maintain good relationships with the business community and the conservative press throughout the retrenchment controversy. In April, Cody appeared before the state legislature to appeal for passage of the $25 million aid package. Although not mentioning Cody by name, *Saturday Night* responded almost immediately by denouncing "the energetic public school lobby that puts song and dance education on a par with home and mother."[138]

Despite this conservative opposition, in the spring of 1935 the legislature passed the aid package that drew revenue from sales, chain stores, and liquor taxes. These taxes formed the core of state school aid for the remainder of the decade and settled the question of whether to increase state aid, at least in principle.[139] Nevertheless, conflict continued over the levels and sources of funding. In 1938, the legislature increased school aid to a total of $40.5 million for 1938–39, yet educators and their allies contended that this was $6.5 million less than was needed to adequately fund public education in the state. Business leaders and their conservative allies, however, argued that the schools could do much more with the available revenues and, for the remainder of the decade, these groups continued to fight to keep taxes low and educational spending down.[140]

In the fall of 1938, the educators and their allies successfully opposed Michigan's powerful automobile and oil interests, who sought to divert state revenues, and thus decrease educational appropriations, through a constitutional amendment. The following year, the automobile and oil companies financed the efforts of the Michigan Public Expenditures Survey, Inc., which, with the aid of the Michigan Chamber of Commerce, conducted a largely successful campaign to hold the line on state appropriations to the schools. Throughout that campaign, leaders of the survey argued that the schools did not deserve more money because they were turning out illiterate students.[141]

These political conflicts over increased taxes and spending were exacerbated by the fears of many rural legislators and conservative politicians that greater state aid would ultimately lead to greater state control of local education. During the late 1930s and early 1940s, these fears were heightened by two pieces of legislation strongly pushed by the Michigan Federation of Teachers and its allies in the labor movement—teacher tenure and minimum teacher salaries. Soon after its founding in 1935, the MFT began a campaign for a statewide tenure plan. Eventually the MEA joined the struggle, and, in 1937 with the support of Governor Frank Murphy, the teacher organizations got the legislature to pass a tenure law.[142] Unfortunately for the teachers, in the final debate on the bill, legislators replaced the provision mandating a statewide tenure process for all teachers with one that set up local referenda to decide on tenure for each district. Fears of "big government" were clearly behind this alteration. As Arthur Elder, chief lobbyist for the MFT, pointed out, "opposition [to the statewide mandate] came chiefly from rural and small town school board members who were under the impression that the passage of the tenure law was a move in the direction of control of our public schools by Lansing."[143]

While the fears of rural and small town educational leaders about state control may have been exaggerated in regard to teacher tenure, they were well founded in regard to the effort by the MFT (and later the MEA) to mandate minimum statewide salaries for teachers. This effort by the MFT and MEA came as a response to the tendency of many rural and small town school boards to use increased revenue from the state as a reason for cutting local taxes rather than as a means to improve salaries and working conditions for teachers. According to the teachers' organizations, these tactics resulted in horribly low salaries for large numbers of teachers in the state. As late as 1938, the MEA reported that nearly 11,000 Michigan teachers, approximately a third of all teachers in the state, earned less than $1,200 annually, more than $300 below the statewide average.[144] Both teachers' organizations believed that minimum salary legislation was the only solution to this problem, and they pressed for a law establishing such salaries for all teachers in the state. But this proposal raised the specter of increased state control of local schools, a prospect that few rural and small town legislators would tolerate. As a consequence of this opposition, the minimum salary legislation, like the campaign for statewide tenure, stalled in the legislature in the 1930s.[145]

More important than the practical failure of statewide tenure and minimum salaries were the philosophical debates that these efforts generated.

Questions about the proper role and size of government dominated political discussions in the 1930s. But in states such as Michigan, where liberal governors like Frank Murphy attempted to implement "little New Deals," these questions became highly charged and politically divisive. Conservative politicians, who valued local control of the schools, clearly recognized that increases in state aid inevitably meant greater state control of local schools. As one Republican legislator stated during the 1939 state aid battle, "increasing contributions for state aid will result in a disintegration of school districts and a concentration of power over education in the hands of the state government." Educators and liberal politicians, on the other hand, argued that increased state aid and control were essential for revitalizing the educational infrastructure that had taken such a beating during the early 1930s.[146] The fact that both sides of this debate were right insured the persistence of the conflict for years to come.

The dramatic growth of state government generally and state school aid specifically helped keep this controversy alive. The total amount of state aid jumped from just over $22 million in 1930 to over $42 million in 1940. In 1930, local property taxes amounted to almost 72 percent of total school revenue in Michigan, with only 20 percent of the total education budget coming from the state. By 1939, the burden was shared more equally, with 47 percent coming from local taxes and 45 percent from the state. These trends were mirrored in Detroit, where revenue from the state grew from $5.7 million in fiscal 1930 to $10.8 million in 1939. Local property taxes for the Detroit schools, which accounted for 76 percent of total revenue in 1930, only accounted for 57 percent in 1939, with state aid accounting for most of the remainder.[147] As schools throughout the state came to depend on these funds for an enormous amount of their operating budgets, the intensity and divisiveness of the political battles about state aid to education increased. As with the financial conflicts on the local level, these battles became one of the enduring legacies of the Great Depression.

Unresolved Issues

The condition of the Detroit school system in 1940 gave educational leaders cause for hope as well as despair. By 1939, the increases in state aid combined with local revenues resulted in an operating budget almost equal to predepression levels. The retrenchment policies articulated by Jamieson in 1931 insured that no teachers were fired and no programs were cut during the worst period of retrenchment. While school leaders certainly could take pride in how the schools had weathered the economic storm, several changes in the system brought about by the depression gave them reason to approach the future with some trepidation.[148]

Four major problems loomed before the school administration: teacher salaries; class size; school construction; and the high school curriculum. Between 1931 and 1935, teachers in Detroit experienced almost a 22 percent reduction in their salaries. This reduction, however, was offset by the increased purchasing power of the dollar during these years, up almost 20 percent from 1929 to 1939. Unfortunately for the teachers, by 1940, the economic boom stimulated by World War II replaced this period of monetary deflation with a period of rapid inflation. While prices and salaries of other workers began to rise dramatically, salaries for teachers barely rose at all. As the depression decade drew to a close, it was obvious to everyone within the school system that salary increases for teachers would soon become an explosive educational issue.[149]

Besides salary increases, the school system desperately needed to find funds to employ more teachers. The hiring freeze put into place in 1931 caused the number of teachers in the system to fall from 7,682 in 1930 to 7,206 in 1933, while the total number of students in the system jumped from 249,031 to 260,113. Consequently, average class size rose, particularly on the secondary level, where enrollment increases were greatest. The average intermediate school class went from just under 40 pupils in 1929 to 43 in 1933; during the same period, high school classes jumped from 33 to 37 students per class. The system began to replenish its depleted teaching staff by 1935, but the hiring did not keep pace with enrollment growth. In 1938, classes in the intermediate school averaged more than 44 students, while high school classes averaged more than 38 students.[150]

As early as 1937, the North Central Association (NCA), which accredited the Detroit high schools, began warning school leaders that such high student-teacher ratios threatened the accreditation of the schools. In 1940, after finding no change in the student-teacher ratios on the high school level, NCA officials privately warned administrators in Detroit of their intention to begin the deaccreditation process unless the city government provided funds to reduce the size of high school classes. By 1943, Detroit did comply with the NCA student-teacher ratios, but not because of funding increases from the city. Only the rapid decline in high school enrollments due to the outbreak of World War II kept the Motor City from facing the threatened NCA action.[151]

Compounding the problem of overcrowded classes was the moratorium on school construction that the board had implemented in 1931. In no other area were the effects of retrenchment so severe. In 1931–32, the board spent $5,225,075 on construction. The following year, the board slashed funds for construction to $91,270, and for the next two years the board allocated only $90,000 annually. As late as 1936–37, the board spent only $523,850 for new buildings or additions. While the school system did get some aid for construction from such New Deal programs as the Public Works Administration, which helped reconstruct Western High School after it had burned and built additions to two other high schools, this aid was not enough to offset the dramatic decline in local funds nor was it enough to meet the housing needs of the growing student population, which had climbed to more than 268,000 in 1935–36.[152]

In June, 1937, Laura Osborn wrote that there was "A Crying Need [for] More Schools" because the mayor and council had simply ignored requests from the board of education for more buildings. Several months later, the administrator charged with trying to placate the NCA on the issue of high school accreditation presented a similar scenario when explaining the overcrowded high school classes. "The building program in Detroit," he noted, "has been stopped entirely during the last six years." When school opened in the fall of 1937, more than 17,000 high school students were on half-day sessions and CIO-backed candidates for city office blasted the mayor and council for their inattention to the problems of overcrowding and the need for new buildings.[153]

As a result of such pressure and the obvious needs of the system, the school board and its allies were able to convince the city government to provide more funds for construction for 1937–38, but the $3,175,000 that the city approved was woefully below the needs of the system. Unfortunately, as a consequence of the sharp economic downturn that began in 1937, the board again slashed capital spending to $1,700,000 for 1938–39 and $1,125,302 for 1939–40.[154] While the onset of World War II had a positive influence on the economy of Detroit, in general, the effects of the war on school construction were almost identical to that of the Great Depression. During the war, resources and labor invariably flowed into the defense industries and such public works projects as school construction virtually came to a halt.

The last looming problem for the schools was the development of a new high school curriculum ostensibly to meet the needs of the changing student body. Like the problems of overcrowded classes and the lack of new buildings, concern with the high school curriculum was a direct result of the sudden increase in secondary school enrollment in the 1930s. One of the most serious consequences of the depression was the collapse of the youth labor market. Prior to the depression, as many as 50 percent of all fourteen-to eighteen-year-olds in Detroit left school without graduating, generally to enter the work force. In 1929, for example, the Detroit Board of Education issued about 100 work permits per month for fifteen-year-olds and over 300 per month for sixteen-year-olds. Since young people were usually the last hired and the first fired, they felt the effects of the depression more swiftly and severely than any other age group. In 1931, the monthly average of work permits issued by the board fell to 15 and 105 for fifteen- and sixteen-year-olds, respectively, and in 1933 the monthly averages hit bottom at 4 and 30.[155]

This collapse of the youth labor market stimulated enormous growth in high school enrollments. In November, 1929, 25,908 students were enrolled in the comprehensive high schools of Detroit. Five years later, the enrollment in these schools had jumped to 37,093, and by 1939 their enrollment swelled to 45,599. Not only did more students attend school, but they remained in school longer. Between 1928 and 1940, enrollment increases were greatest in the eleventh and twelfth grades. Not surprisingly, the numbers of high school graduates soared as well, more than doubling between 1929–30 and 1939–40.[156]

This dramatic jump in the number of students attending high school and the increasing length of time these students stayed in school presented administrators with a series of problems beyond overcrowded classes and insufficient buildings. Equally pressing was the question of adjusting the course of study for these new pupils. Since most of these depression era students probably would have dropped out of high school in normal economic times, educational leaders in Detroit and across the nation assumed that these young people were less academically and vocationally talented than previous generations of students. As a 1934 report by the National Education Association put it, "a very considerable proportion of the new enrollment is comprised of pupils of a different sort—boys and girls who are almost mature physically, who are normal mentally, in the sense that they are capable of holding their own with the ordinary adult, but who are unable or unwilling to deal successfully with continued study under the type of program which the secondary school is accustomed to provide." That same year, a Detroit school principal who chaired the committee charged with developing new curricular guidelines for these students expressed exactly those sentiments. "One of the most important problems of the secondary school in the next decade," he wrote, "will be to formulate curricula and reorganize subject matter for those pupils who have not the ability to master subjects in the college preparatory and commercial curricula. The chief reason for this immediate problem is the economic situation which has forced into the secondary schools thousands of young people who formerly left school at the age of sixteen or seventeen to go to work."[157] Such negative assumptions about the abilities and desires of this new wave of students undoubtedly reflected a considerable amount of class prejudice, since many, if not most, of these young people came from poor or working-class homes.[158]

These biased assumptions *and* the desire to keep students in school and out of the unemployment lines led school authorities to alter the curriculum in order to make high school courses both more relevant and less rigorous for these pupils. As in the 1920s, the principle of equity, specifically the belief that a differentiated curriculum provided the best vehicle for equal educational opportunity, guided these curriculum changes. In this case, however, the principle was seriously distorted as school leaders fashioned a new curriculum that was decidedly inferior to past offerings and ultimately increased educational inequality in Detroit's high schools.[159]

School leaders used the general track to introduce most of these changes, since that track was designed "to take care of pupils that had no particular objective or were unable to meet the rigorous standards of the College Preparatory or the Commercial curricula."[160] Rather than changing graduation requirements for general track students, school leaders replaced the more rigorous courses required for graduation with easier offerings that supposedly weaker students could master. The required laboratory science classes, for example, were replaced with large lecture, "descriptive" science courses that stressed the relevance of science to everyday life. Rather than taking the civics and economic courses required in other tracks, general track students took a course entitled Problems in American Life that concentrated on current events and such issues as finding a job and traffic safety. In addition, because students in the general track could choose more electives than other students, Detroit educators created a host of new classes that were designed to meet "the needs of youth." Many of these new electives were vocational or social studies courses that bore striking resemblances to offerings in the federally sponsored Life Adjustment curriculum of the late 1940s and early 1950s. Two courses, "Personal Standards" and "Applied Economics," were quite popular, focusing on such units as "problems of diet, dress, etiquette, jobs, relations [with the opposite sex], and personal hygiene."[161]

A study on curricular changes in all of Detroit's comprehensive high schools between 1928 and 1940 reveals the consequences of these administrative decisions. During this period, "the proportion of classes devoted to English, art, and the sciences remained stable, the proportion in mathematics and foreign languages declined, and the social studies and vocational classes increased substantially. Over the twelve years, classes in social studies and vocational education increased from about a one-third share to just under one-half." In short, by 1940, Detroit high school students were taking fewer difficult courses and more electives than were students in 1928, and the few difficult courses that they were taking, such as science, had been "watered down" considerably. These curricular developments reveal a major change in the nature and the function of high schools during the 1930s. By 1940, high schools in Detroit were relegating a substantial number of students to a second-rate education primarily to keep them out of the shrunken labor market. In other words, during the depression, Detroit's high schools went from institutions largely concerned with academic and vocational education for most students to institutions in which only some students received such an education while increasing numbers received custodial care.[162]

These enrollment increases and curricular changes appear to have had political as well as educational implications. While neither organized labor nor the business community ever explicitly discussed these developments, it may well be that the political stands about school finance taken by these groups were related to the dramatic changes in the youth labor market of the 1930s. With adult unemployment running at unprecedented levels during this period, organized labor undoubtedly saw an even greater necessity for getting young people into school and out of competition with adults for jobs. Thus, labor had a strong economic incentive to support increased funding for public education. On the other hand, the primary economic motive behind business support for the public schools, the training of prospective managers and skilled workers, was undercut by the economic conditions of the depression. Not only was there less need for managers and skilled workers because of the sluggish economy, but large numbers of well-trained unemployed adults were available to industry when the economy picked up. Thus, from a purely economic viewpoint, the business community could see little "return" for its support of increased educational funding and so fought for lower taxes and reduced educational spending. In essence, the depression helped change the fundamental economic rationale for schooling. Rather than serving the economic interests of business leaders as a training ground for future workers, the schools began to serve the economic interests of unions by keeping large numbers of potential workers out of the labor market. Both the political and curricular changes of the 1930s were rooted in that larger transformation.

One political consequence from the high school curriculum changes of the 1930s was certain. As the "fads and frills" debate of the early 1930s revealed, there was growing dissatisfaction among some conservative opinion makers with "modern" education. While some of the editorial attacks on "fads and frills" by the *Free Press* and *Saturday Night* predated the changes in the curriculum discussed here, the attitudes expressed by these conservative papers about the declining quality of public education and the neglect of basic skills undoubtedly became stronger as the evidence of these curricular reforms became public. Indeed, by the mid-1940s, business leaders were loudly complaining about the inadequate skills of the students who were graduating from the Detroit high schools. Eventually, such questions about the quality of the Detroit public schools would become a central feature in educational politics.

In all, as the 1930s drew to a close, the Detroit schools faced many of the same problems that they had faced in the early 1920s—low teacher salaries, the need for more buildings, and concerns about the school curriculum. Unlike the 1920s, however, the Detroit schools now faced these problems with a deeply fragmented political base and with little hope of restoring the consensus that had characterized educational politics just a decade before.

Conclusion

The transformation of educational politics in Detroit during the 1930s could not have been more complete. In a turbulent five-year period, 1929–34, the essence of educational politics in the Motor City went from consensus to conflict. None of the major interpretations of the history of education in the Great Depression account for that transformation. Little of what occurred in Detroit and Michigan during the 1930s, for example, supports the position articulated by Bowles and Gintis, that during periods of severe social and economic crisis the "advanced corporate economy" uses the schools "to accommodate and deflect thrusts away from its foundations."[163] Indeed, during this period, business leaders and their allies relentlessly sought to slash spending for the schools, a stance that helped turn educational politics into a major arena of class conflict. Similarly, contrary to the arguments put forth by Tyack, Lowe, and Hansot, the 1930s were clearly a watershed era in the educational history of Detroit. Events in Detroit also flatly contradict the

Katznelson and Weir thesis that organized labor abandoned its commitment to public education during this decade. While there is support for the Carnoy and Levin argument that the era witnessed a decline in the influence of business leaders and organizations and a rise in the influence of organized labor and liberal political groups in school politics, a close look at the changes in Detroit reveals that this political transformation had greater consequences in areas such as teacher unionization and school finance than in equalizing educational opportunities for the children of Detroit. Indeed, when school leaders revised the high school curriculum because of the influx of poor and working-class students, in essence agreeing with organized labor that the schools should serve as a mass custodial institution for adolescents, they increased educational inequality.

The great significance of these educational events in Detroit lies in the relationship of the schools to the seismic shift in American politics that took place during the depression decade. Through a combination of circumstances, the degree of support that the most important interest groups in the city gave to the Detroit public schools became contingent upon how these groups addressed the greatest political issue of the era—what is the proper role and size of government? In the 1920s, still flush with the enthusiasm of the Progressive era and certain that the key to the cornucopia had been found, business leaders and their politically conservative allies had strongly supported the expansion and improvement of the schools. Amid the chaos and confusion of the Great Depression, however, these same groups withdrew that support and redefined the schools as another bloated public service whose continued maintenance kept taxes high and profits low. On the other side of the issue, organized labor and its liberal allies saw the schools as a fundamental public welfare service whose expansion and improvement had become even more critical during the economic collapse. Just as these groups endorsed the growing role and cost of the federal government in such areas as public welfare, so they backed efforts to increase taxes and spending for the schools on the state and local levels.

The realignment of these interest groups during the period of retrenchment in the early 1930s and the gradual hardening of the liberal and conservative positions during the New Deal years substantially reduced the political base that had supported the public schools. Business leaders, conservative politicians, and like-minded editorial writers now stood outside the grand public school coalition, critical if not downright hostile to efforts to increase spending and services for the Detroit schools. Organized labor and its liberal allies quickly moved into the political vacuum created by this realignment and endeavored to establish a new base of support for public education. No other developments in the 1930s had such profound consequences for the schools than did this fundamental political transformation.

NOTES

1. Sidney Fine, *Frank Murphy: The Detroit Years* (Ann Arbor: University of Michigan Press, 1975), 246.

2. David Tyack, Robert Lowe, and Elisabeth Hansot, *Public Schools in Hard Times: The Great Depression and Recent Years* (Cambridge, MA: Harvard University Press, 1984), 189; Ira Katznelson and Margaret Weir, *Schooling for All: Class, Race, and the Decline of the Democratic Ideal* (New York: Basic Books, 1985); Martin Carnoy and Henry Levin, *Schooling and Work in the Democratic State* (Stanford, CA: Stanford University Press, 1985). For a detailed critique of Tyack, Lowe, and Hansot's book, see my review, *Educational Studies* 16 (Summer, 1985): 156–65.

3. I use the terms *conservative* and *liberal* in fairly conventional, political ways. By conservative, I mean individuals and groups committed to defending "the status quo against major changes in the political, economic, or social institutions of a society." Conservatives generally oppose governmental intervention to regulate the economy, excessive state spending, high taxes, and governmental programs designed for social amelioration. By liberal, I mean individuals and groups committed to changing the "political, economic, or social status quo to foster the development and well-being" of individuals and groups. Since at least the 1930s, liberals have sought to use governmental intervention "as a means for correcting the abuses and shortcomings of society through positive programs of action" (Jack C. Plano and Milton Greenberg, *The American Political Dictionary* [New York: Holt, Rinehart and Winston, 1989], 6–7, 14–15).

4. For more detailed discussions of the retrenchment issue in Detroit, the development of the Detroit Federation of Teachers, and allegations of radicalism within the Detroit teachers' union, see Jeffrey Mirel, "The Politics of Educational Retrenchment in Detroit, 1929–35," *History of Education Quarterly* 24 (Fall, 1984): 323–58; Jeffrey Mirel, "'Out of the Cloister of the Classroom': Political Activity and the Teachers of Detroit, 1929–39," *Journal of the Midwest History of Education Society* 11 (1983): 49–82; Jeffrey Mirel, "Radicalism and Public Education: The Dies Committee in Detroit, 1938–39," in *Michigan: Explorations in its Social History*, ed. Francis Blouin, Jr., and Maris Vinovskis (Ann Arbor: Historical Society of Michigan, 1987), 1–22.

5. Fine, *Frank Murphy: The Detroit Years*, 201, 245–46, 376; Robert Conot, *American Odyssey: A Unique History of America Told Through the Life of a Great City* (New York: William Morrow, 1974), 260.

6. Fine, *Frank Murphy: The Detroit Years*, 245, 298–99; U.S. Department of Commerce, *Statistical Abstract of the United States, 1931* (Washington, DC: U.S. Government Printing Office, 1931), 871; U.S. Department of Commerce, *Statistical Abstract of the United States, 1933* (Washington, DC: U.S. Government Printing Office, 1933), 755; U.S. Department of Commerce, *Statistical Abstract of the United States, 1935* (Washington, DC: U.S. Government Printing Office, 1935), 781, 789; Detroit Bureau of Governmental Research, *Accumulated Social and Economic Statistics on Detroit* (Detroit: Bureau of Governmental Research, 1937), 5.

7. Fine, *Frank Murphy: The Detroit Years*, 202–4, 307; Detroit Teachers Association, *Executive Council Bulletin* (ca. 1940): 14, in Detroit Council on Public Education Papers, Wallet no. 1, Miscellaneous Papers folder, Burton Historical Collection, Detroit Public Library, Detroit, MI.

8. Fine, *Frank Murphy: The Detroit Years,* 206.

9. The political alignment over cutting the welfare budget was almost identical to the alignment over cutting the school budget. The advocates of retrenchment essentially saw welfare and public education in the same light, as bloated social services that were placing an enormous strain on the taxpayers of the city (see Fine, *Frank Murphy: The Detroit Years,* 299–300, 304–5, 314). The shift from large scale reform to modest, efficiency goals in the Detroit Citizens League, see Raymond Fragnoli, *Transformation of Reform: Progressivism in Detroit—And After, 1912– 33* (New York: Garland, 1982).

10. See, for example, John L. Lovett, "The Tax Raising Orgy Has Reached Its Limit," *Detroit Saturday Night,* 4/29/22. Also see the editorials in *Detroit Saturday Night,* 12/9/23; *The Detroiter,* 10/20/24 and 7/11/27; and Henry Leland, letter to Laura Osborn, 6/26/26, in LFO Papers, box 11A, 1920–29 Correspondence folder.

11. *Detroit Free Press,* 8/13/31.

12. For a detailed discussion of the effort by Williams to fire aliens, nonresidents, and married women teachers, see Jeffrey E. Mirel, "Politics and Public Education in the Great Depression: Detroit, 1929– 40" (Ph.D diss., University of Michigan, 1984), 149–60.

13. Detroit Teachers Association, *Executive Council Bulletin* (ca. 1940): 6–7, 14; Detroit Board of Education, "Cost of Special Subjects—Salaries, 1932–33" (mimeo), in Detroit Council on Public Education Papers, Wallet no. 1, Miscellaneous Papers folder.

14. DBEP, 1931–32, 312; *Detroit Free Press,* 3/25/30, 4/4/30, 11/13/30; *Detroit News,* 2/20/30, 2/22/30, 3/12/30, 3/13/30, 3/14/30, 3/23/30, 3/24/30, 3/25/30, 11/13/30; *Detroit News,* 9/30/30, in Ralph Stone Scrapbook no. 16, Ralph Stone Papers, Michigan Historical Collection, Bentley Historical Library, University of Michigan, Ann Arbor, MI; *Detroit Times,* 4/13/30 and 4/14/30.

15. *Detroit News,* 2/1/30, 2/20/30, 2/26/30; *Detroit News,* 11/14/30, in Ralph Stone Scrapbook no. 16; *Detroit Free Press,* 2/4/31; Detroit Board of Commerce, Governmental Committee Report on the City Budget, Education Subcommittee Report, 2/3/31, in DM Papers, 1931, box 1, Board of Commerce folder. The board of education responded to these attempts by the businessmen to strip the schools of their autonomy by initiating an effort to break free of all fiscal control by city (DBEP, 1930–31, 642, 665; DBEP, 1931–32, 427, 483; *Detroit Times,* 4/27/32).

16. *Detroit News,* 11/14/30, in Ralph Stone Scrapbook no. 16. On Stone's "progressive" credentials, see Ralph Stone, letter to Laura Osborn, 4/7/13, in LFO papers, box 16, 1903–19 Correspondence folder. In addition to supporting school reform, Stone had served as the private secretary to Hazen Pingree, Michigan's most famous Progressive governor (*The Detroiter,* 9/3/28).

17. See, for example, *Detroit Free Press,* 2/21/30, 10/15/30, 10/20/30, 11/20/30; *Detroit Saturday Night,* 3/7/31 and 4/4/31. The shift in the editorial stance of *Saturday Night* was not due to a change in editors. Harry N. Nimmo edited the paper throughout the 1920s and for most of the 1930s, until his death in 1937 (Herbert S. Case, ed., *Who's Who in Michigan* [Munising, MI: Who's Who in Michigan, 1936], 283; *Detroit Saturday Night,* 5/1/37).

18. *Detroit News,* 4/19/31, reprinted in *Michigan Education Journal* 8 (May, 1931): 523; *Detroit Times,* 11/19/30.

19. The Communist party did not really become a strong antiretrenchment advocate until the "Popular Front" period of the later 1930s. Nevertheless, the Detroit party strongly opposed the cuts in teacher salaries, as it did the cuts in salaries of all municipal employees (*Michigan Worker,* 9/2/33; Michigan State Committee of the Communist Party, *Legislative News Letter,* 10/1/38, in Joe Brown Papers, box 13, Labor and Politics folder, Detroit folder, in ALHUA; Richard Frank, "The Schools and the People's Front," *Communist* 16 [May, 1937]: 432–45).

20. Fine, *Frank Murphy: The Detroit Years,* 283–84; Murphy is quoted in *Detroit Labor News,* 4/8/32.

21. The definitive discussion of these political and ideological alignments in Detroit is Fine, *Frank Murphy: The Detroit Years,* 257–339.

22. DBEP, 1930–31, 445; *The Detroiter,* 1/5/31. By December, 1930, Ford Motor Company had fired more than 27,000 employees, almost 22 percent of its total work force (Irving Bernstein, *The Lean Years: A History of the American Worker, 1920–33* [Baltimore: Penguin Books, 1960], 255; Fine, *Frank Murphy: The Detroit Years,* 268–69).

23. The first study was prepared for the mayor by executives from Packard Motor Company, Chrysler Corporation, and a local bank (*Detroit News,* 2/2/31). The second report was prepared by John L. Lovett and G. Oliver Frick (Detroit Board of Commerce, Governmental Committee Report on the City Budget, Education Subcommittee Report, 2/3/31). School officials challenged both the tone and substance of the reports. See *Detroit Free Press,* 2/17/31, 2/18/31, 2/22/31; *Detroit News,* 2/2/31, 2/13/21, 2/14/31, 2/16/31, 2/18/31; *Detroit Times,* 2/17/31 and 2/18/31; *Detroit Labor News,* 2/20/31.

24. The fourteen members of the committee included seven from the school system and seven representing various civic organizations ("The Report of the Salary Schedule Committee, February 17,1931," DM Papers, 1931, box 1, Board of Education folder, no. 1; *Detroit Free Press,* 2/17/31 and 2/24/31).

25. *Detroit Free Press,* 4/3/31.

26. *Detroit Free Press,* 4/6/31; *Detroit Labor News,* 3/20/31 and 4/10/31; *Detroit News,* 4/1/31, 4/5/31, 4/6/31, 4/15/31.

27. The editorial quoted is from *Detroit Labor News,* 3/27/31. See also *Detroit Labor News,* 3/20/31, 4/3/31, 4/10/31.

28. *Detroit Free Press,* 2/28/31, 3/20/31, 4/2/31, 4/6/31; *Detroit Saturday Night,* 3/7/31 and 4/4/31; *Detroit Times,* 3/30/31. Ayres is quoted in *Detroit Times,* 3/30/31.

29. Gorman received 92,531 votes, Webster 75,430, and Krohn 45,371 (*Detroit Times,* 4/7/31; *Detroit Labor News,* 4/10/31; *Detroit News,* 4/19/31). Gorman and Webster remained so popular that, when they ran for reelection in 1937, no other candidates filed to run against them (*Civic Searchlight* 24 [February, 1937]: 4).

30. Bernstein, *Lean Years,* 255; Edmund Wilson, "Detroit Motors," *New Republic,* 3/25/31, 149.

31. DBEP, 1930–31, 702; Fine, *Frank Murphy: The Detroit Years,* 301– 2.

32. Ralph Stone, letter to Frank Murphy, 7/7/31, DM Papers, 1931, box 3, Finance Committee folder; DBEP, 1931–32, 58; *Detroit Free Press,* 7/29/31; *Detroit News,* 7/22/31; *Detroit Times,* 7/22/31.

33. DBEP, 1931–32, 77.

34. DBEP, 1931–32, 77–80. While the vote was unanimous, Laura Osborn immediately protested the recommended leaves of absence for married women teachers. As it turned out, only 19 out of 1,361 married women actually took the leaves. While *this* policy generally did not damage the careers of married women educators, another, less publicized decision by the board seriously set back their careers for over a decade. At about the same time that the board requested the leaves of absence, an unofficial policy froze all married women in the rank they occupied. Whether this was simply a decision on the part of key administrators that continued with the tacit approval of the board or whether it was a directive from the board itself is impossible to say. Whatever its origin, the policy stifled the careers of married women teachers until June, 1942, when the board officially ended the freeze. See DBEP, 1929– 30, 375; DBEP, 1931–32, 77–79; *Detroit News,* 8/25/31 and 9/2/31; author interview with Walter G. Bergman, 8/30/82, Grand Rapids, MI; author interview with Renette Elder, 7/18/83, Detroit, MI; author interview with Florence Sweeney and Helen Bowers, 7/30/83, Detroit, MI; author interview with Lillian Demske and Ruby Hempleman, 8/13/83, Detroit, MI; Orin-Jane Bragg Gardner, "A Study of the

Role of the Teacher in the Evolution of Administrative Personnel Policy in the Detroit Public Schools" (Ed.D. diss., Wayne State University, 1965), 187.

35. Fine, *Frank Murphy: The Detroit Years*, 206, 313–14. See also *Detroit Times*, 12/2/31.

36. DBEP, 1931–32, 283; *Detroit News*, 12/30/31 and 1/13/32; *Detroit Times*, 1/13/32; Fine, *Frank Murphy: The Detroit Years*, 315.

37. Ralph Stone, letter to Frank Murphy, 2/9/32, DM Papers, 1932, box 4, Finance Committee folder; DBEP, 1931–32, 319.

38. Fine, *Frank Murphy: The Detroit Years*, 317–19.

39. Ralph Stone, letter to Frank Murphy, 2/23/32, DM Papers, 1932, box 4, Finance Committee folder; DBEP, 1931–32, 405–13; *Detroit Free Press*, 5/4/32, 5/5/32, 5/6/32; *Detroit News*, 5/4/32, 5/5/32, 5/6/32; *Detroit Times*, 5/4/32, 5/5/32, 5/6/32.

40. Fine, *Frank Murphy: The Detroit Years*, 354–59; Mauritz Hallgren, "Grave Danger in Detroit," *Nation*, 4/3/32, 100; DBEP, 1932–33, 21.

41. DBEP, 1931–32, 21; *Detroit News*, 7/27/32; Fine, *Frank Murphy: The Detroit Years*, 355–59.

42. *Detroit Free Press*, 4/30/32, 6/18/32, 6/19/32, 7/28/32.

43. *Detroit Labor News*, 5/6/32, 5/27/32, 10/14/32, 12/30/32; Arthur Kent, letter to John Dancy, 2/14/32, DUL Papers, Executive Director's Papers, box 2, folder 2-18. Arthur Kent was the Wayne county organizer for the Socialist party (*Detroit Leader*, 2/11/33).

44. Detroit Teachers Association, *Executive Council Bulletin* (ca. 1940): 8, 14–15; U.S. Department of Commerce, Bureau of the Census, *Historical Statistics of the United States: Colonial Times to 1970* (Washington, DC: U.S. Government Printing Office, 1975), 210.

45. Jordan Schwarz, *The Interregnum of Despair: Hoover, Congress, and the Depression* (Urbana: University of Illinois Press, 1970); Fine, *Frank Murphy: The Detroit Years*, 373–75; Conot, *American Odyssey*, 306.

46. DBEP, 1932–33, 216–17, 226, 229, 235–36; Fine, *Frank Murphy: The Detroit Years*, 376–77; *Detroit News*, 3/30/33; *Detroit Times*, 3/30/33. The scrip became another form of salary reduction, because merchants accepted it at discounts as high as 20 to 30 percent (*Detroit Saturday Night*, 5/20/33).

47. Donald W. Disbrow, *Schools for an Urban Society* (Lansing, MI: Michigan Historical Commission, 1968), 122; *Detroit News*, 12/7/32 and 12/14/32; *Detroit Times*, 12/7/32; *Michigan Education Journal* 10 (September, 1932): 2.

48. Ralph Stone, letter to Lent Upson, 1/18/33, Ralph Stone Papers, box 1 (Personal correspondence, 1932–34 folder); *Detroit Free Press*, 1/11/33; *Detroit Times*, 1/16/33, in LFO Papers, box 7, Clippings.

49. *Detroit News*, 1/24/33.

50. DBEP, 1932–33, 319; "Laura Osborn Radio Speech," 1/20/33, in LFO Papers, box 15, Manuscripts folder; *Detroit News*, 7/22/31.

51. DBEP, 1931–32, 284.

52. *Detroit News*, 1/24/33 and 1/25/33; *Detroit Times*, 1/24/33, 1/25/33, 1/31/33.

53. Avis Carlson, "Deflating the Schools," *Harper's*, November, 1933, 713–14; Edward Krug, *The Shaping of the American High School, 1920–41* (Madison: University of Wisconsin Press, 1972), 214.

54. Charles Spain, "Keep Frills—Save Money," *School Life* 18 (March, 1933): 122; Charles Spain, "Economy and the Modern Curriculum," *Detroit Educational Bulletin* 16 (January–February, 1933): 1–3; *Detroit Free Press*, 2/7/33 and 3/26/33; *Detroit News*, 2/6/33 and 4/1/33; *Detroit Times*, 1/24/33, 1/25/33, 1/26/33, 2/6/33.

55. These numbers are based on adding two or three additional teachers to each of the approximately 150 elementary schools in the city.

56. *Detroit Free Press,* 5/5/30, 1/29/33, 3/11/33.

57. The National Economy League was the most prestigious business-dominated organization working to reduce school budgets in the 1930s. Other national organizations with strong ties to the business community, however, were equally vigorous in demanding educational retrenchment. These organizations included the U.S. Chamber of Commerce, the National Organization to Reduce Public Expenditures, and the National Committee for Economy in Government (formed by the National Association of Manufacturers). See William Eaton, *The American Federation of Teachers, 1916–1961* (Carbondale: Southern Illinois University Press, 1975), 46; S. Alexander Rippa, "Retrenchment in a Period of Defensive Opposition to the New Deal: The Business Community and the Schools, 1932–1934," *History of Education Quarterly* 2 (June, 1962): 76–82. On Conlin's speech, see *Detroit Free Press,* 12/14/32.

58. R. E. Prescott, "The Little Brown School," *Detroit Saturday Night,* 8/31/33; *Detroit Saturday Night,* 12/16/33, 12/23/33, 1/12/35. In attacking "fads and frills," the *Free Press* and *Saturday Night* joined ranks with other prominent conservative publications, including the *Atlanta Constitution,* the *Chicago Tribune,* and the *Saturday Evening Post.* The positions these publications espoused probably were among the first expressions of what would be the conservative attack on progressive education (see Edgar Knight, *Fifty Years of American Education* [New York: Ronald Press, 1953], 353–54, 361).

59. *Detroit Free Press,* 3/30/33; *Detroit News,* 3/30/33; *Detroit Times,* 3/28/33 and 3/30/33; *The Detroiter,* 4/10/33; Detroit Board of Education, "Pertinent Facts Relative to the Proposed Increase in Millage: Election of April 4th [1949]," 29, in DFT Papers [inventoried 1/20/83], box 1, Millage and Governmental Aid to Education folder; Detroit Board of Education, *Detroit Public Schools Directory and By-Laws, 1952–53* (Detroit: Board of Education, 1952), 122.

60. "Report of the Committee on Lay Relations [Adopted February 28, 1933]," in *Proceedings of the Seventy-First Annual Meeting of the National Education Association, 1933* (Washington, DC: National Education Association, 1933), 675–76; the quote was reprinted in *Michigan Education Journal* 10 (April, 1933): 371.

61. Murphy is quoted in *Detroit Times,* 2/5/33; Osborn is quoted in *Detroit News,* 1/20/33, in LFO Papers, box 15, Manuscripts and Notes folder; Jamieson and Shurly are quoted in *Detroit News,* 2/22/33. The April 1933 school board election provides some clues about public sentiment on the "fads and frills" issue. Jamieson and Shurly, who defended "fads and frills," polled over 100,000 votes while their antifrills opponent garnered only 55,536 (*Detroit News,* 2/26/33, 3/28/33, 4/1/33, 4/4/33; *Detroit Times,* 3/29/33).

62. *Detroit News,* 2/1/33. See also an undated *Detroit News* editorial, "The 3 R's Not Enough," reprinted in *Detroit Educational Bulletin* 16 (March–April, 1933): 9. The *News* editorial from 2/1/33 was reprinted in *Michigan Education Journal* 10 (February, 1933): 267.

63. *Detroit Leader,* 2/18/33.

64. *Detroit Leader,* 2/11/33. See also *Detroit Leader,* 3/4/33; *Detroit Labor News,* 12/30/32.

65. *Detroit Labor News,* 12/30/32 and 2/3/33.

66. *Detroit Labor News,* 3/3/33, 3/17/33, 3/31/33, 4/7/33. The position Williams took was a good indication of his political opportunism. Knowing that he had solid support from the DFL, Williams took a stand that broadened his base of support by appealing to readers of the *Free Press* and *Saturday Night.* His stand on this issue may have helped him win his race for Wayne County auditor.

67. *Detroit Labor News,* 2/3/33. Other examples of pro–public school, antiretrenchment editorials from this period can be found in *Detroit Labor News,* 3/24/33, 3/31/33, 5/5/33, 5/26/33, 7/7/33. The front page editorials can be found in *Detroit Labor News,* 12/15/33 to 3/16/34. The Michigan Federation of Labor also began agitating for an end to retrenchment at

this time; see Frank Wade, "Organized Labor Wants Adequate Public Schools," *Michigan Education Journal* 10 (February, 1933): 272–74.

68. Kent, letter to Dancy; *Detroit Leader,* 2/11/33, 2/18/33, 2/25/33; author interview with Walter G. Bergman, 8/30/82, Grand Rapids, MI.

69. *Detroit Leader,* 2/11/33; see also 2/18/33. The DFL and, some years later, the Communist party took almost exactly the same position, drawing on the same historical arguments. See *Detroit Labor News,* 2/3/33; Wade, "Organized Labor," 374; Frank, "Schools and the People's Front," 432–33, 443.

70. *Detroit Times,* 1/25/33, 3/3/33, 3/7/33; *Michigan Education Journal* 11 (October, 1933): 93; "Constitution of the Detroit Council on Public Education," and "Minutes of the Detroit Council on Public Education, December 5, 1933," Detroit Council on Public Education Papers, Wallet no. 1, folder no. 1.

71. Board of Education, "Pertinent Facts," 29. The ten-and-ten cuts remained in effect until June 5, 1934, when the school board followed the lead of the common council and eliminated cuts; the board also restored one salary step as of July 1, 1934. The ten-month school year, however, was not restored until the 1936–37 school year. See DBEP, 1933–34, 302–4; DBEP, 1934–35, 2; *Detroit Education News,* 1/31/35, 9/16/35, 1/18/39; *Detroit News,* 1/11/33.

72. Fine, *Frank Murphy: The Detroit Years,* 375, 386.

73. Detroit Teachers Association, *Executive Council Bulletin* (ca. 1940): 14–15; Fine, *Frank Murphy: The Detroit Years,* 386–87; Martin Sullivan, "On the Dole: The Relief Issue in Detroit, 1929–39" (Ph.D. diss., University of Notre Dame, 1974), 126–27. The "windfall" was large enough for the board of education to remove its hiring freeze in 1935, and it slowly began replenishing its depleted teaching staff (*Detroit News,* 2/27/35; *Detroit Labor News,* 2/14/35).

74. Conot, *American Odyssey,* 322; *Detroit News,* 11/25/34, in Joe Brown Papers, box 1, in ALHUA; Sullivan, "On the Dole," 174; U.S. Department of Commerce, *Statistical Abstract of the United States, 1937* (Washington, DC: U.S. Government Printing Office, 1938), 826; U.S. Department of Commerce, *Statistical Abstract of the United States, 1939* (Washington, DC: U.S. Government Printing Office, 1940), 854; Board of Education, "Pertinent Facts," 29.

75. Tyack, Lowe, and Hansot, *Public Schools in Hard Times,* 42–91.

76. DBEP, 1929–30, 620–21; Detroit Public Schools Staff, *Frank Cody: A Realist in Education* (New York: Macmillan, 1943), 446–47.

77. *Detroit Free Press,* 10/2/30, 11/20/30, 2/20/31; *Detroit News,* 3/5/30 and 11/18/30; Public Schools Staff, *Frank Cody,* 457.

78. An announcement of the formation of Detroit local 231 appeared in *American Teacher,* the official voice of the AFT, in April, 1931, but for the rest of the year no other mention was made in either the local press or in the AFT publication. Union members did not publicly declare their affiliation until the fall of 1934. See Anna May Muffaletto, "Detroit Public School Teachers Unions: Organization, Operation, and Activities" (M.A. thesis, University of Detroit, 1958), 35–40; *American Teacher* 15 (April, 1931): 29; *Detroit Labor News,* 8/3/34; Demske and Hempleman interview.

79. *Detroit Free Press,* 4/2/31; *Detroit News,* 4/1/31 and 4/6/31.

80. *Detroit Free Press,* 2/28/31 and 3/20/31; *Detroit Times,* 3/30/31; *Detroit Saturday Night,* 2/28/31, 3/7/31, 4/4/31. On Ayres, see Case, *Who's Who in Michigan,* 12.

81. *Detroit Labor News,* 4/3/31 and 4/10/31. See also *Detroit News,* 4/1/31; *Detroit Times,* 4/7/31.

82. See DBEP, 1931–32, 140; *Detroit Times,* 12/5/31 and 2/9/31; [Wayne County] *Legion News,* 12/11/31; Bergman interview. The Detroit Board of Education and Wayne University had jurisdiction over all the city colleges (known as Wayne University beginning in the early 1930s) until the formation of Wayne State University in 1956. See Leslie Hanawalt, *A Place of Light: The History of Wayne State University* (Detroit: Wayne State University Press, 1968).

83. In 1930, Murphy had appointed Bergman to be the executive secretary of the Mayor's Unemployment Committee, which coordinated relief efforts in the city. See Fine, *Frank Murphy: The Detroit Years*, 396–402; *Detroit Free Press*, 12/5/31; *Detroit News*, 12/8/31; *Detroit Saturday Night*, 3/19/32; Bergman interview.

84. *Detroit News*, 12/6/31.

85. *Detroit Free Press*, 12/9/31; *Detroit Times*, 12/9/31 and 12/23/31; *Detroit Labor News*, 12/11/31 and 12/25/31; Hanawalt, *Place of Light*, 23–24. In addition to representatives from these liberal organizations, Walter and Victor Reuther attended and spoke in defense of Bergman, perhaps the first public speeches by the future labor leaders. See Victor Reuther, *The Brothers Reuther* (Boston: Houghton Mifflin, 1976), 60–61; Bergman interview.

86. DBEP, 1931–32, 247; *Detroit Free Press*, 12/7/31 and 12/9/31; *Detroit News*, 12/9/31; *Detroit Times*, 12/23/31; *Detroit Saturday Night*, 12/12/31. The position expressed by these organizations and newspapers on the rights of teachers to take controversial stands, either outside or inside the classroom, was widespread in the country at the time. See Howard Beale, *Are American Teachers Free?* (New York: Charles Scribner and Sons, 1936), 41–54, 79–97, 167; Willard Waller, *The Sociology of Teaching* (New York: Wiley, 1932), 34–38, 41–45.

87. DBEP, 1931–32, 247; *Detroit Labor News*, 12/11/31; *Detroit News*, 12/6/31, 12/8/31, 12/9/31; *Detroit Times*, 12/8/31; *Legion News*, 12/11/31.

88. Laura Osborn, for example, was the only board member to vote against ROTC (DBEP, 1931–32, 256; *Detroit News*, 12/6/31 and 12/23/31).

89. "Civil Rights for Teachers," *American Teacher* 16 (January, 1932): 13, 20–21; "A Great Victory," *Nation*, 1/6/32, 3; American Civil Liberties Union, *Sweet Land of Liberty, Annual Report for 1931–32* (New York: ACLU, 1932), 12, 34; *Detroit Labor News*, 12/11/31 and 12/25/31; *Detroit News*, 12/9/31; *Detroit Times*, 12/23/31. On the reaction of teachers to the resolution see, for example, Josephine Ettinger, letter to Laura Osborn, 12/12/32, in LFO Papers, box 17, folder 3.

90. James Prickett, "Communists and the Automobile Industry in Detroit before 1935," *Michigan History* 57 (Fall, 1973): 198; Fine, *Frank Murphy: The Detroit Years*, 404–6; *Detroit Free Press*, 4/20/32; *Detroit News*, 4/20/32; *Detroit Times*, 4/27/32. In the early 1930s Detroit schools were used for speeches by such left-wing leaders as Oswald Garrison Villard, Scott Nearing, and Norman Thomas. In addition, the Communist, Socialist, and Proletarian parties all held meetings in the schools. For examples, see *Detroit Labor News*, 11/7/30, 10/30/31, 11/6/31, 12/4/31, 1/8/32.

91. DBEP, 1931–32, 406–7; *Detroit Saturday Night*, 3/5/32; *Civic Searchlight* 19 (March, 1932); Hallgren, "Grave Danger in Detroit," 99. Thereafter, the board denied all requests by the communists and by groups suspected of having communist links (such as the Auto Workers Union). Despite repeated protests by the ACLU and the Communist party, the board maintained the policy throughout the decade. See, for example, DBEP, 1933–34, 65, 214, 216; DBEP, 1938–39, 323.

92. DBEP, 1933–34, 102; DBEP, 1936–37, 359; DBEP, 1937–38, 138; Detroit Federation of Teachers Minutes 1934–38, 5/14/36 and 9/7/37, in DFT Papers.

93. *Detroit Times*, 3/5/32; *Detroit News*, 1/26/33; E. W. McFarland, "Problems of Financing Education," *Detroit Educational Bulletin* 16 (November–December, 1932): 2; Bergman interview.

94. *Detroit Labor News*, 3/31/33; Demske and Hempleman interview; Bergman interview.

95. *Detroit News*, 2/26/33 and 3/12/33; Muffaletto, "Detroit Public School Teachers," 39–40; Demske and Hempleman interview; Bergman interview.

96. Fine, *Frank Murphy: The Detroit Years*, 412–21; Mauritz Hallgren, *Seeds of Revolt* (New York: Alfred Knopf, 1933), 110.

97. *Civic Searchlight*, April, 1927; *Detroit Free Press*, 3/3/33; *Detroit News*, 2/26/33 and 3/31/33; *Detroit Saturday Night*, 3/4/33.

98. *Detroit News*, 2/21/33. The letters from the teachers deplored the attempt by the *News* to deny teachers their fundamental democratic rights (*Detroit News*, 2/26/33). The second editorial attacking the teachers appeared in *Detroit News*, 3/1/33.

99. Chester Culver, letter to John Dancy, 3/1/33, in DUL Papers, Executive Director's Papers, box 2, folder 2-27. On the Employers Association, see Fine, *Frank Murphy: The Detroit Years*, 32; Sidney Fine, *The Automobile Under the Blue Eagle: Labor, Management, and the Automobile Manufacturing Code* (Ann Arbor: University of Michigan Press, 1963), 9.

100. *Detroit Labor News*, 3/31/33; *Detroit Leader*, 2/4/33 and 2/25/33; "Michigan Federation of Teachers Clubs," *Michigan Education Journal* 10 (April, 1933): 386. Regarding the large number of teachers in the Detroit Socialist party during these years, one German Social Democrat who visited the city in 1932 grumbled that "There are too many school teachers coming into the party to do it any good." Such criticism notwithstanding, Walter Bergman ran as the Socialist candidate for state school superintendent in the spring of 1933 and later that year was the Socialist candidate for mayor of Detroit (Hallgren, "Grave Danger," 101; *Detroit Leader*, 3/23/33; "Platform and Declaration of Principles of the Socialist Party, November 1933," in LFO Papers, box 8, folder 3).

101. *Detroit Free Press*, 4/2/33 and 4/5/33; *Detroit News*, 4/3/33 and 4/4/33.

102. The DFT had reason to fear reprisals. Soon after the 1933 election, the school administration, in a clear violation of the free speech policy, demoted Otto Marckwardt and E. W. McFarland, two city college professors who played important roles in the campaign against Shurly and Jamieson (Bergman interview; Demske and Hempleman interview; Elder interview; Sweeney and Bowers interview).

103. Detroit Federation of Teachers Minutes, 1934–38, 10/23/34. Following the announcement of the existence of the teachers' union, *Labor News* coverage of the DFT became quite extensive. See, for example, *Detroit Labor News*, 11/2/34, 12/7/34, 2/8/35, 2/15/35, 2/22/35, 3/1/35, 3/8/35.

104. DBEP, 1934–35, 131; *Detroit Free Press*, 11/6/34 and 11/8/34; *Detroit News*, 10/30/34, 10/31/34, 11/7/34, 11/8/34, 11/19/34; *Detroit Times*, 10/31/34, 11/4/34, 11/6/34; *Detroit Teachers Association News*, 11/13/34. On Pickert's antiunion attitudes, see Sidney Fine, *Sit-Down: The General Motors Strike of 1936–37* (Ann Arbor: University of Michigan Press, 1969), 243.

105. U.S. Congress, House, Special Committee on Un-American Activities, *Investigation of Un-American Activities in the United States, Hearings before a Special Committee on H. R. 282*, 75th Congress, 2d sess., 1938, 1285–92, 1294–95 ; John R. Frye, *The American Legion in Michigan: The Second Decade, 1930–39* (Detroit: American Legion, [1940]), 44; *Legion News*, 2/7/35 and 4/19/35.

106. Detroit Federation of Teachers Minutes, 1934–38, 3/14/35. There was no opportunity to test public sentiment on the issue of DFT involvement in politics in the 1937 school board election either. As noted earlier (n. 29), no candidates filed to run against John Webster and Frank Gorman. The two liberal board members thus retained their seats without an election. By 1939, when Shurly and Jamieson ran for reelection, all of the major unions in the city were deeply involved in local politics and DFT opposition to the reelection of Shurly and Jamieson was not an issue. Some controversy was stirred by the effort of the Communist party to unseat Shurly and Jamieson, whom the party argued were "the chief advocates of Hitlerism in our public school system." Despite the opposition, Shurly and Jamieson easily won reelection. See Michigan State Committee of the Communist Party, *Legislative News Letter*, 1/21/39, in Joe Brown Papers, box 13, Labor and Politics folder.

107. Detroit Federation of Teachers Minutes, 1934–38, 7/28/35, 6/11/36, 11/23/37, 4/12/38, 12/13/38.

108. *Detroit Labor News*, 1/4/35.

109. The size of the DFT is based on the number of members reported to the AFT prior to the annual convention. American Federation of Teachers Papers, "AFT Convention Roll Call, 1938," ser. 13, box 10, in ALHUA; Frances Comfort, "Detroit Teachers [*sic*] Union" (typescript), 2, in DFT Papers, box 2, Miss Comfort, 1948–54 folder.

110. Comfort, "Detroit Teachers Union"; Sweeney and Bowers interview; Elder interview; Demske and Hempleman interview.

111. *Detroit News*, 11/29/37 and 11/30/37; *Detroit Education News* 4/13/37 and 5/11/37; *Detroit Teacher* (May, 1943): 1; Michigan Federation of Teachers Minutes, 1/19/35, in AE Papers, box 11; George Male, "The Michigan Education Association as an Interest Group, 1852–1950" (Ph.D. diss., University of Michigan, 1952), 385.

112. Fine, *Sit-Down*, 341; Carlos A. Schwantes, "We've Got'em on the Run Brothers: The 1937 Non-Automotive Sit Down Strikes in Detroit," *Michigan History* 56 (Fall, 1972): 179–200.

113. DBEP, 1937–38, 1; *Detroit Free Press*, 7/2/37; *Detroit News*, 7/2/37; *Detroit Times*, 7/1/37; *Detroit Labor News*, 7/9/37.

114. Frances Comfort, "Shurly" (undated typescript), in DFT Papers [inventoried 8-12-82], box 2, Miscellaneous History and Memoirs folder; *Detroit Labor News*, 7/16/37 and 7/30/37.

115. *Detroit Free Press*, 7/28/37; *Detroit News*, 7/28/37; *Detroit Times*, 7/28/37; *Detroit Labor News*, 7/30/37.

116. *Detroit Saturday Night*, 7/31/37.

117. Fine, *Sit-Down*, 337–38; Walter Goodman, *The Committee: The Extraordinary Career of the House Committee on Un-American Activities* (New York: Farrar, Straus, and Giroux, 1968), 49–51.

118. U.S. Congress, House, *Special Committee on Un-American Activities, 1938*, 1240.

119. U.S. Congress, House, *Special Committee on Un-American Activities, 1938*, 1241–50, 1266, 1283, 1285–92, 1294–95, 1297, 1332, 1341, 1354, 1357, 1487–88, 1504–10, 1581–95.

120. Richard Reading, letter to Detroit Board of Education, 10/14/38, in DM Papers, 1938, box 1, Board of Education folder; Richard Reading, Executive Order no. 1, October 14, 1938, in DM Papers, 1938, box 1, Board of Education folder; Frye, *American Legion in Michigan*, 58–59; *Detroit Times*, 10/14/38. For more on the educational policies of the American Legion in Detroit, see Mirel, "Politics and Public Education," 234–39.

121. *Detroit Free Press*, 10/13/38; *Detroit Times*, 10/12/38; see also *Detroit Times*, 11/1/38 and 11/2/38. Several days after that first editorial on the Dies Committee and the teachers, the *Free Press* moderated its position somewhat. While still praising the Dies Committee for its "excellent" work, the *Free Press* chastised the committee for the sensationalism that had surrounded the hearings, particularly "the giving out of names of persons in a way which classes them as 'suspects' when, as a matter of fact, there is no suspicion" (*Detroit Free Press*, 10/18/38).

122. *Detroit Free Press*, 10/13/38, 10/14/38, 10/18/38; *Detroit News*, 10/13/38, 10/14/38, 10/17/38, 10/19/38, 10/21/38; *Detroit Labor News*, 10/28/38; *Teachers' Voice*, 10/20/38, in DFT Scrapbook, 1938–40, in Detroit Federation of Teachers Papers; Bergman interview.

123. *Detroit Free Press*, 10/13/38; *Detroit News*, 10/13/38; *Detroit Times*, 10/13/38.

124. DBEP, 1938–39, 119, 271–72; *Detroit News*, 10/26/38 and 2/17/39; Bergman interview. On Rapp-Coudert, see Lawrence Chamberlain, *Loyalty and Legislative Action* (Ithaca, NY: Cornell University Press, 1951), 72–76, 106–8, 125, 127, 172–81; Robert Iversen, *The Communists and the Schools* (New York: Harcourt, Brace and Co., 1959), 211–12, 215–16, 218–19.

125. American Federation of Teachers Papers, "AFT Convention Roll Call, 1940," ser. 13, box 14; *Detroit News,* 3/29/39, in DFT Scrapbook, 1938–40, DFT Papers; *Detroit Times,* 3/29/39, in DFT Papers, Clipping file; Sweeney and Bowers interview; Demske and Hempleman interview.

126. *Detroit Labor News,* 2/23/40 and 3/1/40.

127. The *Detroit Tribune,* one of the two black weeklies in the city, estimated that, on April 1, 1939, about 1,000 blacks joined a mass protest against proposed cuts in the school budget. This was the first evidence I found of substantial black involvement in the school budget process. The same day as that mass protest occurred, the other black weekly, the *Michigan Chronicle,* published an impassioned editorial denouncing the proposed cuts. These actions signaled the beginning of large-scale political activism on educational issues by the black community. See *Detroit Tribune,* 4/1/39; *Michigan Chronicle,* 4/1/39.

128. *Detroit News,* 7/5/33, in DNLB Scrapbooks, 1933; "August 30, 1933" and "November 22, 1933," in Michigan Department of Public Instruction, *News of the Week* (Lansing, MI: Department of Public Instruction, 1933); *Detroit Teacher Association News,* 11/28/33, 4/11/34, 10/2/34; *Detroit Educational News,* 9/10/35; Michigan Federation of Teachers, "History of Fifteen Mill Tax Limitation" (undated typescript), in DFT Papers, box 4, Michigan Federation of Teachers folder; U.S. Department of Commerce, Bureau of the Census, *Historical Statistics of the United States: Colonial Times to 1970,* 210.

129. Because the schools received their money from the city and the city could exceed the limitation, the amendment had little immediate consequence on *local* funding for education in Detroit. See DBEP, 1933–34, 160–63; DBEP, 1945–46, 256–58; *Detroit News,* 1/5/33, 3/9/33, 3/14/33; Michigan Federation of Teachers, "History of Fifteen Mill Tax Limitation." On the impact of the limit on state funding, see E. F. Shepard and William Wood, *The Financing of the Public Schools in Michigan* (Ann Arbor: University of Michigan Press, 1942), 106.

130. State Department of Public Instruction, "Some Significant Data Concerning Michigan Public Schools for the Period 1925 to 1936, Inclusive" (typescript), in MFT Papers, box 4, Michigan Educational Planning Commission, 1936–37 folder; *Detroit News,* 12/28/32 and 6/20/33; *Michigan Education Journal* 15 (September, 1937): 3.

131. *Detroit Free Press,* 2/8/33; *Michigan Education Journal* 10 (February, 1933): 268; *Michigan Education Journal* 10 (September, 1933): 22; DBEP, 1932–33, 199, 212, 298; DBEP, 1933–34, 30–31, 71.

132. The school aid did not materialize because the legislature voted to appropriate school revenue only after $31.7 million had been raised to pay for other state services. In the first year, the sales tax brought in $34.9 million, which left only $3.2 million of additional revenue for education. See *Detroit Free Press,* 2/14/33 and 10/30/34; *Detroit News,* 1/21/33, 2/2/33, 6/15/33; *Detroit Times,* 2/2/33; E. T. Cameron, "State Aid for This Year," *Michigan Education Journal* 10 (September, 1933): 14.

133. *The Detroiter,* 12/18/33. Examples of stands these organizations took on school aid can be found in *Detroit Free Press,* 2/4/33, 2/7/33, 4/2/33, 10/19/34, 10/30/34, 11/4/34; *Detroit News,* 6/15/33; *Detroit Saturday Night,* 12/2/33, 12/16/33, 11/3/34, 11/10/34, 1/12/35; *The Detroiter,* 12/25/33, 1/8/34, 6/4/34; *Detroit Teachers Association News,* 3/20/34; Detroit Bureau of Governmental Research, *Just a Minute,* 10/22/34, in MFT Papers, box 12. See also *Detroit Free Press,* 4/16/37, cited in Male, "Michigan Education Association," 468.

134. MEA Legislative Committee, "M. E. A. Goals and Achievements in School Legislation," *Michigan Education Journal* 12 (January, 1934): 179.

135. *Detroit Teachers Association News,* 5/8/34.

136. *Detroit News,* 10/26/34 and 10/27/34; *Detroit Teacher Association News,* 9/18/34, 10/2/34, 10/16/30, 10/30/34; *Detroit Education News,* 5/14/35, 9/29/36, 10/13/36, 10/27/36, 10/29/36 [special election issue], 11/10/36, 12/8/36, 10/26/38, 11/9/38, 3/29/39; *Detroit Labor*

News, 6/28/40; Disbrow, *Schools for an Urban Society*, 124. George Male describes the campaign in the late 1930s and early 1940s by major Michigan corporations and the Michigan Chamber of Commerce to reduce state appropriations for education in Male, "Michigan Education Association," 476–84.

137. *The Detroiter*, 6/4/34.

138. *Detroit Saturday Night*, 1/12/35 and 4/27/35; Public Schools Staff, *Frank Cody*, 483.

139. Shepard and Wood, *Financing of Public Schools*, 36–37; Eugene B. Elliott, "Michigan's New School Legislation," *Michigan Education Journal* 13 (September, 1935): 15.

140. Shepard and Wood, *Financing of Public Schools*, 36–37; Male, "Michigan Education Association," 468, 476–84; George Male, "A Century of Efforts to Improve the Salaries of Teachers in Michigan," *History of Education Journal* 3 (Winter, 1952): 56–57.

141. *Detroit News*, 10/19/38 and 12/3/38, in DNLB Scrapbooks, 1938; Disbrow, *Schools for an Urban Society*, 124–25.

142. Karl W. Guenther, "On the Battle Lines in Michigan," *Social Frontier* 1 (June, 1935): 27; Male, "Michigan Education Association," 383–401; Sidney Fine, *Frank Murphy: The New Deal Years* (Chicago: University of Chicago Press, 1979), 239, 268, 459; Herbert Coffey, "Teachers Tenure Act," [Ann Arbor Citizen's Council] *Citizen's News*, 12/3/36; *Detroit News*, 10/10/36, 8/7/36, 6/15/37, 7/8/37, 7/29/37, 8/6/37 in DNLB Scrapbooks, 1937.

143. Arthur Elder, "Launching Teacher Tenure," [Ann Arbor Citizen's Council] *Citizen's News*, 8/20/38.

144. Male, "Century of Efforts," 55–58; Michigan Department of Public Instruction, *Ninety-fifth Report of the Superintendent of Public Instruction, 1937–39* (Lansing: Department of Public Instruction, 1940), 96–97.

145. Male, "Century of Efforts," 55–58.

146. The legislator is quoted in *Detroit News*, 4/7/39, in DNLB Scrapbooks, 1939. See also *Detroit News*, 2/9/39, 4/8/39, 5/13/39 in DNLB Scrapbooks, 1939; Fine, *Frank Murphy: The New Deal Years*, 522–26.

147. Shepard and Wood, *Financing of Public Schools*, 26; *Detroit Education News*, 1/18/39; *Detroit News*, 3/10/40.

148. *Detroit Education News*, 1/18/39; *Detroit News*, 3/10/40.

149. U.S. Department of Commerce, Bureau of the Census, *Historical Statistics of the United States: Colonial Times to 1970*, 210; *Detroit Teacher*, 4/5/46.

150. Detroit Teachers Association, *Executive Council Bulletin* (ca. 1940): 8, 10.

151. The NCA threat to strip accreditation from the Detroit high schools due to overcrowding was spelled out in a series of letters from Harlan C. Koch, a professor at the University of Michigan School of Education and Chairman of the Michigan State Committee of the North Central Association, to J. E. Tanis, Principal of Detroit Northern High School, who served as the liaison for the school system to NCA. As the situation grew more serious, Koch began corresponding directly with superintendent Frank Cody and first assistant superintendent Warren Bow. While this threat to strip the accreditation from Detroit did not materialize, the NCA did take this action against Chicago six years later. See J. E. Tanis, letter to H. C. Koch, 10/15/37; Koch, letter to Tanis, 12/22/38; H. C. Koch, letter to Frank Cody, 4/16/40 (draft); Warren Bow, letter to H. C. Koch, 4/17/40; H. C. Koch, letter to Warren Bow, 4/22/40; Tanis, letter to Koch, 4/17/40; Koch, letter to Tanis, 4/22/40. The Detroit high schools did not achieve the NCA recommendation of 30 to 1 student-teacher ratios until 1943 (Ivan Chapman, letter to Edgar Johnston, 3/15/43). These letters from the files of the Bureau of Accreditation and School Services, School of Education, the University of Michigan, are not archived. I am indebted to David Angus for directing me to them. Copies are in my possession. On the NCA action against the Chicago Public Schools, see Julia Wrigley, *Class Politics and Public Schools, Chicago, 1900–1950* (New Brunswick, NJ: Rutgers University Press, 1982), 252–54.

152. That enrollment figure includes children in special programs, not merely those listed in regular K through 12 classes (Detroit Board of Education, *The Superintendent's Annual Report, 1938–39* [Detroit: Board of Education, 1939], 191; Detroit Teachers Association, *Executive Council Bulletin* [ca. 1940], 8). Between 1935 and 1941, federal aid for school construction in Detroit from the Works Project Administration and the Public Works Administration amounted to $1,303,323, of which $216,381 went to rebuild Western High School, and $346,396 and $397,510 went for additions for Mackenzie and Denby high schools, respectively (Detroit Board of Education, "Cost Reports, 1937, 1938, 1939, 1941" [manuscript]; Detroit Board of Education, "Financial Statements, 1940, 1941" [manuscript] in Detroit School Center Building, Detroit, MI).

153. Laura Osborn, "A Crying Need: More Schools," *Detroit Club Woman,* June, 1937, 6, in LFO Papers, box 7, folder no. 2; J. E. Tanis, letter to H. C. Koch, 10/15/37, in the Bureau of Accreditation and School Services Files, School of Education, University of Michigan, Ann Arbor, MI; *Detroit Free Press,* 10/17/37; Political Action Committee [of the Wayne County CIO], *Vote Labor* [election pamphlet] (October 4, 1937), 2, in Joe Brown Papers, box 13, Labor and Politics folder.

154. Board of Education, *Superintendent's Annual Report, 1938–39,* 191; Detroit Board of Education, *The Superintendent's Annual Report, 1939–40* (Detroit: Board of Education, 1940), 121.

155. DBEP, 1929–30, 1930–31, 1931–32, 1932–33, 1933–34, "Employment Permits." The topics of the youth labor market, enrollment increases, and changes in the high school curriculum in Detroit and the nation are discussed in greater detail in Jeffrey Mirel and David Angus, "Youth, Work and Schooling in the Great Depression," *Journal of Early Adolescence* 5 (Winter, 1985): 489–504; Jeffrey Mirel and David Angus, "The Rising Tide of Custodialism: Enrollment Increases and Curriculum Reform in Detroit, 1928–40," *Issues in Education* 4 (Fall, 1986): 101–20.

156. Board of Education, *Superintendent's Annual Report, 1938–39,* 196; Detroit Board of Education, *Detroit Public School Statistics, 1939–40* (Detroit, Board of Education, 1940); Mirel and Angus, "Rising Tide of Custodialism," 107–8.

157. Committee on the Orientation of Secondary Education, *Issues of Secondary Education* (Washington, DC: Department of Secondary School Principals of the National Education Association, 1934), 64; Byron J. Rivet, "Curriculum Revision in Detroit High Schools," *North Central Association Quarterly* 8 (April, 1934): 502.

158. David Angus, "A Note on the Occupational Background of High School Students Prior to 1940," *Journal of the Midwest History of Education Society* 9 (1981): 158–83; Rachel Stutsman Ball, *What of Youth Today?* (Detroit: Board of Education, 1935). The one group of students that still did drop out of school to try to find work to support themselves and their families were young people from the very poorest homes. See Bernard Karpinos, *The Socio-Economic and Employment Status of Urban Youth in the United States, 1935–36,* Public Health Bulletin no. 273 (Washington, DC: U.S. Government Printing Office, 1941), 33–34, 52–54.

159. Rivet, "Curriculum Revision in Detroit," *North Central Association Quarterly* 11 (April, 1937): 453–55. For a more complete discussion of these issues, see Mirel, "Politics and Public Education," 360–89.

160. Rivet, "Curriculum Revision in Detroit High Schools," 502.

161. E. M. Cameron, "Personal Standards Course for High School Girls," *Practical Home Economics* 18 (July, 1940): 205–7; Byron J. Rivet, "Curriculum Revision in Detroit," 455; Detroit Board of Education, *Vitalizing the Experience of Secondary Students in Detroit and Nearby Communities* (Detroit: Board of Education, 1937), 1:111–12, 145; Detroit Board of Education, *Vitalizing the Experience of Secondary Students in Detroit and Nearby Communities*

(Detroit: Board of Education, 1938), 2:273; Mirel, "Politics and Public Education," 375–77. On similar developments nationally, see Diane Ravitch, *The Troubled Crusade: American Education, 1945–80* (New York: Basic Books, 1983), 54–65.

162. Mirel and Angus, "Rising Tide of Custodialism," 110.

163. Samuel Bowles and Herbert Gintis, *Schooling in Capitalist America* (New York: Basic Books, 1976), 5.

Chapter 4

The Expansion of Conflict, 1940–49

In February, 1941, Frances Comfort, president of the Detroit Federation of Teachers (DFT), angrily wrote to William Lovett, executive secretary of the Detroit Citizens League, protesting the decision of the league to withhold its "preferred" endorsement from Laura Osborn in the upcoming school board election.[1] No development reveals more starkly the profound changes that had taken place in educational politics in Detroit than this apparent break between the Citizens League and Osborn. During the Progressive era, Osborn and the League had spoken with one voice, allies in reform who sought the improvement and expansion of the Detroit public schools. Throughout the 1930s, however, as Osborn railed against retrenchment, supported the broadening of civil liberties for teachers, and backed the rights of teachers to join the DFT, she fell into increasing disfavor with her former allies from the Progressive era. By 1941, that estrangement seemed complete.

The controversy about Osborn in 1941 demonstrates how enduring the depression era realignment of interests had became in Detroit. Indeed, even as the city underwent enormous economic and demographic changes in the 1940s, remarkably little changed in the basic positions of the major interest groups concerned with educational issues or in the vehemence of their arguments. Throughout World War II and the postwar years, these positions actually hardened and became institutionalized in the larger political conflicts on both the state and local levels.

Some historians maintain that the 1940s, particularly the postwar years, were a period of relative calm in educational history. Robert Hampel, for example, argues that, during this period, "urban superintendents held firm control of their sprawling systems; open and abrasive confrontation was the exception rather than the rule." Ira Katznelson and Margaret Weir go further, offering a compelling argument that seems to explain that phenomenon.

Drawing largely on the history of the Chicago schools, they contend that battles over public education diminished in intensity because "distinctive working-class positions disappeared from educational politics." Their interpretation may explain developments in cities dominated by political machines, such as Chicago, but it is inadequate for explaining the history of other industrial cities in which local politics were more open and conflicts between organized labor and major business interests were more entrenched. In Gary, Indiana, for example, Ronald Cohen finds educational politics in the 1940s as intense as any period of that city's history.[2]

Similarly, educational politics in Detroit were anything but calm during the 1940s. Unlike the picture offered by Katznelson and Weir, Detroit was the scene of fierce class-based battles over public education. Three main developments kept this political pot boiling. First, virtually none of the educational problems brought about by the Great Depression—particularly problems of school construction, teacher salaries, large classes, and the high school curriculum—had been resolved in the 1930s. Throughout the 1940s, each of these problems became significantly worse. Second, during World War II, both organized labor and the business community increased in power and prestige in Detroit. As a consequence, following the war, both interest groups renewed their political struggle for influence in the city, and the schools remained an important arena of conflict. Finally, the DFT and the African-American community, both of which drew strength from the burgeoning labor movement, stirred controversy by playing a substantially more important role in educational politics.

Throughout the 1940s, but particularly in the postwar years, controversies over local school finance, state aid, the construction of new buildings, teacher salaries, and the transformation of the high school curriculum were as intense and divisive as at any time in the 1930s. In this chapter, I examine the persistence of educational conflict in Detroit, explore how the DFT and the African-American community increasingly influenced educational policy and practice, and discuss the origins of the liberal-labor-black political coalition that came to have an enormous impact on the politics of education in the Motor City.

The Changing Urban Context

World War II transformed Detroit. The late 1930s brought some measure of economic recovery to the city, but the outbreak of war in Europe and the subsequent military buildup by the United States jolted the Motor City into an unprecedented industrial boom. As billions of dollars of military equipment rolled off Motor City assembly lines, Detroit again moved to the center of the national economic stage, now as the "Arsenal of Democracy." "Just as Detroit was a symbol of America in peace," a 1942 story in *Forbes* declared, "so it is the symbol of America at war. Other towns make arms, as other towns make automobiles, but whether we win this war depends in great measure on Detroit." Indeed, no American city produced more military equipment during the war than Detroit.[3]

Jobs were plentiful. By November, 1943, some 867,000 people were employed in the city, more than double the number at work just two years earlier. Between 1937 and 1943, total factory wages in Wayne County jumped from just over $600 million to an estimated $1.8 billion, and weekly earnings of factory workers nearly doubled. As in the 1910s and 1920s, people poured into the city in search of work. In 1943, Harvey Campbell, executive vice president of the Board of Commerce, claimed that "since Pearl Harbor, Detroit has taken aboard a population equal to that of Cincinnati." By 1950, the population of the city had swelled to almost 1.85 million.[4]

By far the most important demographic change brought about by the war was the growth of the African-American community. The black population of Detroit more than doubled in the 1940s, from 149,119, about 9 percent of the total population, to 303,721, more than 16 percent. Moving out from the established black neighborhoods that closely bordered Woodward Avenue during the depression years, the African-American community expanded in the 1940s to include much of the central, southeastern, and southwestern portions of Detroit. As blacks spread out from the core city, white, working-class families increasingly occupied the northeastern and northwestern sections of town. Like many of the blacks, many of these white families were recent migrants from the south, lured by jobs in the booming defense industries. By the late 1940s, these migration and settlement patterns resulted in a highly segregated racial geography that would increasingly influence municipal and educational politics.[5]

The population growth of this period was not confined to Detroit alone. The dramatic growth of the suburbs was another great change of the war and postwar years. Between 1940 and 1950, the population of communities surrounding Detroit climbed from 753,877 to 1,166,629, almost doubling the growth in Detroit during the same period.[6] Many of these new suburbanites were middle- or upper-class Detroiters. In 1950, for example, only a third of the families listed in the Detroit social register still lived in Detroit, down from 46 percent in 1940 and 58 percent in 1930. This out-migration of upper- and middle-class families was further aided by the construction of the John C. Lodge and Edsel Ford expressways, which quickly became two of the major traffic arteries between Detroit and the suburbs.[7]

This migration to the suburbs, especially of elite families, had political as well as demographic ramifications. As early as 1940, the *Labor News* claimed that the Detroit Citizens League, Board of Commerce, and Bureau of Government Research opposed "an adequate school budget" for the city because most of the members of these organizations lived in such swank suburbs as Grosse Pointe. "The rub is that these businessmen and industrialists are more than willing to make their money in Detroit," the labor paper editorialized, "but they do not want to pay taxes on the same basis as in the districts where their children go to school."[8]

Obviously, few of these changes came easily to Detroit. While the sense of national unity inspired by the war muted some of the conflict between business and labor, the tensions between these interest groups continued just beneath the surface of the enormous industrial expansion. Ironically, the war altered the relationship between business and labor by increasing the power and prestige of *both* groups. By putting their management and production skills at the service of the nation, business leaders recovered much of the public confidence they had lost during the Great Depression. Simultaneously, union strength also grew, aided by federal policies and growing labor shortages. Between 1941 and 1945, union membership climbed from 10.5 million to 14.8 million. Detroit was central to all these developments. In 1941, the UAW forced the fiercely antiunion Ford Motor Company into collective bargaining, a victory that set off a wave of organizing and strikes in Detroit and across the nation.[9]

With each union triumph, the Detroit Board of Commerce railed against the Wagner Act, unions in general, and the Congress of Industrial Organizations (CIO), in particular. Throughout the war, businessmen routinely blasted strikers and union leaders for "sabotaging" the war effort. In 1943, Harvey Campbell bluntly declared that "the Wagner Act can lose this war." The unions were equally vitriolic in their attacks on business leaders. That same year, for example, the *Labor News* denounced the members of the Citizens League, the Bureau of Governmental Research, and the Michigan Public Expenditure Survey as "fascists" and "war profiteers."[10] Despite the heated rhetoric, a web of patriotic fervor held these passions in check until 1945. As the war ended, however, that web ripped asunder and what emerged were class politics strikingly similar in tone and content to the political struggles of the 1930s.

Unlike class politics, racial tensions in Detroit, fueled by the large migration of southern blacks and whites, did not wait until the end of the war to explode. Because of the general shortage of housing in Detroit and the widespread segregation of neighborhoods, the need for housing for black families was acute. In 1941, the government announced the construction of the Sojourner Truth housing project for black families on the northeast side of the city. Violence broke out in February, 1942, as the first families attempted to move in. More than thirty people were injured. This violence was a portent of even worse confrontations. An August, 1942, *Life* article on race relations in the city concluded, "Detroit can either blow up Hitler or it can blow up the U.S."[11]

Less than a year later, in June, 1943, Detroit experienced what was then the worst race riot in American history. Following a series of racial disturbances at Belle Isle, blacks and whites fought and looted for almost two days. As the violence escalated, the governor called in federal troops who finally restored order. In the aftermath, 25 blacks and 9 whites lay dead, almost 700 were injured, and more than $2 million in property was destroyed. When the troops finally left on July 9th, the city still smoldered with racial tension.[12]

Like the conflicts between business and labor, these racial tensions also became part of the larger political contests in Detroit. This political evolution took two forms. First, as Meier and Rudwick point out, soon after the riot, the African-American community in Detroit forged a crucial political alliance with the United Auto Workers, "the one important organization willing to take a vigorous stand in support of the black community." Second, as Korstad and Lichtenstein argue, in the 1940s, an important group of African-American leaders emerged within organized labor, particularly the UAW, who sought to advance both a union *and* a civil rights agenda. Korstad and Lichtenstein contend that these leaders made Detroit "a center of civil rights militancy during the war years."[13]

All of these developments had a profound impact on the Detroit public schools. Throughout the 1940s, school leaders expanded vocational programs to meet the enormous demands of the war industries, wrestled with how to accommodate the new waves of emigrants, sought to build schools in the burgeoning new neighborhoods while at the same time maintaining schools in the core city, confronted serious racial tensions within the schools, and tried to adjust the curriculum in response to changing economic and demographic patterns. On the surface, these challenges appear quite similar to those faced by educators in the 1920s. Despite these similarities, however, the task before the school leaders of Detroit in the 1940s was considerably more difficult. Inheriting the fractured political base of the depression years, Detroit school leaders had far less support in dealing with these problems than their counterparts in the 1920s. Throughout the 1940s, educational issues, particularly the battle for increased funding for the schools on both the local and state levels, paralleled the larger struggles between business and labor. Educational issues continued to divide the major interest groups of Detroit and Michigan along the same class and political lines as in the Great Depression. The growing activism of the DFT and the increasing demands by African-Americans for educational equality deepened the divisions and exacerbated these conflicts.

War without Educational Recovery, 1940–46

On the surface, the war seemed to rejuvenate the Detroit public schools just as it had economically transformed the city. Whether one looks at curriculum, programs, or the level of controversy in educational politics, it appeared that the schools had entered into an exciting, new era in the 1940s. Yet beneath the surface, the war actually accelerated many of the troubling educational and political trends that had begun in the 1930s. Most notably, the quality of the high school program deteriorated even further during the war years, and politics fragmented even more than in the depression.

The impact of the war on the high school curriculum provides dramatic evidence of the consistency of educational policy in the face of great economic and demographic change. In the 1930s, as large numbers of working-class youth returned to or remained in high school, school officials expanded the general and vocational programs at the expense of more rigorous academic courses and course content. The war provided even greater impetus for that trend.[14] In a typical statement from the period, Michigan's assistant superintendent for public instruction stated, "We in Michigan committed ourselves to such a program [in practical education] as long ago as 1935, chiefly as a result of the economic depression. Many of the so-called cultural subjects, imbedded in the curriculum by right of tradition, were not fitting the average youngster to go out and earn a living. Now because of the war and possible demand for teen-age boys and girls in the defense industries, many educators are hurrying to revise school programs with an eye to their 'practical' aspects."[15]

By 1943, school leaders in Detroit had completely reorganized the high school program in keeping with the principle that all courses, "especially those in the eleventh and twelfth grades, must demonstrate their validity in terms of military pre-induction value, pre-employment preparation for employment in war industries, or civilian war service."[16] School officials directed virtually the entire Detroit school program to the war effort. Students practiced math skills by computing the sale of war bonds, heard history lessons related to current events, improved their writing by composing letters to GIs, and manufactured crutches and canes for injured soldiers in woodshop. Teachers increasingly used movies and radio broadcasts in class. As part of the preinduction program, physical education requirements were increased to an hour per day in every grade. Behind-the-wheel drivers' education also came of age as a preparedness measure designed to save the military time in training recruits.[17]

One of the most telling developments was the liberalization of high school graduation requirements. Beginning in 1942, with the blessing of the North Central Association, Detroit high schools permitted students in the academic tracks to substitute preinduction and vocational courses for courses required for graduation. In addition, as large numbers of students took after-school jobs, the board of education approved a plan allowing work experience to satisfy as much as one-fifth of the total class credits students could take each semester. In September, 1942, Harvey Campbell of the Board of Commerce noted approvingly that "Detroit's schools will open on a new note. Emphasis on vocational instead of academic instruction."[18] School leaders went so far as to declare that the goal of these changes was the complete transformation of the curriculum "in favor of vocational education." In short, the early 1940s clearly witnessed a significant broadening and deepening of the trend, begun in the 1930s, of offering less academically rigorous instruction in the high schools of Detroit.[19]

In addition to these changes in the regular school program, adult education and vocational programs took on new importance by training huge numbers of workers for the defense industry. From 1940 to 1945, the school system's department of vocational education enrolled 320,000 students in over 800 courses. For most of this period, these courses ran twenty-four hours a day, seven days a week.[20] One visitor to the city exclaimed, " . . . Detroit has become not only the center of war production, but also the greatest training school the nation has ever known." Writing in the midst of the war, one school official boasted, "The Detroit Public Schools have become the arsenal for the arsenal for democracy."[21]

The speed and diligence with which the schools responded to the educational challenges of the war won the Detroit system new respect. Such previously implacable critics of the schools as the *Free Press* and the Board of Commerce once again praised school leaders and programs. When Superintendent Frank Cody retired in 1942 and was replaced by his highly regarded assistant superintendent, Warren Bow, and when, that same year, the school system celebrated its first century of operation, editorial writers and civic leaders applauded the school system and heralded it as a symbol of democracy and freedom.[22]

In the early 1940s, these sentiments, combined with the patriotic fervor and a sense of sacrifice for the war effort, gave the schools a brief, three-year respite from the tumultuous struggles over educational finance that had marked the 1930s. In addition to the relative political calm, the school system also benefited from a substantial decline in school enrollment. During the war, large numbers of teenagers dropped out of high school to find work in the defense industries. In fact, high school enrollments fell almost as quickly in the early 1940s as they had risen in the early 1930s. Between November, 1939, and September, 1942, high school enrollment in Detroit fell from 52,029 to 46,136 students. The high schools lost about 2,500 students in the 1941–42 school year alone. At the same time, the school system experienced a decline in elementary enrollments, from 136,755 to 104,419, due to the drop in the birth rate during the depression. As a consequence of these trends, between November, 1939, and November, 1945, total public school enrollment in Detroit dropped from 260,658 to 227,645. From a financial perspective, this decline was a welcome change, since it gave the board considerably more flexibility in allocating resources.[23]

The kind words from business leaders and positive demographic trends, however, could not hide the fact that the board still faced three crucial financial problems. Probably the most serious of these problems was the moratorium on school construction that the board had approved in 1931. Due to the demands of the war effort, this moratorium essentially remained in effect throughout World War II and, indeed, for several years after. Thus, in the fifteen-year period from 1932–33 to 1946–47, the board spent a total of only $15,847,062 on construction, compared to $88,672,894 spent in the previous fifteen years, 1917–18 to 1931–32.[24] The drop in enrollment should have eased some of the demand for new construction, yet the migration of people to outlying sections of the city actually increased pressures on the board for new buildings. As early as 1939, the board of education and the mayor received petitions signed by hundreds of residents of new neighborhoods demanding schools for their children.[25] As the decade wore on and the first of the baby boomers began to reach school age, this trickle of demands for new schools became a flood.

The second major financial problem facing the board centered on having salaries for teachers keep pace with inflation. By 1940, the teachers had recovered most of the income lost during the depression, but the wartime inflation brought them new economic woes. In August, 1939, the Consumer Price Index for Detroit stood at 98.5 (100 = 1935–39), by June, 1945, it had jumped to 136.4, and by July, 1949, it reached 170.4. Yet as late as 1942, teachers in Detroit still operated under the salary schedule adopted by the board twenty years before. As the 1940s wore on, both the Detroit Federation of Teachers and the Detroit Teachers Association (DTA) vigorously demanded substantial salary increases.[26]

The third major financial problem before the board was overly large classes. Despite the sharp drop in enrollment in the early 1940s, classes in most Detroit schools were overcrowded. One of the most important reasons for overcrowded classes was the general shortage of teachers during the war. Many teachers abandoned the classroom for the higher salaries, better benefits, and better working conditions in the defense industries. In addition, retiring or relocating teachers often could not be replaced because the number of undergraduates majoring in education in Michigan's colleges and normal schools also declined during this era. Thus, in October, 1942, median elementary and junior high school classes in Detroit had more than forty-one students, and median senior high classes had more than thirty-five. Early in 1944, Frances Comfort estimated that it would take an additional 1,500 teachers to reduce the median class size to thirty students.[27]

These three issues would dominate discussions of educational finance throughout the decade. While the solution to each was simple—more money—the means for raising that money and then determining the priorities for spending it continued to generate controversy. Contrary to the findings of historians who contend that "open and abrasive confrontation was the exception rather than the rule," in large, urban school districts during the 1940s, events in Detroit demonstrate that conflicts about educational finance were as divisive and intense as any educational battles during the depression.[28]

The Continuing Conflict over Local School Finance, 1940–46

The early 1940s saw virtually no change from the 1930s in terms of the political alignments, rhetoric, or outcomes of school budget battles. As I indicated in chapter 3, in the spring of 1940, the supporters of increased educational funding, the Detroit and Wayne County Federation of Labor

(DWCFL), the Wayne County CIO, and the UAW were again contesting with the Board of Commerce, the Citizens League, and the Bureau of Governmental Research, who fought to keep school revenues and taxes as low as possible. Ultimately, the mayor and council acceded to the demands of the business and civic leaders, convinced that the national preparations for war would soon force other tax increases. The city cut its appropriation to the schools by more than $1 million, which compelled the board to reinstate several depression era austerity measures, including shortening the 1940–41 school year by one week. Such prewar retrenchment was also common in other large cities. Over the next year, Cleveland, Kansas City, Minneapolis, and Pittsburgh all reported similar cutbacks.[29]

Between 1941 and 1944, debates over educational finance, like other political struggles in the city, lost some of their edge. Nevertheless, the essential alignments and arguments of the interest groups remained unchanged during these years. Occasionally, the groups clashed with the old intensity, as in 1941–42 when the DFT and DTA prevailed on the board to increase teacher salaries with a 10 percent cost of living adjustment and by adopting a single salary schedule that eliminated the salary disparity between elementary and secondary teachers. Business leaders and the Bureau of Governmental Research, however, firmly opposed the increases and convinced the mayor to veto the single salary schedule.[30] The following year, the teachers succeeded in gaining the single salary schedule and a modest 4.5 percent salary increase, but these victories were tarnished by the fact that other city workers, notably police and fire fighters, received increases three times larger than the teachers. School and union leaders were outraged by the inequity. Superintendent Bow demanded "the same treatment for school people as other city employees," but to no avail.[31]

By 1944, tensions over educational finance in general and salaries in particular were ready to explode. As the major interest groups in Detroit prepared for the end of war abroad by jockeying for political position at home, educational issues once again loomed large and polarized the city. Controversy erupted early in 1944, when the Building Owners and Managers Association, the Business Property Association, the Board of Commerce, the Bureau of Governmental Research, the Citizens League, the Detroit Real Estate Board, the Michigan [Public Expenditure] Survey, the Realty Owners and Operators Association, and the Taxpayers Council of Wayne County— virtually the same groups that had made up the Stone Committee in the 1930s—demanded that Mayor Edward J. Jeffries, Jr., sharply cut municipal spending. Apparently convinced that the mayor would acquiesce to these demands, the board of education offered the city a scaled-down budget that made no provisions for new teachers or for salary increases. Yet even this budget, which conservative board member Burt Shurly described as "the minimum on which the schools can operate for the year," was too exorbitant for the mayor and the council. Despite vehement protests from Frank Martel, president of the Detroit and Wayne County Federation of Labor, the DFT, DTA, and such organizations as the League of Women Voters, the mayor and council refused the $3.4 million increase requested by the board. Instead, the city granted the schools only about $1.0 million more than the previous year, an increase that amounted to less than 3 percent when adjusted for inflation. The city government justified this modest increase by citing the sharp decline in enrollments.[32]

As the war neared its end, it became increasingly apparent to school leaders that, in the struggle for adequate funding, they were confronting two distinct sets of opponents—business-led advocates of low taxes, on the one hand, and the hard-pressed city government, on the other.[33] In 1945, as in previous years, vigorous lobbying for larger allocations to the schools by organized labor and various community groups went unheeded, and the city again allocated far less to the schools than the board had requested. Although the $23,511,513 for the 1945–46 school year was the largest amount the city had yet provided for public education, when adjusted for inflation, the funds were actually worth almost 6 percent *less* than the amount the city had allocated in 1944–45. Adding to the woes of the school board at this time was the determination by the corporation counsel of the city that, due to the control of school finances by the city and the restrictions of the 15 mill limit, the Detroit Board of Education could not unilaterally issue bonds for construction.[34]

With each budget battle yielding inadequate resources, school leaders realized that they could not at once meet the incessant demands of teachers for better salaries and smaller classes *and* the growing demands of parents for new or renovated buildings. The situation took on crisis proportions as parent groups that had been placated during the war returned, demanding that the board immediately provide schools for their children.[35] The *Detroit News* estimated that the city needed at least forty new schools and claimed that Detroit had "sections larger than Grand Rapids in area and population, without a high school." Indeed, as school started in 1946, some 25,000 high school students were on half-day sessions and more than 10,000 elementary students were either on half-day sessions, attending school in temporary structures, or being bused.[36]

Following closely on the heels of the parents were the teachers. Teachers certainly recognized the crucial need for new buildings, but surging inflation left many teachers with very different priorities for school spending. As early as 1940, even before the teachers felt the worst of the wartime inflation, the DFT declared that "while physical facilities are unquestionably important they must always be regarded as secondary to personnel in education." As teacher salaries fell further behind those of other city employees and as inflation continued unchecked, such statements became more common.[37]

By 1945, this clash of priorities and the ongoing financial controversy severely strained the relations between the administration and its teachers. In February, as school officials prepared for the budget hearings with the city, the DFT publicly denounced the board for proposing yet another bare-bones budget that failed to even meet the minimal needs of the teachers. This attack was a sharp break with past practices in which the union deferred such criticism during the budget process in order to present a united front to the city government.[38]

The unexpected death of Warren Bow in May, 1945, exacerbated this emerging split between the union and school leadership. Bow, an amiable and conciliatory administrator, had maintained excellent relations with the teachers and the union throughout all the budget controversies. His successor, long-time Detroit administrator Arthur Dondineau, was, however, far less open to the demands of the teachers generally and the DFT in particular.[39] Some of the distrust between Dondineau and the DFT was due to the fact that Dondineau maintained very good relations with prominent business leaders while he was assistant superintendent in charge of the school budget, relations that union leaders believed encouraged him to put the business community's desire for lower taxes ahead of the needs of the school system.[40]

Despite the good relations between Dondineau and prominent business leaders, their basic stand on funding for education did not change following his appointment. Indeed, the budget controversy in 1946 was more bitter than before due to an intense campaign by the DFT to force the city to be evenhanded in its distribution of salary increases. Testifying before the council in January, Frances Comfort warned that "this discrimination is too flagrant for teachers to take lying down." Several weeks later, for the first time in the history of the school district, union leaders threatened to strike if the unequal salary practices continued.[41]

As the controversy continued, business and civic groups lashed out at the union. Following a DFT demand that the board allocate more money for salaries than new buildings, the Citizens League red-baited the union, claiming that the financial problems of the district were caused by individuals bent on fomenting "class warfare." The *Civic Searchlight,* the official voice of the Citizens League, declared that "qualified, unprejudiced observers are raising the question whether the tribulations of our city educational system are due in large part to the top-heavy demands for increased payments to officials, teachers and other employes at the expense of the necessary renewal and rehabilitation of buildings and equipment?" Less than a week after DFT officials had threatened to strike, *The Detroiter* approvingly quoted Mississippi Congressman John Rankin's remark: "When we had the little red schoolhouse we didn't have any little Red school teachers."[42]

Equally pointed was the annual statement on municipal spending issued during the budget hearings by the Board of Commerce, Bureau of Governmental Research, Citizens League, and other major business and civic organizations. Declaring unequivocally that "the survival of cities depends on their economic productivity, not on the munificence of its governmental services," the organizations blasted waste and inefficiency in the city government and demanded that the mayor slash the proposed city budget. In the case of the public schools, the organizations charged that the system was simultaneously squandering funds and lowering educational standards. "In spite of declining enrollments over a period of years," the statement read, "total costs and per pupil costs increase. . . . Facts such as these raise questions about the 'plight' of the schools, and whether best use is being made of available funds to meet more pressing needs."[43]

The board and its allies responded to these attacks with equal fervor. The DFT denounced the Citizens League as a "primeval tax group" that was "the darling of the city's large property holders." The union blasted the other advocates of budget cutting, particularly the signers of the letter to the mayor, as "rich old men, no doubt, in whom the civic spirit stirs listlessly among the ledgers and bank statements. America's bright vision of tomorrow will not be supported by their tax dollars, if they can help it."[44] Hundreds of teachers attended board and council meetings to press their demands and to angrily remind the city leaders that just as teachers had taken an equal share of salary reductions in the 1930s, they now deserved an equal share in salary increases. Pointing to a growing shortage of teachers in Detroit due to low salaries, the DFT warned of educational disaster in the coming years.[45] Joining the DFT in lobbying the mayor and council were Frank Martel, president of the DWCFL, members of the Wayne County Council of the CIO, representatives of the Better Schools Association (a liberal, educational advocacy group), the Consumers League of Michigan, the Council of Jewish Women, the Detroit Council of Social Agencies, the Detroit District Association of the American Legion, the League of Women Voters, and the West Side Human Relations Council.[46]

Despite the formidable array of interest groups favoring an increase in municipal aid for the schools, the city again allocated considerably less money for the schools than the board had requested. The city did increase its allocation by over $2.4 million, but, as in 1945, the increase did not keep pace with inflation. Indeed, when adjusted for inflation, the municipal allocation to the schools was almost 4 percent lower than for the previous year.[47] The mayor and council inflamed passions even further by granting other city employees more than twice the salary increase provided for the teachers. The city justified this action by accurately claiming that the shift to a single salary schedule had given large numbers of teachers raises that other city workers had not received. While admitting that fact, school leaders pointed out that the most experienced teachers, who did not benefit from the new salary schedule, were falling further behind in the race with inflation.[48]

The failure to secure adequate funding for the 1946–47 school year marked a turning point in the history of the district. Between 1936 and 1946, the city had provided the schools with just 49 percent of the increases the board had requested. In 1949, school officials estimated that, over the past ten years, the city had allocated $50 million *less* than the school system was entitled to receive under the 15 mill limitation. Furious over their repeated failure to get badly needed revenue, the board and its allies began an intense search for ways to increase funding from other sources and to win financial independence from the city. Both these efforts ultimately led to Lansing.[49]

In the fall of 1946, in league with other educational interest groups, the Detroit Board of Education strongly endorsed a proposed constitutional amendment earmarking one third of all state sales tax revenues for schools and municipalities. Educational leaders argued that this amendment would substantially increase state aid to education At the same time, Common Council President George Edwards announced his support for efforts to free the school system from municipal control, a position that won the enthusiastic approval of the board members.[50] These two proposals and their ramifications dominated educational politics in Detroit for the rest of the decade and ensured that the bitter political divisions in the city would continue.

Struggle at the State Level, 1940–46

In turning to Lansing for increased funding and financial independence, school leaders from Detroit confronted essentially the same political alignments and issues at the state level that they had encountered since the early 1930s. Throughout the 1940s, the Detroit Board of Education and other mainstream educational organizations such as the Michigan Education Association (MEA) routinely joined organized labor and other liberal organizations in demanding increases in state spending for public education. These demands were challenged with equal regularity by the Detroit Bureau of Governmental Research, Michigan Chamber of Commerce, the Michigan Manufacturers Association, and the Michigan Public Expenditure Survey, an advocacy group sponsored by the automobile and oil industries whose slogan was "Use the ax—cut the tax."[51]

While these coalitions of interest groups clashed on the state and local levels over the same basic issues—the proper levels of taxes and services—four additional factors shaped the struggle for increased state appropriations for the Detroit schools. First, the financial crises brought on by the depression and war had wreaked even greater havoc with rural and small town schools than with Detroit. Second, throughout the 1940s, school leaders from the Motor City became heavily involved in the conflict over legislative reapportionment, a deeply divisive conflict involving strong urban-rural and class tensions. Third, advocates of increased state aid had to contend with widely held fears that with more state money came more state control. Finally, encompassing all these issues were the geographic and partisan biases of the legislators. Throughout the 1940s, educational politics pitted urban Democrats supporting higher taxes and more aid against rural and suburban Republicans attempting to hold the line on taxes and spending.

Across the state of Michigan, the crisis in education was profound. In 1943, as Alan Clive has noted, "one-sixth of the state's rural school districts closed entirely for lack of personnel." The number of emergency teaching certificates issued by the state to stem the growing teacher shortage jumped from 337 in 1939 to over 5,000 in 1944. In 1946, state officials estimated that 12,500 of the almost 32,000 teaching positions in the state would not be filled for the upcoming school year. Everywhere in the state, teachers were scarce because of miserable salaries and working conditions. Teachers who were making $800 per year in rural areas, for example, could earn three or four times that amount working in a factory.[52]

Even if money was found, however, school boards faced the difficult choice of setting their financial priorities. Not only were salaries low, but school boards across the state also desperately needed money to restore their decaying physical plants. In 1947, school leaders estimated that, due to the neglect of buildings during the depression and the war, the state needed to spend $250 million for new schools and major renovations of older buildings.[53] The only positive trend that state education officials found during the war and postwar years was that the pace of school district consolidation accelerated, as hundreds of small rural school systems simply collapsed. Between 1943 and 1950, the number of school districts in Michigan fell by 25 percent from about 6,400 to 4,800.[54]

Given the debilitating condition of so many outstate school districts, school leaders from Detroit faced an uphill battle in their quest for a larger share of state aid. Compounding this problem was the fact that the Michigan legislature, like so many across the nation, was apportioned to favor rural rather than urban residents. A 1942 study conducted by the League of Women Voters found that the urban, industrial areas of the state had over 53 percent of the population but only 31 percent of the House seats and 32 percent of the Senate seats. Four years later, a leader of the Detroit Teachers Association neatly wrapped up the problem, stating that "one third of our population elects two-thirds of the legislators!"[55]

As early as 1930, school leaders in Detroit had fought unsuccessfully for legislative reapportionment in order to protect the city's share of state school aid. By 1941, reapportionment became even more important to educators in the Motor City following a series of legislative actions that dramatically cut Detroit's share of state aid from about 30 to 20 percent of the total amount. Reapportionment, however, was another issue that placed the board of education squarely on the side of organized labor in opposition to major business organizations. By 1942, the political turmoil surrounding the rise of unionism had spilled over into debates about reapportionment. Business leaders, particularly John Lovett of the Michigan Manufacturers Association, opposed any redistricting that would strengthen the hand of organized labor in the legislature. Joining with leaders from rural areas, Lovett and other businessmen vigorously opposed all efforts to apportion more seats to Detroit, Wayne County, and other centers of union activism.[56] The Detroit Board of Education, on the other hand, enthusiastically joined the coalition for reapportionment that included the DWCFL, the Michigan Federation of Labor, the Michigan CIO, the Michigan Federation of Teachers (MFT), and the National Association for the Advancement of Colored People (NAACP).[57]

In 1943, the coalition achieved some success by gaining an increase in the number of house seats for Wayne County (from 21 to 27 out of 100 total seats). Following the next election, the DFT hailed this development, noting that, as a consequence, seven new legislators, all of whom were members of unions, were elected. The teachers' union claimed that "because organized labor consistently supported the improvement and extension of the public school program, the presence inside the railing of numerous laborites will be a distinct advantage when school problems are considered."[58]

Yet even this increase in representation fell far short of the number local political and labor leaders believed was appropriate. In 1948, state representative George Montgomery (D-Detroit), a former teacher and DFT member who maintained strong ties to organized labor, began an effort to increase the number of house seats for the Detroit metropolitan area to 38, and the number of senate seats from 7 to 12 out of 32 total seats. By then, the issue had both class and partisan implications, as Lovett and the Michigan Manufacturers Association joined forces with the Republican party to crush the redistricting effort in 1948 and again in 1949.[59]

The issue of reapportionment was only one of several controversies that hardened the political divisions created during the depression. Questions about increased state control over local schools had a similar impact. According to rural, largely Republican legislators, increased state aid inevitably meant increased control from Lansing. These legislators fought all attempts by the state to impose minimum educational standards as conditions for aid, arguing that such standards were a violation of the principle of local control. Urban and rural legislators also clashed over the common practice of rural school boards using additional state aid as a justification for lowering local taxes rather than for raising teacher salaries or constructing new buildings.[60] Condemning this practice in 1946, Arthur Elder, a Detroit teacher who was president of the MFT, declared that state aid "has now become a subsidy program because pressure groups are more interested in using it as a means of tax relief than for improving schools." Elder also noted that, since Detroit and other urban areas of the state provided far more tax revenue than they received back in state aid, urban residents were subsidizing rural tax relief. The practice of rural tax cutting greatly added to the bitterness of the struggles over reapportionment and state aid and prompted urban educational leaders to redouble their efforts for minimum standards and increased state control over local districts.[61]

In the late 1930s, the Michigan Federation of Teachers had sought unsuccessfully to curb the ability of local districts to cut taxes by advocating minimum salaries for all teachers in Michigan. By 1940, leaders of the more conservative Michigan Education Association joined the campaign for minimum salaries. The discussion of minimum salaries, however, quickly expanded to include debates about minimum millage requirements and maximum class sizes as conditions for state aid. In 1943, the MEA, MFT, and state educational leaders successfully lobbied for a state aid bill that made school districts ineligible for state aid if they reduced their local taxes. A minimum salary bill backed by these groups, however, failed to pass. Nevertheless, the restriction on tax cuts was the first serious step toward increasing the power of the state in this area.[62]

Not surprisingly, some politicians attempted to moderate state power by holding the line on state aid to education. In 1945, for example, legislators deliberately kept the amount of state aid below the amount raised by local taxes in order to avoid having the state provide more than 50 percent of the educational funds. The state superintendent explained, "There is a pretty general feeling that there will be much more rigid State control than in the past, if the State furnishes more than 50 percent of all funds spent."[63]

These political debates about taxes, services, reapportionment, and state power, combined with the general wartime scarcity of resources, severely limited the amount of state aid to public schools in the early 1940s. State aid to education did rise during this period, from over $43 million in 1940 to $50 million in 1945, but the increase did not keep pace with inflation. In this period, Detroit also received somewhat more money from the state, up from over $9 million in 1939–40 to over $10 million in 1944–45, but in this case, too, the gains were wiped out by inflation. School officials certainly understood the need for wartime austerity, but, as the war drew to a close, many educators began demanding substantial increases in state aid.[64]

In 1946, school leaders across the state, especially in urban areas, had run out of patience with the legislature. That summer, educational and municipal leaders formed a coalition to back a constitutional amendment that would earmark an additional third of all sales tax revenue for school districts and local governments (with each agency receiving half, 16.5 percent, of the revenue). Since school districts were already guaranteed 28 percent of the sales tax receipts, the amendment promised to lock in almost 45 percent of sales tax revenue for public education.[65]

The battle over what became known as the "sales tax split" raged for two years and exacerbated all the political tensions about educational issues that had been building for nearly fifteen years. As a leader of the Detroit Teachers Association stated, the need for the sales tax split came about because of "a feud between the cities and a rural legislature with schools caught in between." Equitable reapportionment might have saved the state from the controversy, he noted, but the rural-dominated legislature refused to give up its power.[66] The campaign for the sales tax split did, indeed, divide the state along rural and urban lines but, in addition, the amendment split liberals and conservatives, Democrats and Republicans, and organized labor and the business community. In many ways, the battle over the sales tax split was a microcosm of educational politics in the 1930s and 1940s.

School and civic leaders in Detroit enthusiastically backed the amendment as did the local MEA affiliate, the Detroit Teachers Association, and the *Detroit News*.[67] The DFT, like several other labor organizations, was slow to endorse the proposal, largely because of opposition to the sales tax in principle. Eventually, however, the DFT joined the DWCFL, other public employee unions affiliated with both the AFL and the CIO in solid support of the amendment. On the other side of the issue stood the Detroit Citizens League, the Detroit Bureau of Governmental Research, the Michigan Manufacturers Association, the Michigan State Grange, leading Republican members of the legislature, and the *Free Press*. Several organizations, however, did take uncharacteristic positions on the amendment. The Michigan CIO, for example, fought the measure because of its general opposition to the sales tax. The Detroit Real Estate Board, on the other hand, supported the amendment because it promised to take pressure off property taxes as the main source of school revenue.[68]

More than anything, the vote on the issue confirmed the depth of the urban-rural conflict over school aid. The amendment passed 709,008 to 479,912 with overwhelming support coming from Wayne, Kent, Genesee, Jackson, and Saginaw counties, the major urban areas in the state.[69] Even after the election, however, the controversy did not die down. Opponents of the measure took the issue to court. After a year of litigation, the state supreme court declared that the amendment was constitutional. But even this ruling did not deter the opposition groups. In 1947, the Michigan Farm Bureau called for repeal of the amendment. The following year, a tax study commission set up by Republican Governor Kim Sigler also urged repeal. Spurred by this report, opponents of the split placed a proposal to repeal the amendment on the November, 1948, ballot. Also on the ballot were proposals to amend two key provisions of the 15 mill limitation: the stipulation that millages could only be increased by a two-thirds vote and the five-year limit the amendment placed on bond issues. The amendments proposed that millage increases be decided by a simple majority and that school boards be allowed to increase the terms for bonds up to twenty years. All combined, the repeal proposal and the two millage amendments made the November, 1948, election one of the most important in the educational history of the state.[70]

The alignment of interest groups on these issues was almost identical to that in 1946 with two important changes. The *Michigan Chronicle,* one of the major newspapers in the African-American community, which did not take a position on the original sales tax split, strongly urged voters to retain the split and "safeguard our children's education." The most dramatic about-face on the issue, however, came from the Michigan CIO. Announcing that it still opposed the sales tax in principle, the CIO nevertheless declared that, as long as the sales tax remained in effect, "the CIO favors diverting one-third of the revenue to aid the school districts." The labor organization also strongly backed the proposal to liberalize the 15 mill limit.[71]

The other major difference between the 1946 and 1948 elections was the very partisan nature of the campaign. As early as May, 1947, the legislature had voted for repeal of the tax split along strict party lines. G. Mennen Williams, the Democratic candidate for governor in 1948, who ran with strong labor backing, vigorously campaigned in favor of the tax split and the liberalization of the 15 mill limit. On the other side of the issue, Governor Sigler declared that the tax split was bankrupting the state and campaigned for repeal of the amendment.[72]

The November, 1948, election was a stunning victory for the proponents of the sales tax split and for the efforts to liberalize the 15 mill limitation. The proposal to repeal the sales tax split lost by an enormous margin, 1,446,016 to 343,217. The vote on liberalizing the 15 mill limit was closer but no less decisive, 962,800 to 732,667. In addition, G. Mennen Williams won the governor's race. While the Republicans still controlled the state House and Senate, the election of Williams, who strongly supported increasing state funds for public schools, marked a dramatic change in educational politics in Michigan.[73]

The passage of the sales tax split in 1946 and the defeat of efforts to repeal the split in 1948 went a long way toward ending the almost two decades of financial starvation that public education in Michigan had endured. School leaders in Detroit were jubilant over the victories, especially since legislative support for a bill to grant complete financial independence for the school district was stronger than ever. Yet no sooner did the board set its priorities for spending the additional revenue than a new crisis, which pitted the school board against the increasingly powerful Detroit Federation of Teachers, engulfed the school system.[74]

The Rise of the DFT, 1940–46

The DFT came of age in the 1940s. During these years, the union grew substantially, won major concessions from the board, and emerged as a key player in the politics of education on the state, local, and even the national level. In many ways, the rise to prominence of the DFT in the 1940s not only exacerbated the fragmentation of political support for the schools that began in the 1930s, but it also introduced a dramatic change in the matrix of educational relationships within the school system itself. Just as school leaders had to contend with the clashing interests of city officials, business leaders, and organized labor in the search for adequate funds, so, in the late 1940s, school leaders realized that in deciding how those funds would be spent they also had to contend with an independent and increasingly militant teachers' organization.

Although the DFT did not get any major salary concessions from the board during the early 1940s, the union did win a number of other victories that clearly established its legitimacy and bolstered its reputation as an effective advocate for the teachers of Detroit. Early in 1941, for example, the DFT and several other school-based unions requested that the board "go on record" regarding the rights of all employees to join unions, in effect, asking the board to translate the sentiments expressed at the July 27, 1937, board meeting into policy. One month later, without any controversy whatsoever, the board announced that its employees were free to join "any craft, technical, professional, fraternal or employee organization not subversive in character." The following year, the DFT asked the newly appointed superintendent, Warren Bow, for his views on teacher unionism. The DFT applauded and publicized his reply that "teachers are free to join the teachers' organizations of their choice."[75]

These statements combined with the growing respectability of unionism in general encouraged teachers to join the DFT during the early 1940s. Membership jumped from 169 members in 1939 to 424 members in 1941. These new members dramatically changed the character of the organization. Many of the new DFT members were bread-and-butter unionists, primarily interested in better salaries and working conditions. They had little patience with the socialist or radical left-wing factions of the DFT that frequently had used the union in the 1930s as a platform for addressing large social issues that were often unrelated to education. As the DFT grew in the 1940s, the left-wing factions of the union became increasingly irrelevant. There was no purge of leftists in the 1940s, indeed such key left-wing figures as Walter

G. Bergman and Elinor Laffrey Maki continued to play prominent roles in the union, but their influence unquestionably declined. Nothing better demonstrates the dramatic change in the DFT during this period than the role its leaders played in the expulsion of the communist-dominated locals from the American Federation of Teachers in 1941.[76]

While the 424 members of the DFT accounted for only about 6 percent of the teachers in the Detroit system in 1941, the Detroit local nevertheless was one of the largest in the AFT. As such, the DFT emerged as a powerful force in the AFT at a crucial time in the history of the union. In the late 1930s, American Federation of Labor President William Green urged AFT leaders to take action against several locals, most notably in New York City and Philadelphia, whose political positions appeared to be strongly influenced by the Communist party.[77] In 1935, the DFT opposed the expulsion of these locals from the AFT but, by 1939, the majority of DFT members shifted to support Green's position that communist influence in the New York and Philadelphia locals had to be eliminated. Arthur Elder, president of the Michigan Federation of Teachers and one of the leaders of the liberal wing of the DFT, emerged in the late 1930s as the leader of the anticommunist faction on the AFT executive board.[78]

Early in 1939, Elder traveled to New York to urge Columbia University education professor, George Counts, to run for the AFT presidency on an anticommunist platform. Over the next two years, Elder, DFT President Florence Sweeney, and DFT Executive Secretary Frances Comfort played instrumental roles in Counts's election later that year and the anticommunist takeover of the AFT executive board the following year. These actions culminated in the expulsion of the New York and Philadelphia locals in May, 1941. It seemed altogether fitting, then, in August, 1941, that Detroit hosted the AFT convention in which the liberal anticommunists celebrated their triumph. As the AFT delegates met in the Motor City, the *Detroit News, Detroit Times,* and the *Labor News* hailed the anticommunist stand taken by the AFT.[79]

The ouster of the communist-dominated locals was a pivotal event in the history of the AFT. In a number of ways, the AFT action had a profound and immediate impact on the remaining locals of the union as well. The ouster of the communist-dominated unions strengthened the DFT's ability to combat the charges of radicalism that were frequently leveled at it. During the 1930s, the DFT had been fortunate that the school board took a tolerant view of the radical activities of the local and many of its most prominent members. Following the ouster of the communist-dominated locals in 1941, however, the DFT no longer had to rely on the goodwill of school officials to protect its reputation. DFT leaders had established themselves as committed anticommunists, a stand that paid unexpected political dividends in the McCarthy era.[80]

The most immediate benefit the DFT realized from the anticommunist ouster in the AFT was a dramatic increase in membership. Free from the taint of radicalism and aided by a $5,000 loan from the DWCFL, the DFT began an enormously successful organizing drive. Between 1941 and 1944, the union almost tripled to 1,283 members, representing almost 20 percent of the total teaching staff in the Detroit system. Throughout these years, the union focused on such bread-and-butter issues as improving the retirement system for school employees, ending the unofficial moratorium on promoting married women, gaining a single salary schedule, salary increases, smaller classes, and restoring the sick days lost during the depression. In almost all these areas, the DFT rather than the administrator-dominated DTA, goaded the school board into action.[81]

With the exception of winning higher salaries and smaller classes, the issues that required large amounts of money to resolve, the DFT was remarkably successful in achieving these goals during the early 1940s. The board dropped the moratorium on promoting married women in 1942, adopted the single salary schedule in 1943, gradually increased both the annual number of sick days and the number of sick days teachers could accumulate, and worked with state officials to make the retirement system actuarially sound. The problem with these victories, however, was that the rival DTA also took credit for them.[82]

Throughout the 1940s, the DFT and DTA vied for the loyalty of the teachers, but the struggle really was one-sided. The administrator-dominated DTA simply did not have the freedom of the DFT and, thus, could not take a leading role in these issues. Nowhere was this more apparent than in the fight to restore the teacher salaries that the Stone Committee had forced the board to cut in May and June of 1932. In 1937, at the behest of the DFT, the Detroit and Wayne County Federation of Labor initiated a lawsuit on behalf of all city employees who had lost part of their salary in 1932. The DTA played no role in this suit, and, when it was finally resolved in 1946, the triumph belonged entirely to the DFT. The courts awarded the teachers and other city employees not only the back pay but also interest on the lost salaries. The settlement, amounting to about $2 million, demonstrated to the teachers that the DFT could effectively fight both the board of education and city hall.[83]

The union scored an equally important victory early in 1944, when it won seniority rights for teachers. The union fought for these rights, in part, to protect teachers from arbitrary transfers that union leaders claimed were used to harass teachers who "took part in union activities or who refused to play politics with self-seeking superiors." Several months later, the DFT also successfully negotiated seniority rights for returning service men and women, an action that won high praise from veterans groups.[84]

By 1944, however, the success of the DFT led some school administrators to seek ways to neutralize the union. One attempt was the creation of the Detroit School Employee's Councils, an organization that administrators hoped would represent the teachers and staff in discussions of such issues as salaries and benefits. The DFT, other school-based unions, the DWCFL, and the Michigan CIO immediately denounced the councils as a company union and in September, 1946, after these groups threatened to take the issue to the Michigan Labor Mediation Board, the administration dissolved them.[85]

More than anything, this controversy revealed the growing rift between the unions and the board. Although the board had generally agreed to most of the demands that the DFT and the other employee unions made in the early 1940s, the relationship between the school administration and the unions was increasingly rocky. Throughout this period, the DFT and its allies in the labor movement tried to smooth out that relationship by returning to the strategy of the early 1930s and electing prolabor candidates to the school board. In 1941, the DFT, DWCFL, and Michigan CIO enthusiastically supported Laura Osborn and Howell Van Auken, a liberal attorney whose wife, Clara, was a member of the Democratic national committee. The unions' triumph in electing these two avowedly prolabor candidates was dampened somewhat by the election of Dr. Clark Brooks, who proved to be one of the most antiunion board members in this era. Nevertheless, as union power grew in the city, the DFT became bolder in its attempt to gain a firmer foothold on the school board.[86]

Declining to challenge moderate school board members John Webster and Frank Gorman, who ran for reelection in 1943, the unions once again set their sights on conservatives A. D. Jamieson and Burt Shurly in 1945. The DFT recruited two prominent candidates for the 1945 election, Victor Reuther, the UAW leader, and Robert G. Foster, a psychologist at the Merrill Palmer School and a founder of the liberal Better Schools Association. The DFT-backed candidates drew their strength from the two rival factions of the labor movement in Detroit, with Foster receiving the AFL endorsement and Reuther getting the backing of the CIO. As this compromise reveals, the DFT maintained good relations with both factions of the labor movement during the long period of AFL and CIO conflict.[87] Indeed, throughout the worst years of factional fighting, the AFL and the CIO still stood shoulder to shoulder in their support for the DFT and the public schools. As DFT President Sweeney noted, "No reader of the Detroit papers can be unaware of the unrelenting fight for an adequate school budget which the Federation has maintained and behind which it has marshalled the support of both the AFL and the CIO."[88]

Nevertheless, the split between the AFL and CIO may have cost the DFT the 1945 school board election and, by implication, a prolabor majority on the board. Reuther and Foster were soundly defeated by Shurly and Jamieson in the April election. Almost immediately, the DFT felt the consequences of that defeat as the board debated who should succeed Warren Bow following his untimely death in May. Liberal board members Osborn and Van Auken sought to hire Herold Hunt, the superintendent of the Kansas City schools, while more conservative board members Brooks and Jamieson pushed for Assistant Superintendent Arthur Dondineau. The board gave the position to Dondineau in September on a 5 to 2 vote, with Osborn and Van Auken opposing the appointment.[89]

As I have noted, relations between the DFT and Dondineau were poor even before he assumed the superintendency. Over the next year-and-a-half, relations deteriorated even further as the teachers fell further behind in the race with inflation, as other city workers continued to receive higher salary increases than teachers, as class sizes remained large, and as the Detroit schools went "begging" for teachers. The DFT became increasingly angry over the repeated failures of school leaders to wring more money out of the mayor and common council, a failure that the union attributed, in part, to Dondineau's unwillingness to cross swords with his friends in the business community.[90]

Not surprisingly, the teachers, administrators, and board members all hoped that the sales tax split would be the solution to the crucial financial problems facing the system. The split promised to provide Detroit with a "windfall" of about $10 million, enough, it would seem, to satisfy the demands of the teachers' union and still provide for the other needs of the system. Yet such hopes proved to be illusory. Within weeks of the passage of the sales tax split, the pent-up anger of the teachers about salaries and class size exploded, producing both the most divisive confrontation the system had yet witnessed between the teachers and the board and renewed political battles over school finance.

Conflict over Financial Priorities, 1946–47

The great issues of 1946–47 were rooted in the fundamental problem of financial priorities—how could the board provide decent salaries to the teachers in a period of rapid inflation and still respond to the enormous needs that the depression, war, and the growing urban population had created for new and renovated buildings. Within days of the passage of the sales tax split, the DFT demanded that the board use the money to increase teacher salaries by $500 per year. Frances Comfort warned that "the board should not put school buildings before people."[91] The DFT was particularly incensed over the apparent unwillingness of the board to use the money to bring the salaries of teachers in line with those of other city employees. In an angry letter to the board, DFT President Florence Sweeney declared that a "gross injustice occurred last January when teachers were omitted from the general 15% increase (later adjusted to 18 1/2%) granted all other city employees." Sweeney argued that the board had a moral obligation to use the sales tax money to rectify that injustice. This time, however, the DFT was prepared to do more than appeal to the goodwill of the board. As the controversy escalated, it became increasingly obvious that organized labor's support for the schools did not come without a price.[92]

Dondineau and the board, on the other hand, tried to satisfy both the teachers and the need for buildings, arguing that, as desperately as the teachers needed raises, the system also needed new buildings and major building renovations. The school administration consequently offered the teachers a $265 annual salary increase while pledging most of the sales tax revenue for construction.[93] The DTA quickly endorsed the actions of the board. "We want it made clear that our teachers want increases," DTA president Mary Schultz declared, "but none of us wants to take such a selfish stand that the children themselves or education will suffer." By aligning itself with the board on this issue, the DTA set the stage for a bitter struggle between the rival teachers' organizations in the midst of the larger controversy over the priorities of the board.[94]

Throughout November and early December, the DFT, the DTA, and the board engaged in an intense war of words. The DFT issued a series of statements highlighting the financial plight of teachers and noting that some teachers made less than municipal elevator operators and window washers. The board countered that more than 25,000 high school students were attending half-day sessions and that thousands of children were attending school in buildings over fifty years old. Even with extra revenue, school leaders claimed, the school budget would still be inadequate for the upcoming year.[95]

The first time the DFT confronted the administration face to face was on December 10th, at the board meeting when the finance committee made its recommendations on how to allocate the sales tax money. An overflow crowd of 450 teachers attended the meeting. "Never in all my years in the system," said Florence Sweeney, "have I seen teachers as wrought up as they are now." This show of force, however, failed to influence the board, which, over the strong objection of Laura Osborn, voted just as it had originally intended to, granting the teachers a $265 increase and earmarking the remaining money for school construction. The DFT immediately threatened to submit the issue to the Michigan Labor Mediation Board.[96]

The following day, newspapers carried photographs of DFT members on a "poster walk" outside the board of education building. While the ostensible purpose of the "walk" was to dramatize the financial plight of the teachers, the photographs made it abundantly clear that the DFT could organize a picket line as well as any union in the city and as well as any teachers' union in the country. As all the participants in these events were aware, less than two weeks earlier the 1,200 teachers of St. Paul, Minnesota, struck over the issue of salaries. The DFT, which supported the St. Paul Federation of Teachers with a $1,500 contribution for its strike fund, had every intention of following in the footsteps of the St. Paul union.[97]

Yet even as DFT leaders plotted a strike strategy, the crisis took an unexpected turn. In early December, the *Free Press* began a nine-part series on the Detroit public schools that was unquestionably the most scathing attack on the system since the early 1930s. As in the depression, the *Free Press* claimed that the quality of the school system had declined because educators neglected the basics. Laced with stories of high school graduates who were unable to solve simple math problems, alphabetize files, or make change, the series centered on the refrain expressed in its lead article: "The Detroit schools still are turning out graduates lacking simple 'A-B-C' fundamentals."[98]

By far the most stinging evaluations of the school system came from business leaders. One retail store executive declared that, in Detroit, the three R's had been replaced with the three I's, "illiteracy, illegibility, and inaccuracy." A Chrysler executive claimed that the company rejected half the young applicants for jobs at the Dodge Main plant because of "an obvious lack of training in fundamentals." In almost every case, business and industrial leaders blasted "progressive" or "socialized" education as the cause of the poor student performance. "High school," one businessman insisted, "has become so easy that a flair for the spectacular and a vague notion of how to get along with people constitutes a virtual guarantee of a diploma." What these business leaders failed to see, however, was that many of the reforms they had applauded during the war, particularly the emphasis on "practical" rather than academic education, had encouraged the very trends they now decried.[99]

These criticisms of the Detroit schools marked an important shift in the local debate about funding for the public schools. The *Free Press* and business leaders, traditionally opposed to increases in educational expenditures for the sake of holding down taxes, began to argue against such increases on new grounds. They now claimed that the schools were a bad investment, failing in their primary mission of teaching basic skills. Such an argument was particularly strong in debates about salary increases for teachers, shifting the focus from fiscal issues to concerns about whether the raises were warranted, given the poor quality of the "product" that teachers turned out. Well after the salary controversy had ended, the president of the Economic Club of Detroit asked, "Must We Pay for Education Not Received?" and declared, "The paramount question today in every State is not how we may obtain more money for education systems, but rather how our young people will receive a better education, for money we are now spending to prepare them for their future opportunities, responsibilities, and life work."[100]

Since the initial criticism of school quality came amid the salary controversy, some teachers assumed that these criticisms were part of a "campaign intended to 'kill' teachers' chances for a salary increase." Given the long-standing opposition of the business community to higher school spending and the editorial stance of the *Free Press,* which had warned the board not to be "stampeded" into granting raises early in the controversy, educators had good cause for such fears. Yet the DFT and DTA were well aware that many of the criticisms raised by the *Free Press* were accurate. Indeed, for several years, the union, and to a lesser extent the DTA, had denounced the same practices and programs that the *Free Press* series had highlighted, particularly social promotion, the platoon system, and the general track in the high schools.[101]

Despite longstanding criticisms of many of these policies and practices, the school administration seemed genuinely stunned by the attacks in the *Free Press.* Arthur Dondineau responded to the series with the absurd claim that Detroit had never "accepted the 'progressive' education system." He explained the declining quality of high school graduates as a consequence of increased high school enrollments by less able students. Since the high schools were "[o]perating on democratic principles," he declared, "instead of [serving only] a select, wealthy or highly intelligent group, the educational average is bound to go down."[102]

The school administration also hastily prepared a "progress report," the first of its kind in the history of the system, detailing the recent accomplishments of the schools. The report stated that, in 1943, reading scores of seventh and eighth graders were slightly above the national average and, more significantly, were better than similar test results in 1928 and 1937. In addition, the administrators cited a recent study that found Detroit graduates doing better than average at the University of Michigan. The administrators, however, sidestepped allegations about the general drop in the performance of high school students, the criticism that dominated the *Free Press* series. Like Dondineau, the report maintained that the quality of the students had declined as the number of students had increased. The problem with that argument, however, was that the number of high school students actually declined during the first half of the decade.[103]

Nevertheless, the report appeared to mollify the critics of the schools, at least for a while. Unfortunately, the issue of salaries could not be dealt with as easily. Pressure from the DFT increased in December, when the union demanded $500 raises, presenting the board with petitions purportedly signed by 75 percent of the teachers in the system. Since only 1,750 teachers, roughly 29 percent of the total faculty, were members of the DFT, these petitions indicated widespread dissatisfaction with the salary proposal of the board. Teachers needed the raises, according to the petitions, because the cost of living had risen 50 percent since 1941, while teachers' salaries had only risen 22 percent. Such arguments, however, failed to move the board. At the last meeting of 1946, the members reconsidered the recommendations of the finance committee and again voted to offer the teachers raises of $265. Only Osborn and Van Auken dissented.[104]

The vote provoked a bitter renewal of the war of words between the union and the board. The DFT announced that under, the dictatorial rule of Arthur Dondineau, the school system had become "second-rate and slipshod." The union also claimed that overcrowded classes made individual instruction of pupils virtually impossible.[105] Dondineau dismissed the charges as unfounded, while board member Burt Shurly termed the allegations "un-American." The *Labor News,* in turn, denounced Shurly, stating that he "has wrapped himself in the flag so many times that he looks like an Egyptian mummy."[106]

Behind these exchanges was more serious political maneuvering. On

January 15th, DFT representatives attended the school board meeting and requested that the board permit the Michigan Labor Mediation Board to step in and settle the salary issue. On the advice of the Detroit corporation counsel, the school board refused to mediate, arguing that the mediation board did not have jurisdiction over public institutions. Frances Comfort left the board meeting warning that "this is the kind of treatment that causes teachers' strikes."[107]

From that point on, the DFT executive board began seriously planning a walkout. UAW leader Walter Reuther and DWCFL leader Frank Martel denounced the board for refusing mediation and promised the teachers whatever support they needed in their battle with the board. Other interested parties, such as the Michigan Citizens Council, a liberal advocacy group, and the *Northwest Detroiter,* a community newspaper, also announced their support for the DFT.[108]

With tensions mounting, in late January the board attempted to defuse the situation with a major policy statement. As in 1931, the task of articulating the board's position fell to A. D. Jamieson, who seemed fated to be president during pivotal moments in the history of the school system. In an eloquent and carefully reasoned speech, Jamieson first affirmed the high quality of the Detroit school system, summarized the progress report that the board had issued a month before, and concluded that Detroit still had "one of the outstanding school systems in the country." He then reiterated the board's commitment to higher salaries for teachers, but noted that the board had to balance that commitment against the "needs of the entire system." He urged the teachers to recognize that "the public's demand for new buildings could not be subordinated to the demands for higher wages." Finally, Jamieson took a firm stand against the DFT, declaring that the public employees did not have the right to collective bargaining and reminding the teachers that they were professionals and not industrial workers.[109]

In several ways, this speech is quite similar to the one that Jamieson delivered in 1931. In both cases, the board was reacting to economic and political events well beyond its control. In the depression, the board had to bow to the realities of the economic collapse and the demands of the Stone Committee. In the late 1940s, amid rising inflation, a crumbling educational infrastructure, and the dramatic surge in the birthrate, the board faced the equally difficult task of accommodating justifiable demands of the teachers, the desperate need for new buildings, and the rising power of organized labor in Detroit. In 1931 and 1947, the political and financial crises were exacerbated by claims that the educational quality of the school system had declined.

Yet several important things had changed in the period between the two speeches. Obviously, the greatest shift was that, in 1947, the most serious pressure on the board came from organized labor and liberal organizations, rather than business and conservative groups as in 1931. More important, unlike the 1930s, when the teachers generally accepted that they would bear the brunt of retrenchment, in the 1940s, most of the teachers simply refused to sacrifice their salaries for the good of the system. In preparing his 1947 speech, Jamieson badly underestimated the anger and militance of the teachers, no doubt because he had been assured by Dondineau and the leaders of the DTA that the DFT represented only an embittered minority of teachers.[110]

Two days after Jamieson spoke, the seriousness of that miscalculation became apparent. A thousand teachers braved a snow storm to attend a mass rally called by the DFT. The teachers booed and jeered when a speaker read Jamieson's remarks implying that strikes by teachers were unprofessional. Several unions, most importantly the school custodians, declared that they would honor picket lines set up by the DFT. One week later, a second DFT rally held at the Cass Tech auditorium attracted as many as 1,600 teachers. The crowd cheered as Frank Martel and Victor Reuther blasted the DTA as a "company union" and pledged "labor's solid support in whatever action the teachers decided was necessary." Declaring that "the time for discussion had passed," the DFT leaders told the cheering crowd that next week the union's building representatives would distribute strike ballots to all the teachers in the system.[111]

The agitation for a strike drew an angry response from the DTA, the *Free Press* and the *News*. DTA President Mary Shultz stated, "Teaching is a profession in which dignity and public respect are paramount. We can command neither if we are to be classed with cooks, janitors, and laborers." Schultz claimed that a poll of the teachers conducted by the DTA showed virtually no support for a strike.[112] A *Free Press* editorial acknowledged that the teachers did indeed deserve higher pay, but argued that, at a time when many taxpayers were questioning the quality of the school system, a strike led by the "rabidly vocal" DFT would certainly alienate the community. The editorial concluded with the astonishing statement "that during the depression when most workers who were fortunate to have jobs took wage reductions, Detroit teachers never lacked employment and *never gave up one cent of salary*" (italics added). The *News*, in a less impassioned and more factually accurate editorial, also argued that the teachers needed a raise, but a strike was the wrong way to get it.[113]

The teachers, however, utterly rejected the reminders about professionalism from the DTA and the advice from the *Free Press* and the *News*. In the February 15th strike vote sponsored by the DFT, 5,978 of the 6,130 teachers in the system voted and nearly 69 percent of them supported a strike if negotiations with the board failed. In addition, almost 84 percent said they would honor the picket lines if the teachers struck.[114] Three days later, the DFT filed a thirty-day strike notice with the Michigan Labor Mediation Board. In the following week, every major union in the city from both the AFL and the CIO pledged to support the strike. In addition, the Detroit Federation of Women's Clubs, chapters of the American Veterans Committee, the *Michigan Catholic,* and the *Wage Earner,* official voice of the Association of Catholic Trade Unionists in Detroit, also announced their support for the DFT.[115]

Predictably, Dondineau, several board members, and the DTA denounced the looming strike. The DTA assured the teachers that the people of Detroit supported their salary demands but warned that a strike would utterly destroy the goodwill the community had for its teachers. Yet even as the administration, the DTA, and the DFT jockeyed for position in the battle for public opinion, outside events overtook them. On February 25th, approximately 2,700 teachers in Buffalo, New York, closed down the second largest school system in that state.[116] In a clear warning to the teachers of Detroit, the *News* ran an impassioned editorial that labeled the actions of the Buffalo teachers "An Attack on the Community" and called upon the Michigan legislature to outlaw strikes by public employees. The *Free Press, Times,* and the *Redford Record,* a community newspaper, also denounced teachers' strikes generally and the threatened strike in Detroit specifically. In the midst of this outcry, the Detroit Bureau of Governmental Research released a pair of reports that inflamed the situation even further by claiming that salaries for teachers in Detroit had risen substantially since 1941 and that teachers in the Motor City were among the highest paid in the nation.[117]

The DFT responded to these attacks with a series of initiatives. Declaring that it did not want to strike, the union called for direct negotiations with the board. At the same time, however, a DFT leader left for Buffalo to report firsthand on the situation there. The union also began an intense public relations campaign to counter the claims of the Bureau of Governmental Research about teacher salaries. The union released a report on thirty-five municipal occupations showing that, since 1934–35, all of the cited occupations except dogcatchers had received substantially higher salary increases than teachers. In addition, the union pointed out that while Detroit teachers were well paid in relation to teachers in rural school districts, they were poorly paid in comparison to teachers in other large cities and in several of the booming Detroit suburbs.[118] In advertisements placed in every major paper in the city, the DFT highlighted the financial plight of the teachers and declared that "all the buildings in the world cannot compensate for the lack of teachers." Finally, the union publicized the results of a *Detroit News* poll that found more than 80 percent of the Detroiters surveyed favored higher salaries for teachers.[119]

Two weeks before the strike deadline, the board agreed to negotiate with the DFT. The negotiations, however, proved fruitless. As the strike deadline approached, the union increased the pressure. At a DFT conference, Hubert Humphrey, mayor of Minneapolis and a member of the AFT, blasted the Detroit Board of Education for failing to negotiate in good faith. More ominously, the Teamsters, led by Jimmy Hoffa, announced that they would support the DFT and make no deliveries to the schools if the teachers went on strike. That threat from the Teamsters combined with promises from the custodians to honor the teachers' picket lines meant that the DFT had the power to shut down the school system if it chose.[120]

As the union completed its preparations for the strike, Common Council President George Edwards, who had close ties to the CIO, stepped into the negotiations. On March 19, one day before the strike deadline, Edwards announced that he and Mayor Jeffries would support an additional appropriation of $2.5 million for the schools in order to meet the salary demands of the DFT. At an emergency meeting of the school board members, common council, and the union leaders, eight of the nine councilmen also agreed to support the increase. At a huge rally two days later, an enthusiastic throng of teachers voted to accept the offer. From the point of view of the teachers and the school system, the settlement could not have been better. It provided the teachers with the raises they sought, enabled the board to save face by still earmarking more of the state revenue for buildings than salaries, and it forced the city, finally, into substantially increasing its appropriation for the schools.[121]

Nevertheless, the settlement that pushed the total city budget over $100 million for the first time provoked a furious outcry from major businesses and taxpayer organizations. Within days of the settlement, a new organization, the Home Owners and Taxpayers Co-Ordinating Committee, began a vigorous effort to derail the agreement by distributing 200,000 pamphlets denouncing the high cost of city government and by flooding council members with letters, postcards, and phone calls. Martin Larson, a retail merchant who headed the committee, vehemently assailed the teachers for their high-pressure tactics in gaining the raises. In response, George Edwards, Frank Martel, and Florence Sweeney accused the antitax committee of being a front organization for the major business interests in the city.[122]

Throughout the salaries versus building controversy, the major conservative and business groups, with the exception of the Bureau of Governmental Research, *had* been unusually quiet. Even during the most bitter period of the controversy, Harvey Campbell merely quipped that perhaps teachers should be paid on a "piece-work basis" in order to "tell what they're really worth." The agreement worked out by Edwards and the council, however, seemed to have shocked the business leaders into action. Almost immediately, the Citizens League, the Board of Commerce, the Bureau of Governmental Research, the Michigan Public Expenditure Survey, the Building Owners and Managers, the Business Property Association, the Realty Owners and Operators, the Taxpayers Council of Wayne County, and the Detroit Real Estate Board signed a letter to the council demanding that the members rescind the $2.5 million appropriation for teacher salaries. The *Free Press* also denounced the proposed city budget and castigated the council for knuckling under to the teachers and other pressure groups.[123] Yet for the first time since the depression, the council and the mayor completely rejected the recommendations of the business leaders and voted, instead, to pass the increased appropriations. That action so infuriated the leaders of the Citizens League, Board of Commerce, and Bureau of Governmental Research that they actually considered a campaign to recreate a ward or district system of elections for common council, thus repudiating the at-large system, the very centerpiece of progressive municipal reform.[124]

The salary increase, however, was not an unalloyed victory for the DFT and the unions. In late April, several weeks after the controversy in Detroit had died down, state representative Edward Hutchinson (R-Fennville) introduced a bill in the Michigan legislature to outlaw strikes by public employees. Hutchinson modeled the measure after an anti–public employee strike law that the New York legislature had passed in response to the Buffalo teachers' strike. From the beginning the bill had a great deal of support, but its prospects were boosted considerably when unionized teachers in suburban East Detroit went on strike in May.[125] Amid widespread outrage about the East Detroit strike, the Michigan legislature overwhelmingly passed the Hutchinson bill along with a series of other bills designed to curb the power of unions in general. In July, despite vigorous protests from such union leaders as Walter Reuther, the governor signed the Hutchinson bill into law.[126]

The Hutchinson Act was a serious blow to the DFT, but it did not deter the union from its pursuit of better salaries and smaller classes. The act, however, did force a change in strategy. In 1948, the teachers' union and its allies in organized labor returned to less militant methods for winning raises, namely intense lobbying of the council and the mayor during the budget hearings. They were again successful in securing increases, but in doing so the labor leaders had to fend off sharp attacks from the Board of Commerce and the Bureau of Governmental Research, who also switched tactics by strongly advocating spending money on new buildings rather than on higher salaries for teachers.[127]

The Board of Commerce and the Bureau of Governmental Research unquestionably sensed the growing public unrest about the lack of school facilities in the city. Throughout 1948, Detroiters became increasingly aware that the need for new school construction was every bit as acute as the school administration had claimed during the 1947 salary controversy. As early as 1942, school leaders had noted a sharp increase in the birthrate in the Motor City. In 1947, Detroit experienced its first enrollment increase in eleven years as the first cohort of "war babies" entered kindergarten. The system, however, had not been able to accommodate the number of students it had even before the baby boomers arrived. In 1947, nearly 14,000 elementary students attended school in buildings more than forty years old, over 4,500 were housed in temporary buildings, about 5,000 were bused to less crowded schools, and almost 25,000 high school students were on half-day sessions.[128]

Throughout late 1947 and all of 1948, the board was inundated with demands from parents and community groups for new buildings. In April, 1948, the *Detroit Times* ran a week-long, front-page series on the problems of overcrowded, dilapidated schools in the city. Reporters found kindergartens with as many as sixty children, students sitting in class wearing snowsuits because of inadequate heating systems, and an area of the city the size of Lansing that had no high school. School administrators estimated that the city needed an additional $40 million just to accommodate the present student population. Compounding these problems was the fact that, since 1939, construction costs for schools in Detroit had doubled. No one even speculated on how much it would cost to accommodate the looming tidal wave of the baby boomers in the future.[129]

By late 1948, these escalating financial pressures spurred the school board to redouble its fight for financial independence from the city. It was increasingly apparent to many of the key participants in local educational politics that in order to have sufficient funds for new buildings, new teachers, and adequate salaries, the board had to have the freedom to issue bonds and to bring millage increases before the voters. It is also likely that the mayor and the common council realized at this time that it would be better for the city budget, generally, and their own political fortunes, specifically, to make the school board completely accountable for the financial condition of the schools.

Throughout the year, school leaders, in conjunction with council President George Edwards and Mayor Eugene Van Antwerp, vigorously lobbied the legislature for a bill granting financial independence to the board. In early 1949, that lobbying bore fruit when the legislature finally passed the financial independence act. In announcing the passage of the bill, board President John Webster declared jubilantly that this action "is perhaps the most significant event in the history of the Board of Education since the establishment of the seven member board thirty-one years ago."[130]

Webster was not far off in that assessment. For the first time in its history, the financial fate of the Detroit school system, at least on the local level, rested entirely in the hands of the voters rather than with the mayor, the council, and well-organized interest groups. School leaders and their allies would no longer have to lobby the city government for a larger share of the municipal budget, but now could take their case directly to the people, who would decide on millage increases and bond issues. In that process, the major interest groups would still play an important role in determining the finances, policies, and practices of the Detroit schools. Their power, however, would now be based not only on how much clout they could muster behind the scenes but also on how successfully they could deliver votes. The Detroit schools had indeed entered a new era.

Black Detroit and the Public Schools, 1920–48

By changing the nature of educational politics in the city, the 1949 school law substantially increased the importance of Detroit's African-American community in educational affairs. Until this time, black leaders and interest groups such as the NAACP had played only a minor role in determining the outcome of most school issues. By 1944, however, the Detroit NAACP had over 25,000 members, the largest NAACP chapter in the nation, and it was becoming a serious force in local politics. After 1949, as the focus of school politics shifted from influencing budget hearings to building electoral coalitions, the growing black population of the city established itself as a key participant in the emerging liberal-labor-black coalition in the city.[131]

While the new school law facilitated this process of integration and empowerment, in fact, African-American leaders and organizations in Detroit had been working toward such increased participation for quite some time. David M. Katzman has described the long and ultimately successful black struggle to end segregated schooling in Detroit in the nineteenth century.[132] As late as 1922, with black children comprising approximately 5 percent of the total public school enrollment in the city, that nineteenth-century struggle continued to bear fruit, as the Detroit public schools remained well integrated. Black children were among the top four racial or ethnic groups in 33 of the 141 elementary schools in the city. Only two of these schools were majority black, and both of these schools were still over 40 percent white. In addition, black youths were the fourth largest racial or ethnic group, over 15 percent, in the Sidney D. Miller Intermediate School and they comprised almost 4 percent of the total enrollment in the elite, magnet high school, Cass Tech.[133]

As pleased as many African-Americans might have been with school integration in Detroit, throughout the 1920s and early 1930s several racial issues provoked serious controversy between the community and the board. Black leaders protested against the small number of black teachers, only 40 out of more than 5,800 in 1926, all of whom worked on the elementary level; the board policy of placing black teachers only in schools with large numbers of black students; and such indignities as the singing of discriminatory songs in music programs and separating the pictures of black graduates of Eastern High School from the composite 1934 senior class photograph.[134]

Beginning in 1934, these protests began to have an impact. In February, after the Detroit Civic Rights Committee, led by the Rev. William Peck and Snow Grigsby, a postal worker, appealed to the board of education, Superintendent Frank Cody promised to actively seek more black teachers and counselors for the Detroit schools. Cody lived up to his promise, and, when school opened in September, 1934, the board announced the hiring of Lloyd Cofer, the first black high school teacher and counselor in the system. Within two years, Cody hired a core of black high school teachers, including Edward Benjamin, Alvin Loving, and Harold Harrison, who would become prominent figures in the city and the schools. In addition, Cody gradually increased the total number of black teachers at all levels in the system.[135]

As positive as these developments were, another, more insidious trend was taking place simultaneously. By the mid-1930s, there was growing evidence that the school system was again becoming racially segregated. School leaders publicly maintained that there was no official policy favoring segregation, yet, during the late 1920s and early 1930s, many of the schools that previously had been integrated became almost completely black. Unquestionably, this trend was largely due to the changing racial composition of neighborhoods and practices such as restrictive real estate covenants. Nevertheless, the decision by the board to transform Sidney D. Miller Intermediate School into a high school in 1933 provides strong evidence that the school board also played an important role in segregating the city and the schools.[136]

From its inception, Miller fed into Eastern High School. During the depression, when high school enrollments soared, an increasing number of black students from Miller went on to Eastern. By September, 1933, Eastern, like most of the Detroit high schools, was severely overcrowded. Unlike the other schools, however, Eastern was also racially integrated. Apparently unwilling to maintain Eastern as an integrated high school, the board transformed Miller into a senior high and announced a liberal policy for students who wished to transfer to other schools. Since the Miller attendance area was almost completely black, the transfer policy enabled the few white students still in the area to leave the school. While the board justified the creation of the new high school and the transfer policy as legitimate responses to overcrowding, both actions, in effect, created a segregated, black high school in Detroit. The importance of race in these decisions is underscored by the fact that, despite the severe overcrowding of all the high schools in the city in the 1930s, no other intermediate schools were elevated to senior high status and, with the exception of Western High School (which was rebuilt after a fire in 1936), no new high schools were constructed during this period. In short, the creation of Miller High School was a clear case of deliberate school segregation.[137]

Black Detroiters had no illusions about why the school board had created Miller High School. They were equally aware of the gross inequalities between Miller and other high schools in the city in terms of resources and facilities. As a consequence, during the 1940s and 1950s, Miller became a rallying point and potent symbol for the African-American community of Detroit. Delegations of black leaders and parents, occasionally led by such UAW activists as Coleman Young, routinely attended school board meetings demanding that the board provide the school with facilities equal to those in other high schools in the city. The board, however, just as routinely dismissed these protests or delayed acting on them, usually claiming a lack of funds for capital expenditures. A February, 1949, editorial in the *Michigan Chronicle,* the leading black newspaper in Detroit, noted succinctly, "In a city where non-segregation is the law, the facilities at Miller bespeak a segregated situation in fact if not in principle."[138]

Despite segregation and subsequent inequality, perhaps the most striking thing about Miller was how good a school it became. Excellent educational leadership, high expectations on the part of teachers, and strong community support combined in the early 1940s to help make Miller one of the preeminent high schools in Detroit. In 1942, Charles Daly, one of the most enlightened administrators in the school system, became principal.[139] Daly strongly supported the corps of black teachers—Benjamin, Cofer, Loving—and many of the white teachers who were determined to maintain high standards and expectations in order to assure that students at Miller received a quality education. By 1947, Miller was so academically successful that one black leader estimated that 20 percent of its graduates went on to college.[140]

Indeed, according to one study, during its twenty-four-year history, the school graduated scores of future professionals, including perhaps more teachers and school administrators than any high school in Detroit, as well as many future lawyers, police officers, doctors, and dentists. Miller also produced such nationally known political and civic leaders as Coleman Young and Charles Diggs, Jr. The school was known not only for academic excellence, but for its athletic and music programs as well. In the 1940s and early 1950s, Miller dominated interscholastic sports in the city and launched the careers of two Olympic gold medalists, a number of college All-Americans, and such professional athletes as Eugene "Big Daddy" Lipscomb. The Miller music program produced such towering jazz musicians as Kenny Burrell, Milt Jackson, and Yusef Lateef.[141]

Unfortunately, no other Detroit high school equalled Miller's success in working with black students. Indeed, high schools in changing neighborhoods became flashpoints for racial conflict in the early 1940s. In February, 1940, for example, police were called to quell a near riot that developed as roving groups of black and white youths battled outside Northwestern High School. School officials claimed that the fights were due to the tension of overcrowding, that outsiders started the fights, and that race relations within the school were generally good.

Black leaders, however, took issue with that assessment. Northwestern was notorious in the black community for racist teachers who publicly degraded black students, segregated them within classrooms, and barred them from school clubs and ROTC. At a meeting called to discuss the violent racial conflicts at the school, black parents demanded, at least, a black counselor to work with their children. As late as 1941, with over 700 black students out of a total enrollment of about 4,000, there was not even one black teacher. Over the next year, the board did little to remedy the situation and fights and confrontations between black and white students became increasingly common.[142]

These confrontations at Northwestern foreshadowed the horrible violence that exploded at the Sojourner Truth homes in 1942 and the Detroit riot of June, 1943, in which thirty-four people were killed. Although the schools seemed no more able than any other institution in the city to resolve racial conflict, indeed, one critic labeled the racist teachers as an important cause of the 1943 riot, civic leaders nevertheless expected the schools to play a major role in healing the divided city. "While the problem of inter-racial relations is the concern of all agencies in the community," declared an advisory committee formed soon after the riot, "the school is the greatest force for democratic action and is the logical medium for both children and adults for promoting knowledge and understanding and developing desirable attitudes through the process of learning."[143] Over the next few years, inspired by these beliefs, the Detroit public schools instituted an extensive program of "Inter-cultural Education" that drew praise from the NAACP and the *Michigan Chronicle* for its promotion of racial and religious tolerance on every level of the school system.[144]

For the NAACP and other civil rights groups in the city, however, curriculum reform was not enough. As the national executive secretary of the Urban League stated at a 1946 conference on race relations in the city, "Education? We're for God and education, and for all those things, but we want to know how action goes with it. We're not going to get anywhere by telling little white children how fine some Negro individuals are, the singers and artists. We want to know what action goes with the words." In this case, action meant the commitment of resources to improve the quality of education for black children. One week after the 1943 riot, the NAACP called on school leaders to hire substantially more black teachers, particularly on the high school level, to hire more black counselors, to end the policy of placing black teachers only in schools with predominantly black enrollments, and to elect a black member to the board of education.[145]

Between 1943 and 1945, the administration responded to these demands, to some degree, increasing the number of black teachers in the system from 156 to 286. That number still accounted for only 4 percent of the total faculty in a system that had a 17 percent black enrollment. In addition, only

20 of the 286 black teachers worked on the intermediate or high school levels. Even more troubling was the fact that the board assigned all of the black teachers to the twenty-four predominantly black elementary schools and the three predominantly black secondary schools, Sherrad and Garfield Intermediates, and Miller High School.[146]

The black community was particularly outraged at the continuing failure to hire black counselors. As late as 1949, only 4 of the 147 counselors in the system were black. Black parents believed that the small number of black counselors had a direct relationship to the overrepresentation of black students in special education classes and the general track in high schools and their underrepresentation in the college preparatory track. In the 1930s, school officials had expanded the general track in order to "warehouse" poor and working-class students who flooded into the schools because of the depression. By the 1940s, it appears that school officials were using the general track to fulfill a similar role with blacks. As of May 1945, for example, black students were twice as likely to be in the general track than white students and half as likely to be in the college preparatory track.[147]

Few major civic groups joined with the NAACP and Urban League in pressing for change. The Detroit Federation of Teachers, however, endorsed several of the educational demands of the civil rights groups immediately after the riot and quickly assumed an important role in improving race relations in the schools. Meier and Rudwick have described how the UAW and the African-American community forged a strong political alliance following the 1943 riot. The actions of the DFT during this same period provide another example of how an important union joined forces with black leaders and organizations to pursue a common, liberal agenda in the city. Both the UAW and the DFT would increasingly play a major role in the liberal-labor-black educational coalition that was emerging during these years.[148]

Well before the riot, such DFT members as Walter Bergman, Huldah Fine, and Elinor Laffrey Maki had become leading proponents of civil rights, in general, and curricular revisions designed to promote racial and religious tolerance in the Detroit schools, in particular. Since so many DFT members were also prominent in the civil rights movement in the city, early in 1944, the school administration asked the DFT to prepare materials on black history and culture that school principals distributed throughout the system prior to Negro History Week.[149] The DFT also joined with black organizations to press for a broad array of civil rights demands.[150]

By 1945, these actions paid political dividends for both the DFT and the black community. In that year's school board race, the DFT-backed candidate, Robert G. Foster, ran on a platform calling for more black teachers and ending the transfer policy that enabled white students to withdraw from high schools with large black enrollments. In the same election, Victor Reuther received the endorsement of Urban League leader John Dancy, and both DFT-backed candidates received excellent coverage in the two black weeklies, the *Michigan Chronicle* and the *Detroit Tribune*. In the aftermath of the election, as the school board wrangled over the successor to Warren Bow, the *Tribune* joined the DFT in opposing Arthur Dondineau, although the black newspaper did not support the same candidate for the position as the teachers' union.[151]

These issues and stands brought the DFT and the African-American community closer together during these years, but a number of important issues still divided these liberal allies. One of the most serious problems was the small number of black teachers who belonged to the DFT. While some black teachers, such as Leroy Dues, head of the athletic department at Miller High School, became active, prominent members of the union, most black teachers in the 1940s remained loyal to the DTA.[152] A second, more important point of contention was the clash of priorities between the DFT and African-Americans on the issue of allocating educational resources. During the 1946–47 controversy between the DFT and the board, some prominent black leaders appeared to throw their support to the board rather than union. The *Detroit Tribune* and the *Michigan Chronicle,* for example, did not even report on the salary demands of the DFT. More pointedly, in January, 1947, at the same board meeting at which Jamieson implored the teachers to recognize the desperate construction needs of the system, a delegation of black ministers and parents underscored Jamieson's remarks by demanding that the board allocate additional funds for improving Miller High School.[153]

Blacks were more concerned about buildings than salaries for two very important reasons. First, since most black families lived in the oldest sections of Detroit, the schools their children attended were often in terrible physical condition. Nowhere in the city had the fifteen-year moratorium on school construction and renovation had a more profound impact than in black neighborhoods. In 1945, an editorial in the *Tribune* pleaded with the board to upgrade the schools in the black community, noting that many of these schools had been constructed in the nineteenth century and were now unsafe. Two years later, the *Michigan Chronicle* reported that "in predominantly Negro neighborhoods, buildings, equipment and supervision are far below standard." Thus, any shift in resources from buildings to salaries would probably have been felt most acutely in the black community.[154]

Second, blacks realized that the board was using the issue of over-crowding to increase segregation. The creation of Miller High School demonstrated to the black community how the board could use a legitimate housing issue, the overcrowding of Eastern High School, to mask a decision that further segregated black students within the system. As school opened in the fall of 1947, the black community faced an even more brazen attempt by the school administration to use the issue of overcrowding to transfer black students from a racially mixed school into two other schools that would be predominantly black. The focus of this controversy was Post Intermediate School, situated in the Eight Mile–Wyoming area of the city, where blacks had been moving in large numbers. In August, 1947, school administrators reassigned all of the black seventh and eighth grade students in Post to the largely black Higgenbotham Elementary School. In addition, the board reopened Birdhurst School, which had been closed in 1931 due to its age and poor physical condition, to take in the overflow from Higgenbotham. The reopening of Birdhurst particularly outraged the community, which saw this action as clear evidence of an emerging separate and unequal school system for black children. Leaders of Carver Progressive Club, a black social action group, and Edward Swan, executive secretary of the Detroit NAACP, immediately denounced the Post transfers and the reopening of Birdhurst as blatantly segregationist. Arthur Dondineau, however, declared that these actions were necessary because of a general shortage of classrooms and as a means to avoid half-day sessions for all children in the area.[155]

When the board refused to reconsider the reassignment of the students, black parents took matters into their own hands and pulled their children out of Higgenbotham. Then, they set up picket lines around both Higgenbotham and Birdhurst. The "parents' strike" was remarkably successful. For almost two weeks, the *Detroit Tribune* reported, "not one child between the first and 8th grades attended" Higgenbotham or Birdhurst schools.[156]

Dondineau attempted to defuse the situation by meeting with the parents, members of the Carver Progressive Club, and leaders of the NAACP, but the meeting only inflamed passions further. The superintendent totally rejected the charges of discrimination and, after a heated exchange, threatened the parents with legal action for keeping their children home. Furious, one member of the audience yelled, "There's not enough jails in the state to hold all parents who will keep their children out of school." Following the meeting, the *Michigan Chronicle* pilloried the superintendent as "Mr. (Anti-Negro) Arthur Dondineau" and declared "Indifference to making democracy work was thick in the room and in its presence the spirit of cooperation lay prostrate."[157]

The strike continued for another week. With the parents showing no signs of wavering, Dondineau again met with them, this time in a more conciliatory mood. He agreed not to reopen Birdhurst, to speed up the renovation of Higgenbotham in order to accommodate the new influx of students, and to create a committee to study the larger issue of segregation in the system. Although that last, most important issue remained unresolved, the parents announced victory and agreed to end the protest. Following the meeting, the *Tribune* praised the parents for their "guts" in standing up to the school authorities, but the paper bitterly assailed the administration. "From the action of the Board of Education," the paper editorialized, "anything they can do to help segregation is their policy. When it comes to setting school boundaries, the Board of Education divisions are as fine an example of gerrymandering as you can find in any rotten political set up." One week later the paper blasted the school board again, declaring that "We need some new blood at the top. . . . We need some members of the board who will put a stop to the shilly-shally policy of shifting Negro children around, and allowing other children to go out of their districts, to keep them from being exposed to each other."[158]

Over the next year, the African-American community closely monitored the school system. In November, the *Michigan Chronicle* ran a month-long series on the problems of blacks in the Detroit schools. The series found that virtually every problem identified fifteen years earlier by the Detroit Civic Rights Committee, including small numbers of black educators at every level in the system, segregated attendance boundaries, and overcrowded black schools, either had remained the same or worsened.[159]

Significantly, at this time, the DFT joined in the protests against the most blatant segregationist policies of the board. In February, 1948, the DFT denounced the board policy of shifting school boundaries "to accommodate fleeing white children in districts predominantly Negro" and simultaneously hardening school boundaries "when Negro children attempt to enroll in all-white schools." By 1948, the DFT, the *Tribune,* and the *Chronicle* all concluded that only a change in the leadership of the school system could end these segregationist policies.[160]

While blacks hoped that such new leadership would come with the election of a black school board member, the first real opportunity to influence a change in school leadership came in the spring of 1948, when the board considered the renewal of Arthur Dondineau's contract. As I have noted, the DFT and organized labor also had little love for the superintendent. In 1948, it appeared that this emerging alliance of unions, civil rights organizations, and the liberal Better Schools Association had a serious chance at removing the embattled superintendent.[161]

In 1947, many of these organizations had backed Robert G. Foster in his successful campaign to replace Howell Van Auken (who chose not to seek a second term). As president of the Better Schools Association, Foster had been an outspoken critic of Dondineau, and the liberal organizations knew he could be counted on to forcefully oppose a new contract for the superintendent. In April, when the school board debated the contract, the Better Schools Association along with seventeen other liberal and civil rights organizations issued a scathing press release that blamed Dondineau and the board for the financial plight of the school system. Pointing to overcrowded classes, decaying buildings, and half-day sessions, the press release charged that during the "past seven or eight years" the board "has failed to request monies that might have been granted, and applied to necessary capital costs, as conditions warranted." In addition, the press release concluded that " . . . under [Dondineau's] administration, personnel practices and public relations have been so poor as to affect adversely the education of our children."

This press release marks the formation of what would become known as the liberal-labor-black coalition. In addition to the Better Schools Association, almost every prominent liberal and labor group in the city signed the statement, including the Americans for Democratic Action (ADA), the Joint Board of the United Public Workers–CIO, and the Region 1 and 1A UAW-CIO Women's Auxiliary. Notable on the list of organizations was the Carver Progressive Club, which had organized the Higgenbotham-Birdhurst strike, the black sorority Alpha Kappa Alpha, the largely black, left-wing Michigan Federated Democratic Clubs, and the Higgenbotham PTA. The NAACP was not listed, but, soon after the statement was released, Edward Swan announced that the civil rights organization also opposed the reappointment of Dondineau.[162]

Despite the opposition of this formidable array of organizations and the determined, angry efforts of Robert Foster, the board reappointed Dondineau for a three-year term. Even Laura Osborn abandoned the liberal coalition to vote for reappointment. The failure to oust Dondineau was a serious setback for the groups that sought to introduce more liberal policies and programs into the schools. Yet, like the initial failures to oust Wales Martindale almost forty years earlier, this setback stimulated a reform movement bent on removing a powerful superintendent and implementing major reforms.[163]

Spearheading these efforts was a new organization, Save Our Schools (SOS), which was formed in the aftermath of this controversy. SOS united white liberals, DFT members, labor leaders, leaders of the Jewish community, and African-American activists in the quest for educational change. Like the reformers of the Progressive era, the SOS activists initially focused their efforts on replacing the superintendent, but their agenda, in fact, was much broader. The liberal-labor-black coalition also sought substantially increased funds for public education, an end to racial discrimination in all aspects of the school system, and greater involvement by community groups in shaping school policies and programs. Beginning in 1949, when the board gained control of its own finances and school leaders had to go to the voters for support for millage increases and bond issues, the political fortunes of the coalition rose dramatically.[164]

Independence, 1949

The first election in which the emerging liberal-labor-black alliance played an important role came in the spring of 1949. Immediately after the legislature granted the school board financial independence, the board voted to put a tax increase on the April ballot. In addition, the unexpected resignation of board member Robert G. Foster in December, 1948, meant that three school board seats would also be up for grabs in the same election. Exhorting DFT members to take an active role in the campaigns, Frances Comfort declared that "the opportunity of a lifetime is before us. For the first time in memory a single election holds the possibility of easing the schools' financial plight and at the same time placing *three* new members on the Board of Education."[165]

Even before the campaigning started, organized labor exerted its influence, pressuring the board to increase the size of the millage proposal that would be on the ballot. The board had originally proposed 3 mills for the first year and 2 mills for four additional years. The DFT and the DWCFL attacked that proposal as insufficient and castigated the board for succumbing to pressure from business leaders, who wanted the lowest tax rate possible. Union leaders instead called for a 3 mill increase for five years. The board compromised on 2.5 mills for five years, which would bring in an estimated $10 million annually. To placate the business leaders and many parents groups, however, the board promised that all of the additional money would go for new buildings and additional teachers and that none of the new money would go for teacher salaries.[166]

In March, as the campaigning began in earnest, organized labor enthusiastically got behind the increase. The UAW and the Michigan CIO pledged their support and, in a front-page editorial, the *Labor News* declared "Every trade unionist should do his utmost to promote the passage of Proposition D [the millage increase]." The Americans for Democratic Action, the Better Schools Association, and the League of Women Voters also rallied their members in support of the proposition. Following a request from the DFT, the Detroit Common Council unanimously approved a resolution supporting the tax increase. In a surprise move, the Citizens League also endorsed the increase. The *Detroit News* added its voice to the chorus of support for the tax increase and underscored the need for the increase by running a series of articles highlighting the plight of the school system. Showing photographs of overcrowded, decrepit schools and displaying maps and statistics detailing the shortage of buildings and teachers, the *News* estimated that, over the next five years, the city needed at least $40 million in new school construction and 1,600 new teachers.[167]

In the African-American community, the NAACP solidly supported the tax increase, as did the *Michigan Chronicle.* The endorsement by the *Chronicle,* however, contained more than a hint of concern about whether the board would allocate the additional funds fairly. Just prior to the election, the *Chronicle* ran a damning series of articles and editorials describing how the board had repeatedly failed to live up to its promises to upgrade the physical facilities at Miller High School. In supporting Proposition D, the *Chronicle* declared, "The voters of Detroit can no longer give the Board of Education an excuse of lack of funds to hide behind. . . . The schools must have more money, if for no other reason than to wipe out the glaring inequities which exist here and are so well known to every one."[168]

There was little organized opposition to the millage proposal. Most of the traditional opponents of tax increases for the public schools were essentially neutral on the issue. The *Free Press,* for example, actually endorsed the millage increase, but the paper couched its support in glum, almost cynical terms and berated school leaders for their inefficient and ineffective use of current funds. The *Free Press* also warned its readers that this was just the beginning of the demands for increased taxes. The Bureau of Governmental Research charged the board with obfuscating the actual costs of its proposed building projects and, like the *Free Press,* predicted that the board would seek an additional millage increase five years hence. The Bureau also warned against the possibility that the additional funds would be drained away by excessive salary demands of the teachers, demands that the bureau claimed were "no longer justified." The Board of Commerce echoed the fears about excessive salary demands from the teachers, but the organization did not take an official stand on the tax proposal. The chairman of the education committee of the Board of Commerce, however, was sharply critical of the school system during the millage campaign. The Michigan Public Expenditure Survey also remained noncommittal on the issue. The survey accepted the need for new buildings and more teachers, and even admitted that taxes for schools in Detroit were low. Nevertheless, the survey pointed out that, with the new millage increase, the overall property tax rate in Detroit would be the highest in the state. The only determined opposition came from antitax activist Martin Larson and other property owners who deplored the fact that all registered voters could participate in this election, arguing instead that only property owners should vote.[169]

While the campaign for the millage increase was surprisingly tame, the school board campaign that was going on simultaneously provided some political fireworks. With three seats up for election and only one incumbent, Frank Gorman, seeking to retain his seat, the April balloting offered the possibility for dramatically changing the character of the board. With that in mind, the DFT joined Save Our Schools in setting up ward and precinct organizations to push the exceptionally strong slate of SOS-endorsed candidates—Jane Lovejoy, past president of the Better Schools Association, Patrick V. McNamara, a labor leader and one-term city councilman, and James Lincoln, a law partner of Governor G. Mennen Williams. The ADA, the DWCFL, the Michigan Committee for Civil Rights, the NAACP, and the Wayne County CIO Council enthusiastically endorsed the SOS candidates.[170]

Facing them were Louise Grace, an advertising executive, Richard McRae, an attorney, and Frank Gorman, who was opposed by organized labor for the first time in five campaigns for the board. Despite the nonpartisan nature of Detroit school board races, all three of these candidates received the endorsement of the Wayne County Republican party. In addition, these candidates were strongly supported by the DTA.[171]

With every candidate promising to solve the problems of overcrowded schools and classrooms, little debate centered on genuinely educational issues. Instead, the campaign was dominated by allegations, strikingly similar to those made in 1933, that organized labor was attempting to take control of the board of education. This time, however, rather than coming from the Employers' Association and the Board of Commerce, the charges were leveled primarily by the DTA, which was fiercely trying to win back the loyalty of the teachers from the DFT. In a lengthy press release issued less than a week before the election, the DTA declared that "the public should not only be well informed but gravely concerned about the dangerous note of partisan-ship injected into the current Board of Education election by the pressure of a labor-backed slate of candidates." The DTA claimed the unions were "pav-ing the way for the possible seizure of our educational system by individuals motivated only by a lust for power." Soon after, the *Detroit News* ran an editorial entitled "Union Bosses Aiming at Control of City Schools and University" that blasted both the labor slate for the school board and the labor-backed candidates for the University of Michigan Board of Regents.[172]

These allegations of union-led conspiracies to run the school board election attracted a good deal of attention, but the controversy failed to catch fire as it had in 1933. Certainly, the fear and sense of crisis that had colored that earlier campaign was gone and labor unions had become considerably more respectable in the intervening years. For whatever reason, some of the most vehement critics of union activism in the 1930s failed to be drawn into the conflict. Indeed, the *Free Press* even endorsed Patrick McNamara, and the Citizens League gave James Lincoln its lukewarm, "Qualified," endorse-ment.[173]

On April 4, the voters gave the liberal-labor-black coalition most of what it sought in the election. The tax increase won with more than 58 percent of the vote, a solid victory that gave school officials hope for the future. Combined with the 8.31 mills that the Wayne County Tax Allocation Board allowed the school system as its share of the 15 mill tax, the additional 2.5 mills raised the tax rate in Detroit from one of the lowest for urban school systems in the state to one, at least, on par with other cities. In addition, Patrick McNamara and Jane Lovejoy won their races for the board. Louise Grace, however, beat out James Lincoln, depriving the coalition of a clean sweep.[174]

While the election did not fulfill all the ambitions of the liberal commu-nity in Detroit, it was a watershed in the history of the school system. For the first time in almost two decades, the Detroit public schools had a substan-tial increase in local revenue. Moreover, the retirement of John Webster and the defeat of Frank Gorman signaled a major change in school leadership. Between 1927 and 1949, Webster, Gorman, Jamieson, Osborn, and Shurly had been the backbone of the board. From this point forward, school leader-ship in Detroit would be considerably more fluid and more representative of the changing population of the city. Nothing exemplified that change more than the election of labor leader Patrick McNamara, the first union official ever elected to the position. In addition, Louise Grace and Jane Lovejoy were the first women to join Laura Osborn on the board, a development that

Osborn rejoiced in. All told, the 1949 election signaled that the school system stood on the threshold of a new era, one that school leaders hoped would be less divisive and confrontational than the past two decades had been.[175]

Conclusion

Perhaps the most striking thing about educational politics and policies in Detroit in the 1940s was how closely they mirrored the politics and policies of the 1930s. Certainly in the 1940s, the interest groups involved in educational politics became more adept at articulating and lobbying for their positions, and the relative power of these groups changed amid the economic and demographic transformation of the era. Nevertheless, the positions these groups took and the policies they pursued essentially remained the same between 1929 and 1949.

Nowhere was this more apparent than in the ongoing conflict about school appropriations on the state and local levels. The political alignments over these issues that developed in the 1930s, liberals and organized labor arguing for higher taxes and more spending on education while conservatives and business interests advocated lower taxes and the more efficient use of available resources, remained virtually unchanged during the 1940s. Contrary to the claims of some historians who argue that the deep divisions in educational politics in the 1930s had no long-range impact and that urban school politics in the 1940s were relatively calm, educational politics in Detroit and Michigan were fiercely partisan and divisive for most of the war and postwar years. In effect, the Great Depression hit the Detroit schools with seismic intensity, setting off political and financial aftershocks that lasted almost twenty years. The chief result of these political aftershocks was the slow but certain financial weakening of the school system. Unquestionably, the political, financial, and material condition of the schools was far worse in 1949 than it had been in 1929.[176]

Amid the continuity of political alignments and arguments and the ongoing financial problems of the school system, some important changes in educational politics did emerge during this era—notably the rise to prominence of the DFT, the emergence of the African-American community as a political force to be reckoned with, and the first stirrings of the liberal-labor-black coalition. The driving force behind these developments was the burgeoning power of organized labor in Detroit.

The DFT, particularly, used its strong ties to organized labor to increase its influence over educational decision making in the city. No better example of that influence can be found than the near strike of 1947, when the DFT effectively used its political clout to force the city into approving a large pay raise for the teachers. In taking this action, the teachers of Detroit were in step with thousands of other teachers across the United States. Belying claims that the 1940s were a period of relative calm in educational politics is the large of number of strikes or near strikes by teachers in the last few years of that decade. Between 1946 and 1948, almost 12,000 teachers in forty-eight school districts across the country went on strike, sending an estimated 350,000 students home for unscheduled vacations. In many large cities other than Detroit, including Boston, Chicago, Gary, New York, and St. Louis, teachers threatened walkouts in order to force reluctant school boards into granting salary increases. In all, the late 1940s was the most volatile period of educational labor relations prior to the 1960s.[177]

Black Detroit also began to play an important role in educational politics in the late 1940s. Convinced that school leaders were blatantly segregating black children and neglecting the schools in black neighborhoods, African-American leaders and parents embarked on a series of initiatives, such as the Higgenbotham-Birdhurst strike and joining the effort to oust Arthur Dondineau in order to gain equal, unsegregated education for their children. These actions were among the first steps taken by the civil rights movement in Detroit and they helped provide the basis for one part of the emerging alliance between civil rights organizations, labor unions, and liberal leaders in the city.

Black students and their families, however, had more to contend with from the school system than just highly visible acts of segregation or neglect. School officials placed black students into the academically deficient general high school curriculum at twice the rate of white students, thus dooming them to four years of watered-down required courses and life adjustment–style electives. For some time now, many educational historians have criticized vocational education as the curricular change that introduced substantial inequality into the American high school. Such criticism is clearly warranted. Nevertheless, educational historians are remiss in not examining the development of the general track, whose operation in Detroit appears to be far more insidious in depriving working-class and minority students of access to high-quality education. In many ways, the expansion of the general track in the 1930s and 1940s was as serious a blow to the quality of the Detroit school system as were the many political and financial crises of the era.

In all, the 1940s were a period in which the decline of the Detroit school system accelerated. As a consequence of the economic conditions imposed by the war and the deeply divided political base, the school system plunged even further into fiscal crisis. Similarly, the war stimulated the curricular movement away from solid academic programs and encouraged the expansion of "practical," relevant courses, thus contributing to a serious erosion in the quality of educational offerings. It is important to recognize that this financial, political, and educational decline occurred while the school system was still overwhelmingly serving white students. Class, not race, was still the prime force shaping educational politics and policies in the Motor City in the 1940s. Nevertheless, racial issues were becoming increasingly important and the growing black community, allied with white liberals and labor leaders, was poised to play a much larger role in educational politics.

NOTES

1. Frances Comfort, letter to William P. Lovett, 2/13/41, in AE Papers, box 14, Detroit School Board Election folder.

2. Robert Hampel, *The Last Little Citadel: American High Schools Since 1940* (Boston: Houghton Mifflin, 1986), 30; Ira Katznelson and Margaret Weir, *Schooling for All: Class, Race, and the Decline of the Democratic Ideal* (New York: Basic Books, 1985), 126, 121–49; Ronald Cohen, *Children of the Mill: Schooling and Society in Gary, Indiana 1906–1960* (Bloomington: Indiana University Press, 1990), 157–209; David Tyack and Elisabeth Hansot, *Managers of Virtue: Public School Leadership in America, 1820–1980* (New York: Basic Books, 1982), 218–20; Julia Wrigley, *Class Politics and Public Schools: Chicago, 1900–1950* (New Brunswick, NJ: Rutgers University Press, 1982), 233–60.

3. The *Forbes* article is quoted in Alan Clive, *State of War: Michigan in World War II* (Ann Arbor: University of Michigan Press, 1979), 2.

4. Campbell is quoted in *The Detroiter*, 3/5/45; Clive, *State of War*, 36, 94; Richard Polenberg, *War and Society: The United States, 1941–45* (New York: J. B. Lippincott, 1972), 139; John Morton Blum, *V Was For Victory* (New York: Harcourt Brace Jovanovich, 1976), 93; *The Detroiter*, 6/21/45 and 3/19/50; Sidney Glazer, *Detroit: A Study in Urban Development* (New York: Bookman, 1965), 129.

5. U.S. Department of Commerce, Bureau of the Census, *Sixteenth Census of the United States: 1940, Population, Characteristics of the Population* (Washington, DC: U.S. Government Printing Office, 1943), 2:116; U.S. Department of Commerce, Bureau of the Census, *Seventeenth Census of the United States: 1950, Characteristics of the Population* (Washington, DC: U.S. Government Printing Office, 1953), 2: pt.1, 1–140; City of Detroit Mayor's Interracial Committee, "Distribution of Negro Population in Detroit," *Detroit Focus*, May–June, 1952, 1–3, in MFT Papers, box 2, Detroit Private Organizations folder; see also Dominic J. Capeci, Jr., *Race Relations in Wartime Detroit: The Sojourner Truth Housing Controversy of 1942* (Philadelphia: Temple University Press, 1984), 9–12; Clive, *State of War*, 133–34.

6. Between 1940 and 1950, several suburbs in the metropolitan area soared in population— Allen Park jumped from 3,487 to 12,293, Dearborn from 63,584 to 94,529, Inkster from 7,044

to 16,684, Lincoln Park from 15,236 to 29,265, and Royal Oak from 25,087 to 46,817. *The Detroiter*, 3/19/51; U.S. Department of Commerce, Bureau of the Census, *Statistical Abstract of the United States, 1955* (Washington, DC: U.S. Government Printing Office, 1955), 18, 20.

7. *The Social Secretary of Detroit, 1930* (Detroit: The Social Secretary, 1930); *The Social Secretary of Detroit, 1940* (Detroit: The Social Secretary, 1940); *The Social Secretary of Detroit, 1950* (Detroit: The Social Secretary, 1950); *Detroit News*, 8/31/48, in DNLB Scrapbook, 1948.

8. *Detroit Labor News*, 2/23/40.

9. Steve Babson, Ron Alpern, Dave Elsila, and John Rivitte, *Working Detroit: The Making of a Union Town* (New York: Adama Books, 1985), 103–10; Blum, *V Was For Victory*, 140; Clive, *State of War*, 56–58, 70–71, 86, 89–91; Robert Conot, *American Odyssey: A Unique History of America Told through the Life of a Great City* (New York: William Morrow, 1974), 468–78; Polenberg, *War and Society*, 155.

10. The Campbell quote is from *The Detroiter*, 3/2/42. Such antiunion sentiments can be found in almost every issue of *The Detroiter* during the war years. Some particularly notable examples can be found in *The Detroiter*, 11/3/41, 2/16/42, 8/3/42, 5/17/43, 5/24/43, 6/7/43, 6/14/43, 6/21/43, 7/12/43, 9/20/43, 10/18/43, 11/8/43, 12/13/43, 1/3/44, 1/29/45. *Detroit Labor News*, 1/29/43.

11. The most comprehensive study of the Sojourner Truth controversy is Capeci, *Race Relations*. See also Blum, *V Was for Victory*, 200–202; Clive, *State of War*, 144–50; Conot, *American Odyssey*, 478–82. The *Life* article is quoted in Clive, *State of War*, 156.

12. Blum, *V Was for Victory*, 202–4; Clive, *State of War*, 157–61; Conot, *American Odyssey*, 482–98; Polenberg, *War and Society*, 127–28.

13. August Meier and Elliott Rudwick, *Black Detroit and the Rise of the UAW* (New York: Oxford University Press, 1979), 175, 176–206; Robert Korstad and Nelson Lichtenstein, "Opportunities Found and Lost: Labor, Radicals and the Early Civil Rights Movement," *Journal of American History* 75 (December, 1988): 793. On the role of organized labor, particularly the UAW, in Detroit politics, see J. David Greenstone, *Labor in American Politics* (Chicago: University of Chicago Press, 1977), 110–40.

14. Kandel notes this trend nationally in Isaac L. Kandel, *The Impact of the War Upon American Education* (Chapel Hill: University of North Carolina Press, 1948), 6.

15. *Detroit News*, 12/26/41, in DNLB Scrapbook, 1941.

16. Earl L. Bedell and Walter E. Gleason, "Detroit Public Schools in the War Effort," *Industrial Arts and Vocational Education* 32 (March, 1943): 86.

17. DBEP, 1940–41, 276; DBEP, 1942–43, 166–67; DBEP, 1944–45, 2; DBEP, 1945–46, 4; Detroit Board of Education, *Detroit Public Schools and the War* (Detroit: Board of Education, 1942); Detroit Board of Education, *Superintendent's Annual Report, 1943–44* (Detroit: Board of Education, 1944), vi, 2, 6; Detroit Public Schools Staff, *Frank Cody: A Realist in Education* (New York: Macmillan, 1943), 512–13; Stanley E. Dimond, "Meeting the Threats to Democracy," *Library Journal* 66 (February 1, 1941): 120–22; Eleanor Skimin, "Better Teaching for Better Wartime Service," *Journal of Business Education* 18 (March, 1943), 7–9; *Detroit Education News*, 9/6/40, 2/19/41, 9/17/41, 12/17/41, 9/3/43; *Detroit Free Press*, 9/6/42 and 10/1/42, in Warren Bow Scrapbook, University Archives, Walter P. Reuther Library, Wayne State University, Detroit, MI; *Detroit News*, 9/4/42, 9/6/42, 9/12/42, in Warren Bow Scrapbook; *Detroit Times*, 9/10/42, in Warren Bow Scrapbook.

18. Clive, *State of War*, 206. Campbell is quoted in *The Detroiter*, 9/8/42.

19. Bedell and Gleason, "Detroit Schools," 86. See also *Detroit Times*, 9/9/42 and 10/2/42; *Detroit Free Press*, 10/2/42, in Warren Bow Scrapbook.

20. Earl L. Bedell, Walter E. Gleason, and Herman G. Schumacher, "Vocational Education for National Defense in Detroit," *Industrial Arts and Vocational Education* 31 (March, 1942): 88–90; Bedell and Gleason, "Detroit Schools," 85–88; Earl L. Bedell, "Training Women for

Wartime Industries," *Industrial Arts and Vocational Education* 32 (January, 1943): 1–4; Earl L. Bedell, "Summer Employment for Industrial Education Teachers in Essential War Industries," *Industrial Arts and Vocational Education* 32 (May, 1943): 185–86; Ernest Marshall, "Detroit Schools Train War Workers," *Michigan Chronicle*, 12/12/42.

21. *Detroit Labor News*, 9/18/42; Public Schools Staff, *Frank Cody*, 513; see also *Detroit Education News*, 1/14/42.

22. *Detroit Education News*, 5/6/42; *Detroit Free Press*, 6/22/42, in Public Schools Staff, *Frank Cody*, v; *Detroit News*, 7/3/42; *The Detroiter*, 6/8/42, 6/29/42, 7/6/42, 3/27/44; *DTA News*, 10/22/42 (special edition).

23. DBEP, 1942–43, 2; Detroit Board of Education, *Superintendent's Annual Report, 1938–39* (Detroit: Board of Education, 1939), 196; Detroit Board of Education, *Superintendent's Annual Report, 1954–55* (Detroit: Board of Education, 1955), 4; Detroit Public Schools, Department of Administrative Research, "Tables and Procedures Used in Estimating Future Enrollments for the Detroit Public Schools" [typescript, October 10, 1955], in RGR Papers, box 9; Detroit Public Schools, *Directory and By-Laws, 1952–53* (Detroit: Board of Education, 1952), 122.

24. Detroit Board of Education, *Seventy-fourth and Seventy-fifth Annual Reports, 1917–18* (Detroit: Board of Education, 1918), 190; Detroit Board of Education, *Seventy-eighth Annual Report, 1920–21* (Detroit: Board of Education, 1921), 7; Detroit Board of Education, *Eighty-seventh Annual Report, 1929–30* (Detroit: Board of Education, 1930), 227; Board of Education, *Annual Report, 1938–39*, 191; Detroit Board of Education, *Superintendent's Annual Report, 1949–50* (Detroit: Board of Education, 1950), 31; Detroit Board of Education, "Budget Allocations, 1938–39 to 1944–45" [March 20, 1945], in DFT Papers, box 4, Finances 1941–47 folder.

25. J. V. Butler, letter to the Detroit Board of Education, 11/28/39 with a petition signed by 908 people; N. Sussex, letter to Edward J. Jeffries, Jr., 11/16/40 with a petition signed by approximately 800 people; both in DM Papers, 1940, box 11, Board of Education folder.

26. Detroit Board of Education, Department of Administrative Research, "Consumer Price Index" [August 24, 1950], in LFO Papers, box 18, 1950–53 folder. A summary of the depression era salary cuts and the restoration of those cuts can be found in *Detroit Education News*, 10/15/41.

27. Board of Education, *Annual Report, 1954–55*, 24; Detroit Federation of Teachers, "Cost of Living" [typescript, March, 1942], 4–5; *Detroit Teacher*, September, 1942, January, 1944, March, 1944.

28. Hampel, *Last Little Citadel*, 30.

29. *Detroit Free Press*, 2/24/40 and 2/25/40; *Detroit Labor News*, 2/23/40, 3/1/40, 7/5/40; *Detroit News*, 2/18/40, 2/25/40, 3/1/40; Tracy M. Doll, letter to Edward J. Jeffries, Jr., 2/29/40, in DFT Papers [inventoried 10/30/85], box 5, Wagner-Labor folder. On retrenchment in other cities, see *Detroit Education News*, 10/23/40, 4/30/41, 5/14/41.

30. DBEP, 1941–42, 251–52, 261, 284; *Detroit Education News*, 10/29/41, 11/12/41, 1/14/42; *Detroit News*, 10/16/41; *Detroit Teacher*, November, 1941, January, 1942; Frances Comfort, letter to John Webster, 1/10/42, in DFT Papers [inventoried 1/14/86], box 2, Bureau of Governmental Research, 1942–46 folder; Detroit Bureau of Governmental Research, "Just a Minute" (January 5, 1942), in DFT Papers [inventoried 1/14/86], box 2, Bureau of Governmental Research, 1942–46 folder; F. B. Wittick, letter to Edward J. Jeffries, Jr., 2/9/42, in DM Papers, 1941, box 2, Budget folder; Builders Association of Northwest Detroit, letter to Edward J. Jeffries, Jr., 3/6/41, in DM Papers, 1941, box 2, Budget folder; Northeast Kiwanis Club, letter to Edward J. Jeffries, Jr., 3/26/41, in DM Papers, 1941, box 2, Budget folder.

31. DBEP, 1942–43, 273, 366–67; *Detroit Education News*, 3/19/43, 4/9/43, 9/10/43; *Detroit News*, 3/2/43 and 3/4/43; *Detroit Labor News*, 3/5/43; *Detroit Teacher*, April, 1943, September, 1943, November 23, 1945; Anna May Muffoletto, "Detroit Public School Teachers'

Unions: Organization, Operation, and Activities" (M.A. thesis, University of Detroit, 1958), 112. Bow was quoted in *Detroit Teacher,* April, 1943.

32. Building Owners and Managers Association et al., letter to Edward J. Jeffries, Jr., 2/8/44, in DM Papers, 1944, box 1, Budget folder; DBEP, 1944–45, 422, 473; *Detroit Education News,* 12/17/43; *Detroit Teacher,* January, 1944, February, 1944, March, 1944, April, 1944; Frances Comfort, "Budget Hearing With the Mayor," *Detroit Teacher,* March, 1944, 8; Frances Comfort, "Mayor Cuts the Budget," *Detroit Teacher,* April, 1944, 6; *Detroit Free Press,* 3/2/44, in DFT papers [inventoried 1/30/85], box 5, AFT folder; *Detroit Labor News,* 3/24/44; D. V. Addy [Budget Director, City of Detroit], letter to the Common Council, 3/29/44, in DM Papers, 1944, box 1, Budget folder; Detroit Board of Education, "Pertinent Facts Relative to the Proposed Increase in Millage, Election of April 4th" [March, 1949], 29, in DFT Papers [inventoried 1/20/83], box 1, Millage and Governmental Aid folder; U.S. Department of Commerce, Bureau of the Census, *Historical Statistics of the United States: Colonial Times to 1970* (Washington, DC: U.S. Government Printing Office, 1975), pt. 1, 166.

33. Mayor Jeffries estimated that the city had deferred $437 million of necessary construction during the depression and the war and claimed the city needed $62 million for new sewers alone. Conot, *American Odyssey,* 504; *Detroit News,* 2/8/45; *The Detroiter,* 2/19/45, 2/26/45, 4/16/45.

34. DBEP, 1945–46, 256–58; DBEP, 1946–47, 195; *Detroit Teacher,* 4/13/45; Board of Education, "Pertinent Facts," 29; U.S. Department of Commerce, Bureau of the Census, *Historical Statistics,* pt. 1, 166.

35. For some examples of these petitions for new schools, see DBEP, 1940–41, 234, 271; DBEP, 1942–43, 2; DBEP, 1944–45, 617, 671; DBEP, 1945–46, 2, 153, 166; DBEP, 1946–47, 192, 302; *Detroit Free Press,* 8/5/42; *Detroit News,* 8/5/42, 8/31/46, 9/1/46, 9/9/46; Turner Parents' Club, letter to the Detroit Board of Education, 5/31/45, in DM Papers, 1945, box 3, Education folder; Abe Schmier, letter to A. D. Jamieson, 7/3/46, in DM Papers, 1946, box 1, Board of Education folder.

36. *Detroit News,* 2/8/45, in DNLB Scrapbook, 1945; DBEP, 1945–46, 283–84.

37. Detroit Federation of Teachers, letter to Mayor Edwards, the Board of Education, and Deputy Superintendent Thomas, 2/20/40, in DFT Papers [inventoried 1/14/86], box 2, Miscellaneous 1940–43 folder; Irvine Kerrison, "You and Your Schools," *Detroit Labor News,* 3/29/46.

38. *Detroit Teacher,* 2/19/45.

39. On Bow's death, see *Detroit Times,* 5/12/45. Arthur Dondineau joined the school system in 1921 as supervisor of social studies after serving as a school principal and superintendent in several outstate districts. He received his B.A. and M.A. from the University of Michigan. He co-authored, with J. B. Edmundson, dean of Michigan's School of Education, several widely used civics textbooks. See Donald Disbrow, *Schools for an Urban Society* (Lansing: Michigan Historical Commission, 1968), 238; *Detroit Schools,* 12/3/68.

40. In April, 1944, for example, the DFT blasted Dondineau for declaring that he was "satisfied" with the school budget from which the mayor and council had slashed almost every funding increase the board had requested. The DFT assumed that Dondineau had sold out to the business leaders. Comfort, "Mayor Cuts Budget," 6; Robert G. Foster, letter to Arthur Dondineau, 9/19/45, in DFT Papers [inventoried 10/30/85], box 4, Foster Campaign 1945 folder. On Dondineau's good relationship with business leaders, see *The Detroiter,* 9/24/45; *Detroit News,* 9/12/45.

41. Comfort is quoted in *Detroit Teacher,* 1/14/46; see also *Detroit Teacher,* 11/12/45, 12/3/45, 2/11/46.

42. *Civic Searchlight* was quoted in *Detroit Teacher,* 3/7/46; see also Irvine Kerrison, "You and Your Schools," *Detroit Labor News,* 3/1/46. Rankin is quoted in *The Detroiter,* 2/11/46.

43. Bondholders Management, Inc. et al., letter to Edward J. Jeffries, Jr., 4/12/46, 3, in DM Papers, 1946, box 1, Budget folder.

44. *Detroit Teacher,* 3/7/46.

45. Detroit Federation of Teachers, "Let's Finish the Job!" [poster, 12/13/45], in DFT Scrapbook, 1945–46; *Detroit Free Press,* 1/18/46, 2/21/46, 2/24/46, 2/28/46; *Detroit News,* 1/22/46, 1/24/46, 2/6/46, 2/27/46; *Detroit Labor News,* 12/14/45; DBEP, 1945–46, 276, 356.

46. *Detroit Teacher,* 4/15/46 and 6/14/46.

47. Board of Education, "Pertinent Facts," 29; U.S. Department of Commerce, Bureau of the Census, *Historical Statistics,* pt. 1, 166.

48. DBEP, 1945–46, 384–85, 453, 456, 459; *Detroit Labor News,* 3/1/46; Robert G. Foster [president of the Better Schools Association], letter to the Common Council, 3/19/46, in DM Papers, 1946, box 1, Board of Education folder.

49. *Detroit Teacher,* 4/5/46; *Detroit News,* 3/24/49.

50. DBEP, 1946–47, 194–95; *Detroit News,* 10/23/46 and 11/8/46, in DNLB Scrapbook, 1946.

51. *Detroit Labor News,* 2/26/40; *Detroit News,* 2/4/40, 12/25/40, 4/5/41, 2/7/42, 4/7/43; *Michigan Education Journal,* December, 1940; Michigan Federation of Labor, "Resolutions Adopted by the Convention of the Michigan Federation of Labor, Port Huron, February 1942," in MFT Papers, box 5, Convention folder; *Detroit Teacher,* April, 1942; *Michigan Taxpayer,* 12/10/40, in AE Papers, box 17, Tax Dodgers folder; Arthur Elder, letter to Mrs. Louis Bass, 2/28/44, in AE Papers, box 17, Tax Dodgers folder.

52. Clive, *State of War,* 117; Disbrow, *Schools for an Urban Society,* 147–57.

53. *Detroit News,* 8/29/47 and 10/31/47, in DNLB Scrapbook, 1947.

54. *Detroit News,* 8/14/43, in DNLB Scrapbook, 1943; J. Alan Thomas, *School Finance and Educational Opportunity in Michigan* (Lansing, MI: Michigan Department of Education, 1968), 304.

55. Stanley A. Burns, "Sales Tax Fight Laid to Rural-City Feuds," *Detroit News,* 10/30/46, in DFT Papers, DFT Scrapbook, 1946–47. See also Michigan Council for Representative Government, "Are All Persons Considered Equal?" [1942], in AE Papers, box 11, Michigan Council for Representative Government—July 1942 folder; Michigan League of Women Voters, "What is Re-Apportionment?" (leaflet, May, 1942) in AE Papers, box 11, Michigan Council for Representative Government, August to December, 1942 folder.

56. *Detroit Free Press,* 3/31/42 and 4/24/42, in DFT Papers, Detroit Federation of Teachers Reapportionment Scrapbook. In demanding reapportionment, Detroit's school leaders pointed out that, in 1941, the city educated about 25 percent of the children in the state and that the city paid between 40 and 50 percent of all the taxes collected in the state (DBEP, 1940–41, 258–60).

57. "A Meeting in the Interest of Representative Government in Michigan" (mimeo, 11/1/41), in MFT Papers, box 2, Michigan Council for Representative Government—1941 folder; E. R. Butler [assistant director of administrative research, Detroit Public Schools], letter to Mrs. Edward Bryant [Michigan Council for Representative Government], 5/18/42, in AE Papers, box 11, Michigan Council for Representative Government—1941–43 folder; *Detroit Education News,* 4/15/42 and 5/27/42; *Detroit Free Press,* 3/25/42, 6/7/42, 6/14/42, 7/4/42, in DFT Papers, Detroit Federation of Teachers Reapportionment Scrapbook; *Detroit News,* 11/2/41, 3/8/42, 5/24/42, 7/7/42, 7/5/42, in DFT Papers, Detroit Federation of Teachers Reapportionment Scrapbook; *Detroit Labor News,* 4/24/42 and 5/22/42, in DFT Papers, Detroit Federation of Teachers Reapportionment Scrapbook; *Flint Review,* 4/24/42, in DFT Papers, Detroit Federation of Teachers Reapportionment Scrapbook.

58. *Detroit News,* 3/26/43, 4/5/43, 4/16/43, 4/16/43, 4/22/43, 4/30/43, 9/9/43, 2/25/44, 10/30/46, in DNLB Scrapbook, 1943, 1944, 1946; *Detroit Teacher,* 1/12/45.

59. Detroit Federation of Teachers, Executive Board Minutes, 3/8/48, in DFT Papers; *Michigan CIO News*, 4/21/49, in MFT Papers, box 1, CIO folder; *Detroit News*, 4/2/48, 4/11/48, 9/11/48, 3/21/49, 3/23/49, 5/21/49, in DNLB Scrapbook, 1948, 1949.

60. *Detroit News*, 6/1/40, 1/8/41, 4/10/41, 2/13/43, 3/25/43, 3/29/45, 4/10/45, 4/24/45, 4/27/45, in DNLB Scrapbook, 1940, 1941, 1943, 1945; *Detroit News*, 3/4/43; *Detroit Labor News*, 8/18/44.

61. *Detroit News*, 1/23/46, in DNLB Scrapbook, 1946.

62. *Detroit News*, 6/1/40, 2/13/43, 3/25/43, in DNLB Scrapbook, 1940, 1943; *Detroit Teacher*, March, 1944; Disbrow, *Schools in an Urban Society*, 126.

63. *Detroit News*, 6/9/45, in DNLB Scrapbook, 1945.

64. Michigan Department of Public Instruction, *Ninety-eighth Biennial Report, 1944–46* (Lansing: Department of Public Instruction, 1946), 195; Michigan Department of Public Instruction, *One Hundred and Seventh Biennial Report, 1962–64* (Lansing: Department of Public Instruction, 1965), 136; Detroit Board of Education, *Superintendent's Annual Report, 1939–40* (Detroit: Board of Education, 1940), 116; U.S. Department of Commerce, Bureau of the Census, *Historical Statistics*, pt. 1, 166.

65. Disbrow, *Schools for an Urban Society*, 126–29.

66. Burns, "Sales Tax Fight."

67. *Detroit Times*, 8/10/46, in DFT Scrapbook, 1946–47; *Detroit News*, 8/16/46, 10/8/46, 10/23/46, in DNLB Scrapbook, 1946.

68. *Detroit Free Press*, 1/4/46; *Detroit News*, 8/7/46, 9/27/46, 10/10/46, 10/12/46, 10/16/46, 10/19/46, 10/20/46, 10/22/46, 10/24/46, in DNLB Scrapbook, 1946; *Detroit News*, 9/23/46, 10/8/46, 10/27/46, in DFT Scrapbook, 1946–47; *Detroit Labor News*, 10/25/46.

69. *Detroit News*, 11/4/46; Disbrow, *Schools for an Urban Society*, 126.

70. DBEP, 1946–47, 463; DBEP, 1947–48, 318–20; *Detroit News*, 4/8/47 and 7/20/47, in DNLB Scrapbook, 1947. See also Disbrow, *Schools for an Urban Society*, 127–28; DBEP, 1948–49, 109; Detroit Federation of Teachers, "Notes from Past Papers" (undated typescript), 7, in DFT Papers [inventoried 1/20/83], box 10, DFT 25th Anniversary folder.

71. *Michigan Chronicle*, 10/30/48; *Michigan CIO News*, 10/20/48; *Detroit News*, 10/16/48, 10/17/48, 10/30/48, in DNLB Scrapbook, 1948.

72. *Detroit News*, 5/21/47, 5/23/47, 6/7/47, 6/8/48, 9/29/48, 10/9/48, 10/12/48, 10/2/48, in DNLB Scrapbook, 1947, 1948.

73. Disbrow, *Schools for an Urban Society*, 128; *Detroit News*, 11/3/48 and 11/6/48, in DNLB Scrapbook, 1948.

74. Disbrow, *Schools for an Urban Society*, 127–28; DBEP, 1948–49, 109; Detroit Federation of Teachers, "Notes from Past Papers."

75. DBEP, 1940–41, 274, 310. Bow is quoted in *Detroit Teacher*, October, 1942.

76. The membership figures in DFT are based on the number of members reported to the AFT for determining delegates at the national conference ("American Federation of Teachers Convention Roll Calls, 1939, 1941," American Federation of Teachers Papers, ser. 13, boxes 13 and 16, Convention Roll Call folders, in ALHUA). For evidence of the continuing role of leftists in the union, see John W. Studebaker, letter to Elinor Laffrey, 3/18/42, in MFT Papers, box 6, MFT Education within the Organization folder; Detroit Federation of Teachers, Executive Board Minutes, [June 13,] 1949; author interview with Florence Sweeney and Helen Bowers, 7/30/83, Detroit.

77. William Eaton, *The American Federation of Teachers, 1916–1961* (Carbondale: Southern Illinois University Press, 1975), 99–108; Thomas R. Brooks, "Teachers Divided: Teacher Unionism in New York City, 1935–40" in *Educating an Urban People: The New York City Experience*, ed. Diane Ravitch and Ronald Goodnow (New York: Teachers College Press, 1981), 206–18; Laura D. Muraskin, "The Interests of the Teachers Union, 1913–35," in *Educating an*

Urban People: The New York City Experience, ed. Diane Ravitch and Ronald Goodnow (New York: Teachers College Press, 1981), 219–30.

78. Eaton, *American Federation of Teachers*, 106–9, 114; Sweeney and Bowers interview.

79. Eaton, *American Federation of Teachers*, 112–21; Charles W. Miller, "Democracy in Education: A Study of How the American Federation of Teachers Met the Threat of Communist Subversion Through the Democratic Process" (Ed.D. diss., Northwestern University, 1967), 96, 99–100, 126–27; "American Federation of Teachers 1940 Convention Proceedings," American Federation of Teachers, ser. 13, box 14, 254, 546; Sweeney and Bowers interview. A superb collection of materials on the expulsion of the communist-dominated locals can be found in DFT Papers [inventoried 1/14/86], Helen Bowers Files, box 1, Expulsion folder; *Detroit News*, 8/22/ 41 and 8/27/41 in AE Papers, box 2, 1941 Convention folder; *Detroit Times*, 8/28/41, in AE Papers, box 2, 1941 Convention folder; *Detroit Free Press*, 8/23/41, in AE Papers, box 2, 1941 Convention folder; *Detroit Labor News*, 8/22/41 and 9/15/41.

80. Eaton, *American Federation of Teachers*, 122–52; Robert Braun, *Teachers and Power: The Story of the American Federation of Teachers* (New York: Simon and Schuster, 1972), 50–59.

81. Detroit Federation of Teachers, "An Organizing Drive Among Teachers" (typescript, [1942]) in DFT Papers [inventoried 1/14/86], box 3, Miscellaneous Correspondence folder; *Detroit Labor News*, 1/7/44; *Detroit Teacher*, October, 1941, November, 1941, May, 1943, February, 1944; "American Federation of Teachers Convention Roll Call 1944," in American Federation of Teachers Papers, ser. 13, box 20, Convention Roll Call folder; Orin-Jane Bragg Gardner, "A Study of the Role of the Teacher in the Evolution of Administrative Personnel Policy in the Detroit Public Schools" (Ed.D. diss., Wayne State University, 1965), 117–45, 157–83.

82. An excellent file on the struggle for the single salary schedule can be found in DFT Papers [inventoried 1/14/86], box 3, Single Salary Schedule, 1941–43 folder; on the other issues, see Detroit Federation of Teachers, "Notes from Past Papers" (typescript, [ca. 1956]), in DFT Papers [inventoried 1/20/83], box 10, DFT 25th Anniversary folder; *Detroit Teacher*, January, 1942, September, 1943; DBEP, 1942–43, 78, 112, 209; DBEP, 1943–44, 98, 132.

83. DBEP, 1942–43, 481; DBEP, 1944–45, 425, 654–55; DBEP, 1945–46, 382–83, 423; DBEP, 1946–47, 284–85, 357; *Detroit Labor News*, 5/14/43, 10/8/43, 12/6/46, 1/10/47; *Detroit Teacher*, May, 1943.

84. *Detroit Labor News*, 1/21/44 and 6/9/44.

85. DBEP, 1943–44, 605, 639–40; *Detroit Free Press*, 9/4/46; *Detroit News*, 9/4/45, in DFT Papers, DFT Scrapbook, 1946–47; *Detroit Labor News*, 9/6/46.

86. *Detroit Labor News*, 2/14/41, 2/21/41, 2/28/41, 3/7/41, 4/11/41; *Detroit Teacher*, January, 1943. Brief biographical information on Brooks and Van Auken can be found in Herbert S. Case, ed., *Who's Who in Michigan, 1936* (Munising, MI: Who's Who in Michigan, 1936), 50, 325. Van Auken was listed in the Detroit social register, *Social Secretary, 1940*, 159.

87. *Detroit Labor News*, 2/14/43, 2/8/45, 3/23/45; *Detroit Teacher*, 2/19/45 and 3/16/45; Frances Comfort, letter to Tracy Doll, 11/14/44, in DFT Papers [inventoried 1/14/86], box 3, Miss Comfort, 1944–45 folder; Tracy Doll, letter to Frances Comfort, 11/17/44, in DFT Papers [inventoried 1/14/86], box 3, Miss Comfort, 1944–45 folder; author interview with Victor Reuther, Washington, DC, 4/21/87.

88. Florence Sweeney, "The President's Column," *Detroit Teacher*, September, 1941, 2; May Wolfe Reuther, 1963 Oral History Transcript, in ALHUA; Sweeney and Bowers interview; author interview with Renette Elder, Detroit, MI, 7/18/83.

89. *Detroit Free Press*, 6/1/45 and 9/12/45; DBEP, 1945–46, 127–31.

90. *Detroit Times*, 3/3/45, in Warren Bow Scrapbook; *Detroit Teacher*, 1/12/45, 1/14/46, 12/3/45, 2/11/46.

91. *Detroit Free Press,* 11/20/46, in DFT Papers, DFT Scrapbook, 1946–47.

92. Florence Sweeney, letter to the Detroit Board of Education, 11/23/46, in DFT Papers [inventoried 10/30/85], box 4, 1943–47 Correspondence to Officials folder.

93. *Detroit Free Press,* 11/13/46; *Detroit Times,* 11/13/46, in DFT Papers, DFT Scrapbook, 1946–47; *Detroit News,* 11/7/46; *Detroit Labor News,* 11/22/46.

94. *Detroit Free Press,* 11/20/46, in DFT Papers, DFT Scrapbook, 1946–47; *Detroit News,* 11/20/46, in DNLB Scrapbook, 1946.

95. *Detroit Free Press,* 11/27/46, in DFT Papers, DFT Scrapbook, 1946–47; *Detroit News,* 11/13/46, DFT Papers, DFT Scrapbook, 1946–47; *Detroit Times,* 11/24/46, in DFT Papers, DFT Scrapbook, 1946–47; *Detroit News,* 11/7/46, 11/24/46, 12/5/46, 12/12/46, in DNLB Scrapbook, 1946.

96. Sweeney is quoted in *Detroit Teacher,* 12/16/46. *Detroit News,* 12/11/46, in DFT Papers, DFT Scrapbook, 1946–47; *Detroit Times,* 12/11/46, in DFT Papers, DFT Scrapbook, 1946–47; DBEP, 1946–47, 282–84.

97. Detroit Federation of Teachers, Executive Board Minutes, November 26, 1946, January 13, 1947, February 13, 1947; Renette Elder, letter to Joseph Landis, in MFT Papers, box 7, 1946 Treasurers' folder; *Detroit Teacher,* 12/16/46. For an overview of the St. Paul strike, see Albert Schiff, "A Study and Evaluation of Teachers Strikes in the United States" (Ed. D. diss., Wayne [State] University, 1952), 127–82.

98. *Detroit Free Press,* 12/8/46, in DFT Papers, DFT Scrapbook, 1946–47.

99. *Detroit Free Press,* 12/10/46, 12/12/46, 12/20/46, in DFT Papers, DFT Scrapbook, 1946–47; the retail executive is quoted in *Detroit Free Press,* 12/8/46; the Chrysler executive is quoted in *Detroit Free Press,* 12/11/46; the businessman is quoted in *Detroit Free Press,* 12/9/46.

100. Allen B. Crow, "Must We Pay for Education Not Received?" *The Detroiter,* 4/19/48. In the wake of the salary controversy, Board of Commerce leader Harvey Campbell repeatedly criticized the shoddy "products" produced by the Detroit public schools. See, for example, Campbell's editorials in *The Detroiter,* 8/11/47, 2/6/48, 6/28/48, 7/28/48; Harvey Campbell, "Where is Detroit Going?" *The Detroiter,* 10/18/48.

101. *Detroit Free Press,* 11/14/46, 12/31/46, 1/9/47 in DFT Papers, DFT Scrapbook, 1946–47; *Detroit Teacher,* February, 1944, March, 1944; *Detroit Education News,* 1/14/44, 2/11/44, 2/25/44; Detroit Federation of Teachers, "Educational Policies as Garnered from the Area Conference Suggestions" (October, 1943), 4, in DFT Papers [inventoried 12/20/85], box 2, Building Representatives Meeting Notebook 9/47–10/51.

102. *Detroit Free Press,* 12/14/46, in DFT Papers, DFT Scrapbook, 1946–47; *Detroit News,* 12/22/46, in DFT Papers, DFT Scrapbook, 1946–47.

103. DBEP, 1946–47, 342–46.

104. DBEP, 1946–47, 332–34; *Detroit Teacher,* 2/6/47; a copy of the petition can be found in DFT Papers, DFT Scrapbook, 1946–47; Michigan Department of Public Instruction, *Ninety-ninth Biennial Report of the Superintendent of Public Instruction, 1946–48* (Lansing, MI: Department of Public Instruction, 1948), 108; "AFT Convention Roll Call, 1947," in American Federation of Teachers Papers, box 24, Convention Roll Call folder.

105. *Detroit Times* 1/9/47, in DFT Papers, DFT Scrapbook, 1946–47; see also *Detroit Labor News,* 1/10/47.

106. *Detroit Free Press,* 1/10/47, in DFT Papers, DFT Scrapbook, 1946–47; *Detroit Labor News,* 2/21/47.

107. DBEP, 1946–47, 357–58; *Detroit Labor News,* 1/17/47; see also *Detroit Free Press,* 11/15/47, in DFT Papers, DFT Scrapbook, 1946–47.

108. DFT Executive Board Minutes, 1945–47 (January 16, 1947); *Detroit Teacher,* 1/20/47; *Detroit Free Press,* 1/19/47 and 1/22/47, in DFT Papers, DFT Scrapbook, 1946–47; *Detroit Labor News,* 1/24/47; *Northwest Detroiter,* 1/23/47, in DFT Papers, DFT Scrapbook, 1946–47.

109. DBEP, 1946–47, 378–82; see also *Detroit News,* 1/29/47, in DFT Papers, DFT Scrapbook, 1946–47; *Detroit Times,* 1/29/47, in DFT Papers, DFT Scrapbook, 1946–47.

110. *Detroit Free Press,* 1/31/47, in DFT Papers, DFT Scrapbook, 1946–47; *Detroit News,* 1/31/47, in DFT Papers, DFT Scrapbook, 1946–47.

111. *Detroit Teacher,* 2/24/47; *Detroit News,* 1/30/47 and 2/8/47, in DFT Papers, DFT Scrapbook, 1946–47; *Detroit Times,* 1/30/47, in DFT Papers, DFT Scrapbook, 1946–47; *Detroit Labor News,* 1/31/47.

112. *Detroit Times,* 2/2/47, in DFT Papers, DFT Scrapbook, 1946–47.

113. *Detroit Free Press,* 2/3/47, in DFT Papers, DFT Scrapbook, 1946–47; *Detroit News,* 2/5/47, in DFT Papers, DFT Scrapbook, 1946–47.

114. About 90 percent of the union members said they would honor the picket lines and about 79 percent of the nonunion members said they would not cross the picket lines. Three prominent public officials, Common Council Member and labor leader Patrick V. McNamara, City Treasurer Albert Cobo, and City Clerk Thomas Leadbetter, counted the ballots (*Detroit Teacher,* 2/24/47).

115. *Detroit Free Press,* 2/19/47 and 2/28/47, in DFT Papers, DFT Scrapbook, 1946–47; *Detroit News,* 2/19/47, in DFT Papers, DFT Scrapbook, 1946–47; *Detroit Times,* 2/19/47, in DFT Papers, DFT Scrapbook, 1946–47; *Michigan Catholic,* 2/20/47, in DFT Papers, DFT Scrapbook, 1946–47; *Detroit Labor News,* 2/21/47; *Detroit Teacher,* 2/24/47; Muffoletto, "Detroit Public School Teachers," 141–42.

116. *Detroit Free Press,* 2/20/47, in DFT Papers, DFT Scrapbook, 1946–47; *Detroit Times,* 2/19/47, in DFT Papers, DFT Scrapbook, 1946–47; Detroit Teachers Association, "Let's Continue to Believe in the Public—Which Believes in Us!" (ca. February, 1947), in DFT Papers [inventoried 10/30/85], box 4, DTA folder; Eaton, *American Federation of Teachers,* 146–47.

117. *Detroit News,* 2/27/47, in DFT Papers, DFT Scrapbook, 1946–47; *Detroit Free Press,* 2/26/47, in DFT Papers, DFT Scrapbook, 1946–47; *Detroit Times,* 3/4/47, in DFT Papers, DFT Scrapbook, 1946–47; *Redford Record,* 2/27/47, in DFT Papers, DFT Scrapbook, 1946–47; Detroit Bureau of Governmental Research, "Teachers Salaries," *Bureau Notes,* 3/1/47; Detroit Bureau of Governmental Research, "Figuring Teacher Salaries," *Bureau Notes,* 3/8/47, in AE Papers, box 12, DFT Miscellaneous folder.

118. *Detroit Labor News,* 2/28/47; *Detroit News,* 3/1/47, in DFT Papers, DFT Scrapbook, 1946–47. Detroit, for example, was eleventh out of the thirteen largest cities in terms of maximum salaries. In addition, such suburbs as Ferndale, Gross Pointe, Lincoln Park, Melvindale, and River Rouge all had starting salaries higher than Detroit and several suburbs had higher maximum salaries. Muffoletto, "Detroit Public School Teachers," 122–23; Detroit Federation of Teachers, "A Sampling of City Employees' Salaries" (ca. March, 1947), in DFT Papers [inventoried 10/30/85], box 5, Financial Documents, 1946–47 folder; see also Gerald K. O'Brien, letter to Loren B. Miller ["An Open Letter to Bureau of Governmental Research"], 3/14/47, in AE Papers, box 12, DFT Miscellaneous folder; *Detroit Teacher,* 12/13/48.

119. *Detroit Free Press,* 3/6/46, in DFT Papers, DFT Scrapbook, 1946–47; *Detroit News,* 3/3/47 and 3/6/47, in DFT Papers, DFT Scrapbook, 1946–47; *Detroit Times,* 3/6/47, in DFT Papers, DFT Scrapbook, 1946–47; *Shoppers' Guide,* 3/6/47, in DFT Papers, DFT Scrapbook, 1946–47; *Detroit Labor News,* 3/7/47.

120. *Detroit Free Press,* 3/8/47, 3/10/47, 3/11/47, 3/12/47, in DFT Papers, DFT Scrapbook, 1946–47; *Detroit News,* 3/8/47, 3/11/47, 3/12/47, in DFT Papers, DFT Scrapbook, 1946–47; *Detroit Times,* 3/6/47, 3/7/47, 3/11/47, 3/15/47, in DFT Papers, DFT Scrapbook, 1946–47; *Detroit Labor News,* 3/7/47; *Detroit Teacher,* 3/31/47; DBEP, 1946–47, 473, 483–84.

121. *Detroit Free Press,* 3/19/47 and 3/21/47, in DFT Papers, DFT Scrapbook, 1946–47; *Detroit News,* 3/20/47, 3/21/47, 3/22/47, 3/23/47, in DFT Papers, DFT Scrapbook, 1946–47;

Detroit Times, 3/21/47, 3/22/47 in DFT Papers, DFT Scrapbook, 1946–47; *Detroit Labor News*, 3/28/47; *Detroit Teacher*, 3/31/47; DBEP, 1946–47, 487–88.

122. *Detroit Free Press*, 3/21/47, 3/29/47, 3/30/47, 4/1/47, in DFT Papers, DFT Scrapbook, 1946–47; *Detroit News*, 3/27/47, in DFT Papers, DFT Scrapbook, 1946–47; *Detroit Times*, 3/27/47 and 4/2/47, in DFT Papers, DFT Scrapbook, 1946–47; Home Owners and Tax Payers Co-Ordinating Committee, "You Have Only 4 Days in which to Act" [March, 1947], in AE Papers, box 12, DFT Miscellaneous folder; DFT Executive Board Minutes, 4/1/47.

123. *The Detroiter*, 3/10/47; *Detroit Free Press*, 3/30/47 and 4/4/47, in DFT Papers, DFT Scrapbook, 1946–47; *Detroit News*, 3/30/47, in DFT Papers, DFT Scrapbook, 1946–47; *Detroit Times*, 4/1/47, in DFT Papers, DFT Scrapbook, 1946–47.

124. Arthur Dondineau, letter to Edward J. Jeffries, Jr., 4/10/47, in DM Papers, 1947, box 2, Board of Education folder; *The Detroiter*, 5/26/47.

125. *Detroit News*, 4/22/47, 5/9/47, 5/13/47, 5/27/47, in DNLB Scrapbooks, 1947; *Detroit News*, 4/25/47, in DFT Papers, DFT Scrapbook, 1946–47; *Detroit Times*, 5/13/47, 1/14/47, 5/22/47, in DFT Papers, DFT Scrapbook, 1946–47; *Detroit Labor News*, 5/9/47, 5/16/47, 5/29/47, 6/6/47. For accounts of the East Detroit strike, see Schiff, "Teachers Strikes," 183–207; Florence Estes, "Detroit Teachers—A Selected History, 1920–1965" (seminar paper, Wayne State University, 1980).

126. *Detroit News*, 6/7/47, 6/12/47, 6/26/47, 7/1/47, 7/3/47, in DNLB Scrapbook, 1947. *Detroit Free Press*, 6/8/47, in DFT Papers, DFT Scrapbook, 1946–47; *Detroit News*, 6/4/47, in DFT Papers, DFT Scrapbook, 1946–47; *Detroit Times*, 6/3/47 and 6/4/47, in DFT Papers, DFT Scrapbook, 1946–47.

127. *Detroit Labor News*, 12/19/47, 4/2/48, 4/30/48, 7/9/48; *Detroit News*, 4/8/48; Detroit Bureau of Governmental Research, "Budget Backgrounds," 3/15/48, in DFT Papers [inventoried 2/18/82], box 2, DBGR 1948 folder; Florence Sweeney, letter to Meyer L. Prentis [vice president of the Detroit Bureau of Governmental Research], 4/22/48, DFT Papers [inventoried 2/18/82], box 2, DBGR 1948 folder; *The Detroiter*, 3/15/48; DFT Building Representatives Minutes, 4/26/48.

128. DBEP, 1942–43, 2; *Detroit Free Press*, 4/8/47, 10/1/47, 10/5/47, in DFT Papers, DFT Scrapbook, 1946–47; Detroit Public Schools, "Needs for New Buildings and Additions, Summary of Estimated Costs, 1947," in AE Papers, box 9, Better Schools Association folder, 1947–49; *Detroit Times*, 4/15/48.

129. DBEP, 1946–47, 676; DBEP, 1947–48, 1, 57, 204, 291–92; DBEP, 1948–49, 1, 49, 194, 214, 235, 380; see also College Woods—Southfield Court Civic Association, letter to Mayor Eugene Van Antwerp, 4/13/48, in DM Papers, 1948, box 1, Board of Education folder no. 1; Evergreen Village Civic Association, letter to Mayor Eugene Van Antwerp, 9/19/48, in DM Papers, 1948, box 1, Board of Education folder no. 1; Herman Gardens Community Council, "Report on the Inadequacy of the Herman Gardens School Facilities, 12/9/47" (typescript and graphics), DM Papers, 1948, box 1, Board of Education folder no. 1; *Detroit Times*, 4/13/48, 4/14/48, 4/15/48, 4/16/48, 4/17/48, 4/18/48, 4/19/48; Better Schools Association, "Citizens Questions Regarding Costs of Detroit School Buildings, September 27, 1949" in DUL Papers, box 42, DPS 1949–51 folder.

130. *Detroit News*, 1/12/49, 1/20/49, 1/21/49, 1/26/49, 2/26/49, in DNLB Scrapbook, 1949; *Detroit Teacher*, 1/17/49; DBEP, 1947–48, 355–56, 443, 500, 617–18; DBEP, 1948–49, 171–72, 177–78, 235, 243–44, 262, 276. Webster is quoted in DBEP, 1948–49, 310.

131. *Michigan Chronicle*, 4/14/56.

132. David M. Katzman, *Before the Ghetto: Black Detroit in the Nineteenth Century* (Urbana: University of Illinois Press, 1973), 22–25, 50, 84–90; see also Karl E. Taeuber, "Demographic Perspectives on Housing and School Segregation," *Wayne Law Review* 21 (March, 1975): 843–44.

133. Other historians, such as Michael Homel and Joel Perlmann, have also found northern school districts such as Cleveland, Chicago, New York, and Providence fairly well integrated prior to the 1930s. See Detroit Public Schools, Bureau of Statistics and Research, "Age-Grade and Nationality Survey," *Detroit Educational Bulletin*, Research Bulletin no. 7 (January, 1922): 21–24; Mayor's Inter-Racial Committee, *The Negro in Detroit: Section VII, Education* (Detroit: The Committee, 1926), 2–9; Michael Homel, *Down from Equality: Black Chicagoans and the Public Schools, 1920–41* (Urbana: University of Illinois Press, 1984), x, 6–7, 27, 88–89; Michael Homel, "Two Worlds of Race? Urban Blacks and the Public Schools, North and South, 1865–1940," in *Southern Cities, Southern Schools: Public Education in the Urban South*, ed. David N. Plank and Rick Ginsburg (New York: Greenwood Press, 1990), 240–44; Joel Perlmann, *Ethnic Differences: Schooling and Social Structure among Irish, Italians, Jews and Blacks in an American City, 1880–1935* (New York: Cambridge University Press, 1988), 182, 178–81, 298–99.

134. Mayor's Inter-Racial Committee, *The Negro in Detroit*, 17–20; Detroit Common Council, *Journal of the Common Council, 1932* (Detroit: City of Detroit, 1932), 505; *Detroit Tribune*, 6/27/33.

135. Snow Grigsby, 1967 Oral History, in ALHUA; *Detroit Tribune*, 2/10/34, 2/24/34, 6/16/34, 6/30/34; *Detroit Labor News*, 2/9/40; DBEP, 1933–34, 311, 316. For a detailed account of the hirings of Cofer, Loving, and other black high school educators in Detroit, see Cloyzelle K. Jones, "The Historify of Sidney D. Miller High School with Particular Exploration into those Factors which Resulted in the Inordinately High Incidences of Pupil Successes Considering, and Despite, Existing Socio-Economic Factors which Are Perceived as Being Prime Predictors of High Incidences of Pupil Failure, 1919–1957" (Ed.D. diss., Wayne State University, 1970), 46–66, 230–66; see also *Detroit Tribune*, 8/25/34; *Michigan Chronicle*, 11/8/47.

136. *Detroit Tribune*, 6/16/34, 6/30/34, 1/26/35, 2/2/35, 2/9/35, 4/16/38. In his book on Chicago and in a recent essay, Michael Homel notes a similar pattern in which integrated schools in the 1920s became segregated in the 1930s in other northern, industrial cities such as Cleveland, Chicago, and New York. See Homel, *Down from Equality*, x, 6–7, 27, 88–89; Homel, "Two Worlds of Race," 240–44; Cohen, *Children of the Mill*, 92–100, 146–51.

137. Alfred E. Kauffman, *A Story of Miller* (Detroit: Sidney D. Miller High School, 1938), 12–14, 26–30. By far the best study of Miller High School, based on extensive interviews with teachers and former students, is Jones, "Historify of Miller," 18–48.

138. *Detroit Tribune*, 1/18/41, 2/8/41, 2/16/46, 3/9/46, 2/8/47, 3/12/49; *Michigan Chronicle*, 2/9/46, 9/21/46, 1/25/47, 2/1/47, 2/22/47, 1/22/49, 2/5/49, 2/12/49; DBEP, 1945–46, 384, 427–28; DBEP, 1946–47, 371; Snow F. Grigsby, *Taps or Reveille—?* (Detroit: Snow F. Grigsby, 1956), 44–46.

139. Daly had been principal of the Garfield Intermediate School, which, by the late 1930s, was about 80 percent black. At Garfield, Daly introduced what today would be called black studies into the basic curriculum of the school. See Charles A. Daly, "Racial Enrichment of the Curriculum," *Journal of the National Education Association* 27 (November, 1938): 235–36.

140. A 1970 survey of 373 students who had attended Miller in the 1940s and 1950s found that more than 78 percent believed that school counselors had steered them toward white-collar, skilled white-collar, or professional careers (Jones, "Historify of Miller," 62, 87, 103, 115, 133–53, 217, 224, 258–60, 352–54, 360–61); see also *Michigan Chronicle*, 2/1/47.

141. Other locally prominent Miller graduates include Melvin Chapman, a top administrator in the Detroit schools; Zeline Richards, a leader of the DFT and later New Detroit, Inc.; and Conrad Mallett, a prominent figure in the Cavanagh administration. Jones, "The Historify of Miller," 117, 133, 136, 138, 140, 142, 144, 146, 148, 151, 154, 166–70, 187, 350, 355–56; Conot, *American Odyssey*, 502, 645–46. Coleman Young attended Miller but ultimately graduated from Eastern High School (*Detroit Free Press*, 8/8/73, in Coleman Young Biography File,

vertical file, in ALHUA). Miller was not the only Detroit high school with an exceptional music program. As Gerald Early notes, the music program of the Detroit public schools helped train an astonishing number of successful black groups and performers. These included not only major jazz figures but also the best of Motown. Early points out, for example, that Smokey Robinson and the Miracles, the Supremes, and the Temptations all "were put together and rehearsed at their local high schools." Early contends that "Motown could not have happened without a strong public school music education program in Detroit, even if many of its performers were musically illiterate. Its session musicians, its arrangers, and often its producers were musically literate, and nearly all of them were trained in the public schools" (Gerald Early, "One Nation Under A Groove," *New Republic*, July 15–22, 1991, 36–37).

142. *Detroit Free Press*, 2/28/40; *Detroit News*, 2/29/40; *Detroit News*, 11/27/43, in DNLB Scrapbook, 1943; *Detroit Tribune*, 3/2/40, 3/9/40, 7/26/41, 8/30/41, 9/20/41, 4/4/42, 12/4/43; *Michigan Chronicle*, 3/2/40; Capeci, *Race Relations*, 21–22; Jones, "Historify of Miller," 56–57; DBEP, 1941–42, 70.

143. "The Administrative Committee on Inter-cultural and Inter-racial Education to All Detroit School Principals," 11/2/43, in Detroit Commission on Community Relations Papers, ser. 1, box 17, Board of Education Inter-cultural Program, 1943 folder, in ALHUA. Earl Brown, "The Truth about the Detroit Riot," *Harpers*, November, 1943, 498; Harold J. Harrison, "A Study of the Work of the Coordinating Committee on Democratic Human Relations in the Detroit Public Schools from September, 1943, to June, 1952" (Ed.D. diss., Wayne [State] University, 1953), 28–29.

144. DBEP, 1943–44, 131, 605; DBEP, 1944–45, 316–17; *Michigan Chronicle*, 10/23/43, 11/6/43, 1/29/44, 1/20/45; *Detroit Tribune*, 11/27/43, 1/8/44, 2/5/44, 2/19/44, 11/19/46; *Detroit Teacher*, February, 1944; *Detroit Education News*, 2/11/44; The Administrative Committee on Inter-cultural and Inter-racial Education, "Progress Report on Inter-cultural and Inter-racial Education in the Detroit Public Schools, August 1, 1944," in Detroit Commission on Community Relations Papers, ser. 1, box 1, Board of Education Inter-cultural Program, 1944 folder; The Administrative Committee on Inter-cultural Education, "Progress Report on Inter-cultural Education in the Detroit Public Schools, 1944–45," 9/15/45, in the Detroit Commission on Community Relations Papers, ser. 1, box 1, Board of Education: Intercultural Program, 1945 folder; "Race Relations in Detroit Public Schools," *Interracial Review*, June, 1944, in Joe Brown Papers, box 17, Negroes folder, in ALHUA; Detroit Public Schools, *Promising Practices in Intergroup Education* (Detroit: Board of Education, 1946). On the committee that directed the intercultural program, see Harrison, "Coordinating Committee on Democratic Human Relations."

145. The Urban League leader is quoted in *Detroit Times*, 6/20/46, in Detroit Commission on Community Relations Papers, ser. 1, box 15, Detroit Interracial Committee Clippings, 1945–46. National Association for the Advancement of Colored People—Detroit, "Statement and Recommendations to the Mayor's Committee, June 29,1943," in DNAACP Papers, ser. 1, box 1, Report folder no. 3.

146. Harrison, "Coordinating Committee on Democratic Human Relations," 98, 108, 110.

147. Detroit Public Schools, "Number and Percent of Negro Students, Negro Teachers, and Negro Non-contract Employes of 208 Elementary Schools, 19 Intermediate Schools, 19 High Schools, Technical and Vocational Schools" [ca. May, 1945], in Detroit Commission on Community Relations Papers, ser. 1, box 17, Board of Education: Intercultural/Interracial Program, 1946 folder. See also Harrison, "Coordinating Committee on Democratic Human Relations," 109–10; "Report of the Subcommittee to Study the Practices of the Public Schools with Respect to Intercultural Education in Race Relations, November 30, 1949," appendix 2, 2, in DUL Papers, box A6, Detroit Public Schools folder.

148. *Michigan Chronicle*, 7/10/43; Meier and Rudwick, *Black Detroit*, 175, 176–206; see also Babson et al., *Working Detroit*, 119–21.

149. Harrison, "Coordinating Committee on Democratic Human Relations," 21–24, 70; *Detroit Labor News*, 5/10/40; Detroit Federation of Teachers, Executive Board Minutes, 1943–44, January 11, 1944; *Detroit Teacher*, February, 1944.

150. Detroit Federation of Teachers, Executive Board Minutes, 1945–47, September 24, 1945, October 3, 1945, November 27, 1945, December 4, 1945, March 3, 1946; Detroit Federation of Teachers, Minutes of General Membership Meetings, 1945–47, December 10, 1945, in DFT Papers; *Detroit Tribune*, 4/20/46; Detroit Federation of Teachers, "Toward Better Racial Relations in Detroit," *American Teacher* 32 (February, 1948): 13–16; Frances Comfort, letter to John C. Dancy, 1/1/48, in DUL Papers, box 67, Education—General folder.

151. Robert Foster, letter to James J. McClendon [president of the Detroit NAACP], 3/24/45, in DFT papers [inventoried 12/24/85], box 4, Foster Campaign 1945 folder; "Committee to Elect Victor G. Reuther to the Board of Education" [ca. March, 1945], in DFT Papers [inventoried 12/24/85], box 4, Foster Campaign 1945 folder; *Detroit Tribune*, 3/31/45, 7/28/45, 8/4/45, 8/11/45, 9/12/45; *Michigan Chronicle*, 3/31/45; author interview with Victor Reuther, Washington, DC, 4/21/87.

152. On blacks in the DFT in the 1940s and 1950s, see Elinor Laffrey Maki, Oral History Transcript; Zeline Richard, 1969 Oral History Transcript, in ALHUA. On Leroy Dues, see Jones, "Historify of Miller," 171–72; *Detroit Teacher*, 5/24/49.

153. DBEP, 1946–47, 371; *Michigan Chronicle*, 1/25/47 and 2/1/47; *Detroit Tribune*, 2/8/47.

154. *Detroit Tribune*, 6/2/45; *Michigan Chronicle*, 2/1/47. On other protests to the board about the poor physical condition of schools in the black community, see *Detroit Tribune*, 6/23/45, 2/16/46, 3/9/46; *Michigan Chronicle*, 6/23/45, 12/8/45, 2/9/46, 9/7/46, 9/14/46, 9/21/46; DBEP, 1945–46, 384, 427–28; Capeci, *Race Relations*, 42–43.

155. City of Detroit Interracial Committee, Minutes, 9/11/47, in Detroit Commission on Community Relations Papers, box 10, Minutes August 1, 1947 to December 3, 1947 Notebook; *Detroit Free Press*, 9/6/47 and 9/10/47, in DFT Papers, DFT Scrapbook, 1946–47; DBEP, 1947–48, 122–23; *Detroit Tribune*, 9/19/47.

156. *Detroit Tribune*, 9/20/47.

157. *Michigan Chronicle*, 9/6/47 and 9/13/47. See also *Detroit Tribune*, 9/13/47.

158. *Detroit Tribune*, 9/20/47 and 9/27/47; *Michigan Chronicle*, 9/20/47 and 12/6/47

159. *Michigan Chronicle*, 11/1/47, 11/8/47, 11/15/47, 11/22/47, 11/29/47.

160. Detroit Federation of Teachers, "Toward Better Race Relations," 13.

161. Detroit Federation of Teachers, Executive Board Minutes, 1948, January 2, January 8, January 22, February 26, April 15, May 20; *Detroit Times*, 1/26/48.

162. Detroit Federation of Teachers, Executive Board Minutes, 1945–47, February 10, 1947, March 13, 1947, April 1, 1947; DBEP, 1946–47, 713; DBEP, 1947–48, 1. For the complete text of the press release, see Better Schools Association, "An Open Letter to the Detroit Board of Education, Mrs. Laura Osborn, President," 4/12/48, DM Papers, 1948, box 1, Board of Education folder; see also *Detroit Times*, 4/13/48; *Detroit Tribune*, 4/17/48. Background on some of the organizations can be found in Meir and Rudwick, *Black Detroit*, 92–93. On the NAACP's opposition to Dondineau, see *Michigan Chronicle*, 4/17/48.

163. DBEP, 1948–49, 4–5.

164. *Detroit Teacher*, 1/17/49; Marilyn Gittell and T. Edward Hollander, *Six Urban School Districts* (New York: Praeger, 1968), 149.

165. DBEP, 1948–49, 301–2. Foster resigned in order to take a job in Topeka, Kansas. DBEP, 1948–49, 202, 221–22; *Detroit Teacher*, 1/17/49 and 3/21/49.

166. Frank Martel, letter to John Webster, 2/21/49, in Detroit Metropolitan AFL-CIO Papers, ser. 1, box 5, Board of Education folder, in ALHUA; *Detroit News*, 3/21/49 and 3/24/49; *Detroit Teacher*, 3/21/49 and 4/25/49.

167. DBEP, 1948–49, 331; *Detroit Free Press*, 3/27/49; *Detroit News*, 3/21/49, 3/22/49, 3/23/49, 3/24/49, 4/3/49; Detroit Federation of Teachers, Executive Board Minutes, 1949–50, March 10, 1949; *Detroit Labor News*, 3/11/49; *Detroit Teacher*, 3/21/49.

168. *Michigan Chronicle*, 3/19/49. Another, somewhat less angry endorsement appeared in *Michigan Chronicle*, 4/2/49. The series on Miller ran in *Michigan Chronicle*, 1/22/49, 1/29/49, 2/5/49, 2/12/49, 2/19/49.

169. *Detroit Free Press*, 3/3/49 and 3/28/49; *Detroit News*, 4/3/49; *Detroit Teacher*, 3/21/49; *The Detroiter*, 4/11/49; Michigan Public Expenditure Survey, "You Be the Boss," 3/30/49, in DM Papers, 1949, box 1, Board of Education folder.

170. *Detroit Free Press*, 4/1/49; *Detroit News*, 4/1/49; *Detroit Tribune*, 3/12/49; *Detroit Teacher*, 1/17/49, 2/14/49, 3/21/49; *Detroit Labor News*, 2/11/49 and 3/4/49; Detroit Federation of Teachers, Executive Board Minutes, 1949–50, March 13, 1949.

171. *Detroit Free Press*, 4/4/49; *Detroit News*, 3/30/49; *Detroit Teacher*, 3/21/49.

172. *Detroit Free Press*, 3/31/49; *Detroit Teacher*, 4/25/49; *Detroit News*, 4/1/49. On DFT and liberal response to the DTA, see *Detroit News*, 3/30/49 and 4/1/49; *Detroit Free Press*, 4/1/49; *Detroit Teacher*, 4/25/49; Sidney Woolner [president of Americans for Democratic Action] et al., letter to the Detroit Board of Education, 3/3/49, in Detroit Metropolitan AFL-CIO Papers, ser. 1, box 5, Board of Education folder, in ALHUA.

173. *Detroit Free Press*, 3/30/49; *Detroit News*, 3/27/49.

174. DBEP, 1948–49, 342, 360–61; *Detroit Free Press*, 4/6/49; *Detroit News*, 4/5/49. In 1947–48, the tax rate of 8.31 mills for education in Detroit was the lowest of eight major cities in Michigan. Ann Arbor, for example, levied 14.20 mills; Battle Creek, 9.86 mills; Bay City, 11.08 mills; Kalamazoo, 15.25 mills; and Lansing, 9.00 mills. Even the Detroit suburbs of Hamtramck and Highland Park, which are totally surrounded by Detroit, levied 11.76 mills and 10.90 mills, respectively (Michigan Public Expenditure Survey, "You Be the Boss"; *Detroit Teacher*, 3/21/49).

175. DBEP, 1948–49, 342, 483–87; DBEP, 1949–50, 1.

176. For discussions of political alignments, debates, and outcomes in Gary and St. Paul, similar to what I have found in Detroit, see Cohen, *Children of the Mill*, 120–209; Schiff, "Teachers Strikes," 166–68.

177. *New York Times*, 2/14/47 and 3/2/47, in DFT Papers, DFT Scrapbook, 1946–47; Myron Emanuel, "Why Teachers Strike," *New Republic*, February 24, 1947, 33; "Schools: Struck Buffalo," *Newsweek*, March 3, 1947, 22; "Teacher Strike," *Newsweek*, March 8, 1948, 80; Schiff, "Teachers Strikes," 119, 123–25, appendix A; Cohen, *Children of the Mill*, 199–201.

Chapter 5

The Rise of the Liberal-Labor-Black Coalition, 1949–64

In February, 1951, Walter Reuther addressed the Detroit meeting of the Association for Supervision and Curriculum Development and denounced the business community for its indifference to public education. "Schools are overcrowded," he declared, "teachers are underpaid, facilities are antiquated and inadequate. In Detroit, we took the war factories off the swing shifts, but we put the schools on the swing shifts."[1] As Reuther spoke, union- and business-backed candidates were again bitterly vying for control of the school board. In the election and in educational politics generally it appeared that little had changed from the patterns established in the Great Depression.[2]

This picture of continuing political conflict starkly contrasts to the image of the 1950s that most educational historians convey. Tyack and Hansot, for example, characterize the 1950s as an essentially placid educational era, a period of "business as usual." Indeed, they state that "the basic power alignments . . . did not shift substantially nor did the basically conservative consensus of the period change in any fundamental way." Other historians point to the "red scare" and firings of left-wing teachers, the attacks on "progressive education," and the lack of civil rights challenges to educational segregation in the North as evidence of the generally conservative thrust of this era.[3] While some events in Detroit certainly support these claims, larger developments in educational politics in the Motor City point to a dramatically different interpretation of the 1950s.

Rather than being a period of "conservative consensus" or reactionary oppression, the 1950s in Detroit were an important transition era in which the basic educational power alignments changed substantially. In this decade, the liberal-labor-black coalition that formed in the late 1940s took control of the school system in a process that was neither smooth nor easy. For much of the period, open and abrasive conflict between organized labor and major business interests continued to shape both local and state educational politics. Indeed, it was not until the latter part of the decade that a new educational consensus emerged, and, contrary to the conventional historiography, this consensus was guided by liberal rather than conservative principles. Moreover, Detroit's black community, inspired by the success of the civil rights movement in the South, became a key participant in these political changes.

Spurring all of these developments was the gradual economic decline in the city and the ongoing fiscal crisis of the school system, a crisis made worse by the flood of baby boomers. As a result of these crises, many Detroiters increasingly looked to liberal politicians, union leaders, and civil rights groups to point the way for Detroit and its school system. For a time, it indeed appeared that the liberal-labor-black coalition might rescue the city and the schools from decline. Unfortunately, even the strongest political movement could not arrest the deterioration. Rather than ushering in an educational renaissance in Detroit, the rise of the liberal-labor-black coalition proved to be the last hurrah of the old politics of education in the Motor City.

The Economic and Demographic Transformation
of Metropolitan Detroit, 1950–64

Between 1950 and 1964, the relationship between Detroit and its suburban communities changed profoundly. Even though the suburbs had grown more rapidly than the city in every decade since World War I, until the 1950s, the economic, social, and cultural preeminence of Detroit had remained unchallenged. By 1960, however, the suburbs surpassed the city in population, with approximately 2.09 million residents compared to 1.67 million Detroiters.[4]

Suburbanization, which was taking place at a furious pace in the Midwest and Northeast, was both a blessing and a curse for Detroit. As the demand for cars increased, the Detroit area became the center of a new economic boom. In 1948, auto manufacturers smashed through their 1929 production records and never looked back. The demand for cars, however, put a debilitating strain on the aged industrial infrastructure of the city. Faced with outdated, inefficient plants as well as high land and construction costs within the city limits, many auto manufacturers left Detroit for the open and relatively inexpensive suburbs. In addition, such inefficient auto makers as Packard and Hudson closed their doors in the late 1950s, and the remaining auto companies—General Motors, Ford, Chrysler, and American Motors—began automating existing plants, eliminating thousands of jobs in the city.[5]

There were two immediate consequences of these changes. First, the local property tax base plummeted during these years as businesses and families left the city. Between 1958 and 1963, assessed valuation in Detroit fell from $5.1 billion to $4.6 billion.[6] Second, between 1950 and 1960, Detroit lost more than 34 percent of its manufacturing jobs while the suburbs gained. By 1963, the suburbs had 90,000 more manufacturing jobs than the city. The percentage of white-collar jobs also fell in relation to the suburbs. In 1950, the proportion of white-collar jobs in Detroit and the suburbs was about equal at 30.3 percent and 30.9 percent, respectively. Ten years later, the number of white-collar jobs in Detroit had climbed slightly to 30.5 percent of the work force, but white-collar jobs jumped to 39.1 percent in the suburbs.[7]

These trends cost Detroit dearly in both human and material resources. Between 1950 and 1960, the population of Detroit fell from 1.85 million to 1.67 million, and most of those 180,000 Detroiters who left the city were middle class. As late as 1959, median family income in Detroit was slightly higher than in suburban Wayne, Oakland, and Macomb counties. By 1965, however, median family income in Detroit was $8,707, compared to $9,415 in suburban Wayne County, $9,295 in Macomb County, and $11,751 in Oakland County. This income shift had a profound impact on the local economy. In 1958, Detroit had an edge over the suburbs of about $100 million in retail sales. Five years later, suburban retail sales were almost $700 million greater than in the city.[8]

With these trends, the racial character, socioeconomic status, and even the age range of the remaining population of Detroit utterly changed. Between 1950 and 1960, the proportion of African-Americans in Detroit rose from 16 percent to 29 percent of the total inhabitants. This increase was due to both the in-migration of blacks and out-migration of whites. Between 1950 and 1960, Detroit lost over 23 percent of its white population, while its black population increased by almost 61 percent.[9] These new black residents were generally poorer than whites. Median income for white Detroiters in 1960, for example, was $6,769, but it was only $4,366 for blacks. In addition, blacks moving into the city tended to be young and the birth rate among black Detroiters was high. In 1960, about 32 percent of white Detroiters were nineteen years old or younger compared to almost 43 percent of blacks. In all, between 1950 and 1960, the number of Detroiters between the ages of twenty and forty-nine fell by over 253,000 while the number of inhabitants under twenty and over fifty increased.[10]

Throughout these massive population shifts, the city's racial geography remained virtually unchanged. Despite the 1948 U.S. Supreme Court ruling against restrictive covenants (a suit that was brought by a black Detroit teacher), integrated neighborhoods were still rare. Indeed, in 1960, as a result of redlining, unavailable mortgages, harassment of blacks who purchased homes in white neighborhoods, and white panic selling, blacks were even more segregated in Detroit than they had been thirty years before.[11]

The cumulative effect of these racial, social, and economic changes on the Detroit school system was enormous. Not only did property values, the mainstay of local school finance, decline, but the families who left Detroit for the suburbs during this period were the political backbone of public education—young families in their prime earning years. As their numbers dropped in Detroit, support for the public schools became much more problematic. The loss of young, middle-class families would have been a serious blow to the schools under any circumstances, but the demographic and racial changes that had overtaken Detroit in these years compounded the political and educational problems faced by school leaders.

Exacerbating every problem facing the schools was what the Michigan school superintendent in 1950 called the "tidal wave" of children, the baby boomers. Unlike the city, which was losing population, between 1950 and 1960, the public schools saw enrollment soar from 232,230 to 285,304.[12] While the increase in students ran counter to the general demographic trends in the city, the composition of the student population clearly reflected the larger changes in Detroit. Many of the new students were from poor and minority families.

In 1946, African-American students accounted for 17.3 percent of the 222,391 children enrolled in the Detroit public schools. In 1961, when the school system began taking an annual racial census, African-Americans accounted for 45.8 percent of the students. The number of blacks in the city at the time, however, accounted for only about 29 percent of the total population of Detroit. Five years later, when enrollment in the school system peaked at almost 300,000, nearly 55 percent of the students in the school system were African-American.[13]

These changes had profound political as well as demographic implications. After 1963, the majority of students in the school system were black, but the majority of the voters in the city still were white. Age also became an important factor in school politics as elderly voters, often white retirees on fixed incomes who opposed tax increases, played a larger role in school millage and bond issue elections. Similarly, the exodus to the suburbs introduced a new dimension into state educational politics as well. By 1960, Detroit faced severe competition from suburban, as well as rural, interests in the battle for state aid. Yet at the same time that the political problems of the school system were increasing, civic leaders were increasingly turning to public education as one of the chief means for dealing with the problems of poverty and racial conflict. In short, as the social and educational problems facing the school system grew, the political and financial strength of the system declined.[14]

Communists, Conspiracies, and Control of the School Board, 1951–55

At the beginning of the 1950s, liberal groups, organized labor, and civil rights organizations, though more powerful than in the past, still ranked as "outsiders" in terms of influencing crucial school policies and programs. Five years later, however, the liberal-labor-black coalition had become the most important power bloc in local educational politics. This political transition was neither quiet nor calm. It included accusations of communist infiltration of the classroom and allegations of union-led conspiracies to control the schools. Bitterly contested school board elections still divided the city along established political and economic lines. From each of these struggles, however, the liberal-labor-black coalition emerged with greater power and influence over the school system. As a consequence, by the early 1960s, the coalition had substantially altered the direction of school policies and programs in Detroit.

Initially, the success of this campaign by liberal Detroiters to increase their influence in school politics depended on the degree to which the Detroit Federation of Teachers (DFT) could neutralize the issue of communist infiltration of public education. In the late 1940s, liberal Detroiters had made some progress in electing board members committed to carrying out a more progressive educational agenda. In order to maintain that momentum, leaders of the liberal-labor-black coalition recognized that they had to eliminate the issue of communist involvement in the schools, an issue that their conservative opponents could use with potentially devastating effect. Due to its left-wing roots and the prominent positions several leading leftists still held in the union, the DFT was definitely the weak link in the coalition.

The union had taken an important step toward protecting itself from allegations of communist infiltration by helping oust the communist-dominated unions from the American Federation of Teachers (AFT) in 1941. Nevertheless, the DFT still had much to fear from investigations that relied as much on innuendo and hearsay as fact. As the anticommunist crusade gained strength in Detroit, the union leadership attempted to protect the organization with a policy stating that the DFT would not defend any teacher who espoused totalitarian ideas, whether communist, fascist, or Nazi. Recognizing, however, that right-wingers were often indiscriminate in their charges of communist affiliation, union leaders promised to defend liberal and "nonconformist" teachers wrongly accused of totalitarian ties.[15]

This policy was put to the test three times, once in 1952, when witnesses before the House Un-American Activities committee (HUAC) identified longtime DFT member, Elinor Laffrey Maki as a communist; again in 1953, when the U.S. State Department labeled school administrator Walter G. Bergman a communist; and finally in 1954, when two Detroit teachers and two Wayne University professors were labeled communists during a second HUAC investigation in the Motor City. Of the six educators who were accused of communist affiliation, only Bergman received help from the DFT in fighting the charges, primarily because he flatly denied membership in the Communist party and because he received substantial support from labor leaders and several school board members, particularly Laura Osborn and Patrick McNamara. Maki and the others who were named before HUAC, however, took the Fifth Amendment when asked about Communist party affiliation. In addition, Maki invoked the board's 1931 Free Speech Resolution, claiming that her outside political activities were irrelevant to her effectiveness as an educator. While that defense had worked for Maki in 1938 during the Dies Committee investigation, this time school leaders and union members (in two referenda) rejected it. None of the educators accused before HUAC were supported by the DFT and all lost their jobs. Bergman, however, was totally exonerated and continued with the school system until his retirement in 1959.[16]

In these incidents, the DFT tried to balance its commitments to both anticommunism and academic freedom. As difficult as that stand was, the refusal to provide blanket protection to teachers accused of communist involvement had positive political consequences because it effectively neutralized the issue of communists in the schools. The DFT stand enabled the liberal-labor-black coalition to continue its quest for control of the school board unhindered by allegations of communist conspiracies.

Even without allegations of communist infiltration of the schools, however, accusations about other conspiracies to control the schools played a major part in educational politics in Detroit throughout the early 1950s. In the spring of 1951, for example, when Save Our Schools, now renamed Serve Our Schools (SOS), launched another campaign to win a liberal majority on the board of education, accusations that the unions were trying to take over the schools again became a key issue in the campaign. As in 1933 and 1949, these allegations had some truth.

Members of the SOS steering committee and its later board of directors were, in fact, a veritable "Who's Who" of liberal Detroiters, including, at one time or another, Frank Martel, president of the DWCFL; Al Barbour, a Congress of Industrial Organizations (CIO) leader who later became president of the Wayne County AFL-CIO; Walter Reuther and his wife, May Reuther, a DFT member; Common Council member George Edwards; DFT leaders Frances Comfort and Florence Sweeney; Adelaide Hart, a DFT member and leader of the Michigan Democratic party; Edward Turner, president of the Detroit chapter of the NAACP; Arthur L. Johnson, executive secretary of the Detroit NAACP; John Morning of the Urban League; James Hare, a leader of the Americans for Democratic Action (ADA) and future secretary of state of Michigan; Merle Henrickson, a member of the city planning commission and liberal activist; Leonard Kasle, a self-employed businessman involved in liberal causes; and Thelma Zwerdling, wife of UAW attorney and ADA leader A. L. Zwerdling.[17]

With such broad-based support, SOS leaders approached the 1951 school board election with great expectations. Adding to their optimism was the fact that archconservative board member Burt Shurly had died in October, 1950. With his death, conservatives lost a popular incumbent candidate and liberals believed they now had another golden opportunity to capture a majority on the board. "You can change the whole complexion of the Board this spring," an SOS campaign flyer declared. "Another such chance won't come for years. Let's do it now."[18]

The alignment of interest groups in the 1951 school board campaign demonstrated that, despite such technological breakthroughs as television coverage of the school board campaign, little had changed in school politics in Detroit since the Great Depression. As in 1949, SOS worked closely with the DFT and other unions in the city. The DWCFL solidly backed the liberal candidates, Betty Becker and F. J. Hermann, as did the Wayne County CIO, the NAACP, and the leading black newspaper in the city, the *Michigan Chronicle*. This liberal coalition blasted the conservative candidates, A. D. Jamieson and William Merrifield (an executive at Chrysler Corporation), describing them as ruthless economizers who placed the interests of large tax-payers over the welfare of the children of Detroit. DWCFL president Frank Martel pilloried Jamieson and Merrifield as advocates of "cheap schools."[19]

On the other side of the campaign, the Detroit Citizens League, the

Detroit Board of Commerce, the Detroit Teachers Association (DTA, the local National Education Association [NEA] affiliate), and the *Detroit News* rallied behind Jamieson and Merrifield, touting their commitment to fiscal responsibility and their independence from "special interests" (i.e., unions).[20] As in 1933 and 1949, allegations of a union-led conspiracy to take over the schools, combined with hints about subversion in the classroom, became the main issue in the campaign. The liberal candidates, Becker and Hermann, were routinely denounced as tools of organized labor. In a series of impassioned editorials, the *News* repeated its long-standing allegations that union bosses "patently are seeking to gain control of the public schools . . . [in order to] make the public schools a means of furthering union propaganda."[21] On election day, Harvey Campbell, executive vice president of the Board of Commerce, warned business leaders to get out the vote. "The CIO cares even if you don't," he declared. "Its leaders want a CIO school board."[22]

Liberals responded to these charges with equal vehemence. Amid the campaign, Leonard Kasle, president of SOS, sent out a lengthy report decrying "the attack against public education which is under way in Detroit, as it is in many parts of the country." Kasle specifically decried the "phoney issue of subversion in Detroit's schools" in the current school board campaign. In addition, he highlighted efforts by various "front" organizations allegedly run by business and religious groups that were seeking to cut taxes for public schools, end nonsectarian public education, and, ultimately, "destroy our democratic system which rests on an educated citizenry."[23]

Despite these attempts to polarize the electorate, the voters of Detroit chose to give neither side a complete victory. Jamieson led all the candidates, but the liberal candidate, Betty Becker, ran a close second and thus assumed a seat on the board. SOS hailed Becker's victory, since it seemed to promise a liberal majority. For the first time in the history of the seven-member board, four of the members, Jane Lovejoy, Patrick McNamara, Laura Osborn, and now Betty Becker, had strong ties to the liberal community and organized labor. In addition, for the first time in the history of Detroit, the majority of members of a major policy-making body were women.[24]

Despite this apparent liberal victory, however, the board did not make any immediate shifts in policy. Three months after the election, for example, the board voted to reappoint Arthur Dondineau as superintendent, despite strong protests from Edward Turner, president of the NAACP and a leader of SOS, and A. L. Zwerdling. Osborn and McNamara joined with more conservative board members Brooks, Grace, and Jamieson in voting for reappointment. While this development was not unexpected, Osborn had voted to renew Dondineau's contract in 1948 and few thought she would change her vote in 1951, it did signal to leaders of the liberal-labor-black coalition that their work was far from done.[25]

In 1953, despite another concerted effort by the coalition, the basic political alignment of the board remained unchanged. Incumbents Laura Osborn and Jane Lovejoy, who were supported by SOS, retained their seats while William Merrifield, who had lost in 1951, was elected to replace another conservative, Dr. Clark Brooks. Liberals, however, were heartened by the showing of their one unsuccessful candidate, Dr. Remus G. Robinson, a black surgeon who was also a leader of the Urban League and SOS. Drawing support from all parts of the city, Robinson fell just 2,100 votes short of winning a seat on the board.[26]

Planning for the next campaign began almost immediately but the situation was thrown into confusion by the surprising results of the 1954 general election in which Detroit school board member and labor leader Patrick V. McNamara won a seat in the U.S. Senate, defeating incumbent Homer Ferguson.[27] As delighted as liberal Detroiters were with McNamara's victory, his resignation from the school board left them with a difficult political problem that was compounded, soon after, when Jane Lovejoy unexpectedly announced her resignation from the board. Suddenly, two liberal seats were open in the 1955 school board election.[28]

The liberal-labor-black coalition launched a vigorous campaign to keep the open seats in "safe" hands. SOS, the DFT, the DWCFL, the Wayne County CIO, and the NAACP threw their support behind incumbent Louise Grace, whom they had opposed in 1949, Remus G. Robinson, making his second run for the board, and Leonard Kasle, the past president of SOS and a member of the board of directors of the Detroit chapter of the NAACP.[29] Surprisingly, this strong liberal slate failed to stir much controversy. The sharpest criticism came from the *Free Press,* which editorialized that it did not see how the school system would be improved by "a bloc of candidates having the backing of any special group, or who might be sympathetically inclined toward the political philosophies of that group." Nevertheless, the *Free Press* admitted that all the candidates were of "generally high quality." Indeed, both the *News* and the Citizens League endorsed Grace and Robinson.[30] Moreover, neither the Board of Commerce nor its acerbic spokesman, Harvey Campbell, took a stand on the election. With so little controversy and such widespread support for the SOS candidates, the election proved to be a major success for the liberal-labor-black coalition in Detroit. All three SOS-

and labor-backed candidates won handily. Dr. Remus Robinson thus became the first elected black official in the city. With this election, five of the seven school board members, Becker, Grace, Kasle, Osborn, and Robinson, had ties to the liberal-labor-black coalition. Without question, the character of the school board was now dramatically changed.[31]

While the election itself had not sparked conflict, controversy erupted several months later following the death of Laura Osborn.[32] As the six remaining board members searched for her replacement, a major uproar ensued about who controls the schools. The incident began several weeks after Osborn's death, when school board members Kasle, Grace, Robinson, and Merrifield met in what the *News* later characterized as "secret board sessions" at Kasle's home. These sessions, in which the members ostensibly discussed "educational philosophy," were soon expanded to include a number of school administrators, teachers, and university professors. The first of these larger meetings took place in mid-September at Wayne University and included Mary Kastead, representing the DFT, and Merle Henrickson, president of SOS. Noticeably absent was superintendent Arthur Dondineau, who, the participating board members decided, should not be informed of the meetings.[33]

Word of the meetings, however, leaked out and they quickly became a flashpoint of controversy. Ruth Winters, the head of the Michigan Educational Association, the parent organization of the DTA, and a teacher in the Detroit system, announced to the press that the meetings were "a CIO plot to gain a bigger voice in educational practices." Specifically, Winters claimed that labor leaders were exercising their will through SOS, which, she announced, "is a tool of the CIO."[34] The charges became front-page news. Despite the immediate suspension of the meetings and angry denials of wrongdoing by Kasle, Henrickson, Kastead, and the Wayne County CIO, newspaper stories about the controversy, including a six-part series in the *Times,* continued for almost six weeks.[35] The controversy remained in the public eye largely because it touched something deeper than whether the CIO was trying to take over the school board.

At issue was the changing character of the board and the direction it would take because of this change. In 1950, a majority of the board members—Brooks, Jamieson, Shurly, and Osborn—were listed in the Social Register. Except Osborn, these members were quite conservative in their politics and especially conservative in relation to school finance. In September, 1955, only the aging A. D. Jamieson remained of this original group. Joining him were Becker, Grace, Kasle, Merrifield, and Robinson, who formed the core of a new group of members who would control the board well into the 1960s. These new members were solidly middle class and, while definitely not left-wing, were more open to liberal and labor influences than any group of board members in the history of Detroit. Winters and certainly many other, more conservative Detroiters feared that SOS would pressure the board into filling Osborn's seat with yet another liberal, which would give SOS enormous influence over the policy-making body.[36]

These fears were compounded three weeks later when superintendent Arthur Dondineau announced his intention to resign in June, a full year before his contract was due to expire. In July, 1954, without controversy, the board had reappointed Dondineau to another three-year term.[37] But following the 1955 school board election, Dondineau must have seen the handwriting on the wall. He knew that Kasle and Robinson would aggressively challenge his segregationist policies and must have been stung by being excluded from the "secret" board meetings that he learned about only after reading his morning newspaper. Whatever his reasons for stepping down, Dondineau's resignation marked the realization of one of the major goals of the liberal-labor-black coalition. But the timing of his announcement insured that controversy about who "controls" the schools would become even more intense.

Tempers flared at the October 11th board meeting, at which Dondineau resigned. In an impassioned speech before the board of education, Brendon Sexton, education director for the UAW-CIO and former leader of SOS, vehemently denied that there was a "CIO plot" to take over the schools and argued that the entire uproar had been orchestrated by business groups and conservative politicians who wanted to deny organized labor its right to make its wishes known about new board member and superintendent appointments. Sexton declared that "it seems quite obvious to us that the campaign originated in the deep frustration of certain powerful interests in this city, including the daily newspapers, which for years have worked their will in all of the city's governmental agencies."

Sexton concluded that the entire CIO episode was an effort by these powerful interests to intimidate the board into toeing a more conservative line. He also claimed that the "smear" campaign was an attempt to force organized labor to retreat from its educational agenda, which included electing "a school board representative of the entire community"; new school construction particularly in "slum areas"; higher salaries for teachers; and "[t]he enforcement of the spirit of the United States Supreme Court [*Brown v. Board of Education*] decision dealing with desegregation, which is being outrageously violated by the method of teacher placement in this city's schools." The CIO, he declared, would not be intimidated.[38] The question remained, would the board?

Over the next few months, as the board chose replacements first for Osborn and then for A. D. Jamieson, who died in January, 1956, the liberal community had reason to suspect that the "CIO smear" had indeed intimidated the remaining board members. Neither of the two people whom the board appointed, Gladys Canty and Dr. Warren Cooksey, had strong liberal or labor credentials. Nevertheless, neither Canty nor Cooksey challenged the generally liberal drift of the school board over the next three years and candidates backed by SOS continued to have great success at the polls. Indeed, between 1949 and 1961, eleven out of fourteen SOS-backed candidates won seats on the school board. In 1959, one of the most important changes occurred when SOS candidate Roy Stephens, Jr., replaced Warren Cooksey and substantially strengthened the liberal bloc on the board. Leonard Kasle gradually emerged as the most influential board member, and he guided school policy and practice in a decidedly liberal direction.[39]

The first important change introduced by the new, more liberal board came in 1956 with the appointment of the U.S. Commissioner of Education, Samuel M. Brownell, as superintendent of schools. Several things about Brownell commended him to liberal leaders in Detroit. First, Brownell was an "outsider," the first that the board had hired to head the schools since Charles Chadsey. Because many liberals had believed that Arthur Dondineau had run the schools as a "closed corporation," Brownell's status as an outsider was a considerable virtue. Second, Brownell was committed to increased citizen participation in educational policy discussions, another important liberal concern. Third, he was educationally progressive, favoring innovative programs designed to deal specifically with the problems of inner city children. And finally, as U.S. Commissioner of Education when the Supreme Court handed down its decision in *Brown v. Board of Education*, Brownell was quite familiar with the problems of segregated schools and the outrage in the black community over their continued existence.[40] While he was not the ideal superintendent as far as liberals were concerned, by September, 1958, his work impressed SOS enough to praise him in its monthly newsletter and highlight the accomplishments of his first two years in office.[41] In many ways, Brownell was the perfect representative of the new, middle-class board of education, sensitive to public concerns, cautiously innovative, and far more liberal than Dondineau. Indeed, over the next ten years, Brownell implemented almost every part of the liberal agenda that Brendon Sexton had spelled out in his speech to the board in October, 1955.

The Search for Better Funding and Higher
Educational Standards, 1953–59

The political success of the liberal-labor-black coalition in electing people to the school board was ultimately paralleled by success in increasing funding for the public schools. The road to better funding, however, was considerably more difficult than the road to political power. Despite the growing number of liberal board members, school leaders in the early 1950s remained reluctant to challenge the Board of Commerce and other business organizations in seeking substantial tax increases from the voters. In 1957, amid a major fiscal crisis, the bitter political antagonism about school finance that had colored the 1930s and 1940s was reawakened, and with that controversy came an intensive debate about the quality of education offered in Detroit's high schools. Yet out of these conflicts emerged a broad-based consensus in favor of increasing funds for the schools and a commitment to strengthen, at least, some aspects of the high school curriculum. Unlike the consensus of the 1920s, this new movement to expand and improve the school system was essentially led by liberal leaders and guided by liberal ideals. Business and good government organizations still played an important role in this effort, but they had been reduced to a secondary level.

The early 1950s seemed like the dawning of a bright new financial era for the Detroit public schools. The millage increase that Detroit voters approved in 1949 boosted local revenue from $30,561,000 in the 1948–49 school year to $42,814,480 in 1949–50. The school system began its first major construction program in twenty years, allocating over $15 million in 1949–50 alone. School officials also hired 400 more teachers to reduce class sizes and serve the rapidly growing elementary school population.[42]

As early as 1951, however, the exhilaration that initially surrounded these initiatives had faded before the enormous problems facing the system. It was quickly apparent that even the substantial transfusion of new funds for construction was insufficient. Not only did the existing educational infrastructure need major renovations after nearly two decades of neglect, but the movement of population within the city, largely to new neighborhoods in the northeast and northwest sections of town, increased the demand for new buildings well beyond the limits of the 1949 millage increase. In December, 1952, almost 22,000 students attended school in buildings more than fifty years old, 6,500 were in temporary units, and over 2,100 first and second graders were attending half-day sessions.[43]

The baby boomers compounded these problems, swelling kindergarten and elementary enrollments at unprecedented rates. Between September, 1950, and September, 1952, the number of kindergartners jumped from 23,512 to 32,342.[44] Between renovating or rebuilding decaying buildings and providing classrooms for the baby boomers, school officials estimated that, between 1952 and 1960, they would have to construct enough facilities to house some 70,000 students. Construction was enough of a drain on funds without having to add new teachers' salaries to school costs, as well. Between 1949 and 1952, the system hired almost 1,200 new teachers, but school leaders estimated that, in the next five years, the system would need more than twice that number to accommodate the baby boomers. Indeed, in 1952, even with the added teachers, Detroit had the highest secondary pupil-teacher ratios in the state and one of the highest elementary pupil-teacher ratios. As early as November, 1951, school leaders began planning for another attempt to boost taxes.[45]

Initially, the only debate about this proposed millage increase was over how large it should be. Throughout the fall of 1952, at least forty-five civic, labor, and community organizations met with the board to debate that question. Led by SOS and the DFT, labor and liberal organizations called for a substantial increase of as much as 6 mills above the 2.5 mills approved in 1949 in order to expand and improve the system, keep pace with inflation, and fund the teachers' retirement plan. On the other side of the issue, Arthur Dondineau maintained that the system only needed an additional 2.5 mills. Almost every participant in these discussions agreed that the tax should be in effect for ten years in order to handle the flood of baby boomers that school leaders projected would peak in 1964.[46]

Only one prominent organization opposed the tax increase—the Board of Commerce, which continued its implacable opposition to any tax increase. The Board of Commerce urged the school board to cut expenditures by transferring control of Wayne University over to the state (which the school system eventually did in 1956), by lobbying for additional state aid, and by dropping efforts to reduce class sizes. If the board rejected these measures, the Board of Commerce urged it to, at least, limit the tax increase to five years instead of ten.[47]

Ultimately, the board made the very questionable decision of seeking an increase of only 2 mills, less than even Dondineau thought wise, and for only five years. Laura Osborn, the only board member to protest these decisions, chastised her colleagues for succumbing to pressure from the Board of Commerce. Rising from her seat before she cast her vote on the motion to place the increase on the April ballot, she declared, "I shall vote for this realizing as does everyone here that this will not accomplish what our children deserve and I feel we are letting the children down, but realizing that half a loaf is better than no bread, I shall vote for this and work for it with a heavy heart."[48]

The other board members probably opted for the 2 mill increase because they believed that, by asking for only a modest amount, they could attract broad-based support. On that score they were right. Virtually every major civic organization and labor union backed the measure, as did the daily newspapers. Such long-time advocates of higher taxes for education as the DWCFL, Wayne County CIO, and NAACP were prominent on the list of supporters. But in addition to these organizations, the Detroit Citizens League, the Citizens Research Council of Michigan (formerly the Detroit Bureau of Governmental Research), the Roman Catholic Archdiocese, and the Republican party also urged voters to back the tax increase.[49]

The only real controversy in the campaign came when Bella Dodd, a former communist and New York teacher, declared that there were between 150 and 200 communist teachers in the Detroit schools. The Board of Commerce announced its opposition to the millage increase the same day as Dodd's allegations appeared in the press, and some school leaders feared that the Board of Commerce would use the communist issue in its efforts to defeat the millage. Such fears proved groundless, especially after Senate investigators informed several DFT leaders, who had traveled to Washington to deny the allegations, that no Detroit teachers were actually under suspicion.[50]

Besides the Board of Commerce, a newly organized group called the Small Property Owners of Detroit also opposed the tax increase. Headed by Martin A. Larson, who had led the fight against raising teachers' salaries in 1947 and against the 1949 millage increase, the Small Property Owners denounced the proposed tax in letters to the editors of the *Free Press* and the *News*. The Small Property Owners claimed that the school board had wasted enormous amounts of money on inflated salaries for teachers, had drastically reduced class sizes thereby exaggerating the need for new buildings, and, despite previous funding increases, had allowed educational standards to deteriorate.[51] These arguments, however, had little impact on the Detroit voters, who approved the tax increase by a two-to-one margin.[52]

Nevertheless, as SOS and the other liberal and labor organizations had predicted, the amount of money raised by the increase quickly proved to be inadequate. In October, 1955, school leaders began planning yet another campaign for increased taxes. The seemingly perennial problems of increasing building costs, hiring more teachers, and increasing salaries for teachers remained at the root of the financial crisis. Construction needs alone could have depleted the resources of the school system. Between 1949 and 1956, the board constructed 113 new buildings at a cost of about $67 million, most in the booming outer ring of the city. Despite these efforts, when the school year began in September, 1956, some 24,000 high school students, almost half of the total high school enrollment, and about 5,000 elementary students, mostly first graders, were on half-day sessions due to inadequate classroom space. The future looked even worse as school leaders estimated that an additional 22,000 children would pour into the schools by 1960, bringing the total enrollment to nearly 300,000. Besides the problems caused by the enormous growth in enrollment, school leaders also began to focus on the decay of the educational infrastructure in the "central district" of the school system. In that district, where the black population was rapidly expanding, practically no new schools had been built for three decades. All told, the board estimated that it needed to spend between $33 and $45 million more on construction.[53]

In addition to needing so much additional revenue for construction, school leaders estimated that they also needed to hire at least 800 more teachers to accommodate the continuing surge of baby boomers.[54] Coming up with salaries for these new teachers was one problem; providing adequate salaries for all teachers was another. Since 1952, the rate of annual salary increases for teachers was below other city and county employees and, more important, below that granted by suburban school districts. As a consequence, in 1955, for the first time, Detroit had the lowest starting salary for teachers of any school district in the immediate area—$3,900 in Detroit compared to over $4,000 in the suburbs—a development that prompted outcries from the DFT.[55]

The financial problems of the Detroit schools appeared even worse in comparison to suburban school systems. Detroit lagged well behind these districts in terms of school taxes, levying a total of 12.81 mills (8.31 from the 15 mill distribution and the additional 4.5 mills approved by the voters in 1953) compared to over 19.00 mills in Dearborn, over 20.00 mills in such suburbs as Allen Park, Birmingham, East Detroit, and Garden City, and over 30.00 mills by the Redford Union and Taylor township districts. In 1956, thirty-seven of the forty-five school districts in Wayne County levied higher school taxes than Detroit, and almost half of these districts nearly doubled the Detroit tax rate.[56] In light of Detroit's growing financial problems and the relatively modest taxes the board was then levying, in January, 1957, the board decided to ask the voters to approve a 3 mill increase for two years, primarily for school construction.[57] Unlike the 1949 and 1953 millage campaigns, however, this attempt to raise school taxes generated a battle over school finance as fierce as any that had raged since the Great Depression.

Organized labor, unified by the recent merger of the AFL and CIO, quickly endorsed the millage increase. SOS and the DFT also added their support, despite both groups' dismay that the board had not sought an even larger increase. The *News* and the *Free Press* backed the tax increase, as did the Detroit Council of Churches. The NAACP and the two black weekly newspapers, the *Detroit Tribune* and the *Michigan Chronicle,* also endorsed the proposal but noted, as they had in earlier millage campaigns, that the black community had not received a fair share of new or renovated buildings once the increases had been approved.[58]

Opposition to the increase, however, came from virtually the same coalition of interest groups that had fought increases in school taxes since 1931. Led by the Board of Commerce, the opposition included the Citizens Research Council of Michigan, the Detroit Real Estate Board, the Michigan Manufacturers Association, the Building Owners and Managers Association, the Retail Merchants Association, the Employers' Association of Detroit, and a new organization, linked to the Board of Commerce, called the Citizens' Committee on Public Issues.[59] These groups opposed the proposal for essentially the same reasons they had fought increases in the school budget in the 1930s and 1940s, namely that the tax increase would drive more business and manufacturing concerns out of the city. While recognizing that *school* taxes were indeed low in Detroit, the leader of the Citizens' Committee on Public Issues pointed out that since Detroit had "higher assessments than anywhere else in the state, even with a lower rate, we pay a higher total tax." In addition, business leaders noted that the total tax rate in Detroit, including school, city, and county taxes, was one of the highest in the state. Finally, they dismissed out of hand the contention that the tax would only be levied for two years. As Harvey Campbell stated, "Do you know of any 'emergency' tax that ever ended?"[60]

Despite the striking similarity between these political alignments and earlier clashes over school financing, the 1957 millage campaign differed from past controversies because the opponents objected more to the *method* of raising funds than the need for new revenues per se. Indeed, the business groups unanimously acknowledged the need for new schools and increased revenue for public education. Rather than increasing taxes and using general revenue funds to pay for new building, the business leaders urged the school board to issue bonds for construction, as the board had done in the 1920s.

Just prior to the election, the chairman of the Education Committee of the Board of Commerce urged Detroiters to " . . . vote 'no' on Proposition 'D,' and then lend your support to the financing of much-needed new school construction in Detroit via bond issues."[61]

The problem with this proposal from the Board of Commerce was that the 1949 law that gave the school board financial independence from the city did not include bonding power in its provisions. That power remained with the Detroit Common Council. School officials feared that, even if the council approved the bonds, legal questions about the authority of the council to issue bonds for another independent city agency might lead to court cases that could tie up the desperately needed funds for a considerable time. In addition, school leaders pointed out that their "pay-as-you-go" plan was cheaper than issuing bonds, because the school district would not be burdened with long-term debt.[62]

The election held on April 1st was a total disaster for the school system. Almost 60 percent of the voters rejected the appeal for higher taxes. Whether the debate about the method of financing new schools had a major impact on the election or whether Detroiters were simply in no mood to raise taxes is hard to say. Unemployment, on the rise in the city for almost a year, probably had a major impact on the vote.[63]

The defeat plunged the school system into a political and financial crisis. Less than two weeks after the election, members of the board of education clashed sharply with leaders of the Board of Commerce after the board passed a resolution calling upon the state legislature to approve bonding authority up to $100 million for the board. The school board was essentially seeking the power to issue bonds equal to 2 percent of assessed valuation without voter approval, a power held by every other large school district in the state. The Board of Commerce, however, vehemently opposed this effort, because it gave the board the ability to assume a substantial amount of debt without any check from the voters. The business organization urged the board to simply ask common council approval of $35 million in bonds. The board unfortunately lost on all fronts. It neither got the change in state law nor the $35 million, and the building crisis continued.[64]

One month later, recriminations flew at a meeting of civic leaders called to discuss the crisis. UAW leader Roy Reuther, SOS leader Merle Henrickson, and the chair of the Wayne County Democratic party urged the board to seek another millage increase, while leaders of the Board of Commerce and the Citizens' Committee on Public Issues called on the board to place a bond issue on the November ballot.[65] Unable to resolve this political stalemate, the board simply resigned itself to a severely restricted construction program and cut capital spending almost in half, from $12,200,000 for 1956–57 to $6,746,830, the lowest figure since 1948–49.[66]

Since the money for construction had to be drawn from the board's general revenue funds, militant teachers, once again, demanded a priority for salary increases over new buildings. In early May, DFT President Antonia Kolar repeated the union war cry of the late 1940s, stating that "teachers salaries should have precedence over everything else."[67] When school leaders announced an across-the-board $250 raise that did not keep salaries on pace with inflation, 800 DFT members marched on the board of education in the first serious display of union activism in a decade. Kolar warned the board that teachers would be going to the suburbs "where salaries are more attractive."[68]

Her prediction was accurate. In the first nine months of 1957, 650 teachers left Detroit, outstripping the number who had left during all of 1956 and well above the previous average of about 400. The DFT marked 1957 as the worst single-year loss of teachers in the history of the system. By December, the union believed the salary issue was so serious that it urged the board to put all first graders on half-day sessions in order to provide the teachers with an additional $500 raise. The board rejected the proposal but took no other action. The shortage of teachers grew more severe.[69]

As if the board did not have enough problems, at roughly the same time a new controversy erupted about the quality of education in the Detroit schools. This controversy was part of the national debate about "progressive education" that took place throughout most of the early 1950s.[70] The depression and the war had encouraged school leaders in Detroit and across the nation to shift the focus of the high school curriculum away from rigorous academic courses. This trend continued in the early 1950s in response to three interrelated youth problems: juvenile delinquency, dropouts, and youth unemployment. School officials in Detroit had been increasing their attention to these problems since the end of World War II, especially as dropping out of school and juvenile crime persisted in the postwar years. As late as 1962, for example, approximately 40 percent of high school students in Detroit dropped out. In addition, beginning in the late 1950s, there were mounting concerns about teenage violence and juvenile crime.[71]

Since the 1930s, school and civic leaders generally assumed that the solution to most youth problems was to keep students in school longer, a solution they thought depended on making high school courses more relevant to the lives of young people. In 1947, for example, Arthur Dondineau noted that offering courses in trade and vocational training "will keep in class many children who lack interest in straight, academic schooling."[72] With that strategy in mind, in 1949, the school board began an extensive review of the school curriculum with an eye toward expanding vocational education and programs similar to those gaining national attention in the Life Adjustment movement, programs such as Home and Family Life Education, Drivers Education, and Citizenship Education.[73] Three years later, following a study of dropouts in Detroit, the head of the department of guidance and placement argued for expanding programs in vocational education, driver training, and family living, calling them effective means for keeping young people in school. Other studies, completed over the next few years, reaffirmed educators' faith in these types of curricular innovations. By 1958, the need for these courses was axiomatic among school officials in Detroit. One administrator noted that such "interesting, attractive and constructive courses" were crucial to reducing the dropout rate. As in the past, many of these courses were offered as electives in the general curriculum, in which about a third of all Detroit high school students were enrolled in 1957.[74]

These efforts to curb the dropout problem by offering "relevant courses" unquestionably diluted the quality of the high school program.[75] Debates about this decline in quality were a firmly established part of educational politics in Detroit and the issue of falling standards fitted neatly into larger controversies about financing the school system. Liberals argued for more funds, more "social welfare" programs, and a diversified curriculum, while conservatives called for no new taxes and a return to the teaching of basic skills. In 1951, for example, Leonard Kasle warned members of SOS that business organizations planned to use the issue of eliminating frills and returning to basics as a pretext for slashing funds for public education.[76] Kasle's words seemed prophetic during the 1953 millage election, when Martin A. Larson and the Small Property Owners urged Detroiters to vote down the proposed tax increase in large part because educational standards in Detroit had declined. "It is notorious," the antitax organization declared, "that a majority of present graduates cannot spell many of the simple words in everyday use; they have no grounding in literature, English, arithmetic, discipline, or any practical knowledge. In short, they are totally unprepared for advanced study or the ordinary tasks of life."[77]

Over the next few years, lay leaders and educators in Detroit and across the state leveled similar criticisms at the schools, at times as part of campaigns to cut taxes, but often in sincere efforts to stem what many people feared was a trend toward less rigorous high school programs.[78] By far the most important public debate on this issue in Detroit began with the 1957 millage campaign. Allegations of declining standards had surfaced during the campaign, and, within days of the election, as board members wrestled with the reasons for the defeat, controversy erupted over the issue of curriculum decline.[79] Board President William Merrifield precipitated the controversy with a speech that denounced educational frills and called for a return to a fundamental high school education. Merrifield characterized high schools as a "sort of educational cafeteria where the student is free to choose as he sees fit, and it is felt that if we just have enough courses, regardless of their educational value, surely we can provide something that will appeal to everybody." This "educational grab-bag," he declared, was apparently based on the belief that "mass education necessarily means mass mediocrity." The high schools, he concluded, were neither producing "proficient technicians" nor "ordinary citizens equipped with the fundamentals necessary for living in a scientific age."[80]

Merrifield's remarks became the focus of an intense debate among the board members. The debate ended without any resolution, but it set the stage for a larger and more prolonged discussion of the curriculum that took place following the launch of Sputnik in October, 1957. Throughout late 1957 and 1958, Detroiters, like people across the United States, took a long, hard look at the quality of American education, particularly in the high schools. In March, 1958, both the *Free Press* and the *News* carried scathing, front-page exposés that detailed a serious decline in educational standards in the Detroit high school program. The four-part *Free Press* series began with a litany of complaints from local employers, who found graduates unable to perform jobs requiring basic reading, language, and math skills. These business leaders denounced the "cafeteria-style education" in the high schools that enabled students to choose "snap" courses over rigorous academic ones. The biggest problems, the business leaders claimed, appeared among students who graduated from the commercial, vocational, and, especially, the general track, where students had the greatest latitude in choosing electives. In all, the business leaders urged school officials to scrap every track but the academic one so that all students could get a high-quality, basic education. Vocational training, they argued, should be left to industry.[81]

In the second article in the series, the *Free Press* tried to determine if students did, in fact, choose more electives and easier electives than students had in the past by analyzing transcripts from thirty graduates of Pershing High School in 1933 and comparing them to transcripts of thirty students who graduated from the school in January, 1958. This study showed a dramatic decline in the number of academic courses and a sharp increase in what the *Free Press* called "sandbox and custard" courses. By far the biggest drop in academic coursework occurred in the general track, where the number of academic courses fell from 65 percent in 1933 to 48 percent in 1958. In all, the number of English courses taken by the students dropped by 12 percent, history courses by 10 percent, and both math and science courses by 40 percent. In exchange for these courses, students in all tracks added electives whose content confirmed some of the worst fears of critics of the high school program. Students received credit for graduation from "courses" in stage crew, dance band, football, basketball, track, photography, family living, jewelry making, and helping in the school office and library.[82]

In attempting to assess the consequences of this dilution of the curriculum, reporters from the *Free Press* surveyed the results of 1,000 examinations given over the previous two years by the Wayne County Civil Service Commission. Most of the test takers were recent graduates from Detroit high schools and their test results were appalling. About 90 percent of the graduates failed the test that examined "simple arithmetic, arithmetical reasoning, grammar, alphabetical filing, spelling, name comparisons, and meaning of words." The civil service examiners believed that the test measured skills at the seventh grade level.[83] Less than two weeks later, a five-part series on the Detroit high schools done by the *News* confirmed the findings in the *Free Press* exposé. This series not only targeted the diluted curriculum, but also criticized counselors who made no effort to steer students to more demanding programs and teachers who resented questions, seemed unprepared for class, and appeared bored with their jobs.[84]

As direct and pointed as these criticisms were, school officials unanimously responded to the articles by claiming that the problems of the high schools were rooted almost entirely in the financial crisis brought on by the defeat of the 1957 millage increase. School Board President Leonard Kasle wondered how the public could expect high-quality teaching in "understaffed and overcrowded classrooms." Samuel Brownell noted that half of all the high school students in the city were still on half-day sessions, which unquestionably contributed to poorer quality instruction. Leaders of the DFT and the Detroit Education Association (DEA), the new name for the DTA, in turn dismissed the charges about shoddy and indifferent instruction, claiming that teachers were overwhelmed with large classes and inadequate resources. All these comments seemed to reflect fears that fiscal conservatives and business leaders would use the criticisms of the school program as justifications for opposing further tax increases for the schools.

The problem with these responses was that they were essentially irrelevant to the charges that the quality of the curriculum had declined. Worse than that, in claiming that all that was wrong with the schools was simply a lack of funds, the school leaders placed the responsibility for the deteriorating *program* on the people who voted against the millage increase rather than on the educators who actually designed and implemented the program. For example, the expansion of the general track, one of the most criticized aspects of the high school program, had practically nothing to do with finances and almost everything to do with educational philosophy. Nevertheless, Leonard Kasle went so far as to claim that the students' criticisms really reflected their disenchantment with the community rather than the schools. Referring to the April, 1957, millage defeat, Kasle declared, "Our children know the community does not care enough about about their education to provide the seats and the staff necessary for a full day's educational program."[85] What Kasle and the other educational leaders failed to confront was that even if the school system had been able to comfortably house all its students and teach them in small classes, a large proportion of these high school students would still be receiving, at best, a second-rate, life-adjustment education.

The fact was, in 1958, school leaders who pleaded for additional funds and critics who decried the decline in educational standards were both right. Proof of that fact was soon forthcoming with the publication of a massive community study of the Detroit public schools. This study was the direct result of long-standing pressure from liberal Detroiters for greater community access to policy-making. As a consequence of these demands, when the new, more liberal school board interviewed candidates to replace Arthur Dondineau, board members specifically sought someone who would open the system to input from community groups. The board chose Samuel Brownell, in part because of his willingness to provide such access to the community, and almost as soon as he took office he created the Citizens Advisory Committee on School Needs (CAC).[86]

The mission of the CAC was to survey all aspects of the school system and recommend policy and programmatic changes. In February, 1957, the board appointed George Romney, president of American Motors and a leader of the Michigan Republican party, to chair the survey. Eventually, the CAC included 270 citizens drawn in roughly equal numbers from each of the eight administrative districts of the school system. Norman Drachler, an administrator from the central office, supervised the research activities of the committee.[87]

The board charged the CAC with investigating five aspects of the district as a whole: the school program (curriculum), personnel, the physical plant (buildings), school-community relations, and finance. In addition, each of the eight regional subcommittees researched these areas as they related to their section of the school district.[88] In November, 1958, after eighteen months of study, the CAC issued a report that appealed to both sides of the educational conflict in Detroit by calling for a massive transfusion of funds into the school system and a major transformation of the school curriculum.

Announcing the results of the report in a speech to the Economic Club of Detroit, Romney declared that the CAC study was "perhaps the most complete documentation ever accumulated by citizens on the status of public education in a major American city." In his speech to these Detroit area business leaders, Romney highlighted the problems of overcrowded and decaying schools, thousands of children on half-day sessions, class sizes almost 50 percent larger than the national average, and inadequate curricular offerings in numerous areas. The solution to most of these problems, Romney declared, was additional funds for the schools. As he put it, "I believe Detroit's future depends on investing more money in the education of our children."[89]

Indeed, the CAC discovered that, if anything, the board had been understating its needs in terms of building renovation and new construction. The committee found that almost 70,000 students attended school in buildings that were below national standards in such areas as "adequacy, suitability, safety, healthfulness. . . ." Thirty-two school buildings were over sixty years old. In addition, nearly all of the 153 buildings constructed in the 1910s and 1920s needed costly repairs, due in large part to the suspension of the regular maintenance program during the the 1930s and 1940s. To add, replace, and repair buildings throughout the system, the CAC estimated that, over the next decade, the board would have to spend at least $141 million and perhaps as much as $199 million.[90]

The CAC also found that the building shortage and demographic shifts in the city had wreaked havoc with the general school organization. As of June, 1958, 22,675 high school students were still on half-day sessions. Six high schools, mostly in the outer rim of the city, were above capacity by 751 to 1,711 students. In addition, school officials had virtually abandoned the junior high dimension of the 6–3–3 organizational plan due to lack of space, placing students in grades 7 through 9 wherever there was room for them. In 1958, almost 31 percent of the 51,550 students in grades 7 through 9 attended elementary schools and another 22 percent attended high schools.

In other words, more than half of the junior high school students in the city were *not* in junior high schools. In addition to these secondary students, more than 12,000 elementary students were in temporary buildings or were bused to schools outside their neighborhoods.[91]

The CAC also found the system suffering from a severe shortage of teachers. The committee estimated that the school system would need 813 additional teachers just to handle the more than 25,000 new students who would enter the school system by 1963. In order to replace the "emergency substitutes" who were working without adequate teaching credentials, the board would have to hire 754 more teachers. The CAC also estimated that it would take 225 additional teachers just to reduce the size of classes by one student per class. At the time, classes in the district were averaging about 34 students per teacher.[92] Yet attracting new teachers, especially the best of the recent graduates, was increasingly difficult given the opportunities offered in suburban school systems and in industry. The CAC noted that "surrounding communities are outdistancing the Detroit basic salary scale for teachers" and that local industries were luring away many science and math teachers with far better salaries and benefits.[93]

More money was the only solution to all these problems and the CAC addressed that issue in its most important recommendation.

> We affirm that public education is an investment in Detroit's future, an investment that cannot wait for better times or for more comfortable days. Whatever changes that may take place in Detroit's economy, our most obvious need is more intensive and better education for our children now. . . . Today's child cannot wait for tomorrow to receive his education. *Financial support of education is not primarily a question of resources but—of public attitudes and policy.*[94]

In regard to the curriculum, the recommendations of the CAC were equally sweeping. The committee recommended abolishing the platoon system, intensifying instruction in elementary reading, math, and spelling, and shifting to self-contained classes in all elementary schools. It also urged a renewed commitment to junior high schools and it set goals for housing all students in grades 7 through 9 in their own buildings. Senior high schools, however, received the most attention in the final report. The committee endorsed the concept of the comprehensive high school, but strongly urged the system to increase the amount of math, science, and foreign language courses that students were taking. The committee also recommended that school leaders strengthen vocational programs in the high schools and that they expand initiatives for academically "gifted" students.[95]

These suggestions satisfied some of the demands of critics who sought a more academically rigorous high school curriculum. But none of these recommendations addressed the most problematic area of the high schools, the general track. The consultants who analyzed the high school curriculum *did* label the general track "the most amorphous offered in the high schools." Yet their only suggestion for improvement was to call for more of the kinds of courses introduced in the 1930s and 1940s that created the problems with the track in the first place. The consultants maintained that "relevant" courses offered the best hope for solving the problems of dropouts, youth unemployment, and juvenile crime. They urged school leaders to increase course offerings in "home and family living, home economics, occupational information, health, physical education, hygiene, child care, library reading, job up-grading, and speech." They also urged that many of these courses be expanded from one semester to two and, in some cases, from one year to two. In addition, the consultants called for greater job preparation and "work-experience education" targeted toward getting the students in this track prepared for employment in semiskilled and unskilled jobs.[96]

As in the 1920s and 1930s, the educators used the principle of equity to justify this decidedly unequal education. Indeed, the consultants declared, *"Identical education does not provide equal educational opportunity. It denies it."*[97] Such justifications may have resonated well in conferences of educational experts, but, given the deadening and dead-end nature of the general track curriculum and the dramatic decline in the number of unskilled and semiskilled jobs during this era, these recommendations represented the utter educational abandonment of at least a third of all high school students in Detroit.

The failure to address the problem of the general curriculum was the most serious flaw in the CAC report, but, in the wave of enthusiasm that greeted the document, no one noticed. The board adopted the recommendations of the CAC entirely and quickly geared up for a campaign to get more money for the schools. Despite the fact that the document endorsed virtually all of the major positions liberal, labor, and civil rights groups had taken for the past two decades (such as the need for substantially more money for public education), business leaders also joined this campaign. George Romney and the other business leaders who had been members of the CAC were instrumental in this effort.[98] Despite some initial grousing about higher school taxes by Harvey Campbell, business leaders generally accepted the arguments that Romney presented and, for the first time in over thirty years, many of them actively supported efforts to raise money for the Detroit public schools.[99]

Elated by this show of support from the business community, the board voted in January, 1959, to seek a renewal of the 4.5 mill tax levy that was due to expire that year and a 3.0 mill tax increase. In addition to these 7.5 mills, the board asked the voters to approve $60 million in bonds to fund the first half of a ten-year construction program. The *Free Press* and the *News* immediately endorsed the proposals. Not surprisingly, SOS, the DFT, and the Wayne County AFL-CIO enthusiastically supported both proposals.[100] These groups were joined by the *Detroit Times,* Detroit Citizens League, the Detroit Council of Churches, Detroit Federation of Women's Clubs, the Detroit chapter of the National Council of Jewish Women, the League of Women Voters, the Polish National Alliance, local Democratic and Republican party organizations, and scores of neighborhood organizations, PTAs, churches, and synagogues.[101]

Black Detroiters were among the most enthusiastic supporters of the proposals. The CAC made it abundantly clear that the central and eastern sections of the city, which had the largest concentrations of black families, had the greatest need for new school construction. In addition, the CAC recommended that the board should draw district boundaries without regard to race, a clear slap at the policy of racial gerrymandering pursued by the board of education.[102] The *Michigan Chronicle,* the NAACP, and the Booker T. Washington Trade Association (an organization of black business leaders) gave the millage and bond issue unqualified support. Indeed, one advertisement in the *Chronicle,* linking events locally to the larger civil rights struggle, declared support for the proposals under the headline "Don't Let Detroit Become Another Little Rock."[103]

In all, campaign leaders raised $65,000 for printing and $27,000 for advertising. In addition, there was mass door-to-door canvasing, ward and precinct organizations that included poll watchers working on election day, and "an avalanche of communications to parents through PTA meetings and literature carried home by the children." As two political analysts described it, the 1959 Detroit millage and bond effort was, as far as school tax elections are concerned, "perhaps the most gigantic campaign ever waged in the nation."[104]

Opposition to the proposals, on the other hand, was scattered and disorganized. Neither the Board of Commerce nor any of the groups that had opposed the 1957 millage opposed the 1959 proposals.[105] Not surprisingly, given the dire warnings of the CAC, the huge outpouring of support for the proposals, and the lack of organized opposition, both the millage increase and the bond issues passed by large margins, garnering over 64 percent and almost 60 percent of the vote, respectively.[106] School leaders and their allies were jubilant. For the first time in the memory of most participants in Detroit school politics, it seemed that the school system had enough money to simultaneously provide for better salaries for teachers, hire additional teachers, *and* construct new buildings.[107]

This euphoria, however, was quickly tempered by two unexpected developments. First, the County Tax Allocation Board, which had been providing 8.31 mills out of the annual 15 mill levy to the Detroit public schools, cut the allocation to 8.26 mills. Second, by late 1959, school leaders realized that property assessments in Detroit were declining, which meant that revenue from the extra 7.5 mills would also decline.[108] These developments cut deeply into the revenue that the board had projected from the millage increases. Still, as the 1960s began, the school system was in better financial shape than it had been at any time since the 1920s, and it appeared that a serious effort would be made to improve the quality of the school program in the city.

State Aid and State Power, 1950–64

On New Year's Day, 1950, Michigan Federation of Teachers (MFT) President Arthur Elder wrote a gloomy assessment of educational politics to University of Michigan economist Walter Heller. "On your comment regarding the possibility of resolving the mutual suspicion of labor and conservatives," he stated, "I see little possibility of this so long as middle-of-the-roaders and non-labor people generally are so prone to go along uncritically with business-dictated proposals."[109] Indeed, throughout the early 1950s, the state-level battles between labor and business, urban and rural interests, and Democrats and Republicans continued with the same intensity as in previous decades. Business leaders routinely denounced "CIO socialists" who, they claimed, controlled the Michigan Democratic party, while labor leaders decried the "fascist tendencies" of the Republicans who, they asserted, were simply "stooges" for wealthy industrialists.[110]

Despite this overheated rhetoric, however, the situation in Lansing did change during the 1950s in ways quite similar to what took place in Detroit. By the early 1960s, many of the positions that Elder and other liberal educators had advocated had come to pass—positions such as increased state control over rural schools, the consolidation of school districts, increased taxes and appropriations for schools, and reapportionment of the legislature. Throughout the 1930s and 1940s, urban educators, labor leaders, and liberal politicians had fought for these measures in order to get greater resources for public schools, generally, and to end what they believed was the ongoing subsidy of inadequate and inefficient rural school districts by urban taxpayers. By the mid-1960s, the liberal-labor-black coalition had succeeded in increasing state power over local educational policies and providing urban school districts such as Detroit with a larger proportion of state aid. Unfortunately, even with the increases in state power and appropriations, the Detroit schools continued to receive less funds than schools leaders believed was either adequate or fair.

As in Detroit, the political changes on the state level occurred because of the twin problems of the baby boomers and the chronic underfunding of the schools during the 1930s and 1940s. The increases in state aid in the late 1940s neither met the needs of the times nor prepared the system for the "tidal wave" of baby boomers in the 1950s. Between 1950 and 1956, enrollments in public schools in Michigan soared from approximately 1.08 million to over 1.45 million. By 1958, enrollments hit 1.6 million.[111] Mirroring the situation in Detroit, school districts across the state raced to provide buildings for these children. Despite a furious building program begun in the late 1940s, a 1953 study still found that almost 40 percent of the school buildings in the state had been constructed before 1900. In 1955, school officials estimated that the state still needed to spend an additional $500 million on school construction by 1960 in order to adequately house the continuing flood of children. Like Detroit, the outstate school districts lacked teachers as well as buildings. State officials estimated in 1953 that 7,500 teachers were working without proper training and credentials. Replacing them with qualified instructors was an impossible dream, since the state needed at least 7,000 more teachers just to keep pace with the enrollment increases.[112] In April, 1954, Governor G. Mennen Williams described the teacher shortage in apocalyptic terms, declaring that "the lack of teachers may kill more democracy in 10 years than the H-bomb."[113]

Initially, efforts to solve these problems in Lansing were frustrated by the same controversies about state control and higher taxes that had dominated state educational politics in the 1940s. During the early 1950s, for example, the coalition of liberal and educational groups that had formed in the late 1930s (including the MFT, urban educators, organized labor, and the Democratic party) continued to demand such basic educational standards as minimum millages, minimum salaries, and maximum class sizes as prerequisites for state aid and were countered at every turn by rural interest groups and conservative politicians who feared increased state control of local schools.[114] Yet, these advocates of smaller government finally retreated in the face of the enormous educational problems confronting the state.

In 1951, the Republican-dominated legislature passed a bill requiring 5 mills as the minimum a school district had to levy in order to be eligible for state aid. Two years later, following a scandal in which state officials found some rural districts padding enrollments in order to increase state appropriations, a coalition of Republicans and Democrats began a campaign to increase state control over rural districts and drastically cut the number of school districts in the state. As a result of the scandal, the legislature strengthened the law on enrollment reporting. More important, the scandal gave credence to the arguments of Democrats and union leaders that the state needed to play a larger role in ensuring that state aid was spent appropriately.[115] While action on many of the other demands for greater centralization of power in the state was slow in coming, in 1956, the legislature again raised the minimum millage requirement for state aid to 6.5 mills. This was below the 8 mills that Governor Williams and urban school leaders had requested, but, as far as proponents of greater state power were concerned, it was an improvement.[116]

By far the greatest increase in state control occurred on the one area where labor and business were in substantial agreement, the need for school consolidation.[117] By 1953, all but the most die-hard proponents of local control saw the need for consolidation. A study commissioned by the governor found that 92 percent of the children of the state were being educated in just 11 percent of the school districts. Despite protests from rural leaders, these findings, combined with the massive enrollment increases, the financial scandals, and mounting political pressure made centralization almost inevitable.[118] Between 1950 and 1960, the number of school districts in Michigan fell from 4,841 to 1,989. By 1965, the number had dropped to 993.[119]

Liberals and conservatives may have agreed on the need for school consolidation, but the issue of increasing taxes for education continued to polarize state-level politics. In a number of important ways, the sales tax "split" of 1946 exacerbated this polarization. Liberals, educators, and Democratic Governor G. Mennen Williams hailed the split as the first important step toward adequate funding for education in almost two decades. Conservatives and the majority of the members of the rural and mostly Republican legislature, on the other hand, saw the split as a direct path to massive budget deficits and the eventual bankruptcy of the state. Between 1949 and 1951, in an attempt to avert these catastrophes, the legislature annually voted to take $9 million earmarked for the state teachers' retirement fund out of the sales tax revenues rather than the general fund. This clearly violated the intention of the sales tax split and it ran contrary to a 1947 ruling by the Michigan Supreme Court that had upheld the constitutionality of the split. Nevertheless, the need for fiscal restraint was equally apparent, as the state's budget shortfall nearly doubled to an estimated $70 million in 1952.[120]

As the educational and financial crises grew, Williams and the legislature became deadlocked over attempts to adequately finance the schools and balance the state budget. Williams sought a corporate profits tax, which the legislature and the Michigan Manufacturers Association strongly opposed. The legislature, on the other hand, called for reduced spending, which led to outraged cries from educators, parents, and leaders of organized labor.[121] Beginning in 1953, the public increasingly pressured the state to overhaul the tax system entirely and improve funding for education. As a consequence of that pressure, in 1954, state representative Rollo Conlin (R-Tipton) introduced a measure to increase funding for the schools and resolve the problem of funding the state teachers' retirement system. The Conlin Amendment, as the legislation was called, revised the 1946 sales tax split by allocating two-thirds of all sales tax revenues for the schools. These new revenues, however, carried the stipulation that the schools had to provide enough funds to keep the teachers' retirement system actuarially sound.[122] The Detroit school board, the Michigan CIO, and the Detroit Board of Commerce initially opposed the plan, objecting to the weak eligibility restrictions on rural districts for state aid. Nevertheless, the Conlin Amendment received wide support across the state and was strongly backed by the Michigan Education Association.[123]

In November, 1954, voters approved the amendment overwhelmingly and, over the next few years, funds for education increased. In 1949–50, for example, the state gave public schools over $98.7 million from the general fund and sales tax split. By 1953–54, the amount had climbed to more than $152.6 million. By 1956–57, state aid drawn from the general fund and sales taxes soared to over $256.5 million. Detroit's portion of state aid went from over $28.8 million in 1949–50 to $46.7 million in 1956–57.[124]

School leaders in Detroit obviously welcomed this increase, but they remained dissatisfied. Even with the additional revenue, the state still provided considerably less support for schools in the Motor City than it did for schools in outstate districts. Between 1949–50 and 1956–57, the total amount of state aid jumped almost 160 percent, but the amount allocated to Detroit climbed only 63 percent.[125] In 1958, the CAC reported that the state paid an average of 54 percent of the educational costs of all the districts in Michigan (and, in some cases, as much as 85 percent) but paid only 41 percent of the costs for Detroit. In short, despite some important changes in the amount for state funds provided for public education, school and civic leaders in Detroit firmly believed that the state was still failing in its commitment to support the Detroit schools. Not surprisingly, the CAC strongly endorsed calls for more school consolidation and higher local millage requirements as a prerequisite for state aid.[126]

The ongoing rural-urban conflict represented by these stands kept the political pot boiling well after the passage of the Conlin Amendment. Over the next few years, the governor and the legislature continued to wrangle over appropriations for education and prerequisites for state aid.[127] In June, 1955, for example, Williams reluctantly signed a new state aid package, declaring that "the overwhelming majority of districts now receiving such payments are not carrying a fair share of the state's educational burden. Most of them are taxing themselves far below the statewide averages."[128] Earlier that year, in an attempt to circumvent the legislature and direct more aid to urban districts, Williams and urban educators again went directly to the voters, this time with a constitutional amendment allowing the state to subsidize bond issues for school construction. Despite opposition from rural interests, the amendment, which had the support of both organized labor and the Detroit Board of Commerce, passed largely because of an overwhelming yes vote from Wayne County.[129]

Each new constitutional amendment provided the public schools with badly needed revenue, but each amendment also exacerbated the deeply polarized political situation in Lansing. The amendments highlighted the seemingly impassable gulf between the Democratic governor, who drew most of his support from urban areas and organized labor, and the Republican-dominated legislature that drew much of its support from rural areas and business interests. While Williams and his liberal and educational allies may have delighted in the success of their efforts to circumvent the legislature in these campaigns to amend the constitution, they failed to see that this strategy contained a political and financial time bomb that would explode if the state economy went into recession. In 1958, as business activity slumped, the fuse for that bomb was lit.

Throughout 1958, tax revenues dropped sharply as the economy slowed and the demand for unemployment benefits jumped. By year's end, the state was running a budget deficit of $21 million and was looking ahead to a deficit of $110 million by the end of fiscal 1959. Since an enormous amount of state revenue was earmarked by constitutional amendment for such special purposes as public schools, the legislature was unable to find enough funds to support the normal operations of the state government. Compounding the problem was a $250,000 limit on the amount the state could borrow. As the financial crisis worsened, the governor and his liberal allies once again called for a corporate profits tax and, adding fuel to the fire, proposed a graduated income tax. Republicans and business leaders vociferously protested against these proposals and instead urged the legislature to increase the borrowing power of the state, cut expenditures, and increase the sales tax as well as increasing taxes on beer, tobacco, and telephone calls. As both sides refused to compromise, the state hurtled toward fiscal catastrophe. On May 7, 1959, Michigan ran out of money and state employees suffered a "payless pay day." The impending collapse of state government seemed to bring the politicians to their senses, and a compromise was worked out.[130]

Nevertheless, outrage over the crisis persisted. Business leaders and conservatives immediately led a fight to increase the sales tax and, taking their cue from their political opponents, brought the issue to the voters in the form of a constitutional amendment, narrowly approved in November, 1960.[131] The major consequence of the fiscal crisis, however, was not the sales tax increase but growing sentiment that the entire constitution of the state needed to be scrapped. People were particularly incensed about the proliferation of constitutional amendments and the practice of earmarking funds for education and other special programs. The *Free Press,* for example, argued that, by earmarking funds, state officials could not deal effectively with the financial emergency of 1959. In the wake of the crisis, George Romney, the president of American Motors and former chair of the Citizens Advisory Committee in Detroit, and an organization called Citizens for Michigan launched a successful campaign for a constitutional convention that began deliberations in October, 1961.[132]

Romney, who chaired the convention and headed the subcommittee on elementary and secondary education, played a central role in drafting the educational sections of the new constitution. A liberal Republican with a strong interest in education, Romney fashioned a series of compromises that appealed to a broad spectrum of convention delegates. The new constitution attempted to placate liberals and urban educators by centralizing state power in a new department of education, by allowing property owners to vote to increase the 15 mill limit to 18 mills, and by continuing the practice of earmarking funds for public schools. As one analyst described the new constitution, "It makes an attempt at the co-ordination of all education using the only acceptable tool available to state government, financial control." Rural interests were more satisfied with the compromise since it retained the current apportionment with its disproportionate representation of rural districts.[133]

While controversy erupted on a number of key provisions in the proposed constitution, the most heated debate centered on the failure to apportion the legislature fairly. The Democratic party, the Michigan AFL-CIO, and the Detroit NAACP, which had all fought for reapportionment throughout the 1950s, felt that Romney had betrayed them. Almost immediately after the convention adjourned, the Michigan Democratic party filed briefs in support of the Tennessee suit that eventually led to the *Baker v. Carr* decision of the U.S. Supreme Court. When the court handed down its "one man, one vote" decision in 1962, Michigan Democrats, liberals, and labor leaders were jubilant.[134]

By 1970, however, much of that joy had vanished. *Baker v. Carr* did break the hold rural districts had on the Michigan legislature, but, ironically, it also led to the reduction of the Detroit delegation in the legislature. Because the suburbs had burgeoned and the city had lost population between 1960 and 1970, following *Baker v. Carr,* the Detroit delegation in the Michigan house fell from twenty-six members to twenty-one and Detroit's seats in the senate dropped from nine to seven.[135] Thus, the unexpected consequence of Detroit's victory in this protracted struggle against rural and corporate interests was the loss of representation and power on the state level. Besides losing state representation and power, Detroit suddenly faced a new suburban power bloc in state politics. The traditional rural-urban polarization in the legislature was now replaced by a rural-suburban-urban configuration. In addition, as the demographic character of the Detroit metropolitan area changed, that new political configuration was frequently shaped by racial politics that pitted white suburbs against the increasingly black city in the struggle for power and resources.[136]

The Civil Rights Struggle and the Detroit Public Schools, 1950–60

In May of 1950, the *Detroit News* brought together a panel of African-American leaders to discuss the problems facing their community. When asked if they were satisfied with the education their children were getting in the public schools, the leaders responded with "a loud and unanimous 'No!'"

As evidence that Detroit was operating a separate and unequal school system for black children, they pointed to the continuing school board policy of segregating black teachers in majority black schools and the "disgraceful" physical neglect of schools in black neighborhoods.[137] Black leaders had been protesting these conditions for almost two decades and, as the 1950s began, the problems seemed no closer to resolution. Indeed, as the Detroit schools lurched from one financial crisis to another, schools in black neighborhoods seemed destined to fall even further behind in the battle for equal treatment and equal resources.

Yet, beginning in 1956, following the election of Remus Robinson and Leonard Kasle to the school board, black protests against segregation in the Detroit schools started to have an impact. In alliance with the UAW, SOS, and the Americans for Democratic Action, black Detroiters mounted a sustained and increasingly effective effort directed at six areas: ousting superintendent Arthur Dondineau; adding and physically improving schools in black neighborhoods; increasing the number of black teachers, counselors, and administrators; ending the policy of segregating black educators in majority black schools; upgrading the instructional and the curricular quality in black schools; and stopping the administrative practice of gerrymandering attendance boundaries to segregate schools. With the exception of that last, volatile issue, by 1960, the liberal-labor-black coalition achieved notable successes in all of these areas.

Initially, the black community directed its efforts toward firing superintendent Arthur Dondineau, who had become a symbol of racial intolerance for blacks during the Higgenbotham and Birdhurst controversy in the late 1940s. Following the controversy, the NAACP, the *Michigan Chronicle*, and SOS continued to rail at Dondineau and at what the *Chronicle* labeled "the apparently deliberate discrimination against Negro school teachers and pupils by the Detroit Board of Education."[138] In 1951, after two SOS-backed candidates were elected to the board, black Detroiters urged the board to deny Dondineau another three-year term as superintendent. Edward M. Turner, president of the Detroit NAACP, specifically protested that, under Dondineau's administration, "discriminatory and undemocratic practices . . . have become legendary in the school system." A. L. Zwerdling, representing the Americans for Democratic Action, echoed these denunciations and called for a total reappraisal of the school administration. Despite these protests, the board reappointed Dondineau, but, in a concession to the protestors, the board unanimously passed a resolution mandating a periodic review of the actions of the school administration in such areas as discrimination.[139]

Unfortunately, over the next few years, virtually nothing came of the resolution. Black Detroiters saw it as another example of the board's penchant for what one civil rights leader described as "a lot of say-so but not much do-so."[140] A 1951 study by the Detroit Urban League, for example, found that black children attended the oldest schools in the oldest section of the city, and that the board had done virtually nothing to improve conditions in these schools. Three years later, despite the massive school-building program, schools in black neighborhoods remained physically among the worst in the city. As late as February, 1956, the *Michigan Chronicle* declared that it is the "apparent policy on the part of the Board of Education to allow school facilities in the older areas of the city to deteriorate and decline."[141]

Just as the problems of inadequate school facilities went unresolved, so did the practices of racially gerrymandering attendance boundaries, segregating black teachers in black schools, overloading classes in black schools, and offering an inferior curriculum to black students.[142] The protests of civil rights groups and the black newspapers made no dent in the policies of the school administration. Indeed, Arthur Dondineau responded to the protests with contempt. When asked by a black reporter if he was aware that black teachers were only assigned to black schools, he replied tartly, "I know because I put them there."[143] Such attitudes led the *Michigan Chronicle* to declare that "like the tentacles of some monstrous octopus, the evil of racial discrimination lies entwined about the heart of the Detroit School System."[144]

Three days after that statement appeared, however, the black community gained its most positive victory to date, as Dr. Remus G. Robinson became the first black elected to the Detroit board of education. The election of Robinson and NAACP member Leonard Kasle was the most notable success of the liberal-labor-black coalition until then, and it led the coalition to renew its efforts to end racial discrimination in the Detroit schools. In August, black parents succeeded, for the first time, in getting the board to rescind a decision to change an attendance boundary that would have added to school segregation. In January, 1956, a protest led by longtime black activist Snow Grigsby, Congressman Charles Diggs, Jr., and the DFT succeeded in getting the board to upgrade the facilities at Miller High School. Despite opposition from lame-duck Superintendent Dondineau, in June the board approved a resolution drafted by Remus Robinson that provided $850,000 for the improvement of Miller High School. Black leaders were delighted, but five months later their victory turned bittersweet when the board voted to restore Miller to its previous status as an intermediate school in order to relieve overcrowding at four eastside elementary schools.[145]

While the end results of the struggle to improve Miller High School were less than satisfying, there was growing evidence of a change in the racial attitude of the school board. Indeed, in the fall of 1956, the *Michigan Chronicle* stated that, in the previous six months, the racial situation in the Detroit schools "appears to be considerably improved" due in large part to the "more liberal character" of the board of education. The most dramatic evidence of that improvement was the appointment of Samuel Brownell as the new superintendent, replacing Arthur Dondineau. Almost immediately after his appointment, Brownell won high praise from civil rights leaders by publicly repudiating Dondineau's policy of segregating black teachers and announcing a "color-blind" policy for teacher placements.[146]

The improving racial situation in the Detroit schools was also influenced by the great changes in race relations that were sweeping the country during these years. Many Detroiters, both black and white, were deeply involved in the larger civil rights movement and they increasingly turned their attention to racial problems in the city and its schools. The efforts to desegregate the Little Rock schools in the late 1950s were particularly important, since they provided an object lesson in how a determined group of integrationists could succeed against seemingly insurmountable odds.[147]

The campaign for educational equality in Detroit was not only boosted by events nationally but also by the efforts of the 1958 Citizens Advisory Committee on School Needs. The Center Region subcommittee of the CAC included such civil rights leaders as Mrs. James J. McClendon, wife of a former president of the NAACP, Arthur Johnson, also of the NAACP, and Francis Kornegay, executive secretary of the Urban League.[148] Their investigation provided irrefutable evidence of discrimination against black Detroiters and highlighted many of the problems that African-Americans had been protesting for years, including the deterioration and decay of schools in black neighborhoods and a curriculum in predominantly black secondary schools that clearly shortchanged the students.[149]

Other CAC members, such as Al Barbour of the Wayne County AFL-CIO and Charles Wartman, editor of the *Michigan Chronicle,* also guided various CAC subcommittees in producing reports that went beyond the most optimistic expectations of the black and liberal leaders in highlighting the racial problems of the school system. In late November, 1958, for example, the CAC subcommittee on school-community relations released a study that explicitly detailed the segregationist policies of the school system. The

Michigan Chronicle was jubilant, declaring that "hammer blows have been struck at racial segregation in the Detroit public schools by a subcommittee of the Citizens Advisory Committee on School Needs."[150]

One week later, upon the release of the report of the CAC subcommittee on school buildings, the *Chronicle* editorialized that the report demonstrated unequivocally "that the abandonment of vast areas to inferior buildings and inferior interests has resulted in inferior instruction, handicapped children and has in general lowered the standing of the entire school system." The final report of the CAC did not disappoint the black community either, since it contained a series of recommendations that directly addressed all of these problems. In addition, the CAC strongly recommended that school leaders devote more attention to improving relations between the school system and the black community.[151]

More important than these suggestions was the degree to which the board actually carried them out. During the campaign for the 1959 millage increase and bond issue, Samuel Brownell and other school leaders declared that a large portion of the construction funds would go toward improving conditions in the overcrowded and decaying schools "within the Boulevard," essentially the black section of Detroit that extended south of Grand Boulevard and included the lower east and lower west sides of the city.[152] In a clear signal to liberal Detroiters that the board intended to fulfill that campaign promise, in September, 1959, the board announced the appointment of former SOS president Merle Henrickson as director of planning and school building studies for the system.[153]

Black leaders kept steady pressure on the school administration to insure that the construction program went forward. As a consequence of these efforts, between 1959 and 1962, the board spent over $69 million of the more than $92 million in construction funds, 75 percent of the total, in areas of the city with the largest proportion of black students, particularly in the central and eastern administrative districts.[154]

The increase in the number of black teachers, counselors, and administrators was equally dramatic during these years. In 1949, the 386 black teachers employed by the Detroit public schools accounted for slightly more than 5 percent of the total professional staff. By 1961, according to the first official racial accounting of staff and students since 1949, the number of black teachers had jumped to 2,275, almost 22 percent of the teaching force. This increase was the direct result of a number of fair employment policies and practices instituted by the board and Brownell since September, 1956.[155] The number of black counselors and administrators also increased in this period, but less dramatically. In the 1955–56 school year there were six black counselors; in 1961–62 there were nineteen, and, by 1964–65, there were forty-seven. In the same years, the number of black assistant principals went from nine to fourteen to twenty and the number of black principals went from two to seven to nine. In all, in the late 1950s and early 1960s, as a consequence of combined pressures from the black community, liberal organizations, findings of the CAC report, and increased funds from the 1959 millage, the Detroit schools became a national leader in the number and proportion of black staff members.[156]

In addition to concerns about staffing, black leaders and parents were also determined to upgrade the quality of the educational program their children were getting. In many ways, these curricular concerns were similar to those expressed by the *Free Press* and the *News* in the spring of 1958. Indeed, at precisely the same time that these newspapers were describing the decline in standards generally, a group of black parents with children at McMichael Intermediate School and Northwestern High School led a protest at a board meeting to specifically denounce the lack of college preparatory courses at these schools. The parents also echoed complaints about indifferent and inadequate teachers who were lax in discipline and maintained low academic standards.[157]

Probably nowhere in the school system was the decline in educational standards worse than in the predominantly black schools in the city. Investigating racial and educational changes in Doty Elementary School, one researcher reported, in 1957, "There have been many complaints from parents that their children are not now studying the same curriculum that had been offered to the white children. . . . It is felt that there has been more than just a change in some subjects, that there has been an attempt to change the child's goals in a different direction; that is, away from college preparatory to vocational and frill studies." Not long after the McMichael and Northwestern protests, Remus Robinson, president of the board, also deplored the policy of tracking black students into "watered-down" courses that provided them with none of the knowledge and few of the skills to compete academically.[158]

As in the past, most of the problem lay with the general track of the high schools, into which the administration placed large numbers of poor and black students. In her 1961 study of the Detroit schools, Patricia Cayo Sexton found that 48 percent of the students from the poorest families in the city were in the general track. While Sexton did not analyze these data by race, given the high rate of poverty in the black community, it is likely that many, if not most, of the students assigned to the general track were black.[159]

By 1962, however, it appeared that the problems associated with the general track pervaded almost all aspects of secondary education for black students. In February of that year, a scathing series of articles apparently written by an anonymous black teacher about Northwestern High School showed that the quality of the educational program in the school appeared to have worsened since the McMichael and Northwestern protests in 1958. The teacher declared that, due to massive overcrowding and utter indifference on the part of school administrators, Northwestern had become an "attendance school," which meant that "if a student just keeps going long enough . . . he will be graduated; regardless if he has learned anything or not." The teacher noted that not only had administrators lowered the grading scale so that students could pass more easily, but they also reprimanded teachers who failed too many students. Deploring the lack of academic rigor, the teacher concluded that the lack of "set standards" was a deliberate policy implemented by "people who believe that Negro Children are inferior as students so there is no sense spending a lot of public money trying to educate them as white students are educated."[160]

Unlike the more general criticisms about the deterioration of the school program abroad in Detroit, the author of the article on Northwestern was specifically concerned that the root of the problems in predominantly black schools was racism. Black parents, for example, not only denounced the declining standards but also questioned why these standards seemed to have declined faster in predominantly black schools and why black students were disproportionately represented in the least academically rigorous programs that the school system offered. These concerns led black parents and civil rights leaders to redouble their efforts to end discriminatory policies and practices.

Throughout the 1950s and early 1960s, black leaders had frequently condemned school administrators for their lack of sensitivity to the special educational problems of black children. These concerns were often expressed in protests against culturally biased IQ tests and racially biased textbooks, in demands that black history be included in the Detroit social studies curriculum, and, more generally, in complaints about teachers and administrators who failed to recognize that educating children from poor, black families often demanded different pedagogical strategies than those that worked with other groups of children.[161] The *Michigan Chronicle* noted in 1963, " . . . the Detroit school system, like most of our public school systems, is oriented to the concept that each child should come from a white, Protestant, middle class background." Many black leaders believed that teachers imbued with these attitudes were a primary reason for the poor educational performance of black children.[162] As with black demands for school construction and the appointment of more black teachers and administrators, demands that school leaders become more sensitive to the educational problems of black children also bore some fruit in the late 1950s.

By far the most important effort to redesign educational programs for inner-city children was the Great Cities School Improvement project that Samuel Brownell played a leading role in developing. This "bellwether" program began in September, 1959, when Brownell provided two inner-city elementary schools and one junior high with additional staff members who were to work with teachers and parents to improve educational quality.[163] According to board member Louise Grace, these efforts were a "departure from the accepted pattern of expecting all children to respond to standardized methods of learning and the beginning of an effort to develop new motivations and techniques of learning based upon the child's own special background and experience." The black community applauded the pilot program. The *Michigan Chronicle* declared that the Great Cities project could well mark the dawning of a "new day" in education in Detroit.[164]

Over the next few years, with the aid of grants from the Ford Foundation, the board expanded the pilot program to include seven schools with 420 staff members and 10,400 students. In addition, the Great Cities program expanded into fourteen other large, urban school systems. The program in Detroit provided numerous compensatory education programs, intensive workshops to help teachers bridge the cultural gap between themselves and their students, opportunities to create new curricular materials including a groundbreaking set of preprimers featuring black children, encouragement for teachers to employ novel educational methods, and a concerted effort to involve parents in their children's education. While none of these efforts influenced achievement as powerfully as urban educators had hoped they would, the Great Cities program nevertheless greatly enhanced the national reputation of the school system and served as the prototype for many of the remedial and compensatory education programs of the Great Society.[165]

Like the massive school building campaign in black neighborhoods and the substantial increase in the number of black teachers, the pedagogical changes that Brownell and his staff introduced in the Great Cities program marked a dramatic shift from past practices of the school system. There can be little doubt that, after 1956, school leaders in Detroit were more sensitive to racial issues and more willing to alter policies and programs and provide necessary funds to improve education in black neighborhoods. By the early

1960s, due to the efforts of the liberal-labor-black coalition, the Detroit schools had become a national leader in race relations. Indeed, there appeared to be fairly broad-based support throughout the city for all of these efforts. Yet in the one most important area of race relations, the actual integration of schools, the problems Detroit faced proved to be little different than those in any large city in the nation.

Controversies over Boundaries and Busing, 1959–62

For more than two decades, black Detroiters had strenuously objected to administrative gerrymandering of school attendance boundaries that deliberately segregated black and white children. Following the election of the more liberal board in 1955, the publication of the CAC report in 1958, and the events in Little Rock, black Detroiters hoped to see substantial changes in that policy as well. Indeed, the CAC report had specifically recommended that, in establishing school boundaries, the board should seek "the inclusion of all ethnic, racial and religious groups residing in each school area."[166] By the early 1960s, black leaders were determined to make the school system live up to that recommendation.

Unfortunately, no issue involving civil rights and education was more volatile than the setting of attendance boundaries. Ever since the creation of Miller High School, African-Americans had routinely protested that whenever school leaders drew new boundaries to alleviate overcrowding and reduce half-day sessions, the new boundaries almost invariably increased racial segregation. Many white Detroiters, on the other hand, vehemently opposed any boundary changes that appeared to disturb the racial character of a district. Between 1959 and 1962, there were a number of serious clashes over attendance boundaries and busing, clashes that ominously foreshadowed the fierce, pitched battle over these issues that raged in the 1970s. These early struggles over boundaries and busing were also the first hints of weakness in the liberal-labor-black coalition.

In early October, 1959, the issue of school integration in Detroit burst into the news when school leaders announced plans to transfer 74 black students from the badly overcrowded Pattengill elementary to Houghton school, another predominantly black school that was more than four miles away. A well-organized group of black parents from Pattengill immediately denounced the transfer, noting that two predominantly white schools, which were closer to Pattengill, had space for their children. The parents claimed that the administration had bypassed these schools to avoid integration. When these initial protests yielded no results, the parents refused to allow their children to board the buses for Houghton. In early November, they called a one-day boycott of Pattengill that was observed by more than 1,000 students, about half the student body.[167]

While this protest had some important similarities to the Higgenbotham-Birdhurst controversy in the late 1940s, the results were quite different. In a meeting with the parents and board members, Brownell admitted that the administration had erred in not assigning the students to the nearby schools. He promised to correct the problem at the end of the semester. Board members Robinson and Kasle assured the parents that they would develop a policy to avoid these situations in the future. The parents were overjoyed, and the *Chronicle* and the *News* editorialized that an important step had been taken toward racial equality in the Detroit public schools.[168]

In many ways, however, the most important outcome of the Pattengill controversy was the creation of a new citizens committee to investigate the allegations of racial discrimination in the school system. In January, 1960, the board set up the Citizens Advisory Committee on Equal Educational Opportunities (CAC-EEO), which was chaired by Probate Court Judge Nathan J. Kaufman and included among its members Arthur Johnson, executive director of the NAACP, Circuit Court Judge Wade McCree, the first black elected to countywide office in Wayne County, Al Barbour, president of the Wayne County AFL-CIO, and Roy Eppert, president of Burroughs Corporation. The committee began its work in May and soon found itself embroiled in the renewed controversies about segregation and attendance boundaries.[169]

This time the protests about boundary changes came from the white residents of the northwest section of the city. In mid-October, 1960, the school administration announced that it was going to bus approximately 300 black students from overcrowded schools in the central district to three underutilized schools, Guest, Monnier, and Noble, in the almost entirely white northwestern district. White parents from these three schools immediately attacked the busing plan and threatened to keep their children home when the black students arrived.[170] A front-page editorial in the *Redford Record,* a local newspaper in northwest Detroit, resurrected allegations of left-wing conspiracies in the Detroit schools. Blasting the busing plan as a plot by "leftists within the school system," the editorial also alleged that these conspirators had pressured the board of education to delay building schools "within the boulevard area" so that administrators could use evidence of overcrowding as a pretext for "forced integration." With passions inflamed by these allegations, a group of white parents formed the Northwest Detroit Parents Committee dedicated to fighting the busing plan and committed to recalling all seven members of the board of education.[171]

In an attempt to calm the situation, Samuel Brownell, backed by representatives from the Board of Commerce, AFL-CIO, Detroit Council of Churches, Catholic Human Relations Council, Jewish Community Council, the NAACP, and Urban League met with the parents committee. Before an audience of 2,000 angry community members, Brownell presented a detailed account of how and why the three northwest schools had been chosen for the busing program. His most powerful point was that, over the past ten years, the school administration had routinely bused students to the three schools in question. "The matter of transporting pupils is not new to these schools," he declared. The difference, this time, was that black students would be riding the buses.[172]

The parents, however, would not accept Brownell's explanation nor would they heed blandishments on toleration from the representatives of the Board of Commerce, AFL-CIO, or the religious leaders. This protest was unquestionably a populist revolt that bypassed all of the established interest groups. Tempers flared, and the parents warned Brownell that they would keep their children home if the board persisted with the busing plan. To emphasize their determination, members of the parents committee blatantly circulated recall petitions during the meeting and declared that, with a new board of education, they would get Brownell fired.[173]

Over the next three school days more than 1,300 students boycotted the schools. The Northwest Parents Committee distributed a letter that urged parents to defend their rights and blamed the situation on "Communists and fellow travelers" within the school administration. Brownell, however, refused to budge on the issue and threatened the parents with fines and jail if they continued to keep their children home. Meanwhile, under police protection, the black students were bused to the three schools. In taking this tough stand, Brownell received strong support from the *Free Press,* the *News,* the AFL-CIO, the Detroit Council of Churches, the Jewish Community Council, and the Catholic Archdiocese.[174]

The opposition to the busing plan collapsed by mid-November, perhaps due to Brownell's toughness but also, probably, because the school administration decided to keep the 300 black children segregated within the three schools.[175] In making that decision, however, the school leaders insured that absolutely no one would be satisfied with the outcome of the crisis. In December, for example, Charles L. Wells, a leader of the Detroit NAACP, denounced the Detroit schools before the U.S. Civil Rights Commission, claiming that school leaders were continuing to draw boundaries and make school assignments that reflected a deliberate policy of racial "discrimination and containment."[176]

Pressure for change mounted as the civil rights struggle moved to the center of national attention. Throughout 1960–61, for example, Detroiters took great interest in the campaign to desegregate the New Orleans schools, with black leaders noting the practical irrelevancy of the de jure and de facto distinctions, since schools in Detroit were almost as segregated as those in the South. When someone on the CAC-EEO leaked a story that the committee was uncovering "shocking" evidence of segregation in the Detroit schools, Charles Wartman wondered where these people had been for the past twenty years to suddenly be "shocked" at conditions blacks had been protesting for so long. For Wartman and many other African-Americans, the time for outrage was past and the time for aggressive action had come.[177]

Adding to the sense that blacks could control their own political destiny was the election of the maverick, liberal Jerome Cavanagh as mayor in 1961. Cavanagh had campaigned hard in black neighborhoods, promising, among other things, to appoint a liberal police commissioner who would clean up the notoriously racist Detroit police force. This campaign strategy paid off. Despite running against practically every major interest group in Detroit, including the UAW, Cavanagh won the election handily, thanks in large part to garnering about 85 percent of the black vote. His election signaled a major shift in municipal politics. Traditional power brokers in Detroit were losing control of their constituencies and a new, more independent electorate was emerging. This political change hit the schools with full force less than one year later.[178]

In January, 1962, a group of black parents from the Sherrill school area launched a frontal assault against segregation in the Detroit schools. Three years earlier, school administrators had drawn a new attendance boundary that barred a small number of black students from Sherrill from attending the overcrowded, but overwhelmingly white Mackenzie High School. The new boundary assigned these students to the less crowded but largely black Central and Chadsey high schools. At the time, the NAACP, PTAs from Doty and Sherrill schools, and an ad hoc interracial committee of parents denounced the plan as blatantly discriminatory. Following these protests, Samuel Brownell agreed to indefinitely delay implementing the redistricting plan. In December, 1961, however, the school administration went forward with a new version of the plan, assigning all of the eighth graders at Sherrill to a school in a predominantly black district, thereby insuring that they would not attend Mackenzie High School.[179]

Almost immediately some 300 people formed the Sherrill School Parents Committee to protest the assignments. In January, 1962, the parents filed suit against the Detroit schools alleging that the school administration was operating a separate and unequal school system for black children. In making their case, the parents reiterated virtually every criticism of the school system that blacks had been making since the 1930s, but they particularly emphasized the "drawing and redrawing and gerrymandering of school district lines" in order to segregate black children.[180]

The board responded by categorically denying that it "created or maintained any 'segregated schools.'" Indeed, leaders noted that, since September, 1956, when the present board "was substantially constituted," the school system had made great strides toward equalizing educational opportunity for all children in the city. According to the board, the racial separation that existed in the school system was due to "housing, employment, economic or other practices" outside the control or jurisdiction of the board of education. As evidence of its commitment to racial equality, the board cited the substantial construction program then underway in black neighborhoods, the large increase in the number of black teachers, and the Great Cities program. As the lawsuit proceeded, the board also adopted a series of nondiscrimination resolutions designed to demonstrate its commitment to the goal of equality of educational opportunity.[181]

The board was unquestionably sincere in its commitments to building new schools in black neighborhoods and hiring more black teachers. The troubling question raised by the Sherrill suit, however, focused on the board's commitment to integration itself. A 1969 study of resource distribution and integration between 1940 and 1960, for example, found a very disturbing pattern relating declining resource allocations to rising levels of black students. The study of 164 Detroit elementary schools found that key measures of educational quality—pupil-teacher ratios, the amount of teaching done by emergency substitutes, and teacher turnover rates—deteriorated in schools undergoing racial transition. These schools generally had higher student-teacher ratios, a larger percentage of instruction done by emergency substitutes, and more teacher turnover than schools that remained all-white or all-black.[182] Obviously, these patterns had developed under less liberal school boards and administrations, yet to find them still persisting in 1960 adds credence to the charges brought by the Sherrill parents.

In many ways, the Sherrill case was an early version of the desegregation suits that civil rights groups would bring against northern school systems in the 1970s. Yet two important developments in Detroit set the Sherrill case apart from those later civil rights suits. First, in March, 1962, the Citizens Advisory Committee on Equal Educational Opportunity issued its report that confirmed almost every allegation made by the Sherrill parents. The CAC-EEO found that "school boundaries have been used to further racial and social class segregation" and that there was a "clear-cut pattern of racial discrimination in the assignment of teachers and principals to schools throughout the city." The committee reported that, in February, 1961, 83 percent of the 2,275 black teachers in the school system taught in the predominantly black central, eastern, southeastern, or southern administrative districts. Only 19 black teachers, less than 1 percent, taught in the predominantly white northeastern, northwestern, and western administrative districts.[183]

In addition, one of the most serious findings of the report was that practically no black students participated in the apprenticeship programs that were run cooperatively by the school system, unions, and employers. Since students could not enter these programs without first having a job in the area in which they sought apprenticeships, and unions and employers frequently barred blacks from these jobs, black youths could not take advantage of the programs. As late as 1964, the Construction Trades Apprentice School, for example, enrolled 1,821 students, of whom 34 were black.[184] In all, the CAC-EEO report was a damning indictment of the school system. As George Crockett, Jr., one of the attorneys for the Sherrill parents noted, the "school litigation in Detroit differs from that in every other large Northern urban community bwcause [*sic*] here all of the evidence of the segregated pattern of public school education already has been collected and published in the Citizen's Committee Report."[185]

The second way that the Sherrill case differed from later civil rights suits was that it did not result from charges brought by the Detroit NAACP or any other leading civil rights organization in the city. Indeed, the NAACP initially did not support the lawsuit. As a grass roots effort, the Sherrill suit indicated an emerging split in the African-American community between the established civil rights groups that had proceeded cautiously in alliance with white liberals and a new group of more militant parents and activists who were impatient with the slow pace of change. While the established civil rights groups could point to a number of notable successes, including the election of Remus Robinson to the school board, the substantial increase in the number of black teachers, and the massive building program in black neighborhoods, the more militant groups responded that the Detroit schools still were essentially separate and unequal. In many ways, the CAC-EEO report gave credence to the more militant position. By demonstrating that, despite the successes, the school system was still fundamentally segregated, the CAC-EEO report provided evidence for militants to claim that the incremental approach of the liberal-labor-black coalition was a failure. Perhaps the most damaging findings as far as blacks' faith in the coalition was concerned were the revelations about the apprenticeship programs in which the actions of the unions belied their rhetoric. Nevertheless, the militants failed to acknowledge that, during the six years that the coalition had been able to seriously influence school policy, dramatic changes, including the CAC-EEO report itself, had taken place.

Leading the revolt against the black establishment was Rev. Albert Cleage, Jr., a Congregational minister, whom Sidney Fine has described as the "most articulate spokesman among the black militants and the central figure in the development of a 'strident' black nationalism in Detroit during the 1960s." As early as 1962, Cleage's columns in his family-run weekly, the *Illustrated News,* routinely denounced "condescending" white liberals and labeled Remus Robinson and other members of the black establishment as "Uncle Toms" who lacked "Negro self-pride and racial courage." The Sherrill School case brought Cleage to the forefront of the civil rights struggle in education and clearly established his reputation as a dynamic leader.[186]

Cleage chaired the meetings of the Sherrill School Parents Committee, and he used this platform to excoriate the NAACP and other mainstream civil rights groups for failing to back the lawsuit. Cleage claimed that NAACP executive secretary Arthur Johnson had been utterly co-opted by the white power structure and that "the masses of Negro people will not support this kind of selfish leadership." As an alternative to such "conservative" leadership, Cleage, Richard B. Henry, and other militant blacks formed the Group of Advanced Leadership (GOAL) that, among other things, strongly supported the Sherrill parents and pressured the school board to adopt history texts that recognized the contributions blacks have made to American life and culture.[187] In addition to GOAL, the Trade Union Leadership Council, an organization founded to combat job discrimination that was emerging as a major rival of the Detroit NAACP, provided funds for the Sherrill parents.[188]

The Sherrill case dragged on for two more years. It never came to trial, not because of the merits of the case, but because the parents dropped the suit following a major change in the composition of the school board in 1964.[189] Rather than becoming the first major, northern desegregation case in the country, the Sherrill suit served as a catalyst for the emerging populist trend in educational politics that was affecting black as well as white Detroiters. The Sherrill parents and their supporters had pressed their suit without the blessing or support of established civil rights organizations, much as the white Northwest Parents Committee had ignored established labor, business, and religious leaders when they launched their boycott in 1960.

Significantly, the Sherrill suit was followed by other grass roots protests in the African-American community, notably a campaign against the principal of Balch School and one against overcrowding at Northwestern High School. In each of these incidents, Rev. Albert Cleage, Jr., played an important role. Despite a relatively small following in the black community, by this time, Cleage and his allies were increasingly dominating the debate on educational issues. In doing so, Cleage forced such established civil rights organizations as the NAACP into taking more militant stands. As a consequence, over the next few years educational issues became increasingly polarized along racial lines.[190]

Between 1955 and 1963, the liberal-labor-black coalition had made important strides in the effort to end racially biased policies and practices in the Detroit public schools. Yet, by 1963, the coalition seemed to be in serious trouble due to the disaffection of white, working-class parents opposed to integration and black militants angered over the persistence of segregation. As a consequence of these positions, the politics of education in Detroit entered a period of profound change. Extremists from both sides of the color line were challenging the authority of established leaders. Nowhere were these challenges more apparent than in the campaigns to increase school taxes in 1963 and 1964.

Racial Politics and School Finance, 1963–64

In the early 1960s, educational politics in Detroit were marked by two contradictory trends. On the one hand, the city was one of the most liberal in the nation, a bastion of organized labor and a bulwark of the Democratic party. Such political sentiments, school leaders believed, would translate into strong support for new efforts to improve and expand the schools. On the other hand, by 1963, as the conflicts about boundary changes and busing indicated, some white Detroiters were increasingly resentful of the attention given to black demands and some black Detroiters were furious over the lack of substantive racial change in the school system. Obviously for very different reasons, these individuals were becoming less likely to support school tax increases or bond issues. In 1963 and 1964, as the school board once again went to voters to seek additional funds, these trends became accentuated. Race was emerging as a key factor in educational politics in Detroit.

In March, 1961, school leaders began planning their campaign to renew the 7.5 mill school tax levy that had been passed in 1959. Their planning, however, was filled with foreboding. Even with the enormous increase of funds from the 1959 millage and the bond victories, school leaders saw serious financial problems on the horizon. Enrollments continued to soar, hitting 294,527 in the fall of 1963, but revenue failed to keep pace with that growth. In 1959, when the tax increase was approved, the board had expected property assessments to rise, thus insuring a steady increase in tax revenue. Instead, assessed valuation and, consequently, school revenue declined. Between 1960 and 1965, Detroit lost 5.7 percent of its assessed valuation, while assessed valuation in the rest of state rose 3.4 percent. As a consequence of the decline, between 1960 and 1966, Detroit lost more than $40 million in tax revenue. As early as 1963, the school system was running a $6 million deficit. Some of that lost revenue was made up by federal funds, but the long-term financial prospects of the board were grim.[191]

Other revenue such as state aid did not make up the remaining shortfall. In fact, in the 1962–63 school year, the state provided the Detroit schools with a significantly smaller proportion of its total budget than it had in 1953–54. State and federally mandated expenses, however, such as contributions to the teachers' retirement system and social security, continued to rise. Between 1953–54 and 1962–63, the amount Detroit spent on employee benefits (most of which went to retirement and social security) jumped from $4.12 million to almost $12.50 million, accounting for 4.5 percent and 8.6 percent of the total school budgets, respectively. In addition, inflation was once again taking its toll on the budget, with construction costs rising and the purchasing power of teachers' salaries declining.[192]

As a consequence of these developments, early in 1963, the board decided to ask the voters for an additional 5.3 mills on April 1st, when it sought the renewal of the 7.5 mill tax that was due to expire in 1964. In addition to the 12.8 mill proposal, the board also sought approval of a $90 million bond issue to carry out the second phase of the CAC-recommended building program and eliminate, once and for all, the inadequate housing situation which still found some 65,000 students in substandard buildings or on half-day sessions.[193] Securing these funds, however, proved to be far more difficult in 1963 than in 1959 because of several new factors that were shaping educational politics in the Motor City: increasing tension about racial issues in education, the shift in the racial balance of the schools, and the erosion of the political power of established educational interest groups. In addition, as the board wrestled with these financial problems, the DFT reemerged as a powerful, aggressive force in school politics, a development that placed even greater strain on the board as it attempted to get its financial house in order.

Initially, the board had every reason to be confident of the outcome of the election. All of the major interest groups, including the Board of Commerce, the Wayne County AFL-CIO, the UAW, the NAACP, and the Urban League, as well as both the daily newspapers, strongly endorsed the tax increase and the bond issue. In an impassioned front-page editorial that appeared just before the election, the *Labor News* stated that, as far as the schools were concerned, April 1st was the "Most Crucial Date in Detroit History."[194] Given the fact that this alignment of interest groups had proven to be unbeatable in the past, school leaders paid scant attention to the opponents of the proposals who were appearing in several sections of the city. Yet, the grass roots rumblings among the white working class that had manifested themselves in the Northwest Parents Committee and the rising prominence of black nationalists such as Cleage should not have been ignored.

Opposition to the tax increases came from these two quite different sources: voters in the predominantly white wards in the outlying parts of the city and black nationalists from the inner city. A random survey of generally white westside voters taken about five weeks before the election found heavy opposition to the millage increase and the bond issue. People gave many reasons for their opposition; dismay at the prospect of a large tax hike was high on the list. But the one reason for opposing the propositions that received the most attention was the refusal of many white voters to increase their taxes to pay for schools in black neighborhoods. In a postelection editorial, the *Detroit News* declared that throughout the campaign, the paper had received many letters expressing the blunt, racist sentiment, "I'm not going to vote money for Negro schools." The possibility that the board might use the new tax revenue to promote integration drew an even more vicious response. As a letter quoted in the *Michigan Chronicle* put it, "If you think we're going to vote the Board of Education more money to ship a lot more niggers into white schools, you're nuts."[195]

The second source of opposition to the proposals came from black nationalists led by Albert Cleage, Jr., and GOAL. They argued that despite solid black support for past tax increases, schools in black neighborhoods had received the least amount of benefit from the additional funds. George Crockett, one of the attorneys for the Sherrill parents, strongly opposed the millage, noting that the school board had used additional funds to maintain segregation in the past. Cleage argued that "a vote against the millage will constitute an effective protest against the pattern of racial segregation and discrimination in our Detroit public schools and will force the Board and the Superintendent to take immediate steps to equalize educational opportunity." Prior to the election, Cleage's *Illustrated News* summed up the militants' position succinctly, declaring that "Selling millage to the Negro community will be as hard as selling bleaching cream to Malcolm X."[196]

In the end, however, it was primarily the white opposition to the proposals that determined the outcome of the April 1 millage and bond issue elections. Both proposals went down to staggering defeat, getting only 39 and 33 percent of the vote, respectively. Most of the opposition came from the outlying white wards. Despite the stand taken by Cleage and his supporters, both propositions received majorities in the predominantly black sections of the city, although black voters did not turn out in large numbers to support the measures. Board president William Merrifield declared that the election was a "catastrophe." The failure to renew the 7.5 mill school tax meant that, in June, 1964, the school system would lose about $42 million annually, almost one-third of its budget.[197]

Over the next few months, school leaders scrambled desperately to devise plans, such as shifting to a twelve-month school year, hoping to avert the total financial collapse of the school system.[198] Ultimately, however, they realized that the only "alternative to disaster," as the *News* put it, would have to be a special millage election. In August, the board decided to forgo any attempt to increase revenue or issue bonds and simply placed a ten-year, 7.5 mill renewal on the November ballot.[199]

With school leaders claiming that the very survival of public education in Detroit was hanging in the balance, all major interest groups, including the Archdiocese of Detroit, the Democratic and Republican parties, and even the Detroit Real Estate Board, redoubled their efforts to pass the proposal. No group gave the renewal more solid support than the Board of Commerce, which, by 1963, had made a complete about-face in its attitude on school taxes. Fearing the effects of the utter collapse of the school system on the economic viability of the city, the business leaders gave unqualified support to the proposal. The Wayne County AFL-CIO and the UAW also strongly supported the proposition.[200]

Opposition to the renewal again emerged in predominantly white sections of town, led by the Greater Detroit Homeowners Council. In addition, the *Redford Record* denounced the millage proposal, claiming that the money would be used to promote integration rather than improve educational quality. On the other side of the color line, Cleage and the *Illustrated News* again urged blacks to oppose the renewal, arguing that "we voted for millage once and got 2 million dollars worth of segregation."[201]

This time, however, the opposition failed to move the voters. Proponents of the measure vigorously and successfully argued that the renewal was crucial to the survival of the schools and noted that the proposal would not increase taxes but would merely keep them at the same level they had been for the past five years. These arguments were convincing. The proposal passed with about 63 percent of the vote. Nevertheless, the racial divisions that appeared in the April vote surfaced again in November. Two predominantly white wards in the northeast section of the city were the only sections of the city to vote against the proposition.[202]

The 7.5 mill renewal kept the school system operating, but with no possibility of expanding or improving public education in the city. The second phase of the CAC-recommended building program, for example, was put on hold until the board felt it could again go to the voters to support a bond issue. In the interim, a new problem arose. Detroit's teachers began clamoring for pay raises as their salaries fell further behind those in the suburbs.[203] Faced once more with the twin problems of providing enough buildings and adequately paying teachers, the board kicked off a campaign in August, 1964, to win voter approval of a $75 million bond issue for construction. Once again, all the major interest groups, including the AFL-CIO and the Board of Commerce, supported the campaign. Yet this time, the proponents did not succeed. On September 1, voters defeated this effort to get more money for school construction by a substantial margin. At the same time, two-thirds of all school bond proposals were passing across Michigan, while 70 percent of all bond proposals were approved across the nation. The growing racial polarization in the city was unquestionably compounding the problem of raising adequate revenue for the schools.[204]

The September school bond election was the first in which the majority of the students in the Detroit system were black, while the majority of the voters in the city were white. The political tension that this demographic shift created did not bode well for the financial health of the schools. The proposition lost by over 19,000 votes, most of which were cast in the white northeast and northwest sections of the city. Indeed, almost half of all the no votes came from the predominantly white twenty-second ward, the Redford/Brightmoor area, in the northwest section of the city. A follow-up study of 118 "indicator" precincts confirmed that voters had essentially split along racial lines, with white opponents to the measure turning out in substantially larger numbers than black supporters of the proposal.[205] The only positive outcome of this election was that it spurred the state legislature into beginning work on approving bonding authority for the school system. This authority would enable the board to issue bonds equal to 2 percent of assessed valuation without going to the voters, a power that every other large school district in the state had had for many years. On the negative side, from this point on it was clear that race would play a central role in the struggle to adequately fund the public schools. Further polarization seemed inevitable.[206]

In many ways, the school tax and bond elections of 1963 and 1964 mark the beginning of an important transition in the political history of the school system. Central to this change were the voting patterns of white, largely working-class Detroiters, who exhibited two distinct voting tendencies throughout the early 1960s. In 1960 and 1961, large numbers of white Detroiters backed two prominent liberal Democrats—John Kennedy and Jerome Cavanagh. The fact that both men were Catholic undoubtedly added to their popularity among the large number of white, Catholic Detroiters. Indeed, one researcher argued that the substantial Catholic majorities piled up by John Kennedy in Detroit signaled that the New Deal coalition was "reassembling and revitalizing" in the Motor City.[207] Yet at the same time, another trend, quite contradictory to the first, was emerging in the voting patterns of white Detroiters in school tax elections. As early as the 1957 millage defeat, there were indications that Detroiters were voting along racial lines, with blacks supporting higher school taxes and whites opposing them.[208] The 1959 victories ran counter to that pattern, but it reemerged in April, 1963, and again in September, 1964. These elections provide evidence that large numbers of white, working-class voters, particularly Catholics, were abandoning the liberal-labor-black educational coalition and were the first glimmers of what would come to be known as white "backlash" against school integration, against the Democratic party, and against such liberal union leaders as Walter Reuther.[209]

In addition, the stand taken by militant members of the black community on the millage and bond issues contributed to the importance of these elections in changing the nature of school politics in Detroit. While Cleage and his supporters failed to persuade a majority of black voters to side with them against the measures, their militant stand reflected a growing mood of anger and impatience with the established black and white liberal leadership in the city over the slow pace of change in the school system.

Compounding these growing political and financial problems was the reemergence of the DFT as a major player in school politics. This political resurrection began in 1960 with the election of Mary Ellen Riordan as president of the union. A tough, dedicated advocate for the teachers, Riordan forced the union to shake off the lethargy that settled over it in the 1950s due, in large part, to the Hutchinson Act.[210] The DFT initially focused on winning a substantial salary increase for Detroit's teachers, whose competitive salary advantage with suburban teachers had totally disappeared in the late 1950s. By 1963–64, the maximum salary for Detroit teachers with a master's degree had dropped from the twenty-first highest in the state to the forty-sixth highest. Most of the school systems that surpassed Detroit were in the surrounding suburbs. In addition to agitating for higher salaries, the union broadened its demands to include such emotionally charged issues as better protection for teachers in the increasingly violence-prone schools.[211]

The change in leadership and the immediate problems of deteriorating salaries and working conditions spurred the resurgence of the DFT, but the main catalyst for renewed militance in the DFT was the victory of New York City's United Federation of Teachers (UFT) in a collective bargaining election in December, 1961. The UAW had strongly supported the UFT organizing campaign and the *Detroit Labor News* gave the election front-page coverage. Detroit teachers clearly recognized the significance of the UFT election, which was held after a one-day protest strike in the very state whose anti–public employee strike bill had served as a model for Michigan's Hutchinson Act.[212] Until then, the failure to repeal the Hutchinson Act was one of the most important political setbacks that organized labor suffered in Michigan during the 1950s.[213] The UFT victory, however, seemed to say that the Hutchinson Act was moot. In 1962, with strong support from Walter Reuther, the UAW, and the Wayne County AFL-CIO, the DFT began an intense campaign to force the board to agree to a bargaining election.[214]

What followed were a series of events remarkably similar to those that had taken place in the salary dispute of 1947. In May, 1963, the DFT presented the board with petitions, signed by approximately 70 percent of the Detroit teachers, demanding a bargaining election. In December, angry over the failure of the board to act on the petitions, an estimated 3,000 DFT members carried picket signs, surrounded the board of education headquarters, and demanded a bargaining election.[215] The board, however, rebuffed the teachers once again on the grounds that such an election was illegal. "We want an election and a contract," Riordan declared in response. "Unless we gain these fundamental rights, a strike appears inevitable." On February 27, the DFT members carried that threat one step further and voted to strike by a six-to-one margin. Soon after, the Wayne County AFL-CIO executive committee voted unanimously to support the teachers' union.[216]

In the interim, the board received an opinion from the Michigan attorney general approving the collective bargaining election. Facing enormous pressure from organized labor and with no legal justification to deny the election, the board capitulated.[217] Throughout March and April, the DFT and DEA, the two organizations vying to represent the teachers, waged an angry war of words. The results of the election were, however, a foregone conclusion for three reasons. First, in a union town such as Detroit, the DFT had an enormous advantage over the DEA, which was not affiliated with organized labor. Second, due to events in the 1930s and 1940s, more teachers trusted the DFT as an effective advocate with such proven successes as the restoration of the 1932 salary cut and gaining the 1947 salary increase. Third, for all its appeals to "professionalism," the DEA could not shake the label of being a "company union," a charge the DFT had been making for almost thirty years. In the end, the DFT trounced the DEA, winning almost 60 percent of the total vote.[218] It was a tremendous victory for organized labor, but it could not have come at a worse time for the school board. Just as the school leaders were fighting an uphill battle to get the restive and divided electorate to vote more money for the schools, the DFT emerged as a powerful force that would again play an important role in deciding how new money would be spent.

By mid-1964, the crises of the preceding eighteen months began to take their toll on the members of the school board, particularly the leader of the liberal faction on the board, Leonard Kasle. Despite his strong ties to the liberal community, Kasle was under fire from organized labor for his failure to expedite collective bargaining with the teachers and from civil rights groups for moving too slowly on their demands.[219] In addition, relations between Kasle and Samuel Brownell were becoming increasingly strained. Kasle publicly clashed with Brownell in September, 1963, over the issue of racial discrimination in teacher assignments with Kasle threatening to resign as president of the board if the superintendent did not move more forcefully on that matter. In February, 1964, amid another controversy with Brownell, Kasle, William Merrifield, and Roy Stephens, Jr., all announced that they would not seek reelection to the board. Four months later, in yet one more clash with Brownell, Kasle angrily resigned as president, a last symbolic gesture by a man who was clearly weary of the struggle.[220]

Recognizing another opportunity to dramatically influence the character of the board, leaders of the liberal-labor-black coalition geared up to replace the three resigning members with another group of individuals even more strongly tied to organized labor and civil rights groups. Walter Reuther persuaded his longtime associate, attorney A. L. Zwerdling, to lead the ticket. Joining Zwerdling were Rev. Darneau Stewart, a black minister, and Peter Grylls, an executive at Michigan Bell. Running as a slate, the three received strong backing from the AFL-CIO, the Democratic party, SOS, the DFT, and civil rights groups. The Board of Commerce, on the other hand, took no position on the election, and the Citizens League labeled all three candidates "qualified."[221]

Besides the strong backing from key labor and civil rights organizations and virtually no opposition from major conservative groups, the slate was aided by two fortuitous developments. First, a strike against the daily newspapers during the campaign gave the liberal candidates a marked advantage over their less well known and well connected opponents. The *Labor News,* for example, which *was* published during the strike, gave the liberal slate a great deal of publicity while virtually ignoring the other candidates. Second, the newly revised Michigan constitution shifted school board elections from April to November. As it turned out, the first November school board election in Detroit coincided with the presidential race between Lyndon Johnson and Barry Goldwater. Given the enormous numbers of liberal, labor, and black voters who turned out for Johnson, it was not at all surprising that the entire school board slate swept to victory. Joining Remus Robinson, these new members formed the most solid liberal majority in the history of the school board. The *Michigan Chronicle* hailed their election as "substantial evidence of the effectiveness of a genuine effort on the part of a liberal, labor, church, Negro coalition."[222] The three new members took office on July 1, 1965. After almost four decades of struggle, organized labor and its liberal allies had finally captured the school board.

Conclusion

From 1950 to 1964, the Detroit public schools experienced several profound changes. Far from being a period of "business as usual" or "holding the line," these years mark the time when the liberal-labor-black coalition in Detroit emerged as *the* major force in educational politics in the Motor City.[223] This rise to power occurred despite such events as the red scare and conservative criticism of the deteriorating quality of the school program. The triumph of the coalition, however, was not without irony or surprise.

In the early 1950s, the essential outlines of school politics in Detroit still resembled those of the 1930s. Just as they had for two decades, labor and business organizations continued to clash about school board candidates and the level of educational expenditures. Yet, by 1955, a number of crises coalesced to utterly change these traditional patterns of political conflict. Foremost among these crises was the enormous financial problems facing the school system due to almost twenty years of neglect and the tidal wave of baby boomers. In addition to these problems, the increasingly powerful African-American community began aggressively demanding equal educational opportunities for their children. As Detroiters turned to liberal leaders and ideas to solve all these problems, the political balance of power shifted to the liberal-labor-black coalition. Ironically, however, after the triumph of the liberal school board candidates in the mid-1950s, victories built largely upon appeals to class interests, the basis of school politics in the Motor City began to shift, with race supplanting class as the pivotal feature in educational debates and decisions.

Several factors combined to cause this important change in the basis of school politics. The profound demographic transformation of the city that led to African-American students becoming the majority in the Detroit schools in 1963 certainly was at the heart of this change in the nature of educational politics in Detroit. In addition, the burgeoning civil rights movement focused attention on the separate and unequal educational opportunities in the urban North as well as in the rural South. Black leaders in Detroit were quick to sound that theme and, allied with white liberals and labor leaders, they forced school officials to confront the blatant discrimination that existed in the school system.

The election of the SOS-backed school board candidates in 1955 and the appointment of Samuel Brownell as superintendent in 1956 marked the beginning of dramatic changes in terms of hiring more black teachers, addressing the educational problems of black children, and spending large sums of money for the construction of new buildings in predominantly black neighborhoods. The greater equalization of resources implied by these developments, however, did not really begin until the early 1960s, after the funds from the 1959 millage and bond issues began to flow. In other words, in terms of resources, especially in terms of funds spent on school buildings,

Detroit was clearly operating a separate and unequal school system as late as 1962. The massive building campaign in the early 1960s brought some parity in terms of facilities to black students. Nevertheless, the overall picture in Detroit from the Great Depression to the 1960s was one of large-scale and persistent racial inequality in school construction and renovation.

Perhaps the most insidious aspect of educational inequality in Detroit, however, was largely unrelated to the allocation of resources. Clearly, the quality and availability of the programs in black and white schools was unequal. In predominantly black schools, the dilution of the curriculum proceeded at a faster pace and with a broader stroke than in white schools. Black high school students were channeled more frequently than whites into the insubstantial general track and they were virtually denied apprenticeship opportunities in the most promising vocational programs. Nowhere was the failure to provide equal educational opportunity more pronounced than in these areas.

Unfortunately, by the time leading Detroiters became concerned enough to address these inequalities, the mood of important segments of the Detroit electorate began to change. Precipitating this shift were controversies about school boundaries or, more precisely, school integration. Many white Detroiters vehemently opposed integration. Fearful that racial changes were occurring too swiftly and, after 1963, unwilling to provide financial support for a majority black school system, they began voting heavily against millage and bond issues. On the other side of the color line, some blacks, angry over what they perceived to be the slow pace of change within the system, also opposed increased funding for the schools, arguing that new funds would merely shore up an already segregated system.

In many ways, the April, 1963, and September, 1964, elections were as important to the history of the Detroit public schools as was the formation of the Stone Committee during the Great Depression. These elections signaled the beginning of a sea change in educational politics in the Motor City. Just as the politics of educational retrenchment in the 1930s came to resemble the larger political developments in the nation, so the racial politics of education in the early 1960s would come to resemble the larger political patterns emerging in the 1960s and 1970s. In the 1930s, the business community abandoned its commitment to expanding and improving the Detroit schools. Similarly, during the racial struggles of the 1960s and early 1970s, large numbers of the white working class and a small but vocal segment of the black community would essentially do the same.

NOTES

1. Walter Reuther, "Schools and the American Scene, February 1951," in WPR Papers, box 543, folder F-10.

2. On similar political battles in other cities, see *Labor's Daily*, 11/20/53, in DFT Papers [inventoried 1/20/83], box 13, Teacher Shortage folder.

3. David Tyack and Elisabeth Hansot, *Managers of Virtue: Public School Leadership in America, 1820–1980* (New York: Basic Books, 1982), 221; David Tyack, *The One Best System* (Cambridge, MA: Harvard University Press, 1974), 269–72; Robert Hampel, *The Last Little Citadel: American High Schools Since 1940* (Boston: Houghton, Mifflin, 1986), 30–31, 43–61; David Caute, *The Great Fear: The Anti-Communist Purge Under Truman and Eisenhower* (New York: Simon and Schuster, 1978), 25–81, 403–45; Lawrence Cremin, *The Transformation of the School: Progressivism in American Education, 1876–1957* (New York: Knopf, 1961), 328–53; Gerald Grant, *The World We Created at Hamilton High School* (Cambridge, MA: Harvard University Press, 1988), 16–17; Diane Ravitch, *The Troubled Crusade: American Education, 1945–1980* (New York: Basic Books, 1983), 55–144; Ellen W. Schrecker, *No Ivory Tower: McCarthyism and the Universities* (New York: Oxford University Press, 1986), 3–11, 308–37; James T. Selcraig, *The Red Scare in the Midwest, 1945–1955* (Ann Arbor: University Microfilms International Research Press, 1982), 54–56.

4. Suburban growth in Detroit in the 1950s was even greater than the dramatic expansion that took place in the 1940s. Between 1950 and 1960, for example, Allen Park climbed from 12,329 to 37,052, Dearborn from 94,994 to 112,007, Inkster from 16,728 to 39,097, Lincoln Park from 29,310 to 53,993, and Royal Oak from 46,898 to 80,612. *The Detroiter*, 3/15/65; Reynolds Farley, "Population Trends and School Segregation in the Detroit Metropolitan Area," *Wayne Law Review* 21 (March, 1975): 869; Sidney Glazer, *Detroit: A Study in Urban Development* (New York: Bookman Associates, 1965), 113–14.

5. Nationally, in 1940, almost twice as many people lived in central cities as the suburbs, but, by 1960, the balance had shifted, particularly in the Midwest and northeast, where substantially more people in urban areas lived in the suburbs than in central cities. Robert Conot, *American Odyssey: A Unique History of America Told through the Life of a Great City* (New York: William Morrow, 1974), 550–55; Alan K. Campbell and Philip Mertano, "The Metropolitan Education Dilemma: Matching Resources to Needs," in *Educating an Urban Population*, ed. Marilyn Gittell (Beverly Hills, CA: Sage Publications, 1967), 15–36; John L. Rury, "The Changing Demography of Urban Schooling, 1920–80: Regional Differences" (Paper presented at the annual meeting of the History of Education Society, Chicago, October 29,1989).

6. Expressways in Detroit also facilitated the exodus to the suburbs and removed 1,500 acres with an assessed valuation of $43 million from the Detroit tax rolls. Detroit Board of Education, *Detroit Public Schools Budget, 1962–63* (Detroit: Board of Education, 1963), 106; Conot, *American Odyssey*, 576; *Detroit News*, 6/17/55, in DNLB Scrapbooks; National Education Association (NEA), National Commission on Professional Rights and Responsibilities, *Detroit, Michigan: A Study of Barriers to Equal Educational Opportunity in a Large City* (Washington, DC: National Education Association, 1967), 17–19.

7. Conot, *American Odyssey*, 545, 550–55, 562; *Detroit Labor News*, 5/16/57; Reynolds Farley, "Suburban Persistence," *American Sociological Review* 29 (February, 1964): 42; NEA, *Detroit*, 13; U.S. Department of Health, Education, and Welfare (HEW), Task Force on Urban Education, *Urban School Crisis: The Problems and Solutions Proposed by the HEW Urban Education Task Force* (Washington, DC: Washington Monitoring Service of Education USA, 1970), 10.

8. Conot, *American Odyssey*, 553–54, 562; Farley, "Population Trends," 892; NEA, *Detroit*, 13, 16; HEW Task Force, *Urban School Crisis*, 10.

9. Farley, "Population Trends," 869, 892.

10. Conot, *American Odyssey*, 580; Farley, "Population Trends," 869; Sidney Fine, *Violence in the Model City: The Cavanagh Administration, Race Relations, and the Detroit Riot of 1967* (Ann Arbor: University of Michigan Press, 1989), 3, 5, 71; Elwood Hain, "School Desegregation in Detroit: Domestic Tranquility and Judicial Futility," *Wayne Law Review* 23 (November, 1976): 66–67; Citizens Advisory Committee on School Needs on Equal Educational Opportunities (CAC-EEO), *Findings and Recommendations* (Detroit: Board of Education, 1962), 173–74; NEA, *Detroit*, 13–14; Norman Drachler, "Education in Large Cities, 1950–1970," in *The Politics of Education: The Sixty-sixth Yearbook of the National Society for the Study of Education*, part 2, ed. Jay D. Scribner (Chicago: University of Chicago Press, 1977), 192.

11. "Effects of Population Change on Educational Trends in the Doty School Area, 1947 to 1957" (undated typescript), 9–17, in EG Papers, ser. 2, box 10, Research on Detroit Schools, Report on Doty School folder; Conot, *American Odyssey*, 519–20, 564, 604–5; Fine, *Violence*, 10–11, 58–59; *Michigan Chronicle*, 5/8/48 and 12/4/48; Karl Taeuber, "Demographic Perspectives on Housing and School Segregation," *Wayne Law Review* 21 (March, 1975): 834–35, 838.

12. *Detroit News*, 1/6/50, in DNLB Scrapbooks; Detroit Board of Education, *Data Digest, June 1961* (Detroit: Board of Education, 1961), 1–1, in RGR Papers, box 6, Data Digest folder; Detroit Board of Education, "Preliminary Estimates, 1957–58 Budget" (typescript, 1958), 85, in RGR Papers, box 9, 1957–58 Budget folder; Board of Education, *School Statistics, 1975–76*, 262.

13. Detroit Board of Education, "Number and Percent of Negro Students, Negro Teachers, and Negro Non-Contract Employes of 208 Elementary Schools, 19 Intermediate Schools, 19 High Schools, 8 Technical and Vocational Schools" (typescript, 1946), table 2, in DPS/DCR Papers, box 17, Board of Education Intercultural/Interracial Program folder; Detroit Board of Education, *Detroit Public School Statistics, 1975–76*, vol. 56, pt. 1 (Detroit: Board of Education, 1976), 262; Farley, "Population Trends," 892.

14. NEA, *Detroit*, 13–14.

15. *Detroit Labor News*, 3/14/52.

16. The amount of material on Communist activity in the schools is enormous. For a sample of this material, see Walter Bergman, Ethan Edloff, et al., "An Open Letter to the Members of the DFT" [March, 1952], in DFT Papers [inventoried 1/20/83], box 3, Investigating Committee folder; Detroit Federation of Teachers, "Referendum Information, May 19, 1952," in DFT Papers [inventoried 1/20/83], box 3, Investigating Committee folder; "Walter G. Bergman's Statement of Loyalty, April 28, 1953," in DFT Papers [inventoried 1/20/83], box 2, Bergman folder; Walter Bergman, letter to the Detroit Federation of Teachers, 5/2/53, in DFT Papers [inventoried 1/20/83], box 2, Bergman folder; Walter Bergman, letter to Laura Osborn, 5/2/53, in DFT Papers [inventoried 1/20/83], box 2, Bergman folder; Mary Kastead, letter to Walter Bergman, 5/8/53, in DFT Papers [inventoried 1/20/83], box 2, Bergman folder; Walter Bergman, letter to Laura Osborn, 5/29/53, in LFO Papers, box 4, Papers and Correspondence folder no. 5; U.S. House, *Hearings Before the Committee on Un-American Activities, U.S. House of Representatives, February 25–29, 1952* (Washington, DC: U.S. Government Printing Office, 1952), 2855–60; U.S. House, *Hearings Before the Committee on Un-American Activities of the House of Representatives, April 30, May 3, and May 4, 1954* (Washington, DC: U.S. Government Printing Office, 1954), 4991–5083; Walter G. Bergman, "State Dept. 'McCarthyism': The Passport Division in Action," *Socialist Call*, January, 1954, 19–22, in DFT Papers [inventoried 1/20/83], box 7, Communism in the DFT folder; Caute, *Great Fear*, 187–97, 246–47; Selcraig, *Red Scare*, 12, 72–73, 126–27.

17. Serve Our Schools, "Speakers Handbook, 1951" (mimeo), in DFT Papers [inventoried 1/14/86], box 3, Serve Our Schools folder; Leonard Kasle, letter to Friend [mass mailing], 3/28/51, in Harold Norris Papers, ser. 1, box 8, folder 8, in ALHUA; *Detroit Times*, 11/2/55.

18. DBEP, 1950–51, 179; *Detroit Teacher*, 11/15/50. The SOS flyer was quoted in *Detroit News*, 2/8/51.

19. *Detroit News*, 2/11/51, 2/20/51; *Detroit Labor News*, 12/22/50, 2/9/51, 2/16/51, 2/23/51, 3/23/51, 3/30/51; *Michigan Chronicle*, 2/17/51 and 3/31/51. The DFT leadership, however, was somewhat dissatisfied with the slate of candidates fielded by SOS, since neither of the candidates, Betty Becker and Frederick J. Herrmann, had particularly strong labor or liberal credentials. Becker was a past president of the League of Women Voters and a leader of the Detroit Parents and Teachers Association, and Herrmann was an educator employed by the Ford Motor Company. Despite misgivings about the candidates, the DFT worked hard for the SOS slate. Detroit Federation of Teachers, Executive Committee Minutes, November 2, 1950, November 30, 1950, December 14, 1950, January 4, 1951, in DFT Papers; *Detroit Teacher*, 10/16/50.

20. *Detroit News*, 2/8/51, 2/11/51, 2/14/51, 2/17/51, 3/18/51, 3/25/51.

21. *Detroit News*, 2/8/51, 2/14/51, 2/17/51, 3/25/51, 4/1/51. The *Free Press* essentially remained aloof from the controversy, endorsing Jamieson and ranking Becker and Merrifield as equally qualified (*Detroit Free Press*, 4/2/51).

22. *The Detroiter*, 4/2/51. See also *The Detroiter*, 11/27/50; Kasle, letter to Friend.

23. Kasle, letter to Friend; Serve Our Schools, "The Current Attacks on Public Education: A Fact Sheet," 3/1/51, 1–4, in Harold Norris Papers, ser. 1, box 8, folder 8, in ALHUA. For a good overview of these arguments on the national level, see Ravitch, *Troubled Crusade*, 104–9.

24. The fourth female member of the board was Louise Grace, who had been elected in 1949. DBEP, 1950–51, 387; *Detroit Free Press*, 4/2/51; *Detroit News*, 4/2/51 and 4/4/51; *Detroit Labor News*, 4/6/51; *Michigan Chronicle*, 4/7/51.

25. DBEP, 1950–51, 554–55; DBEP, 1951–52, 5; *Detroit News*, 6/26/51; *Michigan Chronicle*, 6/30/51.

26. *Detroit Free Press*, 4/8/53; *Detroit News*, 3/18/53, 3/22/53, 3/31/53, 4/7/53; *Detroit Labor News*, 2/12/53, 2/19/53, 4/2/53; *Detroit Times*, 11/2/55; *Detroit Tribune*, 2/21/53, 3/7/53, 4/4/53; *Michigan Chronicle*, 3/7/14, 3/21/14, 3/21/53.

27. *Detroit News*, 7/21/54 and 7/22/54, in DNLB Scrapbooks; *Detroit Labor News*, 9/30/54, 10/28/54, 11/4/54, 11/25/54; *The Detroiter*, 11/1/54; *New York Times*, 11/4/54. Over the next decade, McNamara distinguished himself in the Senate as a leading advocate of federal aid to education. As such, he became a focal point of controversy in educational politics in Detroit and the nation. By the end of the 1950s, federal aid to education remained one of the few issues that continued to divide Motor City Democrats and Republicans, liberals and conservatives, labor and business leaders cleanly along the ideological and class lines that had emerged during the Great Depression. For examples of this very partisan, class-based debate about federal aid to education in Detroit, see *Detroit Labor News*, 6/3/54, 6/17/54, 8/12/54, 8/26/54, 9/16/54, 12/2/54, 1/20/55, 2/3/55, 3/24/55, 6/9/55, 10/6/55, 11/3/55, 12/8/55, 12/15/55, 12/29/55, 1/19/56, 1/26/56, 2/2/56, 3/29/56, 6/14/56, 7/12/56, 7/19/56, 2/28/57, 12/19/57, 2/6/58, 7/31/58, 8/28/58, 1/14/60, 2/4/60, 5/25/60; *The Detroiter*, 11/28/55, 3/12/56, 7/23/56, 8/6/56, 8/8/60, 9/11/61; *Michigan Chronicle*, 2/4/56, 7/14/56, 7/1/61.

28. DBEP, 1954–55, 178–79.

29. *Detroit Labor News*, 11/28/54, 12/9/54, 2/10/55, 2/24/55; *Detroit Teacher*, 12/9/54; *Michigan Chronicle*, 2/19/55; "Leonard Kasle, Board of Education Candidate" (typescript, undated [probably 1955]), in DFT Papers [inventoried 1/20/83], box 1, Millage/School Board Elections, 1952–55 folder; Frank Martel and Antonia Kolar, letter to Sir and Brother [form letter], 3/23/55, in DFT Papers [inventoried 1/20/83], box 12, SOS folder.

30. *Detroit Free Press*, 4/1/55; *Detroit News*, 3/27/55 and 3/31/55.

31. *Detroit Free Press*, 4/5/55 and 4/6/55; *Detroit Teacher*, 5/9/55; *Detroit Schools*, May, 1955.

32. DBEP, 1955–56, 68–69; *Detroit Schools*, September, 1955.

33. *Detroit News*, 9/11/52, in DUL Papers, box 42, Detroit Public Schools, 1952–54 folder.

34. *Detroit News*, 9/22/55. Winters repeated these charges about a year later, but the allegations drew little attention and sparked no controversy. See DBEP, 1956–57, 29, 63.

35. *Detroit News*, 9/22/55, 9/23/55, 9/24/55, 10/4/55; *Detroit Times*, 10/30/55, 10/31/55, 11/1/55, 11/2/55, 11/3/55, 11/4/55; *Detroit Labor News*, 10/20/55.

36. *Detroit Times*, 11/2/55; *Michigan Chronicle*, 10/29/55 and 11/19/55.

37. DBEP, 1954–55, 5; DBEP, 1955–56, 141–42.

38. Brendon Sexton, Untitled Statement, 10/11/55, in DFT Papers [inventoried 1/20/83], B of E folder, 4–12; DBEP, 1955–56, 156; *Detroit Times*, 10/30/55; *Detroit Labor News*, 10/20/55.

39. DBEP, 1955–56, 193, 301–2; Marvin R. Pilo, "A Tale of Two Cities: The Application of Models of School Decentralization to the Cases of New York City and Detroit," *Education and Urban Society* 7 (August, 1975): 402; *SOS Newsletter*, June, 1959, in DUL Papers, box 52, SOS folder; *Shopping News*, March, 1959, in ND Papers, box 6, Clippings; *Detroit News*, 4/9/64, 4/15/64, 11/29/64.

40. Brownell had some knowledge of the Detroit area, having served as superintendent in the Detroit suburb of Grosse Pointe. Brownell left Grosse Pointe for Yale University, where he was a professor of educational administration until his appointment as U.S. Commissioner of Education. Conot, *American Odyssey*, 565–68; Fine, *Violence*, 7–10; DBEP, 1955–56, 517–18; *Detroit Labor News*, 1/23/58; *Detroit Schools*, September, 1956.

41. DBEP, 1958–59, 147–48.

42. Detroit Board of Education, *Pertinent Facts Relative to the Proposed Increase in Millage Election of April 4th* (Detroit: Board of Education, 1949), 29; DBEP, 1949–50, 461; DBEP, 1950–51, 2–3.

43. DBEP, 1950–51, 522–23; DBEP, 1951–52, 224–27, 305; DBEP, 1952–53, 205–7, 259; DBEP, 1953–54, 138; *Detroit Schools*, June, 1950, September, 1950, April, 1951, October, 1951, December, 1952; Conot, *American Odyssey*, 564.

44. Detroit Public Schools, Department of Administrative Research, "Tables and Procedures Used in Estimating Future Enrollments for Detroit Public Schools, October 10, 1955," in RGR Papers, box 9, unfoldered.

45. *Detroit News*, 11/21/51, in DNLB Scrapbooks; *Detroit News*, 3/24/53; *Detroit Schools*, December, 1952; *Detroit Labor News*, 3/19/53; Governor G. Mennen Williams, *The Needs of Education in Michigan: Special Message to the 68th Legislature* (Lansing: State of Michigan, 1955), 12, in DFT Papers [inventoried 1/20/83], box 1, 1947–58 Legislation folder.

46. DBEP, 1952–53, 152, 164–66, 256–59; *Detroit Free Press*, 12/10/52, in LFO Papers, Laura F. Osborn Scrapbook; *Detroit Labor News*, 12/11/52 and 12/18/52; *Detroit Schools* (October, 1952); *Detroit Teacher*, 10/15/52.

47. DBEP, 1952–53, 281, 306–8; DBEP, 1956–57, 63, 76–78; *The Detroiter*, 1/19/53; *Detroit News*, 1/13/53.

48. DBEP, 1952–53, 311. See also DBEP, 1953–54, 1–2; *Detroit Free Press*, 12/24/52, in LFO Papers, Laura F. Osborn Scrapbook.

49. DBEP, 1952–53, 305–6; *Detroit Free Press*, 3/31/53; *Detroit News*, 3/22/53, 3/23/53, 3/24/53, 3/29/53, 3/31/53, 4/1/53, 4/5/53; *Detroit Labor News*, 2/5/53, 2/19/53, 2/26/53, 3/19/53, 4/2/53; *Detroit Tribune*, 3/21/53, 3/28/53, 4/4/53.

50. DBEP, 1952–53, 282, 331, 352; *Detroit Free Press*, 2/1/53; *Detroit News*, 1/12/53, 1/13/53, 2/6/53; *Detroit Labor News*, 1/15/53, 1/22/53, 2/5/53, 2/12/53; *Detroit Teacher*, 1/14/53 and 2/11/53; Mary Kastead, letter to Editor [press release], 1/14/53; Caute, *Great Fear*, 131.

51. *Detroit Free Press*, 4/1/53; *Detroit News*, 4/1/53.

52. *Detroit Free Press*, 4/7/53 and 4/8/53; *Detroit News*, 4/7/53.

53. DBEP, 1955–56, 141; DBEP, 1956–57, 194–95, 245; *Detroit Free Press*, 3/26/57; *Detroit News*, 3/27/55,1/27/57, 3/20/57; *Detroit Schools*, April, 1954, February, 1957; *Detroit Labor News*, 2/14/57; Detroit Public Schools, *Superintendent's Annual Report, 1953–54* (Detroit: Board of Education, 1954), 16, 25; Detroit Public Schools, "The ABC's of School Millage Proposition D" (brochure, undated [probably March, 1957]), in DFT Papers [inventoried 1/17/86], box 1, Millages 1957–72 folder; *The Detroiter*, 10/24/55; Conot, *American Odyssey*, 564–66.

54. *Detroit Schools*, February, 1957; Detroit Public Schools, Citizens Advisory Committee on School Needs, *Highlights of Factual Data* (Detroit: Board of Education, 1958), 25.

55. DBEP, 1953–54, 170, 247; DBEP, 1956–57, 1; *Detroit Schools*, June, 1952, June, 1953, February, 1954, June, 1956; *Detroit Labor News*, 7/7/54, 6/9/55, 11/8/56; *Detroit Teacher*, 3/28/55 and 6/13/55; Detroit Federation of Teachers, "Press Release, September 9, 1953," in DFT Papers [inventoried 1/20/83], box 13, Press Releases folder; *Detroit Free Press*, 1/25/57, in DFT Papers [inventoried 1/20/83], box 1, Millage and Government Aid folder.

56. *Detroit News*, 1/27/57; *Detroit Labor News*, 3/21/57.

57. DBEP, 1956–57, 199.

58. *Detroit Free Press*, 2/27/57 and 3/28/57; *Detroit News*, 1/17/57, 1/24/57, 3/20/57; *Detroit Labor News*, 12/8/55, 3/7/57, 3/21/57, 3/28/57; *Detroit Tribune*, 3/16/57 and 3/30/57; *Michigan Chronicle*, 3/23/57 and 3/30/57; Detroit Federation of Teachers, "Vote Yes on D" (brochure, undated [probably March, 1957]), in DFT Papers [inventoried 1/20/83], box 1, Millages 1957–72 folder.

59. *Detroit Free Press*, 3/26/57; *Detroit News*, 1/23/57 and 3/24/57; DBEP, 1956–57, 195–98.

60. *Detroit Times*, [3/?/57], in DFT Papers [inventoried 1/20/83], box 1, Millage and Governmental Aid folder; *The Detroiter*, 3/25/57.

61. DBEP, 1956–57, 195–97; *The Detroiter*, 3/25/57; Howard D. Hamilton and Sylvan H. Cohen, *Policy Making By Plebiscite: School Referenda* (Lexington, MA: D. C. Heath, 1974), 112.

62. *Detroit News*, 3/28/57; DBEP, 1956–57, 194–99, 257–59; *The Detroiter*, 4/8/57.

63. DBEP, 1956–57, 276; *Detroit News*, 9/15/56; *Detroit Labor News*, 5/3/56 and 5/16/57.

64. DBEP, 1956–57, 257–59; *Detroit Free Press*, 4/10/57.

65. DBEP, 1956–57, 295–96; *Detroit Times*, 5/8/57.

66. Detroit Public Schools, Citizens Advisory Committee on School Needs (CAC), *Findings and Recommendations (Abridged) of the Citizens Advisory Committee on School Needs* (Detroit: Board of Education, 1958), 338.

67. *Detroit Labor News*, 5/2/57.

68. DBEP, 1956–57, 305; *Detroit News*, 5/29/57, in DFT Papers [inventoried 1/7/86], box 12, 1957–58 Salaries folder; *Detroit Times*, 5/29/57, in DFT Papers [inventoried 1/7/86], box 12, 1957–58 Salaries folder; *Detroit Labor News*, 6/6/57; *Michigan Chronicle*, 6/8/57.

69. *Detroit Free Press*, 12/17/57; *Detroit News*, 4/10/58; *Detroit Labor News*, 8/15/57 and 12/19/57; *Detroit Teacher*, 9/16/57.

70. On this debate nationally, see Ravitch, *Troubled Crusade*, 43–80; Joel Spring, *The Sorting Machine: National Educational Policy Since 1945* (New York: David McKay, 1976), 1–51.

71. DBEP, 1948–49, 289–90; *Detroit Free Press*, 11/23/47, 11/24/47, 11/25/47, 4/1/49; *Detroit News*, 1/7/44, 1/17/44, 8/26/48, 10/27/50, in DNLB Scrapbooks; *Detroit Labor News*, 8/3/45, 1/4/46; *Detroit Education News*, 3/17/44; *Detroit Teacher*, January, 1944; *Michigan Chronicle*, 7/25/53, 8/1/53, 11/7/53, 12/26/53, 1/23/54, 3/6/54. The 40 percent dropout rate in 1962 was about the same as it had been in 1954 (*Detroit Teacher*, 2/15/54; Detroit Public Schools, *Preparing Pupils for the World of Work* [Detroit: Board of Education, 1962], 9). The DFT also called for increased use of police in schools to control violence and keep "outsiders"

from invading school buildings. See *Detroit News*, 3/30/58 and 4/2/58; *Detroit Times*, 3/26/58 and 4/2/58, in DFT Papers [inventoried 1/20/83], box 10, Police in Schools folder; *Michigan Chronicle*, 5/1/54, 4/26/58, 11/15/58, 11/29/58; *Detroit Teacher*, 1/24/55, December, 1959; *Detroit Labor News*, 10/7/54, 12/23/54, 11/15/56, 3/24/60; "When Violence Hits the Schools," *U. S. News and World Report*, 5/30/58, 64–65.

72. *Detroit Free Press*, 11/25/47.

73. DBEP, 1949–50, 347–49, 438–40, 461; DBEP 1950–51, 2–3, 280–82, 474–76; DBEP, 1951–52, 1–2, 223–24.

74. Warren K. Layton, *Special Services for the Drop-Out and Potential Drop-Out* (New York: National Child Labor Committee, 1952), 14; *Detroit Teacher*, 3/17/54; Citizens Advisory Committee on School Needs, "Factual Report of the City-wide School Program (Curriculum) Sub-committee, 1958," 45–46, in RGR Papers, box 8, Curriculum 1958 folder; *Detroit News*, 4/3/58. It is quite likely that even though a third of the Detroit high school students graduated from the general track, more than a third may have been enrolled in it. Since school officials used the general track to "warehouse" marginal students, it is likely that a large proportion of the students who dropped out of high school before graduation came from that track. Citizens Advisory Committee on School Needs, "Consultants Report on the Curriculum" (ca. 1958), 99, in DPS/DCR Papers, ser. 1, box 2, folder 2-12.

75. Efforts to curb the dropout problem touched the elementary schools as well. By 1952, Detroit school leaders recognized that children who failed elementary grades and were over-age for their classes ran a much higher risk of dropping out of high school than children who advanced through school along the "appropriate" age-grade continuum. Thus, school officials argued, keeping elementary children at grade-level through such policies as social promotion seemed to offer long-term benefits in terms of reducing dropouts. The problem with that policy was that, by increasing the number of children who were socially promoted, school leaders opened themselves to still more charges that they were weakening educational standards. See DBEP, 1946–47, 546; Detroit Public Schools, "Achievement Test Results, November 1958," pt. 3, table 1, in RGR Papers, box 8, Read folder. On social promotion as an antidropout measure, see CAC, "Factual Report," 46; *Detroit Teacher*, 2/15/54; *Detroit Free Press*, 3/18/58; Layton, *Special Services*, 11. On the development of age-grading and social promotion in Detroit and elsewhere, see David L. Angus, Jeffrey E. Mirel, and Maris A. Vinovskis, "Historical Development of Age-Stratification in Schooling," *Teachers College Record* 90 (Winter, 1988): 211–36.

76. Serve Our Schools, "Current Attacks," 1. On these attacks nationally, see Archibald W. Anderson, "The Cloak of Respectability: The Attackers and Their Methods," *Progressive Education* 29 (January, 1952): 66–81; William H. Burton, "Get the Facts: Both Ours and the Other Fellows," *Progressive Education* 29 (January, 1952): 82–90.

77. *Detroit Free Press*, 4/1/53; *Detroit News*, 4/1/53. An editorial entitled "School Problems Need More than Money" appeared in *The Detroiter* two months after the launch of Sputnik in 1957 and reiterated the argument that "[t]he answers to our educational problems are not to be found in federal aid, nor in an increase in the amount of money to spend" (*The Detroiter*, 12/23/57).

78. *Detroit News*, 5/24/54, in DNLB Scrapbooks; *Detroit Teacher*, 1/24/55.

79. Prior to the election, for example, the *Free Press* ran a series detailing the poor quality of math instruction. See *Detroit Free Press*, 2/24/75 to 3/1/57, in ND Papers, box 7, Scrapbook.

80. *Detroit Free Press*, 4/5/57 and 4/9/57.

81. *Detroit Free Press*, 3/17/58.

82. *Detroit Free Press*, 3/18/58.

83. *Detroit Free Press*, 3/19/58.

84. *Detroit News*, 3/31/58, 4/1/58, 4/2/58. In addition to these series, over the rest of the year, both major daily papers ran other lengthy reports on education. The *News* compared U.S.

and foreign schools in August, and the *Free Press* did a detailed exposé of specific educational problems, such as tracking. See *Detroit News*, 8/25/58, 8/26/58, 8/27/58; *Detroit Free Press*, 9/1/58, 9/2/58, 9/8/58, 9/9/58, 9/15/58, in ND Papers, box 55, Curriculum 1958 Scrapbook.

85. *Detroit News*, 4/3/58.

86. Marilyn Gittell and T. Edward Hollander, *Six Urban School Districts: A Comparative Study of Institutional Response* (New York: Praeger, 1968), 144–45. Detailed information about the formation, membership, and deliberations of the CAC can be found in ND Papers, boxes 6 and 7, CAC folders.

87. Paul T. Rankin, ed., *Improving Learning in the Detroit Public Schools: A History of the Division for Improvement of Instruction, 1920–1966* (Detroit: Board of Education, 1969), 1:35–36; Detroit Federation of Teachers, "Resume of Committee Classification," (press release, undated [probably February, 1957]), in DFT Papers [inventoried 1/7/86], box 6, CAC file; *Detroit Schools*, May,1957; DBEP, 1957–58, 1; CAC, *Findings and Recommendations*, 1–8.

88. CAC, *Findings and Recommendations*, 9–10; Citizens Advisory Committee on School Needs, *Regional Findings and Recommendations* (Detroit: Board of Education, 1958); Donald Disbrow, *Schools for an Urban Society* (Lansing: Michigan Historical Commission, 1968), 239–40.

89. George Romney, "Should We Pay More for the Education of Our Children?" 1, 13, 15, 21, 23, in DFT Papers [inventoried 1/7/86], box 6, CAC folder.

90. CAC, *Findings and Recommendations*, 325–28.

91. CAC, *Findings and Recommendations*, 26–29.

92. CAC, *Findings and Recommendations*, 105.

93. CAC, *Findings and Recommendations*, 92.

94. CAC, *Findings and Recommendations*, 6; italics in original.

95. CAC, *Findings and Recommendations*, 13–25; *Consultants Report to the School Program (Curriculum) Subcommittee of the Citizens Advisory Committee on School Needs* (Detroit: Board of Education, 1958), 96–97, in ND Papers, box 8; Disbrow, *Schools for an Urban Society*, 239; *Detroit Schools*, September, 1959.

96. The authors of the consultant's report on the curriculum were not identified in the document. See CAC, *Findings and Recommendations*, iii; *Consultants Report*, 97–99.

97. *Consultants Report*, 100.

98. Romney, "Should We Pay More," 21–23; *Detroit News*, 11/3/58.

99. *The Detroiter*, 11/3/58.

100. DBEP, 1958–59, 207–8, 244–45; *Detroit Free Press*, 1/15/59; *Detroit News*, 1/15/59 and 2/2/59; *Detroit Labor News*, 1/29/59, 2/5/59, 3/19/59, 3/26/59, 4/2/59, 4/9/59; *Detroit Teacher*, February, 1959. Despite the CAC report advocating the abolition of the platoon system, platoon schools continued to be operated in Detroit until well into the 1960s. See Disbrow, *Schools for an Urban Society*, 230; *Detroit Teacher*, January, 1966.

101. *Detroit Free Press*, 4/6/59, in RGR Papers, box 8, Clipping folder; *Detroit News*, 4/5/59; *Detroit Times*, 4/5/59, in RGR Papers, box 8, Clipping folder.

102. Gittell and Hollander, *Six Urban School Districts*, 145; *Michigan Chronicle*, 1/31/59.

103. *Michigan Chronicle*, 1/31/59, 2/21/59, 2/28/59, 4/4/59, 4/11/59; *Detroit News*, 4/5/59, in RGR Papers, box 8, Clipping folder. The Little Rock reference can be found in *Michigan Chronicle*, 4/4/59.

104. Hamilton and Cohen, *Policy Making by Plebiscite*, 113, 112–16.

105. *Detroit Free Press*, 4/7/59, in RGR Papers, box 8, Clipping folder. Just prior to the election, however, a speaker at the Economic Club of Detroit blasted the notion that more money was all that was needed to cure the ills of the schools. The speaker specifically targeted the "cafeteria-style" curriculum as a key aspect of the schools that had to change (*Detroit Free Press*, 3/24/59, in ND Papers, box 6, Clippings).

106. The discrepancy in the millage and bond vote totals is probably due to the fact that only property owners could vote for the bond issue. See DBEP, 1958–59, 338; Citizens for Schools, "Comparison of Election Results on School Millage and Bonds, 1959 and 1963 Elections, June 1963," in RGR Papers, box 13, Citizens for Schools folder.

107. *Detroit News*, 4/15/59, in RGR Papers, box 8, Clipping folder.

108. *Detroit News*, 6/21/59, in ND Papers, box 6, Clippings; Detroit Board of Education, *Pursuing Excellence in Education: The Superintendent's Ten Year Report, 1956–66* (Detroit: Board of Education, 1966), 38; *The Detroiter*, 12/7/59; DBEP, 1960–61, 441–43, 499, 593–96.

109. Arthur Elder, letter to Walter Heller, 1/1/50, in AE Papers, box 15, Minneapolis folder.

110. *Detroit News*, 10/14/50, 10/25/50, 10/31/50, 8/17/52, in DNLB Scrapbooks; *Detroit News*, 3/21/53, 3/22/53, 9/18/55; *Detroit Labor News*, 2/1/52, 2/8/52, 2/29/52, 10/28/54, 10/11/56; *The Detroiter*, 9/22/52, 10/27/52, 11/1/54, 3/14/55, 3/21/55.

111. *Detroit News*, 1/6/50, 8/26/50, 8/12/56, in DNLB Scrapbooks; Disbrow, *Schools for an Urban Society*, 130.

112. *Detroit News*, 1/5/53, in MFT Papers, box 12, Tax Legislation, 1952–53 folder; *Detroit News*, 7/10/53, 11/16/53, 1/20/55, in DNLB Scrapbooks; Disbrow, *Schools for an Urban Society*, 128.

113. *Detroit News*, 4/1/54, in DNLB Scrapbooks.

114. *Detroit News*, 4/6/49, 4/7/49, 8/13/49, 1/17/56, 6/5/56, in DNLB Scrapbooks; Michigan Democratic Party, "Platform Adopted February 2, 1951," in MFT Papers, box 5, Michigan Federation of Labor Political Action 1951 folder; Teachers for Williams, "Who Are the Friends of Education in Michigan?" (campaign brochure, 1951), in MFT Papers, box 5, Michigan Federation of Labor Political Action 1951 folder; G. Mennen Williams, letter to Jessie Baxter [executive secretary of MFT], 10/9/50, in MFT Papers, box 7, MFT Executive Secretary, 1948–50 folder.

115. *Detroit News*, 5/29/51, 4/6/53, 4/11/53, 5/20/53, 8/14/53, in DNLB Scrapbooks; *Detroit News*, 3/27/53.

116. *Detroit News*, 1/17/56 and 3/20/56, in DNLB Scrapbooks.

117. *Detroit News*, 9/15/53, 9/30/53, 3/12/54, 1/1/57, in DNLB Scrapbooks; *Detroit Labor News*, 1/2/57; *The Detroiter*, 12/13/54.

118. *Detroit News*, 1/1/57, in DNLB Scrapbooks; Disbrow, *Schools for an Urban Society*, 128.

119. J. Alan Thomas, *School Finance and Educational Opportunity in Michigan* (Lansing: Michigan Department of Education, 1968), 303–4.

120. *Detroit News*, 3/11/50, 3/16/50, 3/18/50, 3/22/50, 3/23/50, 3/27/50, 4/1/50, 6/3/50, 10/21/50, 10/25/50, 5/4/51, 5/29/51, 10/13/51, 11/3/51, 9/4/52, 10/25/52, in DNLB Scrapbooks; *Detroit Labor News*, 10/30/52; *Michigan Chronicle*, 3/17/51; Williams, letter to Baxter; Teachers for Williams, "Who Are the Friends."

121. *Detroit News*, 1/28/50, 2/19/50, 10/25/52, 2/24/53, 2/26/53, 3/14/53, in DNLB Scrapbook; *Detroit Labor News*, 10/30/52.

122. At first glance, the Conlin Amendment appeared to offer schools a major increase from the 44.77 percent of sales tax revenue guaranteed by the 1946 sales tax split. However, due to a variety of factors, such as providing funding for teachers' pensions, the schools were actually getting close to 65 percent of the sales tax revenues anyway. See *Detroit News*, 1/13/53, 11/2/53, 11/3/53, 11/4/53, 3/25/54, in DNLB Scrapbooks; R. Butler, "Statement on Conlin Amendment," *Detroit Schools*, November, 1954, 3–4; Disbrow, *Schools for an Urban Society*, 128–29.

123. *Detroit News*, 6/4/54, 6/7/54, 6/30/54, 8/19/54, 10/14/54, in DNLB Scrapbooks; *The Detroiter*, 5/31/54 and 6/7/54; Butler, "Statement on Conlin Amendment," 3–4; Disbrow,

Schools for an Urban Society, 128–29; William H. Roe, *Financing Michigan's Schools* (East Lansing, MI: Michigan State University Press, 1957), 18–19.

124. *Detroit News,* 11/3/54; Detroit Board of Education, "Preliminary Estimates, 1957–58 Budget," 80, in RGR Papers, box 9, 1957–58 Budget folder; Detroit Board of Education, *Cost Report, 1950–51* (Detroit: Board of Education, 1951), ii; Detroit Board of Education, *Budget, 1964–65* (Detroit: Board of Education, 1965), 13; Disbrow, *Schools for an Urban Society,* 129; Roe, *Financing Michigan's Schools,* 18–19; Citizens Advisory Committee, *Findings and Recommendations,* 340.

125. Board of Education, *Cost Report, 1950–51,* ii; Board of Education, *Budget, 1964–65,* 13.

126. CAC, *Findings and Recommendations,* 331.

127. *Detroit News,* 3/18/56, 4/18/56, in DNLB Scrapbooks; *Detroit Free Press,* 3/13/57 and 3/?/57, in DFT Papers [inventoried 1/20/83], box 1, Millage and Governmental Aid folder; *Detroit Times,* 3/13/57, in DFT Papers [inventoried 1/20/86], box 1, Millage and Governmental Aid folder; *Detroit Labor News,* 3/21/57 and 5/9/57; *Detroit Teacher,* 2/17/58.

128. *Detroit News,* 1/20/55, 3/21/55, 3/24/55, 5/26/55, 6/22/55, in DNLB Scrapbooks; *Detroit Labor News,* 3/3/55.

129. *Detroit Free Press,* 4/1/55 and 4/5/55; *Detroit News,* 2/8/55, 2/11/55, 2/22/55, 2/23/55, 3/1/55, 3/3/55, 4/5/55, 6/12/55, in DNLB Scrapbooks; *Detroit Labor News,* 3/10/55 and 3/24/55.

130. *Detroit Free Press,* 5/17/59, 5/24/59, 5/26/59, 5/28/59; *Detroit Teacher,* November, 1958; *The Detroiter,* 3/30/59; Disbrow, *Schools for an Urban Society,* 130–31; Conot, *American Odyssey,* 577; Harold H. Martin, "Michigan: The Problem State," *Saturday Evening Post,* 2/25/61, 15, 86.

131. *Detroit Free Press,* 7/22/59, 7/23/59, 7/24/59, 7/25/59, 8/7/59, 8/8/59, 8/11/59; *The Detroiter,* 9/7/59 and 10/31/60; Disbrow, *Schools for an Urban Society,* 131; Martin, "Michigan," 86.

132. Conot, *American Odyssey,* 577, 584; Disbrow, *Schools for an Urban Society,* 128, 251–52; Martin, "Michigan," 86. A wealth of material on the constitutional convention can be found in ND Papers, boxes 15, 17, 18, 182.

133. The analyst is quoted in *Detroit News,* 3/7/63; see also *Detroit News,* 3/5/63 and 3/6/63, in ND Papers, box 17, 1963 Con-Con Scrapbook; *Detroit Free Press,* 2/6/62 and 2/7/62, in ND Papers, box 18, Con-Con Notebook; DBEP, 1962–63, 486–88; Disbrow, *Schools for an Urban Society,* 252–60; J. David Greenstone, *Labor in American Politics* (Chicago: University of Chicago Press, 1977), 127–28.

134. Despite the opposition of these groups, the new constitution was narrowly approved by the voters in April, 1963 (Conot, *American Odyssey,* 584). On the struggle over apportionment in the 1950s, see *Detroit News,* 1/11/50, 2/11/50, 5/3/50, 2/10/52, 2/25/52, 5/25/52, 5/31/52, 6/21/52, 10/14/52, 11/5/52, 3/19/53, 5/16/53, in DNLB Scrapbooks; *Detroit Labor News,* 3/10/50, 2/1/52, 2/15/52, 3/14/52, 4/4/52, 7/2/52, 9/11/52, 10/16/52, 10/23/52, 3/29/62, 3/29/62, 2/7/63, 6/18/64; *Michigan Chronicle,* 11/25/61, 12/9/61, 12/16/61, 1/27/62, 5/9/62, 5/26/62, 6/2/62, 7/21/62, 3/9/63, 3/30/63. Material on the role apportionment played in the 1963 election and the opposition of liberals and organized labor can be found in *Detroit Free Press,* 3/29/63 and 4/11/63; *Detroit News,* 3/10/63, 3/17/63, 3/28/63, 5/9/63, 6/17/63, in ND Papers, box 17, 1963 Con-Con Scrapbook. See also Michigan Democratic Party, "Explanation of Democratic Vote 'NO' on Proposed Constitution" (May 11,1962); United Auto Workers, Citizenship Department, *Con Con: Michigan's Constitution* (ca. 1963), 1–4, in ND Papers, box 182, Con Con folder.

135. Drachler, "Education in Large Cities," 191.

136. As early as 1961, black Detroiters were aware of the political dimensions of the urban-suburban split. In assessing the 1962 gubernatorial race, in which the Democrats lost for the first

time in twenty years, the *Michigan Chronicle* noted that the heavy black vote was almost entirely offset by the suburban white vote (*Michigan Chronicle*, 11/17/62).

137. *Detroit News*, 5/25/50.

138. *Michigan Chronicle*, 1/21/50, 5/12/51, 6/16/51. See also, Serve Our Schools, "Handbooks on Promotional Standards and Discrimination" (typescript, ca.1951), 2–3, in DFT Papers [inventoried 8/18/82], box 3, Serve Our Schools 1951 folder.

139. Dondineau denied most of the charges that Turner and Zwerdling had leveled against him, although he admitted that he did not assign black teachers to white schools. DBEP, 1950–51, 554–55; DBEP, 1951–52, 5; *Detroit News*, 6/26/51; *Michigan Chronicle*, 6/30/51 and 7/7/51.

140. *Detroit News*, 5/24/50.

141. "Memorandum at the Request of the Detroit Urban League" (ca. 1951), in DUL Papers, box A-6, Detroit Public Schools, 1949–51 folder; Harold J. Harrison, "A Study of the Work of the Co-ordinating Committee on Democratic Human Relations in the Detroit Public Schools from September 1943 to June 1952" (Ed.D. diss., Wayne [State] University, 1953), 93; *Michigan Chronicle*, 6/19/54 and 2/11/56.

142. William H. Boone [director of community services of the Detroit Urban League], letter to H. L. Harrington [first assistant superintendent of the Detroit Public Schools], 4/2/52, in DUL Papers, box 42, Detroit Public Schools 1952–56 folder; *Michigan Chronicle*, 4/2/55, 4/9/55, 4/16/55, 4/23/55, 4/30/55, 5/7/55, 5/14/55.

143. *Michigan Chronicle*, 4/16/55.

144. *Michigan Chronicle*, 4/2/55. See the series by Richard B. Henry on segregated teacher placement, school boundaries that increased segregation, and problems with the curriculum. *Michigan Chronicle*, 4/9/55, 4/16/55, 4/23/55, 4/30/55, 5/7/55, 5/14/55.

145. *Michigan Chronicle*, 1/22/55, 2/5/55, 2/12/55, 1/19/55, 2/26/55, 3/5/55, 4/2/55, 5/21/55, 6/25/55, 8/27/55, 1/7/56, 1/14/56, 2/4/56, 2/11/56, 6/16/56, 11/17/56; *Detroit Labor News*, 2/2/56. Miller High School Community Club, "Statement to the Detroit Board of Education, January 24, 1956," in DUL Papers, box 42, DPS, 1952–56 folder.

146. *Michigan Chronicle*, 10/13/56. Dondineau publicly admitted that he segregated black teachers in 1951 during the controversy over his reappointment. See *Detroit News*, 6/26/51.

147. Events in Little Rock drew banner headlines in the *Michigan Chronicle* that highlighted the unprecedented federal intervention in public school desegregation. See *Michigan Chronicle*, 9/7/57, 9/14/57, 9/21/57, 9/28/57, 10/12/57, 10/19/57, 3/1/58, 6/28/58, 8/23/58, 8/30/58, 9/6/58, 9/20/58, 10/4/58, 7/4/59, 8/1/59, 8/15/59. Walter Bergman, who remained with the Detroit schools until his retirement in 1959, became a Freedom Rider in 1961. He was horribly beaten and crippled by the mob that attacked the bus he was on in Anniston, Alabama. Four years later, Viola Liuzzo, a white civil rights worker from Detroit and mother of five, was murdered by Klansmen. See *Ann Arbor News*, 3/2/83, 3/3/83, 3/8/83, 6/9/83, 10/16/83, 2/7/84; *Detroit Free Press*, 11/29/82, 3/8/83, 6/1/83; *Grand Rapids Press*, 12/12/76; *Michigan Chronicle*, 5/27/61; Taylor Branch, *Parting the Waters: America in the King Years, 1954–63* (New York: Simon and Schuster, 1988), 419–21; speech by Walter Bergman, June 28. 1984, in my possession; Albert Matusow, *The Unraveling of America: A History of Liberalism in the 1960s* (New York: Harper and Row, 1984), 185.

148. CAC, *Regional Findings*, 80.

149. CAC, *Regional Findings*, 86, 90, 96, 98.

150. Remus Robinson had urged the board to add the school-community subcommittee to the CAC (*Michigan Chronicle*, 11/22/58).

151. *Michigan Chronicle*, 11/29/58; CAC, *Findings and Recommendations*, 14, 84, 140–44, 197–206.

152. By 1959, class sizes in the central district and other mostly black sections of the city

were the largest in the school system. See DBEP, 1960–61, 190–91; Detroit Public Schools, "Changes in Membership 1959–60" (mimeo, 10/17/60), in DPS/DCR Papers, ser. 1, box 4, folder 14; *Michigan Chronicle,* 12/6/58, 12/13/58, 1/31/59, 2/21/59, 2/28/59, 4/4/59; *Detroit Teacher,* December, 1959.

153. *Detroit Teacher,* September, 1959.

154. *Michigan Chronicle,* 5/7/60, 5/14/60, 5/21/60, 5/28/60, 6/4/60, 6/18/60, 6/25/60, 7/9/60, 9/9/61, 8/18/62; Statement of the Detroit Board of Education, August [14?], 1962, in the case of *Sherrill School Parents Committee et al. v. The Board of Education of the School District of the City of Detroit,* 9, in EG Papers, ser. 2, box 7, folder no. 4. The board also required that the contractors working on schools maintain policies of nondiscrimination against minority employees (Fine, *Violence,* 8).

155. Detroit Urban League, "Report of the Subcommittee to Study the Practices of the Public Schools with Respect to Intercultural Education in Race Relations, November 30, 1949" (typescript), in DUL Papers, box A-6, Detroit Public Schools folder; Statement of the Detroit Board of Education, August, 1962, in *Sherrill School,* 9; *Detroit Teacher,* September, 1963; DBEP, 1963–64, 503; *Detroit Schools,* 6/8/64; Fine, *Violence,* 8–9.

156. Detroit Public Schools, "A Progress Report on the Detroit Program for an Integrated School System, December 1964," in EG Papers, ser. 2, box 9, folder 12.

157. DBEP, 1958–59, 125; *Michigan Chronicle,* 3/22/58 and 4/12/58.

158. "Educational Trends in the Doty School Area," 21; *Michigan Chronicle,* 7/12/58.

159. Only 19 percent of the poorest students were in the college preparatory track and about a third of them were in the vocational/business track. This compares to 79 percent of the children from the wealthiest families in the city being in the college preparatory track, 11 percent in vocational/business, and only 10 percent in the general track (Patricia Cayo Sexton, *Education and Income: Inequalities of Opportunity in Our Public Schools* [New York: Viking Press, 1961], 117).

160. A Northwestern Teacher, "Teacher Continues Northwestern Expose," *Illustrated News,* 2/2/62, 4, in RGR Papers, box 8, *Illustrated News* folder. The other articles in the exposé appeared in *Illustrated News,* 2/5/62 and 2/19/62. Similar sentiments are expressed in an anonymous letter sent to one of the attorneys in the Sherrill School case. See A Concerned Teacher, letter to George W. Crockett, Jr., May, 1962, in EG Papers, ser. 2, box 11, folder 11.

161. *Michigan Chronicle,* 3/3/51, 12/22/51, 2/23/51, 3/8/52, 3/15/52, 3/22/52, 11/15/58, 9/12/59; DBEP, 1962–63, 271–72, 317–20, 388–92; Carl L. Marburger, "Considerations for Educational Planning," in *Education in Depressed Areas,* ed. A. Harry Passow (New York: Teachers College Press, 1963), 304. Many blacks, for example, saw IQ testing and the role standardized tests played in pupil placement as one of the most objectionable practices of the school system. See *Detroit Teacher,* 2/13/50; *Michigan Chronicle,* 7/12/58, 3/11/60, 3/23/63; Mayor's Inter-racial Committee, *The Negro in Detroit: Section VIII, Education* (Detroit: The Committee, 1926), 3–5; DBEP, 1948–49, 1–2; Detroit Public Schools, "Achievement Tests Results in the Detroit Public Schools, November 1957," 5, in RGR Papers, box 8, Read folder; DBEP, 1961–62, 430–31; Sexton, *Education and Income,* 39.

162. *Michigan Chronicle,* 3/2/63.

163. The Great Cities project began as an effort to upgrade vocational programs in order to reduce the high dropout rate of inner-city youth. School administrators quickly decided, however, that this emphasis on vocational education for older students was inadequate, that dropout prevention had to begin in the elementary grades, and that it had to involve parents and the community. See DBEP, 1961–62, 61–62; Conot, *American Odyssey,* 586–87; Frederick Shaw, "Educating Culturally Deprived Youth in Urban Centers," *Phi Delta Kappan* 45 (November, 1963): 93–94. On the national significance of the Great Cities project, see Ravitch, *Troubled Crusade,* 231; Spring, *Sorting Machine,* 218–19.

164. DBEP, 1960–61, 3; *Michigan Chronicle,* 9/12/59; Mary Brand, letter to the DPS Coordinating Committee on Human Relations, December, 1960, 6, in DPS/DCR Papers, ser. 1, box 5, folder 1.

165. On the Great Cities programs, see Carl L. Byerly and Gertrude Whipple, "Detroit's Multiracial Reading Program," *Audio Visual Instruction* 10 (April, 1965): 290–92; Ralph Lee, "Stirrings in the Big Cities: Detroit," *National Education Association Journal* 51 (March, 1962): 34–37; Marburger, "Considerations for Educational Planning," 304–7; Shaw, "Educating Culturally Deprived Youth," 93–94; Gertrude Whipple, "The Culturally and Socially Deprived Reader," in *Education of the Disadvantaged,* ed. A. Harry Passow, Miriam Goldberg, and Abraham J. Tannenbaum (New York: Teachers College Press, 1967), 398–406; *Detroit News,* 9/5/62, in DUL Papers, box 72, Education—General folder; *Detroit Schools,* 10/27/61; *Detroit Teacher,* November, 1960, January, 1964; *Detroit Labor News,* 12/5/63; *Michigan Chronicle,* 9/15/62; Fine, *Violence,* 86. Copies of three of the Great City pre-primers can be found in EG Papers, ser. 2, box 11, folder 24.

166. CAC, *Findings and Recommendations,* 140–41.

167. *Michigan Chronicle,* 10/10/59, 10/31/59, 11/7/59, 11/21/59; *Detroit Teacher,* October, 1959.

168. *Detroit Free Press,* 12/9/59 and 12/17/59, in RGR Papers, box 5, Pattengill folder; *Detroit News,* 12/16/59, in RGR Papers, box 5, Pattengill folder; *Detroit Times,* 12/9/59 and 12/16/59, in RGR Papers, box 5, Pattengill folder; *Detroit News,* 11/27/59 and 12/9/59, in RGR Papers, box 16, Information Volume dated 1/15/60; *Michigan Chronicle,* 12/5/59 and 12/26/59.

169. CAC-EEO, *Findings and Recommendations,* vii; *Detroit Free Press,* 1/13/60, in RGR Papers, box 16, Information Volume dated 1/15/60; *Michigan Chronicle,* 1/13/60, 1/9/60, 7/2/60, 7/9/60, 9/24/60, 10/15/60; *Detroit Teacher,* May, 1960.

170. *Detroit Free Press,* 10/19/60, in DPS/DCR Papers, ser. 1, box 4, folder 12; *Detroit News,* 10/20/60, in DPS/DCR Papers, ser. 1, box 4, folder 12; *Detroit Times,* 10/20/60, in DPS/DCR Papers, ser. 1, box 4, folder 12.

171. *Redford Record,* 10/20/60, in DPS/DCR Papers, ser. 1, box 4, folder 12; *Detroit News,* 10/24/60, in DPS/DCR Papers, ser. 1, box 4, folder 12.

172. *Detroit News,* 10/26/60, in DPS/DCR Papers, ser. 1, box 4, folder 12; *Michigan Chronicle,* 11/5/60; Samuel Brownell, untitled speech, 10/26/60, 4, in DPS/DCR Papers, ser. 1, box 4, folder 13.

173. *Detroit Free Press,* 10/26/60, in DPS/DCR Papers, ser. 1, box 4, folder 12; *Detroit News,* 10/26/60, in DPS/DCR Papers, ser. 1, box 4, folder 12; *Detroit Times,* 10/26/60, in DPS/DCR Papers, ser. 1, box 4, folder 12; *Michigan Chronicle,* 10/29/60.

174. *Detroit Free Press,* 10/27/60, 10/29/60, 10/30/60, 10/31/60, in DPS/DCR Papers, ser. 1, box 4, folder 12; *Detroit News,* 10/27/60, 10/28/60, 10/31/60, in DPS/DCR Papers, ser. 1, box 4, folder 12; *Detroit Times,* 10/27/60, 10/28/60, 10/29/60, in DPS/DCR Papers, ser. 1, box 4, folder 12.

175. *Detroit Free Press,* 10/31/60, 11/1/60, 11/2/60, 11/3/60, 11/18/60, in DPS/DCR Papers, ser. 1, box 4, folder 12; *Detroit News,* 10/31/60, 11/1/60, 11/3/60, 11/18/60; *Detroit Times,* 11/1/60 and 11/3/60, in DPS/DCR Papers, ser. 1, box 4, folder 12; *Michigan Chronicle,* 11/5/60 and 11/12/60.

176. Brand, letter to DPS Coordinating Committee, 5. See also Detroit Public Schools, "Replies to Questions Submitted by the United States Commission on Civil Rights to the Detroit Board of Education, December 1, 1960" in DPS/DCR Papers, ser. 1, box 5, folder 1.

177. *Michigan Chronicle,* 3/25/61 and 5/13/61; Alan Wieder, "The New Orleans School Crisis of 1960: Causes and Consequences," *Phylon* 68 (1987): 122–31.

178. Fine, *Violence,* 16; *Michigan Chronicle,* 7/11/61 and 7/18/61.

179. Sherrill School included seventh and eighth graders. Thus, the issue of which high

school their children would attend was of immediate concern to many parents. See *Michigan Chronicle*, 5/16/59, 5/23/59, 5/30/59, 6/20/59, 7/11/59, 8/29/59; *Sherrill School Parents Committee v. The Board of Education of the City of Detroit*, 7, in EG Papers, ser. 2, box 5, folder 14.

180. See *Sherrill School Parents Committee v. The Board of Education of the City of Detroit*, 4–5; DBEP, 1961–62, 257–60, 375–76; *Detroit Free Press*, 1/23/62, in DUL Papers, box 72, Education—General folder; *Michigan Chronicle*, 1/27/62 and 2/3/62; Hain, "School Desegregation in Detroit," 70.

181. Statement of the Detroit Board of Education, August, 1962, in *Sherrill School*, 3–12; *Michigan Chronicle*, 8/18/62. On the nondiscrimination resolutions, see DBEP, 1961–62, 347–48, 571–72; DBEP, 1962–63, 2; DBEP, 1963–64, 503–5; Detroit Public Schools, "Detroit Program for an Integrated School System, October 5, 1964," in DPS/DCR Papers, ser. 1, box 5, folder 14; *Detroit Schools*, 9/5/62 and 6/8/64; *Detroit Teacher*, September, 1963.

182. The study also found that all-black schools improved the most in terms of pupil teacher ratios between 1940 and 1960. In general, however, the study found that students in all-white, high-income schools had the best total "bundle" of resources devoted to them. See Jay Irwin Stark, "The Pattern Allocation in Education: The Detroit Public Schools, 1940–1960" (Ph.D. diss., University of Michigan, 1969), 2, 23–51, 59. On the volatile nature of the issue of boundary changes, see DBEP, 1958–59, 463–65.

183. In addition to the large-scale segregation of black teachers and administrators, as late as 1960, the central, eastern, and southeastern administrative districts had the largest number of emergency substitutes in regular positions. See CAC-EEO, *Findings and Recommendations*, viii–x, 75–79; *Detroit Free Press*, 3/12/62; *Detroit News*, 2/7/62, 3/11/62, 3/12/62, in ND Papers, box 9, Clippings; Mel Ravitz, "Unequal School Progress in Detroit," *Integrated Education* 1 (June, 1963): 3–9; *Michigan Chronicle*, 3/17/62; NEA, *Detroit*, 26–32; DBEP, 1961–62, 346–48.

184. CAC-EEO, *Findings and Recommendations*, 65–66; DBEP, 1960–61, 181; *Michigan Chronicle*, 7/12/58, 9/28/63, 1/18/64, 8/25/65; NEA, *Detroit*, 48–50.

185. George W. Crockett, Jr., letter to Roosevelt Brown, 11/4/63, 1, in EG Papers, ser. 2, box 11, folder 15.

186. Cleage was the minister at the Central United Church of Christ. He came from a middle-class family and his father was a surgeon in Indianapolis. Cleage received his B.A. from Wayne State and his B.D. from Oberlin. See Fine, *Violence*, 25; J. Anthony Lukas, "Postscript on Detroit: 'Whitey Hasn't Got the Message,'" *New York Times Magazine*, 8/26/67, 52, 56; Lawrence Niblett, "An Illustration of Provocative News" (typescript, 3/1/63), 1, 5–6, in RGR Papers, box 5, *Illustrated News* folder; *Michigan Chronicle*, 6/1/63.

187. Like Cleage, Henry came from a middle-class background, his father was a physician in Philadelphia. Henry was the author of the scathing series on the public schools that appeared in the *Michigan Chronicle* in April, 1955. His main interest in education was curriculum, particularly the racist bias that he found in the teaching of history. *Detroit Free Press*, 1/23/63, in DUL Papers, box 72, Education—General folder; *Michigan Chronicle*, 2/3/62, 2/10/62, 4/21/62; Niblett, "Illustration of Provocative News," 5–8; Albert B. Cleage, Jr., "NAACP Action Threatens Important Sherrill School Suit," *Illustrated News*, 2/26/62, 3, 6, in RGR Papers, box 8, *Illustrated News* folder; see also, *Illustrated News*, 1/29/62 and 2/5/62, in RGR Papers, box 8, *Illusrated News* folder; Lukas, "Postscript on Detroit," 52. On GOAL's demands to the school board, see DBEP, 1962–63, 271–72, 317–20: DBEP, 1962–63, 388–92; *Michigan Chronicle*, 4/14/62, 6/16/62, 7/7/62, 12/1/62, 12/8/62.

188. The NAACP did form a committee to study the Sherrill case, and the organization eventually backed the parents. Nevertheless, because of its initial reluctance to support the parents, the NAACP was relegated to a secondary role in the case. Fine, *Violence*, 6, 25, 47;

Illustrated News, 1/29/62, 3, 6, in RGR Papers, box 8, *Illustrated News* folder; Trade Union Leadership Council, letter to George W. Crockett, Jr., 5/23/63 and 12/20/63, in EG Papers, ser. 2, box 11, folder 15; *Michigan Chronicle*, 2/24/62, 3/24/62, 7/7/62, 12/22/62.

189. DBEP, 1962–63, 63–66, 97–101, 131–36; DBEP, 1964–65, 222–75, 581–83, 609–10; *Detroit Teacher*, November, 1964; *Michigan Chronicle*, 9/26/64, 1/30/65, 5/1/65; George W. Crockett, "Memo to Sherrill School File, March 28, 1962," in EG Papers, ser. 2, box 10, folder 23; Crockett, letter to Brown; Trade Union Leadership Council, letter to Crockett; Hain, "School Desegregation in Detroit," 70.

190. DBEP, 1962–63, 164–69; *Michigan Chronicle*, 6/9/62, 6/16/62, 9/29/62, 10/20/62, 10/27/62, 11/3/62.

191. DBEP, 1960–61, 441–43, 492–99, 593–96; DBEP, 1961–62, 489–98; DBEP, 1962–63, 264–70, 310–16, 346–52; Detroit Board of Education, *1965–66 Budget* (Detroit: Board of Education, 1966), 146; *Detroit Free Press*, 5/9/63; Drachler, "Education in Large Cities," 193; *Detroit Schools*, 9/30/60; NEA, *Detroit*, 19.

192. DBEP, 1960–61, 441–43, 492–99, 593–96; DBEP, 1961–62, 489–98; DBEP, 1962–63, 264–70, 310–16, 346–52; Board of Education, *School Statistics, 1975–76*, 263; Board of Education, *Budget, 1964–65*, 13, 27; Board of Education, *Budget, 1965–66*, 143; *Detroit Schools*, 5/12/61 and 5/14/62; Samuel Brownell, letter to the Members of the Finance Committee of the Detroit Board of Education, 12/4/62, in DFT Papers [inventoried 1/7/86], box 1, 1963 Millage folder no. 1; "The Cost of Building Index, 1967," *School Management* 11 (July, 1967): 56–63.

193. DBEP, 1962–63, 346–54; *Detroit News*, 1/17/63; Detroit Public Schools, "Detroit Schools Financial Needs" (mimeo, 1/15/63), in DFT Papers [inventoried 1/7/86], box 1, 1963 Millage folder; Detroit Board of Education, "Tips for Speakers," DFT Papers [inventoried 1/7/86], box 1, 1963 Millage folder no. 1.

194. *Detroit Free Press*, 1/17/63; *Detroit News*, 1/17/63; *Detroit News*, 2/25/63, in DFT Papers [inventoried 1/7/86], box 1, 1963 Millage folder no. 1; *Detroit Labor News*, 2/7/63, 3/14/63, 3/21/63, 3/28/63; *Detroit Schools* 1/25/63, 2/15/63, 3/1/63, 3/15/63, 3/29/63; *The Detroiter*, 3/25/63; *Michigan Chronicle*, 1/19/63, 1/26/63, 2/2/63, 2/23/63, 3/2/63, 3/9/63, 3/16/63, 3/23/63, 3/30/63; Disbrow, *Schools for an Urban Society*, 245; "Citizens for Schools, City Wide Committee" (mimeo, 2/20/63), in DFT Papers [inventoried 1/7/86], box 1, 1963 Millage folder no. 2.

195. *[West Side and Warrendale] Courier*, 2/21/63, in DFT Papers [inventoried 1/7/86], box 1, 1963 Millage folder no. 1; *Detroit News*, 4/21/63; *Michigan Chronicle*, 3/23/63; Ravitz, "Unequal School Progress," 5; NEA, *Detroit*, 53.

196. *Michigan Chronicle*, 3/16/63, 3/23/63, 3/30/63; NEA, *Detroit*, 53; the *Illustrated News* is quoted in Niblett, "Illustration of Provocative News," 6; Ravitz, "Unequal School Progress," 5–6; Disbrow, *Schools for an Urban Society*, 245.

197. *Detroit Free Press*, 4/3/63; *Detroit News*, 4/3/63 and 4/13/63; *Michigan Chronicle*, 4/6/63; Disbrow, *Schools for an Urban Society*, 245.

198. DBEP, 1962–63, 514–23, 563–74, 688–98, 653–72, 714–18; DBEP, 1963–64, 95–101; *Detroit Free Press*, 4/4/63, 4/21/63, 4/24/63, 4/26/63, 5/9/63, 6/11/63; *Detroit News*, 4/15/63, 6/16/63, 8/25/63; *Detroit Labor News*, 6/13/63; *Michigan Chronicle*, 5/25/63; Mary Ellen Riordan, letter to Samuel Brownell, 4/9/63, in DFT Papers [inventoried 1/7/86], box 11, 1963 Millage folder.

199. DBEP, 1962–63, 607–8; DBEP, 1963–64, 159–61; *Detroit News*, 8/21/63; *Detroit Labor News*, 11/14/63.

200. *Detroit Free Press*, 8/29/63, in RGR Papers, box 16, Information Volume dated 9/13/63; *Detroit News*, 8/21/63, 8/29/63, 9/9/63, in RGR Papers, box 16, Information Volume dated

9/13/63; *Detroit Labor News*, 9/26/63, 10/3/63, 10/17/63, 10/24/63, 10/31/63; *The Detroiter*, 10/14/63, 10/21/63, 10/28/63, 11/4/63; *Detroit Schools*, 9/27/63 and 10/25/63; *Michigan Chronicle*, 10/25/63 and 11/2/63.

201. Disbrow, *Schools for an Urban Society*, 247–48; *East Side Newspapers*, 9/11/63, in RGR Papers, box 16, Information Volume dated 9/13/63; *Illustrated News*, 9/30/63, in RGR Papers, box 6, *Illustrated News* folder.

202. The racial character of the voting becomes even clearer if one looks at the results in terms of high school districts that school officials compiled by analyzing the votes in the precincts that corresponded to the attendance boundaries of the schools. The four districts in which the proposal was defeated (Chadsey, Denby, Osborn, and Finney) were majority white, while the largely black Northern, Northwestern, and Central districts supported the proposal with yes votes of over 90 percent. DBEP, 1963–64, 211–13; *Detroit Schools*, 11/15/63; Disbrow, *Schools for an Urban Society*, 247–48; *Michigan Chronicle*, 11/16/63.

203. *Detroit Free Press*, 4/16/64, in RGR Papers, box 7, Clippings; *Detroit Schools*, 6/17/64; *Detroit Teacher*, January, 1964.

204. DBEP, 1964–65, 64–65, 101–2, 176; *Detroit Labor News*, 12/5/63, 7/16/64, 8/6/64, 8/20/64, 9/10/64; *The Detroiter*, 8/24/64; *Detroit Teacher*, June, 1964, and September, 1964; *Detroit Schools*, 6/17/64 and 9/18/64; Hamilton and Cohen, *Policy Making by Plebiscite*, 286; *Scholastic Teacher*, 11/4/64, in RGR Papers, box 7, 1964–65 Miscellaneous folder.

205. *Redford Record*, 9/24/64, in RGR Papers, box 6, Information Volume dated 10/9/64; *Scholastic Teacher*, 11/4/64, in RGR Papers, box 7, 1964–65 Miscellaneous folder; *Michigan Chronicle*, 8/8/64, 8/22/64, 8/29/64, 9/12/64; Detroit Public Schools, "Racial Distribution of Students and Instructional Personnel in Elementary, Secondary, Special Education and Trade Schools" (typescript, 11/10/64), in RGR Papers, box 7, Clippings.

206. DBEP, 1963–64, 37; Board of Education, *Pursuing Excellence*, 1956–66, 47.

207. Roberta S. Sigel, "Race and Religion as Factors in the Kennedy Victory in Detroit, 1960," *Journal of Negro Education* 31 (Fall, 1962): 447.

208. In the 1957 millage defeat, the largest no vote came from the white north and northwestern section of the city. In terms of racial voting patterns in school elections, Sidney Fine points out that "not a single black precinct cast a negative vote in the six millage elections between 1957 and 1967." See *Michigan Chronicle*, 4/6/57; Fine, *Violence*, 43.

209. For a discussion of the increasing racial polarization of city elections, see *Michigan Chronicle*, 10/12/63 and 9/12/64. A 1965 study of the Detroit SMSA found that, within the city, Catholics were less likely to vote for school millages than Protestants. In the suburban areas, however, religion had no impact. See Philip K. Piele and John Stuart Hall, *Budgets, Bonds, and Ballots* (Lexington, MA: D. C. Heath, 1972), 107. On strikingly similar patterns of white "backlash" voting in school tax and bond elections going on at the same time in Cleveland, see Louis H. Masotti, "Patterns of White and Nonwhite School Referenda Participation and Support, Cleveland, 1960–64," in *Educating an Urban Population*, ed. Marilyn Gittell (Beverly Hills, CA: Sage Publications, 1967), 251–53. On these trends in the larger political arena, see Kevin P. Phillips, *The Emerging Republican Majority* (New Rochelle, NY: Arlington House, 1969), 341–57.

210. "Mary Ellen Riordan, Biographical Sketch" (typescript, undated), in DFT Papers [inventoried 1/7/86], box 11, Biographical Sketches folder; *Detroit Free Press*, 5/10/64; *Detroit News*, 9/3/67, in DFT Papers [inventoried 1/7/86], box 6, Clipping folder.

211. On salaries, see *Detroit Labor News*, 6/16/60, 11/10/60, 12/22/60; *Detroit Teacher*, February, 1960, May, 1960, June, 1960, February, 1961, May, 1961, January. 1964, February, 1964. On the increasing level of violence in the schools, see the major report by Samuel H. Olson, "Inquiry of Complaints for Crimes Committed by Youthful Offenders in and near Public Schools in Detroit" (ca. 1964) in DFT Papers [inventoried 1/7/86], box 12, School Violence,

1963–65 folder; Detroit Federation of Teachers, "Violence in Schools/ TEACHERS NEED HELP!" (press release, 2/15/64), in DFT Papers [inventoried 1/7/86], box 12, School Violence, 1963–65 folder; DBEP, 1964–65, 24–25, 36; *Michigan Chronicle,* 2/9/63.

212. Diane Ravitch, *The Great School Wars* (New York: Basic Books, 1974), 264–65; William Eaton, *The American Federation of Teachers, 1960–61* (Carbondale: Southern Illinois University Press, 1975), 195; *Detroit Labor News,* 1/4/62 and 5/30/63.

213. *Detroit News,* 3/20/53; *Detroit News,* 10/13/52 and 11/11/52, in DNLB Scrapbooks; *Detroit Labor News,* 2/17/50, 3/10/50, 5/5/50, 1/19/51, 6/1/51, 6/8/51, 1/11/52, 3/25/54, 7/28/ 55, 6/12/58.

214. William Eaton argues that when Reuther led the UAW out of the AFL-CIO, teachers lost a powerful advocate for unionism within organized labor. This is simply not the case in Detroit, where both the UAW and the AFL-CIO strongly supported the DFT struggle for collective bargaining. See Eaton, *American Federation of Teachers,* 195; DBEP, 1963–64, 264–65, 293; *Detroit Free Press,* 5/10/64; *Detroit Labor News,* 8/16/62, 8/30/62, 3/14/63, 5/30/63, 6/20/63, 12/5/63.

215. *Detroit News,* 12/17/63; *Detroit Labor News,* 5/16/63, 12/12/63, 12/19/63; *Detroit Teacher,* October, 1963, November, 1963, December 4, 1963 (special issue), December, 1963, January, 1964. There was a racial element to this protest as well. Due to the defeat of the April millage, the board threatened to lay off 1,000 teachers, most of whom were black. Mary Ellen Riordan argued that this threat was one more reason the teachers needed collective bargaining (*Michigan Chronicle,* 5/25/63).

216. *Detroit Labor News,* 2/20/64, 2/27/64, 3/5/64, 3/26/64; *Detroit Teacher,* January, 1964, February,1964, March, 1964.

217. *Detroit Free Press,* 5/10/64; *Detroit News,* 4/9/64; *Detroit Labor News,* 4/30/64. In 1965, Governor George Romney signed a bill allowing public employees the right to collective bargaining. The bill amended the Hutchinson Act, but the provision of the Hutchinson Act that made strikes by public employees illegal was not changed (*Detroit Teacher,* September, 1965).

218. The final vote was 5,739 for the DFT, 3,848 for the DEA, and 59 ballots were void. See *Detroit Free Press,* 5/10/64; *Detroit Free Press,* 5/15/64, in DFT Papers [inventoried 1/7/86], box 6, Clipping folder; *Detroit News,* 5/1/64; *Detroit Labor News,* 2/20/64, 4/30/64, 4/16/64, 5/14/64; *Detroit Schools,* 4/28/64; *Detroit Teacher,* February, 1964, May 5, 1964, May 19, 1964 (special issues); *Michigan Chronicle,* 4/4/64, 4/11/64, 5/9/64; Disbrow, *Schools for an Urban Society,* 249–50.

219. *Detroit Free Press,* 4/21/63, 4/24/63, 4/26/63; *Detroit News,* 4/15/63; *Detroit Labor News,* 5/16/63, 12/12/63, 12/19/63; *Detroit Teacher,* October, 1963, November, 1963, December 4, 1963 (special issue), December, 1963; *Michigan Chronicle,* 2/15/64, 2/22/64, 4/25/64, 6/13/64; Charles L. Wells [chairman of the education committee of the Detroit NAACP], letter to Detroit Board of Education, 4/21/63, in EG Papers, ser. 2, box 10, folder 3; Charles L. Wells, letter to Leonard Kasle, 6/8/64, in EG Papers, ser. 2, box 11, folder 16.

220. *Detroit Free Press,* 8/22/62, in DUL Papers, box 72, Education—General folder; *Detroit Free Press,* 4/21/63, 4/24/63, 4/26/63, 10/18/64; *Detroit News,* 8/22/62, 9/12/62, 6/11/ 63, in DUL Papers, box 72, Education—General folder; *Detroit News,* 4/15/63, 4/9/64, 4/15/64, 4/19/64; *Michigan Chronicle,* 9/14/63, 9/28/63, 10/5/63, 6/20/64; Disbrow, *Schools for an Urban Society,* 249–50.

221. *Detroit News,* 11/19/64, in RGR Papers, box 7, Clipping file; *Detroit Labor News,* 8/27/64, 9/10/64, 10/22/64, 10/29/64; *The Detroiter,* 10/26/64; *Detroit Teacher,* October, 1964, November, 1964; *Michigan Chronicle,* 2/2/63 and 8/22/64; William Grant, "Community Control vs. School Integration—the Case of Detroit," *Public Interest,* Summer, 1971, 63.

222. The three liberal candidates all received over 159,000 votes, more than 12,000 more than their next closest competitor. *Detroit News,* 11/19/64, in RGR Papers, box 7, Clipping file;

Detroit Labor News, 8/27/64, 9/10/64, 10/22/64, 10/29/64; *Detroit Schools,* 11/17/64; *Detroit Teacher,* November, 1964; *Michigan Chronicle,* 8/22/64 and 11/14/64.
223. Tyack and Hansot, *Managers of Virtue,* 217–23; Charles Alexander, *Holding the Line: The Eisenhower Era, 1952–61* (Bloomington: Indiana University Press, 1976), xvi.

Chapter 6

"There Is Enough Blame for Everyone to Share," 1964–81

In the 1920s, Detroit, more than any other city in America, symbolized the nation's seemingly boundless rush into industrial might and material prosperity. Less than a half-century later, following the 1967 riot, one of "the most destructive 'civil disorders' in American history," Detroit symbolized a very different aspect of American life—the violence and decay of the once great industrial centers.[1] In 1975, political analyst William Serrin declared that "nowhere in America can the nation's disregard for its cities and the failure of the nation's economic policies be seen so clearly as in Detroit."[2] The same could be said of the school system, which, by the early 1970s, had slipped to the very edge of financial and educational bankruptcy. In November, 1972, staggered by five years of conflict over decentralization, desegregation, and repeated defeats of crucial millage proposals, the school board prepared to shut the system down. "We cannot believe that such a collapse of public education is inescapable," the *Free Press* editorialized. "We cannot believe it, but it is happening before our eyes."[3]

There is widespread agreement among historians that American education was transformed during this turbulent era, although scholars differ sharply about the nature, causes, and implications of the changes. A number of historians, for example, have argued that these changes occurred primarily because the federal government and the courts asserted greater power over local school districts and, thus, bound public education to often misguided federal policies and programs. Other historians argue that the rise to power of militant teachers' unions produced the most dramatic changes in the modern politics of urban education. Katznelson and Weir speculate that the great political transformation occurred because the civil rights and black power movements vigorously challenged the comfortable educational establishment that had assumed power in the 1940s. Gerald Grant also sees black protests as central to the changes in this era, but he maintains that these revolts so unnerved urban educators that they abdicated their moral authority, diluted the curriculum, and, in general, acquiesced to the "deconstruction" of the old but reasonably effective educational world.[4] The basic problem with these studies, however, is that none of them attempts to unravel the complex interaction between these various developments. Detroit is an ideal site for such an attempt because probably no city in America experienced so many of these changes so profoundly and dramatically as did the Motor City.

At the heart of the problems facing the city and its schools were the massive demographic and economic transformations of the 1960s and 1970s. As major industries relocated to the suburbs and later to the Sun Belt, taking with them jobs, tax revenues, and most of Detroit's middle class, it was increasingly difficult for the city and its schools to provide adequate services to a population that was becoming overwhelmingly black and poor. Intimately linked to the loss of these human and physical resources was the dramatic change in educational politics in the late 1960s brought on by the fragmentation of the liberal-labor-black coalition. The collapse of this powerful educational alliance presaged the larger national crisis of American liberalism in which race supplanted class as a driving force behind political alignments. Indeed, just as educational politics in Detroit during the Great Depression were a bellwether of the emerging New Deal realignment, so educational politics in the Motor City in the late 1960s foreshadowed the often racially based political alignment in the nation today.[5]

In this chapter, I will discuss the political, financial, and educational crises that overwhelmed the school system between 1965 and 1981. I focus on the growing challenges to the authority of the school board and the efforts by various individuals and groups to radically transform the system. Two quite different, indeed contradictory, campaigns to revive the beleaguered system emerged during this era, namely the decentralization and desegregation of the Detroit schools. Rather than resolving the educational crisis in the city, however, both these attempted remedies fueled the bitter racial struggles in the city, worsened the already unstable situation in the schools, and pushed the system toward educational catastrophe.

Urban Blight and Suburban Flight

Throughout the 1950s and early 1960s, Detroit was a city in trouble. In the 1970s, all the problematic trends of earlier decades accelerated so rapidly that by the early 1980s, virtually every statistical measure of urban vitality had fallen dramatically—population growth, industrial output, retail sales, taxable wealth, and so forth. At the same time, such indicators of social and economic decay as the rates of crime, unemployment, single-parent families, and welfare dependency rose with alarming rapidity. Emblematic of these changes was the homicide rate in Detroit, surpassing that of every large city in the nation and earning Detroit the new, frightening sobriquet, the "Murder Capital" of the United States.[6]

During these years, Detroit was a victim of what a group of researchers from the National Education Association (NEA) succinctly described as the process of "urban blight and suburban flight." Between 1960 and 1980, Detroit lost over a quarter of its population, dropping from 1,670,144 in 1960 to 1,203,339. As in the 1950s, most of the people who left Detroit during the 1960s and 1970s were young, white, and middle class, an out-migration that finally changed the racial and economic character of the city completely. In twenty years, the proportion of black residents rose from about 29 percent in 1960 to nearly 44 percent in 1970 to over 63 percent in 1980. In contrast to these trends, the population of Detroit's overwhelmingly white suburbs climbed from 2,814,931 in 1970 to 3,083,377 in 1980. While the number of blacks in the suburbs grew, their proportion of the suburban population remained static at about 4 percent during the entire twenty-year period.[7]

The income disparities between the city and the surrounding communities were as great as the racial disparities. Joe T. Darden and his co-authors noted that, between 1970 and 1977, the income of Detroit homeowners (controlled for inflation) fell by 4.26 percent, while the income of suburban homeowners rose by 4.27 percent. The disparity was even greater for renters. Recent national studies of race and income in major metropolitan areas corroborate these findings. Geographic and social isolation of blacks in Detroit worsened so much that, in 1980, the Detroit metropolitan region was one of the most racially and economically segregated areas in the country.[8]

As always in Detroit, many of these changes were associated with shifts in automobile production and related industries. The early 1960s were good years for automakers. Beginning in 1969, however, a sharp slump in auto production sent the city into an economic tailspin, the effects of which are still felt today. From 1969 to 1973, as plants shut down or moved to new locations outside the city limits, the total number of jobs in Detroit dropped by over 19 percent. Between 1967 and 1985, the city lost 195,000 jobs, almost half of them in manufacturing. In all, Detroit's share of all manufacturing jobs in the metropolitan area fell from just over 40 percent in 1963 to 25 percent in 1982. This steep drop in manufacturing jobs sent shock waves through the local economy.[9]

In the service, retail, and wholesale industries, Detroit's share of jobs in the region also fell sharply. In 1963, Detroiters held almost 66 percent of all jobs in service industries, over 43 percent in the retail area, and 69 percent in wholesale companies in the metropolitan region. Nineteen years later, the city's share of these jobs in each of these industries was cut by more than half, averaging only 24 percent in service, 15 percent in retail, and 30 percent in wholesale. Probably nothing shows the economic impact of these changes as well as the precipitous decline in retail sales. In 1958, Detroit accounted for nearly twice the amount of retail sales as the suburbs, about $524 million compared to $273 million. By 1977, however, retail sales in the suburbs were more than nine times greater than in the city, $2.2 billion compared to just $241 million. Symbolic of these changes, in January, 1983, the Dayton-Hudson Corporation closed the landmark J. L. Hudson store in downtown Detroit.[10]

The most immediate consequence of all these trends was a sharp increase in unemployment. The 5 percent unemployment rate in Detroit in 1967 more than tripled by 1975, reaching 18 percent citywide and as high as 50 percent among blacks. Well into the 1980s, the overall unemployment figures remained in double digits. In 1983, for example, estimates of black unemployment still ranged as high as 40 percent, with a 90 percent rate among black teenagers. The proportion of households headed by females also rose during this period, from 28 percent of the total number of households in 1970 to 40 percent in 1980. Not surprisingly, welfare dependency also rose during this period, increasing from 8.5 percent of all Detroiters in 1967 to roughly 33.0 percent in 1983. One researcher calculated that the combined number of people receiving unemployment benefits, Social Security payments, and welfare assistance in Detroit in 1983 may have reached 600,000, almost half of the population of the city.[11]

All of these social and economic changes and problems were mirrored in the Detroit schools. Property values in the city, the keystone of local school tax revenue, remained stagnant in the 1960s and fell in the 1970s, going from $4.94 billion in 1960 to $5.10 billion in 1970 to $4.27 billion in 1980. During this same period, property values in the suburbs soared. In suburban Oakland County, the assessed valuation rose from $1.35 billion in 1960 to $4.03 billion in 1970 to $10.43 billion in 1980. In all, Detroit's share of assessed valuation in the metropolitan area fell from 49.6 percent in 1960 to 15.5 percent in 1980.[12]

Because of the state equalized valuation (SEV) formula for school districts that adjusted the value of taxable property in Detroit in relation to the generally rising value of property in the rest of the state, the drop in assessed valuation in the city did not hit the schools with full force. Indeed, because of SEV, the value of property available for school taxes actually rose slightly in the early 1970s before starting a steady decline toward the end of the decade. Nevertheless, even with the state adjustment, the value of property eligible for school taxes only rose 8 percent, from $5.37 billion in 1959–60 to $5.81 billion in 1973–74, the highest level the SEV reached between 1951 and 1980. More important, when controlled for inflation, the value of Detroit's SEV plunged during these years. Using 1970 as a base, the Citizens Research Council of Michigan found that Detroit's SEV deflated by more than 40 percent between 1970 and 1980. During roughly the same period, the SEV of many of the school districts in the Detroit metropolitan area nearly doubled, and some rose even more dramatically.[13]

If we consider the value of taxable property over time in Detroit, the picture is just as bleak as in cross-district comparisons. In 1930, for example, Detroit had $24,134 in per-pupil assessed valution (controlled for inflation). In 1967, even after state equalization, Detroit only had $16,247 of taxable property per pupil. Ultimately, these changes in property values forced Detroiters to tax themselves at ever higher rates just to keep local school revenue constant. Given the growing number of poor and unemployed residents in the city, the advocates of tax increases had an increasingly difficult time convincing voters to raise the taxes for the schools.[14]

Complicating this political situation were the changes in the racial and ethnic composition of the student population in the schools, changes that outpaced the demographic transformation of the city itself. In 1963, Detroit's 293,745 students were almost evenly divided between blacks and whites. Seven years later, following what one NAACP official called the "greatest percentage increase of black students of any northern city," 64 percent of the 288,953 students in the system were black, 35 percent were white, and 1 percent were Hispanic. The city population at the time, however, was only 44 percent black. Ten years later, the proportion of blacks rose to 63 percent of the total city population, while a disproportionate 86 percent of the 214,736 students in the public schools were black, 12 percent white, and 2 percent Hispanic.[15]

As a consequence of these demographic changes, school officials seeking additional revenue not only faced uphill battles to convince poor city residents to vote for higher taxes on depreciating property, but they also confronted serious racial and generational issues that were polarizing the electorate. Since the early 1960s, large numbers of white Detroiters had voted against millage increases and bond issues, apparently on racial grounds. As white students became a minority in the schools, white voters became even more reluctant to increase their taxes. Unfortunately for the school system, until the mid-1970s, whites had a *voting* majority in the city because of the age disparity between the races. In 1973, for example, black students accounted for 67 percent of the students in the school system, but blacks accounted for only 40 percent of the eligible voters in the city. Race was not the only variable associated with no votes on school tax increases. Many of the voters in Detroit were retirees on fixed incomes who would not have been eager to increase their taxes even if the racial composition of the schools had not changed. Between 1960 and 1970, the number of Detroiters over the age of sixty-five rose from 158,365 to 173,148, growing from 9.5 percent to 11.5 percent of the total population. Throughout the 1970s, voters over the age of sixty-five played a major role in school politics, because they accounted for more than 20 percent of the electorate. These combined demographic changes, interwoven with the declining economy and the highly charged political atmosphere of the 1960s and early 1970s, created the conditions for what would be the most controversial and violent era in the history of the Detroit public schools.[16]

Growing Dissension in the Black Community, 1965–67

On paper, no school board ever elected in Detroit was better equipped to deal with severe racial and class conflict than the one that took office on July 1, 1965. Organized labor and leading civil rights organizations had enthusiastically supported the three members who took their seats that day: A. L. Zwerdling, a labor attorney; Rev. Darneau Stewart, a black minister; and Peter Grylls, an executive at Michigan Bell. All three men were deeply committed to school integration and, along with Dr. Remus G. Robinson, they formed an unassailable liberal majority on the seven-member board.[17] Over the next two years, these liberal board members undertook a series of bold policy initiatives, such as substantially increasing the number of black administrators and teachers and mandating the use of multicultural materials throughout the curriculum. These actions buttressed the widely repeated claims that Detroit, in the mid-1960s, was a "model city" for race relations.[18] Indeed, in 1967, the *Washington Post* described the Detroit school system as "one of the country's leading examples of forceful reform in education."[19]

Yet just as the glowing accolades about the "model city" hid the reality of neighborhoods quickening to violence, so the liberal reputation of the school system masked fundamental threats to the unity and stability of the district. The most urgent problem was the growing anger and frustration of black Detroiters, who, despite the recent changes in the school system, still saw too little progress in educational reform. In the late 1960s, as the demands of the civil rights movement changed from "Freedom Now" to "Black Power," Detroit's racial controversies in education could no longer remain self-contained debates about resource allocation, integration, or curriculum. During this period, it seemed as if every conflict, no matter how simple, posed a potential threat to the liberal-labor-black coalition and to the moral, political, and educational legitimacy of the school system itself. Rather than ushering in a period of racial harmony, the election of the liberal board of education marked the beginning of a period of unparalleled conflict.

Anger about the poor quality of education in predominantly black schools had been growing for years. Indeed, much of the impetus for creating the liberal-labor-black coalition was the desire among civic leaders to improve educational conditions for black Detroiters. Yet despite the dramatic changes that had taken place in the schools in the previous decade and despite the election of this school board in 1964, improvements were still coming too slowly for many African-Americans. In March, 1965, a new organization, the Ad Hoc Committee Concerned with Equal Educational Opportunity, began agitating "to end the isolation of the Negro from education in Detroit." Headed by Rev. William Ardrey and comprised of such prominent black political and labor leaders as Richard Austin, Rev. Nicholas Hood, Alvin Loving, Horace Sheffield, Rev. James Wadsworth, Charles Wells, and Coleman A. Young, the Ad Hoc Committee relentlessly demanded that the school board implement the recommendations of the already three-year-old Citizens Advisory Committee on Equal Educational Opportunity. Joining with the Ad Hoc Committee, the NAACP redoubled its protests against discrimination in the Detroit schools.[20]

Conditions in the secondary schools were the most important educational issues addressed by the Ad Hoc Committee and the NAACP. The Ad Hoc Committee noted, for example, that the board had taken no concrete action to end the blatant discrimination against blacks in the apprenticeship programs run jointly by the school board, the unions, and employers. In fact, between October, 1964, and March, 1966, the number of black youths enrolled in manufacturing apprenticeship programs had only increased from 73 of 1,050 students to 118 of 1,385, about 7.0 percent to about 8.5 percent. In the building trades program, the situation was even worse.[21]

Secondary education was equally deficient on the academic side. In December, 1965, an NAACP report decried the small number of black guidance counselors in the high schools (17 of 116 positions) and the "inadequate" counseling offered to black students. The report argued that racially biased counselors routinely tracked large numbers of black students out of the college preparatory curriculum. The NAACP report also noted that, in the 1963–64 school year, not a single advanced placement test was given at the predominantly black Central, Northern, Northeastern, and Northwestern high schools. In addition, black leaders repeatedly deplored the failure of school leaders to include units on black history and culture in the curriculum. Finally, not only did black high school students suffer unfairly in academic and vocational programs, many attended schools whose physical conditions, despite some capital improvements, were still as run-down as ever.[22]

In April, 1966, a massive walkout by the students from the largely black Northern High School dramatically focused the attention of the city on these issues. In many ways, the situation at Northern was emblematic of all the problems in the black high schools in the city. As Karl D. Gregory, a Wayne State professor and Northern alumnus, put it, "Northern was THE outstanding high school in Detroit in the 1920s, 1930s, and 1940s." But as the racial composition of the school changed in the postwar years, Gregory stated, Northern became "primarily a custodial institution complete with police as an apparent part of the administration, and was only on the surface an institution where systematic learning took place." By the mid-1960s, Northern and, indeed, most of the majority black high schools in Detroit had essentially become "general track" institutions dominated by the philosophy that the less teachers demanded of students the more tractable the students would be. A study by the Detroit Urban League found that, in 1964, the predominantly black Northwestern and Northeastern high schools had "larger numbers of students enrolled in the 'general' courses than in college preparatory or trade-oriented curriculum." The social promotion policy at Northern was so pervasive, one teacher reported, that "if there is more than a 15 percent failure rate we are called into the principal's office to explain why." As Gregory noted, "It's much easier and cheaper to lower standards to the pupils than to bring the pupils up to standards, especially when parents do or can not protest effectively."[23] The consequences of the curricular dilution and decline in standards were clear. In February, 1965, three-quarters of all tenth and twelfth graders at Northern scored below the national average in math, science, and reading on national standardized tests. Only 20 percent of the graduating class of June, 1966, scored at or above the twelfth grade level on similar exams.[24]

It was precisely this deterioration of the educational program that spurred the Northern students to protest in April, 1966. The catalyst for the walkout was the decision by the chair of the English department, supported by Principal Arthur T. Carty, to ban an editorial in the school newspaper that denounced "inferior education" at Northern. The editorial decried the lack of adequate college preparatory courses at the school, the low academic standards, the policy of social promotion, and it compared Northern unfavorably to Redford High School, a predominantly white school in the northwest section of the city. The suppression of the editorial quickly escalated into a major incident, as Charles Colding, the honors student who had written the article, and two other students, Judy Walker and Michael Batchelor, planned a boycott of Northern to protest Carty's leadership. The students initially sought help from several members of the DFT at the school. The teachers, in turn, advised them to contact the Congress of Racial Equality (CORE), which provided them with offices and helped organize the protest. Some DFT members also provided support for the walkout, seeing it as a golden opportunity to strike at both the principal, whom they wanted removed, and the rival Detroit Education Association (DEA), which supported him. The walkout was set for Thursday, April 7th.[25]

Samuel Brownell heard rumors about the demonstration several days earlier, and he arrived at Northern the morning of April 7th prepared to take action. After failing in his attempt to stop the protest, he "authorized" the walkout by releasing the students from class at 11:30 A.M. Brownell also ordered that Colding's editorial be published in the next issue of the school newspaper. Since Easter vacation began on Friday, Brownell assumed that, by avoiding a confrontation at the moment, he could use the vacation period to resolve the grievances. Buoyed by Brownell's concessions, more than 2,000 students and some parents marched around the school and then proceeded down Woodward Avenue to St. Joseph's Episcopal Church. There, at the invitation of Rev. David Gracie, about a thousand students held a rally at which a list of demands were read. Brownell addressed the students at St. Joseph's and promised to meet with their leaders and discuss their grievances.[26]

Over the next week, the students and a hastily created parents committee met with Brownell and several school board members to try and resolve the problems. Throughout these meetings, the protestors repeated their initial demands, the most important of which were that the school board: (1) replace Arthur Carty as principal but not with the assistant principal, George Donaldson; (2) remove the police officer who had been assigned to Northern to deal with drug and delinquency problems, because the protestors felt the administration used him primarily to coerce students; and (3) provide comparative data on academic standards from other high schools in the city in order to prepare a plan for improving educational quality at Northern. Brownell quickly agreed to remove the police officer and he promised to discuss the other demands. The real sticking point in these deliberations, however, was the question of retaining Carty.[27]

On April 13th, following a negotiating session in which Brownell informed the students that the board would hear their grievances at its meeting on Tuesday, April 19, the students and their supporters turned up the heat by announcing that if Carty returned to Northern on the Monday after the Easter recess, they would not return to school. In response, Brownell temporarily reassigned the principal to the central office, ostensibly to study the situation at Northern, and he placed the school under the direction of two high-level administrators. The students returned to school on the 18th and awaited the results of the board meeting which would take place the next afternoon.

Rather than resolving the issue, however, the April 19 board meeting polarized the situation even further. The students, parents, and the DFT building representative again demanded Carty's removal, but the board refused to take action. One student left the meeting claiming that the board had treated them "like dogs." Following a rally that evening, the students decided to boycott the school. On April 20, only 183 of the 2,307 students enrolled at Northern showed up for class. The following day, students and a group of faculty members from Wayne State set up a Freedom School at St. Joseph's under the direction of Karl Gregory. The Freedom School offered classes throughout the remainder of the crisis and eventually even some teachers from Northern participated in it. By this time, the crisis at Northern totally dominated the front pages of the Detroit newspapers and focused attention on the plight of inner city schools.[28]

The boycott divided Detroiters into two camps. The first argued that the board must be sensitive to the concerns of the community, recognize the legitimacy of the protestors' demands, and fire the principal. The second camp declared that the board had to support Carty, stand firm against "mob rule," and demonstrate that students do not run the schools. This polarization tended to fall along well-established political and racial lines. Most blacks, civil rights organizations such as CORE, the *Michigan Chronicle,* many DFT members, and other liberal Detroiters generally backed the students, while most whites, the Organization of School Administrators and Supervisors (OSAS), the DEA, and conservatives largely supported Carty. For the first group, as Rev. Gracie noted, Carty was the symbol of a system that treated "the ghetto like a colony" in which "outsiders" had all the power. For the latter group, as Brownell put it, Carty had become a "symbol of law and order." As the increasingly conservative *News* stated, "A school system cannot be run by ad hoc committees. The system cannot let its administrators be hired and fired in the corridors and the streets."[29]

As clear as these divisions appeared, however, the issue presented a very difficult problem to the liberal coalition that was still trying to consolidate its power on the school board. The four liberal members, Robinson, Grylls, Stewart, and Zwerdling, were definitely sympathetic to the students. Nevertheless, they recognized the soundness of the argument put forth by the more conservative members, Becker, Canty, and Grace, that the moral authority of the board was on the line in this crisis and that giving in to the students would set a very dangerous precedent. As the representative from OSAS pointed out, if the board removed Carty under pressure, no principal and, indeed, no teacher could make a controversial decision without fear that they would become a target for protestors. Given these concerns, it was not surprising that DFT President Mary Ellen Riordan, though sympathetic to the students, strongly urged them to abandon the strike and trust the school leaders to quietly resolve the issue. Similarly, the NAACP supported the boycott, but its president, Rev. James Wadsworth, favored behind-the-scenes negotiations over mass protests. Not only were these leaders concerned about maintaining authority, they were also quite worried about the impact the boycott was having on the campaign for a school tax increase that was slated for a May 9 vote. As the school leaders saw it, the longer the crisis went unresolved, opponents of the proposal, primarily in white neighborhoods, could claim that the liberal board was coddling the black protestors.[30]

For totally different reasons, some members of the black community also linked their support for the millage to the outcome of the crisis. Rev. Albert Cleage, Jr., a leader of the militant Group of Advanced Leadership (GOAL), stated that "unless the demands of the Northern students are met . . . we will start an intense campaign to defeat the millage proposal in May." Cleage also warned that unless action was taken, the protests would spread to all the other black high schools in the city. Cleage's warning became more ominous on Friday, April 22, as some Eastern High School students joined the more than 1,700 striking students from Northern in the walkout.[31]

Facing this mounting pressure, Brownell, School Board President Remus Robinson, and board members Grylls and Stewart met three days later with the student leaders and their parents, resulting in a decision to reassign Carty to the School Center Building for the duration of the school year. They also agreed to set up a committee to investigate conditions at Northern and another, larger group, the High School Study Commission (HSSC), to report on the conditions at all the other high schools in the city. The next day, Michael Batchelor announced to the 1,000 students at the Freedom School that Carty had been ousted and the boycott was over. The triumphant students then marched back up Woodward Avenue and returned to school.[32]

Rather than ending the controversy, the decision to remove Carty further polarized the community. A group of liberal leaders, including Al Barbour of the Wayne County AFL-CIO, Walter Reuther of the UAW, and Rev. James Wadsworth of the NAACP, immediately issued a statement supporting the actions taken by Brownell and the board. The *Michigan Chronicle* declared that "the total community should say: 'Thank God for Sam Brownell.'" In contrast, the *Free Press*, which had originally supported the walkout, bitterly denounced the board's action. The *Free Press* had initially described the April 7 actions as "One Student Protest That Deserves Applause." Yet once Carty was removed, the paper vilified Brownell and the board, stating that the decision to remove Carty would leave a " . . . bitter legacy. What the community can't support is the removal of a principal under student pressure." Letters to the editor strongly supported that position. One Detroit area legislator stated that by permitting "17-year-old kids to dictate" who their principal should be, the school system had opened the door to "anarchy."[33]

The settlement of the Northern boycott unquestionably contributed to the defeat of the May, 1966, millage proposal. As the associate director of the Citizen's Committee on Equal Opportunity put it, the Northern incident provoked "a punitive vote in the white community which went far beyond the hard core of voters who consistently resist any raise in taxes."[34] Fortunately, the board later recovered from that political setback with a successful millage campaign in November. However, the settlement of the Northern incident had other, more important consequences. Among white Detroiters, the dismissal of Carty was evidence that the board was too weak to deal effectively with student protestors, a perception that added to the feeling of many whites that the key problem in the schools, the city, and the nation was the breakdown of "law and order."

In the weeks and months that followed, black Detroiters, who appeared to have won a great victory in the Northern walkout on first glance, also became increasingly angry with the school board. The crisis at Northern had exposed a deep reservoir of outrage among African-Americans. Several days after the end of the Northern boycott, 150 students at Southeastern High School, a predominantly black school, walked out on the grounds that conditions in their school were "almost as bad as they are at Northern." In late May, Karl Gregory, the Wayne State economics professor who headed the Northern Freedom School, began a scathing series of articles in the *Michigan Chronicle* deploring the fact "that inner city education is inferior education" and, for the first time by a prominent public figure, calling for community control of the schools in the ghetto.[35]

Reinforcing the legitimacy of Gregory's critique of unequal education in the Detroit system was a report issued in June by the Ad Hoc Committee for Equal Educational Opportunity, which took the unprecedented step of publicly analyzing standardized test results in Detroit on a school-by-school basis. Citywide reading achievement scores for fourth, sixth, and eighth graders were all below the national norms. More troubling to the Ad Hoc Committee was the fact that reading scores for black students were far below those of white students. Moreover, the report maintained that "only in predominantly Negro high school areas does the gap widen between the level the child should be reading at and the level at which he is reading as the child progresses from 4th to 6th to 8th grades." The report provided the first hard evidence of unequal educational outcomes on a large scale, and it implied that the longer black children stayed in the Detroit schools, the worse they did academically.[36]

Following closely on the heels of that report, the committee studying conditions at Northern issued its findings. Chaired by veteran civil rights leader Charles Wells, the study confirmed virtually all of the charges made by the student protestors and stated unequivocally that conditions at Northern "reflect a dissatisfied student body, a divided teaching staff, and an estranged community."[37] Attempting to placate the black community, the board immediately adopted a number of the recommendations made by the committee. At the same time, however, perhaps in an attempt to demonstrate to white Detroiters that it had not capitulated entirely to the protestors, the board appointed Northern's assistant principal, George Donaldson, to become the new principal of the school in September. This action was a clear slap at the students, who had specifically demanded that the new principal be someone other than Donaldson, and it insured that both sides in the struggle would remain disgruntled.[38]

Perhaps the most telling blow to the schools at this time was a series of articles in the *Free Press* that appeared soon after the 1966–67 school year began. Unbeknown to the school system, *Free Press* reporter Jim Treloar spent seven days gathering information for the series while substituting at the largely black Jefferson Intermediate School. He described a physically decaying inner-city school, desperately short of the most basic supplies and relying on equipment that appeared to date back to the nineteenth century. He also found an embittered and demoralized teaching staff, some of whom referred to their students as "ADC leeches." "These kids are just plain dumb," other staff members told him. "You'll never teach them anything."

Nearly 40 percent of the students at Jefferson came from impoverished, single-parent families whose daily life, Treloar noted, had little or nothing in common with the teachers or the material in the curriculum. At the heart of the problems at Jefferson, he argued, was the vast gulf between these middle-class teachers and the ghetto students, a gulf made worse by the inability of either side to reach out to the other. Indeed, Treloar reported that the time for bridging that gulf may have passed entirely. The black counselor who served as the community-school agent for Jefferson grimly warned that "someday, the parents are going to come and tear these doors down. But it won't be the administration they'll be after—it'll be the teachers who are cheating their children out of an education who will find their hides nailed to the wall!"[39]

Barraged by criticism, school leaders tried to mollify the angry black community. By far the most important step that the board took in that direction was appointing Norman Drachler to replace Samuel Brownell in July, 1966.[40] Drachler, assistant superintendent for School Relations and Special Services under Brownell, was highly regarded by leaders of Detroit's liberal and civil rights establishment. As a former member of the DFT, he was also warmly endorsed by the teachers and by organized labor, particularly the United Auto Workers. The *Michigan Chronicle* hailed his appointment, calling him a man of "integrity and consistent purpose." Born in Ukraine, where his father had been head of Jewish education for the Czarist government, Drachler was deeply committed to strong intergroup relations. This resolve came, in part, from his personal history. As a child, Drachler and his family had been saved from a pogrom by Christian neighbors. An "aggressive integrationist," his views on race relations coincided well with those of the liberal majority on the board. He was, without question, the most liberal superintendent the city had yet seen.[41]

Drachler acted quickly to secure the loyalty of major civil rights organizations, appointing Arthur Johnson, former executive secretary of the NAACP and then deputy director of the Michigan Civil Rights Commission, as deputy superintendent for School Relations and Special Services. Johnson immediately became the highest-ranking black school administrator in the city. In 1968, Drachler appointed a second black deputy superintendent, Aubrey V. McCutcheon, Jr., an attorney with experience in labor negotiations, who took charge of the Division of Staff Relations.[42]

Not only did Drachler reach out to the established civil rights leaders and organizations, but he also dealt with more radical black leaders and groups. In the fall of 1966, at the urging of Richard Henry, a militant leader of GOAL, Drachler began a thorough review of school texts and curricula with an eye toward eliminating racially biased history books and adding substantially more black history to the social studies program. By the start of the 1968–69 school year, Drachler had banned the most offensive text, started an influential national campaign to get publishers to include materials on black history and culture in their books, and transformed the curriculum along "multicultural" lines, with a strong emphasis on black history and culture.[43]

In addition to these actions, Drachler also announced that companies doing business with the board would have to adhere to new fair employment standards that required them to have larger proportions of black contractors and workers. More dramatically, Drachler pressured the unions participating in the apprenticeship programs, declaring that he would close the programs entirely unless the unions immediately ended their discrimination against black students. By the end of the 1966–67 school year, the Detroit schools had also improved conditions in their own shop. Every school in the district had at least one black teacher, making the staff perhaps the most integrated of any large city in the nation. Similarly, Detroit also led the nation in the number of black school administrators, although this translated into only 9 percent of the department heads, 9 percent of the assistant principals, and 6 percent of the principals in the district.[44]

Yet even as the school administration seemed to be making progress in these crucial areas, new problems emerged. Using the school-by-school results of standardized tests, parents associations and civil rights groups repeatedly demanded that school leaders directly address the inequality of educational achievement between black and white children. In October, 1966, parents at Higgenbotham Elementary threatened to boycott the school when they learned that their students were eighteen months to two years below the national norm on achievement tests. Six months later, parents picketed Winterhalter Intermediate School to protest precisely the same problem. Early in June, 1967, the NAACP added its voice to the protests, with an official leveling an unusually sharp attack at the board about conditions at Northwestern High School, noting that "a significant number of children entering the 10th grade [at Northwestern] were reading at the fifth grade level or below." Amos Wilder, an executive at Motown Records who chaired the HSSC subcommittee investigating Northwestern, called the school "a symbol of the class and racial prejudices the Negro people have been subjected to for many years. It maintains the cycle of systematic neglect of Negro children."[45]

The incremental changes that the board and Drachler were initiating were not enough to quell these long-brewing protests. These criticisms, in fact, signaled the beginning of a distinct change in educational politics in Detroit. Prior to 1967, leading civil rights and liberal activists had maintained that "cultural disadvantages," segregation (of both teachers and students), and unequal finances were the main sources of the educational problems of black children. The solution to these problems lay in such compensatory programs as Great Cities, integrating schools and staffs, and equalizing educational resources throughout the city. Leaders of the liberal-labor-black coalition believed that there was nothing fundamentally wrong with the system, it merely had to shed the vestiges of its discriminatory past and, to paraphrase Martin Luther King, Jr., to live up to the true meaning of its educational creed. In many ways, the Northern High School protest was a perfect illustration of this position, since the students were simply asking for the school to fulfill its fundamental mission of educating them well.

By the middle of 1967, however, that position began to give way before a new set of radical arguments that rested on the premise that the schools *were* fulfilling their fundamental mission, namely to *miseducate* black children. Advocates of this position declared that the schools were part of the white racist establishment, and, as such, they would never contribute to the meaningful education of black children. Indeed, these militant leaders saw the unequal educational outcomes in Detroit as the result of *deliberate* policies and practices of the school board. To paraphrase Black Panther leader Eldridge Cleaver, these leaders saw public education as part of the problem, not part of the solution.[46]

Following the 1965 and 1966 riots in Los Angeles and Cleveland, black nationalists became increasingly vocal, demanding more rapid and profound changes in American society. In 1966, rejecting integration as a ruse for maintaining white supremacy, the Student Nonviolent Coordinating Committee urged "black Americans to begin building independent political, economic, and cultural institutions that they will control and use as instruments of social change in this country." Their goal was "Black Power," not integration. By 1967, the civil rights movement was torn by the struggle between an older generation of integrationists and a younger, more militant generation of separatists.[47]

Gaining control of the schools was a central issue in that debate. In *Black Power*, Carmichael and Hamilton urged black parents to take control of ghetto schools away from the educational "'professionals,' most of whom have long since demonstrated their insensitivity to the needs and problems of the black child." They specifically urged black teachers and administrators for ghetto schools. In May, 1967, at a conference sponsored by the DFT on "Racism in Education," black nationalists advocating this point of view clashed sharply with members of the teachers' union. Reflecting the traditional color-blind position of the civil rights movement, DFT President Mary Ellen Riordan declared "Color is beside the point if the person is doing the job." Black nationalists at the conference, however, countered by demanding "black teachers and principals in black schools."[48]

One month later, on June 13, proponents of these positions clashed again in a hearing at the board of education. Rev. Albert Cleage, Jr., and members of the newly organized Inner City Parents Council presented a blistering report on the condition of black education in Detroit.[49] Cleage and Inner City Parents maintained that the low test scores and high dropout rates of black students in Detroit resulted from deliberate, racist policies and practices of the schools. "We indict the Detroit Board of Education and the school administration for failure to educate inner city children as evidenced by the . . . comparison of achievement levels in Detroit schools . . . " the report began. "Obviously inner city schools do not prepare our children and young people for the world of work or for college entrance. They prepare our children only for ADC and the war in Vietnam."[50]

Following a detailed analysis of standardized test scores, the report charged "that this continuing failure to educate inner city children reflects a deliberate policy of racial discrimination which makes it impossible for the Detroit school system to educate inner city children until basic changes are made in its structure and orientation." Rejecting both "Nazi-like theories of racial inferiority" and the more subtlely racist theories of cultural deprivation, the report stated "that the basic reason for the failure to educate inner city children stems from the schools' deliberate and systematic destruction of the Afro-American child's self-image and racial pride."[51]

Inner City Parents argued that only the following remedies would improve educational quality in black schools: (1) transfer most white teachers and administrators out of predominantly black schools because "consciously or unconsciously, they believe in the inferiority of all non-whites"; (2) remove racially biased texts and materials that "present a distorted picture of the Afro-American child's history and culture . . . [and thereby] rob him of any motivation to learn and develop"; and (3) reorient inner city schools around a curriculum "capable of giving Afro-American children a knowledge of their history, their culture and their destiny."[52]

While the report also called for such noncontroversial reforms as minimum competency exams and regular teachers instead of emergency substitutes, at its heart it was a bold statement of emerging black nationalism. "After 400 years of the white man's enforced separation," the report concluded, "black people are rejecting the dream of integration as the goal for their struggle and are instead finding pride in their own history, culture and power, seeking to develop their own independent leadership, organizations and programs, and determined that the separation which the white man has forced upon them shall now be used for their advancement rather than for their exploitation."[53]

The school leaders, especially the liberal board members, responded to the report with dismay. While the members politely thanked Cleage and the parents for their time and effort, they flatly rejected the basic premise of the report, namely that the school system was deliberately miseducating black children. A. L. Zwerdling chastised Inner City Parents for raising "phony issues" unrelated to the real problems of the school system. Remus Robinson, who had trounced Cleage in the 1966 primary election for school board less than a year before, declared that "we reject bigotry whether it be white or black and I reject the suggestion that all Negro schools such as those in the South are superior to Detroit Schools."[54]

The board issued no new policies or directives as a result of this presentation. In many ways, however, this debate was more than a battle over educational agendas. The civil rights establishment in Detroit, including the school superintendent and the liberal majority on the board, were thoroughly committed to integration. These leaders had fought for over two decades to gain control of the board, and they realized that their strength lay in maintaining the liberal-labor-black coalition. They clearly recognized that appeals to either "white backlash" or "black power" would destroy what AFL-CIO President George Meany described as the "natural alliance" between organized labor, white liberals, and black civil rights activists. Moreover, they could point to a great deal of success, in the past decade, toward realizing the goals of the civil rights movement within the public schools of the city.[55]

Nevertheless, the liberal-labor-black coalition was quite vulnerable to attacks from extremists from both the black and white communities. Even politically moderate African-Americans were outraged at the hypocrisy of union leaders who espoused racial harmony at public forums but whose organizations blocked black students from entering union-controlled apprenticeship programs. In addition, blacks were continually angered over the failure of white Detroiters to support tax increases for the schools. A 1965 survey of 1,175 people in the Detroit area, for example, found that 70 percent of blacks supported increasing school taxes compared to only 48 percent of whites. One of the most striking findings was that blacks without children favored higher school taxes more than whites with children. Such attitudes led many blacks to question the efficacy of any political coalition with whites. As of 1965, the liberal-labor-black coalition had produced only one black city council member and two black school board members in a city that was, at the time, nearly 40 percent African-American. A confidential report received by Remus Robinson that year argued that the coalition was a one-way street for blacks—blacks voted for white candidates but whites rarely voted for blacks. "The Negro-labor-liberal white coalition is a failure" the report concluded.[56]

More than any event in the modern history of the city, the catastrophic Detroit riot that began on July 23 deepened these racial divisions. In six days of violence and destruction, 43 people died, more than 1,000 were injured, and 7,231 were arrested. More than 2,500 stores were damaged, looted, gutted by fire, or destroyed. In all, property damage was estimated at $80–$125 million. Seventeen thousand men, including members of the Michigan National Guard, the State Police, and some 4,700 paratroopers, were required to restore order in the city.[57]

Nowhere was the gulf between the races more apparent than in the totally opposite ways in which blacks and whites interpreted these events. Researchers from the University of Michigan found "for the most part, it was as if two different events had taken place in the same city, one a calculated act of criminal anarchy, the other a spontaneous protest against mistreatment and injustice." Yet one thing was common between both racial groups. After the riot, political extremists from both sides of the color line attracted larger and more receptive audiences.[58]

Indeed, the established liberal leadership in Detroit seemed to be thrown into utter confusion and despair by the riot. The Model City had failed. As Mayor Jerome Cavanagh put it, "Today we stand amidst the ashes of our hopes. We hoped against hope that we had been doing enough to prevent a riot. It was not enough."[59] School leaders were also deeply shaken by the events. Like the members of the Cavanagh administration, they believed that their innovative programs and hiring practices were making significant progress in resolving racial problems in the schools. Nevertheless, while school buildings themselves had escaped serious damage during the riot, anger about the poor quality of education in the ghetto was certainly a factor behind the rioting. A *Free Press* and Urban League survey of blacks in the riot area found that 22.0 percent of the respondents believed that the "failure of the schools" had a great deal to do with the riot, and an additional 24.9 percent stated that the schools had something to do with it. One rioter remarked, "The teachers don't teach a damn thing. . . . They don't give a damn if you don't learn or nothing, you know. . . . Man, I didn't learn shit until I hit the 12th grade."[60]

In the hearings and inquiries that followed the riot, school leaders clung to their basic premise that more money would cure the ailing ghetto schools. Norman Drachler, for instance, stated that the schools in the riot area needed 695 more teachers to reduce class sizes to below 30 pupils per teacher (which would still be above the state average of 25.4), $600,000 for textbooks, and $2 million for new classrooms. Some of the school buildings in the riot area, Drachler noted in testimony before the Kerner Commission, had been dedicated during the administration of President Ulysses S. Grant. Drachler estimated that a minimum of $8.12 million in additional aid was needed to upgrade the quality of education in the riot area.[61]

As accurate as these assessments might have been, their proponents were quickly drowned out by militants who vehemently rejected such liberal strategies as simplistic and inadequate. One month after the riot, Rev. Albert Cleage, Jr., began a weekly column in the mainstream *Michigan Chronicle*. Routinely rejecting liberal reforms, Cleage urged African-Americans to take control of their own communities and institutions. Control of the public schools was a centerpiece of that program. In October, following a violent protest by black students against the white principal at Knudson Junior High, Cleage declared that "there will be no education for black children until the black community controls its own schools."[62]

In essence, Cleage was taking the precedent set by the Northern school boycott one step farther. Rather than hoping that the school board would respond to community pressure about who should administer schools in the ghetto and what the curriculum should be, Cleage sought to bring "power to the people" by having the community run the schools directly. As the issue of community control gained national attention due to the controversy in the Ocean Hill–Brownsville section of New York City, Cleage and his supporters began a simultaneous campaign to radically decentralize the Detroit school system.[63]

The campaign for community control severely attenuated the liberal-labor-black coalition, especially as antagonism mounted toward leaders who remained committed to integration rather than separatism. The campaign also challenged the very cornerstones of the Progressive era reforms that had transformed the Detroit schools in the early part of the century, namely the at-large board of education and the centralized educational bureaucracy.

The Road to Financial Ruin, 1965–68

Just as black militants were mounting their challenge to the school system, two other important groups in the liberal-labor-black coalition, the white working class and the DFT, were mounting challenges of their own. The white working class had always been a shaky member of the coalition. Such union leaders as Al Barbour and the Reuther brothers were unquestionably more liberal on educational issues than many white union members, a fact that had been amply demonstrated by the large number of no votes cast by white Detroiters on school millage proposals even when union leaders had endorsed them. But 1968 marked a turning point in local educational politics because, after that time, union leaders could no longer be assured that they could deliver any substantial white rank-and-file support for school issues, support that had previously played a crucial role in getting millage increases approved in Detroit. In the fall of 1968, amid the tumult of the presidential election, school and union leaders campaigned for the largest school tax increase in the history of the city. But, just as large numbers of white union members defected from the Democratic party and its liberal policies in that election, so a large proportion of Detroit's white working class completely abandoned its political support for the public schools, a development that led to an unprecedented financial crisis for the school system.

Unlike many white working-class Detroiters, the DFT did not abandon the liberalism or the liberal-labor-black coalition during this period. Rather, the union began to aggressively pursue its own financial and professional agenda, often at the risk of alienating both the board and the voters. Unfortunately for the school system, this growing militance of the DFT coincided with the increasing political disaffection from the public schools in both the black and white communities. In short, the DFT began demanding more at precisely the time that the community was offering less.

Ironically, when the liberal board of education took office in July, 1965, the financial prospects for the board seemed to be looking up. In May, Governor George Romney signed into law a bill giving the school board unilateral authority to issue bonds worth up to 2 percent of assessed valuation, equal to about $100 million. Since the Detroit common council had retained this authority since 1949, the new law completed the quest for full financial independence from the city for the board of education. The school board now had the same power to issue bonds that other large school districts in the state had, and, for the first time, school leaders could borrow funds for capital improvement without seeking approval from either the common council or the voters.[64]

The Detroit schools also benefited substantially from the Democratic landslide in the 1964 election, which produced the first majority for that party in the Michigan legislature in thirty years. Throughout the late 1940s and the 1950s, the Democrats led the battle for increased state aid for education generally and spearheaded the fight for additional funding for urban districts specifically. This new Democratic majority voted increases in state aid for the Detroit schools, which received $61.6 million in 1966 compared to $48.8 million in 1964. Nevertheless, as late as 1968, the Detroit schools still received only $193 per pupil from the state, $32 *below* the state average.[65] At about the same time, Detroit also began receiving substantial amounts of federal aid under the Elementary and Secondary Education Act. While restricted, to some extent, by the categorical nature of this aid, school leaders used federal funds to initiate dropout prevention programs, set up day-care and Head Start centers, and expand the scope of the Great Cities project. The increases in state and federal funds played a major role in keeping the Detroit system solvent during the late 1960s and the 1970s.[66]

Despite these increases in state and federal aid, the financial problems of the district remained severe. These financial woes were rooted in a perpetual series of problems: declining property values in the district, inadequate levels of school taxes levied on that property, rising enrollments, and increasingly forceful demands of the DFT for better salaries and working conditions. In the fall of 1965, Detroit levied only 15.76 mills for its schools (8.26 mills allocated by the county and the 7.5 extra mills that had been renewed in 1963). Of the forty-three school districts in Wayne County, only four had tax rates below that of Detroit, and, in most county districts, property assessments were rising. In Detroit, however, the SEV was falling and, consequently, the amount of local revenue raised for the schools from property taxes dropped from almost $90.6 million in 1960–61 to $85.6 million in 1965–66. In all, between 1962 and 1971, school leaders estimated that the district lost over $91 million due to declining property values. Increases in state aid and the arrival of federal aid made up part of that shortfall, but the steady increase in enrollment, which rose from 285,304 in September, 1960, to 299,962 in October, 1966 (the largest enrollment in the history of the school system), kept intense pressure on the board for hiring still more teachers and building additional classrooms. New state and federal laws mandating additional expenditures and rising inflation compounded these financial problems.[67]

The teachers, however, put the greatest financial pressure on the board. In January, 1965, the DFT, now certified as the collective bargaining agent for the teachers, presented the board with a series of demands, including substantial salary increases (ranging from $200 to $700 per teacher) and large cuts in the size of classes. In negotiations that began in February, the DFT argued that only by improving salaries and working conditions could the system end the chronic shortage of regular and substitute teachers in Detroit, a situation that contrasted sharply with suburban school districts that had waiting lists in both categories.[68] While the board sympathized with these demands, projected revenues were neither sufficient to warrant the increases nor for hiring the large number of new teachers necessary to cut class sizes. One researcher estimated that it would take 1,600 more teachers in Detroit just to bring the pupil-teacher ratio in the city equal to the average in the rest of the state. At a June rally, following four months of talks, DFT leaders announced to a thousand union members that negotiations were stalemated. The teachers "roared" their approval as the union leaders declared that they would shut down the school system in September if the board did not meet their demands. As with earlier strike threats, organized labor strongly supported the DFT. Attempting to ward off a crisis, the school board eventually agreed to the major salary demands—maximum salaries rose by $700, from $8,600 in 1964–65 to $9,300 in 1965–66, exactly meeting the DFT demand. Union leaders were jubilant.[69]

While this agreement averted a strike, the additional $7.5 million per year for salaries left the school board in serious financial straits. Early in

1966, following a lengthy analysis of the budget, school leaders estimated that, if they did not raise taxes, the combined impact of declining property values and increasing costs would result in a $12.3 million budget deficit by the end of the 1966–67 school year and a $32.0 million deficit by the end of the decade. In order to head off that fiscal crisis, in January, 1966, the board voted to put a 2.5 mill tax increase for five years on the May ballot.[70]

As with the previous school tax elections in the 1960s, established interest groups unanimously supported the increase. Former school board member Roy Stephens, Jr., chaired the citizens organization that pushed for the proposal, Leonard Woodcock, vice president of the United Auto Workers, served as cochair, and Willis Hall, executive secretary of the Board of Commerce, served on the steering committee. Both the Democratic and Republican parties endorsed the measure. In the African-American community, the proposal drew support from the NAACP, the Trade Union Leadership Council, the organization of black ministers, and the *Michigan Chronicle*.[71]

Despite that broad support, on May 9, the millage proposal went down to defeat, losing by not quite 12,000 votes, 79,746 to 67,815. As in the defeat of the spring 1963 millage, the predominantly white wards in the northeast and northwest sections of the city overwhelmingly opposed the proposal, particularly wards 21 and 22, which, between them, accounted for over 50,000 of the no votes. Indeed, voters in every high school district with a majority of white students voted against the millage, in some cases by nearly a three-to-one margin. In contrast, voters in the primarily black wards and black high school districts generally supported the millage, but voter turnout in these areas was light. In the Northern High School voting district, for example, 82 percent of the people who cast ballots supported the millage, but that translated into only 3,215 yes votes. As the *Michigan Chronicle* argued, the defeat was due as much to apathy and indifference among blacks as it was to ignorance and bigotry among whites. More important than apathy and indifference, however, was the Northern High School boycott. According to the *Free Press*, the sentiment expressed by many opponents of the proposal was summed up in the statement, "Darned if I'll pay for students to run the school system."[72]

The millage defeat left the board badly shaken. Almost immediately the members turned to the difficult task of cutting nearly $12 million out of the 1966–67 budget. At every turn, however, they met resistance. Their plan to reinstate half-day sessions outraged parents, who circulated a petition signed by 35,000 people opposing the action. The parents eventually filed a successful lawsuit that barred the board from implementing the plan. At the same time, the DFT was putting renewed pressure on the board for another salary increase, pointing out that despite the salary increase the previous year, the system was still short 500–600 teachers for the upcoming school year, which one school official claimed was "the most serious shortage of teachers in [the system's] history."[73]

Hamstrung by the millage failure, restricted by the courts in how it could reduce expenses, and facing renewed pressure from the DFT, the board resigned itself to beginning the 1966–67 school year with a large deficit. It was obvious that the only way out of this financial quagmire was to try to pass a millage increase once again. Hoping that anger over the Northern boycott had dissipated, the board voted to place a 5 mill, five-year increase on the November ballot.[74]

School leaders, particularly newly appointed superintendent Norman Drachler, campaigned vigorously for the proposal, especially in black neighborhoods. Viewing black turnout as the key to victory in millage elections, Drachler urged African-Americans to go to the polls in large enough numbers to offset the predicted no vote from the white northeast and northwest sections of the city. Strongly supporting Drachler's efforts, the *Michigan Chronicle* as well as such black leaders as Rev. William Ardrey, chair of the Ad Hoc Committee, enthusiastically endorsed the proposal. Drachler also directly appealed to young voters, calling on them to support the schools and counteract the projected no vote from the large bloc of Detroiters over the age of sixty-five.[75]

As Drachler and others campaigned in the black community, the board also sought to regain support from conservative, white Detroiters. The Detroit Board of Commerce, for example, donated $50,000 toward the millage campaign; *The Detroiter* enthusiastically editorialized in favor of the tax increase and ran a series of full-page ads prior to the election. Leaders of the Wayne County AFL-CIO and the UAW, particularly union presidents Al Barbour and Walter Reuther, also played major roles in the campaign along with the Detroit Citizens League, the Detroit Council of Churches, and the Democratic and Republican parties.[76]

Boosting these efforts was a last-minute settlement of the contract dispute between the board and the DFT. Although a large number of teachers were ready to strike, after a long, stormy meeting, the membership narrowly approved a contract that provided for starting salaries of $5,800 and maximum salaries of $10,000. While the growing militance of the DFT boded ill for the future, Detroiters were thankful that, at least, one problem facing the school district, a possible teachers' strike, had been averted, and proponents of the millage breathed a sigh of relief.[77]

The broad-based and well-financed millage campaign paid off, as voters approved the tax increase by a fairly comfortable margin of 192,240 to 164,897. The strategy of boosting turnout in the black sections of town appeared to have worked, since voters in several of the predominantly white wards of the city rejected the proposal by substantial margins. Wards 21 and 22, for example, together accounted for over 96,000 of the no votes, more than 58 percent of the total no vote. Despite this opposition, the campaign produced the first tax increase for the school system in seven years.[78]

The tax increase promised to raise an additional $21 million in annual revenue and provide the solution to some of the more vexing material problems facing the school system. Yet soon after the election returns were in, the DFT began maneuvering to influence how the board would spend most of that money. In the previous two years, militant teachers in the DFT had been narrowly defeated in their efforts to get the union to strike for even larger salary and benefit packages. Now, with the tax increase assured, the militants demanded a huge, $1,700 annual increase for the teachers.[79] During the millage campaign, however, school leaders had pledged that they would use the bulk of the new revenues for construction. The stage was set for another confrontation between the union and the board over the issue of salaries or buildings in the fall of 1967.[80]

The board planned to use most of the $21 million from the millage increase for 150 new classrooms ($7.5 million), renovating deteriorating older buildings ($3 million), 250 additional teachers to reduce class sizes ($2 million), and the last round of salary increases ($3 million). The remaining $6 million could go for raises averaging $500–600 per teacher. The DFT, however, countered with demands of raises of up to $1,500 and a reduction in the length of the forty-week school year, the longest in the state. The board balked at the demands, noting that the $1,500 increase would absorb about $16.5 million of the $21 million in extra revenue the system was to receive from the tax increase. The board stuck to its offer of $500 and, in June, with the negotiations deadlocked, the teachers voted overwhelmingly to reject the board's offer. Union leaders then declared that they would not reopen negotiations until late August. [81]

By refusing to negotiate until almost the start of the 1967–68 school year, the DFT leaders hoped to intensify the pressure on the board to settle the dispute. They also hoped that, in the aftermath of the riot, the state, which had stepped in earlier in the year to pay off the board's $12 million deficit, would again bail out the school district, this time to demonstrate concern for the devastated city. Indeed, soon after the riot, Gov. Romney *had* called for higher salaries for inner-city teachers as one means for avoiding new disturbances in Detroit. Now, however, Romney adamantly refused to provide any additional financial aid for Detroit, recognizing that giving the city funds in order to avert a strike would set a very dangerous precedent.[82]

As the start of school approached, the DFT reduced its salary demand to $1,200, but the board still rejected that amount as beyond its means. Despite round-the-clock negotiations in the final week, neither side budged and, on September 6, the DFT began picketing the schools. The following day, DFT President Mary Ellen Riordan issued a statement declaring that the teachers would not begin work until a contract was ratified. She stated that higher salaries were crucial to maintaining the viability of the school system, especially in light of the intense competition between Detroit and the suburbs for teachers. In regard to the commitment of the board for more buildings, Riordan reiterated the long-held position of the union, "Mortar and bricks don't teach children. Teachers do." Despite the fact that teachers' strikes were still illegal in Michigan under the Hutchinson Act, the teachers of Detroit were now on strike.[83]

The strike lasted almost two weeks. On September 18, the teachers and the board finally agreed to a package that included increases of $850 in each of the next two years, a one-week reduction in the school year, and a cap on the size of classes. The salary increase, which cost the board about $9.3 million in 1967–68 and $18.6 million in 1968–69, was well above what the school system could afford. The contract forced the school system into a string of unbalanced budgets that eventually pushed the system to the brink of bankruptcy. But in some ways, these consequences were the least significant ones of the strike.[84]

In addition to financial problems, the walkout seriously damaged the reputation of the liberal majority on the board, exposing their impotence in appealing to organized labor to avoid the strike. As both the *Free Press* and the *News* angrily editorialized, the DFT had struck against the most prolabor school board in the history of the city and against a school superintendent who had been a prominent member of the union. Since the Hutchinson Act was too feeble to stop the strike, the *Free Press* called for a new public employee bargaining act to prevent future walkouts.[85]

Not only did the strike weaken the liberal majority on the board, it also severely strained the liberal-labor-black coalition, dividing organized labor, which strongly supported the DFT, from civil rights organizations, which were dedicated to restoring normalcy to ghetto residents after the riot. Prior to the strike, NAACP leaders had pleaded with the union to allow the schools to open while continuing the negotiations. The *Michigan Chronicle,* which was still very sympathetic to the DFT, also urged the union to accept the board's original offer of $500 and get the schools open. The union ignored all such pleas, and, following the settlement of the strike, the *Chronicle* editorialized that "Coming as it did, hard on the heels of 'the week that was' in July, [the strike] seemed like an unnecessary low blow to the city's 300,000 school children—many of whom already had been directly and seriously affected by the rioting."[86]

Perhaps the most important consequence of the strike was the direct challenge the DFT presented to the authority of the school board. In 1966, the Northern High School strike had raised the specter of community control, threatening to eliminate the school board entirely in determining who should administer the schools. The 1967 DFT strike hit the board with an equally powerful blow. The strike demonstrated that teachers were now strong enough to unilaterally force the board to allocate funds according to union demands. Not surprisingly, the *Free Press* used almost the same language to denounce the DFT as it did to chastise the students from Northern. "Who is to run the schools?" the paper editorialized when the strike began. "That's become the crucial question. Is the board of education, elected and responsible to the people, going to exercise the final judgment on how the school district's resources are apportioned among the various needs? Or is the teachers' union?" Unlike similar criticisms of militant teachers in the 1930s and 1940s, these questions were neither rhetorical or polemical.[87]

As the 1967–68 school year progressed, political and financial crises of unparalleled proportions were bearing down on the school system. When the strike was first settled, the *Free Press* noted that the board would not be able to pay for the projected new buildings *and* the new union contract without a "quick and unanticipated" influx of additional funds. In May, 1968, after being rebuffed by the state in a request for more money, Drachler reported that the board would run short by $9 million at the end of the school year and by $19 million at end of 1968–69.[88]

To avert this financial catastrophe, school leaders launched two initiatives. The first was a lawsuit filed against the state that demanded a substantial increase in funding for the Detroit schools. For decades, the state had underfunded public education in Detroit and, by the 1960s, the situation had worsened. At the very time that Detroit was losing the ability to provide more local support for its schools, the disparity in per pupil expenditures between the city and suburbs actually got worse. In its investigation of the causes of the Detroit riot, the Kerner Commission reported that, in 1950, Detroit and the suburbs were fairly close in terms of per pupil aid from the state at $135 and $149 respectively. By 1964, however, the gap between the city and suburbs had widened, with Detroit receiving $189 per pupil while the suburbs received $240. Beginning in 1965, even through the state had channeled more resources to schools in the Motor City, the city's schools were still substantially underfunded. In 1967–68, despite serving 14.23 percent of the students in the state, Detroit received only 11.37 percent of state school aid.[89] Thus, in January, 1968, A. L. Zwerdling announced that the board was filing the first suit of its kind in the nation "to compel the state of Michigan to discharge its constitutional obligation to provide equal educational opportunity for all children attending the public schools in this state."[90]

The board realized that the lawsuit was a long-range strategy. As the case began its slow movement though the courts, school leaders launched their second important financial initiative. On August 27, 1968, the board announced a campaign for a 10 mill, five-year tax increase, the largest school tax increase ever put before the voters. Despite the fact that the board had asked voters to increase taxes less than two years before, the members believed that the situation facing the board was so perilous and the timing for the campaign so favorable as to compel immediate action.

In proposing the millage increase, Superintendent Drachler argued that, because of declining SEV, Detroit ranked eighty-fourth out of the ninety-two tri-county school districts in the amount of revenue raised from every mill levied. He also pointed out that, at the time, Detroit had the worst classroom-to-student ratio in the area (30.9 classrooms for every 1,000 students in Detroit compared to 37.8 for the rest of Wayne County, 37.2 for Oakland County, and 38.2 for Macomb County) and that the city ranked fifty-second out of the fifty-five largest districts in the tri-county area in terms of per pupil expenditures. Only in salaries for teachers did Detroit rank in the top group of school districts.[91]

In addition to believing that they could make a compelling financial case for the tax increase, the school leaders also believed that the increase had a decent chance of passing, because the proposal would appear on the same ballot as the 1968 presidential election. The liberal leaders of the board, who had ridden to victory in 1964 on Lyndon Johnson's coattails, hoped that the large number of Democratic voters who were expected to support Hubert Humphrey would also cast yes votes for the tax increase. Unfortunately for the board, the 1968 election shattered such conventional assumptions. The election, which proved to be a turning point in national politics, was also a watershed in educational politics in Detroit. In precisely the same way that the 1968 presidential election revealed a profound shift toward political conservatism among the white working class, so the millage election that took place on the same day in Detroit marked the virtual end of white working-class political support for the public schools of the Motor City.[92]

Since the mid-1950s, Catholic working-class voters in Midwestern, industrial cities were defecting from the New Deal coalition in substantial numbers. In educational politics in Detroit, that defection was reflected in the substantial opposition by large numbers of white working-class voters to the 1963 and 1966 millage proposals and the 1964 bond proposal. After 1964, when the views of the prointegration majority on the school board became more apparent, the estrangement between the school leaders and white voters became even worse.[93]

The wrenching national events of 1968 compounded the political problems of the board by increasing the racial and political polarization in Detroit as they did the nation. When nationwide riots broke out after the assassination of Martin Luther King, Jr., the gulf between black and white Detroiters became even more apparent. Blacks responded to the assassination and the riots with anger and despair, while many whites responded with calls for more "law and order." Two months later, the murder of Robert Kennedy robbed Democrats of the one candidate who still seemed capable of holding together the New Deal coalition, particularly the Catholic working-class part of the coalition.[94]

By September, it was clear that the Michigan Democratic party and its liberal allies in the labor movement were fighting for their political lives. Large numbers of white union members in metropolitan Detroit were flocking to rallies for George Wallace and Richard Nixon. UAW Local 326 in Flint formally endorsed Wallace, and straw polls in other Detroit area locals found substantial support for Wallace and Nixon. Some UAW members even jeered Walter Reuther as he campaigned for Hubert Humphrey.[95]

At the same time, racial incidents were becoming increasingly common in Detroit's junior and senior high schools. In February, 1968, for example, white parents announced they would boycott Finney High School to protest school board plans to transfer black students from the overcrowded Southeastern High School into Finney. One month later, students at the already integrated Mumford and Cooley high schools walked out after racial clashes.[96] With every incident, "backlash" sentiments among white

Detroiters increased. In covering the 1968 presidential campaign, such political analysts as Samuel Lubell noted that many Wallace and Nixon supporters shared "a common resentment against being 'forced' to accept integration."[97] The schools became a focal point of much of that resentment. In April, after quelling a demonstration at an inner-city high school sparked by the murder of Martin Luther King, Jr., white national guardsmen chalked obscene graffiti throughout the school, applauding the assassination of the civil rights leader. Two months later, white firefighters taunted students from the largely black Durfee Junior High School by draping a Confederate flag on a car parked in front of the school.[98]

Passing a 10 mill tax increase would have been an uphill battle under tranquil circumstances. But these events made the task virtually impossible. As in previous millage elections, all the prominent interest groups in Detroit, ranging from the Board of Commerce to the UAW, strongly endorsed the tax increase.[99] Surprisingly, Rev. Albert Cleage, Jr., who, over the past year, had been impressed by Norman Drachler's sincere commitment to improving the education of black children, also announced support for the proposal. Cleage argued that voters in the northeast and northwest sections of the city, "outlying white racist bigots" as he called them, were opposing the tax increase because Drachler had promised that most of the money would be earmarked for inner-city, black children. For Cleage, the most notable example of this opposition was the unprecedented refusal of the Detroit Parent Teacher Association (D-PTA) to support the proposal. Claiming that the D-PTA was dominated by whites, Cleage charged that the organization opposed the millage precisely because Drachler was trying to equalize education in the inner city. "The November election is going to reveal the largest white racist vote we have ever seen," Cleage wrote in his weekly column in the *Michigan Chronicle*. "This is the Wallace phenomenon. It was always there but [Drachler] has stirred it up and now the stench can no longer be concealed." Warning that black indifference to this issue was as great a threat as white racism, Cleage strongly urged black voters to support the proposal.[100]

Neither Cleage nor leaders of the established interest groups, however, had enough influence with the voters to get this tax increase approved. At a time when almost three-quarters of all proposals to increase school taxes in Michigan were passed, Detroiters rejected the 1968 millage by one of the widest margins ever in a school tax election, with over 62 percent of the voters opposing the increase. Certainly the size of the increase, 10 mills, had a great deal to do with the defeat. More important, however, were the two recurring themes in Detroit school elections, strong white opposition and weak black support.[101]

As in the 1963 and 1966 millage defeats, opposition from the predominantly white northeast and northwest sections of the city was unusually heavy. The seven voting districts that roughly corresponded to the 21st and 22nd wards (districts 4–6 and 16–19 respectively) produced almost 138,000 no votes, nearly enough to defeat the proposal, which won only about 155,000 yes votes citywide. On the other hand, in the predominantly black voting districts in the central part of the city (districts 8–12 and 22–24) the proposal won, in some cases by a two-to-one margin. Yet the total yes vote from these districts amounted to only 48,000 votes.

One of the most striking aspects of the 1968 millage vote was the degree to which it reflected the political divisions that emerged in the presidential election. Detroit went heavily for Hubert Humphrey, the Democratic standard-bearer, winning 71.2 percent of the vote compared to 20.0 percent for Richard Nixon and only 8.4 percent for George Wallace. Yet in a number of voting districts, Wallace received a sizable vote and the combined Nixon and Wallace total was well over 40 percent, 48 percent in district 4 and almost 58 percent in district 17. These Nixon-Wallace districts were all located either in the northeastern or northwestern sections of the city, the very areas that produced the largest antimillage vote. Indeed, the seven voting districts that produced the largest no vote on the millage were also the ones that produced the largest vote for George Wallace and the largest combined Nixon-Wallace totals. A correlation analysis of the votes for the millage and for the presidential candidates by voting district found statistically significant, positive relationships between the votes for Wallace and opposition to the millage, +.86, and the combined Nixon and Wallace vote and opposition to the millage, +.80.

The promillage vote and support for Humphrey were also strongly correlated, +.79. The four voting districts (8, 12, 22, and 23) that produced the highest percentages for Humphrey, over 89 percent, were also among those that produced the highest percentages for the millage, all above 59 percent. The results from the pro-Humphrey districts, however, also reveal the depth of the problem the school board had in terms of convincing blacks and other liberal voters to support increased school taxes. The predominantly black 22nd voting district gave Humphrey over 25,000 votes, the second-highest Humphrey district in the city, yet it produced only 9,291 votes for the millage. This pattern was repeated in nearly every district that Humphrey won. In other words, large numbers of black and liberal voters, whom the board had hoped would spell the difference in this election, did not even mark their ballots on the millage. The failure of these voters to support the tax increase was as much a factor in the defeat of the millage as was the heavy opposition by whites.[102]

Unfortunately for the school board, the 1968 election marked the solidification of these racial voting patterns on school elections. Even as late as 1966, a sizable portion of white voters could be mobilized to support school tax increases. By 1968, however, a variety of factors, including the Detroit riot, the King and Kennedy assassinations, the drop in white school enrollment, and controversy about integration, led many white voters to withdraw their support from the schools entirely. If, as Kevin Phillips and other analysts have argued, the 1968 presidential election marked a watershed in terms of national political trends, then it also marked a turning point in terms of school politics in Detroit.[103] Indeed, a correlation analysis of antimillage votes cast in the 1963 school tax elections and the votes cast for Barry Goldwater in the 1964 presidential election found no statistically significant relationship in the April voting and only a slight relationship (+ .46) in the November voting. Four years later, however, the strong relationship between the antimillage vote and the Wallace-Nixon vote indicates that, between 1964 and 1968, school politics in Detroit had become deeply intertwined with the great changes going on in national politics. Just as strong support for Nixon and Wallace from white, urban voters signaled the fragmentation of the New Deal coalition, so the 1968 millage election pointed to the collapse of the educational wing of that coalition in Detroit. Never again would large numbers of white working-class voters support a tax increase for the Detroit public schools.[104]

This political transformation greatly compounded the problems facing the school system. School leaders not only had to contend with a growing movement among blacks for community control and an increasingly militant teachers' union (which declared that the millage defeat would not affect their new contract demands), but they also faced a looming financial crisis from which there was no apparent escape. After the election, Drachler estimated that, through severe budget cuts (particularly the suspension of most of the building program), the projected deficit for 1968–69 could be reduced to about $3 million. But despite these reductions, the deficit would jump to $10 million in 1969–70 even before teachers' salary increases were figured in.[105] The school system was plunging toward catastrophe.

The Campaign for Decentralization, 1968–70

Following the 1968 election, such white union leaders as Walter Reuther, black union members, and the Detroit Federation of Teachers were about all that was left of the labor component of the liberal-labor-black coalition in education. While the loss of support from most working-class whites was a severe blow to the coalition, the growing number of blacks in Detroit, the increasing power of the DFT, and the emergence of powerful African-American politicians, such as State Senator Coleman A. Young, still offered the possibility of averting the political and financial dissolution of the school system. Unfortunately, during the next few years, deep divisions appeared among these remaining supporters of the school system and destroyed any possibility of a unified approach to solving the problems of the Detroit schools.

The main issue dividing these groups was school governance, specifically whether to retain the current system or redistribute power within it through community control or decentralization. These demands for dramatic change essentially pitted separatists against integrationists and community activists against educational professionals.[106] These plans directly challenged the authority and the priorities of the liberal majority on the school board and implicitly threatened the Detroit Federation of Teachers. As in New York City, which was struggling with these issues at the same time, the conflict over the form of school governance practically tore the school system apart. In both cities, the state legislatures ultimately imposed a compromise plan for decentralization that pleased no one and left the schools in worse shape than before.[107]

Throughout 1968, as the problems of the Detroit schools worsened, the supporters of community control and decentralization became more insistent in their demands for sweeping changes in school governance. In late February, 1968, a conference chaired by Rev. James Wadsworth of the NAACP drew together an impressive array of black leaders from a wide range of political backgrounds, all of whom advocated some form of substantial governance reform. "I am not going to let white educators tell me that our children can't learn," stated Rev. W. C. Ardrey of the Ad Hoc Committee in one of the opening speeches. "I stand here as a member of a community that has the power to see to it that our children get a good education."

In the keynote address, Rev. Albert Cleage, Jr., declared, "Black children cannot be motivated by white teaching. Black children must be motivated by their own sense of dignity and purpose. Black children can only be motivated within the framework of the black revolution." Cleage stated that "Black parents are demanding black teachers, principals, and administrators throughout the city" and he predicted that "we are on the verge of probably the biggest confrontation black parents have ever had with the schools."[108]

Over the next few weeks, violent student demonstrations and walkouts erupted in a number of junior and senior highs. These incidents provided additional ammunition for the decentralizers, who, like the Progressive era reformers a half-century earlier, exploited every apparent weakness of the school board they challenged. Indeed, in his column in the *Michigan Chronicle,* Cleage strongly supported the student demonstrations and urged even greater radicalism. Repeating his position that "the failure of white administrators to educate black children is deliberate," Cleage stated that "the children who are breaking windows are closer to a solution than the parents because they are making it impossible for white administrators to ride out their failures." Following the death of Martin Luther King, Jr., in April, the number of violent disturbances in the schools increased and the educational environment deteriorated even further. By June, when the High School Study Commission released its report, a profound sense prevailed that things were desperately out of control in the schools.[109]

Created in the aftermath of the Northern boycott, the High School Study Commission began its deliberations in May, 1966. It was cochaired by Edward Cushman, a white administrator at Wayne State University who also headed the Detroit Commission on Community Relations, and the Hon. Damon J. Keith, a black U.S. District Court judge. Among its fifty-six other members were such longtime liberal, labor, and civil rights activists as Rev. W. C. Ardrey, Richard Austin, Douglas Fraser, Arthur L. Johnson, Judge Nathan Kaufman, Francis Kornegay, Longworth Quinn, Mary Ellen Riordan, Rev. James Wadsworth, Charles Wells, and Amos Wilder. In all, more than 350 people served on the commission and its twenty-two study groups, one for each high school in the city. For over eighteen months the commission examined the curriculum offerings of every school, the relationship between the schools and the central administration, personnel policies and practices of the board, relations between the schools and the communities they served, and the overall financial plight of the district.[110]

While the membership of the commission and its research agenda were quite similar to those of other citizen advisory commissions, the tone and the recommendations of the HSSC report were dramatically different from all of the earlier studies. The opening chapter of the report declared, "It is the conclusion of the Detroit High School Study Commission that the public schools are becoming symbols of society's neglect and indifference, rather than institutions that serve the needs of society by providing upward social and economic mobility." Evidence of this neglect and indifference were particularly apparent in the majority black high schools that the commission found were offering a decidedly inferior education compared to the largely white schools in the "fringe" areas of the city. "With notable exceptions," the report continued, "individual high school study groups have pointed to poor physical facilities, inadequate school administrations, teachers who perform poorly, an inequitable distribution of qualified teachers, questionable teacher assignment and reassignment policies, faculty uncertainty with respect to students' abilities and needs, programs and curricula that lead nowhere and have little relevance to future goals and employment opportunities."[111] When the report was presented to the board in late June, 1968, Edward Cushman summed up the attitude of the commission, stating that "our high schools are appallingly inadequate, a disgrace to the community and a tragedy for the thousands of young men and women whom we compel and cajole to sit in them."[112]

The solution to these massive problems, Cushman declared, was "nothing less than revolutionary changes in the school system." Specifically, the report endorsed two major changes: the decentralization of administrative authority in the system and increased accountability for teachers. Uniting these two themes was the belief that the very structure of the school system, which permitted poor teaching and administration to continue unchecked, contributed to the educational failure of black children. The commission stated that "many schools are lacking in direction, staffed with teachers and administrators who feel no sense of urgency or accountability to their superiors or to the community for the lack of achievement of their pupils." As a consequence, these students were utterly alienated from their own education and their parents were "in a state of hopelessness and helplessness as the educational deterioration goes unabated." The solution to this alienation and powerlessness was greater parental and community involvement in the schools to insure educational accountability. The report declared, "It is the belief of the High School Study Commission that the era of citizen support and confidence in the public schools which has been based on 'blind faith' in the professional educator has ended."[113]

In no uncertain terms, the report stated that "it is our judgment that the vital interests of this community are not being served by an educational bureaucracy which is characterized by professional inertia and responds only to crisis and demands of community pressure groups." And, in a move that underscored the angry and independent tone of most of the commission members, the HSSC refused to disband once its report was filed in order to make sure that its recommendations were carried out.[114] The sentiment against educational professionals was so pervasive in the HSSC that the only commission member to publicly dissent from these views was Mary Ellen Riordan, president of the DFT.[115]

HSSC demands to decentralize authority and increase teacher accountability were not as radical as those of Cleage and others for community control, but they nevertheless gave an enormous boost to groups that were pressing for the redistribution of power in the school system. In a weekly column in the *Michigan Chronicle* that began soon after the report was published, Amos Wilder, author of the opening chapter of the report, became a passionate advocate of community control of the schools. Unlike the majority of HSSC members, Wilder saw community control, in which parents could take charge of their children's schools, not decentralization, in which the board simply shifted some power to the community, as the only way to improve ghetto schools. Comparing schools in black communities to " 'colonial outposts' manned to a great extent by 'white suburbanite mercenaries' who come into the ghetto at dawn and flee well before dusk," Wilder urged African-Americans to seize power.[116]

Wilder joined Rev. Albert Cleage, Jr., and Dan Aldridge, a leader of SNCC, as regular columnists in the *Michigan Chronicle* who strongly advocated community control of the schools.[117] While they differed in their analyses of the problems facing the Detroit schools, all three based their vision of public education in Detroit on the premise that black children failed educationally because of the organization and actions of the school system and teachers. In late November, 1968, Cleage, for example, quoted approvingly the statement of the newly organized Citizens for Community Control of Schools.

> We citizens of the black community of Detroit, fully conscious of the fact that our children are not receiving a decent education, viewing the increasing deterioration in the educational situation in this city, and after innumerable presentations of our grievances and proposals to the Board of Education, to no avail, have finally come to the conclusion that COMMUNITY CONTROL OF SCHOOLS is the only way to establish real accountability of the school system to the black community.[118]

Neither Wilder, who sought community control to end what he called the "near criminal educational negligence" in ghetto schools, nor Aldridge, who denounced "the educational genocide" taking place in the inner city, would have quarreled with these sentiments.[119]

The fact that by late 1968 three columnists in the mainstream *Michigan Chronicle* were all demanding a major overhaul of school governance clearly indicated the growing popularity of such reforms. Indeed, as the 1968–69 school year began, the political winds in the city seemed to be shifting in favor of some sort of radical educational change. In the 1968 school board election, Andrew Perdue, a black attorney who had strong support from Rev. Cleage, won a seat largely because of his support for community control of schools. In addition, James Hathaway, a white attorney who was also sympathetic to decentralization, was elected. By the end of the 1968–69 school year several other members of the school board cautiously supported the reform, as did the *Free Press*, the *News*, the *Michigan Chronicle*, and the NAACP.[120]

There were several reasons for this trend. The HSSC report certainly added legitimacy to the reform efforts, but, beyond that endorsement, two other factors stand out. First, the redistribution of power, either through community control or decentralization, offered radical change at bargain basement prices. At a time when the school system faced growing budget deficits and stood little chance of winning millage increases, redistributing power seemed like a solution that could placate angry citizens without additional expenditures. Paradoxically, the plan was at once radical and reactionary. By December, 1968, some reform leaders placed a higher priority on changing the way schools were controlled than on gaining additional funds for the system. "We are not attempting to minimize the financial problems facing schools," Amos Wilder wrote, "but we are firmly convinced that until and unless the poor and the black communities demand and acquire responsibility and control of our schools, our children will continue to be served last and worst by that institution."[121]

Finally, the most pressing reason for the growing popularity of political solutions to the city's educational problems was the belief that giving communities more control over their schools might restore order in Detroit's increasingly anarchic junior and senior high schools. The Northern boycott in 1966 and the frequent disturbances in the schools throughout the 1967–68 school year were merely preludes to the even more violent confrontations that began in the fall of 1968 and lasted through 1971. Many of the confrontations were spontaneous protests by students against specific personnel, events, or conditions in the schools. But many other disturbances were orchestrated, or at least exploited, by adult organizations with larger political and social agendas. At least one of these organizations, the Citizens for Community Control of Schools, considered student unrest a means for gaining control of the schools. In 1968, the organization declared that it would be "ready to move to direct action, if necessary, such as pickets, boycotts, sit-ins, liberation of schools and actual takeover of the schoolhouse until the community obtains real decision-making power"[122]

The immediate causes of the high school disturbances fell into three broad categories of conflicts over school personnel, symbols of black nationalism and culture, and verbal and physical violence against administrators, teachers, and students. Regardless of the causes of these disturbances, their ultimate consequence was nearly three years of conflict and confrontation and the virtual destruction of the fundamental basis of authority necessary to operate effective schools.

The first source of conflict, controversies over school personnel, provided the most direct challenge to the authority of the school board. Throughout 1968, Rev. Cleage and members of the Inner City Parents Council staged a number of protests and boycotts against "second class education in the inner city." The central demand in all these efforts was the ouster of white principals in predominantly black schools.[123] Unlike the Northern High School boycott, which had also begun as a protest against a white principal, these protests rested on key tenets of black nationalism and antiprofessionalism as articulated by Aldridge, Cleage, and Wilder. In almost every case, the protestors demanded that white educators be replaced by blacks, who themselves had to pass a political litmus test.

The case of Robert C. Branton, principal of Martin Luther King High School (formerly Eastern), was typical. Branton, a veteran school administrator of thirty years (six at King), was considered by insiders in the system to be one of the best principals in the city. Trouble at King began in late November, 1968, following a *Detroit News* story about the school that, although generally positive, contained statements by Branton that some students found offensive. Soon after the story appeared, a group of militants called the Students for Justice (a group linked to Dan Aldridge) presented the school board with a list of demands that included a public apology from Branton for remarks derogatory to their "upbringing and culture." Particularly, they insisted that Branton acknowledge that the teachers and staff, not the students or their parents, were responsible for the low level of educational achievement at King. In addition, they demanded that a community-controlled governing board select the principal and vice principal of the school.[124]

Publicly supported by such adult leaders as Aldridge, who praised the protest as an effective assault on "white cultural nationalism," militant students introduced an escalating series of demands to the school administration. Each time the administration met the demand or resolved a problem, new demands were presented and more protests and disruptions ensued. The educational environment of the school deteriorated sharply. Several white teachers were assaulted, although none were seriously hurt. In January, Branton reported, "There seemed to be a different temper in the school this fall. The thing that bothers many of us was the constant attitude of disrespect and defiance. . . . I've been told to my face: 'You can't be effective in this school because you're white.'" Before the second semester had begun, Branton requested a medical leave of absence. He was eventually replaced by a black principal.[125]

Unfortunately, the deterioration of the educational environment continued even under the new black principal. Over the next year, police were repeatedly called to the school. A riot in the school cafeteria led to the trashing of the school's administrative offices. Later, students vandalized teachers' offices, a firebomb was set off in a stairwell, and an American flag was torn down. Amid growing chaos in the school, militant students introduced additional demands that included replacing the new black principal because he was an "Uncle Tom." Over the next two years, similar protests against principals, assistant principals, and teachers spread across the inner city. The great fear expressed by some school leaders and the press during the Northern boycott, namely that decisions about who should administer the schools would be usurped by mobs and ad hoc committees, appeared to become a reality.[126]

The second cause of high school disturbances, conflict over symbols of black nationalism and culture, was deeply intertwined with the first. In almost every case where students demanded the ouster of administrators or teachers, they also demanded substantial cultural and curricular changes. The 1971 demands of the Black Student United Front of Northern High School were typical. They reveal the kinds of changes the students sought and the differences between these student protests and the 1966 demonstration at the school. Like the students in 1966, the Black Student United Front wanted to replace specific administrators, in this case two assistant principals. But they made no mention of restoring a traditional academic curriculum at the school. Rather, they demanded that the board totally reorient the educational program along black nationalist lines. Specifically, they called for a community-controlled governing board that would select new administrators and decide on all matters relating to the school, a black studies curriculum including black history, literature, and political education, the recognition of black heroes through "pictures and artifacts," a restocking of the library with books "dealing with the Black experience and true Black history," the renaming of Northern as H. Rap Brown High School, and the flying of the black nationalist flag outside the school.[127]

Some of these demands, such as the introduction of black history and literature, were already being implemented throughout the system. Others, however, such as renaming schools for black nationalist leaders or flying the black nationalist flag, precipitated confrontations between students and the school administration. On March 11, 1969, for example, students and parents from McMichael Junior High School came to a board meeting demanding that their school be renamed to honor Malcolm X. They demonstrated so loudly that the board was forced to adjourn prematurely, perhaps the first time in history that the board had adjourned under pressure.[128] Numerous conflicts between students and administrators at at least six schools also resulted from militants demanding the right to display the nationalist flag or from their raising it in defiance of a 1969 school board ban on flying any flag other than the American.[129]

The third cause of problems in the Detroit high schools was the dramatic and widespread increase in violence. As early as January, 1969, Deputy Superintendent Arthur Johnson reported that "there is growing concern among school staff, pupils and parents about order and personal security in the school environment. This concern is based on substantial evidence of physical assaults by students and non-students on both students and teaching staff members, the high rate of thefts and vandalism against school property, and a significant amount of drug and narcotic traffic in and around school buildings." Three months later, the *Detroit News* urged the board to hire security guards for the high schools to combat the growing "terrorism." Yet even the assignment of unarmed security teams and, later, police to the schools did not solve the problem.[130]

It is impossible to catalog the number of violent incidents in the Detroit schools in this period. Literally hundreds of incidents, including shootings, stabbings, rapes, student rampages, gang fights, assaults, arson, bombings and bomb threats, extortion, and vandalism occurred in the schools or school property. At several points in 1969, 1970, and 1971, Deputy Superintendent Charles Wolfe recorded incidents by the hour. An article in the *Michigan*

Chronicle in December, 1970, entitled "Terror Stalks City's Schools" noted that, in the previous few weeks, at least six people had been either "maimed, beaten, stabbed or shot inside a Detroit public school."[131]

Many of these incidents were caused by "outsiders" who invaded school grounds and buildings looking for trouble. In addition, newspaper and other accounts of many incidents reported that adult agitators from a number of radical organizations were often at the fringes of disturbances exhorting students to action. These organizations included the Citizens for Community Control of Schools; the Black Student United Front (the youth section of the black nationalist/socialist League of Revolutionary Black Workers), which published the *Black Student Voice,* an underground high school newspaper; Breakthrough, an extremist white organization chaired by Donald Lobsinger; the East Side Voice of Independent Detroit (ESVID), a black nationalist group run by an "ultramilitant" community organizer, Frank Ditto; the Republic of New Africa, a black separatist organization headed by Richard B. Henry, who had changed his name to Brother Imari; and the Students for a Democratic Society (SDS). As a consequence of both organized and random disorder, many schools suffered a nearly total breakdown in safety and discipline. Under these circumstances, education was virtually impossible.[132]

Several incidents that took place in the spring of 1969 provide a good picture of the chaotic conditions in the schools in this period. Following a change in attendance boundaries in 1968, Finney High School, located in the northeast section of the city, had become one of the few truly integrated Detroit schools with about 500 black students out of a total enrollment of 2,500. Throughout the 1968–69 school year, black pupils complained of a steady torrent of abuse from whites, including "[r]acial insults, pushing, shoving and other forms of harassment." On May 20, a group of white adults "hot-rodding" around the school attacked several black students. Soon after the attack, violence erupted in the school itself, and police were called. The next day, rumors spread that some black and white students had come to school with guns. Fights again broke out. On May 23, about 125 black parents and students, led by Brother Imari of the Republic of New Africa, showed up at the school to protest the attack. In addition, a number of black-bereted "corpsmen" from the black militant organization ESVID started patrolling the area to protect black students. Some blacks also began boycotting Finney and instead attended a Freedom School sponsored by ESVID. In early June, after school officials suspended a white student for beginning one of the fights, white parents and members of the right-wing extremist group Breakthrough protested what they claimed was a double disciplinary standard that favored blacks.[133] School leaders repeatedly stated that the violence was largely due to "outsiders" and, at most, only a handful of students, but the perception that things were out of control was unavoidable.[134]

Such escalating violence provided the advocates of community control and decentralization with additional evidence in favor of restructuring the school system. They argued that the utter failure of the Detroit system was abundantly clear to anyone who simply picked up a newspaper. In hearings before the Education Committee of the Michigan House of Representatives on March 24, 1969, Rev. Cleage urged the representatives to pass a community control bill because of "increasing chaos and confusion in Detroit schools, and the administration is unable to meet the problem." Rep. James Del Rio (D-Detroit), cosponsor of the bill that would have divided the school system into as many as nineteen independent districts, declared in unalloyed hyperbole that the Detroit board of education "has been responsible for more riots than all the white racism in America."[135]

In addition to the disorders, one last factor also contributed to the success of the decentralization campaign in Detroit, the publication of test scores for fourth, sixth, and eighth graders from the Detroit elementary schools. In June, 1969, Amos Wilder obtained the scores and analyzed them on a school-by-school basis in his column in the *Michigan Chronicle*. Echoing Edward Cushman's assessment of the high schools, Wilder called the elementary schools a "Public Disgrace." Eighty percent of the students in Detroit scored below the national norms on the Iowa Test of Basic Skills. More important, Wilder noted that not a single school that had a majority of African-American or Hispanic students scored above grade level on the exams. "It is incredible to believe that the disgraceful situation in our schools is the result of cultural deprivation, lack of resources, or any of the sophisticated 'excuses' provided by the Detroit school system," Wilder wrote. "We can no longer in good conscience blame the children and the parents for this miserable failure." As he had in the past, Wilder argued that black parents had to take control of their children's schools in order to improve educational quality.[136]

Without question, the worsening condition in the schools made the arguments for redistributing power within the system more appealing to legislators. After several failed attempts by Del Rio and other legislators to draft a viable bill, on April 14, 1969, State Senator Coleman A. Young (D-Detroit), the leader of the black delegation in Lansing, introduced decentralization legislation that attracted wide support. The Young bill was a delicate political compromise, redistributing power within the system but still maintaining some key features of centralized governance. The bill mandated that the present school board divide the district into from seven to eleven regions of 25,000 to 50,000 students each. Each region would have a nine-member school board that would elect one of its members to an expanded central board. In addition to these members, the new central board would also have five members elected from the city at large. Finally, each regional board would set its own budget, determine curricular, testing, and other educational policies, hire and fire its regional superintendent, and "[e]mploy and discharge, assign and promote all teachers, and other employees, subject to review" of the central board, which could "overrule, modify, or affirm" those decisions.[137]

Despite strongly backing community control, Young realized that the legislature would only approve a bill that did not appear too radical. In addition, as he stated in a speech to a community group following the passage of the bill, Young firmly believed that, even in its compromised form, the bill provided the means for "making the system responsible to the people of the community and placing the people of the community in a position to direct, to control and to have input into that system."[138]

Nevertheless, some critics claimed that the bill preserved too many of the powers of the central board and that it was overly sensitive to the demands of the DFT. In fact, Young *had* included two provisions in the bill that sharply restricted the actual power of the regional boards in order to get the board and the DFT to end their opposition to decentralization. The first of these two provisions was that regional boards had to operate under guidelines established by the central board; the second was that the "rights of retirement, tenure, seniority and of any other benefits of any employee transfered to a regional school district or between regional school districts . . . shall not be abrogated, diminished or impaired." In other words, the Young bill protected some of the most important prerogatives of the central board and maintained the collective bargaining arrangements recently won by the DFT. Without these provisions, the bill had no chance of passage.[139]

By the time Young introduced the bill, most members of the Detroit school board realized that some sort of decentralization was inevitable. Pressure from the HSSC, disorder in the high schools, and the continuing failure to improve educational quality in ghetto schools were simply impossible to resist. In early April, even the NAACP, whose leaders were deeply concerned about the potential that community control had for increasing segregation, proposed that the board increase "community participation" in the schools. Board members debated the NAACP proposal with most members agreeing on the principle of decentralization but remaining divided about the degree of control they should turn over to the community. More important, they worried about the effects of decentralization on their goals for school integration.[140]

Two main positions emerged. Andrew Perdue maintained that community control should have a higher priority than integration. "No community can allow its children to be destroyed by the schools," he stated. "The schools must be responsive to the needs of the children and the only way this is going to happen is that the administrators be directly accountable to the community. Power is the name of this game. Power vested in the people whereby they have a voice in the operation of their schools, this is the burning issue of the times." Taking an opposite position, A. L. Zwerdling argued that the burning issue of the times was still integration, not community control. Zwerdling acknowledged the importance of communities having greater input into school decisions (indeed, he had recently proposed that the board create community advisory councils at each Detroit high school), but his priorities were clear. "[I]f I have to vote between a step involving decentralization and integration," he stated, "I would vote against decentralization if it were at the expense of integration."[141]

Despite his misgivings about this reform, Zwerdling also eventually bowed to the inevitable. On May 13, he joined with the six other board members in support of a resolution drafted by Perdue that called for "developing a viable plan for the transference of meaningful power to the community." The resolution did not endorse any specific proposals to redistribute power in the system, but it signaled to the legislature that the board would not oppose a decentralization bill. More important, the board ordered its lobbyist in Lansing, who believed that the Young bill could still be killed in committee, to remain neutral on it. The path was thus cleared for the decentralization of the Detroit schools.[142]

Two months later, both houses of the Michigan legislature passed the Young bill by overwhelming margins, 83 to 18 in the House and 25 to 5 in the Senate. Governor William Milliken signed Public Act 244 into law on August 11. The seven-member board of education elected from the city at large, the keystone of progressive school reform in Detroit, was slated to pass into history on January 1, 1971.[143]

Decentralization versus Desegregation, 1970

The seven-member board did not go gently into that political good night. Even as he promised full support for decentralization, the newly elected board president, A. L. Zwerdling, sparked controversy. "If we are going to have total reform we need two things," he stated, "integrated districts and equal opportunity which means more money for the children who need it most."[144] Of the two issues, the determination of the new regional boundaries proved to be the most volatile political problem the Detroit board of education ever faced. Almost as soon as the governor signed the decentralization law, groups with opposing political and educational agendas began battling over the shape of the new regions. The conflicts between these groups ultimately revealed the utter incompatibility of decentralization and desegregation in Detroit and led directly to the filing of *Milliken v. Bradley I*, one of the most far-reaching school desegregation cases ever decided by the Supreme Court.

The first clashes between advocates of decentralization and desegregation took place in a series of public hearings on regional boundaries in late 1969 and early 1970. During the hearings, three main positions emerged: the first supported black power, the second sought to maintain neighborhood schools, in effect keeping the system segregated, and the third advocated desegregation.[145] A coalition of black activist groups, supported by State Senator Coleman Young, was the most vigorous advocate of the black power position, demanding that the board draw the regional boundaries so as to maximize black voting strength in the regions. Since nearly two-thirds of the students in the Detroit schools were black, the coalition demanded that most of the new regions have black electoral majorities. As a spokesman for the predominantly black First Congressional Democratic Organization put it, "Redistricting must guarantee black control of black schools." These groups rallied behind what became known as the "Black Plan," a boundary proposal drawn up by the West Central Organization (a community activist group with ties to Saul Alinsky) that would have given blacks control of six out of eight regions and authority over the vast majority of black students.[146]

The second position, supported by many white Detroiters, sought to establish boundaries corresponding to the current administrative regions, thereby essentially maintaining racial separation. These whites quickly recognized that decentralization, with its underlying support for neighborhood schools, could be used to protect their communities from integration. In addition, with whites still constituting a majority of the voters in the city (about 56 percent of the total electorate), they conceivably could control at least half of the regions and isolate black students within the regions, blocking any significant attempts at integration. As the hearings progressed, it became increasingly obvious that white segregationists found as many reasons to support racially homogeneous regions as black separatists.[147] William Grant, the education writer for the *Free Press,* noted that "the sentiment of Detroiters who spoke at the public hearings was clearly for districts that included a 'community of interests.' Translated, that means whites wanted to control white schools and blacks wanted to control black schools."[148]

Eschewing segregation and separatism, the liberal majority on the school board, and to some extent the Urban League and the NAACP, backed a third position that sought to use redistricting to encourage integration. Board President A. L. Zwerdling, the most articulate spokesman for this point of view, never wavered in his belief that the highest moral and legal obligation of the board was to integrate the system. Early in 1970, he stated, "For almost a decade the primary consideration of this school board has been integration. We have made our policy on staff, on textbooks, on administration and on everything else conform to our overall goal of seeking the most integration. I don't see why a new program—this time it's decentralization— should not also be made to conform to these goals."[149]

Refusing to be swayed by the separatists and segregationists who dominated the public hearings on boundaries, Zwerdling and the other liberal board members came away from these forums more determined than ever to push for integration. Following the hearings in the fall of 1969, Zwerdling bluntly declared, "It is segregation they ask for whatever they call it. And despite what they ask, I have already decided that I'll have to vote for the decentralization plan that looks like it will create the most integration."[150] To varying degrees, these views were shared by the other liberal board members, Grylls, Robinson, and Stewart. These members remained convinced that they had been elected to integrate the system, that they had made substantial progress toward that goal, and that extremists of either color would not turn them around. Unfortunately, in confronting the extremist threat to their plan, the liberal school leaders chose an equally extreme strategy—not merely drawing boundaries that created integrated regions, but also mandating a high school desegregation plan that far exceeded the requirements of the decentralization law.[151]

When the liberal board members first debated where to draw the regional boundaries, their goal appeared to be merely the creation of integrated regions rather than integrated schools. As late as January 18, 1970, Zwerdling stated, "It is true that decentralization probably will not change where any student goes to school. It is not going to end racial isolation."[152] Nevertheless, soon after Zwerdling made that statement, Remus Robinson was hospitalized, terminally ill with cancer. The liberal bloc suddenly lacked the votes necessary for creating the integrated regions. Of the other board members, Hathaway and Perdue were expected to vote for a plan that maximized black control of schools, while Patrick McDonald, a conservative white attorney who had been elected in 1966, kept his own counsel. According to William Grant, Zwerdling delayed voting on the regional boundaries for weeks, hoping, in vain, that Robinson might recover enough to attend one last board meeting.[153]

In early March, when it was obvious that Robinson would not recover, the liberal school leaders attempted to win over Andrew Perdue, who retained some hope for integration despite his strong support for community control. In the debate about the regions, Perdue, in fact, had challenged the liberal bloc to really demonstrate its commitment to integration by changing *attendance* as well as regional boundaries. With Zwerdling's blessing, Drachler and several aides answered that challenge by quickly fashioning a desegregation proposal for the city's high schools. The superintendent presented the proposal to the board at a secret meeting on March 31. The plan shifted attendance boundaries for 9,000 students (equally divided between blacks and whites) and changed the racial composition of eleven high schools. The most dramatic changes were at Redford, Cody, and Denby, where the proportion of black students would increase from less then 3 percent to 29, 31, and 53 percent respectively. Perdue was impressed, and he agreed to support the whole package, integrated regions and desegregated high schools, at the next official board meeting on April 7. Soon after the meeting, Patrick McDonald, who vehemently opposed the plan, leaked its details to the newspapers. On Sunday, April 5, the *Free Press* and the *News* splashed the story of the board's "sweeping integration plan" across their front pages and all hell broke loose.[154]

The next day the board was inundated with outraged phone calls and telegrams. Angry parents and community leaders demanded to speak at the April 7 board meeting. In addition, parents kept more than 2,000 children at home in protest; at one junior high, only 50 out of 500 pupils came to school. That night a group of white parents formed the Citizen's Committee for Better Education (CCBE). Its chairman, a Detroit police officer, vowed to fight the desegregation plan for "ten years, if necessary."[155]

The April 7 board meeting was probably the most tumultuous in the history of the school system. Nearly 200 people jammed their way into the board room while hundreds more crowded the lobby, stairs, and hallway leading up to it. During the meeting, some protestors, chanting "Hell no, we won't go!" tried to smash down the glass doors into the meeting room.[156]

The situation inside was almost as chaotic. Punctuated by jeers and heckling from the audience and angry exchanges between Zwerdling, Hathaway, and McDonald, the board members tried to discuss the plan. After wrangling among themselves, the board heard from thirty-one speakers. A few individuals, such as Richard Austin, the Wayne County Auditor, Dr. Jesse Goodwin of the NAACP, Francis Kornegay of the Urban League, and Ernest Mazey of the ACLU, praised the board and applauded its courage in drafting the desegregation plan.[157]

The overwhelming majority of the speakers, however, scathingly denounced the liberal board members and their plan. Most of these speakers were whites representing community groups from the northeast and northwest sections of town and almost all of them had only two things to say. First, they deplored the secrecy that surrounded the creation and "announcement" of the desegregation plan. "If this meeting and these procedures are an example of what you intend to achieve in community involvement," one speaker exclaimed, "I must call them a farce." Second, they unequivocally pledged that their children would not participate in the plan. Many speakers declared that they would take whatever measures necessary to stop its implementation. One person urged Detroiters to "recall certain Members of this Board." Another stated simply, "My kid won't go to Mackenzie. I will move out in the suburbs, which I can't afford to live in and I don't want to live in, but I will go there and I will go to work so I can live there because my kids are going to go to the best high school available for them."[158]

Although most of the opponents of the plan were white, one speaker, representing Rev. Cleage, the Inner City Parents Council, the Black Teachers Caucus, and the Action Committee of the Shrine of the Black Madonna, declared that "these organizations, these black organizations, are unalterably opposed to the plan presented here today. . . . So-called integration is not only destructive to the best interests of black people, in fact, it is a form of genocide from our point of view."[159]

After more than three-and-a-half hours of speeches and harangues, the board members made their final statements. Zwerdling repeated his fundamental arguments for integration. "So while we can understand and sympathize with what it is that compels some to call for segregation," he said, "or for some plan that insures black or white political control of our school systems, we cannot yield to it. We have heard the urging, loud and clear, for a return to a divided society, but we cannot in conscience go along with it." Perdue added his endorsement of the plan, stating that "although this does not give the black and the poor the maximum amount of control, maximum integration for our schools is important. Let's support this measure—with its imperfections." Hathaway, on the other hand, denounced his colleagues for ignoring the demands for community control and warned that the plan would spell disaster for the schools. McDonald also declared that the plan "threatens to destroy this very city. This hastily conceived move if adopted will deepen the credibility gap between Detroiters and their schools, between what is said and what is done." After hearing an impassioned letter from Remus Robinson deploring the growing racial divisions in the city and supporting the desegregation plan, the board voted 4 to 2 to adopt the controversial proposals.[160]

Community outrage over the vote was overwhelming and unrelenting. Zwerdling received death threats. Junior and senior high schools across the city were hit with bomb scares, walkouts, and racial clashes. In one particularly destructive incident, militant adults "masterminded" a student rampage at Drew Junior High that resulted in thousands of dollars in damage to the school and the surrounding neighborhood.[161] The *Free Press* blasted the liberal board members, who, despite their noble ideals, had totally undermined public confidence in the schools because of their secret deliberations and their autocratic manner. The *News* echoed these sentiments.[162] Capitalizing on the outpouring of anger, the Citizens Committee for Better Education began circulating petitions to recall Grylls, Perdue, Stewart, and Zwerdling, the members who voted for the plan. Within two weeks they gathered more than half of the 114,000 signatures they needed.[163]

According to Norman Drachler, the board anticipated some of these developments but was totally surprised by "the emotional reaction of the state legislature, prior to a fall election." Two days after the tumultuous board meeting, the Michigan House of Representatives passed a bill, cosponsored by James Del Rio and a white Detroit legislator, that provided for a referendum on decentralization and mandated that the board assign students to their neighborhood schools. Soon after, the Senate passed a bill repealing Public Act 244, the Detroit decentralization law, altogether. An outraged Coleman Young denounced the Detroit school board, whose "chicken shit integration plan" had put his decentralization plan in such jeopardy. He immediately set to work on a new decentralization bill similar to the first but with several key differences. Unlike Public Act 244, the new bill that Young introduced created eight regions, each to be run by a five-member board. It authorized the governor to appoint a commission to draw the regional boundaries, and, most important, Section 12 of the bill nullified the April 7 desegregation plan by forbidding changes in attendance boundaries. The bill unanimously passed in the Senate and received only one negative vote in the House. Governor Milliken signed Public Act 48 into law on July 7, 1970.[164]

This new decentralization law put an abrupt end to the board's plans for desegregation, but it did not derail the campaign to recall the four board members who had voted for the plan. By mid-June, members of the Citizens Committee for Better Education had collected over 130,000 signatures on each of the four recall petitions, far more than they needed to place the issue on the August 4 ballot.[165] Opposition to the recall was, at best, half-hearted. The *Free Press* and the *News* both came out against the effort, but in measured tones. The UAW, still reeling from the sudden death of Walter and May Reuther in May, provided only minimal help to Zwerdling and the others. No editorials against the recall appeared in either the *Labor News* or the *Michigan Chronicle*. Supporters of the embattled school board members, an impressive array of old-line liberal, labor, and civil rights leaders, managed just one newspaper ad urging a no vote. Their appeal, however, had no impact on the outcome of the election.[166]

On August 4, more than 60 percent of the voters approved recalling the four liberal board members. White sections of town voted heavily in favor of the measure, with over 80 percent of the voters in the Cody, Osborn, and Redford high school districts and over 90 percent in the Denby district supporting the recall. Blacks generally opposed the measure but, as in millage elections, turnout in black neighborhoods was low.[167] The recall left the liberal-labor-black coalition in shambles. "Where did everybody go?" Andrew Perdue asked just before the election. "Where are the people who helped get us elected—the UAW, the NAACP, and the others? Don't they care any more?"[168]

Adding insult to injury, on the same day as the recall election, the governor's commission on boundaries presented its map of the eight new, decentralized regions. The commission clearly divided the school system along racial lines, giving political control of four regions to blacks and four to whites. Black pupils, however, were a majority in six of the regions. "The song is 'community control,'" one school official said after seeing the map, "but the tune is 'Dixie.'"[169]

Together, the recall and the segregated regions were the final straws for the NAACP. Having been beaten in the political arena, proponents of school integration now saw the courts as their only recourse. Since early July, the NAACP had been contemplating a suit against the state to restore the April 7 desegregation plan after it was nullified by section 12 of Public Act 48. Indeed, three weeks after the governor signed the bill, Deputy Superintendents Arthur Johnson and Aubrey McCutcheon, Jr., along with the board's attorney, George Bushnell, Jr., secretly traveled to New York to prepare a joint school board–NAACP legal strategy on such a suit. The recall put an abrupt end to that collaboration. Assuming that future school boards would be less sympathetic to integration, the NAACP filed a much broader desegregation suit two weeks after the recall. The suit that became *Milliken v. Bradley I* named not only the governor and the state attorney general as defendants, but the Detroit Board of Education as well. What began as an attempt to reinstate a modest desegregation plan would become one of the most important school desegregation cases in American history.[170]

In 1971, William Grant, perhaps the most astute commentator on these events, noted that, "it may be a significant portent for the future that at no point during the debate on decentralization was education the prime consideration. The arguments were all political."[171] The school board members and the key school administrators were as guilty of that failing as were black nationalists and white segregationists. One member of the Redford Community Council denounced the board's desegregation plan in words that fit virtually *every* group involved in these events, "We all feel this is an attempt by an adult minority to use students for political and propaganda purposes."[172]

Indeed, even in the black community, in whose name black separatists pursued community control and integrationists demanded busing, there was less than enthusiastic support for either of these major reforms. In December, 1971, researchers working for New Detroit, Inc., interviewed a representative sample of 300 black Detroiters over the age of eighteen to obtain their views about the public schools. When asked to rank order sixteen items associated with quality education, the respondents listed good teacher performance, equal educational funding, smaller classes, and good discipline as the four most important items. They listed items associated with community control, black studies, and racial integration of students ninth, eleventh, and twelfth, respectively. Responses to specific questions about these issues provided an even more dramatic picture of black attitudes. For example, 59 percent of the respondents believed that the race of their children's teachers made no difference in terms of student achievement, almost 26 percent wanted a mixed faculty of black and white teachers, and fewer than 9 percent wanted all or a majority of the teachers in predominantly black schools to be black. Of the 81 percent who favored schools with integrated student bodies, more than half (56 percent) *did not* want their children to attend schools outside their own neighborhood in order to have an integrated educational experience. In short, despite over three years of educational debates dominated by demands for community control, black power, and desegregation, black Detroiters rejected radical solutions to their children's educational problems and affirmed their belief that quality education rested on getting good teachers to instruct small classes in well-funded, orderly schools.[173] Unfortunately, these fundamental components of quality education were not part of the political agendas of any of the competing interest groups who used the schools as platforms from which to shout their doctrines. Such attempts to use schools for blatantly political purposes had occurred before in Detroit, but never had the institution been so politicized as it was in the early 1970s.

Busing and Bankruptcy, 1971–77

"It started as dim rumblings from scattered sections of the country," the *New York Times* reported in November, 1971, "but within the last few months opposition to busing of children to achieve school integration has reached a fever pitch all over the United States." Busing was unquestionably one of the most hotly debated issues in the United States in this era, and *Milliken v. Bradley I,* the Detroit desegregation case, was central to that debate.[174]

The basic events in the *Milliken* case are well known. After a year of preliminary legal battles, in April, 1971, the NAACP's suit against segregation in the Detroit school system came to trial. Five months later, Judge Stephen J. Roth ruled that, despite the extensive efforts the Detroit school board had made to integrate the schools, the system was segregated. In addition, Roth found that the state had contributed to the segregation of the Detroit schools, a finding that lay the groundwork for a desegregation order extending beyond the city limits. In June, 1972, Roth issued a metropolitan busing order that Eleanor P. Wolf described as "the most ambitious plan for racial dispersion the nation had ever seen." The plan included three counties and 780,000 students in fifty-two suburban school districts and Detroit.[175] One year later, the Sixth Circuit Court of Appeals affirmed that decision. In July, 1974, however, the Supreme Court struck down the metropolitan remedy on a 5 to 4 vote, declaring that the suburban districts had not caused the segregation of the Detroit schools and should not have to bear the burden of correcting the violation. The *Milliken* decision was the first ruling in more than two decades in which the Supreme Court rejected the arguments of the NAACP regarding school desegregation. As J. Anthony Lukas notes, *Milliken v. Bradley I* "marked an important turning point in the Court's approach to school desegregation." By declaring that desegregation remedies had to stop at the city limits, the Court insured that conflicts over school integration would "increasingly pit poor whites against poor blacks."[176]

The national consequences of these events have been widely discussed and well analyzed. Far less attention has focused on the impact of the *Milliken* case on local school politics. Three key developments characterize that impact on the Detroit school system: the role of the case in intensifying white, working-class opposition to liberal policies in general and to busing and increases in school taxes in particular, the way in which that opposition contributed to the worst financial crisis the school system had faced since the 1930s, and, finally, how the busing controversy accelerated the decline of the school system by increasing the politicization of the schools and diverting attention from more essential, educational issues.

As early as October, 1970, Detroit felt the impact of the *Milliken* case. On October 13, following an NAACP appeal, the Sixth Circuit Court ruled that section 12 of Public Act 48 (which had nullified the April 7 desegregation plan) was unconstitutional. Less than three weeks later, Detroit voters elected the most conservative school board in more than 15 years. If the August recall election marked the death of the liberal-labor-black coalition, then the November school board election buried the remains. Despite the racial gerrymandering that was meant to insure equal black and white control of the regions, whites won control in six of the eight regional boards. White candidates, in fact, captured thirty-two of forty-five school board seats. Of the thirteen members of the new central board, eight elected from the regions and five elected at large, only three were black and only one was elected at large. The only incumbents reelected were Hathaway, McDonald, and Stewart. Besides Hathaway and McDonald, who had voted against the April 7 desegregation plan, six other members of the central board were, according to William Grant, "staunch anti-integrationist conservatives." Indeed, immediately after they were elected, seven of the new members demanded that the board affirm its support for section 12 of Public Act 48 and appeal the Circuit Court's nullification of that section to the Supreme Court. On January 12, these members elected Patrick McDonald, the most vehement opponent to busing on the old board, president of the new one. Two weeks later, facing an impossible political situation, Superintendent Norman Drachler, who still had two years remaining on his contract, handed in his resignation.[177] At the end of the school year, the board replaced Drachler with Deputy Superintendent Charles J. Wolfe, a "quiet, gentle man" who did little to rock the boat during his four years as superintendent.[178]

As McDonald would later remark, the new central board faced three interrelated problems—"deficits, decentralization, and desegregation."[179] Among these problems, the deficit demanded the most immediate attention. Following the defeat of the 1968 millage proposal, the board seemed resigned to operating the school system in the red. Pleas to the state for substantial increases in state aid went unheeded, and, after assessing the mood of voters in the city, the board dropped plans to put another millage proposal on the ballot in 1969. Consequently, the financial problems of the system worsened as the board vainly struggled both to meet their obligations to the teachers arising from the 1967 contract and to keep pace with the inflationary spiral stimulated by the Vietnam War. Between 1969–70 and 1970–71, the deficit jumped from $3.5 million to $20.3 million.[180]

Without some immediate action, the deficit was certain to at least triple in the next two years. The new board members, however, had a limited range of options. They appealed to Gov. Milliken to provide additional funds, noting that implementing decentralization alone would boost costs by about $4 million annually. They revived the 1968 lawsuit against the state that had languished for two years. Unfortunately, neither of these efforts bore fruit. Indeed, soon after the board met with Milliken, due to a worsening outlook for state revenue, the governor announced a two percent *cut* in funding for education. The only options that remained for the board were retrenchment and appealing once again to the voters for tax increases.[181] The board tried both these actions and both proved to be political bombshells.

The issue of retrenchment was particularly volatile, since it heightened the tensions between the majority white school board and the majority black school population. In February, 1971, the board announced $12 million in cutbacks, including the elimination of art and music classes and the firing of nearly 200 long-term substitute teachers. The *Michigan Chronicle* described the cuts as "Another Crippling Blow For Our Schools." Both the DFT, which had agreed to a modest two-year contract in 1969 due to the financial plight of the system, and the OSAS deplored the cuts. More than 2,000 teachers picketed the board, and some DFT militants called for a strike.[182]

By far the most vehement reaction came in the high schools, where the announcement of cutbacks triggered a new wave of student unrest and racial violence. Students at Mumford High School staged a sit-in against the cuts and demanded "real community control," which meant "no majority white boards controlling districts with a majority of Black students." One student leader declared, "When the school was white, the city spent millions of dollars on Mumford. Now that it is black, they can't find a nickel to spend on us."[183] Over the next few weeks, the protests spread to Central, Northern, and Pershing high schools and to several junior highs. Large demonstrations also occurred at Mackenzie and Northwestern, where students took over the schools, and black militants reiterated demands for staff and curricular changes. At Osborn, the police made fifteen arrests after white students used the demonstrations as a pretext for attacking blacks.[184]

The demonstrations had no effect on the board's decisions. Declaring that the school system "is on the edge of a bottomless fiscal chasm," Patrick McDonald warned of still deeper cuts in the future. Indeed, as the *News* accurately editorialized, this was the worst fiscal crisis facing the school system since the 1930s.[185] Retrenchment, however, could only go so far. In the fall of 1971, the board members agreed to propose a tax increase, but they faced two large obstacles in passing the measure. First, the 5 mill levy approved by the voters in 1966 was due to expire in 1972. Thus, the increase and the renewal would be on the ballot together. Getting even one of the measures passed was a difficult proposition; getting both passed was nearly impossible. Second, and more important, in late 1971, developments in the *Milliken* case dramatically diminished the likelihood of passing any tax proposals whatsoever.[186]

The Detroit desegregation trial began on April 6, 1971, and continued until late July.[187] On September 27, 1971, Roth ruled that, while "[t]here is enough blame for everyone to share," the Detroit school board was guilty of de jure segregation. Roth demanded that the board immediately begin work on a desegregation plan for the city. In addition, because he found sufficient state culpability in the segregation of the Detroit schools and because white students comprised less than a third of the total enrollment in Detroit, Roth ordered the state board of education to also prepare a desegregation plan that would include school districts in Wayne, Oakland, and Macomb counties.[188]

The Detroit metropolitan area, already aroused by the unprecedented violence ignited by court-ordered busing in nearby Pontiac, was swept by a wave of "Busing Hysteria."[189] Less than two weeks after Roth's ruling, U.S. Senator Robert Griffin, a Michigan Republican, introduced a constitutional amendment to ban busing for desegregation. Residents of Macomb County began circulating petitions to recall Michigan's probusing, Democratic senator, Philip Hart. Antibusing protest meetings and rallies proliferated across the region. In November, the Michigan House and Senate went into what the *Free Press* called "a frenzy of anti-busing action" and voted overwhelmingly to support the constitutional amendment to ban busing.[190] Governor Milliken announced that he would appeal Roth's decision. President Nixon denounced Roth's desegregation order as a "flagrant" violation of the principle of neighborhood schools.[191]

Emotions also ran high in Detroit, and the board quickly recognized its inopportune timing in seeking additional taxes for the schools. Soon after Roth's September 27 decision, for example, a packed meeting in the northeast section of Detroit broke into applause when a leader from the Citizens Committee for Better Education declared that he would fight any millage increase because "If they have less money, they'll have less money to buy buses."[192] One month later, following a school board debate marked, according to the editor of *Michigan Chronicle,* by appallingly "malicious . . . verbal exchanges among school board members," the white majority on the central board voted to appeal Roth's decision. That action deepened the antagonism between the majority white board and the black community. Black leaders were infuriated by the board's and the governor's decisions to appeal the ruling and by the visceral responses to busing from so many whites. Coleman Young denounced Milliken as a "modern-day equivalent of George Wallace" blocking the door to integration. At a school board hearing on busing, Helen Moore, leader of the newly organized Black Parents for Quality Education (BPQE), accused opponents of busing of "racism in its most vile form." Facing so angry and divided a community and hoping that the governor might rescue the Detroit schools with a state school aid equalization plan, the board shelved its request for a tax increase until the following year.[193]

In February, 1972, however, with the deficit projected to hit $40 million at the end of the school year, the board voted to place the 5 mill renewal *and* a 5 mill (two-year) increase on the May presidential primary ballot. One week later, underscoring the depth of the financial problems facing the system, the board borrowed an additional $23 million, secured by tax anticipation notes, to keep the system operating for the remainder of the school year. To balance the budget, the board voted in April to "pink slip" about 1,550 substitute and probationary teachers, and announced that it would not fill 800 positions vacant due to retirement.[194]

Despite a vigorous campaign to win approval of these tax proposals, Detroiters rejected the renewal and the increase in May, voted them both down again in August, and rejected the renewal that was alone on the ballot in November. In each of these elections, the political alignments and voting patterns reflected trends developing in Detroit since the early 1960s. Established interest groups, including the Detroit Council of Churches, the Metropolitan AFL-CIO, and the NAACP, all the major newspapers as well as several radio and television stations strongly backed the proposals.[195] No prominent organizations opposed the measures. Yet, as in the past, whites in the northeast and northwest sections of the city voted against the proposals and turnout in these neighborhoods was high. New opposition, however, did appear in some black sections of the city, perhaps in protest to the actions taken by the majority white school board. Whatever the reasons, even in areas that strongly supported the millage proposals black turnout was low.[196]

While such factors as rising unemployment contributed to the defeats, anger over busing and desegregation unquestionably played an important role. The May presidential primary and the two millage proposals were on the same ballot. About six weeks before the election, Judge Roth ordered fifty-two suburban school districts included in the desegregation remedy for the city. Touching the city and suburbs alike, the issue of busing dominated the Michigan presidential primary, with support for the main antibusing candidate, George Wallace, soaring in the suburbs and white neighborhoods of the city. Wallace won the Michigan primary, amassing huge totals in suburban Wayne, Oakland, and Macomb counties and in the predominantly white voting districts in the northeast and northwest sections of Detroit. In the city, Wallace votes and antitax votes went hand in hand. Correlation analysis of the returns by voting district found an exceptionally high and statistically significant relationship between the Wallace totals and the antimillage vote, $+.93$ for a no vote on the tax increase and $+.91$ for a no vote on the renewal.[197]

To a considerable degree, antibusing sentiment undergirded voters' rejection of the millage proposals. In February, almost three-quarters of the people responding to a *Detroit News* poll either strongly or somewhat agreed with the statement "School money in Detroit should be spent for better schools and not on bussing." By the spring election, many Detroiters were explicitly linking the tax proposal to the threat of busing. As the new board president, James Hathaway, noted, "Opponents of the millage were saying prior to the election that the money would only be used to buy school buses." The May election indicated that the voters would rather deny the schools any funds than provide money that might be used for desegregation. Following the election, the *News* sharply criticized the negative millage vote as a foolish attempt by Detroiters to punish Judge Roth. Unfortunately for the school system, the voters responded precisely the same way in the August and November elections.[198]

The November effort to renew the 5 mill levy coincided with the 1972 presidential election and provides additional evidence of the relationship between the antimillage and antibusing votes. Throughout the 1972 campaign, busing was a defining issue, clearly dividing Richard Nixon, who opposed busing, and George McGovern, who, despite waffling on the issue, supported it.[199] As with the Wallace vote in the May primary, correlating the results by voting district from the November, 1972, school millage proposals and the presidential election shows a statistically significant, direct relationship, +.83, between support for Nixon and the antimillage votes. The strongest support for Nixon and the greatest opposition to school taxes came from the predominantly white sections of the city. The 1972 election reaffirmed the 1968 trend of white Detroiters shifting allegiance toward conservative presidential candidates, with busing as a strong motivating factor. That same trend also brought the Detroit schools to the brink of bankruptcy.[200]

The failure to renew the 5 mill tax left Detroit levying only 15.51 mills for its schools, well below the 26 mill state average and less than half of what many of the surrounding suburban districts levied. In actual dollars, the schools lost $30 million annually in addition to the $40 million deficit. This combined shortfall was equal to almost a third of the total annual operating budget of the system. After the first millage defeats in May, board member Darneau Stewart declared that "we have just discovered the death of the school system and we don't want to recognize it." In late November, school leaders prepared to shut down the fourth largest school district in the nation, bringing Stewart's grim vision close to reality. As the *Free Press* put it, "We cannot believe that such a collapse of public education is inescapable. We cannot believe it, but it is happening before our eyes."[201]

The board undertook three desperate attempts to avoid the impending catastrophe. First, it borrowed additional money to extend the school year for as long as possible. Second, it slashed the budget and planned to shut the system down completely in March. Since the DFT had already agreed to a "no raise" contract, additional cuts were realized through attrition, dropping orders for new textbooks, and curtailing the maintenance of buildings.[202] In its third attempt to avert disaster, the board also launched a campaign to obtain relief from the state. Spearheading that effort was the Detroit Educational Task Force (DETF), a blue-ribbon commission created by the board (but funded by the Ford Foundation) that was charged with finding ways out of the financial morass. Ultimately, the DETF initiated a successful but controversial effort in which the state legislature authorized the school board to levy taxes without a popular vote.[203]

The DETF pushed the "no popular vote" strategy largely because additional state aid for the Detroit schools was out of the question. In the November election, Gov. Milliken's constitutional amendment to equalize educational funding across the state was defeated, another example of an educational funding measure that fell prey to antibusing sentiment. The amendment would have shifted the burden of support for schools from the districts to the state and from property to income taxes. It unquestionably would have resulted in additional revenue for Detroit. Unfortunately, in the wake of Judge Roth's ruling, many voters believed that because the amendment would have weakened the underlying rationale for local control it would have provided additional legal support for metropolitan desegregation plans. Thus, as William Grant noted, the amendment became another casualty of "the controversy surrounding busing and local control of schools." Following the defeat of the amendment, Milliken showed little inclination to push new educational finance reform, leaving Detroit without any hope of substantially more state aid.[204]

Equal in importance to that defeat was the continuing legislative struggle between the city and state over educational funding. By the early 1970s, that struggle took an ironic turn as outstate legislators began repeating the same arguments about communities that were unwilling to tax themselves sufficiently to maintain their schools that Detroit legislators had been making about rural districts for most of this century. As one suburban legislator put it, "I don't see how you can expect me to tax my people for Detroit when they are already paying their fair share for the schools and Detroit is only paying 15 mills." By 1973, the situation in Lansing had changed so completely that the legislature enacted a minimum millage requirement for full state aid (a long-standing demand of urban educators prior to the 1970s) that was higher than the amount levied in the city of Detroit. Rather than aiding Detroit, as a high minimum millage requirement would have done in the 1940s and 1950s when taxes from the city were funding educational expansion across the state, the new, 25 mill minimum wound up allowing the state to reduce the amount of aid for Detroit due to the penalty for not levying the minimum tax.[205]

As far as the legislature was concerned, Detroit voters had created their own problems. The legislators assumed that if they "bailed out" the district it would only encourage Detroiters to continue shirking their responsibility to their schools.[206] As a consequence of these developments, the relief plan that the DETF and the legislature negotiated was simply a package of loans and pay-back arrangements. According to the agreement, the state advanced the board money to eliminate the deficit, about $73 million; the legislature gave the board the power to impose a 2.25 mill tax to repay the loan and the power to levy a 1 percent income tax on Detroit residents for additional operating revenue. The board could convert the income tax to a 7 mill property tax if the voters approved the change. These remedies, however, had strings attached. The state now had a voice in future school budgets, capable of pressuring the board into specific policy changes in order to avoid further deficits.[207] The financial crisis thus added one more layer of control over a school board that, since 1971, had already lost considerable authority to Judge Roth and his sweeping policy directives.[208]

In addition to complicating already tangled lines of authority, the financial crisis accelerated the disaffection of Detroit's white working class. By 1973, the inchoate political sentiments of many white Detroiters began to form into a clear philosophy that identified many of America's ills with the incursion of liberal government into the lives of ordinary citizens. Busing was the catalyst for that belief. But as Nixon aide Leonard Garment noted at the time, "Busing goes beyond schools and segregation—to all those other areas where people feel threatened in seniority, prestige, identity and begin to ask what are those bastards doing to us?" Opposition to taxes, particularly school taxes, became an equally potent aspect of that philosophy.[209]

When the school board obtained the power to levy taxes without seeking voter approval, white opponents of busing saw one of their worst fears realized. Even before the legislature authorized the board to levy these taxes, Carmen Roberts, a member of the Region 7 board, and a prominent figure in the CCBE and other antibusing organizations, vehemently denounced the "undemocratic" membership of the DETF and warned that these "bankers and big shots" would impose a solution on Detroit regardless of the wishes of the people. When the central board discussed these new powers to tax, Alberta Martin, a white member from the northeast section of the city, blasted the DETF plan as yet another form of state "coercion." The *Northeast Detroiter,* a bitter opponent of busing, roundly condemned the new taxing powers, maligning the DEFT plan as "a blackmail scheme of the most blatant kind."[210] Fueling the anger of these white Detroiters was the fact that in 1973, for the first time in the history of the school system, blacks won a majority of the seats on the central board. With the new powers granted by the state, it appeared that the board could now impose the taxes that so many white Detroiters had been voting against for almost a decade.[211]

The board quickly exercised its new power, imposing the 1 percent income tax and then beginning a campaign to replace that levy with a 7 mill property tax. The case for making the switch was simple. The income tax put most of the burden for supporting the schools on the backs of individuals, while the property tax distributed the load more evenly between individuals and corporations. Between two choices, neither of which the public wanted, the levy on property was better because it meant lower personal taxes. Support for the proposal was overwhelming and included Secretary of State Richard Austin, Mayor Roman Gribbs, mayoral candidate Coleman Young, the Board of Commerce, the Metropolitan AFL-CIO, the Catholic Archdiocese, the Detroit Council of Churches, the Detroit Jewish Community Council, the *Free Press,* the *Michigan Chronicle,* the *News,* and WWJ radio.[212] Despite the opposition from some homeowner groups, the Detroit Real Estate Board, and the *Northeast Detroiter,* the proposal passed easily, winning almost 62 percent of the vote. Yet, as an August editorial in the *Northeast Detroiter* graphically put it, the victory was due more to the knife that the state had put to the throat of Detroit voters than to any improvement in public support for the schools.[213]

Two weeks after the election, the board fulfilled its major campaign promise and rescinded the income tax. Nevertheless, the board still retained the power to reimpose the income tax if Detroit voters failed to maintain the current level of support for the schools. With that in mind, the board placed the renewal of its 7.5 mill tax on the March, 1974, ballot. While the board did not officially threaten to reimpose the income tax, Detroiters were well aware of that consequence if they voted down the renewal. Moreover, as the *News* reported, "the threatened return of a school income tax" was a big part of the pitch of some campaign workers.[214]

The same interest groups and individuals aligned in this election as in September, 1973. All the established business, civic, civil rights, and labor organizations as well as the major media outlets backed the proposal.[215] Carmen Roberts and other antibusing leaders opposed it. The *Northeast Detroiter* succinctly summed up the attitude of the opposition, declaring that "the voters are tired of a non-responsive school board that tells them what their children will learn; where they will go to school; who will teach them; and then forces them to pay for an education that is inferior to almost every school district in the metropolitan area." Despite the opposition, the outcome was never really in doubt. The renewal won almost 72 percent of the vote.[216]

These two millage victories, the first approvals since 1966, saved the school system from bankruptcy. Nevertheless, because they were coerced, the triumphs did not indicate a genuine shift in the mood of the electorate. Nothing reveals the continuing opposition to increased funding for the schools and the ability of antibusing sentiment to scuttle efforts at increasing taxes more than the unsuccessful attempt by the board to boost the tax rate in August.[217]

The September and March millage victories combined with the 2.25 mills imposed by the board to repay the state loans boosted the tax rate to 24.76 mills, slightly below the state average. Unfortunately, the funds generated from these taxes were still insufficient to maintain the system even at its current level. Inflation cut deeply into school revenue, but, in addition, the teachers who had accepted only modest pay increases during the worst of the financial crisis now demanded a substantial hike in salaries. In April, a state arbitrator awarded the teachers a sizable pay increase, 8 percent for experienced teachers and 2 percent for beginning teachers. The board responded with over 1,200 pink slips, essentially firing all first and second year teachers.[218]

Once again, a millage increase seemed to be the only way to keep the system from either huge deficits or even larger classes. Thus, the board placed a 5 mill increase on the August, 1974, ballot. As in previous elections, all the major interest groups supported the measure, although some were not particularly enthusiastic about backing yet a third school tax proposal in less than a year.[219] Opposition, once again, came largely came from the outlying white sections of the city and from the leading opponents of busing. One antibusing state legislator from Detroit, for example, contemptuously dismissed the proposal as "[a]nother effort by those school board blood suckers." Other opponents of the measure introduced what would become a perennial criticism of the school board, denouncing expenses for chauffeur-driven cars and extensive travel that some board members viewed as rightful perks of their office despite the dire financial straits of the school system.[220]

In determining the outcome of the election, however, perhaps the most important factor was not the criticism of the board or even anger over higher school taxes, but, rather, the decision by the Supreme Court on July 25, 1974, to strike down Judge Roth's metropolitan desegregation plan in *Milliken v. Bradley*. The thrust of the decision, as the board's attorney George T.

Roumell, Jr., explained it to the members, was "that in order for there to be a metropolitan remedy it must be proven that school district boundary lines were drawn to foster segregation, and the acts of one district had a segregatory effect in another district." The court found no such situation in Detroit. Rather, it left intact the ruling that Detroit alone was guilty of de jure segregation, thereby confining busing only to students in Detroit.[221] Coming less than two weeks before the millage election, the court's decision combined with the general opposition to higher school taxes led to a sound defeat of the proposal by a 58 to 42 percent margin.[222]

The difficult financial situation facing the board suddenly become perilous again. School leaders faced not only the task of balancing the budget but the added responsibility of finding funds to pay for a massive busing program as well. Over the next nine months, as the board adopted what school leaders called a "suicide budget" and as the scope and cost of the desegregation plan became clearer, criticism against busing escalated. This criticism differed dramatically from earlier protests, however, because the leaders were primarily black and liberal rather than white and conservative. Just as the issue of integration writ large had contributed to the collapse of the liberal-labor-black coalition, so the issue of busing now divided the black community.[223]

In December, 1974, the head of the Michigan Southern Christian Leadership Conference warned that busing "could destroy the whole city." Over the next few months, these sentiments were echoed by other black leaders, particularly Mayor Coleman Young. In a demonstration of biracial solidarity, Nicholas Hood, a black leader of the city council, and the white council president, Carl Levin, issued a statement saying that busing would spur white flight and "defeat the purpose of desegregation."[224] Most of these leaders were pointedly critical of the NAACP, which seemed determined to press ahead with busing regardless of the consequences to the city. In March, 1975, the *Detroit News* editorialized, "you begin to wonder, finally, whether the NAACP speaks for any substantial number of citizens, black or white, on the issue of school desegregation in Detroit." Polls indicated the *News* may well have been right. In May, New Detroit, Inc., found that 89 percent of whites and 50 percent of blacks opposed busing for desegregation.[225]

Underlying these criticisms were fears of increased racial turmoil in the schools and accelerated white flight. By 1975, the majority of Detroiters were black. At the same time, about 70 percent of the students in the Detroit schools were black, but the system was as racially divided as ever. In the 1973–74 school year, 158 schools, about half of all the schools in the city, were over 90 percent black, while 27 schools were 90 percent white and an additional 46 schools were 65 to 89 percent white. If Judge Robert DeMascio, who took over the case following Roth's death in 1974, ordered all schools to have a racial distribution equal to that in the district as a whole, as the NAACP demanded, all of the white students would attend majority black schools. Many civic leaders feared that such an order would lead to an even faster white exodus from the city. These leaders began to emphasize the need for better education and better funding rather than what would be, at best, token desegregation.[226] As School Board President C. L. Golightly, a black philosophy professor at Wayne State, commented, "It is both a joke and a hoax that a school board with a majority of black members is required by law to integrate a minority of white students into a majority of black students in order to bring those black students into the mainstream of American life."[227]

Judge DeMascio had considerable latitude in determining the scale of busing and the scope of other remedies. In the fall of 1975, he outraged the NAACP by ordering a "modest" desegregation plan involving the busing of about 13,200 black students and 8,800 white students and the reassignment of 8,000 students based on boundary changes. One NAACP official denounced DeMascio for not placing all the remaining white students in majority black schools and declared that the order was "racist, evil and a rape of the constitutional rights of black children." Nevertheless, on January 26, 1976, 22,000 children boarded buses and the desegregation of the Detroit schools began.[228]

Besides the pupil transfers, DeMascio ordered major changes in the operation of the school system to focus on "quality education." He demanded that the board establish a tough code of conduct for students as a means for reestablishing order within the schools. He also restructured the system, introducing middle schools for grades 6 through 8 and placing all ninth graders in high schools. Finally, he made substantial changes in the curriculum, mandating a citywide reading program, expanding bilingual education, ordering the construction of five new vocational education centers, and updating testing programs.[229] To cover the cost of these remedies, DeMascio demanded that the state contribute an estimated $70 million. The state appealed that order. Ultimately that appeal led to *Milliken v. Bradley II,* in which the Supreme Court ruled, in June, 1977, that the state was obligated to help for these remedies because state policies had contributed to segregation in the Detroit schools.[230]

Perhaps the most surprising aspect of busing in Detroit was how relatively calm the process was when it actually began. Fears that Detroit would explode, as Boston had, proved unfounded, and what violence did flare up proved to be the exception, not the rule. In part, this success was due to actions by such organizations as PRO-Detroit, a coalition of business, labor, and community groups that worked hard to achieve "peaceful compliance with the court ruling."[231] Yet other factors contributed to the calm as well. William Grant believed that by January, 1976, "there was little fight left in the city's citizens. The anti-busing groups were a shadow of their 1970 strength, and even the city's major anti-busing leader conceded that most of her members had given up the fight." That resignation, however, may have extended beyond the antibusing groups. Reporters from *Newsweek* who watched the beginning of busing in the Motor City commented grimly that

> some thoughtful Detroiters perceived a dark side to the calm; they suspected that the city, desolated by unemployment and almost deserted by the middle class may have accepted busing out of profound resignation and despair. A January poll by the *Detroit Free Press* indicated that a high proportion of residents, both black and white, neither knew nor cared much about the busing order. No matter which side of the busing issue they are on, a good many citizens may simply think that Detroit is no longer worth fighting for.[232]

In 1971, at the beginning of the Detroit desegregation case, an NAACP leader justified the suit, stating "We feel integrated education is automatically quality education. We say the resources channeled into the schools won't be equal unless all in the community are joined in this common goal."[233] Ironically, when *Milliken v. Bradley I* was finally implemented, the Detroit school system was poorer and more racially isolated than ever before. The issue of busing was not the principle cause of the financial problems of the district, nor was the issue the sole reason why whites left the city. Yet busing exacerbated and accelerated both these developments.

White Detroiters had been voting against school tax measures in large numbers since 1963, well before busing was an issue, but opposition to busing unquestionably provided many white voters with a powerful new reason for opposing tax increases for the schools. Such antibusing leaders as Carmen Roberts routinely opposed school tax increases. Indeed, Roberts viewed busing and school tax increases as similar efforts by liberal elitists to impose policies upon a reluctant working class.[234] Such "urban populist" sentiments galvanized white opposition to school tax proposals and, combined with a variety of other economic and social factors, contributed to the unprecedented fiscal crisis of 1968–73 that left the school system in financial ruin. The consequences of these actions were clear. In 1966–67, Detroit ranked forty-fourth in the state in per pupil expenditures. By 1973–74, the system had slipped to seventy-ninth, and, by 1985–86, to ninety-third. Teacher salaries fell even farther during this period, from 12th in the state in 1966–67 to 104th in 1985–86.[235]

Coupled with these negative financial effects was the accelerated exodus of white students from Detroit. Admittedly, even before *Milliken v. Bradley* was filed, white students were leaving in large numbers, with 55,000 fewer whites attending the Detroit schools in 1971 than in 1961. Nevertheless, as soon as the desegregation case went to court, white enrollment fell sharply. Between 1971 and 1976, the peak years of the busing furor, the number of white students in Detroit schools dropped by more than 51,000, almost matching the 1961–71 figure in half the time. In 1971–72 alone, immediately following Roth's desegregation ruling, the system lost twice as many white students as in 1967–68, following the Detroit riot. Parochial and private school enrollments in Detroit also fell substantially during this period, indicating that white families were leaving the city entirely not just enrolling their children in nonpublic schools. Ironically, once busing actually began, the loss of whites slowed somewhat though the outflow continued. By 1980, only 26,320 white students remained in the Detroit public schools, compared to 153,046 in 1961 and 100,717 in 1970. In 1984, the system had fewer than 19,000 white students, a little less than 10 percent of the total student population.[236]

Other than gaining some additional revenue from the state as a result of *Milliken v. Bradley II,* by the late 1970s there were few positive things that anyone could point to about Detroit's experience with busing. Wayne State sociologist Eleanor P. Wolf provided perhaps the best assessment of busing in the Motor City when she wondered "What, then, is the social-policy justification for a costly program that is widely disliked, divisive in its effects on the labor-liberal political coalition, uncertain in its effects on academic achievement and racial attitudes, and leaves demographic sorting-out processes much as before."[237]

From Decentralization to Recentralization, 1971–81

The years of crisis involving busing and the deficit were also punctuated by several dramatic battles over decentralization, as the beleaguered school system found no respite from controversy. While the thirteen-member central board and the five-member boards in the eight regions tried to determine where and how to redistribute power, they encountered problems at every turn. By far the most important and difficult of these problems was the relationship between the boards and the teachers.[238] The decentralization legislation that Coleman Young had drafted was a compromise designed to assuage teachers' fears by preserving the right of the DFT to negotiate its contract with the central board. Nevertheless, the act of decentralization itself planted the seeds of serious conflict between the proponents of community control and the union. In 1973, those seeds matured into a bitter harvest, the longest teachers' strike in the history of the Detroit public schools. The strike provided additional evidence that the collapse of the liberal-labor-black coalition had unleashed a scramble of competing interest groups that had lost a vision of the common good. Like the battles over desegregation, the conflicts engendered by decentralization devastated the school system and sped its descent into educational disaster.

From the beginning of the campaign for decentralization, conflict between the DFT and the decentralized boards seemed inevitable. Many leaders of the decentralization campaign explicitly blamed educators for the poor academic performance of black children. Newspaper exposés such as the one by Jim Treloar in the *Free Press* in 1966 highlighted teachers who despised their students and contributed to the rampant academic failure in the school system. Decentralizers were passionately committed to achieving some form of "accountability" that would enable them to remove such teachers. They were certain that ghetto schools would improve if parents and community groups had the power to hire and fire teachers and principals. As Rev. Cleage put it in 1969, "Contract security must be tied to 'achievement level' in the inner-city. Principals and teachers who cannot TEACH black children cannot have job security in the inner-city." In order to facilitate such staff changes, Helen Moore, the leader of Black Parents for Quality Education, argued that tenure had to be abolished. Recognizing that these issues would spark conflict with the DFT, Amos Wilder argued that, to achieve the goal of accountability, the community control movement had to effectively "neutralize and diminish the power now held by teachers' unions."[239]

In 1968, similar ideas and arguments had helped precipitate the terrible clash between the supporters of community control and the United Federation of Teachers in New York City. That confrontation, which resulted in the longest teachers' strike in the history of the New York schools, centered on the question of whether decentralized school boards had the right to involuntarily transfer teachers out of their schools.[240] In Detroit, the issues that generated conflict were accountability and residency, but the real question was the same as in New York: Did the decentralized boards have the right to determine who would teach in their schools? The logic of decentralization said yes, the boards must have the power to hire and fire educators. As Rev. Cleage argued, "Principals must be 'accountable' to the black community and if this is to be meaningful every teacher must be accountable to his principal. If a teacher is unable to bring the achievement of her class up to the national norm within a reasonable time that teacher must be replaced and all union contracts must be rewritten to recognize this basic 'accountability' of the teacher."[241]

Teachers' unions, in contrast, committed to the protection of tenure and seniority rights, were vigorously opposed to any effort by the central or regional boards to use such issues as accountability or residency to manipulate hiring, firing, or involuntarily transferring teachers. The DFT thus responded to these initiatives with a strenuous defense of the rights and prerogatives the union had fought for since the 1930s. Mary Ellen Riordan repeatedly argued, for example, that even with tenure protection, the contract had ample provisions for removing incompetent teachers. The fact that so few incompetents were removed, she claimed, was due more to a failure of administrative will than union intransigence. The union feared that the new push for accountability was a guise for setting up kangaroo courts to dismiss teachers because of their race or political beliefs. Leaders of Black Parents for Quality Education gave credence to these fears when they announced that they, indeed, planned to use "accountability" to oust "racist" teachers and to insure that "the racial composition of staff reflects that of the students."[242] Such statements, the union argued, showed that " 'accountability' would be a device through which neighborhood vigilante groups could attack teachers on the basis of failing to conform to particular political and racial ideologies." In the strongest possible terms, union leaders denounced both accountability and, later, the residency requirement as efforts to apply racial or political criteria in judging who should teach in the Detroit schools. They asserted that teachers should only be judged by how well they taught.[243]

On the surface, the clash between the DFT and the proponents of decentralization appeared to be simply another battle over racial issues. The conflict did indeed pit Mary Ellen Riordan, the white president of a mostly white union, against the leaders of the mostly black central and regional boards and such black community organizations as BPQE.[244] Nevertheless, the political divisions over these issues were more complicated than that simple racial alignment allows. In 1973, only a bare majority of the teachers in Detroit were white. Almost 47 percent of the teachers in the system at the time were black. In addition, the DFT and its allies in organized labor had prominent black leaders, most notably Tom Turner, president of the Metropolitan AFL-CIO, and John Elliot, executive vice president of the teachers' union and eventual successor to Riordan.[245] On the other side of the conflict, many white Detroiters, particularly such leaders of the antibusing movement as Carmen Roberts, joined Helen Moore and militant blacks in vilifying the DFT and in strongly supporting the board's position on accountability, the elimination of tenure, and residency requirements for teachers.[246]

Almost as soon as the new central board took office in January, 1971, board members and the union clashed over the issues of accountability and residency. Throughout 1971–72, for example, the DFT fought an ongoing battle with the board and the administration over new forms for rating teacher performance. The DFT denounced these forms as the first step toward arbitrary dismissals and "merit pay," while the board defended them as crucial for "teacher accountability." In June, 1971, the controversy heated up to the point that the DFT vowed to strike if the board adopted the new forms. Upon hearing that threat, Helen Moore blasted the union for protecting incompetent and "often abusive" teachers and charged that the DFT had "too much power." She immediately threatened to break any teachers' strike by setting up freedom schools for black children. Neither the strike nor the freedom schools materialized, but, throughout the early 1970s, controversy simmered as several board members enthusiastically supported bills before the Michigan legislature that would have rescinded the 1937 Teacher Tenure Act and compelled Detroit teachers to reside within the district. Such actions, however, only intensified teachers' militancy and loyalty to the union, regarding it as the sole mooring they had in this highly politicized and chaotic educational environment. Given the depth of feeling on both sides, an explosive confrontation over these issues was imminent.[247]

The clash finally occurred in the fall of 1973. Tensions had been building for some time, particularly among the teachers who, in order to help the system though its financial crisis, had accepted a modest salary increase in 1971 and no increase at all the following year. After the legislature provided school leaders with the power to impose the 1 percent income and 2.25 mill property taxes, the DFT asked for an 11 percent pay hike (equal to the increase in the cost of living over the previous two years) and a substantial reduction in class sizes. The board responded that it would not consider these issues unless the DFT agreed to an accountability plan.[248]

The board members and, particularly, their chief negotiator, Deputy Superintendent Aubrey McCutcheon, Jr., believed that the union was vulnerable on the issue of accountability. Over the past year, community outrage about the poor quality of the schools had been increasingly directed at teachers. In January, 1973, for example, Bill Black, a columnist for the *Michigan Chronicle,* wrote an angry column stating that the "Detroit schools are filled to overflowing with nonteachers who rely on that 'socially disadvantaged' bull as the alibi for their own failures. . . . When the people of this city wake up and realize how many alibi artists there are working supposedly as teachers, in our school system, there is going to be hell to pay." By early September, William Grant noted, "Public support for the teachers union [was] at rock bottom." Such perceptions encouraged the board to take a tough stand with the union. In addition, school leaders believed that the DFT would not strike in September, because a strike would have jeopardized the ballot proposal to shift from the 1 percent income tax to the 7 mill property tax. That was a major miscalculation.[249]

The board apparently had learned nothing from the 1968 strike in New York regarding the depth of union opposition to proposals that threatened tenure or seniority. As in New York, union leaders and the vast majority of teachers in Detroit vehemently opposed the accountability initiative. As a DFT broadsheet stated, "McCutcheon's plan amounts to a bludgeon which would keep teachers totally submissive to the whims of administrators and community witchhunters." Moreover, union members believed that the board's stance on accountability and on salaries was vindictive. For the past two years, they argued, the teachers had "subsidized" the schools, forgoing raises in order to keep the system afloat. They were furious that, in return for their forbearance, they were now threatened by a plan that would eliminate the most fundamental job protection they had.[250]

Neither side budged in their demands and, on September 5, 1973, the DFT began a forty-three day strike, the longest and most bitterly divisive strike in the history of the school system. Throughout September, neither side budged on the key issues of accountability or salaries. In addition, no one broke ranks: virtually every teacher in the system remained off the job and the board stood fast behind McCutcheon. Perhaps the only thing the strike accomplished was to reveal still further the fragmentation of the liberal-labor-black coalition as the UAW and the metropolitan AFL-CIO backed the teachers, while the previously pro-union *Michigan Chronicle* urged the board to enforce the Hutchinson Act and end what it called this "blatantly illegal strike charade."[251]

The school board, eventually following that journalistic advice, sought an injunction to force the teachers back to work. In late September, Judge Thomas Foley ordered union leaders Riordan and Elliot to actively urge their members to end the strike. When they failed to do so, he found them and the union in contempt of court, fining the individual leaders $1,000 per day and the union $11,000 per day until they complied with his order. The teachers responded to the contempt citations with a huge rally where thousands chanted "Hell no, we won't go!" At the rally, Metropolitan AFL-CIO President Tom Turner blasted the board for its attempted "union busting" and ripped the accountability plan as an effort "to eliminate due process for teachers and subject them to the whims and harassments of administrators and community groups who want teachers to conform to their particular ideology or attitudes."[252]

As the strike dragged into a second month, state mediators and Gov. William Milliken stepped in to break the impasse. The mediators urged both sides to submit the three key issues to binding arbitration. The board agreed, but the union would only agree to arbitration on salaries and class sizes, not on accountability. At this point, the governor provided a face-saving offer to the board by announcing that he would set up a statewide panel to study accountability and prepare guidelines for the evaluation of teachers. The board accepted the offer, thereby removing what appeared to be the last obstacle to ending the strike.

Unfortunately, by this time, a new issue arose out of the contempt citations issued by Judge Foley, namely fears that after the contract was signed the board would sue the union for "damages arising out of the strike." The DFT, therefore, included a new clause in the contract they voted to accept—no reprisals against striking teachers and no damage claims against the union. On October 17, the board approved these revisions to the contract. Two hours later, the teachers returned to their classrooms, and the students began school the following day. The strike was over, but, incredibly, none of the key issues had been resolved.[253]

BPQE and other activist groups were outraged by the settlement and attempted to "quash" it in court. These efforts were unsuccessful and, as noted earlier, an arbitrator eventually awarded the teachers a sizable salary increase. The accountability issue, however, virtually disappeared from public debate.[254]

Having failed in their attempt to determine who would teach in the schools through the accountability initiative, Helen Moore and BPQE turned their attention to the issue of a residency requirement for teachers. Their arguments for the requirement rested on the belief that Detroit teachers who lived in the suburbs were ineffective in ghetto schools because of their deep cultural differences with their students. As Moore put it, "Our opinion is that the average white, nonresident educator is insensitive to the special problems of inner city black children and has no reason to care about correcting them." At the time, about a quarter of the more than 20,000 employees of the system lived outside the city. Since most of these nonresidents were white, this issue appeared to be more racially motivated than the issue of accountability.[255]

In the wake of the strike, the debates about residency bristled with barely concealed anger and bitterness.[256] In late February, 1974, for example, the board flatly denied Martin Kalish, president of the Organization of School Administrators and Supervisors, permission to voice his opposition to the residency proposal at a board meeting. Claiming that this was the first time the board had ever refused to allow a representative of an employee organization the right to speak on an issue of concern to its members, Kalish accused a group of black board members of "racism of the vilest sort." Noting "growing hostility toward the school system 'staff,' particularly white members," he warned that "catastrophe is just down the road."[257] Despite continued protests by Kalish and Riordan, the board passed the residency requirement in March, mandating that all central administrators, all candidates for promotion, and all new teachers live in Detroit. The DFT and OSAS immediately filed suit against the requirement and, in 1975, the courts struck it down.[258]

The DFT was the clear winner in all these struggles, but the cost was high. Following the strike, the *Michigan Chronicle* editorialized that the forty-three-day walkout "may very well be an even more costly tragedy" than the 1967 riot. The *News* was equally pointed. "Public education is a partnership between the public and the educator," the paper declared. "If that partnership is dissolved in acrimony, the public schools as we know them will cease to exist." The editor of the *Free Press* made similar observations in an Op-Ed column that appeared several days later. Arguing that public outrage at the the union was rooted in a "desperate hatred of the teachers," he wrote, "Militancy may have its uses, but so does mutual confidence, and there is little feeling in the schools that teachers and parents are working together for common goals."[259]

While it is difficult to precisely assess the impact these controversies had on the schools, it appears that these editorial writers were right on the mark. Unquestionably, the charges of racism and insensitivity hurled by both sides in these conflicts contributed to the deterioration of the educational environment in the city. Mutual distrust did seem to replace mutual confidence, and the most basic interpersonal requirements for a decent education were badly undermined. In December, 1973, Helen Moore charged that some "students have been subjected to abuses by school personnel, perhaps in retaliation for efforts to force the end of the teachers' strike by the Black Parents for Quality Education." At the same time, student violence, often specifically directed against teachers and administrators, continued unabated.[260]

The violence in the mid-1970s, however, seemed different than the incidents that dominated the late 1960s. In the earlier period, many incidents were rooted in political or social protest. By the mid-1970s, those underlying rationales were less apparent. Unrestrained hostility and naked aggression appeared to have superseded political challenges and attacks. Assaults in and around the schools were common, vandalism was rampant, and it was widely rumored that teachers were so intimidated by students that discipline within the some schools was nonexistent. In late 1974, following two shooting deaths of students in or near school, the board asked the city to provide armed police patrols in the junior and senior highs. But even that drastic step and a later code of conduct mandated by Judge DeMascio did not stem the violence. As late as 1977, newspapers were reporting "near anarchy" in many buildings. Exacerbating these problems, absenteeism among teachers became chronic. In the first semester of the 1977–78 school year, the number of teachers failing to show up for work was almost double the normal rate.[261]

Cumulatively these developments had dire educational consequences. Standardized test scores for Detroit high school students, slowly falling since the mid-1960s, plunged sharply in the 1970s. Between 1972 and 1979, the scores of ninth and eleventh graders on the Sequential Test of Educational Progress fell from the thirty-third to the twenty-fourth percentile in reading and from the forty-third to the twenty-ninth percentile in math. The same pattern characterized sixth and seventh graders, although the drop in scores was not as pronounced as on the high school level. Between 1972 and 1979, only children in Detroit's first and second grades consistently tested at grade level, but in 1978–79 even those children fell below national norms. It was clear that decentralization was either having a negative impact on student achievement or, at best, no impact whatsoever.[262]

Indeed, at this time, many Detroiters sensed that decentralization was headed nowhere. The number of candidates for regional board seats dropped sharply, as did voter participation in the regional elections, indicating a serious decline in public support for and interest in the reform. William Grant reported that Detroit's black middle class was increasingly dissatisfied with the quality of education in the public schools and with the leadership of the district. In fact, at the time, many middle-class blacks, including a large number of public school employees, simply gave up on public education altogether and enrolled their children in Catholic schools.[263]

As a consequence of these developments, some Detroiters began to seek new approaches to solving the desperate educational problems of the schools.[264] In January, 1977, Superintendent Jefferson issued "A Call to Action," a comprehensive set of educational initiatives specifically designed to deal with poor student performance and to "restore public trust in Detroit's schools." Jefferson, who became the first black superintendent of schools when he replaced Charles Wolfe in 1975, argued that the board had to set new priorities and standards for the system. He urged a greater commitment of energy and resources to improve the middle schools and high schools, sought minimum competency requirements for promotion at every grade level, and advocated more challenging "performance objectives" for all students to meet. Little was educationally groundbreaking in these proposals, but they indicated an important change in the approach to school improvement in Detroit. Combined with Judge DeMascio's earlier decision to favor "quality education" over maximum integration, Jefferson's "Call to Action" signaled a fundamental change in the approach to educational problems in Detroit. For the first time in almost a decade, pedagogical concerns appeared to be replacing politics as the guiding force behind educational reform in Detroit.[265]

As a "top down" initiative, the "Call to Action" was also another indication that decentralization had failed. By 1978, opposition to decentralization was widespread. Critics included both daily newspapers, the *Michigan Chronicle,* major television and radio stations, the Coalition of Black Trade Unionists, the Detroit City Council, the Detroit Association of Black Businessmen, the Detroit Parent Teacher Association, the DFT, the Metropolitan AFL-CIO, OSAS, the NAACP, the Teamsters Union, the UAW, the Urban League, and Judge Robert DeMascio. These opponents argued that not only had the reform failed to improve educational quality, but it was costly and inefficient as well. In many ways, the arguments these critics put forth mirrored those of the educational reformers of the Progressive era. As one analyst stated, decentralization had "creat[ed] a system clogged with trivia that, at best, provides petty offices for aspiring politicians, at a cost some estimate to be $3 million or more per year." Moreover, blacks now controlled the schools and the city government. As a vehicle for black power, decentralization had outlived its usefulness.[266]

Public opinion mirrored the stand taken by the media and these organizations. Between 1977 and 1980, New Detroit, Inc., commissioned three surveys on school governance, each showing declining public support for decentralization although as late as 1980 a plurality of respondents described themselves as "prodecentralization." Given this growing opposition to decentralization, it was only a matter of time before the legislature once again considered the issue. In 1981, the legislature passed and the governor signed Public Act 96, which mandated that Detroit citizens vote on the future of decentralization. On September 15, Detroiters voted overwhelmingly, 104,312 to 37,694 to recentralize the system.[267]

Recentralization, however, did not solve Detroit's educational problems. The economic collapse of the city, the attendant social crises, and the preceding fifteen years of educational conflict had left the schools in disarray. Like the controversies over busing, whatever merits decentralization might have had were overwhelmed by the passions that it unleashed. Ironically, decentralization, which was designed to bring the schools closer to the community, shattered much of what remained of the relationship between educators, students, and parents.

Given the philosophy that guided the reform, it is unlikely that it could have gone any other way. The political battles between community groups and the teachers over the issues of accountability and residency were implicit in the very act of decentralization. In 1972, Kenneth Clark chastised proponents of school decentralization in New York City, noting that the reform encouraged political and racial issues to take precedence over more pressing educational concerns. Rather than concentrating on getting the schools to provide the best education, he said that advocates of decentralization were more concerned with teaching "the glories of racial separatism or pride or whether a black liberation flag should be flown in a school or classroom." Unfortunately, he added, when schools focus on "these problems of immediate, direct racial psychology and conflict, it seems to me that this can only be at the expense of teaching these children to read and to write and to speak and to think." The conflicts over accountability and residency in Detroit fit that analysis as well. Though less focused on racial issues than in New York, the battles ignited by decentralization in Detroit clearly centered around political rather than educational issues. As Clark envisioned, the children paid the price of those conflicts.[268]

Conclusion

In the early 1960s, many Detroiters believed the city and the schools stood poised on the edge of a bold, new era. Touted as a model city for race relations, led by a dynamic, progressive mayor, and boasting perhaps the most liberal school board of any big city in the nation, it seemed that if racial harmony and urban educational progress could be achieved anywhere, Detroit was the place. Yet by the early 1970s, these hopes were shattered beyond salvation. In that regard, Detroit mirrored the nation. The hopes for a great society, for a newer world, lay among the ruins of that turbulent decade.

None of the educational histories of the era fully account for that development. No single change, not the increased role of the federal government, the rise of teachers' unions, the challenges of the civil rights and black power movements, nor the collapse of moral authority within the schools can alone explain what occurred. All these factors clearly played a role in the great educational transformation of this era. But from the perspective of Detroit, the most important change of the 1960s and early 1970s was the massive political shift in which the remnants of the New Deal coalition broke asunder. Just as the period from 1929 to 1934 marked the collapse of the Progressive educational consensus in Detroit, so the period from 1968 to 1973 signaled the end of the liberal-labor-black coalition. Like the Progressive consensus at its best, the coalition was inspired by a vision of the common good, and it presented Detroiters with an educational agenda broad enough to attract support from diverse interest groups. With its demise, the school system seemed to come apart politically, financially, and educationally.

The coalition fell beneath a series of hammer blows—the economic decay of the city, pervasive white racism, the rise of black nationalism, insistent demands from the DFT, the unyielding position of the NAACP on busing, and the disastrous experiment with decentralization. From the ruins of the coalition emerged a new politics of education dominated by blatant bigotry and self-seeking interest groups. In this highly politicized atmosphere, the education of children became a secondary rather than a primary concern. In the late 1960s and early 1970s, so many groups sought to impose their particular orthodoxy upon the schools that the true function of public education—the mastery of sufficient knowledge and skills to assume the rights and responsibilities of American citizenship—was lost.

Nowhere can this trend be seen more readily than in comparing the initial Northern High School walkout in 1966, rooted as it was in the desire for better academic preparation, and later student protests, often orchestrated by adult extremists and precipitated by political agendas that had little to do with education. Indeed, after the Northern boycott, discussions about raising academic standards virtually disappeared from educational debates in Detroit. In 1969, amid protests calling for more black history and literature, Remus Robinson wondered why the students weren't also clamoring for more physics and math. But by then, no one was listening either to moderates such as Robinson or to such questions. The schools had simply become another arena where embittered interest groups battled for supremacy. In 1849, Horace Mann warned "that if the tempest of political strife were to be let loose upon our Common Schools, they would be overwhelmed with sudden ruin." By 1973, Mann's prophecy had become Detroit's reality.[269]

Perhaps no one in this era captured the essence of these problems better than Joseph Featherstone, whose observations about school decentralization in New York City fit Detroit precisely. Indeed, his insight regarding the unresolved crises in urban public education still rings true today. "Sooner or later discussions of these matters come round to the need for national political coalitions," he wrote, "for which there would seem to be no realistic immediate prospects. The decentralization crisis is in part a reflection of this political failure. Behind the struggle for community control of the ghettoes lies the somber truth about America in 1969; here, as St. Paul says, we have no continuing city, only groups pursuing self-interest to the edge of self-destruction."[270]

NOTES

1. J. Anthony Lukas, "Postscript on Detroit: 'Whitey Hasn't Got the Message,'" *New York Times Magazine*, 8/27/67, 24; see also Sidney Fine, *Violence in the Model City: The Cavanagh Administration, Race Relations, and the Detroit Riot of 1967* (Ann Arbor: University of Michigan Press, 1989), 291.

2. William Serrin, "The Detroit Disease: An American Infection," *Urban Review* 8 (Summer, 1975): 153.

3. *Detroit Free Press*, 11/11/72, in ND Papers, box 46, no folder.

4. Robert Hampel, *The Last Little Citadel: American High Schools since 1940* (Boston: Houghton, Mifflin, 1986); Hugh Davis Graham, *The Uncertain Triumph: Federal Education Policy in the Kennedy and Johnson Years* (Chapel Hill: University of North Carolina Press, 1984); Gerald Grant, *The World We Created at Hamilton High School* (Cambridge, MA: Harvard University Press, 1988), 11–113; Ira Katznelson and Margaret Weir, *Schooling for All* (New York: Basic Books, 1985), 178–206; Marjorie Murphy, *Blackboard Unions: The AFT and the NEA, 1900–1980* (Ithaca, NY: Cornell University Press, 1990); Diane Ravitch, *The Troubled*

Crusade: American Education, 1945–1980 (New York: Basic Books, 1983), 145–81, 267–320; Joel Spring, *The Sorting Machine: National Educational Policy Since 1945* (New York: David McKay, 1976), 186–258; David Tyack, *The One Best System: A History of American Urban Education* (Cambridge, MA: Harvard University Press, 1974), 255–91; David Tyack and Elisabeth Hansot, *Managers of Virtue: Public School Leadership in America, 1820–1980* (New York: Basic Books, 1982), 224–37; Wayne Urban, *Why Teachers Organized* (Detroit: Wayne State University Press, 1982), 173–78. See also, Robert Lowe and Harvey Kantor, "Considerations on Writing the History of Educational Reform in the 1960s," *Educational Theory* 39 (Winter, 1989): 1–9.

    5. Thomas Byrne Edsall with Mary D. Edsall, "Race," *Atlantic Monthly,* May, 1991, 53–86; Diane Ravitch, *The Schools We Deserve: Reflections on the Educational Crises of Our Time* (New York: Basic Books, 1985), 261; Paul Peterson, *School Politics, Chicago Style* (Chicago: University of Chicago Press, 1976), 51, 39–55. On the collapse of the liberal-labor-black coalition in Detroit and Michigan generally, see J. David Greenstone, *Labor in American Politics* (Chicago: University of Chicago Press, 1977), 256–60.

    6. Robert Conot notes that the two-year total in 1971 and 1972 (1,109) was larger than the total number of homicides in the city during the entire decade of the 1950s (988). See Robert Conot, *American Odyssey: A Unique History of America Told through the Life of a Great City* (New York: William Morrow, 1974), 817–18; Fine, *Violence,* 459; William R. Grant, "Letter from Detroit: The Courts and the Schools," *Urban Review* 8 (Summer, 1975): 146.

    7. National Education Association (NEA), *Detroit, Michigan: A Study of Barriers to Equal Educational Opportunity in a Large City* (Washington, DC: National Education Association, 1967), 14; U.S. Department of Commerce, Bureau of the Census, *1970 Census of Population, Characteristics of the Population, Michigan,* vol. 1, pt. 24 (Washington, DC: U.S. Government Printing Office, 1973), 11, 59, 77; U.S. Department of Commerce, Bureau of the Census, *1980 Census of Population, Metropolitan Statistical Areas (as defined by the Office of Management and Budget in 1983): Supplementary Report* (Washington, DC: U.S. Government Printing Office, 1984), 50; Reynolds Farley, "Residential Segregation and Its Implications for School Integration," *Law and Contemporary Problems* 39 (Winter, 1975): 171. Conot notes that, between 1950 and 1970, Detroit "lost two out of every three whites between the ages of twenty-five and forty-four" (Conot, *American Odyssey,* 840).

    8. Joe T. Darden, "The Residential Segregation of Blacks in Detroit, 1960–1970," *International Journal of Comparative Sociology* 17 (March-June, 1976): 85–86, 88–89; Joe T. Darden, Richard Child Hill, June Thomas, and Richard Thomas, *Detroit: Race and Uneven Development* (Philadelphia: Temple University Press, 1987), 67, 99–100; Douglas S. Massey and Mitchell L. Eggers, "The Ecology of Inequality: Minorities and the Concentration of Poverty, 1970–1980," *American Journal of Sociology* 95 (March, 1990): 1162, 1167, 1175; Douglas S. Massey and Nancy A. Denton, "Hypersegregation in U.S. Metropolitan Areas: Black and Hispanic Segregation Along Five Dimensions," *Demography* 26 (August, 1989): 382, 388.

    9. Conot, *American Odyssey,* 632–33; Fine, *Violence,* 18, 456, 458–59; Darden et al., *Detroit,* 22; Walter Guzzardi, Jr., "A Determined Detroit Struggles to Find a New Economic Life," *Fortune* 101 (April 21, 1980): 74; Cornish R. Rogers, "Penalizing the Poor," *Christian Century* 91 (August 21, 1974): 789.

    10. Darden et al., *Detroit,* 22, 24–26.

    11. Darden et al., *Detroit,* 76; Fine, *Violence,* 18, 456, 458–99; Guzzardi, "Determined Detroit," 82; Kevin Moss, "Joblessness in Detroit is 'Devastating,'" *Crisis* 90 (April, 1983): 14; Serrin, "Detroit Disease," 153; *Michigan Chronicle,* 11/21/70; James Harris, Jr., "Decentralization and Recentralization of the Detroit Public Schools: A Study of the Transitions of a School System, 1969–83" (Ph.D. diss., University of Michigan, 1985), 208.

    12. Darden et al., *Detroit,* 20–22.

13. Between 1962–63 and 1972–73, for example, the SEV of Allen Park rose from $59 million to $121 million; Dearborn from $620 million to $1.01 billion; Grosse Pointe from $247 million to $467 million; Inkster from $23 million to $44 million; Livonia from $316 million to $838 million; and Taylor from $99 million to $380 million. Across the nation, many large, urban school systems faced stagnation or decline of assessed valuation while real property values in suburban school districts rose sharply. See Citizens Research Council of Michigan, *Fiscal Trends of the City of Detroit* (Detroit: Citizens Research Council, 1991), 14; Detroit Public Schools, *1965–66 Budget* (Detroit: Board of Education, 1966), 143; Detroit Public Schools, *1979–80 Budget* (Detroit: Board of Education, 1980), 8; U.S. Department of Health, Education, and Welfare (HEW), Task Force on Urban Education, *Urban School Crisis: The Problems and Solution* (Washington, DC: Washington Monitoring Service, 1970), 9–12; Detroit Metropolitan Bureau of School Studies, *Membership, Financial Data, and Costs Per Pupil in Metropolitan Detroit Schools, 1962–63* (Detroit: Metropolitan Bureau of School Studies, 1964), 17; Metropolitan Bureau of School Studies, *Public School Membership, Financial Data, and Costs Per Pupil in the Metropolitan Detroit Six County Area, 1971–72 (with related data for 1972–73)* (Detroit: Metropolitan Bureau of School Studies, 1973), 29.

14. In controlling for inflation, 1967 = 100. Detroit Bureau of Governmental Research, *Accumulated Social and Economic Statistics on Detroit* (Detroit: Bureau of Governmental Research, 1937), 5; Detroit Public Schools, *Directory and By-Laws* (Detroit: Board of Education, 1952), 122; Detroit Public Schools, *Facts about Detroit Schools* (Detroit: Board of Education, 1974), 3, in DUL Papers, box 83, Educational Services, 1974 folder.

15. Detroit Board of Education, *Detroit Public Schools Statistics, 1975–76*, vol. 56, pt. 1 (Detroit: Board of Education, 1976), 263; Detroit Board of Education, *Detroit Public Schools Statistics, 1979–80*, vol. 61, pt. 1 (Detroit: Board of Education, 1976), 607; Denton L. Watson, "The Detroit School Challenge," *Crisis* 81 (June-July, 1974): 189.

16. Norman Drachler, "Education and Politics in Large Cities, 1950–1970," in *The Politics of Education,* Part 2, ed. Jay Scribner (Chicago: University of Chicago Press, 1977), 192, 205, 208; Harris, "Decentralization and Recentralization," 78; Maris A. Vinovskis, "An Historical Perspective on Support for Schooling by Different Age Cohorts" (paper presented at The New Contract Between Generations Conference, University of Southern California, 1991).

17. Ironically, because these new members shifted the political outlook of the board so noticeably to the left, two of the veteran board members, Betty Becker and Louise Grace, who had been supported by the liberal-labor-black coalition in the 1950s, were now labeled, along with Gladys Canty, as conservatives (*Detroit News,* 11/29/64, in RGR Papers, box 7, Clippings).

18. On Detroit's reputation as a "model city," see Fine, *Violence,* 32–34.

19. *Washington Post,* 7/25/67, quoted in Fine, *Violence,* 32.

20. DBEP, 1964–65, 645–46, 649–51, 722–24; DBEP, 1965–66, 163–64, 192–93, 324–25; *Detroit News,* 6/23/65; *Detroit News,* 2/16/65, in DFT Papers [inventoried 1/7/65], box 6, Clippings; *Michigan Chronicle,* 3/6/65, 4/17/65, 5/22/65, 5/29/65, 7/3/65, 2/5/66; *Detroit Teacher,* June, 1965; Coleman Young and David S. Holmes, Jr., letter to Fellow Citizens [form letter], 3/3/65, in EG Papers, ser. 2, box 9, folder 18; "Agenda of the Ad Hoc Committee Concerned with Equal Educational Opportunity, March 29, 1965," in EG Papers, ser. 2, box 9, folder 19; Fine, *Violence,* 44.

21. DBEP, 1964–65, 722–24; DBEP, 1965–66, 192–93, 236–37, 324–25; Detroit Public Schools, "Racial Count, Manufacturing Trades—Apprentice School, 1965–66" and "Racial Count, Building Trades—Apprentice School, 1963–66" (Detroit: Board of Education, 1966), in EG Papers, ser. 2, box 11, folder 19. See also Roy Gene Phillips, "A Study of Equal Opportunity in the Construction Trades Apprenticeship Training Program Sponsored by the Pipefitting Indus-

try of Metropolitan Detroit Within the Detroit Public Schools" (Ph.D. diss., University of Michigan, 1971).

22. Sub-Committee on Guidance and Counseling of the Education Committee of the Detroit NAACP, "A Report on Counseling and Guidance to the Board of Education of the City of Detroit, December 1965," 1–4, in the NAACP Papers, pt. 2, ser. 2, box 29, folder 1; *Detroit Teacher*, June, 1965; *Michigan Chronicle*, 3/20/65, 11/6/65, 11/13/65, 2/12/66, 2/19/66, 3/5/66, 3/12/66, 3/19/66; Young and Holmes, letter to Fellow Citizens.

23. Karl D. Gregory, "The Walkout: Symptom of Dying Inner City Schools," *New University Thought* 5 (May-June, 1967); 29, 40, 48–49, 51; Detroit Urban League, *A Profile of the Detroit Negro, 1959–67* (Detroit: Detroit Urban League, 1967), 7, in DUL Papers, box 65, 1967 Research Reports: "Profile" folder; NEA, *Detroit*, 81. The policy of placing black students in the general track at rates far exceeding whites was evident throughout the system. A 1967 report on Mumford High School, one of the most academically oriented schools in the city, found 22 percent of the black students in the general track, compared to only 2 percent of the whites. Forty-seven percent of the blacks *were* enrolled in the college prep track at Mumford, but that compared to 91 percent of the whites. See Mumford High School Study Committee, "Final Report, October 1967," 57, in DUL Papers, box 24, Mumford folder.

24. *Detroit Free Press*, 5/1/66; Fine, *Violence*, 52; Gregory, "The Walkout," 30–31; David Gracie, "The Walkout at Northern High," *New University Thought* 5 (May-June, 1967): 13; NEA, *Detroit*, 74.

25. *Detroit Free Press*, 4/8/66, in RGR Papers, box 16, NHS folder; *Detroit Free Press*, 4/19/66, in ND Papers, box 41, NHS folder; *Detroit Free Press*, 5/1/66; *Detroit News*, 4/8/66, 4/19/66, 4/20/66, in ND Papers, box 41, NHS folder; Gracie, "Walkout at Northern," 15; Fine, *Violence*, 52–53. The Colding editorial, entitled "Educational Camouflage," is reprinted in NEA, *Detroit*, 74–75.

26. *Detroit Free Press*, 4/8/66, 4/9/66, 4/13/66, in RGR Papers, box 16, NHS folder; Samuel Brownell, "Statement Concerning the Northern High School Situation, April 29, 1966" (press release), 5, in RGR Papers, box 16, NHS folder; Gracie, "Walkout at Northern," 15–16; Fine, *Violence*, 52–53; NEA, *Detroit*, 76–77.

27. *Detroit Free Press*, 4/9/66 and 4/16/66, in ND Papers, box 41, NHS folder; *Detroit News*, 4/11/66 and 4/13/66, in ND Papers, box 41, NHS folder; Judy Walker, Michael Batchelor, and Charles Colding, letter to Samuel Brownell, 4/15/66, in RGR Papers, box 16, NHS folder; Samuel Brownell, letter to Judy Walker, Michael Batchelor, and Charles Colding, 4/15/66, in RGR Papers, box 16, NHS folder; Detroit Public Schools, "Background—Northern High School" (5/3/66), 1, in RGR Papers, box 16, NHS folder; Fine, *Violence*, 53–54; Gracie, "Walkout at Northern," 16–17; NEA, *Detroit*, 76–78.

28. *Detroit Free Press*, 4/18/66, 4/19/66. 4/20/66, 4/21/66, 4/22/66, 4/23/66, in ND Papers, box 41, NHS folder; *Detroit News*, 4/18/66, 4/19/66, 4/20/66, 4/21/66, 4/22/66, 4/23/66, in ND Papers, box 41, NHS folder; *Michigan Chronicle*, 4/16/66 and 4/23/66; *New York Times*, 4/21/66 and 4/22/66, in ND Papers, box 41, NHS folder; Detroit Public Schools, "Background—Northern High School," 2; Fine, *Violence*, 54–55; Gracie, "Walkout at Northern," 18–20; NEA, *Detroit*, 79.

29. *Detroit News*, 4/19/66 and 4/20/66, in ND Papers, box 41, NHS folder; *Michigan Chronicle*, 4/23/66; NEA, *Detroit*, 79–80; Fine, *Violence*, 55; Gracie, "Walkout at Northern," 22, 24–26; Brownell, "Statement Concerning Northern," 1.

30. DBEP, 1965–66, 526, 534; DBEP, 1966–67, 4; Brownell, "Statement Concerning Northern," 1; *Detroit Free Press*, 4/23/66, in ND Papers, box 41, NHS folder; *Detroit Free Press*, 5/1/66, in DFT Papers [inventoried 1/7/86], box 6, Clippings; *Detroit News*, 4/23/66 and 4/25/66, in ND Papers, box 41, NHS folder; *Detroit News*, 4/25/66, in RGR Papers, box 7, Clipping file; Fine, *Violence*, 55; Gracie, "Walkout at Northern," 20–23.

31. *Detroit Free Press*, 4/21/66, 4/25/66, 5/4/66, 5/5/66, 5/10/66, in ND Papers, box 41, NHS folder; *Detroit News*, 8/3/66, in RGR Papers, box 7, Clippings; *Michigan Chronicle*, 5/14/66 and 5/21/66; Gracie, "Walkout at Northern," 21.

32. *Detroit Free Press*, 4/26/66 and 5/5/66, in ND Papers, box 41, NHS folder; *Detroit News*, 4/26/66, in ND Papers, box 41, NHS folder; Gracie, "Walkout at Northern," 24; Detroit Public Schools, "Background—Northern High School," 2; NEA, *Detroit*, 78.

33. *Detroit Labor News*, 5/4/66; *Michigan Chronicle*, 4/30/66 and 5/7/66; *Detroit Free Press*, 4/9/66, in RGR Papers, box 16, NHS folder; *Detroit Free Press*, 4/30/66, 5/3/66, 5/4/66, 5/5/66, in ND Papers, box 41, NHS folder; NEA, *Detroit*, 79.

34. Fine, *Violence*, 55; NEA, *Detroit*, 79.

35. *Michigan Chronicle*, 5/7/66. The Gregory series ran weekly from 5/28/66 to 8/27/66 (Charles Colding wrote the last article in the series). Many of the views that Gregory expressed in the series were summarized in Gregory, "The Walkout."

36. The Ad Hoc Committee may have been right regarding the declining levels of achievement by black children between fourth and eighth grade, but the data they presented did not prove that claim. The Ad Hoc Committee report commits the classic error of assuming longitudinal results from cross-sectional data. See Ad Hoc Committee of Citizens Concerned with Equal Educational Opportunity, "An Open Letter to the Detroit Board of Education and to the Public," 6/2/66, 1–2, in EG Papers, ser. 2, box 9, folder 19; *Detroit Free Press*, 5/26/66; Mayor's Inter-Racial Committee, *The Negro in Detroit, Section VII Education* (Detroit: The Committee, 1926), 2–9.

37. Northern High School Study Committee, "Interim Report, June 1966,", in ND Papers, box 79, no folder; *Michigan Chronicle*, 7/2/66.

38. Samuel Brownell, letter to the Board of Education, 5/3/66, in RGR Papers, box 16, NHS folder; Gracie, "Walkout at Northern," 27.

39. *Detroit Free Press*, 9/25/66, 9/26/66, 9/27/66, 9/28/66, in RGR Papers, box 7, 1959–66 Material folder.

40. In July, 1965, soon after the liberal majority on the board took office, Brownell announced that he would retire at the end of the school year. Like his predecessor, Arthur Dondineau, Brownell realized that the new, liberal board members would want to put their own philosophical stamp on the school administration. On reaction to Brownell's resignation, see DBEP, 1965–66, 54; *Detroit Free Press*, 8/31/66, in ND Papers, box 9, 1966 Clippings; *Detroit News*, 7/15/65; *Michigan Chronicle*, 7/24/65, 11/13/65, 5/7/66; Fine, *Violence*, 50.

41. Drachler was born in Ukraine in 1912. His family came to the United States in 1918 and moved to Detroit in 1929. Graduating from Detroit Central High School and Wayne University, he began work in the Detroit schools in 1936. He was a teacher, assistant principal, and then principal in various schools before he entered the central administration. He received a Ph.D. in the social foundations of education from the University of Michigan in 1951, and he directed the research for the Citizens Advisory Committee in 1958. Soon after the CAC finished its work, Brownell appointed him to be assistant superintendent for school-community relations. In 1966, the board appointed Drachler as Acting Superintendent and, in March, 1967, the board confirmed him as General Superintendent. DBEP, 1966–67, 48–49; *Detroit Free Press*, 1/27/71, in ND Papers, box 44, Schools in the News folder; *Detroit Schools*, 9/9/66 and 3/21/67; *Michigan Chronicle*, 8/6/66, 9/10/66, 9/17/66; Conot, *American Odyssey*, 745–46; Fine, *Violence*, 50; Elwood Hain, "School Desegregation in Detroit: Domestic Tranquility and Judicial Futility," *Wayne Law Review* 23 (November, 1976): 72; Edgar Logan, "Norman Drachler: Defender of Decentralization," *Clearing House* 46 (April, 1972): 497–501.

42. Arthur Johnson was born in Alabama and held a B.A. from Morehouse College and an M.A. from Atlanta University. He came to Detroit in 1950 to be the executive secretary of the Detroit NAACP. He held that post until 1964, when he became deputy director of the Michigan

Civil Rights Commission. Johnson was well acquainted with the problems of the school system, having served on both the CAC and the CAC-EEO (*Detroit Labor News,* 9/21/66; *Detroit Schools,* 9/16/66). Aubrey McCutcheon, Jr., was educated in the Detroit schools. His law degree was from the Detroit College of Law (*Detroit Schools,* 4/2/68).

43. Richard Henry began his campaign against racist textbooks well before Drachler became superintendent. As early as 1962, Henry had denounced *Our United States,* an American history text, as racist. His efforts were eventually supported by the Anti-Defamation League of the B'Nai B'Rith, which demanded better representation of both blacks and Jews in the texts. Out of this original protest, the schools created a 53-page supplement on black history for eighth grade American history teachers. On the earlier protest, see DBEP, 1961–62, 271–72, 317–20; DBEP, 1962–63, 330–31, 388–92, 442–43; DBEP, 1963–64, 2; DBEP, 1964–65, 89; *Detroit Free Press,* 4/24/63; *Detroit Free Press,* 12/19/62, 1/23/63, 5/2/63, in DUL Papers, box 72, Education—General folder; *Detroit News,* 12/9/62, 1/28/63, 5/2/63, 11/13/63, in DUL Papers, box 72, Education—General folder; *Detroit Labor News,* 3/5/65; *Michigan Chronicle,* 4/14/62, 6/16/62, 7/7/62, 12/1/62, 12/8/62, 3/2/63; Hain, "School Desegregation in Detroit," 70; Detroit Public Schools, *The Struggle for Freedom and Rights: Basic Facts about the Negro in American History* (Detroit: Board of Education, 1963), in EG Papers, ser. 2, box 12, folder 2. On the later protests and Drachler's efforts to get book companies to substantially change their texts, see Richard Henry, letter to Norman Drachler, 9/13/66; Norman Drachler, letter to Richard Henry, 9/16/66; Richard Henry, letter to Norman Drachler, 10/17/66; Norman Drachler, letter to Richard Henry, 10/20/66; Norman Drachler, letter to Richard Henry, 11/3/66, in ND Papers, box 98, GOAL folder; *Michigan Chronicle,* 11/26/66, 7/6/68, 9/20/69; Intergroup Relations Department, School-Community Relations Division of the Detroit Public Schools, *Textbook Report* (Detroit: Board of Education, 1968), 3–10, in DFT Papers [inventoried 12/24/85], box 1, *Bradley v. Milliken,* 1971–80 folder; *Detroit Teacher,* 10/2/68; Freeman Flynn and Max Rosenberg, "One Textbook, One Publisher, One School System," *Quest: The Detroit Public Schools Staff Journal* (Autumn, 1971): 44–48, in DPS/DCR Papers, ser. 2, box 10, folder 6.

44. *Detroit News,* 6/16/67, in DFT Papers [inventoried 1/20/86], box 1, envelope 6; *Detroit Labor News,* 5/28/67; *Michigan Chronicle,* 1/28/67, 2/4/67, 7/1/67, 7/22/67, 8/31/68, 9/14/68; Fine, *Violence,* 50; Phillips, "Study of Equal Opportunity," 14–28, 34–40.

45. *Detroit News,* 4/6/67, in ND Papers, box 79, NWHS folder; *Michigan Chronicle,* 10/1/66, 2/11/67, 4/15/67, 6/10/67.

46. On the shift from "color-blindness" to "color consciousness" in education during these years, see Ravitch, *Troubled Crusade,* 145–81; Tyack and Hansot, *Managers of Virtue,* 224–37.

47. One of the most striking events that illustrated the fragmentation of the civil rights movement came in late 1966, when black members of the Student Nonviolent Coordinating Committee ousted whites from the organization in order to facilitate the struggle for black power. Black Detroiters followed that event closely; see *Michigan Chronicle,* 8/28/65, 5/28/66, 6/4/66, 6/11/66, 7/2/66, 7/23/66; Clayborne Carson, *In Struggle: SNCC and the Black Awakening of the 1960s* (Cambridge, MA: Harvard University Press, 1981), 191–210, 236–42; Conot, *American Odyssey,* 684–88, 690–91; Allen J. Matusow, *The Unraveling of America: A History of Liberalism in the 1960s* (New York: Harper and Row, 1984), 354–55.

48. Stokley Carmichael and Charles V. Hamilton, *Black Power: The Politics of Liberation* (New York: Random House, 1967), 166–67; *Michigan Chronicle,* 5/13/67, 5/27/67, 6/20/67; *Detroit Labor News,* 4/12/67; Fine, *Violence,* 56.

49. As early as 1964, Cleage had urged African-Americans to "think black, vote black and buy black." In March, 1967, he renamed his church the Shrine of the Black Madonna and announced a radical reinterpretation of Christianity based on the premise that "Jesus was the non-white leader of a non-white people struggling for national liberation against the rule of a

white nation, Rome." Conot, *American Odyssey,* 685–86; Fine, *Violence,* 25; *Michigan Chronicle,* 4/1/67.

50. Inner City Parents Council, "Inner City Parents Program for Quality Education in Inner City Schools" (typescript, June, 1967), 1, in RGR Papers, box 5, Miscellaneous Papers folder.

51. Inner City Parents Council, "Program for Quality Education," 4.

52. Inner City Parents Council, "Program for Quality Education," 8, 11–12.

53. Inner City Parents Council, "Program for Quality Education," 12; *Michigan Chronicle,* 6/17/67. In addition to the Inner City Parents Council, a second organization, the Positive Neighborhood Action Committee, which was centered in the Northeastern High School area, also began pressing the board with demands for increased community control of the schools. See Sidney J. Berkowitz, "An Analysis of the Relationship Between the Detroit Community Control of Schools Movement and the 1971 Decentralization of the Detroit Public Schools" (Ph.D. diss., Wayne State University, 1973), 92–95.

54. DBEP, 1966–67, 614–16; *Superintendent's Pipeline,* 6/13/67; Fine, *Violence,* 45–46; Berkowitz, "Analysis," 92–94. In the school board primary election, Robinson received 96,548 votes, compared to Cleage's 40,736. In addition to this run for the board, in the preceding few years, Cleage had run unsuccessfully for various offices, including U.S. Congress, governor, Detroit Common Council, and the Board of Trustees of the Wayne County Community College. In all of these races, he finished near the bottom of the list of candidates. See *Detroit Free Press,* 8/4/66, in ND Papers, box 9, 1966 folder; *Detroit News,* 6/15/66, in ND Papers, box 9, 1966 folder; *Michigan Chronicle,* 7/30/66; *Detroit News,* 8/3/66, in RGR Papers, box 7, Clipping file; Lukas, "Postscript on Detroit," 56.

55. *Detroit News,* 6/15/66, in ND Papers, box 9, 1966 Clipping file; *Detroit Labor News,* 7/20/66 and 11/30/66; *Michigan Chronicle,* 6/25/66, 7/2/66, 7/23/66.

56. DBEP, 1965–66, 532–33; *Detroit News,* 4/27/66; Anonymous, "An Analysis of the 1965 Detroit Primary Election" (typescript, ca. 1965), 3, in RGR Papers, box 1, Miscellaneous Reports to 1970 folder; *Michigan Chronicle,* 1/15/66, 5/28/66, 6/11/66, 7/23/66; Ralph V. Smith, "Behind the Riots," *American Education* 3 (November, 1967): 31; Peter K. Eisinger, *The Politics of Displacement: Racial and Ethnic Transition in Three American Cities* (New York: Academic Press, 1980), 60–61; Fine, *Violence,* 55.

57. Without question, the finest and most comprehensive account of the 1967 riot is Sidney Fine's recent study; see Fine, *Violence,* 233, 249, 291, 297, 299, 291–301. See also Conot, *American Odyssey,* 679–706; Lukas, "Postscript on Detroit"; Matusow, *Unraveling of America,* 363; *Report of the National Advisory Commission on Civil Disorders* (New York: Bantam Books, 1968), 85–108.

58. Quoted in Fine, *Violence,* 369–73.

59. Cavanagh is quoted in Fine, *Violence,* 301; The Editors, "The Riot—Why?" *Michigan Education Journal* 45 (September, 1967): 4; Conot, *American Odyssey,* 705; Lukas, "Postscript on Detroit," 51–52, 58.

60. The survey of people in the riot area was conducted August 5–12, 1967. See *Detroit Free Press* and Detroit Urban League, *1967 Survey of Negro Attitudes* (Detroit: The Free Press, 1967), 13, in DUL Papers, box 65, 1967 Survey folder; *Detroit News,* 8/20/67. The rioter is quoted in Fine, *Violence,* 46.

61. DBEP, 1967–68, 44–45, 67–69, 95–96; Norman Drachler, *A Report on the Immediate Needs of Public Schools in Areas Affected by Civil Disturbances of July 1967* (Detroit: Board of Education, 1967), 1–2, in ND Papers, box 81, Detroit Disturbance folder; *Report on Civil Disorders,* 433; *Detroit Labor News,* 8/16/67.

62. On the Knudson protest, see *Detroit Free Press,* 10/10/67, in DFT Papers [inventoried 1/20/86], box 3, Miscellaneous Clippings; *Detroit Free Press,* 10/11/67, in ND Papers, box 56, 1966–67 Clippings; *Detroit News,* 10/10/67, in DFT Papers [inventoried 1/20/86], box 3, Mis-

cellaneous Clippings; *Michigan Chronicle,* 10/14/67. Cleage's call for community control can be found in *Michigan Chronicle,* 10/28/67, 11/4/67, 11/11/67. See also Fine, *Violence,* 372.

63. On Ocean Hill–Brownsville see Diane Ravitch, *The Great School Wars: New York City, 1805–1973* (New York: Basic Books, 1974), 292–378; Daniel Perlstein, "Visions of Reconciliation: Bayard Rustin and the 1968 New York School Crisis" (Paper presented at the American Educational Research Association Conference, Chicago, 1991).

64. DBEP, 1964–65, 707, 711; DBEP, 1965–66, 13–14; *Detroit News,* 4/2/65; *Detroit Teacher,* February, 1965, March, 1965; *Superintendent's Pipeline,* 5/11/65.

65. DBEP, 1968–69, 3; Detroit Public Schools, *Annual Financial Reports of the Board of Education of the City of Detroit, 1966* (Detroit: Board of Education, 1966), 17; *Detroit Teacher,* February, 1965; *Detroit Labor News,* 12/30/65.

66. DBEP, 1964–65, 480–81; *Detroit News,* 2/12/65; *Detroit Schools,* 5/14/65 and 4/2/68; *Michigan Chronicle,* 7/10/65; *Superintendent's Pipeline,* 9/28/65 and 11/9/65.

67. In addition to such problems as rising enrollments and falling SEVs, beginning in the 1966–67 school year, a new state law mandated that the school system distribute free textbooks to high school students, adding $1.56 million to the budget. Rising Social Security costs also hit the schools during this period, boosting the annual budget by some $2.23 million. Inflation added to the financial problems facing the board, as well, rising over 31 percent in the 1960s. DBEP, 1964–65, 686; DBEP, 1965–66, 498–503; DBEP, 1968–69, 2; Board of Education, *1965–66 Budget,* 143; Detroit Public Schools, *Facts about Detroit Schools,* 3; Detroit Board of Education, *Detroit Public Schools Statistics, 1975–76,* pt. 1 (Detroit: Board of Education, 1976), 263; *Detroit News,* 4/13/66, in DFT Papers [inventoried 1/7/86], box 6, Clippings; *Detroit Schools,* 2/11/66; U.S. Department of Commerce, Bureau of the Census, *Historical Statistics of the United States: Colonial Times to 1970* (Washington, DC: U.S. Government Printing Office, 1975), 210.

68. *Detroit Free Press,* 1/22/65, 1/23/65, 3/31/65; *Detroit News,* 3/31/65; *Detroit Labor News,* 4/8/65; *Detroit Teacher,* 1/27/65 (special issue) and November, 1965.

69. *Detroit Free Press,* 6/22/65, 6/30/65, 7/1/65; *Detroit News,* 6/22/65 and 6/30/65; *Detroit Labor News,* 6/24/65 and 7/1/65; *Detroit Teacher,* June, 1965, September, 1965, October, 1966; Gregory, "The Walkout," 36. The contract negotiated by the DFT was only the third, following New York in 1962 and Philadelphia in 1964, signed between an AFT local and the board of education of a large, urban district. See *Detroit Teacher,* December, 1965.

70. DBEP, 1964–65, 733–34; DBEP, 1965–66, 359–63, 396, 498–503; *Detroit News,* 4/13/66, in DFT Papers [inventoried 1/7/86], box 6, Clippings; *Detroit Schools,* 2/11/66 and 4/15/66.

71. DBEP, 1965–66, 438; *Detroit Labor News,* 2/10/66, 3/2/66, 3/23/66, 3/30/66, 4/6/66, 4/20/66, 5/4/66; *Detroit Schools,* 3/25/66; *Detroit Teacher,* March, 1966; *Michigan Chronicle,* 2/12/66, 3/26/66, 4/9/66, 4/30/66, 5/7/66; *Superintendent's Pipeline,* 2/8/66 and 3/8/66.

72. DBEP, 1965–66, 555–56; DBEP, 1966–67, 595; Detroit Public Schools, "Yes and No Votes on Millage—May 1966 and November 1966" (typescript, November 8, 1966), vi–vii, 6, in ND Papers, box 183; *Detroit Free Press,* 5/1/66; *Detroit Free Press,* 5/10/66, in ND Papers, box 41, NHS folder; *Detroit Labor News,* 5/11/66; *Detroit Schools,* 5/13/66; *Michigan Chronicle,* 5/14/66, 5/21/66, 7/23/66; *Superintendent's Pipeline,* 5/10/66; Detroit NAACP, "Report on Counseling," table 1; Fine, *Violence,* 55; NEA, *Detroit,* 79. School officials analyzed elections by high school districts by totaling the votes in the precincts that roughly corresponded to the high school attendance areas.

73. DBEP, 1965–66, 630–33; DBEP, 1966–67, 16, 39–42, 44, 67, 136; *Detroit Free Press,* 6/10/66; *Detroit Free Press,* 9/4/66, in ND Papers, box 9, 1966 Clippings folder; *Detroit Schools,* 9/6/66; *Superintendent's Pipeline,* 5/10/66 and 6/14/66; *Michigan Chronicle,* 7/16/66 and 9/3/66; "Detroit's Sick Schools," *Newsweek,* 9/5/66, 87. Karl Gregory summed up the feeling of the parents who protested the half-time sessions stating, "Half day schools will reduce

the financial deficit [but they will also] increase the educational deficit." See Karl Gregory, "Parents Must Now Carry School Battle to Legislature," *Michigan Chronicle*, 6/25/66.

74. DBEP, 1966–67, 69–83; "Detroit's Sick Schools," 87.

75. *Detroit Labor News*, 10/19/66; *Michigan Chronicle*, 10/22/66, 10/29/66, 11/5/66.

76. DBEP, 1966–67, 83, 160–61, 234; *Civic Searchlight*, November, 1966; *Detroit News*, 11/6/66; *Detroit Labor News*, 10/19/66 and 10/26/66; *Detroit Schools*, 9/30/66, 10/28/66, 11/14/66; *The Detroiter*, 10/10/66, 10/17/66, 10/24/66, 10/31/66, 11/7/66, 11/14/66; *Superintendent's Pipeline*, 9/27/66; "Detroit's Sick Schools," 88.

77. *Detroit News*, 9/11/66, in DFT Papers [inventoried 1/7/86], box 6, Clipping file; *Detroit Labor News*, 11/14/66; *Detroit Teacher*, October, 1966.

78. DBEP, 1967–68, 254; Detroit Public Schools, "Yes and No Votes," vi–vii, 6; Detroit Public Schools, "Report on the Election of November 8, 1966," 2–7, in RGR Papers, box 7, Election folder; *Detroit Free Press*, 11/10/66, in RGR Papers, box 7, Clipping file; *The Detroiter*, 11/14/66; *Michigan Chronicle*, 1/19/66 and 11/26/66. The millage campaign completely overshadowed the school board election that took place at the same time. The race itself was fairly lackluster, and the outcome did virtually nothing to change the political character of the board. Dr. Remus Robinson was easily reelected and a conservative, white attorney, Paul McDonald, replaced Louise Grace, who retired from the board after serving eighteen years. *Detroit Free Press*, 8/3/66 and 8/4/66, in ND Papers, box 9, 1966 Clipping folder; *Detroit Free Press*, 11/10/66, in RGR Papers, box 7, Clipping file; *Detroit Free Press*, 7/2/67, in DFT Papers [inventoried 1/20/86], box 1, folder 8; *Detroit News*, 6/15/66, in ND Papers, box 9, 1966 Clippings folder; *Detroit News*, 8/3/66, in RGR Papers, box 7, Clipping file; *Detroit Labor News*, 9/14/66; *Detroit Teacher*, November, 1966; *Michigan Chronicle*, 7/30/66, 11/5/66, 11/19/66.

79. *Detroit Labor News*, 4/26/67; *Michigan Chronicle*, 2/18/67; *Detroit Teacher*, May, 1967. On the impact of DFT vs. DEA competition in encouraging the 1967 strike, see *Christian Science Monitor*, 9/9/67, in DFT Papers [inventoried 1/7/86], box 6, Clippings folder; *Detroit Free Press*, 9/20/67, in DFT Papers [1/20/86], box 1, envelope 6.

80. DBEP, 1966–67, 643–44; *Detroit Free Press*, 6/22/67 and 6/25/67, in DFT Papers [inventoried 1/20/86], box 1, envelope 6; M. Jeffries, letter to Walter Reuther, 9/8/67, in WPR Papers, box 54, folder 8.

81. DBEP 1967–68, 69, 91; *Detroit Free Press*, 6/22/67, 6/25/67, 9/2/67, in DFT Papers [inventoried 1/20/86], box 1, envelope 6; *Detroit News*, 6/16/67, 6/22/67, 8/2/67, in DFT Papers, box 1, envelope 6; *Detroit Labor News*, 3/22/67.

82. DBEP, 1967–68, 100; *Detroit Free Press*, 8/15/67, 8/16/67, 8/19/67, in DFT Papers [inventoried 1/20/86], box 1, envelope 6; *Detroit News*, 8/15/67 and 9/11/67, in DFT Papers [inventoried 1/20/86], box 1, envelope 6; *Detroit Labor News*, 8/23/67; *Michigan AFL-CIO News*, 8/9/67, in DFT Papers [inventoried 1/20/86], box 1, envelope 6.

83. The Hutchinson Act was still on the books, but the law had been amended in 1965 to the point that, in the event of a strike, the only punitive recourse left to school boards was to fire the striking teachers. DBEP, 1967–68, 99–100; *Detroit Free Press*, 8/23/67, 9/2/67, 9/3/67, 9/4/67, 9/5/67, 9/6/67, in DFT Papers [inventoried 1/20/86], box 1, envelope 6; *Detroit News*, 8/23/67, 9/4/67, 9/5/67, in DFT Papers [inventoried 1/20/86], box 1, envelope 6; *Detroit News*, 9/3/67, in DFT Papers [inventoried 1/7/86], box 6, Clippings folder; *Detroit Labor News*, 8/9/67 and 9/6/67; Mary Ellen Riordan, "Statement by Mary Ellen Riordan, President of the Detroit Federation of Teachers, September 7, 1967," 2, in ND Papers, box 181, no folder; *Christian Science Monitor*, 9/9/67, in DFT Papers [inventoried 1/7/86], box 6, Clippings folder.

84. *Detroit Free Press*, 9/8/67, 9/18/67, 9/20/67, in DFT Papers [inventoried 1/20/86], box 1, envelope 6; *Detroit News*, 9/9/67, 9/14/67, 9/18/67, 9/19/67, in DFT Papers [inventoried 1/20/86], box 1, envelope 6; *Detroit Labor News*, 9/20/67; *Detroit Teacher*, October, 1967;

Martin Buskin, "Strikes: Now that the Big Ones Are Over What's Left? What's Ahead?" *School Management* 11 (November, 1967): 66.

85. *Detroit Free Press*, 9/6/67 and 9/20/67, in DFT Papers [inventoried 1/20/86], box 1, envelope 6; *Detroit News*, 9/6/67, in ND Papers, box 56, 1966–67 Clippings.

86. *Detroit Free Press*, 9/2/67, in DFT Papers [inventoried 1/20/86], box 1, envelope 6; *Michigan Chronicle*, 9/16/67 and 10/7/67.

87. DBEP, 1968–69, 2; *Detroit Free Press*, 9/6/67, in DFT Papers [inventoried 1/20/67], box 1, envelope 6.

88. New Detroit, Inc., a group of prominent civic leaders formed after the riot to help rejuvenate the city, played a role in the unsuccessful attempt to get more money from the state. DBEP, 1967–68, 568–73; *Detroit Free Press*, 9/20/67, in DFT Papers [inventoried 1/20/86], box 1, envelope 6; *Detroit Labor News*, 1/24/68; *Detroit Teacher*, June, 1968; New Detroit Committee, *Progress Report of the New Detroit Committee* (Detroit: The Committee, 1968), 45, in ND Papers, box 15, no folder. The board did scale back the amount of money from the millage increase that it would use for construction to only $7.5 million. Using its 2 percent bonding authority, it then borrowed $43 million for new construction (Detroit Public Schools, Press Release, 1/23/68, in DFT Papers [inventoried 1/20/86], box 1, envelope 1; *Detroit Schools*, 2/13/68).

89. *Report on Civil Disorders*, 435. In 1967–68, the National Center for Educational Statistics figured that Detroit should be receiving 17.98 percent of state school aid based on an equalization model that adequately took into account the decline in the assessed valuation in the city and the large number of disadvantaged children in the school district. See Detroit Commission on Community Relations, "Statement before the Michigan Senate Committee, January 18, 1973," 1, in DUL Papers, box 83, Desegregation 1973–74 folder.

90. Zwerdling is quoted in *Detroit Labor News*, 2/7/68. On the lawsuit, see DBEP, 1969–70, 438; *Detroit Labor News*, 1/24/68; *Detroit Schools*, 2/13/68; *Detroit Teacher*, March, 1968; *East Side Shopper*, 2/7–13/68, in DFT Papers [inventoried 1/20/86], box 3, Miscellaneous Clippings; *Michigan Catholic*, 2/15/68, in DFT Papers [inventoried 1/20/86], box 3, Miscellaneous Clippings; *Michigan Chronicle*, 2/3/68; *Wall Street Journal*, 2/6/68, in DFT Papers [inventoried 1/20/86], box 3, Miscellaneous Clippings; *West Side and Warrendale Courier*, 2/2/68, in DFT Papers [inventoried 1/20/86], box 3, Miscellaneous Clippings; George Bushnell, letter to Mrs. Alan Canty [president of the board of education], 1/30/68, in ND Papers, box 85, no folder; "Detroit Sues Michigan," *Saturday Review*, 3/16/68, 74–75; Thomas F. Wilbur, "The Quality of Inequality: Ghetto and Suburban Schools," *Nation*, 12/23/68, 691; *Superintendent's Pipeline*, 2/24/70. The Detroit suit was the first of a series of similar lawsuits initiated by large cities for additional revenue. By January, 1969, Chicago, Los Angeles, and San Antonio followed Detroit's lead in this action (*Washington Post*, 1/9/69, in ND Papers, box 19, no folder).

91. DBEP, 1967–68, 571, 626–33; DBEP, 1968–69, 119–26; *Detroit Schools*, 9/17/68.

92. Kevin Phillips, *The Emerging Republican Majority* (New Rochelle, NY: Arlington House, 1969).

93. Norman Drachler, letter to the Board of Education, 6/30/67, in ND Papers, box 81, no folder; *Michigan Chronicle*, 10/8/66; *Northeast Detroiter*, 6/22/67, in ND Papers, box 81, no folder; William V. Shannon, "The Vietnam Election," *Commonweal* 85 (December 2, 1966): 250; Phillips, *Emerging Republican Majority*, 341–57.

94. J. Anthony Lukas, *Common Ground: A Turbulent Decade in the Lives of Three American Families* (New York: Random House, 1985), 262–63; Matusow, *Unraveling of America*, 395–97, 404–22; Charles Kaiser, *1968 in America* (New York: Weidenfeld and Nicholson, 1988), 130–49,167–89; Phillips, *Emerging Republican Majority*, 25–42.

95. *Detroit Free Press*, 8/23/68 and 9/12/68, in WPR Papers, box 437, folder 5; *Detroit News*, 9/11/68, 9/21/68, 11/6/68, in WPR Papers, box 437, folder 6; *Detroit Labor News*,

9/18/68 and 10/2/68; *New York Times,* 9/22/68, 9/23/68, 11/1/68, in WPR Papers, box 437, folder 9; *St. Louis Globe-Democrat,* 9/30/68 and 10/15/68, in WPR Papers, box 437, folder 7; Joseph Kraft, "Problem Lies in Shift to Right of Vital Center of Opinion," *Washington Post,* 6/13/68, in WPR Papers, box 437, folder 2; "Worrying about the Wallace Impact," *Business Week,* 8/17/68, 98; "Can Unions Hold Their Votes in Line in November?" *U.S. News and World Report,* 9/9/68, 101; "Labor's Battle Cry Now: Stop Wallace," *U.S. News and World Report,* 10/14/68, 108–9; "Wallace Rides Wave of Hate in His Campaign for Power," *AFL-CIO News,* 9/21/68, 7, in WPR Papers, box 437, folder 3; Matusow, *Unraveling of America,* 426. Anonymous UAW Pollster, "Who Would Be Your Choice for President of the U.S. Now?" [a straw poll of seven locals], in WPR Papers, box 7, 1968 Presidential Campaign folder.

96. *Michigan Chronicle,* 2/24/68, 3/23/68, 3/30/68, 4/13/68, 6/15/68, 6/22/68, 6/29/68, 7/20/68, 9/14/68; *North End News,* 1/25/69, in DFT Papers [inventoried 1/20/86], box 1, envelope 1.

97. Samuel Lubell, "Nixon Called the No. 1 Second Choice of Wallace Voters," *Detroit Free Press,* 8/23/68, in WPR Papers, box 437, folder 5.

98. James Ross Irwin, *A Ghetto Principal Speaks Out: A Decade of Crisis in Urban Public Schools* (Detroit: Wayne State University Press, 1973), 11–14; *Michigan Chronicle,* 6/22/68.

99. DBEP, 1968–69, 134, 167–68, 193–94, 264; *Detroit News,* 9/3/68 and 11/3/68, in DPS Archives, Schools in the News clipping book; *Detroit Labor News,* 10/23/68; *Detroit Schools,* 10/15/68 and 10/29/68; *The Detroiter,* 9/30/68; *Michigan Chronicle,* 9/21/68 and 9/28/68; *North End News,* 10/31/68, in DPS Archives, Schools in the News clipping book.

100. *Michigan Chronicle,* 10/26/68. Early in 1968, Cleage invited Drachler to speak at his church. Cleage was delighted with the talk, in which Drachler discussed his commitment to hiring more black teachers and administrators as well as his desire to see the curriculum include more material on black history and culture. Cleage, however, criticized Drachler for his continued belief in integration (*Michigan Chronicle,* 3/9/68).

101. The final tally was 258,207 no to 154,971 yes. DBEP, 1968–69, 310; Ira Polley, "The Financial Crisis in Michigan Education" (typescript, 3/31/69), in ND Papers, box 85, no folder.

102. I am indebted to John Rury for this correlation analysis and the one on the 1972 elections. The correlation between the Nixon vote and the antimillage vote was +.67. These results are significant at the .05 level for all values above .40. The data were taken from Detroit Public Schools, "Report of the Vote, November 5, 1968," 81–104, in ND Papers, box 183, no folder; Richard M. Scammon, ed., *America Votes 8, 1968* (Washington, DC: Governmental Affairs Institute, 1970), 185, 188.

103. Phillips, *Emerging Republican Majority;* Matusow, *Unraveling of America,* 395–439; Edsall with Edsall, "Race," 62–63; E. W. Kenworthy, "Some Democrats, After Sifting '68 Vote, Fear Coalition is Dead," *New York Times,* 1/31/69, in WPR Papers, box 437, folder 6.

104. Unlike the analyses of the 1968 and 1972 elections, the correlations for 1963 and 1964 were by wards rather than by voting districts. I did not use the 1964 bond issue vote in this analysis because only property owners could vote in bond issue elections. Data for the correlation of the 1963 and 1964 election came from *Detroit Schools,* 11/15/63; Richard M. Scammon ed., *America Votes 6* (Washington, DC: Congressional Quarterly, 1966), 201.

105. DBEP, 1968–69, 282–84; *Detroit News,* 11/6/68 and 11/7/68, in DPS Archives, Schools in the News; *Michigan Chronicle,* 11/23/68; *Detroit Teacher,* December, 1968; Alvin Skelly [deputy superintendent for school housing], letter to Norman Drachler, "Recommended Priorities for $40 million Construction Program," 11/12/68, in RGR Papers, box 3, Reports folder.

106. Even within the campaign to redistribute power there were deep divisions. Such radical groups as the Citizens for Community Control of Schools, one of the major reform organizations, demanded "the right of local governing boards, elected by the community, to control the budget,

hire and dismiss teachers and administrators, and determine curriculum." More moderate groups, such as the majority of the members of the High School Study Commission, merely sought to reduce the role of the central bureaucracy by granting principals more power and creating citizen advisory councils in every school. See *Detroit Free Press,* 11/23/68, in DPS Archives, Schools in the News; *Detroit News,* 11/9/68, in DPS Archives, Schools in the News; *Michigan Chronicle,* 11/23/68; Detroit High School Study Commission, *Report of the Detroit High School Study Commission* (Detroit: Board of Education, 1968), 4–6, 244–45; Berkowitz, "Analysis," 104.

107. On the decentralization of the New York City schools, see Ravitch, *Great School Wars,* 385–87.

108. *Michigan Chronicle,* 3/9/68 and 3/16/68.

109. *Michigan Chronicle,* 3/30/68; Irwin, *Ghetto Principal Speaks Out,* 11–14.

110. Prof. Frederick W. Bertolaet from the School of Education of the University of Michigan served as the research director for the commission. I am indebted to him for loaning me his copy of the final commission report and the complete set of subcommittee reports. High School Study Commission, *Report,* iii, v–vii; *Detroit Free Press,* 2/28/66, 5/5/66, 7/21/66, 9/8/66, 9/22/66, 9/24/66, in ND Papers, box 41, NHS folder; *Detroit Free Press,* 5/17/66, in EG Papers, ser. 2, box 12, folder 5; *Detroit Labor News,* 4/27/66; *Detroit Schools,* 5/27/66; *Michigan Chronicle,* 5/28/66; Irwin, *Ghetto Principal Speaks Out,* 265.

111. High School Study Commission, *Report,* 4, 6.

112. *Michigan Chronicle,* 7/6/68; "Detroit's Disgrace," *Newsweek,* 7/8/68, 46–47; *East Side Shopper,* 7/9/68, in DFT Papers [inventoried 1/20/86], box 1, envelope 3.

113. Detroit High School Study Commission, *Report,* 4–6; *Michigan Chronicle,* 7/6/68; "Detroit's Disgrace"; *East Side Shopper,* 7/9/68, in DFT Papers [inventoried 1/20/86], box 1, envelope 3. By focusing on these two changes, I am not implying that the report ignored other, more traditional problems. In fact, the majority of the 213 recommendations made by the commission concerned such long-standing problems as the lack of resources to repair deteriorating buildings and to hire enough educational staff. All these recommendations, however, were less significant in their ultimate impact on the system than the call for decentralization and accountability. See DBEP, 1967–68, 300; DBEP, 1968–69, 18–21, 42–44, 52–61, 91–97, 205–48, 274–80, 312–18, 390–92, 411–16, 528–34, 551, 586–99, 624–32, 670–81, 711–27, 785–96; High School Study Commission, *Report,* 6, 186, 228, 231, 243, 316, 326, 345.

114. High School Study Commission, *Report,* 7, 345; *Michigan Chronicle,* 7/6/68; "Detroit's Disgrace"; *East Side Shopper,* 7/9/68, in DFT Papers [inventoried 1/20/86], box 1, envelope 3; Leonard S. Demak, "Impact of Social Forces on Public Schools in Cities," *Educational Leadership* 26 (November, 1968): 129–30; Norman Drachler, "Education in Large Cities," 200–202.

115. *Detroit Labor News,* 7/3/68. In addition to Mary Ellen Riordan, commission member Lester K. Kirk also denounced the report, but for different reasons than Ms. Riordan. Lester K. Kirk, "Re: The Co-chairmen's Summary of the High School Commission Report, July 1, 1968," in DFT Papers [inventoried 12/24/85], box 3, *Bradley v. Milliken* folder no. 4.

116. For some examples of these columns on education and decentralization, see *Michigan Chronicle,* 7/20/68, 7/27/68, 8/10/68, 8/17/68, 11/23/68, 11/30/68, 12/7/68, 12/14/68, 12/21/68.

117. On Aldridge, see Fine, *Violence,* 285–86, 380, 403; Berkowitz, "Analysis," 103, 116–17.

118. Cleage did criticize this statement, however, for being too vague in terms of how these goals would be implemented (*Michigan Chronicle,* 1/23/68).

119. *Michigan Chronicle,* 7/20/68 and 1/16/68. On the Citizens for Community Control of Schools and Wilder's link to them, see Berkowitz, "Analysis," 104–7.

120. Perdue and Hathaway replaced Betty Becker and Gladys Canty. This marked the first time in the history of the small board of education that there were no women on the Detroit school board. *Detroit Schools,* 11/19/68; *Michigan Chronicle,* 7/13/68, 10/12/68, 11/2/68,

11/16/68; DBEP, 1968–69, 599–603; *Detroit Free Press*, 11/23/68, in DPS Archives, Schools in the News; *Detroit News*, 10/16/68, in DFT Papers [inventoried 1/20/86], box 1, envelope 3; *Detroit News*, 11/9/68, in DPS Archives, Schools in the News; *Detroit News*, 4/6/69; *Michigan Chronicle*, 12/14/68 and 1/18/69; Calvin H. Smith, *Decentralization in Detroit: A Study of a School System in Transition* (Detroit: Board of Education, 1977), 6.

121. *Michigan Chronicle*, 12/14/68 and 5/24/69.

122. Quoted in Berkowitz, "Analysis," 105.

123. DBEP, 1968–69, 244–46; *Detroit Free Press*, 9/28/68, in DFT Papers [inventoried 1/20/86], box 1, envelope 3; *Detroit Free Press*, 10/22/68 and 10/23/68, in RGR Papers, box 7, Clipping folder; *Detroit News*, 9/25/68, in DFT Papers [inventoried 1/20/86], box 1, envelope 3; *Michigan Chronicle*, 2/24/68, 3/23/68, 3/30/68, 4/13/68, 6/15/68, 6/22/68, 6/29/68, 7/20/68, 9/14/68, 10/5/68, 10/26/68; *North End News*, 1/25/69, in DFT Papers [inventoried 1/20/86], box 1, envelope 1; *Northwest Publications*, 10/31/68, in RGR Papers, box 7, Clipping folder; *Redford Record*, 10/31/68, in RGR Papers, box 7, Clipping folder.

124. For the article that set off the protests, see Beverly Craig, "Anatomy of an Inner City High School," *Detroit News*, 11/25/68. See also *Michigan Chronicle*, 12/7/68 and 12/14/68; Irwin, *Ghetto Principal Speaks Out*, 153–54; Berkowitz, "Analysis," 116.

125. *Detroit Free Press*, 1/?/69 and 1/30/69, in DFT Papers [inventoried 1/20/86], box 3, Miscellaneous Clippings; *Michigan Chronicle*, 12/7/68 and 12/14/68.

126. *Michigan Chronicle*, 2/8/69; Irwin, *Ghetto Principal Speaks Out*, 156–58. During the second semester of the 1968–69 school year, for example, in addition to the resignation of the principal of King, protest and controversy forced out the principals of Butzel Junior High School, Guest Elementary School, and Mackenzie High School. See DBEP, 1968–69, 244, 246, 441–42; *Detroit Free Press*, 10/22/68 and 10/23/68, in RGR Papers, box 7, Clippings; *Detroit Free Press*, 1/?/69, 1/30/69, 5/20/69, 5/26/69, in DFT Papers [inventoried 1/20/86], box 3, Miscellaneous Clippings; *Detroit Free Press*, 5/26/69, in ND Papers, box 45, Schools in the News binder; *Detroit Schools*, 2/11/69; *Michigan Chronicle*, 10/26/68, 1/25/69, 2/8/69, 2/22/69, 5/24/69; Irwin, *Ghetto Principal Speaks Out*, 158–62. Between 1968 and 1971, protests erupted against the new black principal of Butzel and against the white administrators and teachers at Barton Elementary School, Cass Technical High School, Cooley High School, Edmunson Elementary School, Mackenzie High School, Northeastern High School, Northern High School, Pershing High School, and Southwestern High School. See DBEP, 1970–71, 185–86; *Cooley Black Student Voice*, 4/20/70, in ND Papers, box 79, Cooley folder; "Demands of Students from Southwestern High School, March 23, 1971," in ND Papers, box 79, Cooley folder; *Cooley Black Student Voice*, 4/28/71, in DFT Papers [inventoried 1/7/86], box 7, Community Control folder; Charles Wolfe [deputy superintendent], letter to Norman Drachler, 9/23/69, in ND Papers, box 79, no folder; Harry Goldstein [principal of Mackenzie], letter to Charles Wolfe, 3/12/71, in ND Papers, box 80, Mackenzie folder; Department of Intergroup Relations, Detroit Public Schools, "Summary Report From Various Detroit High School Student Groups Since September 1970" (April 7, 1971), in DPS/DCR Papers, ser. 2, box 8, folder 14; *Michigan Chronicle*, 10/18/69, 10/25/69, 12/13/69, 9/26/70, 1/23/71.

127. Black Student United Front of Northern High School, "We Demand" (leaflet, 1971), in DPS/DCR Papers, ser. 2, box 8, folder 14 (this folder contains a number of these lists of demands from various schools); see also Intergroup Relations, "Summary Report," Black Student United Front of Cooley High School, "We Demand" (leaflet, 1970), in ND Papers, box 79, Cooley folder; *Northern High School Black Student Voice*, March, 1969, November, 1969, in RGR Papers, box 5, 1969 folder; *Superintendent's Pipeline*, 3/25/69.

128. See DBEP, 1968–69, 524–25, 541, 546–49, 558–60; *Detroit Free Press*, 3/22/69, in RGR Papers, box 5, Clipping file; *Detroit News*, 3/26/69, in RGR Papers, box 5, Clipping file; *Michigan Chronicle*, 3/15/69, 3/22/69, 3/29/69; *Superintendent's Pipeline*, 3/25/69; *Black Stu-*

dent Voice 2, no. 9 [no date, ca. April, 1969], in RGR Papers, box 5, 1969 Miscellaneous folder; Irwin, *Ghetto Principal Speaks Out*, 213–15. On later efforts to change school names, see *Michigan Chronicle*, 3/27/71; *The Malcolm X [Northwestern] Senior High School Black Voice*, 3/23/71, in ND Papers, box 79, Cooley folder.

129. DBEP, 1968–69, 729–31, 755–61, 782; *Detroit Free Press*, 5/17/69 and 5/20/69, in ND Papers, box 80, Northeastern High School folder; *Detroit News*, 5/18/69 and 5/20/69, in ND Papers, box 80, Northeastern High School folder; *Northeast Detroiter*, 5/?/69, in ND Papers, box 45, Schools in the News folder; The Black Student Association of Northeastern High School, letter to Peter F. Grylls, 5/21/69; Ruth Cox, letter to Norman Drachler, 5/23/69, and Norman Drachler, letter to Ruth Cox, 6/4/69, in ND Papers, box 79, no folder; see also the collection of other letters and telegrams on the flag issue in ND Papers, box 80, Northeastern High School folder. On the prevalence of the demand to fly the nationalist flag in student manifestos, see "The 20 Demands of the Black Community and Black Students of Detroit, Michigan, Presented to the Board of Education March 25, 1969," in ND Papers, box 81, no folder; also see Intergroup Relations, "Summary Report."

130. Arthur L. Johnson, letter to Norman Drachler, 1/3/69, in ND Papers, box 81, no folder; Irwin, *Ghetto Principal Speaks Out*, 120, 183–84.

131. DBEP, 1969–70, 179–84, 441; Wolfe, letter to Board of Education, 9/19/69; Charles Wolfe, letter to Norman Drachler, 9/23/69, in ND Papers, box 79, no folder; Wolfe, letter to Board of Education, 9/21/70; see also Detroit Public Schools Staff, "Incidents" (typescript, 1969), in DPS/DCR Papers, ser. 2, box 8, folder 14; a set of more than two dozen memos detailing incidents in 1970–71 can be found in ND Papers, box 81, Incidents notebook; *Michigan Chronicle*, 12/12/70; *Superintendent's Pipeline*, 9/23/69.

132. The descriptions of these radical organizations were compiled from *Detroit Free Press*, 9/27/69 and 9/28/69, in ND Papers, box 40, Schools in the News binder; Breakthrough, "They Charge 'White Racism'/ They Promote 'Black Racism'" (undated, probably 1970), in ND Papers, box 80, Finney High School folder; Fine, *Violence*, 380–81, 383; Dan Georgakas and Marvin Surkin, *Detroit: I Do Mind Dying* (New York: St. Martin's Press, 1975), 91–93, 83–99; Irwin, *Ghetto Principal Speaks Out*, 121–23. Samples of the *Black Student Voice* for Central, Cooley, Northern, and Northwestern high schools can be found in DFT Papers [inventoried 1/7/86], box 7, Community Control folder. On incidents in which members of these groups were identified as playing a part, see *Detroit Free Press*, 9/18/69, in ND Papers, box 79, no folder; *Detroit Free Press*, 2/21/70, in DFT Papers [inventoried 1/20/86], box 1, envelope 3; *Detroit Free Press*, 4/30/70, in DFT Papers [inventoried 1/20/86], box 1, envelope 1; *Detroit News*, 6/6/69, in ND Papers, box 80, Finney folder; *Detroit News*, 9/18/69, in ND Papers, box 79, no folder; *Detroit News*, 4/17/70, in DFT Papers [inventoried 1/20/86], box 1, envelope 1; *East Side Shopper*, 6/4–10/69, in ND Papers, box 45, Schools in the News binder; *Northeast Detroiter*, 7/3/69, in ND Papers, box 45, Schools in the News binder; *Michigan Chronicle*, 6/14/69, 2/28/70, 4/18/70, 10/3/70; Public Schools Staff, "Incidents"; Wolfe, letter to Board of Education, 9/19/69; Wolfe, letter to Drachler; Constance Cooper, letter to Arthur Johnson, 5/23/69, in ND Papers, box 80, Finney folder; B. J. Sandweiss, letter to Dr. Marvin Greene, 9/24/69, in ND Papers, box 79, no folder; Irwin, *Ghetto Principal Speaks Out*, 164.

133. *Detroit Free Press*, 5/28/69, in ND Papers, box 45, Schools in the News binder; *Detroit News*, 6/6/69, in ND Papers, box 80, Finney folder; *East Side Shopper*, 6/4–10/69, in ND Papers, box 45, Schools in the News binder; *Michigan Chronicle*, 6/7/69; Stanley Webb and Constance Cooper, letter to Arthur Johnson, 5/23/69, in ND Papers, box 80, Finney folder.

134. *Detroit News*, 6/10/69, in DFT Papers [inventoried 1/20/86], box 1, envelope 4; *Michigan Chronicle*, 6/14/69; Charles Wolfe, letter to Board of Education, 6/9/69, in ND Papers, box 80, Finney folder.

135. *Detroit Free Press*, 3/25/69, in RGR Papers, box 5, Clipping file; *Detroit News*,

3/25/69, in RGR Papers, box 5, Clipping file; *Detroit Teacher,* April, 1969; Berkowitz, "Analysis," 125.

136. *Michigan Chronicle,* 6/28/69. See also DBEP, 1969–70, 82–84; *Michigan Chronicle,* 7/5/69, 8/16/69, 8/23/69, 8/30/69; *Detroit Free Press,* 8/3/69 and 8/6/69, in ND Papers, box 40, Schools in the News binder; *Detroit News,* 8/3/69 and 8/6/69, in ND Papers, box 40, Schools in the News binder; *Courier Newspapers,* 8/7/69, in ND Papers, box 40, Schools in the News binder; Department of Research and Development, Detroit Public Schools, "Achievement of Pupils in the Detroit Public Schools as Measured by Nationally Standardized Tests, July 31, 1969," in DPS/DCR Papers, ser. 1, box 7, folder 1.

137. Harris, "Decentralization and Recentralization," 90–91, 261–62. See also Berkowitz, "Analysis," 138–48; Smith, *Decentralization in Detroit,* 8–9; "Detroit Decentralization Law," *Integrated Education* 7 (November-December, 1969): 37–38.

138. Berkowitz, "Analysis," 125–26.

139. Harris, "Decentralization and Recentralization," 90–91, 261–62. See also Berkowitz, "Analysis," 138–48; Smith, *Decentralization in Detroit,* 8–9; "Detroit Decentralization Law," 37–38; William Grant, "Community Control vs. School Integration—the Case of Detroit," *Public Interest,* no. 24 (Summer, 1971): 69.

140. Berkowitz, "Analysis," 112–13.

141. DBEP, 1968–69, 634–46.

142. DBEP, 1968–69, 704–6; *Michigan Chronicle,* 5/24/69.

143. DBEP, 1969–70, 49–54, 57; *Michigan Chronicle,* 8/16/69.

144. *Michigan Chronicle,* 8/16/69.

145. DBEP, 1969–70, 295–301; Norman Drachler, "Some Legal and Practical Implications of Decentralization" (typescript, November 20, 1970), 7, in ND Papers, box 86, no folder.

146. The West Central Organization worked with the Detroit Geographical Expedition and Institute to draw up the "Black Plan." The West Central Organization eventually joined with twenty other militant groups, including the Black Student United Front, to lobby for the plan. For an excellent description of this effort, see Berkowitz, "Analysis," 108, 107–12; Smith, *Decentralization in Detroit,* 9–10; *Michigan Chronicle,* 11/22/69; Grant, "Community Control," 69–70. The study that formed the basis of the "Black Plan" appeared as Michael A. Jenkins and John W. Shepard, "Decentralizing High School Administration in Detroit: An Evaluation of Alternative Strategies of Political Control," *Economic Geography* 48 (January, 1972): 95–106.

147. *Detroit Free Press,* 1/18/70, in RGR Papers, box 16, Schools in the News folder; Harris, "Decentralization and Recentralization," 97–99; Grant, "Community Control," 69.

148. *Detroit Free Press,* 12/7/69, in RGR Papers, box 1, Clippings; Grant, "Community Control," 63; *Michigan Chronicle,* 11/15/69.

149. *Detroit Free Press,* 1/18/70, in RGR Papers, box 16, Schools in the News folder. In their quest to integrate the district, the board had made some dramatic strides. Between 1966 and 1970, the proportion of black teachers in Detroit jumped from 31.7 percent to 41.2 percent and every school in the city had some black teachers. During the same period, the proportion of black administrators climbed from 11 percent to 37 percent. Between 1965 and 1970, the number of schools that had no black pupils dropped from thirty-five to eleven. In addition to these efforts, the board also created a "shared-experience" program at 100 schools in which black and white students joined together in in various extracurricular activities, such as band concerts, student council sessions, cheerleading workshops, and cultural events. See DBEP, 1969–70, 59–60; Detroit Public Schools, "Racial and Ethnic Distribution, October 1970," 2–3; Grant, "Community Control," 65; Sol M. Elkin, "Shared-Experiences Creates Better Understanding between White and Negro Students," *Clearing House* 42 (May, 1968): 550–52. For more on the shared experience program, see DPS/DCR Papers, ser. 1, box 6, folders 3, 4, 12. Under the prodding of the liberal board, even the apprenticeship programs, the bastion of racial exclusivity, made

some progress toward integration, as the number of black apprentices increased from only 10 of 1,219 in the building trades program to 115 of 2,335 in 1969. There was better progress in the manufacturing trades program, where the numbers climbed from 72 of 1,037, in 1964 to 214 of 947 in 1969. Despite the improvement, the board was still very unhappy with the slow pace of change in these programs (*Detroit News,* 6/28/69, in ND Papers, box 45, Schools in the News binder).

150. *Detroit Free Press,* 1/18/70, in RGR Papers, box 16, Schools in the News folder. See also Grant, "Community Control," 69. See also Zwerdling's speech upon being elected president of the board on July 1, 1969, in DBEP, 1969–70, 4–6. On the stand of the Urban League and the NAACP, see Francis A. Kornegay, "A Statement of the Detroit Urban League at the Detroit Board of Education Hearing: Osborn High School, November 18, 1969," 2, in DUL Papers, box 68, Racial Composition of the Schools folder; Harris, "Decentralization and Recentralization," 97–99.

151. DBEP, 1969–70, 208–10, 240–41, 265, 288–89, 295–304, 458–60, 470, 494–95; *Detroit Free Press,* 11/2/69; *Detroit Free Press,* 12/7/69, in RGR Papers, box 1, Clipping file; *Detroit News,* 3/19/70 and 3/20/70, in ND Papers, box 12, Decentralization Scrapbook; *Detroit Labor News,* 2/25/70; *Michigan Chronicle,* 12/13/69, 12/20/69, 12/27/69, 1/17/70; William Grant, "The Detroit School Case: An Historical Overview," *Wayne Law Review* 21 (March, 1975): 855.

152. *Detroit Free Press,* 1/18/70, in RGR Papers, box 16, Schools in the News folder.

153. Grant, "Community Control," 70–71; Grant, "Detroit School Case," 856–57.

154. *Detroit Free Press,* 4/5/70, in ND Papers, box 12, Decentralization Scrapbook; *Detroit News,* 4/5/70, in ND Papers, box 12, Decentralization Scrapbook; Grant, "Community Control," 70–71; Grant, "Detroit School Case," 856–57.

155. DBEP, 1969–70, 497, 501, 538; *Detroit Free Press,* 4/7/70, in ND Papers, box 12, Decentralization Scrapbook; *Detroit News,* 4/8/70, in ND Papers, box 12, Decentralization Scrapbook; Grant, "Community Control," 72; Grant, "Detroit School Case," 857; Harris, "Decentralization and Recentralization," 100; Drachler, "Some Implications of Decentralization," 9. A log of some of the phone calls and telegrams can be found in ND Papers, box 94, Detroit Decentralization folder.

156. An excellent description of all these events can be found in Grant, "Community Control," 72. A transcript of the meeting can be found in DBEP, 1969–70, 497–555. See also *Detroit Free Press,* 4/8/70, in ND Papers, box 12, Decentralization Scrapbook; *Detroit News,* 4/8/70, in ND Papers, box 12, Decentralization Scrapbook.

157. DBEP, 1969–70, 515, 516, 519, 521. Eventually, the UAW, the Metropolitan AFL-CIO, the Detroit PTA, the Detroit Council of Churches, and the *Michigan Chronicle* announced support for the measure as well. See DBEP, 1969–70, 557–63; *Detroit Labor News,* 4/15/70; *Michigan Chronicle,* 4/18/70 and 5/2/70; "The Battle for Integrated Quality Education," *Human Touch* 5 (October, 1970), in DFT Papers [inventoried 12/24/85], box 3, *Bradley v. Milliken,* folder no. 3.

158. DBEP, 1969–70, 527, 528, 532.

159. DBEP, 1969–70, 522–23. A representative from the West Central Organization also spoke at the meeting and opposed the plan. Her statement, however, was somewhat ambiguous (DBEP, 1969–70, 527).

160. DBEP, 1969–70, 543, 550–51, 545, 554; Detroit Public Schools, "Boundary Plan," 5–8; *Detroit Free Press,* 4/8/70, in ND Papers, box 12, Decentralization Scrapbook; *Detroit News,* 4/8/70, in ND Papers, box 12, Decentralization Scrapbook; *Courier Newspapers,* 4/15/70, in DPS Archives, Schools in the News binder; *Superintendent's Pipeline,* 4/7/70. Robinson died on June 14, 1970. He was replaced by Dr. Cornelius Golightly, a black philosophy professor and administrator at Wayne State University and former member of the Milwaukee School Board.

See DBEP, 1969–70, 34–35; DBEP, 1970–71, 6; *Detroit Labor News,* 6/17/70; *Michigan Chronicle,* 6/20/70 and 6/27/70; Detroit Public Schools, "Central and Regional Board members, January 1, 1971," in DPS/DCR Papers, ser. 2, box 8, folder 18.

161. *Detroit Free Press,* 4/11/70, in DPS Archives, Schools in the News binder; *Detroit Free Press,* 4/13/70, in ND Papers, box 12, Decentralization Scrapbook; *Detroit News,* 4/10/70, in DPS Archives, Schools in the News binder; *Detroit News,* 4/30/70, in DFT Papers [inventoried 1/20/86], box 1, envelope 1; *Northeast Detroiter,* 4/15/70, in DPS Archives, Schools in the News binder; *Michigan Chronicle,* 5/7/70.

162. *Detroit Free Press,* 4/8/70, 4/9/70, 4/13/70, in ND Papers, box 12, Decentralization Scrapbook; *Detroit Free Press,* 4/11/70 and 4/12/70, in ND Papers, box 179, no folder; *Detroit News,* 4/8/70, in ND Papers, box 12, Decentralization Scrapbook; *Detroit News,* 4/11/70, 4/12/70, 4/13/70, in DPS Archives, Schools in the News binder; *Redford Record* 4/15/70, in ND Papers, box 12, Decentralization Scrapbook.

163. *Detroit News,* 5/4/70, in ND Papers, box 12, Decentralization Scrapbook; *Courier Newspapers,* 4/30/70, in ND Papers, box 12, Decentralization Scrapbook; Grant, "Community Control," 74–75.

164. Drachler, "Some Implications of Decentralization," 9; *Detroit Free Press,* 5/28/70, 5/29/70, 6/1/70, 6/4/70, 6/6/70, 6/11/70, 6/17/70, 7/1/70, in ND Papers, box 12, Decentralization Scrapbook; *Detroit News,* 4/10/70, 4/15/70, 5/3/70, 5/27/70, 5/28/70, 6/2/70, 6/14/70, 6/20/70, 7/1/70, 7/4/70, 7/8/70; Grant, "Community Control," 74–75; Grant, "Detroit School Case," 857–58; "Text of Act 48—Public Act of 1970," in DPS/DCR Papers, box 7, folder 32; Berkowitz, "Analysis," 137–48; Harris, "Decentralization and Recentralization," 100–102.

165. *Detroit Free Press,* 4/5/70, 5/22/70, 5/29/70, 6/15/70, 7/21/70, 7/23/70, 7/25/70, 7/27/70, in ND Papers, box 12, Decentralization Scrapbook; *Detroit News,* 5/4/70 and 7/11/70, in ND Papers, box 12, Decentralization Scrapbook; *Courier Newspapers,* 4/30/70, in ND Papers, box 12, Decentralization Scrapbook; *Redford Record,* 7/1/70, in ND Papers, box 12, Decentralization Scrapbook; Drachler, "Some Implications of Decentralization," 9; Grant, "Community Control," 74–75; Grant, "Detroit School Case," 858.

166. *Detroit Free Press,* 5/6/70 and 7/29/70, in ND Papers, box 12, Decentralization Scrapbook; *Detroit News,* 5/24/70, 7/18/70, 8/2/70, in ND Papers, box 12, Decentralization Scrapbook; "Can We Risk Putting Our School System into Chaos? Vote 'No' to the Recall Question," in DFT Papers [inventoried 1/7/86], box 14, Decentralization folder; William Grant, "Where Did Everyone Go?" *New Republic* 163 (September 12, 1970): 20; Grant, "Community Control," 74–75.

167. Detroit Public Schools, "Recall Votes by High School Constellations, August 4, 1970," in ND Papers, box 184, no folder; Grant, "Community Control," 74–75.

168. Grant, "Where Did Everyone Go?" 20. Following the election, Governor Milliken appointed four new members who served until January 1, 1971, when the new, thirteen-member central board took office. DBEP, 1970–71, 63–67, 117–19; *Detroit News,* 8/6/70 and 8/31/70, in ND Papers, box 12, Decentralization Scrapbook; *Michigan Chronicle,* 8/15/70, 8/22/70, 9/5/70; *Superintendent's Pipeline,* 9/8/70.

169. *Detroit Free Press,* 8/5/70, in ND Papers, box 79, no folder; DBEP, 1970–71, 80–87; *Detroit Free Press,* 5/24/70, in ND Papers, box 12, Decentralization folder; *Michigan Chronicle,* 8/22/70; Grant, "Community Control," 76–77, 79.

170. *Detroit Free Press,* 5/24/70, in ND Papers, box 12, Decentralization folder; *Detroit Teacher,* 9/28/70; *Michigan Chronicle,* 8/22/70; Drachler, "Some Implications of Decentralization," 11; Grant, "Community Control," 76; Grant, "Detroit School Case," 858. News of the secret trip by Bushnell, Johnson, and McCutcheon did not become public until September, 1971 (*Detroit Free Press,* 9/29/71 and 9/30/71, in DFT Papers [inventoried 1/20/86], box 1, envelope 4).

171. Grant, "Community Control," 78.

172. *Detroit News,* 4/8/70, in ND Papers, box 12, Decentralization Scrapbook.

173. Market Opinion Research, "Quality of Education Study in the Black Community of the City of Detroit for New Detroit, Inc." (typescript, 1971), 7, 10–11, in DPS/DCR Papers, ser. 2, box 12, folder 10. The survey is summarized in *Detroit Free Press,* 1/21/72, in DFT Papers [inventoried 1/20/86], box 1, envelope 4.

174. *New York Times,* 11/14/71, in DPS Archives, Schools in the News binder; Gary Orfield, *Must We Bus? Segregated Schools and National Policy* (Washington, DC: Brookings Institution, 1978), 319–38; Spring, *Sorting Machine,* 237, 242, 245–50.

175. The ruling against the state was due, in part, to section 12 of Public Act 48, which outlawed the board's integration plan. A number of other state actions regarding school construction and pupil transportation in Detroit, however, also figured into the decision. See Eleanor P. Wolf, *Trial and Error: The Detroit School Segregation Case* (Detroit: Wayne State University Press, 1981), 17.

176. The best account of *Milliken v. Bradley* is Wolf, *Trial and Error.* A partial list of other discussions of the case and its implications include Victor T. Adamo, "Integration and the Burger Court: The New Boundaries of School Desegregation," *Intellect* 103 (March, 1975): 387–90; Charles T. Clotfelter, "The Detroit Decision and 'White Flight,'" *Journal of Legal Studies* 5 (January, 1976): 99–112; Eugene E. Eubanks and Daniel U. Levine, "Big City Desegregation Since Detroit," *Phi Delta Kappan* 56 (April, 1975): 521–22, 550; Grant, "Detroit School Case"; Thomas F. Pettigrew, "A Sociological View of the Post-Bradley Era," *Wayne Law Review* 21 (March, 1975): 813–32; Hain, "School Desegregation in Detroit," 65–165; Wolfgang Pindur, "Integration and Education: The Supreme Court's View of Detroit," *Education* 96 (Spring, 1976): 245–50; Denton L. Watson, "The Detroit School Challenge," *Crisis* 81 (June-July, 1974): 188–92; Bilione Whiting Young and Grace Billings Bress, "A New Educational Decision: Is Detroit the End of the School Bus Line?" *Phi Delta Kappan* (April, 1975): 515–20; Lukas, *Common Ground,* 242–43; Orfield, *Must We Bus?* 30–35, 336–37; Ravitch, *Troubled Crusade,* 178–79; U.S. Commission on Civil Rights, *Milliken v. Bradley: The Implications for Metropolitan Desegregation* (Washington, DC: U.S. Government Printing Office, 1974); Mark G. Yudof, David L. Kirp, Tyll van Geel, and Betsey Levin, *Educational Policy and the Law* (Berkeley, CA: McCutchan Publishing, 1982), 478–91.

177. DBEP, 1970–71, 305–6, 455–60, 464; *Detroit Free Press,* 1/27/71, in ND Papers, box 44, Schools in the News binder; *Detroit News,* 1/27/71, in ND Papers, box 44, Schools in the News binder; *Detroit Labor News,* 12/23/70; *Detroit Schools,* 2/17/71; *Detroit Teacher,* September, 1972; *Michigan Chronicle,* 2/6/71; Detroit Public Schools, "Central and Regional Board Members"; Grant, "Community Control," 77.

178. Wolfe was a longtime Detroit educator. He was a graduate of Northwestern High School, and earned his B.A., M.A., and doctorate at Wayne State. He served as Acting Superintendent from December, 1971, to October, 1972, and then assumed the position of General Superintendent, which he held until June, 1975. See *Detroit Free Press,* 10/11/72, in ND Papers, box 46, no folder; see also *Detroit News,* 10/12/72, in ND Papers, box 46, no folder; *Detroit News,* 6/6/75, in ND Papers, box 50, no folder; *Superintendent's Pipeline,* 12/12/71 and 10/12/72.

179. DBEP, 1975–76, 732.

180. DBEP, 1969–70, 338–44, 389; *Detroit Free Press,* 1/20/70, in DFT Papers [inventoried 1/20/86], box 3, Miscellaneous Clippings; *Detroit Labor News,* 1/22/69, 5/14/69, 1/21/70; *Detroit Schools,* 1/21/69, 3/20/69, 5/20/69, 2/3/70; *Michigan Chronicle,* 1/18/69 and 2/14/70; *Courier Newspapers,* 1/15/70, in DPS Archives, Schools in the News binder; *Northwest Detroiter,* 1/22–28/70, in DPS Archives, Schools in the News binder. The amount of the deficit varied with just about every press account of the issue. I have chosen to present the figures listed in the official annual budgets prepared by the board. See Detroit Public Schools, *Annual Budget For*

the Year Ending June 30, 1970 (Detroit: Board of Education, 1970), 1; Detroit Public Schools, *Annual Budget For the Year Ending June 30, 1971* (Detroit: Board of Education, 1971), 1.

181. DBEP, 1970–71, 483, 512, 568–79; *Detroit Free Press*, 1/30/71, in DFT Papers [inventoried 1/20/86], box 1, Clipping file; *Detroit News*, 1/31/71 and 2/26/71, in DFT Papers [inventoried 1/20/86], box 1, Clipping file; *Detroit Teacher*, 3/15/71.

182. DBEP, 1970–71, 568–79, 592–95, 608–11; *Detroit Free Press*, 6/13/69 and 6/14/69, in ND Papers, box 45, Schools in the News binder; *Detroit Free Press*, 2/27/71 and 3/2/71, in DFT Papers [inventoried 1/20/86], box 3, Clipping file; *Detroit News*, 2/24/71, in DFT Papers [inventoried 1/20/86], box 3, Clipping file; *Detroit Labor News*, 2/24/71; *Detroit Teacher*, September, 1969; *Michigan Chronicle*, 2/27/71 and 3/13/71; "Detroit," *Integrated Education* 9 (July-August 1971): 59.

183. *Detroit Free Press*, 3/3/71, in DFT Papers [inventoried 1/20/86], box 1, envelope 7; *Northwest Detroiter*, 3/4/71, in DFT Papers [inventoried 1/20/86], box 1, envelope 7; M. Beresh, letter to Mumford Staff [with verbatim list of student demands], 3/4/71, in DPS/DCR Papers, ser. 2, box 8, folder 15.

184. DBEP, 1970–71, 644–50, 679–84; *Detroit Teacher*, 3/29/71; *Michigan Chronicle*, 3/27/71 and 5/1/71; Ben S. Chinitz, letter to Julia McCarthy [regarding events at Northwestern], 3/22/71, in ND Papers, box 79, Cooley High School folder; Black Student United Front of Northern High School, "We Demand" (leaflet, 1971), in DPS/DCR Papers, ser. 2, box 8, folder 14.

185. *Michigan Chronicle*, 5/29/71; *Detroit News*, 6/1/71, in DFT Papers [inventoried 1/20/86], box 1, envelope 6.

186. DBEP, 1971–72, 59–60, 90–93, 119–20, 124–25, 152–62, 216–18.

187. Following the October, 1970, ruling by the Sixth Circuit Court that section 12 of Public Act 48 was unconstitutional, Judge Roth ordered a new trial on segregation in the Detroit schools. At that point, the Detroit case began in earnest. The most damning evidence against the board concerned actions by the board in locating new buildings, drawing attendance boundaries, student transfer policies, and transportation practices, all of which, in one way or another, encouraged racial segregation. See *Detroit Free Press*, 4/7/71, 5/24/71, 7/16/71, in DFT Papers [inventoried 1/20/86], box 1, envelope 4; *Detroit Free Press*, 10/7/71 in DPS Archives, Schools in the News binder; *Detroit News*, 4/25/71, in DFT Papers [inventoried 1/20/86], box 1, envelope 4; *East Side Shopper and Community News*, 7/21/71, in DFT Papers [inventoried 1/20/86], box 1, envelope 4; *Michigan Chronicle*, 5/1/71; *Northeast Detroiter*, 7/22/71, in DFT Papers [inventoried 1/20/86], box 1, envelope 4; Grant, "Detroit School Case," 862–64; Wolf, *Trial and Error*, 159–207, 211–38.

188. The complete text of Roth's September 27 ruling can be found in DUL Papers, box 79, Roth's Decision folder, and in Wolf, *Trial and Error*, 303–28. See also "The Detroit School Decision," *Integrated Education* 9 (November-December, 1971): 3–8. For reaction to the decision, see DBEP, 1971–72, 168–69; *Detroit Free Press*, 9/28/71, 9/29/71, 10/2/71, 10/3/71, 10/4/71, 10/7/71, 10/11/71, in DPS Archives, Schools in the News binder; *Detroit News*, 9/28/71, 9/29/71, 9/30/71, 10/5/71, in DPS Archives, Schools in the News binder; *Michigan Chronicle*, 10/2/71 and 10/9/71; *New York Times*, 10/3/71, in DPS Archives, Schools in the News binder; *Superintendent's Pipeline*, 9/28/71; George E. Bushnell, Jr., letter to James Hathaway, 10/4/71, in DPS/DCR Papers, ser. 2, box 10, folder 5.

189. *Detroit Free Press*, 9/9/71, 9/20/71, 10/2/71, 10/3/71, 10/4/71, 10/7/71, in DPS Archives, Schools in the News binder; *Detroit News*, 10/5/71, in DPS Archives, Schools in the News binder; *East Side Shopper and Community News*, 9/22/71, in DPS Archives, Schools in the News binder; *Michigan Chronicle*, 8/21/71, 9/11/71, 9/18/71, 9/25/71; *New York Times*, 9/8/71, 9/10/71, 9/15/71, 10/3/71, in DPS Archives, Schools in the News binder; *Washington Post*, 9/10/71 and 9/15/71, in DPS Archives, Schools in the News binder; Breakthrough, "Citi-

zens of Pontiac, Resist Forced Busing, Boycott the Public Schools" (ca. September, 1971), in CR Papers, box 1, Anti-Busing Materials.

190. *Detroit Free Press,* 10/2/71, 10/10/71, 10/16/71, 10/28/71, 10/31/71, 11/1/71, 11/2/71, 11/7/71, in DPS Archives, Schools in the News binder; *Detroit News,* 9/30/71, 10/7/71, 10/20/71, 10/27/71, 10/28/71, 10/29/71, in DPS Archives, Schools in the News binder; *Michigan Chronicle,* 10/16/71; *New York Times,* 10/3/71, 10/18/71, 11/14/71, in DPS Archives, Schools in the News binder.

191. *Detroit Free Press,* 10/19/71, 11/4/71, 11/7/71, in DPS Archives, Schools in the News binder; *Detroit News,* 10/27/71, in DPS Archives, Schools in the News binder; Watson, "Detroit School Challenge," 191.

192. *Eastside Shopper and Community News,* 10/6/71, in DFT Papers [inventoried 1/20/86], box 1, envelope 4.

193. DBEP, 1971–72, 216–19, 335–36, 382–86; *Detroit Free Press,* 10/10/71 and 11/4/71, in DPS Archives, Schools in the News binder; *Eastside Shopper and Community News,* 10/6/71, in DFT Papers [inventoried 1/20/86], box 1, envelope 4; *Michigan Chronicle,* 11/20/71 and 12/11/71; *Superintendent's Pipeline,* 10/12/71. The quote from Coleman Young is from *Detroit Free Press,* 11/4/71, in DPS Archives, Schools in the News binder. The quote by Moore is from *Michigan Chronicle,* 12/11/71.

194. DBEP, 1971–72, 508–20, 546–50, 617–28; *Detroit News,* 1/21/72, in DFT Papers [inventoried 1/20/86], box 1, envelope 6; *Detroit News,* 5/18/72, in DFT Papers [inventoried 1/20/86], box 3, Miscellaneous Clippings; *Detroit Labor News,* 4/19/72; *Detroit Teacher,* 3/24/72; *Detroit Teacher,* September, 1972; *Superintendent's Pipeline,* 2/22/72.

195. DBEP, 1971–72, 749–51; *Detroit Free Press,* 3/5/72, 5/18/72, 8/26/72, 11/5/72, in DFT Papers [inventoried 1/20/86], box 3, Miscellaneous Clippings; *Detroit Free Press,* 5/9/72, in ND Papers, box 46, no folder; *Detroit News,* 5/12/72 and 11/8/72, in ND Papers, box 46, no folder; *Detroit News,* 8/4/72, in DFT Papers [inventoried 1/20/86], box 1, envelope 2; *Detroit Labor News,* 3/8/72, 4/12/72, 4/19/72, 5/3/72, 5/10/72, 8/2/72; *Detroit Teacher,* 5/9/72; *Detroit Teacher,* September, 1972, October, 1972; *Superintendent's Pipeline,* 6/13/72; *Michigan Chronicle,* 11/4/72.

196. City of Detroit, "Report of the Board of Canvassers on the Primary and Special Elections of May 16, 1972," in ND Papers, box 184, no folder; City of Detroit, "Report of the Board of Canvassers on the Primary and Special Elections of August 6, 1972," in ND Papers, box 184, no folder; City of Detroit, "Report of the Board of Canvassers on the Election and Special Elections of November 6, 1972," in ND Papers, box 184, no folder; "Detroit Schools Head Toward Disaster," *Time,* 2/19/73, 72–73.

197. Stephen E. Ambrose, *Nixon: The Triumph of a Politician, 1969–1972* (New York: Simon and Schuster, 1989), 541–42; Theodore H. White, *The Making of the President 1972* (New York: Atheneum, 1973), 98, 128, 170; *Detroit News,* 5/17/72; *Detroit News,* 5/18/72, in ND Papers, box 46, no folder; *Detroit Labor News,* 5/25/72. Data for this correlation came from Wayne County Board of Canvassers, *Statement of the Election Returns, Presidential Primary Election, May 16, 1972,* 87; City of Detroit, "Report on the Elections of May 16, 1972."

198. *Detroit Free Press,* 8/26/72, in DFT Papers [inventoried 1/20/86], box 3, Miscellaneous Clippings; *Detroit News,* 2/7/72, in ND Papers, box 86, no folder [in the poll, 29 percent "somewhat agreed" and 45 percent "strongly agreed" with the statement "School money in Detroit should be spent for better schools and not on bussing"]. Hathaway is quoted in *Detroit News,* 5/17/72, in DFT Papers [inventoried 1/20/86], box 3, Miscellaneous Clippings; *Detroit News,* 5/18/82, in ND Papers, box 46, no folder; *Detroit Teacher,* September, 1972; "In the North Now: An Order to Mix City, Suburban Schools," *U.S. News and World Report,* 4/10/72, 58; William Serrin, "The Most Hated Man in Michigan," *Saturday Review,* 8/26/72, 13–15.

199. Ambrose, *Nixon*, 460–61, 523–24, 542, 555, 586–87, 657; White, *Making of the President, 1972*, 170, 190, 222–23, 241–42; Spring, *Sorting Machine*, 242, 245–50; David O. Sears, Carl P. Hensler, and Leslie K. Speer, "Whites' Opposition to 'Busing': Self-Interest or Symbolic Politics?" *American Political Science Review* 73 (June, 1979): 373, 379, 381.

200. The correlations between the antimillage votes in the other 1972 elections and Nixon's totals were also strong, ranging from + .83 and + .87 in the May renewal and increase votes, respectively, and + .57 and + .89 for the August renewal and increase, respectively. Sources for the analysis of the 1972 elections are: Detroit, "Report on the Elections of May 16, 1972"; Detroit, "Report on the Elections of August 6, 1972"; Detroit, "Report on the Elections of November 6, 1972"; Richard M. Scammon, ed., *America Votes* 10 (Washington, DC: Congressional Quarterly, 1973), 194. These findings fit nicely into other analyses of the role of the busing issue in the 1972 presidential election. See Sears, Hensler, and Speer, "Whites' Opposition," 378–83.

201. DBEP, 1971–72, 684; *Detroit Free Press*, 11/11/72, in ND Papers, box 46, no folder; *Detroit Free Press*, 11/21/72, in DFT Papers [inventoried 1/20/86], box 3, Miscellaneous Clippings; *Detroit News*, 11/9/72 and 11/13/72, in ND Papers, box 46, no folder; *Detroit News*, 11/9/72, 11/22/72, 11/23/72, in DFT Papers [inventoried 1/20/86], box 3, Miscellaneous Clippings; *Detroit News*, 11/21/72, in DFT Papers [inventoried 1/20/86], box 1, envelope 7. Stewart is quoted in "Struggle to Survive," *Newsweek*, 6/19/72, 42.

202. *Detroit Free Press*, 11/16/72, 11/20/72, 11/23/72, in DFT Papers [inventoried 1/20/86], box 3, Miscellaneous Clippings; *Detroit News*, 11/21/72, in DFT Papers [inventoried 1/20/86], box 1, envelope 7; *Detroit News*, 10/9/72, 11/9/72, 11/22/72, 11/23/72, 12/6/72, 12/27/72, 12/28/72, 12/29/72, in DFT Papers, box 3, Miscellaneous Clippings; *Detroit Labor News*, 12/6/72; *Detroit Teacher*, February, 1973; *Superintendent's Pipeline*, 11/28/72, 1/23/73, 2/27/73; *Michigan Chronicle*, 11/18/72, 12/2/72, 12/9/72, 12/16/72, in DFT Papers [inventoried 1/20/86], box 3, Miscellaneous Clippings. The desperate straits of the system forced the DFT into yet another modest contract agreement, which ran until 1973. See *Detroit Free Press*, 5/29/72 and 6/14/72, in DFT Papers [inventoried 1/20/86], box 1, envelope 6; *Detroit News*, 6/14/72 and 8/31/72, in DFT Papers [inventoried 1/20/86], box 1, envelope 6; *Detroit News*, 9/5/72 and 9/6/72, in DFT Papers [inventoried 1/20/86], box 3, Miscellaneous Clippings; *Detroit Teacher*, September, 1972; *Superintendent's Pipeline*, 9/12/72.

203. The task force was chaired by Albert M. Pelham, a former city controller, and Stanley Winkelman, the head of Winkelman's Department Stores. Its executive director was Luvern Cunningham, dean of the College of Education of Ohio State University. See *Courier Newspapers*, 1/10/73, 3/21/73, 4/3/73, in DFT Papers [inventoried 1/20/86], box 1, envelope 6; *Community News–East Side Shopper*, 1/31/73, in DFT Papers [inventoried 1/20/86], box 1, envelope 6; *Detroit Free Press*, 2/7/73, 3/16/73, 4/20/73, 4/25/73, 5/23/75, 8/4/73, 7/5/75, in DFT Papers [inventoried 1/20/86], box 1, envelope 6; *Detroit News*, 12/2/72, in DFT Papers [inventoried 1/20/86], box 3, Miscellaneous Clippings; *Detroit News*, 2/6/73, 4/25/73, 5/25/73, 1/14/74, 5/28/75, in DFT Papers [inventoried 1/20/86], box 1, envelope 6; *Michigan Chronicle*, 2/10/73; James E. House, "Urban Educational Problems: Whose Responsibility?" *Educational Leadership* 32 (April, 1975): 437–40.

204. The proposal was jointly sponsored by the governor and the Michigan Education Association. It would have funneled more money to Detroit because it required the state to assume primary responsibility for educational funding and to distribute the funds more equitably. The proposal allowed districts to vote no more than 10.5 mills for education, 6.0 mills for enrichment, and 4.5 mills for special school operations. Since the average school tax levied across the state was 26.0 mills, the lost revenue would be made up by the legislature through other taxes, mostly likely an income tax. The amendment also demanded that the funds be distributed equally, to

assure "quality educational opportunity for all students." That provision would certainly have meant an increase in revenue for Detroit, which was still getting less than its fair share of state revenue. The proposal lost by a 58 to 42 percent margin. See *Detroit Free Press,* 10/29/72, 11/5/72, 11/6/72, in DFT Papers [inventoried 1/20/86], box 3, Miscellaneous Clippings; *Detroit News,* 9/22/72, 10/4/72, 10/22/72, 10/23/72, 10/31/72, 11/5/72, in DFT Papers [inventoried 1/20/86], box 3, Miscellaneous Clippings; *Detroit Labor News,* 10/18/72; William R. Grant, "Detroit School Finance: A Perils of Pauline Melodrama," *Phi Delta Kappan* 59 (February, 1978): 383; Citizens Research Council of Michigan, *School Finance Reform in Michigan* (Detroit: Citizens Research Council, 1989), 4; C. Philip Kearney, "The Courts: An Alternative to Solving Michigan's Current School Finance Crisis?" (unpublished paper, 1982, in my possession), 8.

205. *Detroit Free Press,* 12/1/72, 12/7/72, 12/14/72, in DFT Papers [inventoried 1/20/86], box 3, Miscellaneous Clippings; *Detroit News,* 8/28/73, in DFT Papers [inventoried 1/20/86], box 1, envelope 6; *Detroit News,* 8/21/73, in DFT Papers [inventoried 1/20/86], box 1, envelope 7; *Detroit Labor News,* 1/31/73; *Oakland Press,* 11/13/72, in DFT Papers [inventoried 1/20/86], box 3, Miscellaneous Clippings; Grant, "Detroit School Finance," 383. The legislator is quoted in "Detroit Schools Head Toward Disaster," 74.

206. The accusation that Detroiters did not adequately support their schools ignored the fact that, when all city taxes were totaled, Detroiters paid one of the highest rates in the state, approximately 70 mills. See *Detroit News,* 11/22/72 and 12/21/72, in DFT Papers [inventoried 1/20/86], box 3, Miscellaneous Clippings; *Detroit Labor News,* 1/31/73; *Michigan Chronicle,* 1/18/72, in DFT Papers [inventoried 1/20/86], box 3, Miscellaneous Clippings.

207. DBEP, 1973–74, 3–5, 73–77, 130–35, 198–99, 259–61, 401–3, 514; *Detroit Free Press,* 2/7/73 and 4/20/73, in DFT Papers [inventoried 1/20/86], box 1, envelope 6; *Detroit News,* 2/6/73 and 2/7/73, in DFT Papers [inventoried 1/20/86], box 1, envelope 6; *Detroit News,* 4/4/73, 6/6/73, in DFT Papers [inventoried 1/20/86], box 1, envelope 7; *Detroit Labor News,* 3/14/73; *Detroit Teacher,* 3/23/73; *Michigan Chronicle,* 2/24/73, 3/24/73, 6/2/73; *Superintendent's Pipeline,* 5/22/73; Grant, "Detroit School Finance," 383.

208. Roth, for example, feared that new school construction in specific areas of the city might increase segregation and he thus issued a moratorium on all school construction. Ironically, that order forced a number of black children to continue attending schools that were badly deteriorated. See *Detroit Free Press,* 6/9/71, in DFT Papers [inventoried 1/20/86], box 1, envelope 4; *Detroit News,* 6/9/71, in DFT Papers [inventoried 1/20/86], box 1, envelope 4; *Superintendent's Pipeline,* 6/8/71.

209. White, *Making of the President, 1972,* 241.

210. Carmen Roberts Biography File, in CR Papers; *Community News—East Side Shopper,* 1/31/73, in DFT Papers [inventoried 1/20/86], box 1, envelope 6; *Detroit News,* 4/4/73, in DFT Papers [inventoried 1/20/86], box 1, envelope 6; *Northeast Detroiter,* 9/6/73, in DFT Papers [inventoried 1/20/86], box 1, envelope 7.

211. *Detroit Free Press,* 1/9/72, in ND Papers, box 46, no folder; Harris, "Decentralization and Recentralization," 82.

212. DBEP, 1973–74, 47–51, 58, 69–71, 80, 159–60; *Detroit Free Press,* 7/12/73, 7/24/73, 7/25/73, 7/27/73, 8/15/73, 8/16/73, 9/4/73, 9/12/73, 9/13/73, in DFT Papers [inventoried 1/20/86], box 1, envelope 7; *Detroit News,* 7/12/73, 8/15/73, 9/1/73, 9/12/73, in DFT Papers [inventoried 1/20/86], box 1, envelope 7; *Detroit News,* 7/25/73, 8/2/73, 8/21/73, 8/28/73, 9/6/73, in DFT Papers [inventoried 1/20/86], box 1, envelope 6; *Detroit Labor News,* 8/8/73 and 8/29/73; *Michigan Catholic,* 9/5/73, in DFT Papers [inventoried 1/20/86], box 1, envelope 7; *Michigan Chronicle,* 7/21/73, 8/25/73, 9/1/73.

213. DBEP, 1973–74, 159–60; *Detroit Free Press,* 9/12/73 and 9/13/73, in DFT Papers

[inventoried 1/20/86], box 1, envelope 7; *Detroit News,* 9/8/73 and 9/12/73, in DFT Papers [inventoried 1/20/86], box 1, envelope 7; *Northeast Detroiter,* 7/19/73, 8/9/73, 9/6/73, in DFT Papers [inventoried 1/20/86], box 1, envelope 7.

214. DBEP, 1973–74, 374–77; *Detroit News,* 3/15/74 and 3/20/74, in DFT Papers [inventoried 1/20/86], box 1, envelope 7; *Northeast Detroiter,* 1/3/74, in DPS Archives, Schools in the News binder.

215. DBEP, 1973–74, 427, 469; *Detroit Free Press,* 2/28/74, 3/3/74, 3/11/74, 3/16/74, 3/17/74, 3/18/74, in DFT Papers [inventoried 1/20/86], box 1, envelope 7; *Detroit News,* 3/20/74, in DFT Papers [inventoried 1/20/86], box 1, envelope 7; *Detroit News,* 2/20/74, 3/3/74, 3/18/74, in DFT Papers [inventoried 1/20/86], box 1, envelope 7; *Detroit Labor News,* 2/28/74, 3/7/74, 3/14/74, 3/21/74; *Michigan Chronicle,* 2/16/74 and 3/9/74, in DPS Archives, Schools in the News binder; *Michigan Chronicle,* 3/16/74, in DFT Papers [inventoried 1/20/86], box 1, envelope 7; *Superintendent's Pipeline,* 2/26/74.

216. *Northeast Detroiter,* 2/7/74, in DFT Papers [inventoried 1/20/86], box 2, Schools in the News folder; DBEP, 1973–74, 502; *Northeast Detroiter,* 3/14/74, in DFT Papers [inventoried 1/20/86], box 1, envelope 7; *Detroit Free Press,* 3/21/74, in DFT Papers [inventoried 1/20/86], box 1, envelope 7; *Detroit News,* 3/20/74 and 3/21/74, in DFT Papers [inventoried 1/20/86], box 1, envelope 7.

217. A revision of the law giving the board the power to levy the income tax allowed the board to reimpose the tax if the level of local support dropped below 24.76 mills. Because the August proposal called for an increase rather than a renewal, the board did not have the power to reimpose the tax if the measure failed. See *Detroit Free Press,* 3/7/74, in DFT Papers [inventoried 1/20/86], box 2, Schools in the News folder; *Detroit Free Press,* 3/15/74 and 3/18/74, in DFT Papers [inventoried 1/20/86], box 1, envelope 7; *Detroit News,* 3/15/74, in DFT Papers [inventoried 1/20/86], box 1, envelope 7; Grant, "Detroit School Finance," 384.

218. DBEP, 1973–74, 578–600, 608; *Detroit News,* 3/15/74 and 3/20/74, in DFT Papers [inventoried 1/20/86], box 1, envelope 7; *Detroit News,* 4/30/74 and 7/2/74, in DPS Archives, Schools in the News binder; *Detroit Labor News,* 4/18/74; *Detroit Teacher,* 4/8/74, 4/22/74, 5/13/74.

219. DBEP, 1973–74, 687–89, 722; DBEP, 1974–75, 17–18; *Detroit Free Press,* 6/1/74, 6/4/74, 6/23/74, 7/31/74, 8/1/74, in DFT Papers [inventoried 1/20/86], box 1, envelope 7; *Detroit News,* 5/29/74, 6/1/74, 7/3/74, 7/19/74, 7/29/74, 7/30/74, 7/31/74, in DFT Papers [inventoried 1/20/86], box 1, envelope 7; *Detroit Teacher,* 7/1/74; *Michigan Chronicle,* 6/15/74 and 8/3/74, in DFT Papers [inventoried 1/20/86], box 1, envelope 7; WXYZ Radio Editorial, 6/18–19/74, in DPS Archives, Schools in the News binder; WWJ Radio Editorial, in DPS Archives, Schools in the News binder.

220. This is the first election that I came across in which the issues of the chauffeur-driven cars and board travel were important issues. In 1974, the estimates of the cost of the cars was about $200,000 and the travel was about $150,000 annually. See *Detroit Free Press,* 7/2/74, in DPS Archives, Schools in the News binder; *Detroit Free Press,* 7/6/74, in DFT Papers [inventoried 1/20/86], box 1, envelope 7; *Detroit News,* 6/15/74, in DFT Papers [inventoried 1/20/86], box 1, envelope 8; *Northeast Detroiter,* 6/6/74, in DFT Papers [inventoried 1/20/86], box 1, envelope 7; *Suburban Newspapers,* 7/4–10/74, in DFT Papers [inventoried 1/20/86], box 1, envelope 8.

221. George T. Roumell, Jr., letter to Dr. Golightly and Ladies and Gentlemen of the Detroit Board of Education, 7/25/74, in DPS/DCR Papers, ser. 2, box 15, folder 7.

222. DBEP, 1974–75, 55–56; *Detroit News,* 8/7/74, in DFT Papers [inventoried 1/20/86], box 2, Schools in the News folder; *Northeast Detroiter,* 8/15/74, in DFT Papers [inventoried 1/20/86], box 1, envelope 7.

223. DBEP, 1974–75, 498–501, 537–38; Grant, "Letter from Detroit," 145.

224. *Detroit Free Press,* 1/17/75, 2/13/75, 3/16/75, 3/23/75, in DFT Papers [inventoried 1/20/86], box 1, envelope 4; *Detroit Free Press,* 4/3/75, in ND Papers, box 50, no folder; *Detroit News,* 12/5/74, 3/15/75, 3/18/75, 6/29/75, in DFT Papers [inventoried 1/20/86], box 1, envelope 4; *Detroit News,* 4/7/75, in DFT Papers [inventoried 1/20/86], box 1, envelope 7; *Michigan Chronicle,* 12/21/74, in DFT Papers [inventoried 1/20/86], box 1, envelope 7.

225. *Detroit News,* 3/15/75 and 5/3/75, in DFT Papers [inventoried 1/20/86], box 1, envelope 4; *Detroit News,* 5/14/75, in ND Papers, box 50, no folder. The NAACP appeared unphased by these criticisms. Roy Wilkins stated that Mayor Young's statements were similar to those made "by the worst Southern racists." Other NAACP leaders dismissed the "white flight" argument as self-fulfilling prophecy. See *Detroit Free Press,* 6/28/75, in DFT Papers [inventoried 1/20/86], box 1, envelope 4; *Detroit News,* 5/21/75, in DFT Papers [inventoried 1/20/86], box 1, envelope 4. A survey of 1,000 blacks in two cities done at about the same time found that 56 percent of the respondents had "negative feelings toward busing." See William J. Wilson, Castellano B. Turner, and William A. Darity, "Racial Solidarity and Separate Education," *Social Review* 81 (May, 1973): 366–68.

226. *Detroit Free Press,* 4/7/75, in ND Papers, box 50, no folder; *Detroit News,* 3/15/75, in DFT Papers [inventoried 1/20/86], box 1, envelope 4; Grant, "Letter from Detroit," 147, 151.

227. Grant, "Letter from Detroit," 145.

228. DBEP, 1975–76, 148–54, 254–55, 278–82, 313–14, 341–48; *Detroit News,* 9/19/75, in DFT Papers [inventoried 1/20/86], box 2, Schools in the News folder; *Detroit Teacher,* 9/16/75, 10/21/75, 11/18/75, 1/13/76; Arthur Jefferson, "Detroit's Educational Renaissance," *Crisis* 86 (March, 1979): 88. The NAACP official is quoted in Eleanor P. Wolf, "Northern School Desegregation and Residential Choice," in *The Supreme Court Review, 1977,* ed. George B. Kurland and Gerhard Caspar (Chicago: University of Chicago Press, 1978), 84; Roger L. Webb, "A Study of the Socio-Political Process that Preceded and Followed the Federal Court Order Calling for Remedies to Post-Desegregation Problems: Detroit, 1975" (Ph.D. diss., University of Michigan, 1978), 56.

229. DBEP, 1975–76, 278; *Detroit Teacher,* 6/12/75 and 1/13/76; William R. Grant, "Detroit," *Integrated Education* 15 (November-December, 1977), 3; Webb, "Study of the Socio-Political Process," 55–58.

230. DBEP, 1976–77, 772–73; *Detroit Free Press,* 3/22/77 and 6/28/77, in DFT Papers [inventoried 1/20/86], box 1, envelope 5; *Detroit News,* 6/28/77, in DFT Papers [inventoried 1/20/86], box 1, envelope 5; Thomas J. Flygare, "Federal Desegregation Decrees and Compensatory Education," *Phi Delta Kappan* 59 (December, 1977): 265–66; Jefferson, "Detroit's Educational Renaissance," 89; Merrill Sheils, Christopher Ma, and James C. Jones, "Tale of Two Cities," *Newsweek,* 7/11/77, 54; Yudoff et al., *Educational Policy and the Law,* 476–78.

231. DBEP, 1975–76, 399–402; *Detroit Free Press,* 2/1/76, 2/6/76, 2/9/76, in ND Papers, box 50, no folder; *Detroit Free Press,* 3/9/76, in DFT Papers [inventoried 1/20/86], box 1, envelope 1; *Detroit News,* 3/17/76 and 3/19/76, in DFT Papers [inventoried 1/20/86], box 1, envelope 1; *Michigan Chronicle,* 2/7/76, in ND Papers, box 5, no folder; Kathleen Straus and Scott Schrager, "PRO-Detroit: A Pragmatic Approach to School Desegregation," *Theory into Practice* 17 (February, 1978): 86; Metropolitan Coalition for Peaceful Integration, "What's It All About" (typescript, 1972), in DFT Papers [inventoried 1/20/86], box 2, Metro Coalition folder.

232. Grant, "Detroit," 2; Merrill Sheils and James C. Jones, "Smooth Ride in Detroit," *Newsweek,* 2/9/76, 45.

233. *Eastside Shopper and Community News,* 1/27–2/2/71, in DFT Papers [inventoried 1/20/86], box 1, envelope 4.

234. The emerging "urban populism" that first found its voice in the George Wallace campaigns and, later, in the Nixon and Reagan campaigns was deeply rooted in opposition to "liberal elitists."

See, for example, John Warnock, letter to Carmen Roberts, 1/1/76, in CR Papers, Correspondence 1973–76; *Northeast Detroiter*, 11/20/75, in CR Papers, Correspondence 1973–76.

235. *Detroit News*, 2/16/76, in DFT Papers [inventoried 1/20/86], box 1, envelope 8; Fine, *Violence*, 489.

236. Detroit Board of Education, *Detroit Public School Statistics, 1980–81*, pt. 1 (Detroit: Board of Education, 1981), 607; Harris, "Decentralization and Recentralization," 80. Parochial and private school enrollment fell from 88,266 in 1963 to 53,850 in 1970 and to 30,763 in 1980. Detroit Board of Education, *Detroit Public School Statistics, 1964–65* (Detroit: Board of Education, 1965), 697; Detroit Board of Education, *Detroit Public School Statistics, 1971–72*, pt. 2 (Detroit: Board of Education, 1972), 511; Board of Education, *School Statistics, 1980–81*, 183. On the issue of white flight and desegregation, see Clotfelter, "Detroit Decision," 99–112; Orfield, *Must We Bus?* 91–94, 99–101; Diane Ravitch, "The 'White Flight' Controversy," in *The Public Interest on Education*, ed. Nathan Glazer (Cambridge, MA: Adt Associates, 1984), 93–107.

237. Wolf, "Northern School Desegregation," 85.

238. *Detroit Free Press*, 2/10/71, in DFT Papers [inventoried 1/20/86], box 1, envelope 1; *Detroit News*, 2/10/71, in DFT Papers [inventoried 1/20/86], box 1, envelope 1; *Michigan Chronicle*, 11/28/71, 3/20/71, 5/27/71, 7/24/71; Berkowitz, "Analysis," 137–74; Harris, "Decentralization and Recentralization," 105–23.

239. *Michigan Chronicle*, 3/8/69; DBEP, 1971–72, 226–27; Amos Wilder, "Client Criticism of Urban Schools: How Valid?" *Phi Delta Kappan* 51 (November, 1969): 130. An excellent discussion of the accountability issue in Detroit, based on extensive interviews with the participants, can be found in Thomas E. Glass and William D. Sanders, *Community Control in Education: A Study of Power in Transition* (Midland, MI: Pendell Publishing, 1978), 65– 106.

240. Ravitch, *Great School Wars*, 292–378.

241. *Michigan Chronicle*, 3/1/69.

242. DBEP, 1973–74, 107. See also *Christian Science Monitor*, 10/20/73, in DFT Papers [inventoried 1/20/86], box 2, Schools in the News folder; *Detroit Free Press*, 9/20/73, in DFT Papers [inventoried 1/20/86], box 2, Schools in the News folder; *Detroit News*, 6/17/71, in DFT Papers [inventoried 1/20/86], box 3, Miscellaneous Clippings; *Detroit Teacher*, 11/26/73; *Michigan Chronicle*, 3/24/73.

243. *Detroit Teacher*, 11/26/73; Mary Ellen Riordan, "Residency: Detroit Federation of Teachers Position Paper, June 1974," in DFT Papers [inventoried 12/24/85], box 1, Residency folder no. 1; see also DBEP, 1973–74, 406–7; Detroit NAACP, "Position on Residency for Detroit Board of Education Employees, April 16, 1973," in DFT Papers [inventoried 12/24/85], box 1, Residency folder no. 3.

244. Harris, "Decentralization and Recentralization," 81, 165–69.

245. Board of Education, *School Statistics, 1975–76*, 263. Even within the union there was dissension between an integrated group of more radical union members and the equally integrated majority of more moderate union members. On divisions within the union over these issues, see Zeline Richards Oral History Transcript, 15, 21, 29, 36, in ALHUA.

246. In a statement to the Republican Platform Committee in August 1976, Carmen Roberts stated that she was "for more accountability by administrators and teachers, for paying teachers on the basis of performance, against teacher tenure, against student privileges and against busing for racial integration" (Carmen Roberts, "Speech to the Republican Platform Committee, August 10, 1976," in CR Papers, Speeches folder). See also Northeast Mothers Alert, "Brief in Support of Petition of Intervention, April 17, 1975," 8, 9, in CR Papers, box 1, NEMA-Antibusing folder.

247. DBEP, 1971–72, 114, 225–27, 257–58, 269–70, 291–93, 690–91, 754–55, 774–75; *Detroit Free Press*, 7/17/71, in DFT Papers [inventoried 1/20/86], box 3, Clipping folder; *Detroit*

News, 2/25/71 and 3/27/71, in DFT Papers [inventoried 1/20/86], box 3, Clipping folder; *Detroit News*, 5/18/71, 6/23/71, 7/18/71, in DFT Papers [inventoried 1/20/86], box 1, envelope 6; *Detroit Teacher*, 2/8/71, 2/22/71, 9/23/71, 10/27/71; *Michigan Chronicle*, 3/13/71. Moore is quoted in *Michigan Chronicle*, 6/12/71, in DFT Papers [inventoried 1/20/86], box 3, Miscellaneous Clippings. Irwin, *Ghetto Principal Speaks Out*, 104–6.

248. *Detroit Free Press*, 3/27/73, 6/24/73, 8/28/73, in DFT Papers [inventoried 1/20/86], box 3, Miscellaneous Clippings; *Detroit News*, 8/25/73, in DFT Papers [inventoried 1/20/86], box 3, Miscellaneous Clippings; Harris, "Decentralization and Recentralization," 166–67.

249. *Michigan Chronicle*, 1/6/73; *Last Man Free*, March, 1973, in DFT Papers [inventoried 1/7/86], box 7, Community Control folder; *Detroit Free Press*, 9/8/73, in DFT Papers [inventoried 1/20/86], box 2, Schools in the News folder. See also L. Haitn, letter to F. Kornegay, 10/5/72, in DUL Papers, box 83, Miscellaneous folder.

250. *Detroit Free Press*, 9/8/73, in DFT Papers [inventoried 1/20/86], box 2, Schools in the News folder. The DFT argued that, under the McCutcheon plan, the only appeal a teacher with a negative evaluation had was to the school board. In other words, no case had to be presented against an allegedly incompetent teacher. In addition, the principal could dismiss a teacher on the ground that the "community found the teacher unacceptable" (Detroit Federation of Teachers, "McCutcheon's Bludgeon" [leaflet, 1973] in DFT Papers [inventoried 1/17/86], box 2, 1973 Strike folder). Not all DFT members, however, supported the union on this issue. In March, 1974, a dissident group of teachers published a proresidency tract that declared, "Are there good reasons for selecting teachers only from the city? We think so. After all, our schools were established by the business/industry controlled political powers of the past and because of this they necessarily stand in contradiction to many of the basic needs and interests of neighborhoods" (*Intercomm* 1 [March 1974]: 5, in DFT Papers [inventoried 12/24/85], box 1, Residency folder no. 1).

251. DBEP, 1973–74, 103–10, 113, 163–65, 170, 175–78; *Detroit Free Press*, 9/6/73, in DPS Archives, Schools in the News binder; *Detroit News*, 9/2/73, 9/3/73, 9/4/73, 9/5/73; *Detroit News*, 9/18/73, in DPS Archives, Schools in the News binder; *Detroit Labor News*, 9/5/73 and 9/12/73; *Michigan Chronicle*, 9/29/73 and 10/6/73.

252. *Detroit Labor News*, 10/10/73; *Michigan Chronicle*, 10/13/73 and 10/17/73.

253. *Christian Science Monitor*, 10/20/73, in DFT Papers [inventoried 1/20/86], box 2, Schools in the News folder; *Detroit Free Press*, 10/21/73, in DFT Papers [inventoried 1/20/86], box 2, Schools in the News folder; *Detroit News*, 10/18/73, in DFT Papers [inventoried 1/20/86], box 3, Miscellaneous Clippings; *Detroit News*, 10/19/73, in DPS Archives, Schools in the News binder; *Detroit Labor News*, 10/17/73 and 10/24/73; *Detroit Teacher*, 10/29/73, 11/26/73, 1/14/74; *Michigan Chronicle*, 10/20/73.

254. DBEP, 1973–74, 328–29; *Michigan Chronicle*, 10/20/73, 10/27/73, 11/3/73, 11/10/73.

255. Moore is quoted in *Detroit News*, 2/13/74, in DFT Papers [inventoried 1/20/86], box 2, Schools in the News folder. The argument that residency would provide more jobs for Detroiters put forth by Moore and others in the 1970s is quite similar to the position that Edward Williams urged in the 1930s with strong support from the Detroit Federation of Labor. In the 1970s, however, the arguments had a strong racial rather than class component. Proponents of the residency requirement in the 1970s argued that if jobs in the school system were reserved for Detroit residents, more minorities would be employed. They also claimed that if all employees of the system lived in the city, their property taxes would boost revenues for the schools and their votes would help swing school millage elections. See DBEP, 1971–72, 226–27, 690, 754, 775–76; *Detroit Free Press*, 2/13/73, in DFT Papers [inventoried 1/20/86], box 3, Miscellaneous Clippings; *Detroit News*, 4/19/72 and 6/27/72, in DFT Papers [inventoried 1/20/86], box 3, Miscellaneous Clippings; *Michigan Chronicle*, 3/8/69; *Shrine of the Black Madonna Newsletter*, 10/30/70, in DFT Papers [inventoried 1/7/86], box 7, Community Control folder; Detroit Coali-

tion for School Employees District Residency, "Press Release, May 22, 1972," in DFT Papers [inventoried 12/24/85], box 1, Residency folder no. 1; Detroit Coalition for School Employees District Residency, "Press Release, April 2 1973," in DFT Papers [inventoried 12/24/85], box 1, Residency folder no. 1; Detroit Coalition for School Employees District Residency, "To the Members of the Detroit Board of Education, January 22, 1974," in DFT Papers [inventoried 12/24/85], box 1, Residency folder no. 3.

256. For a sample of some of the debate, see DBEP, 1973–74, 388–93, 406–7, 421–23, 451–52; *Detroit Free Press,* 2/15/74, in DPS Archives, Schools in the News binder; *Detroit News,* 2/3/74, in DFT Papers [inventoried 1/7/86], box 3, Miscellaneous Clippings; *Detroit News,* 2/11/74, 2/13/74, in DFT Papers [inventoried 1/7/86], box 2, Schools in the News folder; *Detroit Teacher,* 2/11/74; Detroit Coalition, "To the Board of Education."

257. Martin Kalish, "The Bates, Rutherford, Quinn Axis and the New Central Board of Education" (typescript, 1974), 2–3; *Detroit News,* 3/5/74, in DFT Papers [inventoried 1/7/86], box 2, Schools in the News folder. See also *Detroit Free Press,* 3/14/74, in DFT Papers [inventoried 12/24/85], box 1, Residency folder no. 1.

258. DBEP, 1973–74, 490–94; *Detroit Free Press,* 10/29/74 and 2/10/75, in DFT Papers [inventoried 1/20/86], box 3, Miscellaneous Clippings; *Detroit Free Press,* 1/30/75, in DFT Papers [inventoried 12/24/85], box 1, Residency folder no. 1; *Detroit News,* 10/29/74, 1/29/75, 1/30/75, in DFT Papers [inventoried 1/20/86], box 3, Miscellaneous Clippings; *Detroit Teacher,* 2/25/74, 3/25/74, 5/13/74, 7/1/74, 2/24/75, 10/21/75, 11/4/75; *Superintendent's Pipeline,* 2/12/74 and 3/12/74, in DFT Papers [inventoried 12/24/85], box 1, Residency folder no. 1.

259. *Michigan Chronicle,* 10/20/73, 10/27/73, 11/3/73, 11/10/73; *Detroit News,* 10/19/73, in DFT Papers [inventoried 1/20/86], box 3, Miscellaneous Clippings; Joe Stroud, "Can Schools Recover from the Strike?" *Detroit Free Press,* 10/22/73, in DFT Papers [inventoried 1/20/86], box 2, Schools in the News folder.

260. Helen P. Moore, letter to the Detroit Board of Education, 12/17/73, in DFT Papers [inventoried 1/7/86], box 7, Community Control folder

261. DBEP, 1974–75, 371–76, 383–85; DBEP, 1976–77, 205; *Detroit Free Press,* 1/21/75 and 5/8/75, in DFT Papers [inventoried 1/20/86], box 1, envelope 1; *Detroit Free Press,* 1/30/75, in DFT Papers [inventoried 1/20/86], box 3, Miscellaneous Clippings; *Detroit News,* 2/26/74, in DFT Papers [inventoried 1/20/86], box 1, envelope 1; *Detroit News,* 1/8/75, 1/9/75, 1/10/75, 1/15/75, 8/14/75, in DFT Papers [inventoried 1/20/86], box 3, Miscellaneous Clippings; *Detroit News,* 10/13/76, in DFT Papers [inventoried 1/20/86], box 1, envelope 5; *Detroit News,* 11/23/77, in DFT Papers [inventoried 1/20/86], box 1, envelope 3; *Detroit Teacher,* 3/25/74, 5/12/75, 6/12/75, 3/9/76, 4/6/76, 1/26/77; *Michigan Chronicle,* 1/25/75, in DFT Papers [inventoried 1/20/86], box 3, Miscellaneous Clippings; *Michigan Chronicle,* 5/17/75, in DFT Papers [inventoried 1/20/86], box 1, envelope 1; Grant, "Letter from Detroit," 147. Truancy was also high during this period. In 1972–73, the truancy rate in Detroit was twice that of a decade earlier. Indeed, despite a decline in the total number of students in the district, in 1972–73, the schools were annually investigating over 9,000 *more* reports of truancy than in 1963–64. See *Detroit Free Press,* 1/14/78, in DFT Papers [inventoried 1/20/86], box 3, Miscellaneous Clippings; *Detroit News,* 1/24/74, in DPS Archives, Schools in the News binder; *Detroit News,* 10/12/77, in DFT Papers [inventoried 1/20/86], box 3, Miscellaneous Clippings.

262. On the various tests given to Detroit students and the scores, see Harris, "Decentralization and Recentralization," 144–46; see also, DBEP, 1976–77, 130–31.

263. DBEP, 1975–76, 759–62; DBEP, 1976–77, 39–40, 69–72, 123–26, 160–61, 166–67, 199, 249–42; *Detroit Free Press,* 9/1/76, in CR Papers, June-December, 1976 Clippings folder; *Detroit Free Press,* 11/19/76 and 11/21/76, in DFT Papers [inventoried 1/20/86], box 1, envelope 5; *Detroit News,* 3/21/76, in DFT Papers [inventoried 1/20/86], box 1, envelope 7; *Detroit News,* 7/8/76 and 11/9/76, in CR Papers, June-December, 1976 Clippings folder; *Detroit News,*

9/29/76, 11/19/76, 11/22/76, in DFT Papers [inventoried 1/20/86], box 1, envelope 5; *Detroit Teacher,* 10/13/76 and 11/27/76; Jefferson, "Detroit's Educational Renaissance," 89; Grant, "Detroit School Finance," 383–84; Harris, Decentralization and Recentralization," 175–85.

264. Compounding this educational crisis was another fiscal disaster brought about by the defeat of two millage proposals in August and November 1976. The millage defeats forced the board to trim the already tight budget even further. See DBEP, 1975–76, 278–79; *Detroit News,* 6/3/77, in DFT Papers [inventoried 1/20/86], box 3, Miscellaneous Clippings; *Detroit Teacher,* 11/24/76.

265. Arthur Jefferson was a product of the Detroit schools who rose through the ranks to become superintendent. A graduate of Northeastern High School, Jefferson earned his B.A. in 1960, M.A. in 1963, and Ed.D. in 1973 from Wayne State University. He became Interim Superintendent in June, 1975, and General Superintendent later that year. Prior to assuming the general superintendency, he served as a regional superintendent. On Jefferson, see DBEP, 1975–76, 2–5; *Detroit News,* 6/6/75, in ND Papers, box 50, no folder; *Detroit Public School Reporter,* September, 1975, December, 1975; *Detroit Teacher,* 11/18/75; *Michigan Chronicle,* 6/14/75, in ND Papers, box 50, no folder. On the "Call to Action," see DBEP, 1976–77, 401–5, 563–64; *Detroit Teacher,* 2/9/77; Jefferson, "Detroit's Educational Renaissance," 89–94.

266. *Detroit Teacher,* 3/23/76, 6/1/76, 5/1/77, 5/25/77; *Michigan Chronicle,* 3/4/78, in DPS Archives, Schools in the News binder. The analyst is quoted in Harris, "Decentralization and Recentralization," 215, 187–94.

267. Harris, "Decentralization and Recentralization," 197–204, 218, 215–29.

268. *New York Times,* 11/30/72, in ND Papers, box 12, General Clippings folder.

269. On Robinson's question, see *Detroit News,* 4/6/69; Horace Mann, "Twelfth Annual Report," in *The Republic and the School: Horace Mann on the Education of Free Men,* ed. Lawrence Cremin (New York: Teachers College Press, 1957), 94.

270. Joseph Featherstone, "The Problem is More than Schools," *New Republic,* 8/30/69, 22.

Epilogue

In November, 1987, while visiting Chicago, U.S. Secretary of Education William Bennett declared that its schools were the "worst in America." Citing a 43 percent high school dropout rate and the "dismal" performance by Chicago students on nationally standardized tests, Bennett described the situation as close to "educational meltdown." Sadly, his assessment would have been equally valid if he had been discussing Detroit, Cleveland, Los Angeles, or any of the large urban school systems in the nation.[1]

This book began with a question directly related to Bennett's assessment—what caused urban public schools to change from among the best in the nation early in this century to among the worst in the nation today? The history of a single school system, even one as representative as Detroit's, cannot answer that question definitively. Yet this study does provide some insights into the process of decline. First among these is that none of the current interpretations of urban educational history adequately explains the transformation of the Detroit schools.

While some elements of the revisionist model, for example, are sustained by developments in the Motor City, this study challenges many of the basic tenets of that interpretation. Elite control of the at-large board of education in Detroit did not overturn the schools' democratic mission, spread alienation, or encourage overt dissatisfaction with the system. Indeed, between 1917 and 1931, the years of strongest control by elite board members and educational experts, all the major interest groups in the city, including the Communist and Socialist parties, the Detroit Federation of Labor, the growing immigrant communities, the Board of Commerce, and the Citizens League, strongly backed expanding and improving the schools. These groups may have sought different and, at times, contradictory things from public

399

education, but all of them were committed to maintaining high quality schools in Detroit.

Just as revisionist arguments are not borne out by developments in Detroit, neither are some aspects of the antirevisionist stance. Evidence from Detroit unquestionably supports the argument that a major factor in the deterioration of urban schools was the decline in quality of secondary education. Yet the mechanisms that were instrumental to that deterioration, the differentiated curriculum and the class and racial biases of educators, are associated more with revisionist works than antirevisionist ones. Where both revisionist and antirevisionist scholars err, however, is in their common failure to recognize the importance of the general track (rather than tracking or vocational education per se) as the primary vehicle for the dilution of academic standards and the increase in educational inequality.

Educators in Detroit responded to the collapse of the youth labor market in the 1930s and to the influx of black students in the post–World War II years by steering many of these students into the general track, in essence using it as a "warehouse" for unemployed youth. The nature and function of high schools thus changed from institutions primarily preparing young people for college and skilled work to institutions designed to keep teenagers out of the labor market. As educators embraced that custodial mission by diluting educational standards and introducing supposedly relevant and practical courses, urban public schools began to slide into what Arthur Bestor called the educational wasteland.[2] No groups were more damaged by these developments than working-class and minority youth.

The arguments of postrevisionist scholars that schools are "contested terrain" are also supported to some extent by the history of the Detroit schools. Yet as with the other interpretations, events in the Motor City demand a reconsideration of at least the claim made by Katznelson and Weir that in the 1930s working-class organizations abandoned their commitment to urban public education. From the early 1930s to the mid-1960s, precisely the opposite occurred in Detroit, as organized labor played an increasingly prominent role in educational politics. Katznelson and Weir are correct in seeing the collapse of white working-class support for public education as a key development in the political decline of urban schools, but so far as Detroit is concerned, they miss both the timing of that development and its primary cause. Rather than occurring because of the "domestication" of organized labor in the 1930s, white working-class support of the Detroit schools collapsed in the mid-1960s and early 1970s primarily because this group opposed racial desegregation and higher taxes for the predominantly black school system.

The racial transformation of Detroit and its schools has also encouraged two other explanations for the decline of urban education that are rarely addressed by historians but certainly are abroad in the land. First is the reductionist, racist assertion that the once great urban school systems went downhill when blacks moved in and whites moved out. This study flatly contradicts that claim. The Detroit public schools began to deteriorate politically, financially, and educationally as early as the 1930s, a period in which school leadership, staff, and student populations were overwhelmingly white. Similarly, some black nationalists argue that Detroit and its schools declined because of a wide-ranging white racist conspiracy. That theory is equally suspect. Substantial black voter turnout and support, for example, in the crucial millage elections of the late 1960s and early 1970s would have ensured passage of the tax increases and spared the system from the crushing fiscal crises of those years. When considering the decline of the Detroit schools, there is, as Judge Roth noted, enough blame for everyone to share.[3]

If none of these interpretations adequately explains what occurred in Detroit, what does? This study points to at least two factors that historians of urban education have sidestepped but must consider in exploring the decline of urban public schools—resources and politics. As I noted at the beginning of the book, studies showing that levels of funding have little correlation to school achievement appear to have persuaded historians to ignore questions of resources and finances in explaining the modern history of urban school systems. Correlating spending and achievement is outside the scope of this study. Yet this study does demonstrate a strong relationship between levels of funding, the intensity of political conflict, and the viability of the school system itself. Severe shortages of funds at key periods in the history of the Detroit schools created serious fiscal problems that exacerbated battles between major interest groups, weakened political coalitions in support of public schools, and, ultimately, shook the moral foundation of the system. One cannot understand the rise and fall of the Detroit schools without factoring in the effects of shifting levels of funding.

At no time was this relationship clearer than during the Great Depression and World War II. The economic crises of these years generated battles over school finance that shattered the consensus of the 1920s. Business leaders forced city and school leaders into major budget cuts, in turn forcing educators into painful choices that had debilitating long-term effects on the

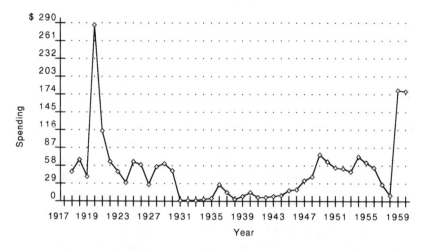

Fig. 1. Per pupil capital spending, 1917–59. (Amounts are given in 1967 dollars.)

system. These effects were particularly severe in the area of capital expenditures. Unlike the operating budget, which rebounded by the early 1940s, the capital budget remained moribund throughout most of the 1930s and 1940s. As figure 1 shows, except for a brief rise in 1936–37, between 1931 and 1947 per pupil expenditures on construction were but a shadow of previous years' spending. During these years, the board's decision to defer maintenance and construction was a reasonable response to the fiscal crises caused by the depression and war. By the late 1940s, however, as a result of this neglect, the school system's physical plant was in utter disrepair. It was challenge enough for school leaders to find funds to renovate decaying schools in the older neighborhoods of the city. But as tens of thousands of baby boomers reached school age and as large numbers of families moved to the burgeoning neighborhoods in the outer areas of the city, school leaders had to locate funds literally to build, from the ground up, another school system almost equal to the one constructed during the halcyon days of the 1920s.

   The capital budget problem was complicated by a fierce struggle between the school board and the teachers' union over salaries, which had not kept pace with postwar inflation. Conflicts about placing spending priorities on buildings or salaries became a defining feature of postwar educational politics. Unable to adequately fund both of these vital components of the educational enterprise, school leaders had to choose between two equally important priorities, knowing full well that either choice would exacerbate political problems and damage the system. Unfortunately, even in relatively good financial times, the issue of salaries versus buildings remained, and, as the Detroit Federation of Teachers gained power, the board's ability to balance these competing priorities diminished.

Insufficient funds also contributed to mounting racial tensions in the city. Children from Detroit's growing African-American community attended the oldest and most run-down schools in the district. Faced with limited capital funds and the need for new schools in the outer sections of the city, school officials allowed buildings in the ghetto to deteriorate as they scrambled to build new schools for whites. While school leaders justified these actions by claiming that black children at least had schools to go to, the dreary, crumbling structures in the ghetto became daily reminders for black Detroiters of their separate and unequal status in the city and the schools. The lack of capital funds ensured that black children would study in the worst buildings in the city, and the persistent failure of school officials to address the miserable conditions in these schools became one of the main issues behind the civil rights protests in the 1950s and 1960s.

Rather than occupying a separate political sphere, since the 1930s, these battles over school finance and resource allocation have become deeply intertwined with American politics writ large. During the depression, the elite-dominated educational consensus of the 1920s split cleanly along the emerging fault lines of the New Deal realignment. Educational politics became another arena of social, class, and partisan conflict; debates about funding for the public schools paralleled raging national struggles about the proper size and role of government. As the economy collapsed, the conservative, business-oriented interest groups that had strongly supported greater funding for the schools in the 1920s abandoned that commitment and demanded major cuts in education budgets to keep the city from bankruptcy. Liberals and labor leaders, on the other hand, fought to maintain funding levels because they believed the schools were providing a vital public service in a time of economic and social crisis.

These divisions deepened in Detroit following the triumph of the United Auto Workers in the Flint Sit-down Strike of 1937. The opposing stands taken by business and labor leaders on educational issues in the early 1930s quickly became integrated, in the 1940s and early 1950s, into the larger political struggles between capital and labor. On both the local and the state levels in the 1940s, educational politics in Detroit and Michigan were as fierce and divisive as they had been during the Great Depression.

Only in the late 1950s did the intense political feuding subside. As school and civic leaders began to face the enormous problem of educating the baby boomers, the dominant interest groups again set aside their differences and sought a new political consensus on public education. Unlike the elite-dominated efforts of the 1920s, however, this new consensus was led by a coalition of liberal, labor, and black organizations.

Formed in the late 1940s, the liberal-labor-black coalition came to power in the late 1950s and, by the mid-1960s, its leaders had transformed the Detroit public school system into a national leader in interracial educational progress. The coalition succeeded, in large part, for the same reasons that the earlier elite-dominated consensus succeeded—the major interest groups shared a vision of the public schools broad enough to satisfy all concerned. These individuals and groups firmly believed that the school system would thrive if they raised revenues, substantially increased the numbers of black teachers and administrators, integrated the administration and faculty of all schools in the district, strengthened the teachers union, implemented a more multicultural curriculum, and eliminated the most egregious manifestations of racial segregation among students. By 1970, almost all of these goals had been achieved, but the coalition was in shambles, a victim of a declining local economy, fractious racial politics, and the emergence of what Kevin Phillips called the new Republican majority.

Just as educational politics divided along pro– and anti–New Deal lines in the 1930s, so in the late 1960s educational politics in Detroit fractured along the racial and ideological lines that have come to characterize American politics in the last part of this century. The liberal-labor-black coalition collapsed primarily because two important constituent groups, a large contingent of working-class whites and a small but vocal group of militant blacks, rejected the coalition's sustaining vision of a common, integrated school system. As noted earlier, white working-class Detroiters abandoned their commitment to the city schools because of their opposition to integration, and they struck a major blow against the school system by opposing higher school taxes. Black nationalists struck the second major blow by advocating the adoption of separatist policies and practices within the system. Partially achieving their goals through the decentralization of the system, the separatists inevitably clashed with school administrators and teachers who feared that race and politics would become determining factors in pedagogical issues. These confrontations ripped apart the fragile bonds between educators, parents, and students and contributed to the collapse of moral authority within the schools themselves. If the actions of the white working class pushed the system toward financial ruin, the black nationalists contributed to its political dissolution. Having abandoned the vision of a common, integrated school system, both of these groups vied for the power to impose their particular racial agendas on the children of the city.

By the early 1970s, every other constituent member of the liberal-labor-black coalition was similarly engaged in a quest for power. Integrationists, led by the liberal members of the school board and the NAACP, were as intransigent in their efforts to transform the system as were the racial extremists. The Detroit Federation of Teachers pursued its self-interest as well, battling far more strenuously to protect tenure and seniority than it did to protect children from cynical and incompetent teachers.

In many ways, the recent political history of the Detroit schools parallels the modern history of political liberalism in the United States. After coming to power in the early 1960s, the liberal coalition collapsed amid crises and quarrels that led its constituent groups to abandon their common principles and pursue separate, often contradictory agendas. This collapse has left America's cities both politically isolated and deeply fragmented along racial, ethnic, and class lines.

In the past decade, the conditions in major American cities and in urban public schools have continued to deteriorate at an alarming rate. Life for many urban residents has become an ongoing nightmare of welfare dependency, crime, violence, and despair. Tragically, the urban family, the one institution that traditionally provided refuge from these problems, has itself fallen prey to the pervasive economic and social decay of recent years. Since 1960, the number of children born to unwed mothers, the divorce rate, and the number of fatherless families has risen substantially in urban America. The serious problems of teenage pregnancies and the consistent failure of the fathers of these children to provide adequate emotional or financial support for their children stand as enormous obstacles to educational and ultimately social progress.[4] Strong families are the most fundamental of all educational institutions. When they deteriorate schools face enormous new burdens.

The ability of public schools to shoulder these burdens, however, has been undermined by the continuing economic decay of major cities and the persistent financial, political, and curricular problems of city schools. Economically, the shift from an industrial to a service economy has led to the closing of still more factories in central cities, the additional loss of thousands of high paying jobs, and the worsening of social conditions in urban areas. Between 1972 and 1987 Detroit lost over 40 percent of its manufacturing and almost half of its wholesale and retail jobs. In 1989, the city's unemployment rate stood at 15.3 percent, twice the state and three times the national average.[5]

The extent of the city's decline was summed up recently by Sidney Fine, who observed that if Detroit could somehow "return to the conditions prevailing in the city in 1967 with regard to the state of the economy, the level of unemployment, the percentage of inhabitants living in poverty and on welfare rolls . . . , it would undoubtedly be hailed as a remarkable and happy achievement." Other urban areas have suffered a similar fate. Early in 1991, a leader of the National League of Cities declared that "cities are caught in a death spiral."[6]

This study has identified a strong relationship between the health of the local economy and the general condition of the public schools. Given that relationship, these negative economic developments point to a grim future for urban education. Admittedly, more than a healthy economy is required for high quality public education. Strong schools can be found even in the most difficult circumstances. But the economic collapse of major American cities over the past two decades has been so unremitting and the social consequences of that collapse so severe that urban public schools today are routinely engaged in an unequal battle against powerful outside forces that are aggressively hostile to children's lives, let alone their education.

How an urban economic revival could be created, by New Deal–style work programs as some liberals suggest, through enterprise zones as some conservatives maintain, from a national industrial policy, or by some other means, remains open to debate. But something must be done. Without an economic transformation of our cities, urban public schools will continue to spend inordinate amounts of time addressing social problems that they are ill equipped to solve and too little time dealing with the educational problems that they can alleviate.

As this study has shown, however, even in such good economic times as the 1940s and 1950s, urban schools still faced serious political, financial, and curricular problems. Solving these problems today may be even more difficult than in the past, in large part because of the increasing significance of racial and ethnic issues. The politics of school finance cogently exemplify this situation. In the past two decades, as cities have declined economically, they have increasingly needed and relied on state funding for vital services, particularly education. This reliance on states, however, has led to fierce legislative battles over resource allocation that often pit predominantly white suburbs and rural communities against predominantly black and Hispanic cities. In many of these battles the cities come up short.[7]

Levels of funding do not determine the quality of educational achievement. Yet, as this study has shown, that finding does not encompass all the ways in which financial issues affect a school district. Repeated fiscal crises unquestionably have taken a serious toll on urban schools. Although many urban districts saw funds increase in the 1980s, severe financial problems remain. Often, these problems are rooted in the continuing buildings-versus-salaries dilemma that has so plagued Detroit. In Chicago, for instance, long-standing neglect of capital expenditures in favor of salary increases has created a $1.1 billion backlog of necessary new construction, renovation, and repair. How the Chicago schools, already running deficits between $100 and $200 million, will raise that staggering sum and still provide the salary increases demanded by the teachers and other staff members is anybody's guess. Increasing funds to pay for reforms that might improve student achievement such as expanded early childhood education or lengthening the school day or the school year seem hopelessly out of the question.[8]

The one aspect of urban education that has seen some positive developments in the last decade is curriculum. Here also, however, the forces of social fragmentation and racial antagonism threaten to derail the progress that has been made. In the late 1960s, such farsighted school leaders as Norman Drachler sought to revise substantially the traditional curricula and compel publishers to portray minorities, women, and working people accurately—in all aspects of the school curricula, but especially in history and literature. Over the past few decades, these efforts have been remarkably successful. Vestiges of past practices certainly remain. But the trend toward a curriculum guided by a vision that celebrates the diversity of American life while stressing the common values that bind the nation together, what Diane Ravitch has called pluralistic multiculturalism, is gaining strength. Moreover, educational leaders have increasingly recognized the need for national educational standards and assessment, which, if implemented wisely, could lead school districts to offer *all* students a high quality academic education.[9]

Unfortunately, as in Detroit in the late 1960s and early 1970s, racial, ethnic, and religious ideologues have rejected such changes as insufficient and have demanded instead that public schools adopt essentially separatist curricula. Basing their demands on questionable hypotheses and less-than-convincing research, the proponents of Afrocentrism, cultural maintenance, and religious fundamentalism, like their predecessors in the 1960s and 1970s, propose educational programs guided by politics rather than pedagogy. These efforts seem fated to travel the same fruitless path marked out in the late 1960s, namely increased racial tension and social fragmentation with few, if any, educational gains for urban students. Compounding that problem is the fact that the most widely discussed urban educational reforms—Afrocentric immersion schools, politically controlled local school councils, and voucher (choice) initiatives—threaten to institutionalize the very racial, ethnic, class, and religious divisions that have ripped America apart since the late 1960s. Each of these reforms seem rooted in the belief that the common school and the common good are impossible dreams.[10]

The revitalization of urban public schools cannot be based on reforms that threaten to divide Americans further along racial, ethnic, class, or religious lines. Restoring these systems to previous levels of excellence can only come from broad-based campaigns that seek common ground. At least two components are crucial to any such efforts to rebuild urban schools. The first, as Joseph Featherstone noted more than twenty years ago, must be to strive for national, state, and local political coalitions that can unite diverse interest groups in the quest for adequate funding and the establishment of high academic standards for all schools and all students.

The second effort must work from the ground up to create what David Tyack and Elisabeth Hansot have called "a new social contract between the people and their public schools."[11] This new social contract must reestablish the vital bonds of trust and respect between parents, students, and educators that were torn asunder in the late 1960s. One of the most promising efforts in this direction can be found in the work of James P. Comer. Guided by a philosophy that stresses consensus building between families and educators, Comer and his colleagues have succeeded in boosting achievement levels in a number of previously troubled urban schools. At the heart of the Comer model is cooperation and mutual support between parents and educators. Institutionalizing this vision, Comer and his colleagues have established "governance and management teams" in neighborhood schools that agree "to focus efforts on problem solving and not waste time and energy placing blame." By getting parents and educators to work together toward the common goal of improved educational outcomes, Comer and his colleagues have recreated "organic" educational communities that are worlds apart from the dreary, stagnant school environments that characterize most other urban schools across the nation. These new educational communities offer hope that things can be different.[12]

The decline and fall of America's urban public school systems is the greatest educational tragedy of this century. Reversing this trend must become one of the dominant social and political initiatives of our time. To do otherwise, to allow urban schools to continue their slide into desperation and despair, will not only blast the hopes of another generation of urban youth, it will also signal the end of our national quest for a just society in which all Americans are full participants.

NOTES

1. *Chicago Tribune*, 11/7/87.

2. Arthur Bestor, *Educational Wastelands: The Retreat from Learning in Our Public Schools* (Urbana: University of Illinois Press, 1953).

3. Ze'ev Chafets presents examples of both of these racially reductionist explanations for the decline of Detroit in his *Devil's Night and Other True Tales of Detroit* (New York: Random House, 1990).

4. On these issues see, for example, William Julius Wilson, *The Truly Disadvantaged: The Inner City, the Underclass, and Public Policy* (Chicago: University of Chicago Press, 1987); Christopher Jencks and Paul Peterson, eds., *The Urban Underclass* (Washington, DC: Brookings Institution, 1991).

5. Citizens Research Council of Michigan, *Fiscal Trends of the City of Detroit* (Detroit: Citizens Research Council, 1991), 75–81.

6. Sidney Fine, *Violence in the Model City: The Cavanagh Administration, Race Relations, and the Detroit Riot of 1967* (Ann Arbor: University of Michigan Press, 1989), 461; *New York Times*, 1/6/91.

7. Detroit simply cannot financially support its own schools. Between 1970 and 1990, state equalized valuation of property in Detroit plunged from $5.3 billion to $1.8 billion when controlled for inflation (Citizens Research Council of Michigan, *Fiscal Trends*, 14). On similar problems in Chicago and Illinois, see Patrick T. Reardon, "Hundreds Lose Jobs as Chicago Schools Cut $42 Million," *Chicago Tribune*, 9/1/91.

8. Chicago, for example, still operates over 100 schools that were built before 1900. On the problems of physically deteriorating schools, see *Chicago Sun Times*, 4/14/91 and 4/15/91; Thomas E. Glass, "Deteriorating School Buildings: And the Walls Come A-Tumblin' Down," *Illinois Issues* 16 (November 1990): 21–24; Thomas E. Glass, "America's Deteriorating School Infrastructure: The Most Expensive Reform Problem," *NCPEA Record* (Fall/Winter, 1991): 94–98. See also Jonathan Kozol, *Savage Inequalities: Children in America's Schools* (New York: Crown Publishers, 1991).

9. On these curricular trends see James P. Comer, "Ignorance is Not Bliss," *Parents* 66 (March, 1991): 193; E. D. Hirsch, Jr., *Fairness and Core Knowledge* (Charlottesville, VA: Core Knowledge Foundation, 1991); Diane Ravitch, "Multiculturalism: E Pluribus Plures," *American Scholar* 59 (Summer, 1990): 337–54; Marshall Smith, Jennifer O'Day, and David K. Cohen, "National Curriculum, American Style: What Might It Look Like?" *American Educator* 14 (Winter, 1990): 10–17, 40–47.

10. A superb critique of the trend toward educational and social fragmentation is Arthur M. Schlesinger, Jr., *The Disuniting of America: Reflections on a Multicultural Society* (New York: Norton, 1992).

11. Tyack and Hansot, *Managers of Virtue: Public School Leadership, 1820–1980* (New York: Basic Books, 1982), 249.

12. James P. Comer, "Educating Poor Minority Children," *Scientific American* 259 (November, 1988): 58–59. Comer and his colleagues very explicitly attempted to recreate "the kind of climate of relationship that existed between home and school in the pre–World War II period." See James P. Comer, "Home-School Relationships as They Affect the Academic Success of Children," *Education and Urban Society* 16 (May, 1984): 335, 323–37.

A Note on Sources

This bibliographic note does not include all the materials cited in this study. Rather, I have listed only those sources that were particularly important to the book.

Manuscript Collections

Archives of Labor History and Urban Affairs, Walter P. Reuther Library, Wayne State University, Detroit, Michigan

The most extensive collection of materials on the Detroit Public Schools from the 1930s to the early 1980s can be found in the Detroit Federation of Teachers Papers. An extremely large collection, the DFT Papers include personal reminiscences, correspondence, city and state governmental documents, union and board publications, scrapbooks, and hundreds of newspaper clippings. The DFT Papers are as rich an array of sources on urban public schools as one could find anywhere. The only drawback to the collection is that it is unprocessed. The Arthur Elder Papers and Michigan Federation of Teachers Papers contain materials on essential state-level politics and the role the DFT and organized labor played in Lansing. The Remus G. Robinson Papers, which cover the period from the early 1950s to the late 1960s, is a rich collection of sources on the school system generally and on issues of concern to black leaders specifically.

One of the best collections of materials on race relations in the schools is the Ernest Goodman Papers. This collection is particularly valuable in regard to the Sherrill School Case. The Detroit Public Schools Division of Community Relations Papers covers the period from the 1940s to the 1960s and has some superb materials on efforts by the school system to deal with racial problems. The Detroit National Association for the Advancement of Colored People Papers also contain some useful materials on race relations.

The Joe Brown Papers have important information on left-wing activism in school politics and on allegations of radicalism among teachers in the 1930s and 1950s. The Walter P. Reuther Papers contain some important information on the relationship between organized labor, particularly the United Auto Workers, and the public schools.

Burton Historical Library, Detroit Public Library, Detroit, Michigan

The Laura F. Osborn Papers are the best collection of materials on the Detroit schools from the turn of the century to the early 1950s. This invaluable collection contains personal and board-related correspondence, speeches, board publications, and reports, photographs, and hundreds of newspaper clippings. Unfortunately, like the DFT Papers, this collection is unprocessed.

The Detroit Mayors Papers contain essential documents related to school finance and several other issues up to 1949. The Detroit Council on Public Education, a small but vital collection, has information on state-level politics in the late 1930s. The Frank Cody Clipping File contains some useful material on Cody's years as superintendent.

Paul and Jean Hanna Collection, Hoover Institution on War, Revolution and Peace, Stanford, California

The Norman Drachler Papers are an outstanding collection of materials on the Detroit schools from the 1950s to the early 1970s. Particularly useful are the materials on the growing racial problems in the district from 1966 to 1971. Like the DFT and Osborn Papers, this large and valuable collection suffers from the fact that it is unprocessed.

Michigan Historical Collection, Bentley Historical Library, University of Michigan, Ann Arbor, Michigan

The Ralph Stone Papers have only a few useful items relating to the Detroit schools. The Detroit Urban League Papers, on the other hand, contain absolutely essential information on blacks in the Detroit schools from the 1920s through the 1970s. The *Detroit News* Lansing Bureau Scrapbooks are a handy source of newspaper clippings describing state-level politics from the 1930s through the 1950s. For specific details on the antibusing movement in Detroit, the Carmen Roberts and Shirley Wohlfield Papers offer a rare collection of materials on the conservative, grass roots politics of the late 1960s and early 1970s.

Wayne State University Archives, Walter P. Reuther Library, Detroit, Michigan

Charles Spain, a top administrator of the school system for more than two decades, deposited some papers and scrapbooks in the Wayne Archives. These contain some outstanding materials on Progressive era politics and educational innovations.

Other Manuscript Collections

The Joseph A. Labadie Collection in the Graduate Library of the University of Michigan, Ann Arbor, was the best source for materials on left-wing political organizations.

The Detroit public schools maintains an archive of historical materials with some documents dating back to the founding of the school system in the mid-nineteenth century. Ranging from school board *Proceedings,* to reports, to photographs, this collection contains many indispensable materials. Unfortunately, the collection has no permanent home in the Detroit School Center Building. Finding the collection and gaining access to it often depended on tracking down a compassionate administrator who was both aware that the collection existed and, as important, had a key to the room where it was stored.

Newspapers

The wealth of articles in the *Detroit Free Press* and the *Detroit News* provide an excellent longitudinal picture of the development of the Detroit schools in the twentieth century. The *Detroit Times,* which stopped publishing in 1960, is also a useful source. During the Progressive era, the *Detroit Journal* played an important role in educational politics and the paper contains a great deal of information on the schools. Copies of both the *Times* and the *Journal* are available at the Detroit Public Library. *Detroit Saturday Night* (which ceased publication in 1937) and *The Detroiter,* the official voice of the Detroit Board of Commerce, offer insights into the attitudes of wealthy, business-oriented Detroiters. Both these weeklies are available in the Burton Historical Collection in the Detroit Public Library. The best source of information on the attitudes of organized labor toward the schools is the *Detroit Labor News,* which has been published since 1914. The relationship between the black community and the schools in the 1930s and 1940s can be gauged from the weekly *Detroit Tribune,* which is available in the Burton Historical Library. The *Tribune* is much less useful for the 1950s. Fortunately, the weekly *Michigan Chronicle* emerged during the 1950s as the most important newspaper in the black community. The *Chronicle* focused extensively on the schools throughout the 1950s and 1960s. Copies of Rev. Cleage's *Illustrated News* can be found in the Remus G. Robinson Papers. The DFT, Drachler, and Robinson Papers also have copies of the militant *Black Student Voice.* Copies of the *Northeast Detroiter, Redford Record,* and other Detroit community newspapers are also scattered throughout the DFT, Drachler, and Robinson Papers. The views of the Detroit Socialist party can be gleaned from the *Detroit Leader* and the *Michigan Socialist,* while those of the Detroit Communist party can be found in the *Michigan Worker.* These left-wing papers are available in the Labadie Collection of the Graduate Library of the University of Michigan.

The official voice of the Detroit Teachers Association (later the Detroit Education Association), the *Detroit Teacher Association News* (later the *Detroit Education News*) illuminate local- and state-level educational politics from the 1930s to the late 1950s. Similarly, the official voice of the Detroit Federation of Teachers, the *Detroit Teacher,* which has been published continuously since the late 1930s, is a vital source. Bound volumes of these weekly teachers' publications are available in the Religion, Education, and Sociology Department of the Detroit Public Library. Copies of the official voice of the school administration, the *Detroit Schools,* can be found in the Purdy Library at Wayne State University. The *Superintendent's Pipeline,* a weekly newsletter begun by Samuel Brownell and continued by his successors, is also an excellent source. Copies of the *Pipeline* can be found in the DFT Papers, Drachler Papers, and Robinson Papers.

During the 1960s and 1970s, the Detroit public schools compiled copies of newspaper articles about the system that were filed in volumes called *Schools in the News*. A disorganized but seemingly complete set of these volumes can be found in the school archives in the School Center Building. Copies of some volumes of *Schools in the News* can be found in the Drachler and Robinson Papers. There are also a number of extremely helpful scrapbooks of newspaper clippings and clipping files in the DFT Papers, the Norman Drachler Papers, the Frank Cody Clipping File, the Laura Osborn Papers, the Remus G. Robinson Papers, and the Charles Spain Papers.

No discussion of newspapers in Detroit would be complete without mentioning the work of William Grant, the education writer for the *Free Press* in the 1960s and 1970s. His regular articles in the *Free Press* and his occasional publications in such journals as the *New Republic,* the *Public Interest,* and the *Wayne Law Review* were unfailingly thorough, insightful, and immensely helpful in unraveling the contentious and complex developments of the era.

Local and State Board of Education Documents

Detroit Board of Education

The *Proceedings of the Detroit Board of Education* were the most valuable single source for this study. This compendium of speeches, discussions, data, reports, and decisions from the board's bimonthly meetings offers unparalleled information about the inner workings of the school system and the ideas and attitudes of school leaders. In addition, the *Annual Reports of the Superintendent of Schools* provides statistical data about the schools until the mid-1950s. Unfortunately, at that time, the function of the reports changed from one of conveying large amounts of information about the schools to one of improving public relations by touting various achievements. Nevertheless, most of the statistical information that had been contained in the Superintendent's *Annual Reports* was still available in the 1950s and early 1960s in the *Annual Budgets of the Detroit Board of Education,* copies of which can be found in the Purdy Library of Wayne State University. In the mid-1960s, however, the format of the *Budgets* changed. The new *Annual Financial Reports of the Board of Education,* which can be found at the Purdy Library, contained important financial data but the reports no longer contained other statistical information about the school system. Some of the data dropped from the *Financial Reports* could still be found in a board publication entitled *Facts about the Detroit Schools,* copies of which are available in the Detroit Urban League Papers and the Remus G. Robinson Papers.

Another outstanding source of quantitative data is *Detroit Public Schools Statistics,* an annual, multivolume collection that includes information down to the building level. Until recently, copies of the *Statistics* from the 1920s to the present were available in the School Center Building. Unfortunately, the early volumes now have been moved to a warehouse that is inaccessible to anyone not employed by the board. Copies of the *Statistics* from the early 1960s to the present are available at the Purdy Library.

Besides these annual publications, occasional studies of the system are excellent sources of material. A number of early studies are summarized in the *Detroit Educa-*

tional Bulletin, which was published during the 1920s and early 1930s. Copies are available at the Purdy Library and the University of Michigan Graduate Library. Later studies that were vital to this project include the *Report of the Citizens Advisory Committee on School Needs* (1958), *The Findings and Recommendations* of the Citizens Advisory Committee on Equal Educational Opportunity (1962), and the *Report of the High School Study Commission* (1968). Copies of these reports can be found at the Purdy Library and the University of Michigan Graduate Library. Some of the studies of individual high schools that were conducted in conjunction with the High School Study Commission can be found in the Detroit Urban League Papers.

The State of Michigan

The *Annual Report of the State Superintendent of Instruction for the State of Michigan* provides some useful information on Detroit in relation to other districts in the state as well as data on the evolution of state aid to education. The main problem with these reports is that Detroit school officials apparently used very different criteria in determining what statistical information should go to the state than they used in preparing local reports. These criteria are never made clear and, thus, local and state annual reports often differ substantially on numerous items.

Dissertations and Theses

J. Elenbaas, "Detroit and the Progressive Era: A Study of Urban Reform, 1900–1914" (Ph.D. diss., Wayne State University, 1968) traces the evolution of Progressive political reform in Detroit. Allan Robert McPherson, "The Introduction and Development of the Detroit Public Schools Adult Education Program: A Historical Study" (Ph.D. diss., University of Michigan, 1988) specifically details the development of evening schools during the Martindale years. An excellent analysis of how the national standardized testing movement influenced educational policy and practice in Detroit in the 1920s and 1930s is Stephen Scott Williams, "From Polemics to Practice: IQ Testing and Tracking in the Detroit Public Schools and Their Relationship to the National Debate" (Ph.D. diss., University of Michigan, 1986). One chapter in Timothy Mark Pies, "Historical and Contemporary Analyses of the Financing of Lutheran and Catholic Education in Michigan's Saginaw Valley" (Ph.D. diss., University of Michigan, 1983) offers a concise view of the effort to ban parochial education in Michigan in the early 1920s. Concentrating mainly on Detroit, Leon S. Waskiewicz, "Organized Labor and Public Education in Michigan, 1888–1938" (Ph.D diss., University of Michigan, 1939) is a solid overview of the role organized labor played in local educational politics prior to the Flint Sit-Down Strike.

A detailed examination of the impact of the Great Depression on the Detroit schools is found in Jeffrey E. Mirel, "Politics and Public Education in the Great Depression: Detroit, 1929–40" (Ph.D. diss., University of Michigan, 1984). The political battles about funding welfare in Detroit during the Great Depression, which were as volatile as the battles over educational retrenchment, are discussed in Martin Sullivan, "On the Dole: The Relief Issue in Detroit, 1929–39" (Ph.D. diss., University of Notre Dame, 1974) .

There are a number of important studies on the development of teachers' organizations and unions in Detroit and Michigan. George Male, "The Michigan Education Association as an Interest Group, 1852–1950" (Ph.D. diss., University of Michigan, 1952) is a comprehensive view of the political activities of the MEA during the years that it was dominated by school administrators rather than teachers. Orin-Jane Bragg Gardner, "A Study of the Role of the Teacher in the Evolution of Administrative Personnel Practices in the Detroit Public Schools" (Ed.D. diss., Wayne State University, 1965) and Anna May Muffaletto, "Detroit Public School Teachers Unions: Organization, Operation, and Activities" (M.A. thesis, University of Detroit, 1958) have a great deal of information on early efforts to form a teachers' union in Detroit and on the beginnings of the DFT.

Charles W. Miller, "Democracy in Education: A Study of How the American Federation of Teachers Met the Threat of Communist Subversion Through the Democratic Process" (Ed.D. diss., Northwestern University, 1967) discusses the role of the DFT in ousting the communist-dominated unions from the American Federation of Teachers. Albert Schiff, "A Study and Evaluation of Teachers Strikes in the United States" (Ed.D. diss., Wayne [State] University, 1952) is an excellent overview of the wave of teacher strikes that swept the nation during the post–World War II years.

Harold J. Harrison, "A Study of the Work of the Coordinating Committee on Democratic Human Relations in the Detroit Public Schools from September, 1943 to June, 1952" (Ed.D. diss., Wayne [State] University, 1953) has a great deal of useful data on the early efforts of the school system to deal with racial problems. A fascinating look at Miller High School, based on surveys and interviews of former faculty and students, can be found in Cloyzelle K. Jones, "The Historify of Sidney D. Miller High School with Particular Exploration into those Factors which Resulted in the Inordinately High Incidences of Pupil Successes Considering, and Despite, Existing Socio-Economic Factors which Are Perceived as Being Prime Predictors of High Incidences of Pupil Failure, 1919–1957" (Ed.D. diss., Wayne State University, 1970). Jay Irwin Stark, "The Pattern Allocation in Education: The Detroit Public Schools, 1940–1960" (Ph.D. diss., University of Michigan, 1969) is a quantitative study of the distribution of resources for Detroit elementary schools.

Ray Gene Phillips, "A Study of Equal Opportunity in the Construction Trades Apprenticeship Program Sponsored by the Pipefitting Industry of Metropolitan Detroit with the Detroit Public Schools" (Ph.D. diss., University of Michigan, 1971) analyzes the patterns of racial discrimination in one of the Detroit apprenticeship programs. Roger L. Webb, "A Study of the Socio-Political Process that Preceded and Followed the Federal Court Order Calling for Remedies to Post-Desegregation Problems: Detroit, 1975" (Ph.D. diss., University of Michigan, 1978) is a rather thin study that nevertheless contains some useful information on the impact of the *Milliken* decision on the school system. Sidney J. Berkowitz, "An Analysis of the Relationship Between the Detroit Community Control of Schools Movement and the 1971 Decentralization of the Detroit Public Schools" (Ph.D. diss., Wayne State University, 1973) is a comprehensive, well-researched study of the political efforts to decentralize the school system. Berkowitz also offers an insightful look at the early years under the new regime. Another strong treatment of decentralization that considers educational as well as political implications of the reform is James Harris, Jr., "Decentralization and

Recentralization of the Detroit Public Schools: A Study of the Transitions of a School System, 1969–83" (Ph.D. diss., University of Michigan, 1985).

Published Materials

Sources on Urban Education

The historiography of twentieth-century American public education has largely focused on the history of urban schools. Lawrence Cremin's classic study, for example, *The Transformation of the School: Progressivism in American Education, 1876–1957* (New York: Knopf, 1961) primarily analyzes reforms in urban districts. Similarly, Raymond Callahan's influential study, *Education and the Cult of Efficiency* (Chicago: University of Chicago Press, 1962), focuses almost exclusively on city schools.

The best single introduction to the political, administrative, and curricular changes in twentieth-century urban education is David Tyack, *The One Best System: A History of American Urban Education* (Cambridge, MA: Harvard University Press, 1974). In addition, parts 2 and 3 of David Tyack and Elisabeth Hansot, *Managers of Virtue: Public School Leadership in America, 1820–1980* (New York: Basic Books, 1982) focus mainly on urban school systems and offer some excellent insights into changes and challenges confronting urban school leaders. David Tyack, Robert Lowe, and Elisabeth Hansot, *Public Schools in Hard Times: The Great Depression and Recent Years* (Cambridge, MA: Harvard University Press, 1984) provides a helpful overview of urban schools in the depression years.

Revisionist historians also have devoted most of their attention to urban public schools. The most sweeping revisionist work is Samuel Bowles and Herbert Gintis, *Schooling in Capitalist America* (New York: Basic Books, 1976), a provocative Marxist interpretation of the political and curricular changes in the Progressive era. Other examples of revisionist studies that concentrate primarily on urban schools are: Clarence Karier, Paul Violas, and Joel Spring, *Roots of Crisis: American Education in the Twentieth Century* (Chicago: Rand McNally, 1973); Michael Katz, *Class, Bureaucracy and Schools* (New York: Praeger, 1972); Joel Spring, *Education and the Rise of the Corporate State* (Boston: Beacon Press, 1972); and Paul Violas, *The Training of the Urban Working Class* (Chicago: Rand McNally, 1978).

Diane Ravitch, whose *The Great School Wars: New York City, 1805–1973* (New York: Basic Books, 1974) offers a a detailed look at several large political controversies in the New York City schools, critiqued the revisionist interpretation in *The Revisionists Revised: A Critique of the Radical Attack on the Schools* (New York: Basic Books, 1978). Some revisionists, in turn, challenged her critique in Walter Feinberg, Harvey Kantor, Michael Katz, and Paul Violas, *Revisionists Respond to Ravitch* (Washington, DC: National Academy of Education, 1980).

Postrevisionist scholars similarly have concentrated primarily on the history of urban schools. They focus, however, mostly on single districts rather than on overviews of urban education. David Hogan's study of Chicago, *Class and Reform: School and Society in Chicago, 1880–1930* (Philadelphia: University of Pennsylvania Press, 1985), is both theoretically sophisticated and meticulously researched. Martin Carnoy and Henry Levin, *Schooling and Work in the Democratic State* (Stanford, CA: Stanford University Press, 1985), offer some intriguing speculations on the modern history of urban education, but they base their speculations entirely on secondary sources.

Ira Katznelson and Margaret Weir's *Schooling for All* (New York: Basic Books, 1985) is a masterful discussion of events in Chicago and San Francisco. Despite my criticisms of their work, I have found *Schooling for All* to be one of the most intriguing efforts to understand the historical problems of urban education to date. Similarly, Paul Peterson, *The Politics of School Reform, 1870–1940* (Chicago: University of Chicago Press, 1985) is an engaging look at Chicago, San Francisco, and Atlanta. Katznelson and Weir and Peterson draw heavily from Julia Wrigley's very rich study of Chicago, *Class Politics and Public Schools: Chicago, 1900–1950* (New Brunswick, NJ: Rutgers University Press, 1982).

An outstanding study of Progressive era school politics in several medium-sized cities is William Reese, *Power and the Promise of Progressive School Reform* (Boston: Routledge and Kegan Paul, 1986). Bryce E. Nelson, *Good Schools: The Seattle Public School System, 1901–1930* (Seattle: University of Washington Press, 1988) contains important material on various interest groups involved in school politics, particularly the socialists. Ronald Cohen and Raymond Mohl, *The Paradox of Progressive Education: The Gary Plan and Urban Schooling* (Port Washington, NY: Kennikat, 1979), offer a well-crafted portrait of the history of the Gary plan. Ronald D. Cohen, *Children of the Mill: Schooling and Society in Gary, Indiana, 1906–1960* (Bloomington: Indiana University Press, 1990) is a beautifully researched study of the Gary schools with a wealth of information on the history of an important urban school system. Cohen has some excellent sections on racial issues in the Gary schools. In addition to Cohen, the best studies of African-Americans in urban public schools are Michael Homel, *Down from Equality: Black Chicagoans and the Public Schools, 1920–41* (Urbana: University of Illinois Press, 1984); Vincent P. Franklin, *The Education of Black Philadelphia* (Philadelphia: University of Pennsylvania Press, 1979); and the chapter on blacks in Joel Perlmann, *Ethnic Differences: Schooling and Social Structure among the Irish, Italians, Jews, and Blacks in an American City, 1880–1935* (New York: Cambridge University Press, 1988).

The early history of teacher unions in Atlanta, Chicago, and New York is thoughtfully presented in Wayne Urban, *Why Teachers Organized* (Detroit: Wayne State University Press, 1982). William Eaton, *The American Federation of Teachers, 1916–1961* (Carbondale: Southern Illinois Press, 1975), offers a useful introduction to the history of the AFT. A more detailed and sophisticated look at the history of teacher unionism can be found in Marjorie Murphy, *Blackboard Unions: The AFT and the NEA, 1900–1980* (Ithaca, NY: Cornell University Press, 1990). The anticommunist crusade in the late 1940s and early 1950s is described in Ellen W. Schrecker, *No Ivory Tower: McCarthyism and the Universities* (New York: Oxford University Press, 1986) and David Caute, *The Great Fear: The Anti-Communist Purge Under Truman and Eisenhower* (New York: Simon and Schuster, 1978).

A helpful study on the changes in the nature and function of the high school can be found in Robert Hampel, *The Last Little Citadel: American High Schools Since 1940* (Boston: Houghton Mifflin, 1986). Arthur Powell, Eleanor Farrar, and David K. Cohen, *The Shopping Mall High School: Winners and Losers in the Educational Marketplace* (Boston: Houghton Mifflin, 1985) also contains a very insightful chapter on the history of the high school in the twentieth century. Gerald Grant's study of a single high school from the early 1950s to the early 1980s, *The World We Created at Hamilton High School* (Cambridge, MA: Harvard University Press, 1988), has some powerful insights on the collapse of moral and educational authority within the institution during the late 1960s and early 1970s. Diane Ravitch, *The Troubled Crusade: American Education, 1945–1980* (New York: Basic Books, 1983) contains the single best description and analysis of the deterioration of the twentieth-century high school curriculum as well as outstanding chapters on the McCarthy era, racial issues, and federal educational initiatives.

Federal educational policies also are well described in both Hugh Davis Graham, *The Uncertain Triumph: Federal Education Policy in the Kennedy and Johnson Years* (Chapel Hill: University of North Carolina Press, 1984) and Joel Spring, *The Sorting Machine: National Educational Policy Since 1945* (New York: David McKay, 1976).

J. Anthony Lukas's study of three families caught in the conflict over busing in Boston, *Common Ground: A Turbulent Decade in the Lives of Three American Families* (New York: Random House, 1985) is a riveting analysis of the human consequences of social policy. Gary Orfield's *Must We Bus? Segregated Schools and National Policy* (Washington, DC: Brookings Institution, 1978) is a well-researched, powerful study supporting court-ordered busing for desegregation.

Sources on Detroit

Despite its lack of adequate documentation, Robert Conot's *American Odyssey: A Unique History of America Told through the Life of a Great City* (New York: William Morrow, 1974) is a very useful overview of the history of the city. Although brief, Sidney Glazer, *Detroit: A Study in Urban Development* (New York: Bookman Associates, 1965) is also helpful. Melvin Holli, ed., *Detroit* (New York: New Viewpoints, 1976), offers a fine array of original source documents. A description of Progressive era politics in Detroit by one of the key participants in the reform effort is William Lovett, *Detroit Rules Itself* (Boston: Gorham Press, 1930). Complementing Lovett's work are two excellent studies of Detroit politics in the Progressive era: Raymond Fragnoli, *The Transformation of Reform: Progressivism in Detroit—And After, 1912–1933* (New York: Garland Publishing, 1982) and Melvin Holli, *Reform in Detroit: Hazen S. Pingree and Urban Politics* (New York: Oxford University Press, 1969). Olivier Zunz's *The Changing Face of Inequality: Urban Industrial Development and Immigrants in Detroit, 1880–1920* (Chicago: University of Chicago Press, 1982) is an outstanding analysis of the importance of class and ethnicity in the development of the city.

Absolutely indispensable to any research on the history of Detroit in the twentieth century, particularly investigations of local and state politics, are Sidney Fine's superbly researched studies. These works include: Sidney Fine, *Sit-Down: The General Motors Strike, 1936–37* (Ann Arbor: University of Michigan Press, 1969); Sidney Fine, *Frank Murphy: The Detroit Years* (Ann Arbor: University of Michigan Press, 1969); Sidney Fine, *Frank Murphy: The New Deal Years* (Chicago: University of Chicago Press, 1979); Sidney Fine, *Violence in the Model City: The Cavanagh Admin-*

istration, Race Relations, and the Detroit Riot of 1967 (Ann Arbor: University of Michigan Press, 1989).

The transformation of Detroit during the early 1940s is thoroughly discussed in Alan Clive, *State of War: Michigan in World War II* (Ann Arbor: University of Michigan Press, 1979). Dominick Capeci, Jr., *Race Relations in Wartime Detroit: The Sojourner Truth Housing Controversy of 1942* (Philadelphia: Temple University Press, 1984), focuses on the first major incident of racial violence in Detroit in the 1940s. August Meier and Elliott Rudwick, *Black Detroit and the Rise of the UAW* (New York: Oxford University Press, 1979) is the standard work on the relationship between African-Americans and organized labor up to the early 1940s. J. David Greenstone, *Labor in American Politics* (Chicago: University of Chicago Press, 1977) has some outstanding sections on the role of organized labor in local politics in Detroit and the increasingly difficult time organized labor had with racial issues in the 1960s and 1970s. Similarly, Peter K. Eisinger's *The Politics of Displacement: Racial and Ethnic Transition in Three American Cities* (New York: Academic Press, 1980) is quite helpful in exploring the battle between blacks and whites for control of Detroit's city government. Kevin P. Phillips, *The Emerging Republican Majority* (New Rochelle, NY: Arlington House, 1969) was an extremely important source for analyzing the changing voting patterns of the white working class in Detroit and Michigan in the 1960s.

Detroit Bureau of Governmental Research, *Accumulated Social and Economic Statistics on Detroit* (Detroit: Bureau of Governmental Research, 1937) has a wealth of data on Detroit through the late 1930s. Similarly, the Citizens Research Council of Michigan, *Fiscal Trends of the City of Detroit* (Detroit: Citizens Research Council, 1991) is a useful compendium of data from the 1920s through the 1980s. Joe T. Darden, Richard Child Hill, June Thomas, and Richard Thomas, *Detroit: Race and Uneven Development* (Philadelphia: Temple University Press, 1987) is far and away the best source of information about the economic and social changes that occurred in Detroit and the metropolitan area in the the 1960s and 1970s.

Sources on Public Education in Detroit and Michigan

Arthur B. Moehlman was a key participant in the Progressive transformation of the Detroit schools. His *Public Education in Detroit* (Bloomington, IL: Public Schools Publishing, 1925) is a helpful overview of the history of the school system through the early 1920s. Ironically, it is weakest in precisely those areas in which Moehlman played the most important role, namely the introduction of progressive changes by the small board. Although embarrassingly hagiographic and poorly documented, the Detroit Public Schools Staff's *Frank Cody: A Realist in Education* (New York: Macmillan, 1943) provides a wonderful picture of Cody's long career and the development of the school system under his leadership. A well-researched history of Wayne State, Leslie Hanawalt, *A Place of Light: The History of Wayne State University* (Detroit: Wayne State University Press, 1968), has some valuable information on the Detroit board of education from the 1910s through the 1950s, the period in which the board controlled the city colleges that became Wayne State University. Paul T. Rankin, ed., *Improving Learning in the Detroit Public Schools: A History of the Division for*

Improvement of Instruction, 1920–1966, 2 vols. (Detroit: Board of Education, 1969) contains some important information on the evolution of major curricular programs in the Detroit schools.

James T. Selcraig, *The Red Scare in the Midwest, 1945–1955* (Ann Arbor: University Microfilms International Research Press, 1982), has some excellent material on the anticommunist crusade against teachers in Detroit and Michigan. Marilyn Gittell and T. Edward Hollander, *Six Urban School Districts: A Comparative Study of Institutional Response* (New York: Praeger, 1968) effectively compares the problems facing Detroit and other large-city systems in the 1950s and early 1960s. Howard D. Hamilton and Sylvan H. Cohen, *Policy Making By Plebiscite: School Referenda* (Lexington, MA: D. C. Heath, 1974) has a helpful section of the 1957 millage campaign. Patricia Cayo Sexton, *Education and Income: Inequalities of Opportunity in Our Public Schools* (New York: Viking Press, 1961) is a first-rate study of class-based inequality within the Detroit system. Its one major drawback is that Sexton does not analyze her data in terms of race as well as class. Another outstanding study is National Education Association, National Commission on Professional Rights and Responsibilities, *Detroit, Michigan: A Study of Barriers to Equal Educational Opportunity in a Large City* (Washington, DC: National Education Association, 1967). This is rich in information about the rapidly changing racial landscape in the city and the school system. James Ross Irwin, *A Ghetto Principal Speaks Out: A Decade of Crisis in Urban Public Schools* (Detroit: Wayne State University Press, 1973), provides a grim picture of the violence and protests that led to the deterioration of educational authority within the high schools in the late 1960s. The best study of the *Milliken v. Bradley* trial, with special attention to the role of social science testimony in the case, is Eleanor P. Wolf, *Trial and Error: The Detroit School Segregation Case* (Detroit: Wayne State University Press, 1981).

Donald Disbrow, *Schools for an Urban Society* (Lansing, MI: Michigan Historical Commission, 1968) has some excellent chapters on Detroit and on state-level politics and controversies. E. F. Shepard and William Wood, *The Financing of the Public Schools in Michigan* (Ann Arbor: University of Michigan Press, 1942), provides a brief, informative picture of the growth of state aid in the 1930s. J. Alan Thomas, *School Finance and Educational Opportunity in Michigan* (Lansing: Michigan Department of Education, 1968) is the basic work for understanding the debate over state aid in Michigan in the 1960s.

Appendix: Longitudinal Data on the Detroit Public Schools

TABLE 1. Fall Enrollment by Grades, 1911–49

Year	K	1–6	7–9	10–12	Total
1911–12	4,217	35,048	8,069	2,771	50,105
1912–13	4,562	38,599	8,776	3,013	54,950
1913–14	5,246	42,531	9,495	3,237	60,509
1914–15	6,392	46,989	10,473	3,518	67,372
1915–16	7,313	52,735	12,426	3,786	76,260
1916–17	8,396	58,144	13,621	4,149	84,310
1917–18	8,939	62,815	15,415	4,621	91,790
1918–19	10,151	67,688	17,149	5,012	100,000
1919–20	11,197	73,924	19,424	6,122	110,667
1920–21	11,447	76,198	20,721	7,023	115,389
1921–22	12,463	80,684	24,948	9,036	127,095
1922–23	13,254	85,076	26,923	10,752	136,005
1923–24	14,016	93,799	29,145	12,132	149,092
1924–25	13,216	99,565	32,342	13,710	158,833
1925–26	15,209	107,941	35,738	15,183	174,071
1926–27	17,900	117,239	41,953	16,857	193,949
1927–28	17,852	119,227	46,084	19,049	202,212
1928–29	18,883	127,386	50,100	21,549	217,918
1929–30	20,928	132,802	52,738	25,542	232,010
1930–31	20,869	130,369	53,830	30,011	235,079
1931–32	20,070	129,291	52,920	35,182	237,463
1932–33	20,529	129,023	53,257	37,062	239,871
1933–34	19,832	128,943	56,100	38,895	243,720
1934–35	20,136	129,968	59,178	38,189	247,471
1935–36	20,842	129,302	60,933	38,877	249,954
1936–37	19,870	128,355	59,514	40,758	248,497
1937–38	18,269	125,739	60,182	42,552	246,742
1938–39	17,403	119,876	60,872	46,159	244,310
1939–40	17,463	114,272	60,332	48,850	240,917
1940–41	17,930	110,049	58,703	49,189	235,871
1941–42	18,350	107,706	57,261	46,988	230,305
1942–43	18,979	105,087	55,442	43,810	223,318
1943–44	19,981	105,925	54,056	39,747	219,709
1944–45	NA	NA	NA	NA	NA
1945–46	NA	NA	NA	NA	NA
1946–47	20,834	102,767	43,978	42,602	210,181
1947–48	23,917	103,984	42,188	40,909	210,998
1948–49	26,105	108,072	42,218	37,559	213,954

Sources: Detroit Board of Education, *Superintendent's Annual Report, 1943–44*, pts. 2–6 (Detroit: Board of Education, 1944); Detroit Board of Education, *Superintendent's Annual Report, 1947–48* (Detroit: Board of Education, 1948); Detroit Board of Education, *Superintendent's Annual Report, 1954–55* (Detroit: Board of Education, 1955).

Notes: Enrollments do not include apprentices or vocational, trade, special, veterans institute, and adult day students. NA = not available.

TABLE 2. Fall Enrollment by Divisions, 1949–64

Year	Kindergarten	Elementary	Junior High	Senior High	Other[a]	Total
1949	23,512	127,245	23,426	41,707	12,798	228,688
1950	23,512	130,592	24,240	42,041	12,150	232,230
1951	27,059	133,812	23,843	42,473	11,570	238,757
1952	32,342	138,495	23,994	43,769	11,758	250,358
1953	31,533	150,253	23,276	45,342	11,685	262,089
1954	31,088	152,602	23,507	45,964	12,012	265,173
1955	31,200	158,038	23,790	47,470	12,030	272,528
1956	31,512	160,293	23,643	49,788	12,111	277,347
1957	31,359	160,704	24,871	53,179	11,338	281,451
1958	30,555	159,078	28,407	53,862	11,948	283,850
1959	30,600	153,819	35,332	51,597	12,051	283,399
1960	30,092	154,844	38,268	49,883	12,217	285,304
1961	30,575	153,808	41,023	50,038	12,702	288,146
1962	30,091	152,563	42,728	53,586	13,151	292,119
1963	28,822	149,052	48,590	55,971	12,092	294,527
1964	27,599	141,602	60,708	52,625	12,733	294,727

Sources: Detroit Public Schools, Preliminary Budget Estimates, 1957–58 (Detroit: Board of Education, 1958), in RGR Papers, box 9, no folder; Detroit Public Schools, 1962–63 Budget (Detroit: Board of Education, 1963); Detroit Public Schools, 1965–66 Budget (Detroit: Board of Education, 1966).

[a]Includes vocational, trade, special, veterans institutes, adult day students, and apprentices.

TABLE 3. Fall Enrollment by Grades, 1964–73

Year	K–6	7–9	10–12	Other[a]	Total
1964	168,661	60,708	52,625	14,100	296,094
1965	168,970	61,209	52,307	14,096	296,582
1966	170,340	62,096	53,069	14,457	299,962
1967	166,591	62,008	53,704	13,604	295,907
1968	163,860	63,219	53,254	11,764	292,097
1969	162,531	64,320	52,019	11,309	290,179
1970	158,059	66,259	50,810	10,929	286,057
1971	157,595	65,324	51,800	10,779	285,498
1972	152,903	63,723	50,553	10,363	277,542
1973	145,349	61,236	47,564	9,434	263,583

Source: Detroit Public Schools, "Facts About Detroit Schools" (February 1, 1974).

[a]Includes vocational, trade, special, veterans institutes, adult day students, and apprentices.

TABLE 4. Enrollment by Race and Ethnicity, 1921–80

Year	Black	White	Hispanic	Other	Total
1921	5,680	123,302	NA	NA	128,982
1946	38,529	183,862	NA	NA	222,391
1961	130,765	153,046	NA	1,701	285,512
1963	150,565	141,240	NA	1,940	293,745
1964	155,852	136,077	NA	2,037	293,966
1965	161,487	130,957	NA	2,378	294,822
1966	168,299	126,354	NA	2,382	297,035
1967	171,707	120,544	NA	2,614	294,865
1968	175,474	115,295	NA	4,531	295,300
1969	180,630	108,264	NA	4,965	293,859
1970	184,214	100,717	3,092	930	288,953
1971	187,966	96,269	4,382	840	289,457
1972	189,192	86,555	4,562	767	281,076
1973	185,362	74,965	4,434	817	265,578
1974	184,118	67,833	4,757	988	257,696
1975	187,640	56,855	4,268	833	249,596
1976	189,617	44,614	4,022	961	239,214
1977	187,498	36,227	3,933	1,113	228,771
1978	186,293	31,317	3,341	1,162	222,113
1979	184,722	29,377	3,728	1,249	219,076
1980	183,694	26,230	3,614	1,198	214,736

Sources: Detroit Public Schools, Bureau of Statistics and Reference, *Detroit Educational Bulletin,* January, 1992; Detroit Public Schools, "Number and Percent of Negro Students, Negro Teachers, and Negro Non-Contract Employees of 208 Elementary Schools, 19 Intermediate Schools, 19 High Schools, 8 Technical and Vocational Schools, 1946" in Detroit Commission on Community Relations Papers, box 17, Board of Education: Intercultural/Interracial Program, 1946–47 folder in ALHUA; Detroit Board of Education, *Detroit Public School Statistics, 1975–76,* vol. 56, pt. 1 (Detroit: Board of Education, 1976); Detroit Board of Education, *Detroit Public School Statistics, 1980–81,* vol. 61, pt. 1 (Detroit: Board of Education, 1981).

TABLE 5. Enrollment by Race and Ethnicity, 1921–80

Year	Black	White	Hispanic	Other	Total
1921	4.4%	95.6%	NA	NA	128,982
1946	17.3	82.7	NA	NA	222,391
1961	45.8	53.6	NA	0.6	285,512
1963	51.3	48.1	NA	0.6	293,745
1964	53.0	46.3	NA	0.7	293,966
1965	54.8	44.4	NA	0.8	294,822
1966	56.7	42.5	NA	0.8	297,035
1967	58.2	40.9	NA	0.9	294,865
1968	59.4	39.1	NA	1.5	295,300
1969	61.5	36.8	NA	1.7	293,859
1970	63.8	34.9	1.0	0.3	288,953
1971	64.9	33.3	1.5	0.3	289,457
1972	67.3	30.8	1.6	0.3	281,076
1973	69.3	28.2	1.7	0.3	265,578
1974	71.4	26.3	1.8	0.4	257,696
1975	75.2	22.8	1.7	0.3	249,596
1976	79.3	18.6	1.7	0.4	239,214
1977	82.0	15.8	1.7	0.5	228,771
1978	83.9	14.1	1.5	0.5	222,113
1979	84.3	13.4	1.7	0.6	219,076
1980	85.5	12.2	1.7	0.6	214,736

Sources: See table 4.

TABLE 6. Number of Professional Personnel by Race and Ethnicity, 1946–80

Year	Black	White	Hispanic	Other	Total
1946	286	6,976	NA	NA	7,262
1961	2,275	8,210	NA	31	10,516
1962	2,472	8,325	NA	NA	10,797
1963	2,700	7,669	NA	33	10,402
1964	2,961	7,757	NA	32	10,750
1965	3,292	7,828	NA	37	11,157
1966	3,628	7,792	NA	39	11,459
1967	4,125	7,747	NA	47	11,919
1968	4,490	7,733	NA	71	12,294
1969	4,879	7,373	NA	69	12,321
1970	5,106	7,189	47	46	12,388
1971	5,248	6,893	44	44	12,229
1972	5,380	6,366	51	51	11,848
1973	5,797	6,478	69	62	12,396
1974	5,676	5,704	59	60	11,499
1975	5,790	5,470	66	60	11,386
1976	5,485	4,929	58	58	10,530
1977	5,647	4,784	67	50	10,548
1978	5,896	4,682	57	58	10,693
1979	6,443	5,148	63	56	11,710
1980	6,223	4,800	62	51	11,136

Sources: See table 4.

TABLE 7. Professional Personnel by Race and Ethnicity, 1946–80

Year	Black	White	Hispanic	Other	Total
1946	3.9%	96.1%	NA	NA	7,262
1961	21.6	78.1	NA	NA	10,516
1962	22.9	77.1	NA	NA	10,797
1963	26.0	73.7	NA	0.3	10,402
1964	27.5	72.2	NA	0.3	10,750
1965	29.5	70.2	NA	0.3	11,157
1966	31.7	68.0	NA	0.3	11,459
1967	34.6	65.0	NA	0.4	11,919
1968	36.5	62.9	NA	0.6	12,294
1969	39.6	59.8	NA	0.6	12,321
1970	41.2	58.0	0.4	0.4	12,388
1971	42.9	56.4	0.4	0.3	12,229
1972	45.4	53.7	0.4	0.5	11,848
1973	46.8	52.2	0.6	0.4	12,396
1974	49.4	49.6	0.5	0.5	11,499
1975	50.9	48.0	0.6	0.5	11,386
1976	52.1	46.8	0.6	0.5	10,530
1977	53.5	45.4	0.6	0.5	10,548
1978	55.1	43.8	0.5	0.6	10,693
1979	55.0	44.0	0.5	0.5	11,710
1980	55.9	43.1	0.6	0.4	11,136

Sources: See table 4.

TABLE 8. Local Funding for the Detroit Public Schools, 1900–1950

Year	Funds	Year	Funds
1900–1901	$813,270	1925–26	$13,029,668
1901–02	876,068	1926–27	16,673,030
1902–03	989,773	1927–28	17,301,594
1903–04	1,003,714	1928–29	16,326,602
1904–05	781,049	1929–30	17,890,136
1905–06	601,499	1930–31	17,884,821
1906–07	598,300	1931–32	16,403,413
1907–08	889,532	1932–33	12,875,173
1908–09	592,359	1933–34	12,185,452
1909–10	944,318	1934–35	13,300,981
1910–11	1,337,772	1935–36	13,571,000
1911–12	1,468,031	1936–37	14,146,992
1912–13	1,333,697	1938–39	15,306,000
1913–14	2,071,921	1939–40	14,256,473
1914–15	2,341,599	1940–41	16,185,920
1915–16	2,431,599	1941–42	17,458,236
1916–17	3,615,495	1942–43	21,447,625
1917–18	4,654,635	1943–44	21,852,625
1918–19	6,137,468	1944–45	22,927,625
1919–20	6,207,851	1945–46	23,511,513
1920–21	11,983,671	1946–47	25,964,246
1921–22	10,923,678	1947–48	27,665,246
1922–23	11,575,223	1948–49	30,561,000
1923–24	11,701,428	1949–50	42,814,480
1924–25	12,494,516		

Sources: Detroit Board of Education, *Annual Reports;* Detroit Board of Education, "Pertinent Facts Relative to the Proposed Increase in Millage Election of April 4th, 1949."

Note: Data do not include revenue from the sale of bonds.

TABLE 9. State Equalized Valuation, 1951–80 (in millions)

Year	SEV	Year	SEV
1951	$4,201.2	1966	$4,991.1
1952	4,498.0	1967	4,807.7
1953	5,307.2	1968	4,925.6
1954	5,173.6	1969	5,188.2
1955	5,156.7	1970	5,306.3
1956	5,304.6	1971	5,719.3
1957	5,598.6	1972	5,770.6
1958	5,486.5	1973	5,806.7
1959	5,372.0	1974	5,762.4
1960	5,672.2	1975	5,792.1
1961	5,508.0	1976	5,046.4
1962	5,285.4	1977	4,930.2
1963	5,264.6	1978	4,852.5
1964	5,229.9	1979	5,051.6
1965	5,196.9	1980	5,227.4

Sources: Detroit Board of Education, *Budgets 1960–61, 1969–70, 1979–80;* Citizens Research Council of Michigan, *Fiscal Trends in the City of Detroit* (Detroit: Citizens Research Council, 1991).

TABLE 10. Millage Proposals and Outcomes, 1949–77

Date	Proposal	Majority Vote	Total Extra Voted Millage[a]
April, 1949	2.5 mills	Yes	2.5 mills
April, 1953	2.5 mill renewal	Yes	
	2.0 mill increase	Yes	4.5
April, 1957	3.0 mill increase	No	4.5
April, 1959	4.5 mill renewal	Yes	
	3.0 mill increase	Yes	7.5
April, 1963	7.5 mill renewal	No	0.0
November, 1963	7.5 mill renewal	Yes	7.5
May, 1965	2.5 mill increase	No	
November, 1966	5 mill increase	Yes	12.5
November, 1968	10 mill increase	No	
May, 1972	5 mill renewal	No	7.5
	5 mill increase	No	
August, 1972	5 mill renewal	No	7.5
	5 mill increase	No	
November, 1972	5 mill renewal	No	7.5
November, 1973	7 mill increase to replace	Yes	14.5
	1 percent income tax		
March, 1974	7.5 mill renewal	Yes	14.5
August, 1974	5 mill increase	No	14.5
August, 1976	5 mill increase	No	14.5
November, 1976	5 mill increase	No	14.5
September, 1977	3 mill increase	Yes	17.5
November, 1977	7 mill renewal	Yes	17.5

Sources: Detroit Public Schools, "Data Digest" (1962); Detroit Public Schools, "Facts About Detroit Schools" (1974); DBEP, 1973–74, 1974–75, 1976–77, 1977–78.

[a]These extra voted taxes are in addition to the approximately 8 mills allocated annually to the Detroit Public Schools from Wayne County out of the 15 mill tax. During these years, the county allocated as much as 8.34 mills in 1951–52 and as little as 7.58 mills in 1953–54. Throughout most of the later period, however, the county allocated a steady 8.26 mills.

TABLE 11. Sources of Revenue, 1947–66

Year	Local	State	Federal	Other[a]	Total
1947–48	$27,665,246	$25,021,000	—	$3,137,827	$55,824,073
1948–49	30,561,000	27,619,707	—	5,719,568	63,900,275
1949–50	42,814,480	28,762,000	—	4,101,593	75,678,173
1950–51	42,528,499	29,155,391	—	4,525,121	76,209,011
1951–52	45,149,789	30,933,614	—	3,673,673	79,760,076
1952–53	48,838,762	35,950,500	—	4,840,736	89,629,998
1953–54	49,642,812	37,913,600	—	4,939,246	92,495,658
1954–55	60,748,821	39,716,150	—	3,826,000	104,290,971
1955–56	66,057,737	41,130,000	—	4,144,000	111,331,737
1956–57	67,951,629	46,732,500	—	1,853,000	116,537,129
1957–58	71,718,426	45,482,920	—	2,334,425	119,535,771
1958–59	70,281,555	46,055,000	—	2,655,425	118,911,990
1959–60	85,151,368	42,710,000	—	2,552,000	130,413,368
1960–61	90,575,141	43,282,432	—	4,260,465	138,118,038
1961–62	88,879,748	43,359,012	$1,044,135	4,368,800	137,651,695
1962–63	85,658,373	48,334,032	539,500	9,111,850	144,643,755
1963–64	86,663,027	49,242,163	495,500	3,302,800	139,703,490
1964–65	86,114,327	52,002,231	515,500	10,141,155	148,773,213
1965–66	85,592,510	58,812,926	525,000	8,533,556	153,463,992

Sources: Detroit Board of Education, *Preliminary Budget Estimates, 1957–58* (Detroit: Board of Education, 1957), in RGR Papers, box 9, no folder; Detroit Board of Education, *1960–61 Budget* (Detroit: Board of Education, 1961); Detroit Board of Education, *1965–66 Budget* (Detroit: Board of Education, 1966).

Note: Data do not include revenue from the sale of bonds.

[a]Includes funds received from Wayne County, tuition, lunchroom, and bookstore sales.

TABLE 12. Sources of Revenue, Operating Budget, 1962–80 (in thousands)

Year	Local	State	Federal	Other[a]	Total
1962	$75,642	$44,622	$1,388	$7,704	$129,356
1963	80,260	47,981	1,439	7,851	137,531
1964	83,345	48,773	2,186	7,808	142,112
1965	81,932	52,114	4,826	8,885	147,758
1966	81,920	61,673	18,733	10,359	172,686
1967	76,180	71,636	19,736	15,111	182,664
1968	90,901	78,706	14,474	13,648	200,728
1969	103,052	82,362	25,990	13,504	224,907
1970	107,817	89,857	23,989	13,780	235,444
1971	110,861	106,106	35,223	12,839	265,029
1972	117,951	113,642	42,429	10,797	284,818
1973	88,909	123,414	43,117	9,854	265,294
1974	128,841	136,637	43,725	13,340	322,542
1975	130,051	156,485	52,490	17,745	356,771
1976	130,381	164,299	53,845	15,590	364,115
1977	111,502	188,236	58,453	18,338	376,529
1978	125,111	225,580	70,802	13,539	435,032
1979	124,362	250,962	77,143	16,758	469,225
1980	138,206	269,609	87,884	19,169	514,869

Sources: Detroit Public Schools, *Annual Financial Reports of the Board of Education of the City of Detroit, 1966, 1970, 1973, 1977, 1980* (Detroit: Board of Education, 1966, 1970, 1973, 1977, 1980).

[a]Includes funds from investments, tuition, lunchroom, and bookstore sales, as well as other miscellaneous revenue.

Index

Aaron, Henry, vii

Accountability, teacher, 360–63, 394n.246, 395n.250

Accreditation, and class size, 130, 147n.151

ACLU. *See* American Civil Liberties Union (ACLU)

Action Committee of the Shrine of the Black Madonna, 341

Activism, teacher, 111–14, 115–16, 117–18, 121–22

ADA. *See* Americans for Democratic Action (ADA)

Ad Hoc Committee Concerned with Equal Education Opportunity, 299, 305, 374n.36

Administrators, black, 298, 307

Adult education, 18, 157

Advanced placement tests, 300

AFL. *See* AFL-CIO; American Federation of Labor (AFL)

AFL-CIO, 243, 260, 267, 268, 272, 273, 350, 354, 367

African-Americans. *See* Blacks

AFT. *See* American Federation of Teachers (AFT)

Age-grading, xii, 8

Aid, state, 90, 115, 124–29, 146n.132, 166, 167, 168, 221, 245, 247–48, 266, 314, 347, 352–53, 379n.89

Aldridge, Dan, 329, 331, 332

Alfred, Frank, 28, 41n.118

Alinsky, Saul, 338

Allen Park, 232

Alpha Kappa Alpha, 195

American Association of University Women, 109, 113

American Book Company, 12, 13, 22, 30, 53n.125

American Civil Liberties Union (ACLU), 113, 114, 143n.91

American Federation of Labor (AFL), 45, 118, 169, 172, 175, 182. *See also* AFL-CIO

American Federation of Teachers (AFT), 47, 57, 114, 118, 119, 123, 172, 221

Americanization, 18–19, 52

American League Against War and Fascism, 118

American Legion, 109, 113–14, 121, 122, 125

American Motors, 219

American party, 113–14

Americans for Democratic Action (ADA), 195, 197, 198

American Veterans Committee, 182

Angell, Alexis, 41n.118, 46

Anticommunism, 119–20, 120–23, 172–73, 221–22

Apportionment, legislative, 166, 250

Apprenticeship programs, 263, 299–300, 311

437

Citizen's Committee for Better Education
(CCBE), 340, 342, 343
Citizens' Committee on Public Issues,
233, 234
Citizens for Community Control of
Schools, 329, 331, 334,
380–81n.106
Citizenship, 369–70
Citizenship Education, 236
Citizen's Research Council of Michigan,
231, 233, 297
City council. *See* Detroit Common Coun-
cil
Civic Searchlight (journal), 163
Civil liberties: and school use, 45, 46–
47, 114–15; and teacher activism,
113–14
Civil rights movement, xi, 243, 299,
307, 375n.47; impacts of, 261, 263–
64, 293–94; on integration, 310–11;
law suits on, 262–63
Clark, Kenneth, 368
Class, xi, xiv, 42n.130, 93, 165; and
school reform, 31–32; and suburb
growth, 153–54. *See also* Middle
class; Working class
Class conflict, 6–7, 27–28, 163
Class size, 130–31, 147n.151, 159, 179,
285–86n.152
Cleage, Albert, Jr., 264, 265, 288n.186,
341, 360, 376n.54, 380n.100; on
black education, 326–27, 329; on
community control, 330, 331, 335; on
educational quality, 309, 310; on
Northern boycott, 303–4; on social reform, 312–13, 375–76n.49; on tax issues, 267–68, 269, 323
Cleaver, Eldridge, 308
Clergy, 1, 5
Cleveland, 160
Clive, Alan, 165
Coalition of Black Trade Unionists, 367
Cody, Frank, 18, 47, 52, 61, 98, 122,
127, 158, 187; on curriculum, 104–5;
on intermediate schools, 71–72; promotion of schools by, 68–69, 70–71;

as school superintendent, 29–31,
42n.125, 53–54, 78; on teacher sala-
ries, 56, 57, 112
Cody, Fred, 30, 42n.125, 46
Cody High School, 340
Cofer, Lloyd, 187, 189
Cohen, Ronald, 88n.111, 152
Colding, Charles, 301
Coleman Report, viii–ix
Collective bargaining, 271–72,
291nn.215, 216
Comer, James P., 408, 409n.12
Comfort, Frances, 117, 119–20, 159,
172, 180, 223; on school board activi-
ties, 151, 162, 176, 196
Committee on Military Training in the
Schools, 46
Common Council. *See* Detroit Common
Council
Communism, 77; investigation of, 121–
22; unionism as, 118, 120–21; in
unions, 172, 221–22
Communist party, 46, 49, 81n.23, 114,
138n.19, 143n.91, 399
Community, control of schools by, 329,
330–37, 338–39, 360, 376n.53
Condon, George, 17, 32, 38n.71
Congress of Industrial Organizations
(CIO), 154, 166, 175, 182, 227; on
school board elections, 174, 196–97;
school support by, 118, 119, 123, 125;
on tax issues, 169, 170; Wayne County
Council of, 160, 163. *See also* AFL-
CIO
Congress of Racial Equality (CORE),
301, 303
Conlin, Rollo, 247
Conlin, Thomas, 106
Conlin Amendment, 247, 283n.122
Conot, Robert, 371n.6
Constitutional convention, 249–50
Constitutional rights, 113–14
Construction Trades Apprentice School,
263
Consumers League of Michigan, 164
Cooksey, Warren, 228